Solar Cell Array Design Handbook

The Principles and Technology of Photovoltaic Energy Conversion

Solar Cell Array Design Handbook

The Principles and Technology of Photovoltaic Energy Conversion

H. S. Rauschenbach

Special Assistant for Advanced Technology
TRW Defense and Space Systems Group

VNR VAN NOSTRAND REINHOLD COMPANY

NEW YORK   CINCINNATI   ATLANTA   DALLAS   SAN FRANCISCO
LONDON   TORONTO   MELBOURNE

Van Nostrand Reinhold Company Regional Offices:
New York Cincinnati Atlanta Dallas San Francisco

Van Nostrand Reinhold Company International Offices:
London Toronto Melbourne

Library of Congress Catalog Card Number: 79-9389
ISBN: 0-442-26842-4

Manufactured in the United States of America

Published by Van Nostrand Reinhold Company
135 West 50th Street, New York. N.Y. 10020

Published simultaneously in Canada by Van Nostrand Reinhold Ltd.

15 14 13 12 11 10 9 8 7 6 5 4 3 2 1

Library of Congress Cataloging in Publication Data

Rauschenbach, Hans S
  Solar cell array design handbook.

  Includes index.
  1. Solar batteries. 2. Photovoltaic power
generation. I. Title.
TK2960.R35   621.47′5   79-9389
ISBN 0-442-26842-4

Preface

Solar cells and solar cell arrays—photovoltaic converters of solar energy into electric energy—are a reality. In a time period of two decades, solar cell arrays have grown in size from less than 1 watt to hundreds of kilowatts of electrical output in terrestrial applications and to over 10 kilowatts of output in space. New designs are on the drawing boards and in development laboratories all over the world for terrestrial and space arrays having hundreds and thousands of kilowatts of electric power output. Solar cell efficiency has increased from just a feeble response to sunlight to nearly 20%, surpassing the luminous efficiency of the incandescent light bulb on the way. Solar cell array costs are decreasing rapidly, making photovoltaic electric energy affordable and competitive today in remote areas.

In the same two-decade time span, the solar cell array design effort has matured from a spirited pioneering effort into a sophisticated, systematized, computer-aided process. While it has not been possible to adequately define or improve, or otherwise influence the creative design activity, all other aspects of the design process have been formalized and, for good reason, subjected to documentation, control, and verification.

As the 1970's draw to a close, we find ourselves engulfed by flurrying activities in photovoltaics. While we stand at the threshold of an unprecedented economical exploitation of this particular solar energy conversion technology, we should also realize that all the "easy" inventions have perhaps been made already. From here on, the going can be expected to get tougher. It is hoped that this book will be helpful to those who are going to keep on working for the benefit to all of use who consume energy.

Hans S. Rauschenbach

Purpose and Scope of this Handbook

This handbook intends to diseminate as much current and practical information relating to photovoltaic energy conversion technology for earth and space applications as practical. The emphasis is on the presentation of many different concepts and detailed techniques for several reasons:

- To introduce non-technical persons to the subject
- To aid students of the subject and younger workers in this field in mastering it
- To help specialists already working in the field to get their jobs done more effectively
- To inspire the creativity of advanced designers
- To document those concepts, data, and information that are of interest today but are not readily available in the open literature
- To define the entire field of solar cell array design and its multidisciplinary nature.

This handbook is written on several levels, ranging from the illustrative and introductory to the detailed technical. Most of the text should be understandable to advanced high school students and senior technicians. Few sections, if any, are expected to pose difficulties for college graduates or practicing engineers.

The mathematical treatment has been held simple. Differential and integral equations are used sparingly, but are included to permit computer programming. Most mathematical problems can be handled with today's scientific pocket calculators.

This handbook recounts some of the more important historical events that led to today's advanced solar cell array technology and includes sufficient references for locating more detailed accounts. Subjects that are treated elsewhere and readily available, such as general structural design, heat transfer and thermodynamics, civil engineering, and electrical wiring codes and practices, are not included here. Rather, only the special considerations for solar cell arrays are treated.

design, composition, or any other feature of any article may fall within a claim of an existing patent. It is not the intent of any of the authors, editors, and publishers of and contributors to this handbook—nor is it the intent of any of the sponsoring or performing organizations involved in the preparation of this or the original handbook—to induce anyone to infringe upon any existing patent. It is the responsibility of the prospective user of any of the information, material, data, and descriptions herein to determine whether such usage constitutes infringement or noninfringement of any patent or otherwise legally protected or proprietary right.

Specifically, neither the United States, the National Aeronautics and Space Administration, the California Institute of Technology, the Jet Propulsion Laboratory, nor the TRW Defense and Space Systems Group; nor any of the employees of these organizations; nor the pre-

parers, editors, approvers, or publishers of this or the earlier document; nor any other person:

1. Makes any warranty or representation, expressed or implied, with respect to the accuracy, completeness, or usefulness of the information contained in this document, or that the use of any information, apparatus, method, or process disclosed in this document may not infringe upon privately owned rights;
2. Assumes any liabilities with respect to the use of, or for damages resulting from the use of, any information, apparatus, method, or process disclosed in this document;
3. Sanctions, approves or recommends any designs, practices, selections, or procedures contained in this document for a specific purpose, use, or project.

SAFETY NOTICE

Solar cell assemblies, modules, panels, or arrays are sources of electric power and may, under certain circumstances, constitute a potential hazard. Even under conditions of low ambient lighting, a sufficient number of solar cells connected in series may produce voltages and currents that may cause electrocution. Appropriate safety procedures for handling and installing such assemblies must be used and followed (see also the entries under Safety in the Index).

A larger array, when exposed to bright sunlight and short-circuited with a conductor having inadequate cross-section, may start a fire.

Any solar cell assembly, even in low ambient light, when accidentally short-circuited, may cause a spark that is capable of igniting explosive atmospheres, such as may be found in solvent cleaning operations.

Acknowledgments

This handbook is a completely revised, updated, and expanded issue of an earlier, space technology oriented document published in October 1976 and now available as NASA CR-149365 [N77-14193 (Vol. 1) and N77-14194 (Vol. 2)] : *Solar Cell Array Design Handbook*, from the National Technical Information Service, Springfield, Virginia 22151.

The earlier handbood was prepared by the Power Sources Engineering Department of TRW Defense and Space Systems Group, Space Vehicles Division (author and editor, H. S. Rauschenbach), under Contract No. 953913 with the California Institute of Technology, Jet Propulsion Laboratory, Pasadena, California. The active support in the creation of the original document of E. Cohn at NASA Headquarters, J. V. Goldsmith and R. Josephs at JPL, and the following at TRW is gratefully acknowledged and appreciated:

W. R. Brannian and P. Goldsmith, editing and review; A. Kaplan, material properties, stress and fatigue; R. M. Kurland, mechanical systems and components; W. Luft, solar cell and array technology and analysis; A. N. Munoz-Mellows, thermo-dynamics and heat transfer; H. Riess, electrical systems and array analysis; D. W. Rusta, electrical systems, array and orbital analysis; W. R. Scott, corrosion; R. K. Yasui, array technology and material properties.

Also acknowledged and deeply appreciated are the many contributors to the original manuscript drafts and their extensive reviews by numerous personnel in industry and government, especially by L. Slifer of the NASA Goddard Space Flight Center. The typing and editing of the many drafts by M. J. Gustetto, M. C. Winn, and E. A. Harper of TRW, and by my wife Marianne are also greatly appreciated. A special word of appreciation and thanks goes to my resourceful wife and understanding children, Christian, Isabella, Angelina, and David, who provided a home environment that not only made the preparation of this book possible, but also made it a unique experience.

Credit goes also to the literally thousands of workers who, over the years, have created the large body of photovoltaic knowledge and technology from which this author has drawn, and to the institutions of higher learning, private industry, and government which contributed to it in some indispensable way. Since a book of this nature cannot name them all, and naming of only a few would be highly inequitable, names of individuals and organizations have been deleted entirely, except where essential, from the text. Those included in the references were not selected according to the significance of their work, but rather to provide the researcher with leads for a greater in-depth pursuit of a particular topic.

Contents

Solar Cell Array Design Handbook

The Principles and Technology of Photovoltaic Energy Conversion

PART I

Solar Cell Arrays

1
Array Systems

ARRAY CONCEPTS

1-1. Arrays and Batteries

An *array* constitutes an orderly arrangement of elements in rows and columns. A *solar cell array* is an arrangement of solar cells, electrically connected into circuits, that have the appearance of rows and columns. Solar cell arrays are also known as *solar batteries* and, colloquially, as *solar arrays*. The term *battery* means a group of cells connected together to furnish electricity. Therefore, the use of either term would be correct to describe an array of solar cells. However, to distinguish clearly between solar cells of the photovoltaic type and other "battery" cells of the galvanic or electrochemical types, the term *array* will be used throughout this book in connection with solar cells and the term *battery* in connection with electrochemical cells.

Solar cells produce electricity from sunlight *directly* without utilizing a chemical process, while electrochemical cells produce electricity without sunlight by chemical conversion of one substance into another. Examples of electrochemical batteries are the batteries used in flashlights, transistor radios, cameras, and automobiles.

1-2. Arrays, Panels, Parts, and Components

Except for the smallest of them, solar cell arrays are fabricated and installed in several pieces, known as solar cell subassemblies, modules, panels, subarrays, and others. To minimize the use of the same term for describing different items, the term *solar cell panel*, or simply *panel*, will be used to denote either a small array or a portion of a larger array that is a self-contained mechanical entity as far as fabrication, testing, and assembly is concerned, regardless of its electrical characteristics.

A solar cell panel is comprised of the following parts or components: solar cells, wiring, solar cell covers, solar cell support, and support structure. The solar cells are the "heart" of the array, converting solar energy in the form of sunlight into electricity. (For descriptions of how solar cells produce electricity, see the beginning sections of Chapter 4.) The panel wiring collects the electricity from all the solar cells and routes it to the panel *terminals*. Transparent solar cell covers protect the solar cells from adverse environmental influences, while permitting the sunlight to shine right through them. The solar cell support, typically a flat plate-like *substrate*, holds the solar cells mechanically in place. The support structure mounts the cell support (substrate or panel) to the ground, to a vehicle, or to a sun-tracking mechanism.

1-3. Array Types

Solar cell arrays may be classified into different types according to their intended use, construction, sun orientation, use of sunlight concentration, or application, as follows:

Terrestrial arrays are designed to operate within the earth's atmosphere and withstand all weather related environmental influences. *Space arrays* are designed to operate primarily outside of the earth's atmosphere and withstand the space environment. *Non-concentrator arrays*, sometimes also called *flat plate arrays* (even though they may actually be curved), simply utilize the sunlight as it falls naturally onto the solar cells. The solar cells may or may not be fully oriented toward the sun. *Concentrator arrays* utilize some devices for increasing the sunlight intensity on the solar cells. Increasing the intensity, called solar or sunlight concentration, is done primarily by mirrors (reflectors) or lenses (refractors). Concentrator arrays can convert more solar energy with a smaller number of solar cells than can non-concentrator arrays, but not without some penalties. *Flat arrays* are, as the name implies, flat plate-like structures having all solar cells face into the same direction. Used for terrestrial and space applications, they may be mounted in a fixed, approximately sun-pointing direction, or may be attached to sun-tracking equipment. *Curved arrays* utilize structural solar cell supports that are portions of cylindrical, conical, or spherical shells. The solar cells may point *outward* from their convex sides or *inward* from their concave sides. Their application includes both terrestrial and space, sun-tracking and non-tracking concepts. *Body-mounted arrays*, rigidly held to the internal structure of a vehicle, are contrasted by arrays that are mounted on protruding structures such as on rigid or articulated frames, cantilevers, or booms. *Fixed arrays* are rigidly held to a spacecraft or to a terrestrial structure. The angle between the solar cell surfaces and the sun varies continually. *Oriented arrays* are being pointed into the direction of the sun to maximize the electrical power output from the arrays. Array orientation toward the sun, also known as *sun-following*, *sun-tracking*, or *steering*, is done with *orientation drive mechanisms*, also known as *sun-trackers* or *heliostats*. Sun-tracking may be facilitated by continuous slewing of the array or by intermittent, stepwise movements. The equipment that performs the array orientation may utilize sun sensors in complex feedback circuits or simple clock drives that execute preprogrammed motions. For some specific array designs and applications, the array may have

to be oriented toward the sun very precisely, while for other designs and applications, only very approximate orientation, if any, may suffice. *One-axis oriented arrays* follow the sun by rotating about a single axis. Perfect sun-tracking cannot be achieved by this method, except for a few days out of the year. The axis about which the array rotates may make any convenient angle with the ground or spacecraft; likewise, the array may be inclined relative to this axis at any convenient angle. *Two-axes oriented arrays* follow the sun by rotating about two different axes. Perfect sun-tracking is possible. The two axes may make any convenient angle with the ground, spacecraft, or array, and need not be orthogonal (perpendicular) to each other. *High-voltage arrays* produce nominal operating voltages that are significantly greater than the 24 to 30 volts of typical systems of the past and present. While there are no agreed upon limits, some workers in the field classify arrays producing 100 volts as high-voltage arrays, but others reserve this classification for arrays producing at least 1000 volts. *Hardened arrays*, especially designed to withstand nuclear weapons or laser weapons attack, are used on some military equipment.

Other array types, making up an almost endless list, include high-altitude balloon arrays (half terrestrial, half space); submersible arrays for under-water applications; ground-based extraterrestrial arrays for Lunar or Martian surface stations; lightweight arrays having exceptionally high power per unit weight (kilowatts/kg) performance; low-cost arrays having unusually low cost per power output ($/watt); hybrid systems, producing both electric and thermal (hot water, etc.) output; and many others.

1-4. The Array as Part of the Power System

In most practical applications, the solar cell array constitutes the power generating subsystem within the framework of a power system, as illustrated in Fig. 1-1.

The array orientation subsystem aids in maximizing the array output capability by orienting the solar cells toward the sun. The output from

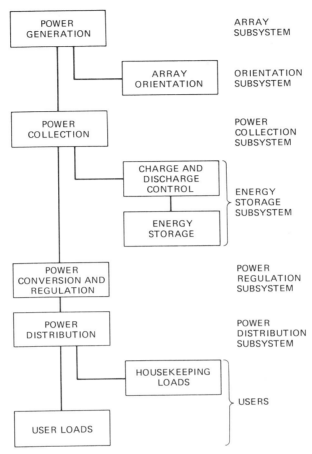

Fig. 1-1. The array as part of a power generation system.

the solar cell circuits and solar cell panels is gathered by the power collection subsystem, and routed in part to the energy storage subsystem and in part to the power conversion and regulation subsystem. The energy storage subsystem provides electricity during periods when the array is not (or is only insufficiently) illuminated. The power conversion and regulation subsystem smoothens the typically varying raw output power from the solar cells and provides a steady flow of controlled power, via the power distribution subsystem, to the loads. The housekeeping loads are those needed by the power system for the array orientation drive motors, for powering status and monitoring circuits, for operating cooling equipment, and for performing other, similar duties. The user loads are those electricity consumers for which the entire power system was created in the first place.

Not all power systems have the same block diagram as that shown in Fig. 1-1. Some have no orientation mechanism, some have no energy storage, some have no regulation, and some have no housekeeping requirements. Of those which have energy storage, some may have just enough to provide only for essential housekeeping needs, while others may be able to supply more than the user loads require. Some power systems are very simple, and others are very complex, even requiring computer control for efficient operation. Some power systems, for either space or terrestrial application, are designed to operate automatically for many years without attention; others may require frequent operator activity. Non-automatic power systems on unmanned spacecraft are operated from the ground by remote control via radio communication.

1-5. The Array as a System

A solar cell array can also be thought of as a system that is made up of a number of subsystems, as shown in Fig. 1-2. The optical subsystem includes sunlight concentrators (if used) and the solar cell or array coverglass. All solar cells and their wiring make up the electrical subsystem. The solar cell mechanical support constitutes the mechanical subsystem, and the structural supports and sun-tracking mechanisms are parts of the orientation and structural subsystem. Array temperature transducers (remote control thermometers), orientation sensors, voltage and current transducers (remote control voltmeters and ammeters), and other status or performance monitoring devices are encompassed, with their circuits, by the status sensor subsystem. The thermal control subsystem is comprised of heat radiators, cooling fins, thermal control coatings, and other items that reduce the solar cell operating temperature as much as is practical. The environmental protection subsystem is represented by the solar cell packaging material that minimizes adverse environmental effects on the solar cells.

1-6. Hybrid Systems

A solar cell array hybrid system is one which is composed of elements from different techno-

logical fields. The following hybrid systems have been designed:

- Photovoltaic/thermal energy conversion systems
- Body mounted/deployable solar cell arrays (see Section 7-18)
- Rigid/flexible deployable solar cell arrays (see Section 7-18).

In photovoltaic/thermal hybrid systems, solar cells convert sunlight into electricity, utilizing the photovoltaic energy conversion process (see Section 4-2) while the cell's heat (thermal) energy is extracted by a thermal system. Depending upon their energy conversion efficiency and their operating conditions, solar cells convert between approximately 5% and 20% of the incident solar energy into electricity. Most of the remainder of the incident solar energy is converted by the cells into heat. The thermal energy is typically carried away by a cooling fluid. The relatively low temperature (less than that of boiling water) of the fluid does not lend itself to driving rotating machinery, but is usable for water heating and for the heating and cooling of buildings (see Sections 7-8 and 7-9).

HISTORICAL DEVELOPMENTS

1-7. History of Terrestrial Arrays

The first practical solar cell was developed in 1954 (see the historical review in Chapter 4). However, the relatively high cost and low efficiency of these early cells, together with the consumer skepticism that is a typical reaction to many new products, prevented their widespread use. During the mid-1950's, a number of remotely located low-power radio-telephone stations were operated with small solar cell arrays, and several experimental solar cell arrays were constructed. Overall success, however, was limited, because the protection of the solar cell circuits from adverse environmental effects was inadequate, and the application's engineering approaches to solar cell powered systems were still in their infancy. Several novelty items appeared on the market during this time, including "Solar Packs" to power transistor radios, and small arrays built into the frames of eye-

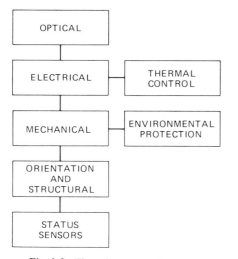

Fig. 1-2. The subsystems of an array.

glasses to recharge batteries that powered integrally attached hearing aids.

The largest solar cell panel during these early years was assembled from 10640 silicon solar cells of 1 × 2 cm size and mounted above the roof of a 1912 Baker Electric automobile to recharge its batteries.[1] The solar cell powered car toured the world and made international front page news, but failed to open a large terrestrial market.

Solar cell array applications in Japan started in 1960. Between 1963 and 1973, 720 photovoltaic systems were installed with a cumulative array output of 13 kilowatts. One-half of the installed power was used for lighthouse equipment (Fig. 1-3), the other half on land stations.[2] Economic analyses showed solar cell arrays with storage batteries and associated electronics for 4 to 8 watt loads to be of greater advantage than the installation of new power lines to the public utility system over distances of 1 km or greater.

The evolution of terrestrial solar cell arrays in France started in 1961 with the fabrication of a system for a copper electrolysis experiment in Chile, producing 26.5 amperes at 3.3 volts at 6% efficiency (Fig. 1-4).[4] Solar cells were 19 mm diameter n-on-p silicon cells having paint-on silver contacts. An improved array design was developed in 1965, using 10% efficient cells of 30 mm diameter. Another improvement, using 40 mm diameter cells, was completed in 1969. Various problems were encountered on

Fig. 1-4. Chilean Installation of 1961. (*Courtesy North American Philips*)

the earlier models, primarily solar cell contact problems and cracking of epoxy seals between the plate glass covers and aluminum box frames. The seal problems were solved by replacing the epoxy with a rubber seal.

Photovoltaic installations in the U.S.S.R. date back to the late 1960's. Attractive especially for use in the remote, semi-arid southeastern areas of that country, a variety of systems, ranging in size from 1 to 500 watts output for powering irrigation pumps, water gates, communications equipment, and light buoys on waterways, have been installed. Some installations utilize solar concentration of up to 1000 times, aided by highly accurate tracking equipment. Array configurations include fixed and sun-tracking flat plate arrays without and with low-concentration ratio mirrors, and long, narrow arrays contained in transparent, sealed glass and non-glass tubes. The tubes are dried out and filled with an inert gas before sealing. The solar cells are made from silicon, cadmium sulfide, and cadmium telluride. A typical temperature rise of 30°C between the solar cells and the ambient air temperature has been observed.[5]

The growing awareness of limited world fossil fuel resources during the 1970's led to the creation of the U.S. Department of Energy (formerly

Fig. 1-3. Early Japanese installation. (*Courtesy Sharp Corp.*)

the Energy Research and Development Agency). The Department has been funding at an increasing rate basic and applied research to make large-scale solar energy utilization economically viable. In 1977, an experimental solar array system was completed that operated seasonally alternating irrigation pumps, grain drying fans, and other equipment.[7] The array consists of 2 rows of 14 solar cell panels each, containing a total of 97,000 solar cells and producing a peak power output of 25 kilowatts (Fig. 1-5). The panels are tilted for optimal array performance. A 10 horsepower (7.5 kilowatt) dc irrigation pump motor operates directly from the 120 to 140 volt dc array bus. An energy storage subsystem, consisting of two parallel-connected strings of 19 series-connected 6 volt lead-acid batteries, having a capacity of approximately 80 kilowatt-hours, is connected directly to the dc bus.

In 1978, a 60 kilowatt peak output solar cell array started to accumulate military experience with such systems.[8] Designed for the U.S. Air Force, the array of 190,000 solar cells, located in Southern California, is fixed and tilted for optimum performance. Array dc output power is converted into ac, regulated and made available for supplying power into the public utility grid.

Earlier Department of Defense (DoD) projects included solar cell arrays of 35 to 74 watt peak output for radio relay stations, a 150 watt solar cell charger for rechargeable nickel-cadmium batteries, a 12 kilowatt array for a remote radar site at China Lake, California, a 10.8 kilowatt array water purification system at Fort Belvoir, Virginia, and a 2.4 kilowatt array for a telephone communications system (Fig. 1-6). Each of the two arrays consists of 2,592 cells, each 3 inches in diameter, and produces nominally 56 volt output.

1-8. History of Space Arrays

The space age arrived on October 4, 1957, when the U.S.S.R. launched into earth orbit Sputnik 1, a 23 inch aluminum sphere weighing 184 lb, returning density, temperature, cosmic ray, and meteoroid data for 21 days. This satellite and its successor, Sputnik 2, were powered by electrochemical batteries only. The first solar cell array that successfully operated in space was launched on March 17, 1958, on board Vanguard I, the second U.S. earth satellite. This solar cell array consisted of six solar cell panels distributed over and mounted to the outer surface of an approximately spherical spacecraft body. Each panel was made of 18 p-on-n solar cells of 2×0.5 cm size, having approximately 10% energy conversion efficiency at 28°C. This solar array system provided less than 1 watt of power for more than 6 years.

Fig. 1-5. Installation at Nebraska, U.S.A. (*Courtesy Massachusetts Institute of Technology, Lincoln Laboratory*)

Fig. 1-6. Solar powered mobile communications station, deployed and stowed. (*Courtesy of the U.S. Army Mobility Equipment Research and Development Command, Fort Belvoir, Virginia*)

Tables 1-1 and 1-2 show the total number of spacecraft successfully launched between 1957 and 1977.[9] Most of these spacecraft have used solar cell arrays as the primary power source.

Since 1957, solar arrays have grown in size and complexity. The largest U.S. solar array flown was on Skylab 1, launched on May 14, 1973, into near-earth orbit. Skylab carried two separate solar cell array systems: the Orbital Workshop (O.W.S.) array and the Apollo Telescope Mount (A.T.M.) array (Fig. 1-7). The Orbital Workshop array design consisted of two deployable wings. Each wing carried 73,920 n-on-p solar cells of 2 × 4 cm size, providing in

Table 1-1. U.S. Space Launches as of December 31, 1977.[9]

Year	Successes*	Failures	Total
1957	0	1	1
1958	7	10	17
1959	11	8	19
1960	16	13	29
1961	29	12	41
1962	52	7	59
1963	37	8	45
1964	54	5	59
1965	62	6	68
1966	70	4	74
1967	59	3	62
1968	47	3	50
1969	40	1	41
1970	28	1	29
1971	29	4	33
1972	30	0	30
1973	23	2	25
1974	25	2	27
1975	28	2	30
1976	26	1	27
1977	24	2	26

*Payload(s) injected into orbit. Included are International payloads if launched by U.S. booster and classified as U.S. payloads.

excess of 6 kilowatts of electric power in orbit. The O.W.S. array in flight actually consisted of one wing only; during launch, a meteoroid/thermal shield tore loose from the O.W.S., ripping away the second wing.

The A.T.M array consisted of four deployable wings, carrying a total of 123,120 solar cells of 2 X 2 cm and 41,040 cells of 2 X 6 cm size, and provided in excess of 10 kilowatts of electric power in orbit.

Typical early satellites were approximately spherical (Fig. 1-8). At first, as for Vanguard I, relatively small solar cell assemblies were attached to the satellite housing. Soon, however, the entire usable exterior surface of satellite housings was being utilized for the mounting of solar cells to accommodate increasing power requirements. To extend the available solar cell array area, the satellites were fitted with so-called solar cell *paddles* (Fig. 1-9). Explorer 6, launched in August of 1959, was the first spacecraft to use paddles. Of the four 51 cm² paddles, one failed to extend fully and lock. The

solar cells of the resultant three paddle array rapidly degraded in the Van Allen radiation belt and all transmission was lost in two months.

This failure was followed by a string of successes, and solar cell arrays become the preferred power supply. Then, on July 9, 1962, a high-altitude nuclear explosion, "Starfish," released an estimated 10^{25} fission electrons that became trapped in the lower region of the Van Allen belt. The resultant damage to solar cell arrays, evident in Fig. 1-10, rapidly caused a number of spacecraft to cease transmission, degrading both the solar cells and the on-board electronics.

Radiation damage became a subject of intense interest, and changes were implemented to improve the radiation resistance of arrays. These changes included a switch from p-on-n to n-on-p solar cells, increased base resistivity, and more careful shielding of the cells by coverslides. As power requirements increased, detailed design criteria for the array were evolved. Ranger Block II, Mariner 4, Nimbus 1 (1964), and Pegasus (1965) were among the first that were designed to accommodate thermal expansion differences between the solar cells and the substrate. But new problems were encountered: On several spacecraft launched in 1967 and 1968, coverslides slightly smaller than the solar cells were used for ease in construction and because of tolerances necessary in cell and coverslide size. Any adhesive that extruded around the coverslide was carefully cleaned away. As a result, on Intelsat 2-F4, the Applications Technology Satellite A.T.S.-1, and on the Gravity Gradient Test Satellite (G.G.T.S.), about 5% of the solar cell front area was bare or covered only by a thin contact bar, leading to an anomalous 10 to 30% array degradation in a very short time. The rapid degradation of those solar cell arrays was caused by low-energy protons of the outer region of the Van Allen belt entering the bare solar cell surface and damaging the junction (see Section 4-38 for a design solution).

Satellite designs soon required more powerful solar cell arrays than could be provided by paddles. Oriented or semi-oriented solar cell panels (Fig. 1-11) provided one answer, while cylindrical and other body-mounted solar cell panels for larger diameter vehicles provided another (Fig. 1-12).

The highest-power solar cell array designed in

Table 1-2. Spacecraft Orbited, Totals as of December 31, 1977.[9]
(Reprinted with permission of TRW)

Sponsor	Earth Orbit	Lunar Missions	Planetary	Solar Orbit	Totals
Indonesia	2	–	–	–	2
Australia*	2	–	–	–	2
Canada*	8	–	–	–	8
E.S.A. (E.S.R.O.)*	10	–	–	–	10
France*	20	–	–	–	20
Germany*	4	–	–	2	6
Intelsat*	21	–	–	–	21
Japan	12	–	–	–	12
N.A.T.O.*	4	–	–	–	4
People's Republic of China	7	–	–	–	7
U.K.*	8	–	–	–	8
U.S.**	774	36	13	4	827
U.S.S.R.†	1151	33	27	–	1211
Netherlands*	1	–	–	–	1
Spain*	1	–	–	–	1
Italy*	5	–	–	–	5
India	1	–	–	–	1
Totals	2031	69	40	6	2146

*Includes launches from the U.S. or by U.S. boosters, of satellites built by sponsors or built jointly under cooperation agreements with the U.S.

**U.S. totals consist of exclusively U.S.-sponsored satellites, including unidentified satellites, but not including Atlas-Centaur, Saturn, or Titan III non-functional payloads.

†U.S.S.R. totals include unidentified Russian spacecraft; do not include earth-parking platforms used for injecting payload spacecraft into other orbits. Lunar spacecraft now in solar orbit are included in "Lunar Mission" column. Planetary spacecraft now in solar orbit are included in "Planetary" column. Spacecraft failing to reach any orbit are not included in this tally.

the late 1970's for operation in geosynchronous orbit is that for the Tracking and Data Relay Satellite System (T.D.R.S.S.), illustrated in Fig. 1-13. Both wings of the array carry 31062 solar cells of 11.4% efficiency at 28°C. If the array were to be tested in the laboratory, it would produce 3.9 kilowatts of power output. In orbit, its initial power output capability of 3.1 kilowatts is expected to diminish to 2.2 kilowatts after ten years.[11]

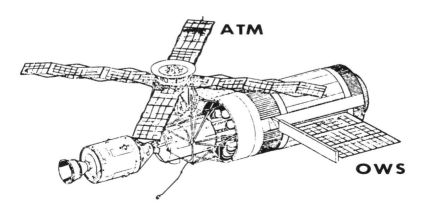

Fig. 1-7. NASA's Skylab.

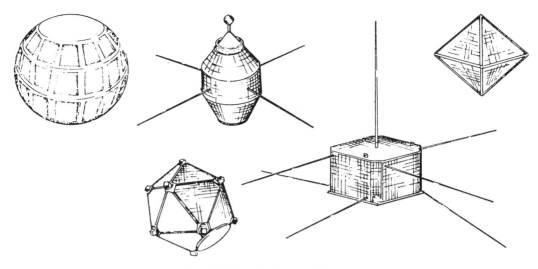

Fig. 1-8. Early body-mounted arrays.

1-9. The Future of Solar Cell Arrays

All indications are that solar cell arrays will have a bright future on earth as well as in space. It can be expected that solar cells will not only continue to be making contributions to providing much needed energy, but also that their contributions will increase importantly in the future in those areas in which solar cells offer unique advantages over other methods of energy generation. It should not be expected that solar cells will replace most other forms of generating electricity, nor should it be assumed that solar cells, because of their relatively high cost at the present time, will not find increasingly widespread use. There are already many applications in remote locations in the U.S. and elsewhere in the world where solar cell power, even at its present high cost, is economically more viable than a diesel-generator system or the construction of a connecting line to a distant utility power feeder. Many such remote sites are now being provisioned with solar cell arrays and associated energy storage and regulation equip-

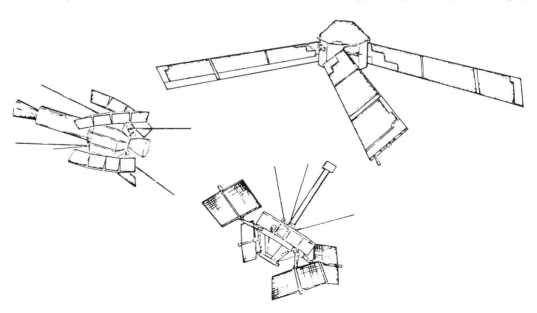

Fig. 1-9. Paddle-wheel arrays.

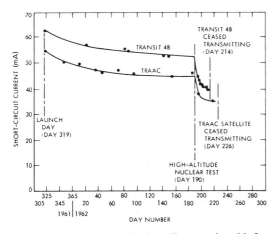

Fig. 1-10. Degradation of solar cell output in orbit for transit 4B and TRAAC satellites.

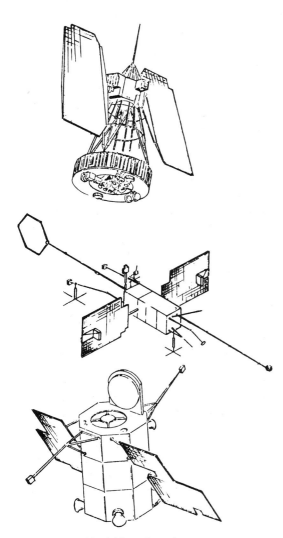

Fig. 1-11. Oriented arrays.

Fig. 1-12. Body-mounted arrays on spinning satellites; antennas are despun. (*Courtesy Comsat Corp.*)

ment to power radio transmitters, television receivers, irrigation pumps, and electrolytic corrosion prevention equipment used to protect bridges and other metallic structures.

The economic factors that operate in favor of an increasing use of solar cell power are increasing fossil fuel prices and decreasing solar cell costs. Fossil fuel prices will rise because most readily accessible and practically usable deposits either have been or are being rapidly depleted, while less accessible or less usable deposits are simply more costly to exploit. Solar cell costs will drop because new processes, requiring less energy and manpower for raw material refining and cell fabrication, are being developed.

The role of nuclear power in the future is not clear. However, it seems certain that safety considerations will add increasingly growing cost penalties to nuclear energy production, both regarding nuclear power plant operations and the safe-guarding and disposing of the dangerous radioactive waste products. Furthermore, a developing world, still made up of many industrially underdeveloped countries, will bid for a

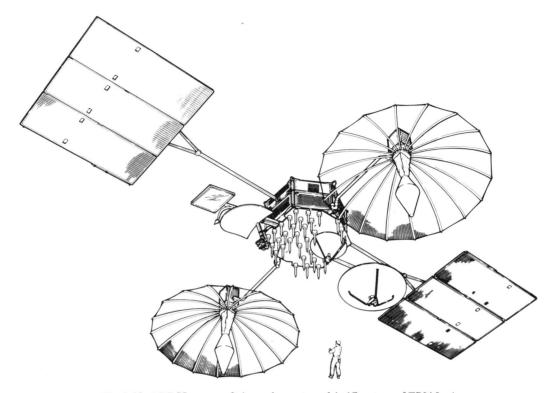

Fig. 1-13. TDRSS spacecraft (man shown to scale). (*Courtesy of TRW Inc.*)

greater share of the world's energy supply than it has in the past. The use of solar energy, of which conversion into electricity by solar cells is only one aspect (see Section 4-2) is one of the most viable, long-range alternate approaches to the international energy shortage problem. The feasibility of huge power stations in space, placed into permanent orbits around the earth, is now being investigated. Electric power, generated by solar cells from sunlight, would be beamed down to earth by wireless transmission at about the turn of the century, providing millions of kilowatt-hours annually to the world's energy consumers.

During the coming years, solar cells will continue to power unmanned and manned spacecraft as the most economical and safest source of electric energy. Communication satellites are already relaying data, messages, and news across countries and continents, reaching parts of the world that would otherwise be inaccessible. Direct-broadcast satellites will beam radio and television programs literally to the last man on earth. Landsat earth resources satellites will sweep over our globe, locating new mineral deposits, identifying crop and forest diseases, mapping water resources, and checking pollution patterns. Weather satellites will monitor oceanic environmental and meteorological data, effluxes from rivers, cloud formations, and developing centers of destructive storms. Navigation satellites will guide ships and aircraft safely along their routes. In the weightless environment of space laboratories, new materials and medical products may be manufactured that cannot be produced in the gravity field of the earth. And while large space telescopes will search the skies for a key to the knowledge of man's origin and destiny, military reconnaissance and defense communication satellites will keep watch on weapons satellites and foreign military operations. The international participation in space exploration is already growing, and the international competition for a greater share of space enterprises, already in full swing, can be expected to sharpen.

The solar cell array technology required for future missions, both for space and earth applications, will be characterized by much lower cost and greater size than is possible today. Cost reductions are being sought primarily in the areas of solar cells and other components through utilization of lower-cost materials and fabrication processes.

ARRAY APPLICATIONS

1-10. Terrestrial Applications

Solar cell arrays are suited for any applications that require electric power and energy. They are especially suited for remote applications where there is no direct tie-in to an electric utility feeder, or where the transportation of fuel to the generator site is impractical. In conjunction with an electrochemical storage battery and suitable charge control electronics, solar cell power supplies can be designed to provide energy for night time operation as well as for operation during several weeks of intense cloud cover. Arrays for maintenance-free applications can be mounted in a fixed position without requiring orientation mechanisms.

Solar cell arrays, when properly designed, are not subject to self-destruction due to electrical load conditions, minor array failures, orientation drive malfunctions, or other influences. Solar cells are quite rugged and resistant to electrical and mechanical damage. The most severe environmental threats to solar cell arrays are long-term corrosion due to weather influences, direct lightning strikes, and vandalism (see Chapter 9 for details and other environmental considerations).

Solar cell arrays can be designed for systems having any reasonable voltage level, ranging from less than 1 volt to many kilovolts of output. No special precautions need be taken (except for solar cell hot spot problems, as discussed in Sections 2-45 and 2-46) when interfacing with electronic equipment and batteries. Applications for terrestrial solar cell arrays include, but are not limited to, the following:

- Television and radio receivers (mobile and stationary)
- Radio transmitters and transponders (mobile and stationary)
- Weather and earthquake monitoring stations
- Irrigation and other pump motors
- Refrigerators and fans
- Electronic (galvanic) corrosion protection of metal structures (bridges, towers, etc.)
- Electronic and optical beacons and warning devices
- Rechargeable battery chargers for military devices and recreational vehicles and boats
- Emergency, surveillance, and security systems
- Hydrolysis (electrolysis of water, separating water into hydrogen and oxygen gas, and others)
- Electrochemical processes.

1-11. Space Applications

Solar cells are especially suited for space applications because they consume no fuel, do not exhaust themselves, and do not emit exhaust products or radiation. Most satellites and space vehicles launched to date have utilized solar cell energy to operate the internal equipment as well as to power the communiation equipment.

A new applications area presently being explored is electric propulsion, also known as solar-electric propulsion. High-voltage electric energy from a solar cell array is utilized by an ion engine, or ion-drive, to ionize a substance (i.e., to break apart its molecular or atomic arrangements) and to eject a stream of ionized particles. The acceleration and ejection of the particles causes a thrust (force) that propels the engine and the attached spacecraft in a manner similar to the working of a jet engine.

1-12. Power From Space

The largest solar cell array system proposed is a part of the Satellite Solar Power Station (S.S.P.S.) concept. Now actively being studied and developed by industry and government agencies, satellite solar power stations would be large platforms placed in stationary earth orbits. Solar cells would convert solar energy into electricity for microwave transmission to earth. On the ground, the microwave energy would be rectified, converted, and fed into the existing utility power grid. There are several advantages to converting solar energy in space rather than on the ground: in space, approximately ten times as much energy can be converted than on the most suitable terrestrial sites; there are no weather limitations; and there are almost no night time limitations. Relatively short eclipse periods (72 minutes maximum) during two seasons in the year amount to an average loss of about 1% of energy during one year as compared to full illumination.

One of the recent S.S.P.S. studies shows the solar array having an overall size of 19.2 km in length by 3.85 km in width, intercepting 82,200 megawatts (megawatt = 10^6 watts) of solar energy. Six troughs, comprised of flat reflector walls and solar cell bankets at their bottoms, contain 30.6 km^2 of solar cells of the gallium arsenide (GaAlAs/GaAs) type. The solar cells operate at 125°C, owing to 2-to-1 geometrical concentration ratio, at which they are predicted to achieve an energy conversion efficiency of 17.6% (20% efficiency at 28°C). Aluminum bus bars collect 218 amps at 45.5 kilovolts at end of life from the solar cell circuits. 8700 kilowatts of this power reaches the microwave transmitter. At the ground, the microwave energy is received and converted into dc, resulting in 5000 kilowatts of electricity that is fed into the public utility grid system. The overall system efficiency is 6.1%. The solar cells, the blankets, and the concentrators are estimated to weigh 5.0, 2.6, and 1.1 million kg, respectively, and have a design life of 30 years.[12]

ARRAY SYSTEMS PERFORMANCE

1-13. Array Ratings

Solar cell arrays are designed to provide certain amounts of electricity under certain constraints. The amount of electricity required may be defined by any one or combination of the following performance criteria (for definitions of the electrical parameters, see the beginning sections of Chapter 2).

Power Output. Also specified as current output at a certain voltage, it refers to the power (watts) available at the power regulator or load circuit input terminals, and is specified either as *peak* power or *average* power produced during one day or one orbit. It is specified under certain conditions of illumination, solar cell temperature, degradation, and other factors.

Energy Output. Being the time-integrated value of power, the energy (watt-hour) output indicates the amount of energy produced by the array during one day or one orbit. Energy output may be defined under the same conditions as power output.

Ampere-Hour Output. Arrays delivering electricity primarily into energy storage batteries are rated more conveniently in terms of the ampere-hour capacity.

Efficiency. Also known more precisely as *energy conversion efficiency*, this parameter is usually given as a *power* efficiency by

$$\eta_p = \frac{\text{Power output from array}}{\text{Power input from sun}} \times 100\%.$$

The array *power* output may be the peak or an average output. The true *energy* conversion efficiency is defined by

$$\eta_e = \frac{\text{Energy output from array}}{\text{Energy input from sun}} \times 100\%.$$

Power is given in units of *watts*, and energy in units of *watt-hours*. Either of these parameters can be indicative of the highest efficiency at which a system could operate under ideal conditions, or of the actual operating conditions.

While power and energy output can readily be measured, the power or energy input from the sun into the solar cell array is not a uniquely defined quantity. Ambiguities arise from defining the array area. Some manufacturers or users of solar cell modules define the incoming energy as falling on the entire, gross array area, others on the overall module area, still others on the solar cell area, and a few even on the active area of the solar cell that is not covered by contacts and gridlines.

Weight or Mass. The weight, or (technically more precise) mass, of an array, expressed in kg, indicates how much material is contained in a given array system.

Cost. Usually broken down into acquisition and maintenance costs, these figures permit evaluation of the economics of a given system.

Specific Power. Three specific power parameters are in use: power per unit array area (watts/m^2), power per unit array mass or weight (watts/kg), and power per unit array cost (watts/$).

Specific Energy. The parameters are, correspondingly, watt-hours/m^2, watt-hours/kg, and watt-hours/$.

Specific Mass or Weight. The parameters in use are: mass per unit area (kg/m^2), mass per unit power (kg/watt) or energy (kg/watt-hour), and area per unit mass (m^2/kg).

Specific Cost. The units in use are: cost per unit power ($/watt) or energy ($/watt-hour), cost per unit mass ($/kg), and cost per unit area ($/$m^2$).

Illustrative Example No. 1-1

Problem: Calculate all previously discussed power efficiencies for an array that is comprised of ten modules of Type I as defined in Table 7-2 of Section 7-3. The modules are mounted to an open frame as described in Section 7-4, having outside dimensions of 5.5 X 0.60 m, and therefore, an area $A_a = 5.5 \times 0.60 = 3.3$ m^2. Assume that the solar cells actually operate at 65°C, and the solar intensity S is 1.0 kilowatts/m^2 and illuminates the solar cells perpendicularly. Assume further that at 65°C, the modules produce only 75% of their 25°C output.

Solution: The solar energy (actually power) falling onto the entire array is $P_a = SA_a = 1.0 \times 3.3 = 3.3$ kilowatts. The energy falling onto the ten modules is $P_m = SA_m = 1.0 \times 10 \times 0.533 \times 0.581 = 3.10$ kilowatts. The energy falling onto the solar cells, P_s, is found by using the fraction "Cell Area/Module Area" from Table 7-2: $P_s =$

0.53 X 3.10 = 1.64 kilowatts. Since about 5% of the cell area is covered by contacts, only 95% of the 1.64 kilowatts illuminate the active cell area; hence, the power falling onto the active areas is $P_i = 0.95 \times 1.64 = 1.56$ kilowatts. From Table 7-2, the module power output at 25°C cell temperature is 22 watts. For an array comprised of ten modules, the power output is 220 watts or 0.22 kilowatts. The array efficiencies, using the same subscripts for η as were used for P above, are as follow:

	At 25°C	At 65°C
$\eta_a = \dfrac{0.22}{3.30} \times 100\%$ =	6.7% × 0.75 =	5.0%
$\eta_m = \dfrac{0.22}{3.10} \times 100\%$ =	7.1% × 0.75 =	5.3%
$\eta_s = \dfrac{0.22}{1.64} \times 100\%$ =	13.4% × 0.75 =	10.1%
$\eta_i = \dfrac{0.22}{1.56} \times 100\%$ =	14.1% × 0.75 =	10.6%.

In actual installations, these efficiencies may be further reduced by wiring losses, dust accumulations, and other factors.

Illustrative Example No. 1-2

Problem: Assume that a flat, oriented space array is required to supply 1000 watts (1.0 kilowatt) of electric power during the sunlight period of the orbit. The eclipse duration is 10% of the orbit time, and the array life is 10 years. Also assume that solar cells are available at a cost of $1.0/$cm^2$, having in-orbit efficiencies of 10%, and weighing 0.1 g/cm^2. Other solar cell array materials cost $5000/$m^2$ and weigh 400 g/m^2. The array structure and orientation drive weighs 20 kg and costs $5000/kg. All assembly and test costs amount to $10,000/$m^2$. Determine the array system's general and specific performance, mass, size, and cost figures.

Solution: From Section 9-3, the solar power in space is 1.35 kilowatts/m^2. The solar cells convert 10% of this power, or $0.10 \times 1.35 = 0.135$ kilowatts/m^2 = 135 watts/m^2. Since 1000 watts of output are required, we need

$$\frac{1000 \text{ watts}}{135 \text{ watts/m}^2} = 7.4 \text{ m}^2 = 74,000 \text{ cm}^2$$

of solar cell area. At a cost of $1/cm^2$, the total cell cost is $74,000. At a cell weight of 0.1 g/cm^2, the total cell weight is 0.1 $(g/cm^2) \times$ 74,000 (cm^2) = 7400 g = 7.4 kg. The other material cost is 5000 $(\$/m^2) \times 7.4 (m^2)$ = $37,000, and the weight is 400 $(g/m^2) \times 7.4 (m^2)$ = 2960 g = 3.0 kg. The cost of the structure and orientation drive is 5000 $(\$/kg) \times 20 (kg)$ = $100,000. Assembly and test costs are 10,000 $(\$/m^2) \times$ 7.4 (m^2) = $74,000.

The amount of energy produced in 10 years, with 10% eclipse time (or 90% illumination time) is

10 (years) $\times$ 365 (days/year) $\times$ 24 (hours/day)

$\times$ 0.90 (illumination time ratio) $\times$ 1000 (watts)

   = 78,840,000 watt-hours

   = 78,840 kilowatt-hours

   = 78.84 megawatt-hours

The cost for this energy, ignoring launch and development costs, is

$$\frac{285,000\ (\$)}{78,840\ (\text{kilowatt-hours})} = \$3.6/\text{kilowatt-hour.}$$

By comparison, U.S. domestic energy consumption costs were about 3 to 6¢/kilowatt-hour during the late 1970's. Summarizing the above data, we can prepare the following specification sheet:

1-14. Terrestrial Flat-Plate Arrays

Operational photovoltaic power systems in the field have shown performances that ranged from exhilarating successes to dismal failures. Success was typically achieved by over-designed systems located in dry, desert-like areas, while failures occured largely in marginally designed systems that were subject to adverse environments. Marginal designs include systems that have insufficient output voltage at their actual operating temperature, insufficient corrosion protection, or both. In some cases, materials have deteriorated from ultraviolet sunlight, in others by corrosion due to the effects of humidity. However, even though the total terrestrial photovoltaic experience is still small, it has been clearly demonstrated—largely outside the U.S.—that photovoltaic power generators can operate for many years—indeed, even for decades—in high-cloud and high-fog areas, in salty ocean air environments, at low and high geographic latitudes, and at low and high elevations. Prerequisite for successful operation at any location is sound engineering, selection of the best materials available for the job, good fabrication process control, and appropriate consideration to adequate design margins.

Only a relatively small amount of reliable performance and degradation data for existing photovoltaic power systems is available. How-

Power output in sunlight		1000 watts
Orbital lifetime (90% sun time)		10 years
Array mass (weight)		30.4 kg
Solar cells	7.4 kg	
Other materials	3.0 kg	
Structure and orientation	20.0 kg	
Array size		7.4 m^2
Array cost		$285,000
Solar cells	$ 74,000	
Other materials	$ 37,000	
Structure and orientation	$100,000	
Assembly and test	$ 74,000	
Power per unit mass: 1000/30.4 =		32.9 watts/kg
Power per unit area: 1000/7.4 =		1.35 watts/m^2
Cost per unit power: 285,000/1000 =		285 $/watt
Energy per unit cost: 78,840,000/285,000 =		277 watt-hours/$
Energy cost: 285,000/78,840 =		3.61 $/kilowatt-hour
Mass per unit area: 30.4/7.4 =		4.11 kg/m^2

ever, these data are typically not applicable to today's technology; therefore, they are not presented here. Data of general applicability are reflected throughout this handbook, where appropriate (as in the following).

Some of the experience gained in the U.S. since 1976 includes the performance of a total of 16 photovoltaic systems that were installed as part of the Department of Energy Photovoltaic Program.[13] These systems were used to power seven different load types. After a two year period, the status (as of May 1978) was as described below. (All systems use a shunt regulator and are equipped with ampere-hour meters in the array and battery circuits.)

System 1 (see Table 1-3) was located for four months at a remote site at Isle Royale National Park, Michigan, and operated a small refrigerator. Of the six 100 ampere-hour automotive batteries, one was broken by accidental dropping and a second was found dry after four months. The array delivered only 59% of its rated output; however, the refrigerator consumed only 76.5% of its predicted consumption (see Table 1-3), so that the system was able to perform its function.

System 2 also powered a small, recreational vehicle type of refrigerator, located in a remote

Table 1-3. Performance of 16 U.S. Installations.[13]

System	Design Ratings			Actual Conditions (Percentage of Rating)	
	Watts	Volts	Ampere-hours	Power %	Load %
1	220	12	600	59	76.5
2	220	12	600	81	48
2 (modified)	330	12	600	78	48
3	294	12	3000	84	58
4	294	12	3000	85	64
5	116	12	200	95	92
6	111	24	60	N/A*	N/A*
7	74	24	60	88	N/A*
8	74	24	60	N/A*	N/A*
9	148	24	1060	86	N/A*
10	111	24	60	N/A*	N/A*
11	74	24	60	74	N/A*
12	163	12	400	82	79
13	163	12	400	82	79
14	23	12	100	82	79
15	23	12	100	82	79
16	446	120	100	71	10

*Percentages not available.

Indian village in Arizona. Initially, the system consisted of a 220 watt array mounted about 5 meters above ground, and six 100 ampere-hour automotive batteries. A defective refrigerator destroyed the initial set of batteries. During the winter months, two 20 watt, 12 volt dc fluorescent lights were installed, requiring the array size to be increased to 330 watts during the warmer season. Extensive deep discharge cycles had caused shorted cells in two of the batteries, and all batteries were replaced. Additional problems encountered were an ampere-hour meter that gave erroneous readings at low bus voltages, dust accumulation on the array (causing an estimated 10% power loss), and one defective module, showing growing encapsulant voids beneath the solar cells.

Systems 3 and 4 are installed on U.S. Forest Service lookout towers in the Lassen and Plumas National Forests in California. The batteries are of the lead-calcium type. The loads consists of a 3 ft^3 refrigerator, a water pump to supply household needs, fluorescent and incandescent lights, and radio and television equipment. No operational problems have occurred.

System 5 is installed on Interstate Highway 10 between Tucson and Phoenix, Arizona, powering a changeable message sign. The electrical loads consist of a continuously operating transmitter/receiver, an occasionally operating motor that drives the message display, flashing strobe lights, and a bank of fluorescent lights which illuminate the sign. Problems encountered included a complete discharge of the electric vehicle type batteries while the motor had stalled (due to jamming of the sign mechanism) and two other battery discharges caused by excessive sign use during long periods of cloudy weather.

Systems 6 through 11 power remote automatic meteorological observation systems (R.A.M.O.S.) located at Long Island, New York; Clines Corners, New Mexico; South Point, Hawaii; Point Retreat (Admiralty Island), Alaska; Halfway Rock, Maine; and Dry Tortugas, Florida. All systems use their original 50 ampere-hour gelled electrolyte type batteries, except the Point Retreat system, which is augmented with 1000 ampere-hours of lead-calcium batteries. The South Point station is not operating for non-power system related difficulties. The Clines Corner array suffered seven fractured cells, distributed over three modules, apparently from hailstones, without loss of power. On the Point Retreat array, three modules were damaged by vandals, requiring replacement. The complete installation at Halfway Rock was swept into the sea by 12 meter high waves in 1978. After one year, the Long Island station array was found to exhibit opens in two of the three series strings, due to encapsulant delamination, cell contact corrosion, and shorting. Damage to other parts of this weather station from high seas or high wind was also observed. All operating stations have performed well in a functional sense, even though exact ampere-hour data were not taken because of the remoteness of most stations.

Systems 12 through 15 are installed to power insect survey traps in East Central Texas. The traps are remotely located in fields, operate only at night, and are moved from season to season. Two systems use 40 watt ultraviolet lamps and two systems are of the electrically charged grid type. Problems encountered included one open-circuit failure of a module, one ampere-hour meter failure, and discharged batteries of one system due to a shorted trap, caused by a nest built by wasps during daylight hours.

System 16 powers a 120 volt dc water cooler at an Interagency Visitor Center at Lone Pine, California, near the Mt. Whitney entrance portal. The system is designed as an educational attraction. The solar cell array operation is adversely affected by deposits of dust and alkaline materials from nearby Owens Lake, and by short afternoon hours caused by the towering Sierra Nevada Mountains, but not sufficiently to cause problems. The battery is of the electric vehicle type.

The primary lessons learned from these installations are that environmental protection of the modules is of paramount importance and that the system must be adequately sized (or oversized) relative to the anticipated load profile. (For a description of the modules discussed above, see Section 7-3. For sizing calculations, see Chapters 2 and 3.)

1-15. Terrestrial Concentrator Arrays

Long-term performance data from operational photovoltaic concentrator systems have not been reported. Preliminary experimental results are encouraging and indicate that potentially lower fabrication and installation costs compared to those for fixed flat plat arrays may be achievable. However, the reliability characteristics of the solar cells operating at higher temperatures and the maintenance requirements for the sun-tracking mechanisms are totally unknown at this time and may adversely affect the long-term cost posture of concentrator arrays. A reasonable experimental data base for terrestrial concentrator arrays should become available by about 1980.

1-16. Space Flat Plate Arrays

The power output per unit area of oriented and semi-oriented flat plate arrays in space is determined primarily by the inherent solar cell efficiency and by the solar cell orbital operating temperature. The latter is related to the cell's heat absorption and the heat emission properties of the coverglass and the substrate.

Factors which determine the array's power output per unit mass (weight) include, primarily, the mass of the array's structural components and, secondarily, the mass of the solar cells and coverglasses and the solar cell packing density.

The power output per unit mass of a number of arrays are shown in Fig. 1-14 in relation to their sizes. This figure reflects published information that is not necessarily self-consistent. This is because power, radiation fluence, mission duration, solar cell and cover type, temperature, and natural frequency all have an effect on the specific weight and power density characteristics. The numbers reported in the literature reflect these effects, but usually they are not stated explicitly. Therefore, when making comparisons between different designs, it should be realized that most arrays were designed to meet some very specific mission requirements within some very specific design and, frequently, schedule and cost constraints.

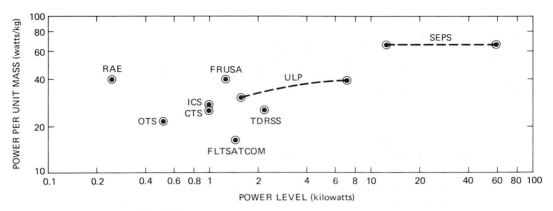

Fig. 1-14. Comparative space array end-of-life performance.

Only a few arrays were designed to accommodate an entire class of missions; but even these are usually modified considerably from one application to the next. (For further details on array designs, see Chapter 7.)

1-17. Spinning Space Arrays

Body-mounted solar cell arrays on spin-stabilized satellites, depicted in Fig. 1-12, have grown in diameter and length as the available launch vehicles grew in size.[14,15] Recently, telescoping cylindrical arrays that deploy in space have been developed. Typical array electrical and performance characteristics are shown in Table 1-4.

The 10 ohm · cm silicon solar cells for Intelsat I were of the electroless nickel contact type, solder dipped, and assembled into rigid five cell shingles. The cell AR coating was SiOx.

Table 1-4. Spinning Array Characteristics and Synchronous Orbit Performance.[14,15]

Satellite	Flight	Launch Date (months/year)	Solar Cell Size (mm)	Main Array NS	Main Array NP	Weight (kg)	Predicted Power (watts)	Predicted Power (years)	Power Degradation in Orbit After Number of Years 1	2	3	4
Intelsat I	(Early Bird)		10 × 20	60	92					0.85		0.79
Intelsat II	F-3		10 × 20	60	180					0.82		
	F-4		20 × 20	60	102					0.81		
Intelsat III	F-2		20 × 20	67	160		180			0.89	0.88	
	F-3									0.90	0.89	
	F-4									0.90	0.86	
	F-6									0.91		
	F-7									0.89		
Intelsat IV	F-1	5/75	20 × 20	64	660	72.9	400	7				
	F-2	1/71							0.94	0.90	0.88	0.87
	F-3	12/71										
	F-4	1/72										
	F-5	6/72										
	F-6	8/73										
	F-7	11/74										
Intelsat IV A		9/75	20 × 62	64	220	71.9	522	7				
T.A.C.S.A.T.		2/69	20 × 20	71	840	83.6	750	3	0.96	0.94	0.925	
Telesat	F-1	11/72	20 × 20	72	270	33.1	217	7	0.94	0.925	0.91	
	F-2	4/73										
	F-3	5/75										
Western Union	F-1	4/74	20 × 20	72	270	23.1	217	7	0.94	0.925	0.91	
	F-2	10/74										

For Intelsat II, the solar cell contacts were changed to solder dipped TiAg and the solar cell interconnectors became flexible. The cells for Flight 2 used corner dart contacts, but the cells for Flight 4 used bar contacts. Bar contact cells were also used for the later Intelsat arrays.

All solar cell covers for the arrays shown in Table 1-4 were made from 0.30 mm thick fused silica (Corning Type 7940 glass) and carried both a magnesium fluoride anti-reflective coating and an ultraviolet reflective filter having a 410 nm cut-on wavelength.

1-18. Space Concentrator Arrays

Concentrator arrays for space applications have been proposed many times but have never actually been flown. The proposed concepts for space are similar to the terrestrial concepts except that they must be very light and either be folded and stowed for launch or fabricated and assembled in space. A number of proposed concentrator concepts are discussed in Sections 7-23 and 7-24.

1-19. Space Array Orbital Performance

There is generally a considerable lapse of time between solar cell procurement for a given project and completion of orbital data analysis, typically ranging from three to seven years. Adding two years for the design and development phase, the solar cell array designer can typically be expected to wait for from five to ten years (conceptual design to array end-of-life) or more before he has full confirmation of the adequacy (or inadequacy) of his design efforts.

The orbital performance of solar cell arrays can be obtained from two sources: solar cell flight experiments (discussed in Chapter 4) and operational satellite array performance. The orbital performance of solar cells and their rate of degradation has been found to differ somewhat between different satellites in the same orbit and under the same environmental stress.

Table 1-5. Pioneer Solar Orbits.

Parameter	Pioneer VI	Pioneer VII	Pioneer VIII
Perigee (AU)	0.814	1.010	0.992
Apogee (AU)	0.985	1.125	1.089
Inclination (degrees)	0.1695	0.097	0.057
Period (days)	311.3	402.9	387.5

Pioneer VI, VII, and VIII.[15,16] The array consisted of 10,368 conventional n-on-p silicon solar cells of 1 ohm · cm base resistivity mounted on a cylindrical substrate of 94 cm diameter and 89 cm height. The cells, 1×2 cm in size, are covered by 0.15 mm thick microsheet covers with blue reflective coatings. The covers were attached to the cells after the overlapping type modules were assembled and were then mounted to the substrate. Sufficient excess adhesive provided protection of those active solar cell areas not shielded by coverglass. At 1.0 AU,* the array operated at +5°C and produced 80 watts at its maximum power point; at 1.2 AU, it operated by -21°C and produced 60 watts. The array, spinning at 60 rpm, was oriented with its spin axis normal to the ecliptic plane. The three spacecraft are in solar orbits outside the earth's radiation belts; the orbital parameters are noted in Table 1-5.

The solar cells were connected into 48 strings, each of 54 cells in series by four cells in parallel. Each string was connected to the bus through an isolation diode with approximately 1 volt forward drop. The nominal operating bus voltage of the spacecraft was 31 volts at 1.0 AU. The power subsystem used a storage battery but no voltage regulators.

The performance data was obtained from onboard telemetry. Bus current, bus voltage, and array temperature were measured in succession. The telemetry resolution introduced resolution errors up to the following magnitudes: voltage, 1.8%; voltage error due to temperature error, 1.2%; current, 2.4%.

*AU = astronomical unit.

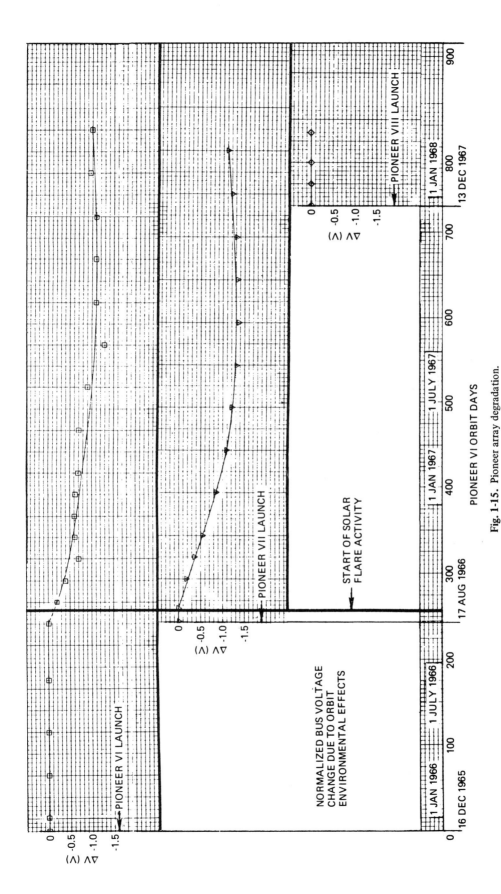

Fig. 1-15. Pioneer array degradation.

Figure 1-15 shows the changes in output voltage of three different Pioneer solar arrays launched at different times. This figure indicates that "free space" environments—within the accuracy and resolution of the data—had no measurable effects on the voltage of the Pioneer VI array for 259 days, and on the Pioneer VII array for 15 days. After this time (September 2 through 4, 1966), a large solar flare, consisting predominantly of protons, was observed. The flare was characterized by a total integrated flux of 17.2×10^7 protons/cm^2 of >25 million electron volts (MeV) over a three day period, occurring in two peaks, one on September 3, 1966, and the other on September 4, 1966.

In addition to this solar flare, two other major solar events, consisting mostly of electrons, occurred in a period from August 28 through September 10, 1966.

Figure 1-15 shows significant voltage degradation commencing immediately following the proton flare of September 2 to 4, both on the Pioneer VI and VII arrays. It is interesting to note that the flare apparently started a solar cell degradation process which continued for approximately 200 days after the event, then stopped, and about 450 days after the flare, converted into an improvement indicative of radiation damage annealing.

Based on the foregoing, it may be concluded (with considerable caution) that a solar flare proton dose of 17.2×10^7 protons/cm^2 of 25 MeV energy may produce a voltage degradation as high as 4%. Figure 1-16 shows the array operating points for various orbit conditions.

Initial Defense Satellite Communications System (I.D.S.C.S.).[17, 18] A study of the solar arrays on 19 U.S. Air Force I.D.S.C.S. satellites in a drifting, near-synchronous orbit showed that the best and worst case degradations projected to five years, encompassing all cell and non-cell (i.e., coverslide system) losses, were 12.5% and 16.8% for short-circuit current, and 1.7% and 5.5% for open-circuit voltage, respectively.

The calculated cell degradations due to electrons and flare protons penetrating the coverslide shield indicated that maximum damage regions appeared at electron energies near 0.7 MeV and at proton energies near 3 MeV. The ratio of calculated electron to proton cell damage was about 5 to 2.

Interpretation of these results and calculations within the limits of the statistical uncertainties involved and a knowledge of ground cell irradiation data, led to the following conclusions: non-cell losses affecting I_{sc} ranged from 6 to 12%, while cell losses were only about 6% (projected to 5 years). The basic V_{oc} loss was about 2%, but an additional 0 to 3% was observed and credited to low-energy proton damage. The best equivalent fluence for the 5 year projection was 1.2×10^{14} electrons · cm^{-2} of 0.8 MeV energy.

The solar cells were a 1×2 cm conventional n-on-p boron doped silicon cell of 1964 vintage with a base resistivity ranging between 7 and 13 ohm · cm. All cells were shielded by 0.51 mm thick fused silica covers applied with Dow Corning XR-6-3489 adhesive. The solar cells were assembled in overlapping (shingled) fashion and excessive cover adhesive was not removed from glassed cell assemblies, thus providing some low-energy proton protection.

The I.D.S.C.S. satellite shape was a symmetrical polyhedron consisting of two octahedral truncated pyramids joined by an octagonal cylindrical center section. The height of the satellite body was 79 cm, and the diameter of the circle circumscribing the octagonal cylinder was 91 cm.

The nominal orbits for the three launches, together with their launch dates, are given in Table 1-6. The individual satellite orbits differed slightly because each had a slightly different initial velocity to ensure separation and eventual distribution around the earth. The satellites tumbled in orbit.

Surprisingly large variations were observed in presumably identical satellite solar cell arrays, both as to initial array outputs and to cell degradation rates on-orbit. Initial short-circuit currents and open-circuit voltages showed a near Gaussian distribution, spanning 10.1% and

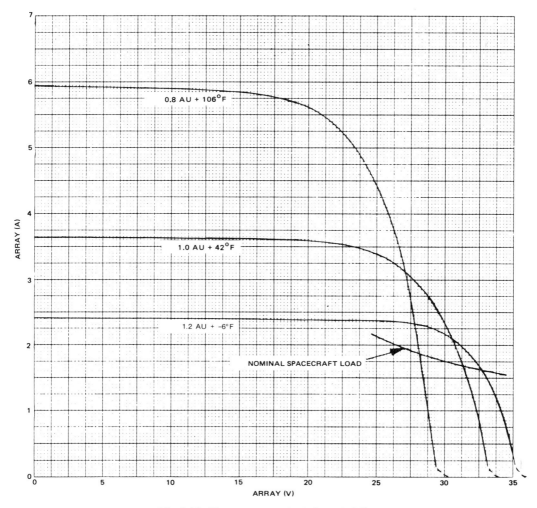

Fig. 1-16. Pioneer array output characteristics.

Table 1-6. I.D.S.C.S. Satellite Earth Orbits.

Orbital Parameter	First Launch June 16, 1966	Second Launch Jan. 18, 1967	Third Launch July 1, 1967
Number of satellites	7	8	4
Apogee (km)	34458	33947	33758
Perigee (km)	33716	33634	33690
Eccentricity	0.0092	0.0039	0.00086
Inclination (degrees)	0.042	0.41	6.998
Period (minutes)	1350	1335	1332

1.8%, respectively. This spread was attributed to the random solar cell panel selection used in the satellite construction and, in part, to telemetry sensor variations. When all initial parameters were normalized to unity, subsequent degradation levels over five years were again observed to span 5.0% for I_{sc}, and 4.0% for V_{oc}. Figure 1-17 presents the best and worst case cell short-circuit current degradation curves, extrapolated to five years, for the first two launches (15 satellites). All cell and non-cell losses were included. Figure 1-18 presents similar open-circuit voltage curves and includes a curve which corresponds to the calculated

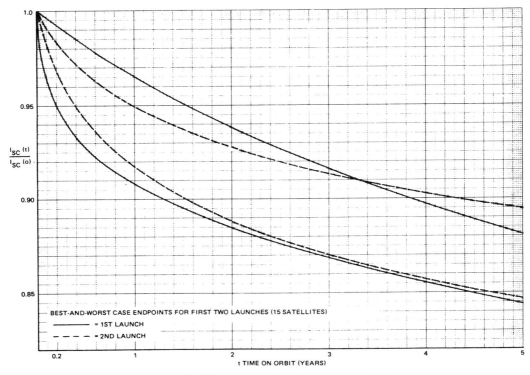

Fig. 1-17. IDSCS array short-circuit current degradation.

V_{oc} degradation, based on the updated radiation environment and best available damage coefficient data. This curve is observed to present an average path between the mea-sured extremes. Figure 1-19 presents the calculated I_{sc} degradation of the cells alone, due to radiation. Comparing this curve with the two extreme curves of Fig. 1-17, the best

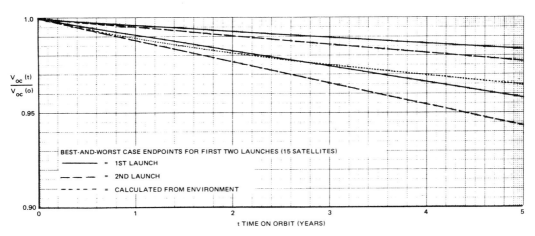

Fig. 1-18. IDSCS array open-circuit voltage degradation.

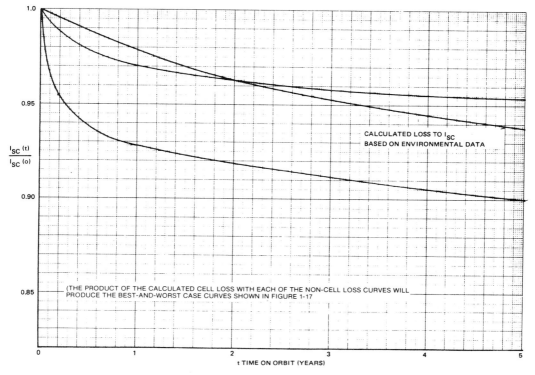

Fig. 1-19. IDSCS array non-cell and short circuit current degradation.

and worst case estimations of non-cell (i.e., coverslide) losses projected to five years is presented.

Spinning Arrays in Synchronous Orbit.[20, 21, 22] The characteristics of a number of cylindrical arrays, body-mounted to spin-stabilized com-munication satellites that have been operating successfully in geosynchronous orbit, are shown in Table 1-4. The degradation data should be viewed with regard to solar cycle-related solar proton events, as described in Section 9-46. However, significant differences in degradation rates still exist and cannot be explained satis-

Table 1-7. Typical Solar Cell Array Degradation in Orbit.[20]
(Reprinted with permission of the IEEE)

Type of Degradation	Time in Synchronous Equatorial Orbit		Time in 1000 km Circular Polar Orbit	
	1 year	7 years	1 year	7 years
1 MeV fluence (electrons · cm^{-2})*	4.3×10^{13}	3.0×10^{14}	2×10^{14}	1.0×10^{15}
Solar cell degradation (%)	3	15	8	20
Non-cell losses (%)	4 to 10	4 to 10	4 to 10	4 to 10
Total losses (%)	7 to 13	19 to 25	12 to 18	24 to 30

*Note: Calculated values for infinite back shielding thickness.

factorily. The best estimate of array degradation, based on a large number of spinning as
well as flat plate arrays and solar cell ground
and orbital experiments, is summarized in
Table 1-7.

All of the Intelsat I and II arrays degraded
at a slightly greater rate than was expected
from penetrating charged particle radiation
considerations. Low energy proton degradation
was presumed for Intelsat I and Intelsat II F-3
and F-4, in addition to a possible solar cell
contact deterioration on F-4 due to humidity
effects on the solderless Ti-Ag contacts and/or
thermal stresses on the cell interconnectors
(silver mesh), arising from an epoxy cell to
substrate adhesive. On F-4, a damage reversal
was noted that is similar to that observed in
laboratory low-energy proton testing. No
anomalous degradations were observed on the
Intelsat III and later solar cell arrays.

The damage-equivalent 1 MeV fluence due to
geomagnetically trapped radiation environment
alone, for the 0.30 mm thick conventional
n-on-p silicon solar cells, protected by 0.30 mm
thick fused silica covers, was determined to be
2.1×10^{13} electrons/cm^2/year.[14] The large
solar flare proton event of August 4, 1972 was
estimated to be equivalent to a 1 MeV dose of
4.7×10^{13} electrons/cm^2. The effect of this
flare on the Intelsat IV F-2 array performance is
illustrated in Fig. 1-20.

The optical transmission degradation of the
covers and the cover adhesive was assessed to be
in the order of 2% and was estimated to occur
during the first two months in orbit. This

degradation is contrasted by laboratory ultraviolet radiation testing, which showed a 4%
degradation.[14]

REFERENCES

1. *International Rectifier Solar Cell and Photocell Handbook*, International Rectifier Corp., 1960.
2. *Technical Information on Sharp Solar Battery Power Supply System*, Sharp Corporation, Osaka, Japan.
3. *Proceedings of the Photovoltaic Power and its Applications in Space and on Earth International Congress*, "The Sun in the Service of Mankind," Paris, July 1973.
4. B. Dalibot (p. 565) in *Proceedings of the Photovoltaic Power and its Applications in Space and on Earth International Congress*, "The Sun in the Service of Mankind," Paris, July 1973.
5. N. S. Lidorenko and B. V. Tarnizhevski (p. 533) and A. P. Landsman and N. V. Pulmanov (p. 545) in *Proceedings of the Photovoltaic Power and its Applications in Space and on Earth International Congress*, "The Sun in the Service of Mankind," Paris, July 1973.
6. *Proceedings of the ERDA Semiannual Solar Photovoltaic Program Review Meetings*, Silicon Technology Programs Branch, San Diego, California, Jan. 1977. Document No. CONF-770112.
7. M. D. Pope, "Solar Photovoltaic Field Tests and Applications Project," (p. 165) in *Proceedings of the Semiannual Review Meetings*, Silicon Technology Programs, compiled by the Solar Energy Research Institute, Golden, Colorado, March 1978.
8. D. D. Faehn, "Military Applications of Photovoltaic Systems," (p. 617) in *Proceedings of the ERDA Semiannual Solar Photovoltaic Program Review Meetings*, Silicon Technology Programs Branch, San Diego, California, Jan. 1977, Document No. CONF-77012.
9. TRW Space Log 1977, TRW Systems Group, TRW, Inc., 1978.
10. *Conference Records of the 13th IEEE Photovoltaic Specialists Conference*, Washington, D.C., June 1978.
11. Rauschenbach *et al* (p. 232) in *Conference Records of the 13th IEEE Photovoltaic Specialists Conference*, Washington, D.C., June 1978.
12. A. D. Tonelli and W. V. McRae, "Design and Analysis of a 5000-MW GaAlAs Satellite Power System," (p. 1412) in *Proceedings of the 12th Intersociety Energy Confersion Engineering Conference*, *Vol.* II, August 1977.
13. A. F. Ratajczak (p. 1272) in *Conference Records of the 13th IEEE Photovoltaic Specialists Conference*, Washington, D.C., June 1978.
14. L. G. Goldhammer and S. W. Gelb (p. 562) in

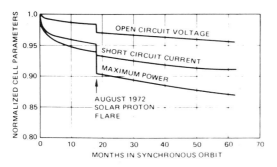

Fig. 1-20. Normalized performance of Intelsat IV F-2
solar cell array. (Reprinted with permission from the
Institute of Chemical Engineers)[23]

Conference Records of the 13th IEEE Photo-voltaic Specialists Conference, Washington, D.C., June 1978.

15. Based on data from TRW DSSG, TRW, Inc.

16. W. R. Baron, "The Solar Array for the Pioneer Deep Space Probe," TRW Systems, January 1967.

17. "Flight Data Analysis of Power Subsystem Degradation at Near Synchronous Altitude," Report No. **WDL-TR4223,** Philco-Ford Corp., July 1970.

18. W. T. Picciano et al (p. 221) in Conference Record of the 8th IEEE Photovoltaic Specialists Conference, 1970.

19. Conference Record of the 8th IEEE Photovoltaic Specialists Conference, 1970.

20. D. J. Curtin and R. L. Statler, "Review of Radiation Damage to Silicon Solar Cells," in IEEE Transaction on Aerospace and Electronic Systems, Vol. **AES-11,** No. 4, July 1975.

21. D. J. Curtin and J. F. Stockel, "Evaluation of the Performance of Solar Arrays in INTELSAT Spacecraft at Synchronous Altitude," (pp. 736–742) in Proceedings of the Intersociety Energy Conversion Engineering Conference, 1969.

22. W. H. Wright, "Design and Orbital Performance of the INTELSAT III Power System," in Proceedings of the 7th Intersociety Energy Conversion Engineering Conference, 1972.

23. L. G. Goldhammer and S. W. Gelb (p. 1379) in Eleventh Intersociety Energy Conversion Engineering Conference Proceedings, Vol. **II,** 1976.

2
Array Analysis

ANALYTICAL CONCEPTS

2-1. The Role of Analysis

The process of breaking something complex down into simpler elements and subjecting them to scrutiny is called analysis. In engineering, systems are broken down into subsystems, and subsystems into components. Everything is broken down until it becomes simple enough to be understood and to be converted into mathematical expressions that describe its properties, behavior, or function. The process of describing something physical by mathematical formulas is called analytical or mathematical *modeling*. The "model" represents something real and physical in abstract, mathematical terms.

The great advantage of having analytical models of a design and its elements is two-fold: 1) by studying the models, it is possible to figure out how to change, improve, and optimize the design, and 2) the performance and behavior of a design under a great variety of operational and environmental conditions can be predicted analytically long before the design is actually constructed and taken into service.

2-2. Atoms and Electrons

All matter is composed of atoms, also known as elements. An atom is the smallest particle of an element. Atoms, in turn, are composed of sub-atomic particles of which protons, neutrons, and electrons are the most important. An atom can be visualized as consisting of a small nucleus, made up of protons and neutrons, that is surrounded by orbiting electrons. The nucleus is made up of the same number of protons as there are electrons in the atom. This is because each proton carries a unit positive charge and each electron a unit negative charge, and both charges must be equal in magnitude (i.e., they must neutralize each other) by the principle of charge neutrality. The positive and negative charges in the atoms attract one another and hold the atom together. There are over 90 naturally occurring and over 10 man-made elements, and each one has a different number of electrons, protons, and neutrons.

Most of the mass (weight) of an element, or atom, is concentrated in its nucleus. A proton and a neutron each have a mass of 1.67×10^{-27} kg, while an electron has a mass of only 9.11×10^{-31} kg. Therefore, a proton is 1840 times as heavy as an electron.

In an atomic, or nuclear, process or reaction, atoms are broken up and thereby changed from one configuration into another. This change manifests itself as a transformation of one substance (element) into another.

The electrons that are part of an atom can be found in certain well-defined regions surrounding the nucleus; these regions are known as electron shells. Each shell can hold only a certain maximum number of electrons. The number of electrons in the various shells, and their relationship to the number required to completely fill the shells, determines the chemical activity of the element. The electrons in the outermost, incompletely filled shells are also known as the valence electrons. Atoms having completely filled shells, such as helium, neon, or xenon, are chemically very stable. All other elements are chemically unstable, or reactive, in different ways, so that they combine with others to form chemically stable compounds (molecules), such as water (hydrogen oxide), rust (iron oxide), or sand (silicon oxide, a raw material used for making silicon solar cells). Electrons also play roles in the processes of generating, conducting, and consuming electricity, and in defining the magnetic properties of materials.

2-3. Electric Charge

The experience of being electrically charged during periods of extremely low humidity is at time fascinating, but at other times annoying. Electric charging may result from walking across certain carpets while wearing certain foot gear. The subsequent electrical discharge to another person or metallic object can indeed be a shocking experience. Lightning flashes, like miniature thunderstorms, can be provoked by vigorous combing and brushing of hair. Inflated toy balloons, rubbed slightly, may cling tenaciously to walls and clothes. These phenomena are technically called *charging by friction*. During the close surface contact of two dissimilar surfaces, such as a hard rubber rod being rubbed by a catskin, electrons are transferred from one material to the other. The material that gains electrons (the rubber) is said to have become negatively charged, while the material that has lost electrons (the catskin) has become positively charged. Charging by friction due to strong air currents in the atmosphere during weather changes leads to charging of the clouds, followed by violent electric discharges from cloud to cloud or from clouds to the earth. Less spectacular, but not necessarily negligible, electric charging phenomena can occur on larger, non-conductive surfaces of terrestrial and space solar cell arrays.

The quantity of electric, or electronic, charge that one electron carries is 1.6×10^{-19} coulomb. This is the smallest quantity of charge that can exist. This charge is negative for electrons and positive for protons. Neutrons carry no charge; they are electrically neutral.

2-4. Conductors

A crystalline atomic structure and an abundance of freely moving valence electrons make most metals good conductors of electricity and heat. The different atoms are located in precise and symmetrical arrangements, forming an orderly lattice structure. The atomic nuclei with their inner, filled electron shells are visualized as being immobile, except that they may vibrate about their center positions, while the outer valence electrons are "free" to move about throughout the lattice similar to an electron "gas." Ordinarily, the electron gas is uniformly distributed throughout the conductor, because at any time and at any place in the material, the positive and negative charges must exactly equal one another, i.e., there must be charge neutrality.

Electrical conduction in a conductor arises from the application of an electric or magnetic force field when the electric circuit is completed. Thermal conduction arises from the application of a source of heat. Electrical or thermal conduction will take place only if there is energy transport from a higher to a lower potential.

The measure of a material's ability to conduct electricity is its conductance. Some materials are better conductors than others; i.e., they possess a higher conductance, even though they may be of the same physical size. Also, thicker conductors have a higher conductance than do thinner conductors made from the same material. Let l denote the length of a conductor, w the width, and t the thickness, as illustrated in Fig. 2-1a. The conductance of this

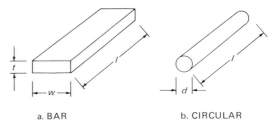

a. BAR   b. CIRCULAR

Fig. 2-1. Conductor shapes.

piece of conductor, denoted by the letter G, is given by

$$G = \sigma wt/l$$

where the Greek letter σ (sigma) stands for the material's specific conductance, also known as conductivity. The units of conductance and conductivity are "per ohm" and "per ohm · meter," also written "ohm^{-1}" and "ohm^{-1} · meter^{-1}" or "Ω^{-1}" and "$\Omega^{-1} \cdot m^{-1}$," respectively. For a conductor having an arbitrarily shaped cross-section denoted by A, wt is replaced by A. For round conductors, as shown in Fig. 2-1b, the cross-sectional area is $A = r^2\pi = d^2\pi/4$, so that the conductance becomes

$$G = \sigma d^2\pi/4l.$$

2-5. Insulators

Insulators, also known as dielectrics, do not conduct electricity under ordinary circumstances (see Section 2-6 for ionic current). Unlike metals, insulators have only few, if any, valence electrons available for the conduction of electricity.

The measures of an insulator's quality are its dielectric constant and its breakdown voltage. The dielectric constant, a dimensionless quantity, indicates how effective a material is relative to air when it is used in the construction of a parallel-plate capacitor. The breakdown voltage, also known as dielectric strength, indicates how much voltage a material, having given thickness, can withstand. Dielectric strength is usually given in units of kilovolts/mm or kilovolts/mil (1 mil = 0.001 inch = 0.025 mm).

2-6. Current

The flow of electric charges constitutes an electric current. For example, the movement of electrons through a conductor is a current. Electric current is analogous to a current of water: the electrons correspond to the water molecules (H_2O), and the quantity, or magnitude, of the current is in a direct relationship to the number of electrons, or water molecules, respectively, passing by a given point in a given time interval (the magnitude of the current does not depend upon how fast the particles are moving).

Electric current is measured in units of ampere or amps, denoted by the letter A. A current of 1.00 A is equivalent to the flow of 1.24×10^{20} electrons/second past a given point on a conductor. For comparison, water flow can be measured in units of cm^3/second. A water flow of 1 cm^3/second corresponds to the passage of 0.334×10^{20} water molecules/second.

In a conductor, electric current is always associated with the flow of electrons. In vacuum, current may result from the flow of electrons, protons, or ions. In dielectric materials and in conductive liquids, current is essentially carried by ions. In semiconductors, current is carried both by electrons and by holes (see Section 2-27).

The molecules of a substance may be split apart into ions by a chemical or electrical process called ionization. One of the two ions of each molecule is positively charged and the other is negatively charged by the same amount of charge. For example, a molecule of table salt is made up of one atom of sodium and one atom of chlorine. When dissolved in water, the molecules "dissociate" themselves into negatively charged chlorine ions and positively charged sodium ions that are free to move in response to an electric field applied to the solution (i.e., when an electric current is passed through the solution). The positive ions move in the direction of the electric field (see Section 2-7) while the negative ions move in the opposite direction. In the process of moving, chemical changes take place that depend upon the ions and the solution substance. Typically, gas atoms or molecules are liberated in the process, and the electrodes (i.e., the current lead-ins into the solution) are being chemically attacked (corroded). In the above example, the chlorine ion moves toward the anode (the positive electrode) and, upon its arrival, gives up an electron (i.e., contributes to current flow) and thereby becomes a chlorine atom. The sodium ion moves toward the cathode and, upon its arrival, picks up an electron (i.e., contributes to current flow) and becomes a sodium atom.

2-7. Electric Field

Sources of electricity, and conductors connected to them, are surrounded by electric fields, regardless of whether there is current flowing or not. When electric current flows in a circuit, magnetic fields are also present. Electric fields exert forces on electric charges. For illustration, consider the space between the two plane-parallel conductive plates in Fig. 2-2. A voltage source connected to the plates sets up an electric field, denoted by E, between the plates. The value of the field is

$$E = V/d$$

where d is the distance between the plates and V is the voltage. Now let a proton, labeled P and carrying a positive charge q, be placed into the space between the plates. Immediately, the proton will experience a force F which will accelerate it in the direction of the E-field from the positively charged plate toward the negatively charged plate. An electron in the same space will experience a force of the same magnitude as the proton, but this force will act in the opposite direction because the electron carries a negative charge (i.e., $-q$). The force acting on any charged particle in an electric field is given by

$$F = qE$$

or, in vector notation,

$$\mathbf{F} = q\mathbf{E}.$$

The charge q is measured in coulombs, the electric field E in volts/m or newtons/coulomb, and the force F in newtons.

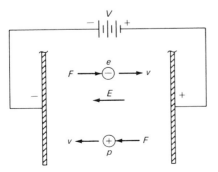

Fig. 2-2. Proton and electron in electric field.

Illustrative Example No. 2-1

Problem: For illustration, consider the upper plate in Fig. 2-2 to represent a solar cell (in cross-sectional view) and the bottom plate a solar array substrate. Let us assume that the solar cell is only partially bonded to the metallic substrate (not shown in the figure) so that we are actually looking at the air gap between the cell and the substrate. Let us assume further that the voltage difference between the cell and the substrate is 100 volts and that the gap width is 1 mm. What is the electric field strength in the gap? What is the force on an electron that sits loosely on the surface of the substrate? How long does it take for the electron to fly to the solar cell?

Solution: The electric field strength is

$$E = V/d = 100/0.001 = 100,000 \text{ volts/m}$$
$$= 10^5 \text{ volts/m.}$$

The force on the electron, having a charge of -1.6×10^{-19} coulombs, is

$$F = qE = -1.6 \times 10^{-19} \times 10^5$$
$$= -1.6 \times 10^{-14} \text{ newtons}$$

and is constant anywhere between the plates. The electron accelerates under the influence of the constant force. From physics, we know that a mass of "m" kg accelerates by "a" meters/second/second (m/s^2) under the influence of a force of F newtons according to Newton's law:

$$F = ma.$$

Rearranging terms,

$$a = \frac{F}{m} = \frac{1.6 \times 10^{-14}}{9.1 \times 10^{-31}} = 1.8 \times 10^{16} \text{ m/s}^2.$$

After having traveled the distance $d = 1$ mm $= 1 \times 10^{-3}$ m, its velocity v is

$$v = \sqrt{2ad} = \sqrt{2 \times 1.8 \times 10^{-3}} = 5.9 \times 10^6 \text{ m/s.}$$

The time t is

$$t = \frac{v}{a} = \frac{5.9 \times 10^6}{1.8 \times 10^{16}} = 3.3 \times 10^{-10} \text{ seconds}$$
$$= 0.33 \text{ nanoseconds.}$$

2-8. Potential and Voltage

The force that is able to push electrons through a conductor or a current through a circuit is known alternately as electromotive force (abbreviated EMF), electric potential, or voltage. In any source of electricity, voltage is always present and ready to push an electric current through a circuit as soon as that circuit is completed. Voltage is analogous to water pressure (also known as "head") in a water supply line, always ready to push a stream of water molecules through the pipe as soon as a faucet is opened. The presence of voltage in electrical circuitry is popularly referred to as the "wires being hot."

Voltage, or potential, is always measured between two points in a circuit. If the two points are labeled a and b, respectively, the voltage measured between these two points is denoted by V_{ab}. In this notation, it is understood that the positive voltmeter probe is connected to point a (presented by the first subscript) and the negative probe to point b. When voltages are measured relative to ("against") a common bus or ground, the subscripts are dropped. In electronic equipment, the "ground" may be connected to either the negative or to the positive power supply voltage terminal.

Voltage can be generated by a number of different processes: chemically, electromagnetically, and quantum mechanically. Chemical voltage generators include all types of battery cells, whether they are rechargeable or not, such as flashlight and automobile batteries. Generators of the rotating machinery type, such as those used in steam and hydroelectric

power generation stations, and automobiles ("dynamos" and "alternators") produce voltage electromagnetically. Quantum mechanical generators include solar cells, solar electric devices, and others (see Section 2-26 through 2-30).

Different materials develop electrical activity with respect to each other when in immediate contact or when immersed together in an electrically conductive medium. This phenomenon leads to electrolytic corrosion (see Chapter 9).

2.9. Electrical Circuits

Electrical circuits are designed to handle energy or information: their generation, their conversion from one form into another, their transmission from the source to the user, and finally, their utilization. One of the key features of an electrical circuit is that is must be a closed loop for it to function. This is illustrated in Fig. 2-3; the light bulb and switch are connected to the battery, and all points of the circuit are "hot." However, there is no current flow (current $i = 0$) as long as the switch remains open. With the switch open, the electric potentials, or voltages, measured at points a and b relative to point c, are identical, namely +3 volts. Similarly, the voltages at points c, d, e, and f, measured against point a, are identical and equal to −3 volts. Inasmuch as the voltages at d and e are the same, the voltage drop V_R across the light bulb (R) is zero.

With the switch closed, current i will flow out of the positive battery terminal, through the switch, through light bulb, and into the negative battery terminal: the circuit loop is

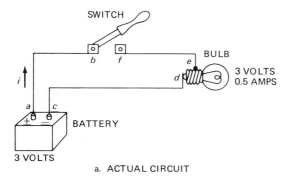

a. ACTUAL CIRCUIT

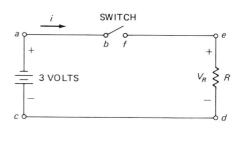

b. SCHEMATIC DIAGRAM

Fig. 2-3. Simple electric circuit.

completed. The same current i also flows internally in the battery, the battery's electromotive force being an "electric current pump." While the switch is closed, points a, b, f, and e are at the same voltage relative to points c and d. Hence, the voltage across the light bulb is $V_R = 3$ volts.

2-10. Sources and Generators

Solar cells, batteries, alternators, generators, and dynamos are all sources of electricity. Strictly speaking, they are all *energy converters*, "making" electricity out of solar, chemical, or mechanical energy. Different sources, or generators, of electricity exhibit different behavior under different loading conditions. Some sources show relatively little voltage output variation when different size electrical loads are connected, while other sources show relatively little current output variation. In circuit analysis, these two types of sources are idealized, the former as a voltage source and the latter as a current source. These sources are also known as *constant voltage generators* and *constant current generators*, respectively. In their idealized form, *voltage sources* are capable of supplying or absorbing infinite current, power, and energy, all at a constant voltage value. *Current sources* are capable of supplying or absorbing infinite voltage, power, and energy, all at a constant current value.

To more closely represent physical sources, voltage sources are always used in connection with a series resistance and current sources with a shunt resistance, as illustrated in Fig. 2-4. This figure also shows how one source can be changed into another.

Examples of voltage sources are electrochemical batteries such as those used for flashlights,

transistor radios, and automobiles. Solar cells are current sources.

Power (and energy) is "taken in" by an ideal source when either the voltage or the current is opposite in algebraic sign to the condition when the source "puts out" power. When a source "takes in" power, one portion of it is dissipated (converted into heat) in the resistance associated with that source, and the other portion is "absorbed" by the ideal source. The amount of power that is absorbed is equal to the product of the voltage across the current through the source. To find out where this power goes, one must write and solve an energy balance equation, utilizing the principle of conservation of energy (see Section 2-46).

2-11. Current Flow Convention

Consider the circuit containing an electrochemical battery shown in Fig. 2-5. By long-established convention, the current flow is from the positive battery terminal through the external circuit to the negative battery terminal, and then inside the battery from the negative to the positive battery terminal. Current always flows from a higher (more positive) potential to a lower (more negative) potential. A voltmeter connected to the battery with its positive lead attached to the positive battery terminal will provide a positive ("right") reading. An am-

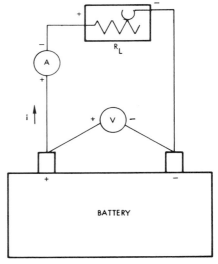

Fig. 2-5. Simple battery circuit.

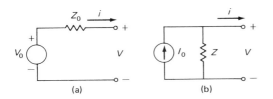

Fig. 2-4. Equivalent sources. Sources (a) and (b) are equivalent sources if $Z_0 = Z$ and $V_0 = ZI_0$.

meter connected into the circuit with its positive terminal to the positive battery terminal will also provide a positive ("right") reading (the positive terminal of an ammeter is always connected to the higher voltage point).

The flow of electrons is exactly opposite to that of the conventional current. For instance, the current flows "into" the anode (or plate) of a vacuum tube and comes "out" the cathode (filament), but the electrons are emitted by (come out of) the cathode and propagate to the anode.

A semiconductor diode is *forward biased* when the conventional current flows through it in the direction of the arrow of the printed-on diode symbol. This happens when the positive side of a voltage source is connected to the diode p-layer and the negative side to the n-layer. Hence, the diode symbol arrow points from p to n or from the anode to the cathode (Fig. 2-6).

The diode symbol printed on a zener diode is in the same direction and has the same physical meaning as that on the ordinary (rectifier) diode except that in use, zener diodes are reverse biased (i.e., the positive voltage is connected to the n-layer).

A non-illuminated solar cell is forward biased like a diode, by connecting the positive terminal of a bias supply to the cell p-contact. An illuminated solar cell develops a *forward output*; i.e., its p-contact is the positive voltage terminal. When the negative terminal of an overpowering external bias supply is connected to a cell p-contact, the cell becomes *reverse biased* regardless of the illumination level.

Solar cell and array I-V (current-voltage) characteristics are typically shown in the first quadrant of the voltage-current (abscissa-ordinate) coordinate system (Fig. 2-7b). This presentation is consistent with the theoretical solar cell model in which current is a function of voltage. It is equally consistent with electrical measurement techniques where positive voltage, current, and power output are obtained from the cell working into a resistive (positive conductance) load. Some presentations of the I-V curve in the fourth quadrant of the same coordinate system lead to negative current, positive voltage—and hence, confusingly, to negative power output from the cell into a negative conductance load.

2-12. Resistance and Resistors

Any conductor of electricity resists the flow of electrons; hence the name *resistance*. Different materials conduct electricity more or less readily; i.e., they exhibit different values of resistance, even if they are formed into the same physical size. Also, thinner conductors have greater resistance than do thicker conductors made from the same material. Let l denote the length of a conductor, w its width, and t its thickness, as illustrated in Fig. 2-1a. The *resistance* of this piece of conductor, denoted by

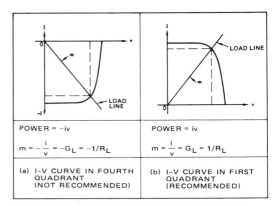

POWER = −iv	POWER = iv
$m = -\dfrac{i}{v} = -G_L = -1/R_L$	$m = \dfrac{i}{v} = G_L = 1/R_L$
(a) I–V CURVE IN FOURTH QUADRANT (NOT RECOMMENDED)	(b) I–V CURVE IN FIRST QUADRANT (RECOMMENDED)

Fig. 2-7. Solar cell I-V curve presentations.

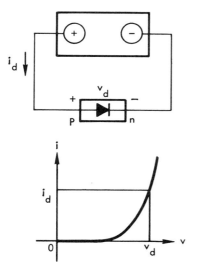

Fig. 2-6. Forward-biased p-n junction device.

the letter R, is given by

$$R = \rho l/wt$$

where the Greek letter ρ (rho) stands for the material's specific resistance, also known as *resistivity*. The units of resistance and resistivity are ohm and ohm · meter, also written Ω and Ω · m, respectively. For a wire having a arbitrarily shaped cross-section denoted A, wt is replaced by A. For round wires, as illustrated in Fig. 2-1b, the cross-sectional area is given by

$$A = r^2\pi = d^2\pi/4$$

and the foregoing equation becomes

$$R = 4\rho l/d^2\pi.$$

Circuit components designed to possess a given resistance value are called resistors. Resistors are identified according to their resistance value (ohms) and their maximum safe power handling capability (watts). In circuit analysis, resistors are assumed to behave ideally; that is, they can dissipate infinite amounts of energy without burning up and they always keep their assigned value. Physical resistors, however, change their value of resistance with temperature and are otherwise sensitive to a variety of influences. Physical conductors behave like physical resistors, even though in circuit analysis they are assumed to possess zero resistance and infinite current-carrying capability. (The effects of connecting resistors in parallel and in series are discussed in Section 2-22.)

A comparison of resistance with conductance G (see Section 2-4) reveals that one is the inverse of the other:

$$R = 1/G \text{ and } G = 1/R$$

$$\rho = 1/\sigma \text{ and } \sigma = 1/\rho.$$

The resistivity ρ is also known as the *bulk resistivity* of a material. For very thin sheets of conductive material for which the thickness t cannot be readily ascertained, the concept of *sheet resistivity*, denoted by ρ_s, is useful. For illustration, consider the conductive film in Fig. 2-8. The sheet resistance is given by

$$R_s = \rho_s e/w$$

and the sheet resistivity by

$$\rho_s = wR_s/l.$$

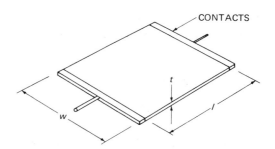

Fig. 2-8. Sheet resistance of a thin conductor.

The sheet resistivity ρ_s, measured in units of ohms or "ohms/square," is related to the bulk resistivity ρ through the film thickness t:

$$\rho = \rho_s t.$$

Illustrative Example No. 2-2

Problem: A thin conductive paint layer is used on a dielectric solar panel facesheet to conduct solar substorm related electric charges to spacecraft ground (see Section 3-40). A small sample was painted at the same time that the actual solar cell panel was painted. The small sample was 5 cm in width and 10 cm in length. Contacts were applied to either end, as shown in Fig. 2-8, and the resistance measured was 1000 ohms. The actual solar panel was 100 cm in width and 2 m in length. Contacts were applied along the edges of the 2 m dimension. What resistance reading do we expect on the actual panel?

Solution: For the small sample,

$$\rho_s = wR/l = 5 \times 1000/10 = 500 \text{ ohms/square.}$$

For the actual panel, we note that w and l are now interchanged, and that w and l must be in the same units:

$$R = \rho_s l/w = 500 \times 1.0/2.0 = 250 \text{ ohms.}$$

We expect to read 250 ohms.

2-13. Ohm's Law

The current I in a circuit is related to the voltage V that drives the circuit and its resistance R by Ohm's law:

$$I = V/R.$$

Conversely, if the current and the resistance are known, the voltage can be found from

$$V = IR.$$

If I and V are known, we can find

$$R = V/I.$$

Ohm's law always holds for any circuit under any condition, even though its mathematical expression may become quite complex at higher frequencies such as those used in radio communication.

2-14. Power

Power is the product of voltage and current. No power is drawn from a battery when the switch is open and current does not flow. Plenty of current, but not enough power, is drawn by the starter motor from an automobile battery whose voltage is low: it cannot crank the engine over. Power, requiring both voltage and current, is measured in watts, denoted by the letter W.

Illustrative Example No. 2-3

A solar cell array producing an output of 120 volts and 10 A produces a power of 120 × 10 = 1200 W. This is approximately the same amount of power a steam iron consumes. One horsepower is equivalent to exactly 746 W. Hence, the array power output is equivalent to 1200/746 = 1.61 horsepower.

The load resistance for this array can be calculated from Ohm's law:

$$R = V/I = 120/10 = 12 \text{ ohms}.$$

The power P dissipated in R can be calculated in different ways:

$$P = VI = I^2R = V^2/R.$$

For example, $I^2R = 10^2 \times 12 = 1200$ W and $V^2/R = 120^2/12 = 1200$ W.

2-15. Energy

Energy is the product of power and time. Energy, or work, is measured in units of watt-hours (Wh), kilowatt-hours (kWh), joules (J), or British Thermal Units (BTU). One kWh equals 1000 Wh or 3.6×10^6 J or 3412 BTU.

Illustrative Example No. 2-4

If the array described in Illustrative Example No. 2-3 were to produce 1200 W for 8 hours, it would produce an energy of 1200 × 8 = 9600 Wh or 9.6 kWh or $9.6 \times 3.6 \times 10^6 = 35 \times 10^6$ J or 9.6 × 3412 = 32,800 BTU. A typical, modest home air conditioner swallows up 32,800 BTU in about one hour. Therefore, if a solar cell array were to drive such an air conditioner, it would have to be eight times as large as the one described above.

2-16. Capacitance and Capacitors

Capacitors are electrical circuit components that have the capability of accumulating and storing electric charge. The amount of charge q (in coulombs) that can be stored in a capacitor depends upon its physical size and the material of which it is made, and is related to the capacitor's capacitance C (in farad) and the voltage V (in volts, abbreviated V) across the capacitor's terminals by

$$q = CV.$$

The capacitance of a parallel plate capacitor is given by

$$C = K\epsilon A/d$$

where K is the dielectric constant of the insulator between the two plates, the permittivity (a constant) is $\epsilon = 8.85 \times 10^{-12}$ coulomb^2/newton · m^2, A is the area of either plate in m^2, and d is the distance between the plates in m. The electric field strength (see Section 2-7) between the plates, away from the edges, is

$$E = V/d = q/K\epsilon A.$$

Capacitors resist a change of the voltage across them. A change in voltage across the capacitor, denoted by dV/dt (in units of volts per seconds) occurs when charges flow into the capacitor at a rate of i A(A = amps); i.e., i coulombs/second:

$$i = C\frac{dV}{dt}.$$

This equation indicates that the voltage across the capacitor increases as long as current feeds into it. Also, for a given value of current, larger capacitors, having a greater value of C, charge more slowly than smaller capacitors. The energy W stored in a capacitor is given by

$$W = CV^2/2 = qV/2 = q^2/2C$$

where the units of W are joules (watt · seconds), those of V are V (volts), q is in coulombs, and C is in farads (abbreviated F). The effects of connecting capacitors in parallel and series are discussed in Section 2-22.

Illustrative Example No. 2-5

Problem: Assume that a certain solar cell array has a capacitance of 100,000 pF = 1×10^{-7} F, and that a nearby lightning bolt feeds a current of 100 A for 1 second into the positive array bus. Calculate the rate of rise of the bus voltage and determine if there is a problem.

Solution: Assume the lightning bolt is a constant current source. From the above,

$$\frac{dV}{dt} = \frac{i}{C} = \frac{100}{10^{-7}} = 10^5 = 100,000 \text{ V/second.}$$

Hence, in 1 second, the voltage has risen by 100,000 V, which is indeed a problem, potentially destroying solar cells and cables. Note that a current of 100 A due to lightning assumes that the main bolt, carrying many thousands of amps, has been shunted by a lightning arrester.

2-17. Magnetism

Magnetic fields emanate from permanent magnets as well as from current-carrying conductors, exerting forces on magnetic materials and on moving electric charges. Let a charge q (coulombs) move with velocity v (m/second) in a magnetic field having a flux density (field strength) B (weber/m^2). The force on the charge (in newtons) is:

$$F = qvB \sin \phi.$$

The angle ϕ is measured between the direction of v and the direction of the flux B. In vector notation,

$$\mathbf{F} = q\mathbf{v} \times \mathbf{B}.$$

Parallel conductors through which currents flow attract or repel each other, depending upon

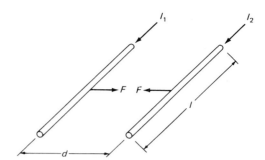

Fig. 2-9. Attraction force between two parallel current-carrying conductors.

whether the current is in the same or in the opposite direction. The force F (in newtons) per unit conductor length l (in meters) is given by

$$F/l = 2 \times 10^{-7} I_1 I_2 /d$$

where the currents I_1 and I_2 are measured in amps (A) and the separation between the conductors is d, measured in meters (m); see Fig. 2-9. This equation holds strictly only for infinitely long wires and in the absence of magnetic materials such as iron.

The magnetic properties of a material are related to the orbital motions of the electrons spinning about the atomic nuclei. If the electrons possess certain spin moments, the material exhibits a certain magnetic property. In solar cell array engineering, we differentiate between magnetically hard, magnetically soft, and non-magnetic materials.

Copper, aluminum, and stainless steel are non-magnetic. Construction (or carbon) steel, most low-expansion alloys containing iron and nickel, and materials used for transformer cores, are magnetically soft. Magnetically soft materials exhibit strong magnetism only while they are being magnetized, but lose almost all of their magnetism after the excitation stops. Magnetically hard materials remain strongly magnetic after having been magnetized.

Magnetic fields penetrate non-magnetic materials, but are shielded by magnetically soft materials.

Illustrative Example No. 2-6

Problem: To minimize magnetic moments, the positive and negative flat conductor bus bars on a space roll-out solar cell array are attached to the front and back sides of a 0.050 mm thick Kapton substrate blanket. The bus strips are 10 cm wide, are lined up over each other, and carry 100 A. Calculate the stress in the adhesive that holds the bus strips to the blanket.

Solution: The currents I_1 and I_2 are equal in magnitude, so that $I_1 = I_2 = 100$ A. The distance between the 10 cm (0.1 m) wide strips is 0.05 mm $(5 \times 10^{-5}$ m). Substituting these values into the above equation, the force per unit length is

$$F/l = 2 \times 10^{-7} \times 100^2 / 5 \times 10^{-5}$$

$$= 40 \text{ newtons/m.}$$

From Section 10-7, stress σ is force per unit area:

$$\sigma = \frac{40 \text{ newtons/m}}{0.1 \text{ m}} = 400 \text{ newtons/m}^2$$

$$= 0.06 \text{ psi.}$$

Since the currents flow in opposite directions, the force in the adhesive is in tension, trying to rip the bus strips away from the blanket. This force, however, is negligibly small.

2-18. Inductance and Inductors

Inductors are electrical circuit components that consist essentially of coils of wire. The inductor's property of interest is its inductance, denoted by the letter L and measured in units of henry. Any coil, or even a piece of straight wire, has a self-inductance that resists the change of current in a circuit. A change in current, denoted by di/dt, in units of A/second (amperes per second), results in an EMF, or voltage E developing across the inductor of magnitude

$$E = -L \, di/dt.$$

The minus sign relates the direction of the current with the polarity of E as depicted in Fig. 2-10, showing that E opposes the change in current. The energy W (in joules or watt-seconds) stored in an inductor's magnetic field is related to the current I (in A) flowing through it by

$$W = LI^2/2.$$

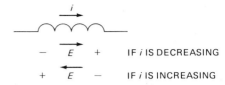

Fig. 2-10. Polarity of self-induced EMF.

The effects of solar cell array wiring inductance are of interest to the power control electronics designer, but usually play no role in array design. (The effects of inductors connected in parallel and in series are discussed in Section 2-22.)

2-19. AC and DC Current

The electrical output from a solar cell array is direct current, denoted by dc. Likewise, electrochemical batteries produce dc current; that is, the current is one direction only. By contrast, the public utility delivers alternating current, abbreviated ac, to operate our appliances and lighting equipment. Alternating current reverses its direction continually, at a rate of 60 times a second in the utilities, and millions of times a second when in the form of a television signal that enters a receiver from an antenna.

The advantage of ac over dc current is that it can readily be transformed from one voltage level to another. To utilize the power from a solar array for most applications, the array output must be changed from dc to ac current by a process known as *conversion*. Dc-to-dc or dc-to-ac converters are considerably more expensive than ac transformers, for the same power ratings.

2-20. Impedance

The term impedance indicates that a circuit analysis is concerned not only with dc (direct current), but also with ac (sinusoidally alternating current). The concept of impedance expands that of resistance, and includes the effects of capacitors and inductors on the current in a circuit in the analysis. The units of impedance, denoted Z, are also ohms, but there is a "real" and an "imaginary" part. The imaginary part is identified by j. The real part is identical to the resistance value, while the imaginary part is called reactance, denoted X. The inverse of impedance is admittance, Y, which consists of the real conductance, G, and the imaginary susceptance, B. These are written as

$$Z = R + jX \quad \text{(ohm)}$$

$$Y = G + jB \quad \text{(ohm}^{-1}\text{)}.$$

The physical significance of impedance is that in a circuit containing reactive components (capacitors and/or inductors), and connected to a source of alternating current (ac), the voltage typically observed across a circuit element varies differently than the current, both of them being time-wise *out of phase*.

The amount by which they are out of phase is known as the phase angle, denoted by the Greek letter ϕ (phi, pronounced as "fee"). The phase angle is given by

$$\tan \phi = \frac{X}{R} \quad \text{and} \quad \cos \phi = \frac{R}{|Z|}$$

where tan (tangent) and cos (cosine) are trigonometric functions that are tabulated in many texts, and are now preprogrammed into many medium-priced pocket calculators. The notation $|Z|$ indicates the *magnitude* of Z, given by

$$|Z| = \sqrt{R^2 + X^2}$$

and also measured in ohms. The power P dissipated in a resistor that is connected with a capacitor and/or inductor across an ac current source is

$$P = IV \cos \phi = IVR/|Z|.$$

The term "cos ϕ" is also known as the *power factor*, abbreviated "p.f." For a purely resistive circuit, p.f. $= \cos 0° = 1$. For a purely reactive circuit, p.f. $= \cos 90° = 0$.

The reactance X depends upon the frequency f and the type of circuit. For an inductive circuit,

$$X_L = 2\pi fL.$$

For a capacitive circuit,

$$X_c = -\frac{1}{2\pi fC}.$$

For a circuit having both inductance and capacitance,

$$X = X_L + X_C = 2\pi fL - \frac{1}{2\pi fC}.$$

The *output impedance* of an electric circuit is also its *internal impedance*. (The impedance of solar cells and arrays is treated in Section 2-35.)

Illustrative Example No. 2-7

Problem: A certain 120 V, 60 hertz ac motor is to be operated by day from a solar cell array and by night from the 120 V public utility. A dc-to-ac converter is available that changes the array power dc output into 120 V, 60 hertz ac, with 90% efficiency independent of load phase angle. While running, the motor has a dc resistance of 300 ohms and an inductance of 0.3 henry. How much power output must the array provide?

Solution: The reactance of the motor is

$$X = X_L = 2\pi fL = 2 \times \pi \times 60 \times 0.3 = 113 \text{ ohms.}$$

The motor impedance is

$$Z = 300 + j113 \text{ ohms.}$$

The magnitude of the impedance is

$$|Z| = \sqrt{R^2 + X^2} = \sqrt{300^2 + 113^2} = 320 \text{ ohms.}$$

The motor current is

$$I = V/|Z| = 120/320 = 0.375 \text{ A.}$$

The power drawn by the motor is

$$P_M = I^2R = 0.375^2 \times 300 = 42.2 \text{ W.}$$

The power could also be calculated using the phase angle:

$$P_M = IVR/|Z| = 0.375 \times 120 \times 300/320$$
$$= 42.2 \text{ W.}$$

Since only 90% of the array power reaches the motor, the array power output must be

$$P_A = P_M/0.90 = 42.2/0.90 = 46.9 \text{ W.}$$

CIRCUIT ANALYSIS

2-21. Circuit Modeling

Circuit analysis is concerned with the macroscopic behavior of electrical circuits and devices

Table 2-1. Current-Voltage Relationships of Circuit Elements.

Element	Parameter	Unit	Symbol	Current-Voltage Equation	Relationships
Resistor	Resistance R	Ohms		$v = Ri$	Power $P_R = Ri^2 = Gv^2$
	Conductance G	Ohms^{-1}		$i = Gv$	
Inductor	Inductance L	Henrys		$v = L\dfrac{di}{dt}$	$v = \dfrac{d\lambda}{dt}$, $\lambda = Li$
	Inverse Inductance Γ	Henrys^{-1}		$i = \dfrac{1}{L}\displaystyle\int_o^t v(t)dt + i(o)$	Stored energy $W_L = \dfrac{1}{2}Li^2 = \dfrac{1}{2}i\lambda = \dfrac{1}{2L}\lambda^2$
Capacitor	Capacitance C	Farads		$i = C\dfrac{dv}{dt}$	Stored energy $W_c = \dfrac{1}{2}Cv^2 = \dfrac{1}{2}qv = \dfrac{1}{2C}q^2$
	Inverse Capacitance D	Farads^{-1}		$v = \dfrac{1}{C}\displaystyle\int_o^t i(t)dt + v(o)$	$i = \dfrac{dq}{dt}$, $q = Cv$
Current Source	Current	Amperes		$i = i_g$	
Voltage Source	Voltage	Volts		$v = v_g$	

at their terminals and is based on the principle of conservation of energy and the validity of all physical and chemical laws. Real circuits and devices are modeled by a selection of, or combination of, the two active elements (sources) and the three passive elements shown in Table 2-1. All conductors are ideal (i.e., without resistance or impedance). The five circuit elements in Table 2-1 are abstractions which have no physical meaning in terms of their *I-V* characteristics as given in this table. Similarly, real components are never "pure" elements and are never linear over all ranges of voltages and current. Because of the non-linear behavior of real compoments, it is usually necessary to develop different circuit models to describe the actual hardware as truthfully as possible for the specific case to be analyzed. Specific models of the same physical circuit that may be considered are dc (direct current), low frequency, high frequency, small signal, and large signal analyses.

2-22. Circuit Simplifications

Before any circuit is analyzed mathematically, it is expedient to simplify the circuit as much as possible. Table 2-2 defines the relationships that hold for combining passive and active circuit elements in parallel and in series. In circuit analysis, current sources cannot be directly connected in series, and voltage sources cannot be directly connected in parallel, unless the sources so connected have identical output characteristics.

Complex ladder networks may be simplified by step-by-step combinations of series and parallel elements. Sometimes circuits may be simplified by looking for equipotential junctions and connecting them with conductors. Table 2-3 lists voltage and current dividers helpful for circuit simplification. Networks may often be simplified by using one of the three theorems below (the theorems are stated here for dc circuit analysis; however, they can be expanded for ac analysis).

Thevenin's Theorem. Any network that is connected to a terminal pair *a-b* and is comprised of active and passive elements can be replaced

Table 2-2. Combination of Elements.

$R = R_1 + R_2$	
$R = \dfrac{R_1 \cdot R_2}{R_1 + R_2}$	$\dfrac{1}{R} = \dfrac{1}{R_1} + \dfrac{1}{R_2}$
$C = \dfrac{C_1 \cdot C_2}{C_1 + C_2}$	$\dfrac{1}{C} = \dfrac{1}{C_1} + \dfrac{1}{C_2}$
$C = C_1 + C_2$	
$L = L_1 + L_2 + 2M$	*
$L = L_1 + L_2 - 2M$	*
$L = \dfrac{L_1 L_2 - M^2}{L_1 + L_2 - 2M}$	*
$L = \dfrac{L_1 L_2 - M^2}{L_1 + L_2 + 2M}$	*
$V = V_1 + V_2$	
$I = I_1 + I_2$	

*Equations apply also for M = 0.

by a voltage source *V* in series with a resistance *R*. The voltage *V* is the open-circuit voltage of the network (i.e., no external elements are connected to the terminal pair *a-b.*). The resistance *R* is measured across the terminal pair *a-b* with all internal voltage sources shorted and all current sources opened.

Norton's Theorem. Any network that is connected to a terminal pair *a-b* and is comprised of active and passive elements can be replaced by a current source *I* in parallel with a resistance *R*. The current is the short-circuit current of the network. The resistance *R* is measured across

Table 2-3. Voltage and Current Dividers.

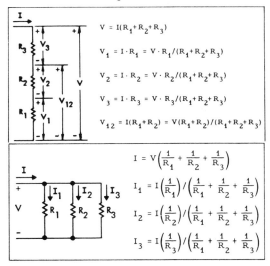

$$V = I(R_1 + R_2 + R_3)$$

$$V_1 = I \cdot R_1 = V \cdot R_1 / (R_1 + R_2 + R_3)$$

$$V_2 = I \cdot R_2 = V \cdot R_2 / (R_1 + R_2 + R_3)$$

$$V_3 = I \cdot R_3 = V \cdot R_3 / (R_1 + R_2 + R_3)$$

$$V_{12} = I(R_1 + R_2) = V(R_1 + R_2) / (R_1 + R_2 + R_3)$$

$$I = V\left(\frac{1}{R_1} + \frac{1}{R_2} + \frac{1}{R_3}\right)$$

$$I_1 = I\left(\frac{1}{R_1}\right) / \left(\frac{1}{R_1} + \frac{1}{R_2} + \frac{1}{R_3}\right)$$

$$I_2 = I\left(\frac{1}{R_2}\right) / \left(\frac{1}{R_1} + \frac{1}{R_2} + \frac{1}{R_3}\right)$$

$$I_3 = I\left(\frac{1}{R_3}\right) / \left(\frac{1}{R_1} + \frac{1}{R_2} + \frac{1}{R_3}\right)$$

the terminal pair *a-b* with all internal voltage sources shorted and all current sources opened.

Equivalent Sources. Any voltage source V_0 in series with a resistance R_0 is equivalent to a current source I_1, in parallel with a resistance R_1 if $R_1 = R_0$ and $V_0 = R_1 I_1$.

NOTE: A voltage source must always be connected to a series element and a current source to a parallel element if infinite currents and voltages are to be prevented. It should also be noted that solar cell circuits are non-linear and, therefore, more difficult to analyze than linear circuits. For this reason, the above three theorems must be applied with great caution.

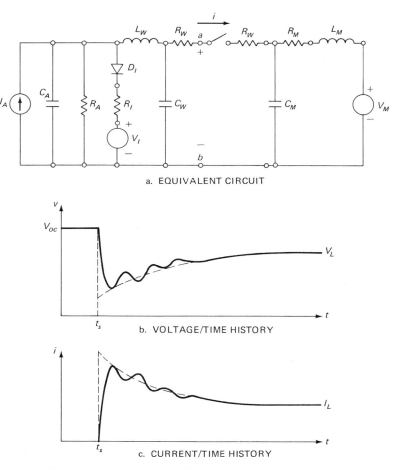

a. EQUIVALENT CIRCUIT

b. VOLTAGE/TIME HISTORY

c. CURRENT/TIME HISTORY

Fig. 2-11. Response of simplified array and DC-motor circuit.

2-23. Circuit Responses

A circuit can be analyzed for steady state operating performance or for transient effects. Most solar cell array analysis is concerned with steady state performance. Array electrical systems analysis, however, is also concerned with steady state ac and transient performance. For example, consider the circuit of Fig. 2-11a. The array current generator I_A provides all load current. The voltage source V_I in series with R_I and an ideal diode D_I represent the internal solar cell junctions which limit the array's open-circuit voltage. The diode D_I prevents current flow from V_I into the load. All elements carrying subscript W represent the wiring. The motor winding resistance, inductance, and capacitance is labelled R_M, L_M and C_M, respectively. The voltage source V_M represents the *back-EMF* of the motor. V_M is zero when the dc motor armature does not turn, and increases with increasing armature speed of rotation. At a given rotating speed, V_M decreases when the work done by the motor (i.e., its load) increases, causing an increase in the current drawn by the motor. Let the switch initially be open, so that at the array terminals *a-b* the source circuit's open-circuit voltage, V_{oc}, develops. Consequently, the current i is zero. Now let the switch be closed at time t_s. It will be observed (Fig. 2-11b and c) that both voltage and current will swing up and down for a while, a phenomenon known as *ringing*, before they reach their final, steady state values of V_L and I_L, respectively. A similar *transient response* will be elicited when an additional electrical load is connected, or when a load is disconnected, or when an additional source circuit is connected or disconnected.

Now let the dc sources in the above example be replaced by ac sources. Again, there will be transient and steady state responses, but they will be different from the dc cases cited because the alternating currents and voltages continually change both magnitude and direction. In the steady state, currents and voltages have settled to constant *effective* values. The voltage and current waveforms typically do not exactly coincide, time-wise, but are slightly out of phase (see Section 2-20).

Of some interest to the solar cell array de-

signer and analyst are circuit responses to step functions. Such network responses are calculated using differential equations, giving solutions as shown in Fig. 2-12.

2-24. Circuit Equations

Electrical circuits, or networks, are usually made up of a large number of individual electrical components. For illustration, consider the portion of a network depicted in Fig. 2-13. The three components labeled 1, 2, and 3 form two branches and a *closed loop*. The points at which the components are connected together, labeled a, b, and c, are called nodes.

Any network may be analyzed by writing either node equations or loop equations for the circuit under consideration and solving those for the desired quantity. These network equations are based on *Kirchhoff's laws*, which are as follow:

Kirchhoff's *current law* states that the algebraic sum of all currents leaving or entering any junction (node) at any time is zero. His *voltage law* states that the algebraic sum of all branch voltages around any closed loop at any time is zero.

Example of Analysis by Loop Equations

Consider the circuit of Fig. 2-14. It has four branches and three nodes. As a first step, we arbitrarily assign branch currents and node voltages to the circuit. Their direction and polarity will always come out right; i.e., when a value comes out positive, it is as initially assumed. If it comes out negative, it is opposite to that initially assumed. Also, we assign the (also arbitrary) artificial loop currents i_a and i_b. We now apply Kirchhoff's voltage law and write the loop equations:

$$-V_0 + i_1 R_1 + i_2 R_2 = 0$$
$$-i_2 R_2 + i_3 R_3 + i_4 R_4 = 0.$$

We can reduce the number of unknowns from three to two, by noting that $i_a = i_1$ and $i_3 = i_4 = i_b$, and make the equations solvable:

$$-V_0 + i_a R_1 + (i_a - i_b)R_2 = 0$$
$$-(i_a - i_b)R_2 + i_b R_3 + i_b R_4 = 0.$$

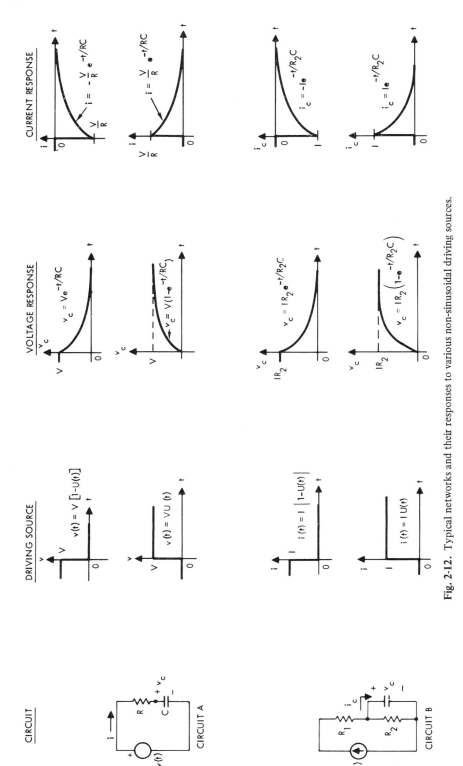

Fig. 2-12. Typical networks and their responses to various non-sinusoidal driving sources.

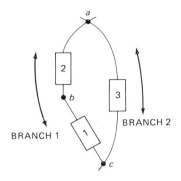

Fig. 2-13. A loop with two branches and three nodes.

Example of Analysis by Node Equations

Using Kirchhoff's current law, we see in Fig. 2-14 that at nodes a, b, and c

$$-i_1 + i_2 + i_3 = 0$$

$$-i_3 + i_4 = 0$$

$$+i_1 - i_2 - i_4 = 0.$$

We also note that $V_1 = V_0 - V_2$ and $V_3 = V_2 - V_4$, so that

$$-\frac{V_1}{R_1} + \frac{V_2}{R_2} + \frac{V_3}{R_3} = 0$$

$$-\frac{V_3}{R_3} + \frac{V_4}{R_4} = 0.$$

This pair of equations can be written as

$$-(V_0 - V_2)G_1 + V_2G_2 + (V_2 - V_4)G_3 = 0$$

$$-(V_2 - V_4)G_3 + V_4G_4 = 0,$$

which can again be solved. Simultaneous equations in several unknowns are usually solved by the method of substitution, by determinants, or by modern, high-level language computer codes.

If the foregoing circuit had contained capacitances and/or inductances, the analysis would

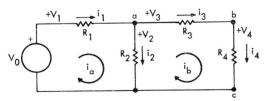

Fig. 2-14. Two-loop circuit with current directions and voltage polarities arbitrarily assigned.

have been similar, except that the *I-V* relationship of Table 2-1 would have been used. For convenience, the operational forms $p \equiv d/dt$ and $1/p \equiv \int_0^t dt$ are frequently used.

2-25. Operating Points

Operating points, also known as *quiescent* points, are formed by the intersections of the *I-V* (current-voltage) characteristics of two or more elements connected in series or parallel. Typically, the operating point is determined by a dc analysis, and further interest exists to examine the circuit's small signal ac response.

For a resistively loaded solar cell, the operating point is defined by the intersection of the load line and the cell's *I-V* curve (Fig. 2-7). For arrays loaded by a combination of resistive and constant-power loads, two intersections exist and the power system operation may be unstable, flipping back and forth between the two operating points, Q_1 and Q_2 in Fig. 2-15. The combination of loads is obtained by summing the load's current at constant voltages, as illustrated in Fig. 2-16.

In the simple power system of Fig. 2-17, the three components—array, battery, and load—are all connected in parallel, so that V is common to all of them. First it is necessary to assign a direction to the positive current flow. Either charging or discharging may be associated with "positive" current flow; it depends only on the

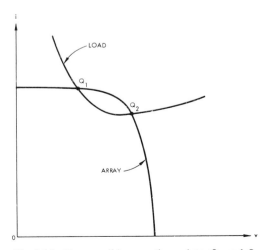

Fig. 2-15. Two possible operating points, Q_1 and Q_2.

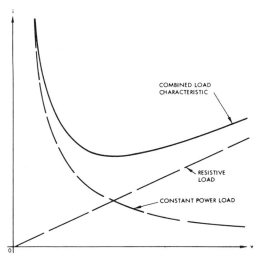

Fig. 2-16. Combining load characteristics.

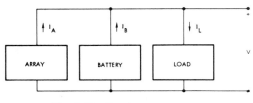

Fig. 2-17. Simple power system.

viewpoint. For convenience, let us (arbitrarily) define "positive" current as coming out of the positive battery terminal. Since by Kirchhoff's law, $I_L = I_A + I_B$, the bus voltage V must adjust itself. There is only one solution for this case and if it has been found, all branch currents and voltages are known. The graphical solution of a simple power subsystem problem is illustrated in Fig. 2-18. In the case of the battery being charged (left graph of Fig. 2-18), the available array current, I_A, is greater than the load current, I_L, and the magnitude of the battery charging currents is $|I_B| = I_A - I_L$. In the case of the battery being discharged (right graph of Fig. 2-18), the available array current, I_A, is less than the required load current, I_L, requiring a current from the battery of magnitude $|I_B| = I_L - I_A$.

SEMICONDUCTORS AND SOLAR CELL MODELS

2-26. Quantum Mechanics

Solar cells operate on quantum mechanical principles. Quantum mechanics is a field of

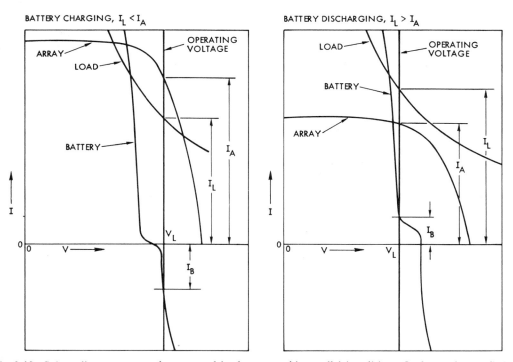

Fig. 2-18. Solar cell array, storage battery, and load connected in parallel (condition $\Sigma I = 0$ must be satisfied in all cases).

physical science that deals on the atomic level, among other things, with the emission (giving off) and absorption of radiant energy. Radiant energy, such as heat and light, is carried along (i.e., transmitted) by waves. Each type of radiant energy, also known as electromagnetic radiation, has a different wavelength λ (lambda, a Greek letter) given by

$$\lambda = \frac{c}{f}$$

where c is the speed of light ($c = 300,000,000$ m/second = 3×10^8 m/second) and f is the frequency of the radiation in units of hertz, meaning cycles/second. One cycle is one complete vibration, or amplitude variation, of the wave. For example, visible light has wavelengths around one-half of one-billionth of a meter (0.5×10^{-9} m) and frequencies of around $600,000$ gigahertz (6×10^{17} hertz). Other forms of radiant energy include infrared and ultraviolet radiation, X-rays, television waves, microwaves, and laser beams.

Electromagnetic radiation is comprised of alternating electric and magnetic fields, and is characterized by the intensities of the electric field E and the magnetic field H, the spatial relationship between E and H, and the frequency (i.e., the wavelength) of the alternating fields (both E and H vibrate at an identical frequency f). The instantaneous energy contained in, or transported by, the electromagnetic field is given by the product of the E and H fields, known as the Poynting vector S:

$$S = EH.$$

In vector notation, this equation is written as

$$\mathbf{S} = \mathbf{E} \times \mathbf{H}.$$

In general, **E** and **H** are perpendicular to each other and perpendicular to the direction of **S**. The Poynting vector (after J. H. Poynting) points in the direction of the rays into which the electromagnetic radiation, or the wave, travels. In vacuum, the waves propagate with the speed of light, c. In penetrable substances, the speed of propagation, s, is reduced by the ratio of the index of refraction, n (see Section 5-1):

$$s = c/n.$$

The time-average energy transported by the wave is given by the average Poynting vector:

$$S_{av} = EH/2$$

where E and H represent the maximum instantaneous amplitudes, as before.

Even though radiated electromagnetic energy appears to be leaving a source in a continuous, uniform flow, the radiant energy actually departs from the source in small increments, known as quanta, or photons. One *quantum* (*photon*) is the smallest, indivisible amount of energy that can be emitted from any source in the form of electromagnetic radiation. The amount of energy E in a photon is related to the wavelength λ of the radiation, and therefore also to the frequency f, by

$$E = hf = \frac{ch}{\lambda}$$

where h is Planck's constant ($h = 6.63 \times 10^{-34}$ joule-seconds). Light, or any other form of electromagentic radiation, falling upon a surface, is similarly a situation of individual energy quanta, or photons, impinging upon that surface. Some of these photons penetrate just a minute distance into the surface before they are adsorbed, while others are reflected from the surface, bouncing back like a billards ball from the side rails of a pool table.

A photon is absorbed in a material by its collision with an atom of that material. The collision leads to an annihilation of the photon, and the photon energy E is imparted to the atom, according to the principle of the conservation of energy that applies in atomic as well as in classical physics. In metals and in most other materials, the energy received by the atom causes it to vibrate, which, in turn, causes other, adjacent atoms to vibrate. The atomic vibrations manifest themselves as the temperature of the material. An increase in the magnitude of the vibrations, caused by photon absorption, is correspondingly an increase in the material's temperature.

Photons may also ionize materials (destroy organic molecules), cause electrons to leave metal surfaces (electron emission), and, in semiconductors, create "carriers" that participate in the solar cell's energy conversion process discussed later in this chapter.

Another property of electromagnetic, as well as corpuscular, radiation is momentum, denoted by the Greek letter μ (mu) and given by

$$\mu = mv$$

where m is the mass of the particle (corpuscle) and v is its velocity. In the case of electromagnetic radiation, m is the mass of the photon and v becomes c, the speed of light. When impinging upon a surface, the radiation is either absorbed or reflected. In a perfect absorption process, the entire momentum μ is imparted to the absorber, according to the principle of conservation of momentum. In a perfect reflection process, the incident mass is recoiled at the same velocity as it came in, so that the total change in momentum of the particle is 2μ. This same quantity of 2μ is imparted to the reflector. The force on a surface arising from the exchange of momentum is also known as *radiation pressure* (see Section 9-5).

2-27. Semiconductor Materials

Semiconductors are a class of crystalline materials that are neither conductors nor insulators. At room temperature, their resistivity lies in the range between approximately 10^{-3} and 10^9 ohm $\cdot$ cm, which is between that of metals (less than 10^{-4} ohm $\cdot$ cm) and insulators (greater than 10^9 ohm $\cdot$ cm). Practical values of semiconductor resistivities for solar cell applications range from 10^{-3} to 10^2 ohm $\cdot$ cm.

Semiconductor materials come in two types: p-type and n-type. For example, consider silicon, the most widely used semiconductor material for fabricating solar cells today. Silicon is made by refining silicon compounds to a high degree so that essentially all impurities are removed. The refined silicon is then molten, and a single crystal of silicon is made by carefully withdrawing an ingot of solidifying silicon from the melt. This process is called the Czochralski method of growing artificial crystals. As the molten silicon freezes, the atoms arrange themselves into a well-ordered structure, known as the *crystal lattice*.

To make the silicon useful for the construction of solar cells (or transistors or other devices), the silicon is made either p-type or n-type

by the controlled addition of desirable impurities to the silicon melt, a process known as *doping*. Silicon of the n-type is created by the addition of a Group V element from the periodic chart of elements, such as phosphorous, to the melt. Phosphorus has five electrons in its outer shell, while silicon, a group IV element, has only four electrons. In the crystal growing process, an occasional phosphorus atom takes the place of a silicon atom and therefore donates one extra electron to the lattice. Group V elements are therefore also called *donor* or *n-type* impurities.

To produce p-type silicon, p-type impurities from Group III, such as boron, are added to the melt. The boron atom, having only three electrons in its outer shell, has a "shortage" of one electron compared with the silicon atom it replaces. This absence of an electron is called a *hole* and carries a positive charge. Consequently, *p-type* impurities are *acceptor* impurities.

Electrons and holes are free to move about in a piece of semiconductor. An electron can "fall" into a hole, a process known as *recombination*, but a new hole would exist where the electron was located originally. Under the influence of an electric field, the electrons move into one direction and the holes into the opposite direction.

2-28. Semiconductor Junctions

Physical semiconductor devices are made either from p-type or from n-type base material into which one or more impurities of the opposite polarity are introduced to form p-n layers. The interface between layers having opposite polarity is called the *p-n junction*. For an illustration of the design of a modern n-on-p solar cell, consider the piece of semiconductor material containing a p-n junction as depicted schematically in Fig. 2-19. For a silicon solar cell, both the p-side and the n-side consisted originally of so-called intrinsic silicon. During the silicon crystal growing process, the p-material was created by adding a relatively small quantity of a Group III element to the melt (see Section 2-27). The n-side was created during the *junction formation* or *diffusion* process. During this process, slices of p-type silicon material (solar cell wafers) were exposed at elevated tempera-

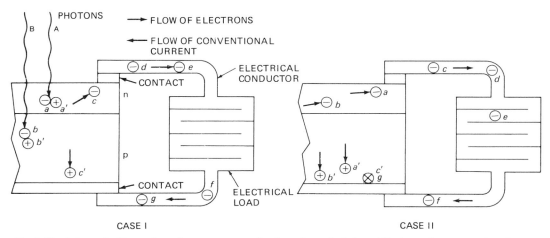

Fig. 2-19. Schematic illustration of current generation by solar cell. Solar cell is shown in cross-section, but not to scale. *Case I:* Photons A and B generate electron-hole pairs at a and b. Electron c and hole c', created by a previous photon, are drifting toward cell contacts. Electrons d, e, f and g move in external circuit, demonstrating flow of electric current. *Case II:* Hole from photon A has crossed junction and drifts toward + contact. Electron from photon B also has crossed junction and drifts toward negative contact. Electron c has moved from semiconductor to metal conductor. Electron g has entered semiconductor and recombined with previous hole c'.

tures to an environment containing a Group V element. The n-type impurities diffused into the surface, substituted themselves into the silicon lattice, and, because of their higher concentration, *overdoped* the already present p-type impurity. The changeover from p-type to n-type material occurs in the less than 1 μm thick *transition region* or *transition zone*. The p-n junction, an idealized electrical concept which does not directly represent the physical change from p-type to n-type material, actually is located somewhere in the volume enclosing the transition region.

Application of metallic contacts to the semiconductor layers completes the fabrication of the solar cell. When non-illuminated, the solar cell will conduct an electric current that is supplied by an eternal source only in one direction, but not in the other. Hence, a solar cell, like any semiconductor p-n junction, acts like a "check valve." This directional property of p-n junctions is utilized, for example, by rectifier diodes.

2-29. Solar Cell Operation

Let the solar cell described in Section 2-28 be illuminated with sunlight. Photons having dif-

ferent energy will be absorbed at a different depth from the front surface, as depicted schematically in Fig. 2-19. An external load (a resistor, for example) is shown connected to the cell's contacts. The actual proportions of all items in this figure are heavily distorted for the purposes of illustration. In the upper part of the figure, both photons, labeled *A* and *B*, have just knocked electrons from their respective semiconductor atoms. Photon *A* has a higher energy (shorter wavelength) than photon *B*. The departed electrons have left two electrical vacancies, known as holes, at the collision sites. Thus, it is said that the photons have created electron-hole pairs. The electrons and holes are now able to move through the semiconductor material under the influences of electric fields in the material set up by the electrical effects of the p-n junction. The electrons are attracted into the n-layer and the holes into the p-layer. Hence, the solar cell layer structure acts like a pump, "pumping" electrons into the n-contact, through the external circuit, and back into the solar cell p-contact. At the interface between the metallic p-contact and the semiconductor p-layer, the electrons "fall into the holes"; that is, electrons and holes recombine. This process renders them electrically neutral, until another photon separates electrons and holes again.

2-30. Solar Cell Equation

Theoretical models of the solar cell are derived from solid-state physics theory. Such derivations are lengthy and result in models which are especially useful for the solar cell researcher. However, most solar cell array workers are more interested in "how a solar cell works"; therefore, only the essential elements of the derivation of a solar cell mathematical model and the associated semiconductor terminology are highlighted below.

The starting point for the derivation of the basic solar cell equation is the p-n junction discussed in Section 2-28 and depicted in Fig. 2-20a. At temperatures above $0°K$, thermal agitation of the atomic lattice structure generates mobile (i.e., "free") electrons and holes in both the p-type and n-type material. These free electrons and holes move through the material in random fashion. Due to the effects of doping with impurities, the concentration of free holes in the p-material, p_p, is much greater than the concentration in the n-material, p_n, and the concentration of free electrons in the n-material, n_n, is much greater than in the p-material, n_p (Fig. 2-20). Consequently, the holes in the p-material and the electrons in the n-material are called "majority carriers" and the holes in the n-material and the electrons in the p-material are called "minority carriers." The operation of p-n junction diodes and solar cells depends upon the behavior of the minority carriers; hence, such devices are "minority carrier devices."

Because there is an excess of "carriers" (i.e., holes or electrons) on either side of the transition region (Fig. 2-20b), there exists a hole density gradient, dp/dx, across the transition region, which tends to cause holes to "diffuse" from the p-region into the n-region. Similarly, an electron density gradient, dn/dx, tends to diffuse electrons from the n-material into the p-region. The "diffusion currents" (actually current densities) J_p and J_n, for holes and electrons, respectively, are of the magnitude

$$J_p = -eD_p \frac{dp}{dx} \text{ and } J_n = eD_n \frac{dn}{dx}$$

where e is the electronic charge, and D_p and D_n are the diffusion constants (material properties) for holes, p, and electrons, n, respectively. (The minus sign indicates flow to the left in Fig. 2-20).

The actual concentration of holes in the n-material, as well as the concentration of electrons in the p-material, decreases with increasing distance from the transition region, as shown in Fig. 2-20c, due to a "recombination" process consisting of "electrons falling into holes." The time period between the instant of "injection" of a carrier into a type of material where it is a minority carrier, and the instant it recombines with a majority carrier, is called the "minority carrier lifetime"; the distance it travels between injection and recombination is called its "diffusion length." Lifetime, τ, and diffusion length, L, are related by

$$L_p = \sqrt{D_p \tau_p} \text{ and } L_n = \sqrt{D_n \tau_n}$$

where D_p and D_n are the diffusion constants for the holes and electrons, respectively.

In solar cells, the important process is to "inject" minority carriers by utilizing the energy of incident photons (sunlight) to "create" electron-hole pairs" and to "collect" the minority carriers. The number of incident photons per unit area and time (i.e., the light intensity) is referred to as the "injection level."

As a result of the diffusion currents across the transition region, the high concentration of free electrons coming from the n-region provides great opportunity for recombination with holes associated with the acceptor atoms in the p-material. Conversely, the holes coming from the p-material recombine with electrons in the n-material. As a consequence of this recombination process in the transition space, the donor and acceptor ions are depleted of free electrons and holes. Hence, the transition region is also called the space charge region or the depletion region (Fig. 2-20d). The electric charges of the immobile ions in the depletion region provide an electrostatic potential which opposes the diffusion currents. This electrostatic potential, V_0, called the potential barrier, causes holes to drift from the n-material to the p-material and

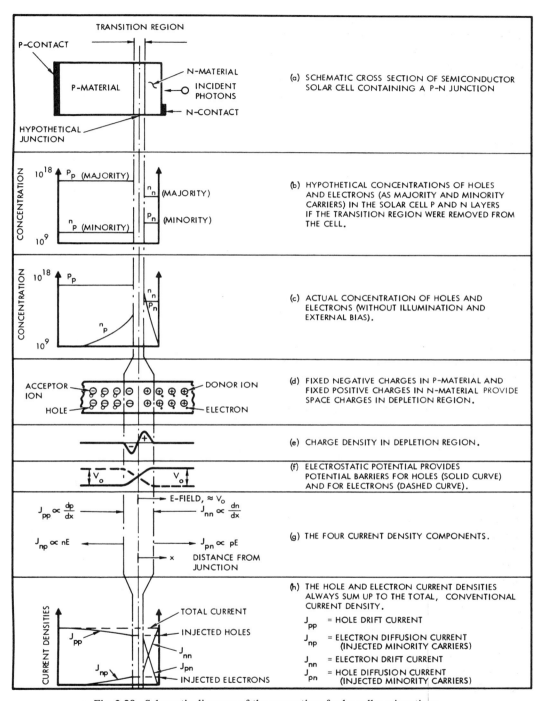

Fig. 2-20. Schematic diagrams of the properties of solar cell p-n junctions.

electrons to drift in the opposite direction (Fig. 2-20f). This is to be expected, because a piece of matter in equilibrium with its environment must have charge neutrality. The drift current (in opposite direction to the diffusion current) for electrons (n) and holes (p), respectively, is

$$J_n = ne\mu_n V_0 \text{ and } J_p = pe\mu_p V_0$$

where μ is the mobility of electrons and holes, respectively. The mobilities are material constants and are related to the diffusion constants by the Einstein equation

$$\frac{D_p}{\mu_p} = \frac{D_n}{\mu_n} = \frac{kT}{e}$$

where k is Boltzmann's gas constant, T is the absolute temperature, and e is the electronic charge.

The dynamic equilibrium of diffusion and drift of holes and electrons at any time, t, and at any distance, x, from the hypothetical p-n junction must satisfy the principle of conservation of charge (Fig. 2-20g). This principle is expressed by the equation of conservation of charge or the continuity equation as follows for holes in the n-region (a similar equation can be written for electrons in the p-material):

$$\frac{\partial p_n}{\partial t} = -\frac{p_n - p_{no}}{\tau_p} + D_p \frac{\partial^2 p_n}{\partial x^2} - \mu_p \frac{\partial(p_n V_0)}{\partial x}.$$

This equation states that the increase in minority carrier hole concentration in the n-material due to all processes at a distance x with time t (the left-hand term of the equation) equals the externally injected hole concentration (due to bias or exposure to light) in addition to the thermal equilibrium concentration, p_{no}, (the first term on the right-hand side) plus the contributions from the diffusion and drift currents (the second and third terms on the right-hand side, respectively).

The solution of the continuity equation (non-illuminated case) requires two boundary conditions. One boundary condition is that the injected hole concentration decreases away from the junction, i.e., $p_n(x) \to 0$ as $x \to \infty$. For the other boundary condition, it can be shown that the hole concentration $p_n(0)$ at the junction (i.e., at $x = 0$) depends upon the thermal equi-

librium (minority carrier) hole concentration p_{no} and the externally applied voltage, V, by the relationship

$$p_n(0) = p_{no} \exp \frac{eV}{kT}.$$

This equation and a similar one for electrons are the key equations in rectifier theory. Using both of the above boundary conditions in the solution of the continuity equation and applying the fact that the total, conventional current through the device must be constant at any distance x, the diode equation (dc case) results:

$$J = J_0 \left(\exp \frac{eV}{kT} - 1 \right)$$

where the saturation current density is given by

$$J_0 = \frac{eD_p p_{no}}{L_p} + \frac{eD_n n_{po}}{L_n}.$$

It can be shown that the temperature dependence of the saturation current is

$$J_0(T) = eA_0 \left(\frac{D_p}{N_d L_p} + \frac{D_n}{N_a L_n} \right) T^3 \exp \left(\frac{-eV_g}{kT} \right)$$

where N_a and N_d are the acceptor and donor concentration, respectively, and V_g and A_0 are material constants.

For the case of an illuminated p-n junction (i.e., a solar cell), solution of the continuity equation leads to an additional term in the diode equation which represents the "light-injected" minority carrier concentrations (i.e., holes in the n-material and electrons in the p-material). These light-generated minority carriers, or these carrier productions by the solar cell, give rise to the light-generated current, I_L (or current density, J_L), which is available for flowing in an external electric circuit. The complete cell equation is then as follows (per unit area):

$$J = J_L - J_0 \left(\exp \frac{eV}{kT} - 1 \right).$$

For this theoretically derived equation, an equivalent idealized electrical circuit may be synthesized, as shown in Fig. 2-21. The current source produces a current of magnitude J_L equal to the "injection level" (i.e., light inten-

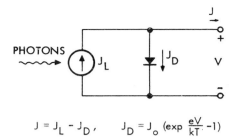

$$J = J_L - J_D, \qquad J_D = J_o \left(\exp \frac{eV}{kT} - 1\right)$$

Fig. 2-21. Ideal solar cell model.

sity), while the cell *I-V* (or *J-V*) curve shape is defined by 1) the value of J_L and 2) the current J_D flowing internally across the cell's ideal semiconductor junction at a particular cell absolute temperature, T, and terminal voltage, V.

In the continuity equation, the quantity $p_n(0)$ (i.e., $p_n(x)$ for $x = 0$), represents the concentration of holes in the n-material due to either an external forward bias or minority carrier holes injected into the solar cell n-material by incident photons. As soon as an external forward bias is applied or photons are incident, causing, in turn, the p-n junction to become forward biased, the internal electric field (Fig. 2-20d) causes holes to drift from the p-side to the n-side. While crossing the junction, the hole drift current becomes an injected hole current in the n-material. Similarly, the electron drift current in the n-material becomes an injected electron current in the p-material. At any distance x the sum of the hole and electron currents equals the total current density, J (Fig. 2-20h).

As the holes approach the junction (J_{pp} in Fig. 2-20h), some of them recombine with the injected electrons (J_{np}), thereby lowering the total current density, J. Solar cell manufacturers, in an attempt to maximize the cell output, J, expend significant amounts of effort to reduce such recombination. Long diffusion length, L, and long lifetime, τ, aid in reducing recombination losses. On the other hand, charged-particle irradiation produces crystal defects which reduce the effective diffusion length and lifetime. Effective diffusion length in unirradiated cells is also reduced when the cell base width (cell thickness) is made equal to or smaller than the mean diffusion length. This is a actually the

case for modern silicon cells thinner than approximately 350 μm and explains the reduction in short-circuit current output when cell thickness is reduced.

2-31. Solar Cell DC Model

The basic solar cell equation derived from solid-state physics theory (shown in Section 2-30) does not represent the actual solar cell *I-V* characteristics with sufficient accuracy to be useful for engineering analysis. Observations of the solar cell terminal characteristics under a variety of test conditions have led to the inclusion of three additional parameters—A, R_S, and R_{SH}—in the solar cell equation (illustrated in Fig. 2-22) as given below.

$$I = I_L - I_0 \left\{ \exp\left[\frac{e(V + IR_S)}{AkT}\right] - 1 \right\} - \frac{V}{R_{SH}}$$

$$(2\text{-}1)$$

The symbols are defined as follows:

A = an arbitrary curve-fitting constant between 1 and 5

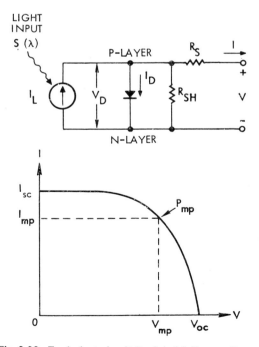

Fig. 2-22. Equivalent circuit (top) and *I-V* curve (bottom) of solar cell.

R_S = cell's series resistance
R_{SH} = shunt resistance
I = cell's output current
I_L = light generated current
I_0 = diode saturation current
e = electronic charge
V = cell's terminal voltage
k = Boltzmann's constant
T = absolute temperature.

This solar cell model has been widely used for solar cell and array analysis; however, it still exhibits some minor but occasionally objectionable deviations from actual solar cell characteristics. One of the reasons for such deviations is the difficulty in accurately measuring the cell series resistance (see Section 8-21). Therefore, more detailed cell models have been developed, as discussed below. No single model exists at this time which accurately represents all currently available solar cells over all ranges of temperature, illumination intensity, and radiation damage.

The term "$(V + IR_S)$" in the above Eq. 2-1 is sometimes shown as "$(V - IR_S)$." This term represents the diode voltage V_D inside the solar cell. The magnitude of this diode voltage is greater than the cell terminal voltage V when power is delivered by the cell to an external load. If the flow of positive current for the cell model is defined (arbitrarily) as in Fig. 2-22, then $V_D = (V + IR_S)$. On the other hand, if the positive current flow would be defined opposite to that shown in Fig. 2-22, the sign would reverse so that $V_D = (V - IR_S)$ would become the correct form (see also Section 2-11 for conventions).

2-32. Distributed Parameter Solar Cell Model

In most solar cells, the p-n junction, series resistance, and other cell parameters are distributed over a relatively large area, leading to voltage gradients and varying current densities throughout the device. As a first step of improvement, a second order lumped parameter model was developed (Fig. 2-23).[1] Earlier p-on-n cells, as well as modern n-on-p cells, were found to exhibit two distinctly different, dominant p-n junction characteristics which are related to

minority carrier diffusion and recombination effects.[2]

Many more fully distributed parameter solar cell models were developed, using transmission line theory[3] and other approaches, primarily intended for solar cell contact and grid-line optimization work.[4]

None of the distributed parameter models lend themselves in a practical way to solar cell or array performance analysis because essentially all of the solar cell parameters vary with any one or any combination of temperature, illumination intensity, and radiation damage, and the parameters I_0, A, and R_S are very difficult to measure over all ranges of interest.

2-33. Analytical Models for Computer Work

Analytical expressions of the solar cell I-V curve shape generally are derived from the solar cell model described in Section 2-31. The equation is altered such that the computer can derive its own curve-fitting constants from the experimental solar cell test data input. Three typical models are discussed below.

Model 1. The solar cell model given in Eq. 2-1 is rewritten as follows:[5]

$$I = I_L - I_0 \{\exp [k_0(V + R_S I)] - 1\} - V/R_{SH}$$

$$(2\text{-}2)$$

where

I = current through the load
I_L = photovoltaic current across the junction
R_S = series resistance
R_{SH} = shunt resistance
k_0 = e/AkT = coefficient of the exponential
k = Boltzmann's constant
T = absolute temperature, °K
e = electronic charge, 1.6×10^{-19} coulombs
A = a curve fitting constant
I_0 = reverse saturation current of the ideal diode characteristic.

Next, Eq. 2-2 is solved for V:

$$V = R_{SH}(I_L - I - I_0 \{\exp [k_0(V + R_S I)] - 1\})$$

$$(2\text{-}3)$$

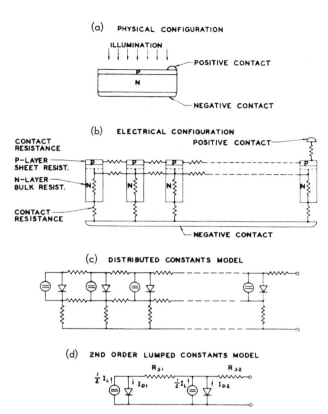

(a) PHYSICAL CONFIGURATION

ILLUMINATION

POSITIVE CONTACT

P

N

NEGATIVE CONTACT

(b) ELECTRICAL CONFIGURATION

CONTACT RESISTANCE

POSITIVE CONTACT

P-LAYER SHEET RESIST.

N-LAYER BULK RESIST.

CONTACT RESISTANCE

NEGATIVE CONTACT

(c) DISTRIBUTED CONSTANTS MODEL

(d) 2ND ORDER LUMPED CONSTANTS MODEL

Fig. 2-23. Distributed solar cell model and simplification to second-order lumped parameter model; illustrated for p-on-n cells. (Reprinted with permission of the Pergamon Press)[1]

Now the following parameters are defined,

$$v = \frac{V}{V_{oc}} \quad i = \frac{I}{I_{sc}} \quad i_0 = \frac{I_0}{I_{sc}} \quad i_L = \frac{I_L}{I_{sc}}$$

$$r_p = \frac{R_{SH} I_{sc}}{V_{oc}} \quad r_s = \frac{R_S I_{sc}}{V_{oc}} \quad \alpha = k_0 V_{oc}$$

and substituted into Eq. 2-3, with V_{oc}, I_{sc} and R_{SH} as defined in Section 2-31. This gives the set of equations below.

$$v = r_p (i_L - i - i_0 \{\exp [\alpha(v + r_s i)] - 1\})$$

$$i = i_L - \frac{v}{r_p} - i_0 \{\exp [\alpha(v + r_s i)] - 1\}.$$

Since $i = 0$ when $v = 1$, and $v = 0$ when $i = 1$, the following two equations result:

$$1 = r_p [i_L + i_0 - i_0 \exp (\alpha)]$$

$$1 = i_L + i_0 - i_0 \exp (\alpha r_s).$$

Hence, only three parameters need be independently chosen. For reasons of convenience, r_s, r_p, and α were chosen as independent, with i_L and i_0 determined by

$$i_0 = \frac{r_p - 1}{r_p} \left[\frac{1}{\exp (\alpha) - \exp (\alpha r_s)} \right]$$

$$i_L = 1 + i_0 [\exp (\alpha r_s) - 1].$$

Consequently, only three points on the normalized I-V characteristic curve are sufficient to determine the three parameters, r_s, r_p, and α. From these three parameters and measured values of I_{sc} and V_{oc}, one can derive a complete mathematical model based on Eq. 2-2. These five parameters are temperature dependent and must be determined from empirical data.

Model 2. Starting with Eq. 2-1, the V/R_{SH} term is neglected and Eq. 2-1 is redefined through a change in variables.[6] Let $K_1 V_{oc} = AkT/e$,

$K_2 I_{sc} = I_0$, and $I_L = I_{sc}$. Then

$$I = I_{sc} - I_{sc} K_2 \left[\exp\left(\frac{V + IR_S}{K_1 V_{oc}}\right) - 1 \right] \quad (2\text{-}4)$$

With reference to Fig. 2-22 and Eq. 2-4, an expression for cell output power P can be written.

$$P = IV = V I_{sc} \left\{ 1 - K_2 \left[\exp\left(\frac{V + IR_S}{K_1 V_{oc}}\right) - 1 \right] \right\} \quad (2\text{-}5)$$

At the cell maximum power point, $V = V_{mp}$, $I = I_{mp}$, and $dP/dV = 0$. Also

$$\frac{dP}{dV} = I_{sc} \left\{ 1 - K_2 \left[\exp\left(\frac{V_{mp} + I_{mp} R_S}{K_1 V_{oc}}\right) - 1 \right] \right\}$$
$$- K_2 I_{sc} V_{mp} \left[\exp\left(\frac{V_{mp} + I_{mp} R_S}{K_1 V_{oc}}\right) \right]$$
$$\cdot \frac{1}{K_1 V_{oc}} \left(1 + R_S \frac{dI}{dV} \right). \quad (2\text{-}6)$$

But from Eq. 2-4, we find Eq. 2-7.

$$\frac{dI}{dV} = \frac{-\dfrac{K_2 I_{sc}}{K_1 V_{oc}} \exp\left(\dfrac{V + IR_S}{K_1 V_{oc}}\right)}{1 + \dfrac{R K_2 I_{sc}}{K_1 V_{oc}} \exp\left(\dfrac{V + IR_S}{K_1 V_{oc}}\right)} \quad (2\text{-}7)$$

Evaluating Eq. 2-7 at the maximum power point, substituting the result into Eq. 2-6, and dividing by I_{sc}, we get Eq. 2-8.

$$0 = K_2 + 1 - K_2 \exp\left(\frac{V_{mp} + I_{mp} R_S}{K_1 V_{oc}}\right) - \frac{V_{mp} K_2}{K_1}$$
$$\cdot \left[\frac{1}{V_{oc} \exp\left(\dfrac{V_{mp} - I_{mp} R_S}{K_1 V_{oc}}\right) + \dfrac{R_S K_2 I_{sc}}{K_1}} \right] \quad (2\text{-}8)$$

Now, under open-circuit conditions when $I = 0$ and $V = V_{oc}$, Eq. 2-4 can be solved for K_1:

$$K_1 = \left[\ln\left(\frac{1}{K_2} + 1\right) \right]^{-1} \quad (2\text{-}9)$$

By substituting Eq. 2-9 into Eq. 2-8, noting that $\exp(A \ln B) = B^A$, we get Eq. 2-10.

$$0 = K_2 + 1 - K_2 \left(\frac{1}{K_2} + 1\right)^{[(V_{mp} + I_{mp} R_S)/V_{oc}]}$$
$$- \frac{V_{mp} K_2 \ln\left(\dfrac{1}{K_2} + 1\right)}{\left\{ V_{oc}\left(\dfrac{1}{K_2} + 1\right)^{[(-V_{mp} - I_{mp} R_S)/V_{oc}]} \right\} + R_S K_2 I_{sc} \ln\left(\dfrac{1}{K_2} + 1\right)} \quad (2\text{-}10)$$

However, by substituting Eq. 2-9 into Eq. 2-4, we find Eqs. 2-11 and 2-12.

$$R_S = \frac{V_{oc} \left\{ \dfrac{\ln\left[\dfrac{1 + K_2 - (I_{mp}/I_{sc})}{K_2}\right]}{\ln\left[(1/K_2) + 1\right]} \right\} - V_{mp}}{I_{mp}} \quad (2\text{-}11)$$

$$\frac{V_{mp} + I_{mp} R_S}{V_{oc}} = \frac{\ln\left(\dfrac{1}{K_2} + 1 - \dfrac{I_{mp}}{K_2 I_{sc}}\right)}{\ln\left(\dfrac{1}{K_2} + 1\right)} \quad (2\text{-}12)$$

Substituting Eq. 2-12 into Eq. 2-10 results in an equation for K_2 as a function of I_{sc}, I_{mp}, and V_{oc}:

$$0 = \frac{I_{mp}}{I_{sc}} - \frac{\left(\dfrac{V_{mp}}{V_{oc}}\right) \ln\left(\dfrac{1}{K_2} + 1\right)}{\left[\dfrac{1}{1 + K_2 - (I_{mp}/I_{sc})}\right] - \dfrac{I_{sc}}{I_{mp}} \left[\dfrac{V_{mp}}{V_{oc}} \ln\left(\dfrac{1}{K_2} + 1\right) - \ln\left(\dfrac{1}{K_2} + 1 - \dfrac{I_{mp}}{K_2 I_{sc}}\right)\right]} \quad (2\text{-}13)$$

Equation 2-13 cannot be solved in closed form for K_2 but a numerical solution can be obtained in a conventional manner. Equation 2-13 has more than one root and care must be taken to select the proper K_2 value, which usually corresponds to the smallest absolute value of R_S. Equations 2-9 and 2-11 define R_S and K_1 as functions of K_2. The final model is formed by substituting the numerical values of K_1, K_2, and R_S from Eqs. 2-9, 2-11, and 2-13, respectively, into Eq. 2-4, which defines the cell I-V curve. The required inputs to fully define the model are the four common cell parameters, I_{sc}, I_{mp}, V_{mp}, and V_{oc}. The translation of these quantities with temperature, illumination intensity, and radiation dose follows the same procedures discussed in Section 2-48.

The model represented by Eq. 2-4 is valid only for the forward operating region of the solar cell. An avalanche breakdown occurs for reverse bias potentials. This region of the solar cell I-V characteristic is not controlled by the cell manufacturers, and, typically, a considerable variation will be found in the breakdown voltage. Equation 2-14 is a general model for both operating regions. For a tpyical cell, $V_b = 30$ V and $B = 15$.

$$I = I_{sc}\left\{1 - K_2\left[\exp\left(\frac{V + IR_S}{K_1 V_{oc}}\right) - 1\right]\right.$$
$$\left. + K_2 \exp\left(\frac{-V - V_b}{BK_1 V_{oc}}\right)\right\} \quad (2\text{-}14)$$

The avalanche breakdown effect is of importance in high voltage array design.

The accuracy of this model in the forward bias operating region over an environmental range from $10°$ to $90°$C and for radiation doses between 0 and 10^{15} 1 MeV electrons/cm^2 is better than 2%.

Model 3. The solar cell I-V curve is also based on Eq. 2-1 and is represented by the equation below.[7]

$$I = I_{sc}(1 - C_1\{\exp\,[V/(C_2 V_{oc})] - 1\})$$
$$(2\text{-}15)$$

where

$$C_1 = [1 - (I_{mp}/I_{sc})]\,\{\exp\,[-V_{mp}/(C_2 V_{oc})]\}$$
$$(2\text{-}16)$$

and

$$C_2 = [(V_{mp}/V_{oc}) - 1]\,[\ln\,(1 - I_{mp}/I_{sc})]^{-1}$$
$$(2\text{-}17)$$

Equation 2-15 results in a considerable error at light intensities above two solar constants. Empirical investigation revealed that a better agreement between the calculated and actual characteristics can be obtained at higher intensities with the equation below.

$$I = K_6 - [\exp\,(K_4 V^m - K_5)] \quad (2\text{-}18)$$

Expressing the constants again in terms of the three characteristic cell points results in Eq. 2-19.

$$I = I_{sc}\{1 - C_3\,[\exp\,(C_4 V^m) - 1]\} \quad (2\text{-}19)$$

The constants are defined in Eqs. 2-20, 2-21, 2-22, and 2-23.

$$m = [\ln\,(C_5/C_6)]\,/[\ln\,(V_{mp}/V_{oc})] \quad (2\text{-}20)$$

$$C_4 = C_6/(V_{oc})^m \quad (2\text{-}21)$$

$$C_5 = \ln\,\{[I_{sc}(1 + C_3) - I_{mp}]/(C_3 I_{sc})\}$$
$$(2\text{-}22)$$

$$C_6 = \ln\,[(1 + C_3)/C_3] \quad (2\text{-}23)$$

The constant C_3 could not be expressed in terms of the three characteristic points, but through trial and error it was found that a value of 0.01175 for C_3 will produce the least errors over the range of illumination and temperature considered. With this value substituted for C_3, the other constants are reduced as shown below.

$$m = [\ln\,(C_5/4.46)]\,/[\ln\,(V_{mp}/V_{oc})] \quad (2\text{-}24)$$

$$C_4 = 4.46/(V_{oc})^m \quad (2\text{-}25)$$

$$C_5 = \ln\,[(1.01175\,I_{sc} - I_{mp})/0.01175\,I_{sc}]$$
$$(2\text{-}26)$$

$$C_6 = 4.46 \quad (2\text{-}27)$$

2.34. Nonanalytical Computer Models

An analytical expression of the solar cell I-V curve is not required for computer work. Discrete sets of I-V data points representing the otherwise smooth I-V curve may be stored in the computer memory. These sets of points may be translated point-by-point to operating conditions different from those for which test data exists.

2-35. Selecting the Proper Model

Any solar cell model used for computerized array analyses must meet the following criteria:

1. It must, with sufficient accuracy, simulate I-V curves over the range of interest of temperature, illumination level, and environmental degradation; and
2. It must permit, with sufficient accuracy, the manipulation of the I-V curves, as required, for predicting the array performance under certain specified array operating conditions.

Both the "range of interest" and the numerical definition of "sufficient accuracy" are mission and program peculiar. A "sufficiently accurate" analysis, in general, is one in which the probable error of the analysis is equal to or less than the design margin. For power output predictions, the accuracy of the analysis should be highest at the maximum power point, but may be lower at the I_{sc} and V_{oc} "ends" of the I-V curve. However, for the sizing of power regulating electronic equipment, knowledge of I_{sc} or V_{oc} may be required more accurately than knowledge of P_{mp}. If one solar cell model cannot (with sufficient accuracy) predict the entire I-V curve, separate computer runs may have to be made using slightly different input values to achieve the desired results.

The accuracy of any computerized array analysis is typically highest for those operating conditions for which direct solar cell test data are input into the computer. For these direct input conditions, an accuracy of better than $\pm 0.1\%$ should be expected. For extrapolations toward the extremes of the range of interest, with an absence of test data, the accuracies tend to deteriorate to $\pm 1\%$ or, in extreme cases, to $\pm 10\%$. Inasmuch as the actually occurring inaccuracies are highly computer-program and case dependent, the array analyst should attempt to ascertain the most likely accuracy of his analysis.

2-36. Solar Cell AC Model

The solution of the continuity equation which resulted in the dc diode equation, as shown in Section 2-31, is actually complex for the general case and contains both a dc and an ac part.[8] The ac part is of the form

$$J = (G_p + jS_p)v \exp(j\omega t)$$

where $(G_p + jS_p) = A_p$, the complex admittance for holes diffusing into the n-layer. The real part, G_p, is the conductance; the imaginary part, jS_p, is the susceptance; v is the magnitude of the sinusoidal signal at the cell terminal superimposed on the dc terminal voltage V; $\exp(j\omega t) = (\cos \omega t + j \sin \omega t)$; and $\omega = 2\pi f$ where f is the frequency.

The numerical value of A_p at low frequencies indicates a conductance paralleled by a capacitance. At higher frequencies, both the conductance the susceptance increase, approximately one-half an order of magnitude for each order of magnitude increase in frequency.

Such solar cell behavior has been verified experimentally, even though the numerical results turned out quite different. Also, at higher frequencies, inductive components not predicted theoretically come into play.

The theoretical ac model of semiconductor junctions described above has been applied to alloyed junctions[9] and to diffused p-n junction, silicon photodiodes.[10] For small ac signals (compared to the dc bias voltage of the junction), these references have shown that the ac output voltage component, v_{ac}, that is superimposed on the dc output voltage, V_{dc}, is

$$v_{ac} = \frac{qM(1-r)QAF(\alpha, \omega)\exp(j\omega t)}{Y_{ac} + Y_L}$$

where

q = electronic charge
M = degree of modulation of the input light level
ω = angular frequency of modulation of the input light level ($\omega = 2\pi f$)
r = front surface reflectivity
Q = steady-state illumination level (photons per cm^2 per second)
A = illuminated surface area

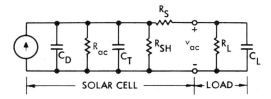

Fig. 2-24. Solar cell small-signal AC model.

$F(\alpha, \omega)$ = function independent of time
Y_{ac} = internal admittance of the junction
Y_L = admittance of the load.

For the frequency range of interest, Y_{ac} is a parallel combination of R_{ac} and C_{ac} such that

$$R_{ac} = (kT/qJ_0 A) \exp(-qV_{dc}/kT)$$

and

$$C_{ac} = W(sR_{ac})^{-1}$$

Table 2-4. Approximate Low-Frequency ac Parameters for Conventional 2 × 2 cm Silicon Solar Cells (One Solar Constant AMO Intensity, 28°C Cell Temperature).

V_{dc} (mV)	R_{ac} (Ω)	R_s (Ω)	R_{SH} (kΩ)	C_D (μF)	C_T (μF)
550	0.2–2	0.1–0.5	5–50	2	0.06
350	1–10	0.1–0.5	5–50	0.2	0.06

where

k = Boltzmann's constant
T = absolute temperature
J_0 = reverse saturation current density
s = surface recombination velocity

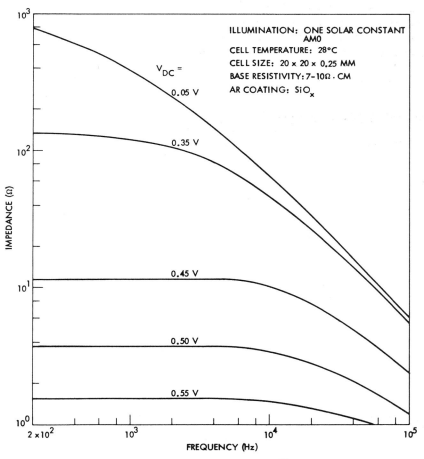

ILLUMINATION: ONE SOLAR CONSTANT AMO
CELL TEMPERATURE: 28°C
CELL SIZE: 20 x 20 x 0.25 MM
BASE RESISTIVITY: 7–10Ω · CM
AR COATING: SiO$_x$

V_{DC} =
0.05 V
0.35 V
0.45 V
0.50 V
0.55 V

IMPEDANCE (Ω)

FREQUENCY (Hz)

Fig. 2-25. Solar cell impedance.[11]

and

$$W = (2.46\, D_n/\omega_0)^{0.5}$$

with

D_n = minority carrier diffusion constant in the p-region of a p-on-n junction

ω_0 = cutoff frequency of the junction.

Experimental investigations have shown that for photodiodes operated in the photovoltaic mode, the transition capacitance, C_T, (measured under conditions of zero illumination and zero reverse bias) and the shunt resistance, R_{SH}, must be included in addition to R_{ac} and C_{ac}. For solar cells, the series resistance R_S must also be included. The small-signal ac equivalent circuit including all terms is shown in Fig. 2-24.

The capacitance, C_{ac}, is also known as the diffusion capacitance, C_D. The values for C_D, C_T, and R_{ac} vary with the incident light level, the cell temperature, the cell operating voltage, and the solar cell material constant and processing parameters. For conventional n-on-p, 2×2 cm, 0.25 mm thick silicon solar cells (defined in Section 4-11) of 10 ohm cm base resistivity produced during 1967 through 1969, the parameters discussed above were found[11, 12] to have the approximate values shown in Table 2-4. The values in this table are for frequencies up to approximately 5000 hertz. Above this frequency, minority carrier storage effects cause the value of C_D to diminish with increasing frequency until $C_D = 0$ and C_T is the only capacitance remaining at the higher frequencies. The value of C_T depends upon V_{DC} as follows:

$$C_T = K(V_{dc})^{-0.5}$$

where K is a constant for a given solar cell. The experimentally determined impedance and phase angle values for the solar cells discussed above are shown in Figs. 2-25 and 2-26. The impedance, Z, and the phase angle, ϕ, are given by

$$Z = v/i$$

and

$$\cos \phi = Z/R_D$$

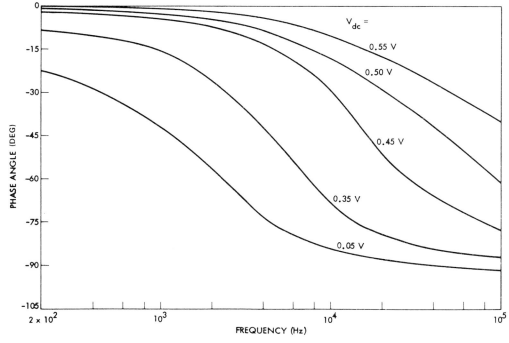

Fig. 2-26. Phase angles for impedances of Fig. 2-25.

respectively, and the capacitances are related by

$$C_D + C_T = \sin \phi/(2\pi f Z)$$

where v and i are the cell small-signal ac voltage and current, respectively, the other symbols are as previously defined, and the incremental diode dc resistance, R_D, is defined as

$$R_D = |dV/dI|$$

at any point of the photovoltaic output portion of a photodiode or solar cell under steady-state illumination. R_D is related to R_{ac} as follows (see Fig. 2-24):

$$R_D = \frac{R_{ac} \cdot R_{SH}}{R_{ac} + R_{sc}} + R_S.$$

The variation of R_D as a function of the cell bias voltage, V_{dc}, for the cell I-V curve illustrated in Fig. 2-27 is given in Fig. 2-28. Near short-circuit current R_{ac} becomes very large and R_{SH} dominates the cell impedance. Near open-circuit voltage, R_{ac} becomes small and R_S exerts a large influence on the impedance.

The Nimbus B solar cell array is one example on which the impedance was measured on an entire array.[13] The array consisted of two parallel-connected panels having a total of 98 cells in series and 112 cells in parallel. The cells

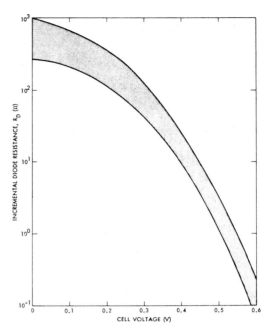

Fig. 2-28. Range of incremental solar cell diode resistances for solar cells of Fig. 2-27.

(conventional SiO_x-coated, 1 to 3 ohm cm cells of $20 \times 20 \times 0.35$ mm size) were grouped into 12 strings that were connected through parallel-redundant blocking diodes to the array bus. The array was tested in natural terrestrial sunlight of 104 mW/cm^2 intensity. The array temperature was $20°C$ and its output values were as follows: $I_{sc} = 10.55$ A, $V_{oc} = 56$ V, and $V_{mp} = 46$ V. The ac impedance was measured

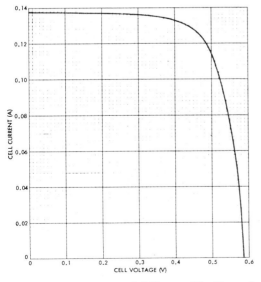

Fig. 2-27. Average solar cell I-V curve (11-cell sample, conventional $20 \times 20 \times 0.2$ mm, n-on-p, 10 $\Omega \cdot$ cm, one solar constant AM0, 28°C).

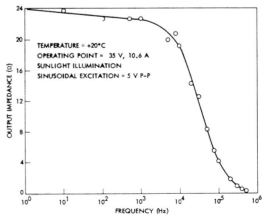

Fig. 2-29. Nimbus-B solar cell array output impedance versus frequency.[13]

at $V_{dc} = 35$ V (a point on the I-V curve that is at 76% of V_{mp}) with an ac voltage of $v_{ac} = 5$ V peak-to-peak. The test results are shown in Fig. 2-29.

ARRAY MODELS

2-37. Solar Cells in Parallel and Series

The relatively small power output from an individual solar cell is multiplied by the number of solar cells in an array. The cell's output current is multiplied by the number of cells connected in parallel, and its voltage output by the number of cells connected in series. Figure 2-30 illustrates the concepts of series and parallel connection. Let us define the following quantities:

N_s = number of cells connected in series
N_p = number of cells connected in parallel
N_t = total number of cells on the array
V_c = cell output voltage
V_a = array output voltage
I_c = cell output current capability
I_a = array output current capability
P_c = cell output power capability
P_a = array output power capability.

Then we have the following relationships:

$$V_a = N_s V_c$$
$$I_a = N_p I_c$$
$$P_a = N_t P_c$$

and, of course, $P_a = V_a I_a$, $P_c = V_c I_c$, and $N_t = N_s N_p$.

Illustrative Example No. 2-8

Let a certain solar cell type have an output capability of 0.5 A at 0.4 V. Assume that we build an array of such cells with 100 cells connected in parallel by 300 cells in series. The array will have an output capability of $100 \times 0.5 = 50$ A at $300 \times 0.4 = 120$ V, or a power of $50 \times 120 = 6000$ W = 6 kW. As a check, we find that one cell can provide $0.5 \times 0.4 = 0.2$ W, and the array $100 \times 300 \times 0.2 = 6000$ W, as before.

The foregoing example is repeated below in algebraic notation.

Given: $V_c = 0.4$ V, $I_c = 0.5$ A
           $N_s = 300$, $N_p = 100$
Find: V_a, I_a, and P_a.
Solution: $V_a = N_s V_c = 300 \times 0.4 = 120$ V
           $I_a = N_p I_c = 100 \times 0.5 = 50$ A
           $P_a = N_t P_c = N_s N_p V_c I_c$
              $= 300 \times 100 \times 0.4 \times 0.5$
              $= 6000$ W or $P_a = V_a I_a$
              $= 120 \times 50 = 6000$ W.

Illustrative Example No. 2-9

Problem: A solar cell array is required to deliver 100 W peak output at 120 V dc bus voltage. The solar cells to be used are rated for 0.1 W peak output at 0.4 V. Assuming that there are no assembly losses, define the array.

Solution: Each cell produces $P_c = 0.1$ W, therefore $N_t P_c = N_t \times 0.1 = 100$, or $N_t = 100/0.1 =$

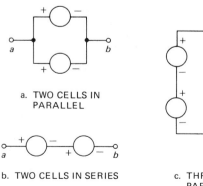

a. TWO CELLS IN PARALLEL

b. TWO CELLS IN SERIES

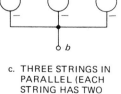

c. THREE STRINGS IN PARALLEL (EACH STRING HAS TWO CELLS IN SERIES)

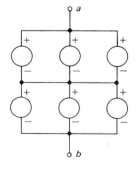

d. TWO SUBMODULES IN SERIES (EACH SUBMODULE HAS THREE CELLS IN PARALLEL)

Fig. 2-30. Parallel and series-connection of solar cells. (also applicable to solar cell modulus, panels, and electrochemical batteries, but not to *ideal* voltage or current sources.)

1000 cells. Also, $0.4 N_s = 120$, or $N_s = 120/0.4 = 300$ cells in series. Since $N_t = N_p N_s$, $N_p = N_t/N_s = 1000/300 = 3.33$ cells in parallel. A decision must be made to use either three or four cells in parallel, resulting in either one of these arrays:

$N_p = 3$:

$$N_t = N_p N_s = 3 \times 300 = 900$$
Array power $= P_c N_t = 0.1 \times 900 = 90$ W;

$N_p = 4$:

$$N_t = N_p N_s = 4 \times 300 = 1200$$
Array power $= P_t N_t = 0.1 \times 1200 = 120$ W.

2-38. Illuminated Arrays

To be useful for solar cell array analysis, the solar cell models discussed previously must be electrically connected in series-parallel matrices to represent an entire array. Typically, an additional series resistance component representing the solar cell interconnectors and the array wiring, and a voltage drop to a account for blocking diode losses, are considered. Depending upon the purpose of the array analysis to be performed, different array models may be required. For the assessment of solar cell mismatch losses or for the computation of the output from partially shadowed arrays, much more detailed models are required than for the computation of the output of a uniformly illuminated array that is free of thermal gradients.

For the purposes of the following discussion, the solar cell I–V curve is expressed as $I(v)$ to show explicitly that I is a function of v.[14,15] The cell $I(v)$ relationship may be any of the models given in Section 2-33 or may be obtained from measurements at some standard test conditions. The solar cell is considered a two-port black box with light energy entering one port and current, voltage, and impedance being offered at the other. The equivalent circuit of this black box is of no further interest in this model. The cell's exit port $I(v)$ characteristics are defined by the externally measurable quantities of terminal current, I_c, as a function of terminal voltage v, at a given light intensity, Q, cell temperature, and state of charged-particle irradiation. Implicit in these

output characteristics is the internal cell series resistance, R_S, which causes the familiar voltage translation as Q is varied (see Section 4-19).

It is assumed that the cell temperature and charged-particle irradiation are held constant for the following. The black box output at some standard conditions (i.e., at light level Q) may be given functionally by

$$I_c(v) = I_L - I_0(v_0) \qquad v \geqslant 0$$
$$= I_L - vG(v) \qquad v < 0 \qquad (2\text{-}28)$$

where I_c is the terminal current, v the terminal voltage, and I_L a constant current equal to the terminal short-circuit current. $I_0(v_0)$ is a function responsible for the typical solar cell curve shape and corresponds conceptually to the diode conduction current in the simple, lumped-constants solar cell model frequently given by Eq. 2-1.

$G(v)$ is a non-linear conductive element in parallel with the output port terminals which affects the cell characteristics only when v is negative. This element represents the cell reverse characteristics which are important when solar cells are connected into arrays where they are subjected to external bias.

It has been determined experimentally that, within a range of intensities about the cell's nominal design intensity Q, the solar cell $I(v)$ curve shape is nearly invariant with intensity and translates only along the current and voltage axes. Using this finding, Eq. 2-28 may be written for any light intensity different from Q (i.e., at kQ).

$$I_c(v) = kI_L - I_0(v_0 - \Delta v) \qquad v \geqslant 0$$
$$= kI_L - vG(v) \qquad v < 0$$
$$(2\text{-}29a)$$

where

$$\Delta v = (1 - k)I_L R_S \qquad (2\text{-}29b)$$

The significance of Eqs. 2-28 and 2-29 is made clear in Fig. 2-31. Curve A in this figure shows a cell curve at intensity Q, while curve B shows the same cell curve at zero intensity; i.e., at $k = 0$. Any point on the A curve has shifted along the current axis by the amount of $(1 - k)I_L = I_L$ and along the voltage axis by an amount of $\Delta v = (1 - k)I_L R_S = I_L R_S$. The negative sign in front of Δv is consistent with the observation that the current to be subtracted from the short-circuit current at a given voltage becomes smaller and smaller as the light intensity is reduced to lower and lower values; i.e., the $I(v)$ curve shifts to higher and higher voltages.

The intensity modifier, k, may reflect changes in the solar distance, coverglass transmission losses, or angle of incidence effects. For most terrestrial and space silicon solar cells for flat plate applications, Eq. 2-29 is accurate for $0 \leqslant k \leqslant 2$ to $0.5 < k < 1.5$. For concentrator cells, the permissible range of k can be expected to be less.

Submodules and Strings. A number of solar cells connected in parallel form a *submodule*, and a number of submodules in series which provide power directly to the bus is called a *string*. A submodule composed of p equal cells of Eq. 2-29 connected in parallel has the characteristics shown below.

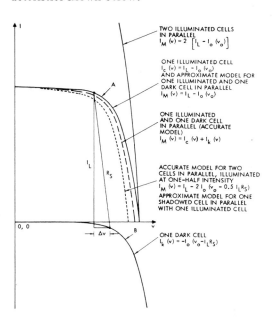

Fig. 2-31. Effects of illumination and shadowing on the current-voltage relationships of a solar cell and a submodule with two cells in parallel.[15] (Reprinted with permission of the IEEE)

$$I_M(v) = p[kI_L - I_0(v_0 - \Delta v)] \qquad v \geqslant 0$$
$$= p[kI_L - vG(v)] \qquad v < 0$$
$$(2\text{-}30\text{a})$$

where

$$\Delta v = (1 - k)I_L R_S \qquad (2\text{-}30\text{b})$$

The first-quadrant portion of the $I(V)$ curve of a string with s submodules in series is obtained by first expressing Eq. 2-30 in terms of v and then forming the sum at constant current values of I_s.

$$V_s(I_s) = \sum_{i=1}^{i=s} [v(I)_i]_{I_s} \qquad (2\text{-}31)$$

Eq. 2-31 may now be expressed in terms of I and written functionally as given in Eq. 2-32a.

$$I_s(V_s) = p[kI_L - I_0(V_s - \Delta V)] \quad (2\text{-}32\text{a})$$

where

$$V_s = sv \text{ and } \Delta V = (1 - k)I_L s R_S$$
$$(2\text{-}32\text{b})$$

The reverse characteristics of the string $I(V)$ curve are of no importance for array output considerations if isolation diodes connect the string to the bus, but are required to determine cell reverse bias.

Array. The array consists of all the strings feeding a particular bus system. Its equation is obtained by forming the sum of all string currents at constant voltage values and accounting for the isolation diode drop. If the array voltage V_A is forced by an energy storage battery, by a power regulator, or by a number of other power-producing strings, the string voltage V_s is also forced, so that

$$V_s = V_A + V_D \text{ and } I_s = I_D \qquad (2\text{-}33)$$

where V_D is the isolation diode drop and I_s and I_D are the string and diode currents, respectively.

For an array comprised of m strings, each generally being illuminated at a different intensity, the array current I_A is as described in Eq. 2-34.

$$I_A(V_A) = \sum_{j=1}^{m} [I_s(V_A)_j]_{V_A}$$

$$= p \sum_{j=1}^{m} [k_j I_L - I_0(V_S - V_D - \Delta V)_j]_{V_A}$$

$$(2\text{-}34)$$

2-39. Partially Shadowed Cells in Parallel

A shadow falling on a portion of a single cell or a submodule will reduce the total output by two mechanisms: 1) by reducing the energy input to the cell, and 2) by increasing internal energy losses in the non-illuminated cell portions.[15] If the energy conversion capability is uniform over the entire active cell area, the short-circuit current will be proportional to the non-shadowed (illuminated) area, regardless of the shape or position of the shadow (at least for up to two solar constants intensity and contemporary solar cells). If the total active cell area is A_t and the illuminated, active portion thereof is A_i, the short-circuit current output of the partially shadowed cell becomes rI_L.

$$r = \frac{A_i}{A_t} \qquad (2\text{-}35)$$

Hence, a partial shadow on a cell will have the same effect on I_L as reduced light intensity on a non-shadowed cell. The remainder of the cell $I(v)$ curve will, however, not follow this relationship, as will be shown by the examples below.

For illustration, let a submodule at normal incidence, consisting of $p = 2$ identical cells in parallel, be partially shadowed with $r = 0.5$, and such that one cell is illuminated and the other is dark. From Eq. 2-29, the illuminated cell equation with $k = 1$ is $I_c(v) = I_L - I_0(v_0)$, and that of the shadowed or dark cell with $k = 0$ is $I_k(v) = -I_0(v_0 - I_L R_S)$. The partially shadowed submodule characteristics are the current sum of these two equations at constant voltage values:

$$I_M(v) = I_c(v) + I_k(v)$$

$$= I_L - I_0(v_0) - I_0(v_0 - I_L R_S)$$

$$(2\text{-}36)$$

Both the single cell components and their sums are illustrated in Fig. 2-31.

While Eq. 2-36 represents the correct solution to the example given, there are other, approximate solutions available which may solve certain problems more rapidly. These approximations are shown below.

First, assume that the above submodule of two cells in parallel is represented by the illuminated cell only. In this case, the submodule equation is identical to a single cell equation and the losses in the dark cell are neglected:

$$I_c(v) = I_M(v) = I_L - I_0(v_0) \qquad (2\text{-}37)$$

Curve A in Fig. 2-31 shows that this approximation calculates the power output as too high from this partially shadowed submodule.

Next, assume that the above submodule of two cells in parallel is represented by two equally illuminated cells at one-half of the original intensity. The submodule equation is the sum at constant voltages of two cells of Eq. 2-29 with $k = 0.5$.

$$I_M(v) = I_L - 2I_0(v_0 - 0.5\,I_L R_S)$$

$$(2\text{-}38)$$

This curve, also shown in Fig. 2-31, is lower than the correct curve.

Before proceeding, Eq. 2-36 shall be generalized. If the submodule contains p cells in parallel, and rp of them are illuminated (i.e., $p(1 - r)$ of them are shadowed), then the submodule equation becomes

$$I_M(v) = I_{\text{illum}} + I_{\text{dark}}$$

where

$$I_{\text{illum}} = rpkI_L - rpI_0(v_0 - \Delta v_1)$$

and where

$$\Delta v_1 = (1 - k)I_L R_S.$$

The dark component is

$$I_{\text{dark}} = -(1 - r)pI_0(v_0 - \Delta v_2)$$

where

$$\Delta v_2 = I_L R_S.$$

The dark current component is, of course, independent of the illumination factor k.

Equations 2-37 and 2-38 may be similarly generalized. All three models, shown in Fig. 2-31, are then expressed as in Eqs. 2-39 to 2-42. From Eq. 2-36, the *accurate model* becomes:

$$I_M(v) = rp\left[kI_L - I_0(v_0 - \Delta v_1)\right.$$

$$\left. - \frac{1-r}{r}I_0(v_0 - \Delta v_2)\right]$$

$$\Delta v_1 = (1 - k)I_L R_S$$

$$\Delta v_2 = (1 - r)I_L R_S$$

$$v \geqslant 0 \qquad\qquad (2\text{-}39a)$$

From Eq. 2-37, the *optimistic approximation* becomes:

$$I_M(v) = rp\left[kI_L - I_0(v_0 - \Delta v)\right]$$

$$\Delta v = (1 - k)I_L R_S$$

$$v \geqslant 0 \qquad\qquad (2\text{-}40a)$$

From Eq. 2-38, the *pessimistic approximation* becomes:

$$I_M(v) = rp\left[kI_L - \frac{1}{r}I_0(v_0 - \Delta v)\right]$$

$$\Delta v = (1 - rk)I_L R_S$$

$$v \geqslant 0 \qquad\qquad (2\text{-}41a)$$

For all three, *reverse characteristics* (Eqs. 2-39b, 2-40b, and 2-41b).

$$I_M(v) = p\left[rkI_L - vG(v)\right] \qquad v < 0$$

$$(2\text{-}39b)$$
$$(2\text{-}40b)$$
$$(2\text{-}41b)$$

To facilitate writing of Eqs. 2-39 through 2-41, all three equations for partially shadowed submodules are expressed simply as shown in Eq. 2-42.

$$I_M(v) = I(0) - J(v') \qquad v \geqslant 0$$

$$= I(0) - vG(v) \qquad v < 0 \quad (2\text{-}42)$$

$I(0) = rpkI_L$, and $J(v')$ provides the same function for the submodule that $I_0(v_0)$ serves in the cell Eq. 2-28, except that $J(v')$ may represent

any of the corresponding terms in Eqs. 2-39 through 2-41.

The validity of the above accurate models has been established experimentally.[16,17]

2-40. Partially Shadowed Cells in Series

In Fig. 2-32, two cells of unequal output are shown connected in series. The terminal behavior of this cell pair, requiring $I_1 = I_2$, is obtained by summing the cell voltages at constant current values, as illustrated. It is clearly seen that the lower output cell number 1—i.e., a shadowed cell—limits the output from the higher output cell number 2. The amount of the limiting depends, of course, on the reverse characteristics of cell number 1. In order to analyze cells connected in series, the reverse breakdown characteristics must be considered as expressed by the term $G(v)$ in Eq. 2-29.

The general current-voltage characteristics of an entire unshadowed solar cell string (Eq. 2-32) are nearly identical to the average individual cell characteristics, except for the coordinate scales, some additional series resistance due to cell interconnections, and some minor alterations of the cell $I(V)$ curves due to the string assembly techniques. For simplicity, these effects are understood to be included in the basic cell model and, hence, are omitted in this discussion. The blocking diodes are considered later in the array analysis.

In this section, it is assumed that the solar cells have infinite breakdown voltages and zero reverse currents. This assumption is an excellent one as long as the cell reverse currents remain negligible (compared to the cell output currents) up to voltages in the order of the magnitude of the bus voltage. The model for a partially shadowed submodule with p cells in parallel was shown in Eq. 2-42 to be $I_M(v) = I(0) - J(v')$ and the string $I_s(V_s)$ curve was obtained by summing all the s submodule characteristics of that string at constant current values as shown for Eqs. 2-31 and 2-32 for the non-shadowed case. By substitution, we get Eq. 2-43.

$$I_s(V_s) = I(0) - J(V_s + \Delta V) \qquad (2\text{-}43)$$

Three solutions to Eq. 2-43 are outlined for a partially shadowed string consisting of $s = 48$

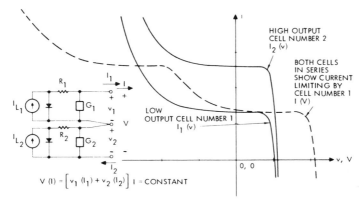

$$V (I) = \left[v_1 (I_1) + v_2 (I_2) \right] I = \text{CONSTANT}$$

Fig. 2-32. Current-voltage characteristics of two unequal solar cells connected in series.[15] (Reprinted with permission of the IEEE)

series-connected submodules of $p = 8$ parallel-connected cells each, illuminated with intensity Q. From the infinite number of possible shadow patterns, three distinct cases of special interest may be isolated: A, B, and C.

Case A. The same portions of active cell areas are shadowed in each submodule.

Case B. One submodule is completely shadowed, all others are illuminated.

Case C. Several submodules are shadowed, each by a different amount. The most heavily shadowed submodule is illuminated by the ratio r of Eq. 2-35.

The solutions to Eq. 2-43 for the cases above, (illustrated in Fig. 2-33) are given below.

For Case A. Eq. 2-43 is directly applicable, since r in this equation is identical to all the r's in the $s = 48$ submodule equations.

For Case B. According to the assumption of negligible reverse current flow through dark cells, the string output is nearly zero.

For Case C. By the foregoing, the most heavily shadowed submodule limits the string output. Hence, the string output is equal to the sum of $(s - 1) = 47$ fully illuminated submodules plus one partially shadowed submodule, all of the type of Eq. 2-42. The graphical solution of this sum is

given for submodules according to Eq. 2-41 (for a number of values of r by the dashed curves) in Fig. 2-33. The solid curves in this figure show experimental data.

The test results included in Fig. 2-33 were obtained from a typical string consisting of 1×2 cm size cells with very low breakdown voltages in the order of 2 to 4 V and of 1963–1964 vintage. Very similar results were reported in 1965 for other, more recently manufactured cells[18] with 20 to 30 V breakdown voltages for which the string model of Eq. 2-43 without reverse characteristics is indeed a very realistic model, leading to much less conservatism in power assessments than may be deduced from Fig. 2-33.

2-41. Solar Cell Strings with Shunt Diodes

From Figs. 2-32 and 2-33, it becomes readily apparent that if a cell in a series string is shadowed, the amount of current limiting can be reduced; i.e., the output will be increased if cells with low breakdown voltages are used. This thinking has led to the use of *shunt*, or *bypass*, diodes connected across shadowed cells or submodules.[19,20] The addition of these shunt diodes across shadowed submodules artificially produces a very low breakdown voltage. The diodes are connected across the submodules such that the shunt diode goes into forward conduction when the submodule is subjected to

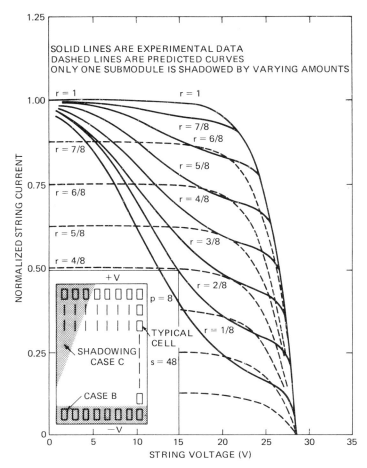

Fig. 2-33. *I-V* curves of a partially shadowed string without shunt diodes.[15] (Reprinted with permission of the IEEE)

reverse bias. A submodule becomes reverse biased when the remainder of the series string containing this submodule tries to force a greater current through this submodule than its short-circuit current permits.

In the following, a precise string model with shunt diodes is developed as a logical extension of the discussions in the foregoing sections. An approximation is then made which leads to one of the earlier models.[21] This is accomplished by first substituting the shunt diode characteristics, $I_d(v)$, for $G(v)$ in Eq. 2-42, so that the submodule equation with p cells and d shunt diodes in parallel becomes Eq. 2-44.

$$I_M(v) = I(0) - J(v') \qquad v \geqslant 0$$

$$= I(0) + dI_d(v) \qquad v < 0 \quad (2\text{-}44)$$

It is implied in Eq. 2-44 that the shunt diode forward conduction current flows only when v is negative. The string voltage is obtained similarly, as shown earlier, by first expressing Eq. 2-30 in terms of v.

$$V_s(I_s) = \sum_{i=1}^{s} [v(I)_i]_I \qquad (2\text{-}45)$$

This can be expressed in terms of I.

$$I_s(V_s) = f(I_M, v, p, s, d, r, \cdots) \quad (2\text{-}46)$$

For a partially shadowed string with shunt diodes, the same three shadowing cases studied for a string without shunt diodes are discussed again here.

Case A. Since this case is independent of the reverse characteristics, the results obtained with Eqs. 2-43 and 2-46 are identical.

Case B. The string curve is the sum of $(s - 1) = 47$ fully illuminated submodules plus one non-illuminated submodule of Eq. 2-30 as illustrated in Fig. 2-34 for $r = 0$. It will be noted that only the power (and voltage drop) dissipated in the shunt diode is lost. (Figure 2-35 also illustrates the resulting summation for eight discrete steps of r, as well as the experimental data.)

Case C. The effect of a general shadow pattern on a string consisting of twenty submodules of seven parallel-connected cells each is illustrated in Fig. 2-35.

The experimental data substantiate the validity of the model.[21] The somewhat higher experimental current output as compared to the prediction was caused by incomplete shadowing

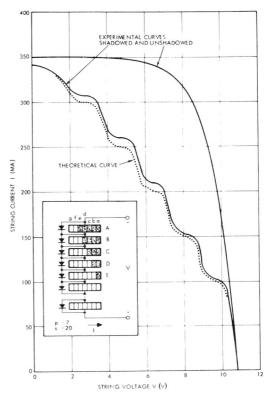

Fig. 2-35. Partially shadowed string characteristics for illustrated shadow pattern (shadowing Case C of Fig. 2-33). (Reprinted with permission of the IEEE)[15]

of the cells during the experiment. The theoretical curve of Fig. 2-35 was obtained by digital computer computations[22] carried out according to Eqs. 2-44 through 2-46.

Inspection of Figs. 2-34 and 2-35 reveals a certain pattern according to which the string $I(V)$ curve shape is altered when cells in a submodule are shadowed. If one submodule is completely shadowed, the $I(V)$ curve will, in general terms, be lowered in voltage by $\Delta V = v + V_d$, where v is the submodule photovoltaic voltage under full illumination and V_d is the voltage drop of the shunt diode connected across this now shadowed submodule. If ΔV could be assumed a constant, then a family of curves, each displaced by ΔV to the left of adjacent curves, could be drawn. The highest voltage curve, of course, is the unshadowed output curve, Eq. 2-45, and increasing number of entire submodules shadowed (shadowing *Case B* above)

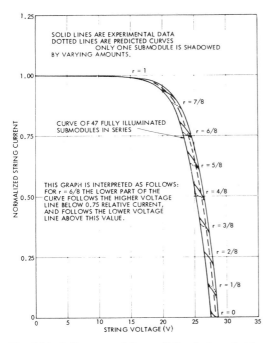

Fig. 2-34. I-V curves of the partially shadowed string of Fig. 2-33 with shunt diodes.[15] (Reprinted with permission of the IEEE)

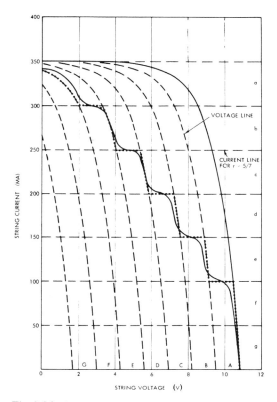

Fig. 2-36. Accurate and approximate I-V curves of the partially shadowed string.[15] Solid line is the theoretical curve of Fig. 2-35. Dotted line is the approximate model output. $\Delta V = 1.3$ volt. (Reprinted with permission of the IEEE)

would be represented by the lower voltage lines shown in Fig. 2-36.

Similarly, shadowing of series-connected columns of cells (shadowing *Case A* above) reduces the unshadowed string output by $\Delta I = (1 - r)I(0)$ as shown by the current lines in Fig. 2-36. Any particular shadow pattern on the string can then readily be transformed into the corresponding $I(V)$ curve by the method suggested by and illustrated in Fig. 2-36. By determining the value for ΔV experimentally, this approximation may become a highly accurate one. To improve the accuracy even more, the sharp corners may be rounded off to approximate the submodule $I(V)$ curve shape knee and the shunt diode knee.

It should be noted that string $I(V)$ curves, as shown in Figs. 2-33 through 2-36, vary their shape with both intensity or angle of incidence;

i.e., all characteristics become $I_s(V_s) = J(V_s + \Delta V_s)$ with $\Delta V_s = I(0)pR_s$ at zero intensity.

2-42. Shadowing Factors

A so-called *shadowing factor*, F, can be defined as the ratio of the output of an entire, partially shadowed, arbitrarily sized and shaped solar array to the hypothetical unshadowed output of this same array.[15]

The creation and use of the shadowing factor has been found to be particularly helpful in the analysis of solar arrays with a relatively large number of strings arranged in complicated fashion and subjected to substantial, diverse, and rapidly varying shadow patterns for which the detailed knowledge of the effects discussed earlier would lead to prohibitively large amounts of data to be generated and processed. While the shadowing factor could be used in the analysis of arrays using shunt diodes, it is developed here only for arrays not using them. Blocking diodes, however, are required.

For the following, consider a solar array of a spinning satellite. Define a coordinate system, xyz, such that its origin is located at the center of mass of the arbitrarily shaped satellite. The z-axis coincides with the satellite spin axis, and the center of the sun is always located in the yz-plane. Let the solar array be divided into zones A, each characterized by its typical zone temperature and zone angle α. Let each zone be divided into flat panels (facets) N, symmetrically distributed and separated by panel angle λ. The first panels of different zones are displaced from the reference panel by an angle χ. The solar vector makes an angle θ with the spin axis, and the normal to each panel makes an angle γ with the solar vector. In terms of the given definitions, for each panel of each zone (see illustration in Section 2-49) we find Eq. 2-47.

$$\cos \gamma = \cos \theta \cos \alpha$$
$$+ \sin \theta \sin \alpha \cos [\psi + (N - 1)\lambda + \chi] \quad (2\text{-}47)$$

It should be noted that for naturally shaded panels $\cos \lambda$ of Eq. 2-47 is negative. Panels with such negative outputs must either be discounted if they connect through blocking diodes to the bus, or they must be considered as loads (as discussed in Section 2-39).

The output from a partially shadowed array was given by Eq. 2-34. If we define the relationship, as in Eq. 2-48, for the most heavily shadowed submodule in each string and negligible cell reverse currents, then Eq. 2-34 may be restated as Eq. 2-49.

$$rI(0) \cos \gamma = 0 \qquad 0 \leqslant r < 0.5$$
$$= I(0) \cos \gamma \qquad 0.5 \leqslant r \leqslant 1$$
$$(2\text{-}48)$$

$$I_Z(V_A)_{\theta,\psi} = p \sum_{i=1}^{m} \rho_i [I(0) \cos \gamma_i - J(V_A)_i]_V$$
$$(2\text{-}49)$$

V_A is still given by Eq. 2-34, but ρ_i may be either 0 or 1, depending on whether r in Eq. 2-48 is smaller or larger than 0.5. The choice of 0.5 will statistically result in zero error for a large number of strings and random shadow patterns. The unshadowed zone output, $I_{Z0}(V_A)_{\theta,\psi}$, is also given by Eq. 2-49, except that all $\rho_i = 1$. The ratio, F, of the partially shadowed zone output to the unshadowed output (Eq. 2-50) indicates the fraction of actually available current.

$$F(V_A)_{\theta,\psi} = \frac{I_Z(V_A)}{I_{Z0}(V_A)}\bigg|_{\theta,\psi}$$

$$= \frac{\sum_{i=1}^{m} \rho_i [I(0) \cos \gamma_i - J(V_A)_i]}{\sum_{i=1}^{m} [I(0) \cos \gamma_i - J(V_A)_i]}$$
$$(2\text{-}50)$$

Since, for a given zone, the total (as well as this fraction of) available current is uniquely determined by the short-circuit currents, Eq. 2-50 may be restated as Eq. 2-51.

$$F(0)_{\theta,\psi} = \frac{I_Z(0)}{I_{Z0}(0)} = \frac{\sum_{i=1}^{m} \rho_i \cos \gamma_i}{\sum_{i=1}^{m} \cos \gamma_i}$$
$$(2\text{-}51)$$

The $I(0)$ terms have cancelled out, and F has been reduced to a geometric projected area relationship. Equation 2-51 may be stated in words: *The shadowing factor, F, is the ratio of the actual short-circuit current output to the theoretical output from the total number of strings which would be illuminated in the absence of shadowing.*

The instantaneous shadowing factor, F, may be averaged over any range of the spin angle ψ, and/or sun angle θ. Assume that an average shadowing factor, $\overline{F}$, is to be determined for n values of ψ, all at one θ. Then, from the integral definition of the average, we find, Eq. 2-52.

$$\overline{F}_Z(0)_\theta = \frac{\sum_{i=1}^{m} \sum_{j=1}^{n} \rho_{ij} \cos \gamma_{ij}}{\sum_{i=1}^{m} \sum_{j=1}^{n} \cos \gamma_{ij}}$$
$$(2\text{-}52)$$

Only for special cases, such as when $\Delta\psi = \lambda$, or when n is very large, Eq. 2-52 may be written as Eq. 2-53.

$$\overline{F}_Z(0)_\theta = \frac{\sum_{j=1}^{n} \sum_{i=1}^{m} \rho_{ij} \cos \gamma_{ij}}{n \sum_{i=1}^{m} \cos \gamma_i}$$
$$(2\text{-}53)$$

The application of the shadowing factor to array analysis is outlined below. First, the shadowing factors are determined, either according to Eq. 2-51 or Eq. 2-52. Next, the shadowing factors are applied for calculating the ratios of the instantaneous or average zone outputs, respectively, to the hypothetical, unshadowed zone output according to Eq. 2-32 with $r = 1$:

$$I_Z(V_A)_{\theta,\psi} = pF(0)_{\theta,\psi}$$

$$\cdot \sum_{i=1}^{m} [I(0) \cos \gamma_i - J(V_A)_i]_V \quad (2\text{-}54)$$

$$I_Z(V_A)_\theta = p\overline{F}(0)_\theta$$

$$\cdot \sum_{i=1}^{m} [I(0) \cos \gamma_i - J(V_A)_i]_V. \quad (2\text{-}55)$$

2-43. Non-Illuminated Array Models

The I–V curves of non-illuminated (i.e., dark) solar cell arrays are well represented in the array models described in Section 2-38, except that $I_{SC} = 0$ when the illumination is zero. Temperature gradients and non-uniform solar cell I–V curves do not influence the accuracy of this model for engineering purposes. (Further details of non-illuminated arrays are given in Chapter 8 in connection with dark forward testing of solar cell arrays.)

2-44. Blocking Diode Models

Isolation diodes can be treated as series network elements having the general form[14] given in Eq. 2-56.

$$I_d = I_{od} \left\{ \exp\left[\frac{q(V_d - I_d R_{Sd})}{DkT} \right] - 1 \right\} \quad (2\text{-}56)$$

where

$\quad I_d$ = diode current
$\quad I_{od}$ = diode saturation current
$\quad q$ = electronic charge
$\quad V_d$ = diode terminal voltage
$\quad R_{Sd}$ = diode series resistance
$\quad D$ = curve-fitting constant
$\quad k$ = Boltzmann's constant
$\quad T$ = absolute temperature.

However, for most practical array analysis cases, the blocking diode equation can be approximated by the piecewise linear model in Eq. 2-57.

$$V_d = V_{od} + I_d R_{Sd} \quad (2\text{-}57)$$

V_{od} is the diode threshold voltage (about 0.6 V for silicon).

2-45. Reverse-Biased Solar Cells

This section describes the circuit analysis aspects of the so-called *hot spot* problem and the analytical methods of solution.[23] In general, the solar cell array is electrically subdivided into a number of solar cell *modules* (also called *strings*) which are connected through blocking diodes to the main array bus. The bus voltage, V_B, is held relatively constant by some kind of

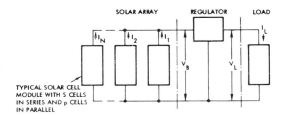

Fig. 2-37. General block diagram of solar cell array power subsystem.

regulator independently of the solar cell array output capability. The nomenclature is defined in Fig. 2-37. A single submodule containing an *affected* cell (i.e., a failed-open or shadowed cell) may be isolated from the remainder of the string, as illustrated in Fig. 2-38.

The reverse voltages on the cells connected in parallel with the affected cell are obtained by writing suitable loop and node equations and solving them. The node equations for current and the loop equations for voltage, taken in the direction of current I_1 are given below.

$$\text{At node A:} \quad I_A - I_U = 0 \quad (2\text{-}57\text{a})$$

$$\text{At node B:} \quad I_U - I_1 = 0 \quad (2\text{-}57\text{b})$$

$$\text{Loop } I_1: \quad V_A + V_U - V_B = 0 \quad (2\text{-}57\text{c})$$

These non-linear equations, existing in the first and second quadrant of the I–V coordinate system, must now be solved simultaneously. This can be accomplished with numerical (computerized) or graphical methods. The latter method is illustrated here.

First, the current-voltage (I–V) characteristics of the three circuit elements of Fig. 2-38 are constructed, based on actual solar cell test data. For example, Fig. 2-39 shows these combined I–V curves for two variations of a particular design, namely, two and four cells in parallel by 154 cells in series. Also shown for each case are two different reverse leakage values; one is based on a very low leakage current (at any voltage); the other cell is based on a very high leakage current which had been measured on a sample of cells. The method for constructing I–V curves of partially shadowed (or open) solar cell circuits is based on Sections 2-38 through 2-40.

The graphical solutions of Eqs. 2-57a, b, and

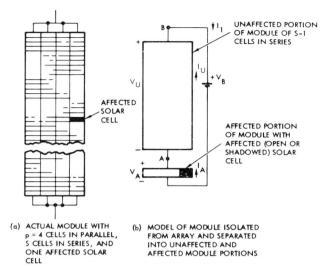

(a) ACTUAL MODULE WITH
    p = 4 CELLS IN PARALLEL,
    S CELLS IN SERIES, AND
    ONE AFFECTED SOLAR
    CELL

(b) MODEL OF MODULE ISOLATED
    FROM ARRAY AND SEPARATED
    INTO UNAFFECTED AND
    AFFECTED MODULE PORTIONS

Fig. 2-38. Module design and model.

c are effected with reference to Fig. 2-39 as follows. From Eqs. 2-57a and b, it is obvious that the current in all circuit elements is the same; i.e., $I_A = I_U = I_1$. The objective is now to find that current for which Eq. 2-57b is satisfied; that is, for which $V_A = V_U - V_B$ (note that V_A is a negative quantity and the signs are consistent). The graphical solution can be simplified by plotting $I_U(V_U - V_B)$ instead of $I_U(V_U)$ and inverting the sign of V_A. This is shown in Fig. 2-40. The intersections of the curves readily provide the operating points Q_1 through Q_4.

In Fig. 2-40, only four operating points are

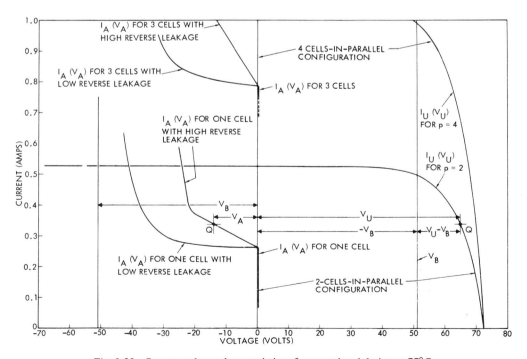

Fig. 2-39. Current-voltage characteristics of conventional design at 77°C.

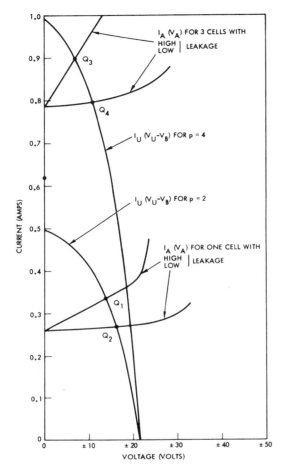

Fig. 2-40. Graphical solution for the two designs at 77°C.

shown. In practice, however, things are more complicated. For the design with two cells in parallel ($p = 2$), the not-failed or unshadowed cell in an affected submodule may be biased at any point between Q_1 and Q_2, provided of course, that its reverse characteristics lie within that range. For the design with four cells in parallel ($p = 4$), the affected submodule may be biased between Q_3 and Q_4; however, the dissipation in each of the three unaffected cells is one-third of that indicated by Q_3 and Q_4 only if all three cells have the same (i.e., perfectly matched) reverse characteristics. If the reverse characteristics are mismatched, one cell may dissipate a greater amount than is the case when the dissipation is equally shared by the cells.

2-46. Power Dissipation in Reverse Biased Solar Cells

The total energy input which contributes to heating of a reverse biased solar cell consists of both the solar radiation input and the full electrical energy input as measured by the product of cell terminal current and terminal voltage. This conclusion can be derived independently, either from energy balance or from electrical circuit considerations.

Energy Balance Considerations. In the steady state and in space, the solar cell temperature, T (absolute), is determined by the energy flow balance (or power balance) equation derived from Fig. 2-41 (Eq. 2-58).

$$P_R = P_S - P_E \qquad (2-58)$$

From Stefan-Boltzmann's law, we get Eq. 2-59 (where ϵ is the emissivity and σ is Boltzmann's constant).

$$P_R = \epsilon \sigma T^4 \qquad (2-59)$$

The solar input, P_S, and the electrical output from the cell, P_E, are independent variables. The radiant heat energy outflow from the cell, P_R, is the resulting or dependent variable. P_E depends on the load but is limited to $\eta_{max} P_S$ if the load is passive (η_{max} is the maximum solar cell efficiency at the actual operating conditions). If the load contains an energy source, P_E may take on large negative values, indicating heat dissipation in the cell.

If the cell operates in its normal power output mode, the wattmeter in Fig. 2-42 measures the cell output. If the cell becomes reverse biased, V (in Fig. 2-42) and, therefore P_E become negative (i.e., power flows into cell). From Eq. 2-58, we find Eq. 2-60.

$$P_R = P_S - (-P_E) = P_S + P_E \qquad (2-60)$$

The above equation confirms that, as far as the cell is concerned, it "sees" both the solar input,

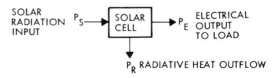

Fig. 2-41. Energy balance model.

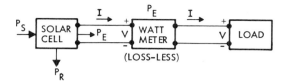

Fig. 2-42. Measurement of P_E.

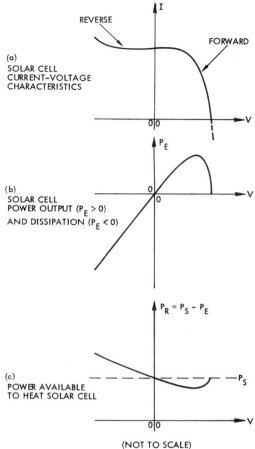

(a)
SOLAR CELL
CURRENT-VOLTAGE
CHARACTERISTICS

(b)
SOLAR CELL
POWER OUTPUT ($P_E > 0$)
AND DISSIPATION ($P_E < 0$)

(c)
POWER AVAILABLE
TO HEAT SOLAR CELL

(NOT TO SCALE)

Fig. 2-44. Relationships between solar cell bias voltage and power dissipation.

P_S, and the electrical input, $P_E = VI$, as read on the wattmeter or on independent voltage and current meters. The product VI in the dc steady state always gives the correct dissipation.

Electrical Circuit Considerations. For positive solar cell output voltages according to the convention of Fig. 2-43, the cell current and power output varies as shown to the right of the vertical axes in Figs. 2-44a and b; Fig. 2-44c illustrates that when the cell operates at its maximum power point, the amount of power available for cell heating, P_R, is at a minimum.

For negative cell voltages—i.e., reverse bias (achieved with a generator within the load)—the power output from the cell is negative according to the convention of Fig. 2-43, which means that the power is dissipated within the cell (this is consistent with the previous figure). Figure 2-44c shows the increase in P_R for increasing reverse bias.

It is also evident from Fig. 2-43 that if the polarity of V reverses, all current greater than I_L (i.e., $I - I_L$) must flow through R_{SH} because the diode blocks the current flow. Again, the dissipation in the cell is independently determined by P_S and P_E, and $P_R = P_S - P_E$. In the fully shadowed case, $P_S = 0$ and $P_R = P_E$. Hence, in the fully shadowed case, the curve of $P_R(V)$ (Fig. 2-44c) exists only to the left of the origin.

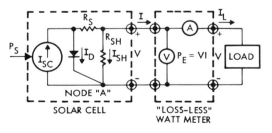

Fig. 2-43. Solar cell and load model (see text for limitations of this model).

ARRAY PERFORMANCE PREDICTION

2-47. Array Output Analysis

The electrical performance of a solar cell array is defined as the electrical power output *capability* (as contrasted by the actual output that depends upon the load demand) of an array at some specified operating conditions and before or after some specified environmental exposure. Array performance prediction is also known by other terms, such as *performance analysis* or *output computation*.

The process of electrical performance prediction contains the following elements:

• Solar cell electrical performance characterization

- Determination of the degradation factors related to solar cell array design and assembly
- Conversion of environmental considerations and criteria into solar cell operating temperatures
- Calculation of solar cell array power output capability.

Of course, not all of the input data and design parameters given in this section are applicable for all designs or all missions. For some other array designs or missions, additional input data may be required or other design parameters may have to be considered.

The general analytical approach followed in this section presupposes the existence of a detailed solar cell array design which is intended for a specific terrestrial or space application. (The procedures for creating and developing a detailed array design are given in Chapter 3.) The detailed array performance prediction consists of three major activities:

- Gathering of input data
- Performing supporting analyses
- Performing the array output analysis.

Figure 2-45 illustrates the general analytical approach and the flow of data between the various analyses. While shown for space arrays, most parameters also apply to terrestrial arrays. The array output computation is based on the commonly used computerized shifting of I-V curves within an I-V coordinate system to account for environmental and operational effects. The performance prediction for space arrays is developed using the damage-equivalent, normal incident (DENI) 1 MeV fluence method for determining solar cell degradation (see Section 3-32), and using orbital data to determine the optical array degradation; however, any other method for determining solar cell and optical (cell cover and cover adhesive) degradation may be substituted for the methods shown here.

The input data can be gathered from Chapters 4 through 10; the design process is illustrated in Chapter 3. The supporting and array output analyses are described in this chapter, and their applications are illustrated in Chapter 3.

The input data listed under "INPUTS" in Fig. 2-45 are defined as follows, with reference to this figure, and in the same sequence as in the figure—from top to bottom.

Solar Cell Cover Factors. The optical transmission factor, F_τ, includes anything that may affect the amount of light reaching the solar cell active surface (Eq. 2-61).

$$F(\theta, \phi_{uv}, \phi_p) = F_{\tau a}(\phi_{uv}, \phi_p) \cdot F_{\tau c}(\phi_{uv}, \phi_p)$$
$$\cdot R_{sc}(\theta, \phi_{uv}, \phi_p) \cdot F_d(t)$$

$$(2-61)$$

where

$F_{\tau a}$ = adhesive darkening factor, defined as the ratio of the solar cell short-circuit current after adhesive darkening to that before darkening

$F_{\tau c}$ = cover darkening factor, defined as the ratio of the solar cell short-circuit current after darkening to that before darkening

R_{sc} = relative short-circuit current, defined as the ratio of the glassed solar cell short-circuit current actually measured at a given sun off-point angle, θ, to that expected from the cosine of θ (i.e., R_{sc} is the cosine correction factor)

F_d = light transmission loss factor due to deposits and their darkening with time, defined as the ratio of the solar cell short-circuit current after darkening of the deposits to that before deposits were present

$F(\theta, \phi_{uv}, \phi_p, t)$ = indication that the factor, F, is a function of $\theta, \phi_{uv}, \phi_p, t$

ϕ_{uv} = ultraviolet radiation dose

ϕ_p = particulate radiation dose

t = time in service or in orbit.

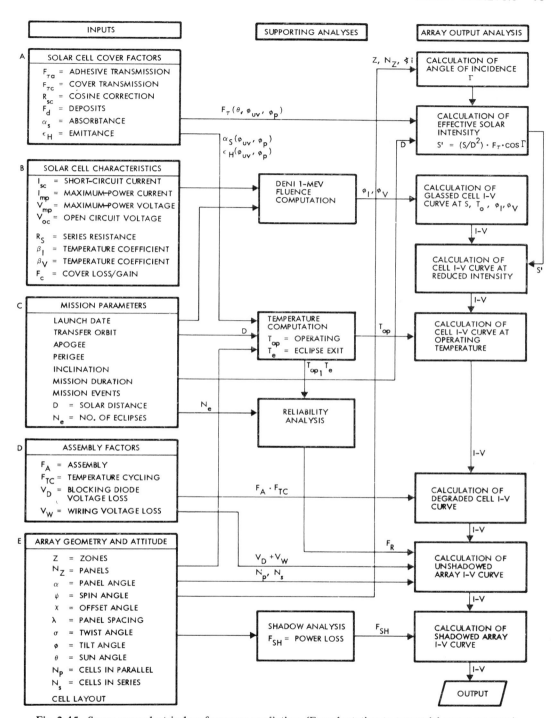

Fig. 2-45. Space array electrical performance prediction. (For adaptation to terrestrial arrays see text.)

The radiometric properties, α_S and ϵ_H are functions of both ϕ_{uv} and ϕ_p. For terrestrial arrays, the array *convective* heat transfer coefficient also enters in.

Solar Cell Characteristics. The electrical characteristics of the specific solar cells or modules considered for a design may be obtained from Chapter 4. The following solar cell characteristics are required for the analyses described herein:

- Solar cell *I-V* curves at standard test conditions (typically, 25°C cell temperature, one solar constant intensity and air-mass-one or air-mass-zero spectrum) and, for space arrays, before and after irradiation with 1 MeV electrons
- Temperature coefficients for solar cell or module current (β_I) and voltage (β_V), and power (β_p) before and (for space) after irradiation with 1 MeV electrons
- Cover installation factor, F_c
- Cell series resistance, R_s.

The cover installation factor, F_c, is defined as

$$F_c = I_{sc}(C)/I_{sc}(U)$$

where the indices (C) and (U) indicate the *covered* and *uncovered* cell short-circuit current output, I_{sc}, respectively. Typically, for SiO_x-coated solar cells, F_c is less than unity and for Ta_2O_5-coated cells, F_c is equal to or greater than unity.

Mission Parameters. The mission or service parameters listed in Fig. 2-45 determine or contribute to the following:

- Solar cell radiation dose (in space only)
- Cover and cover adhesive radiation dose (in space only)
- Solar cell illumination level
- Solar cell operating temperature
- Solar cell array temperature cycling stress levels.

The launch date for space arrays is of significance in establishing the solar flare proton environment.

Assembly Factors. Assembly factors reflect a reduction in solar cell or module output capa-

bility due to unavoidable or deliberately chosen design, assembly, and installation process parameters. Assembly factors may be expressed as dimensionless ratios to be applied to output power, current, or voltage, or as incremental series resistances, or as voltage differences. A common practice is to use both ratios and voltage drops.

The values of assembly-related factors may change with time in service or in orbit. For example, blocking diodes, when exposed to particulate radiation, will exhibit lower forward voltage drops but higher reverse leakage currents after irradiation. As another example, solder coatings on solar cell interconnectors may cease to be electrically conductive in the current flow direction after extensive temperature cycling. The assembly and assembly degradation factors may be defined as follows:

F_A = assembly factor (solar cell power output degradation due to soldering, welding, etc.)

F_{TC} = solar cell array power output degradation due to temperature cycling

V_D = blocking diode voltage losses

V_W = interconnector and wiring voltage losses due to resistance and changes in resistance (increases with increasing temperature).

Array Geometry and Attitude. The solar cell array configuration and its physical orientation relative to the sun determines the amount of sunlight intercepted by the solar cells and, hence, both the array operating temperature and the solar cell output.

2-48. Sequence of Shifting *I-V* Curves

The best method for predicting solar cell and array performance is shifting the cell or array *I-V* characteristics along their current and voltage coordinates and adjusting the curve shape when required. The proper sequence for such curve is given below:

1. Start with initial, bare cell characteristics obtained under standard test conditions (i.e., 25°C cell temperature, one solar constant intensity, air-mass-zero spectrum for space arrays or air-mass-one for terrestrial arrays).

2. Adjust, I_{sc}, I_{mp}, V_{mp}, and V_{oc}, measured under standard test conditions for particulate radiation damage, as expressed for a given damage equivalent 1 MeV fluence. (This applies for space arrays only.)

3. Adjust the I-V curve for the operating solar intensity actually incident on the solar cell through degraded optical elements and at off-point angles. Include any cover installation loss or gain. Correct the curve shape, if required.

4. Adjust the I-V curve for the operating temperature. Correct the curve shape again, if required.

5. Scale up the cell characteristics to the array level and include isolation diode and wiring losses, and external series resistance effects.

2-49. Calculation of Angle of Incidence

Let the solar cell array be centered in a Cartesian coordinate system such that the array's spin axis or axis of symmetry is coincident with one of the axes of the coordinate system, as illustrated in Figs. 2-46 through 2-48 for a variety of general array configurations.[22]

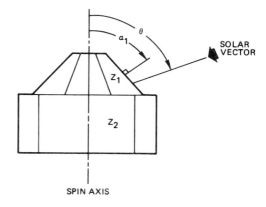

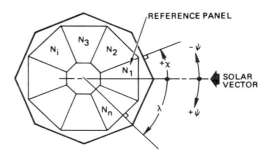

Fig. 2-47. Solar cell array geometry for flat or body-mounted solar panels.[7]

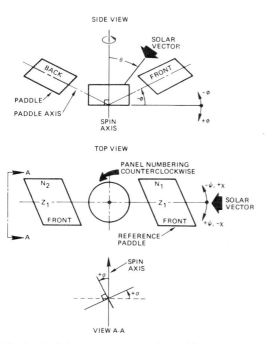

Fig. 2-46. Solar array geometry for paddle-wheel solar array configurations.[7]

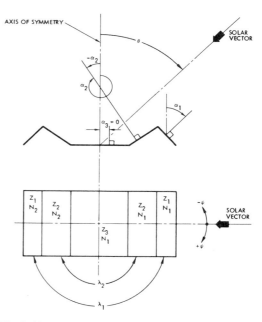

Fig. 2-48. Solar cell array geometry for flat solar cell panels.

The array is subdivided into Z zones. Each zone contains only those solar cell panels whose normal unit vector* projections on the spin axis are equal; i.e., they all have the same angle α.

Each zone is subdivided into N solar cell panels or paddles. Each panel or paddle is angularly displaced from its neighbor by an angle λ. The angle λ is measured in a plane which is perpendicular to the spin axis (i.e., when viewed in the direction of the spin axis) and is always positive.

The normal unit vector of the first panel or paddle in the first zone is (for convenience) placed in a plane defined by that unit vector and the array-sun line (the *solar vector*).

The projection (on a plane perpendicular to the spin axis) of the unit vector of the first panel of the second zone makes an angle χ with the projection of the unit vector of the first panel of the first zone. When the projections of both unit vectors are parallel, $\chi = 0$.

The array may be spinning in the coordinate system through the spin angle ψ. Initially, $\psi = 0$, for convenience.

For a paddle wheel array configuration, the axis through each paddle in a direction pointing away from the spin axis may be inclined (raised up) from a plane which is perpendicular to the spin axis by an angle ϕ. When a paddle axis is perpendicular to the spin axis, $\phi = 0$.

Each paddle is twisted relative to being plane-parallel to a plane which is perpendicular to the spin axis by an angle σ. This angle is measured in a counterclockwise direction when viewed along the twist axis in the direction of the spin axis.

For a body-mounted or flat panel array configuration, all normal unit vectors in a given zone make an angle σ with the spin axis.

The angle of incidence, Γ, for each panel or paddle on the array, for a given angle θ (sun angle) between the array spin axis (spin vector) and the array-sun line (sun vector), can be found from Eqs. 2-62a or 2-62b, respectively. The angles are defined above and in Figs. 2-46 through 2-48.

*For a definition of vectors, see Appendix A.

Paddle-Wheel Configuration. For the ith panel, Eq. 6-62a.

$$\cos \Gamma_i = \sin \sigma \cdot \sin \theta \cdot \sin [\psi + (N_i - 1)\lambda + \chi]$$
$$+ \cos \sigma \cdot \sin \phi \cdot \sin \theta$$
$$\cdot \cos [\psi + (N_i - 1)\lambda + \chi]$$
$$+ \cos \sigma \cdot \cos \phi \cdot \cos \theta \qquad (2\text{-}62a)$$

Body-Mounted and Flat Configurations. For the ith panel, Eq. 2-62b.

$$\cos \Gamma_i = \cos \theta \cdot \cos \alpha + \sin \theta \cdot \sin \alpha$$
$$\cdot \cos [\psi + (N_i - 1)\lambda + \chi] \qquad (2\text{-}62b)$$

2-50. Calculation of Effective Solar Intensity

The effective solar intensity, S', is defined as the actual, *effective* light level which is incident upon the active surface of the solar cell and is given by Eq. 2-63.

$$S' = (S/D^2)F_\tau \cos \Gamma \qquad (2\text{-}63)$$

The terms in Eq. 2-63 are defined as follows:

S = sunlight intensity (in units of solar constants)
D = array-sun distance (in units of AU)
F_τ = solar cell cover transmission factor
Γ = angle of incidence.

2-51. Calculation of Cell and Array I-V Curves

Glassed Solar Cell I-V Curve. The $I\text{-}V$ curves for unglassed cells are shifted parallel to the current axis until the value of the cell short-circuit current after glassing is

$$I_{scg} = I_{scu}F_c$$

where I_{scu} is the unglassed short-circuit current of the radiation-damaged cell and F_c is the cover installation factor. Since Fc is typically within a few percent of unity, the other three solar cell parameters after glassing are

$$I_{mpg} = I_{mpu} + (I_{scg} - I_{scu})$$
$$V_{mpg} = V_{mpu}$$
$$V_{ocg} = V_{ocu}$$

where

I_{mp} = current at maximum power
V_{mp} = voltage at maximum power
V_{oc} = open-circuit voltage.

The additional subscripts, g and u, refer to "glassed" and "unglassed" conditions, respectively. The output parameters of terrestrial flat plate modules are the same as those for glassed cells, except, of course, that the modules contain several solar cells.

Solar Cell I-V Curve After Intensity Change. The solar cell I-V curves for a particular radiation damage are shifted in the I-V coordinate system along the current and voltage axes by the amounts ΔI_1 and ΔV_1, given by

$$\Delta I_1 = (S' - S)I_{scg}$$

$$\Delta V_1 = -\Delta I_1 R_S$$

where

I_{scg} = original cell short-circuit current after glassing before the intensity was changed
R_S = cell series resistance
S' = effective solar intensity
S = solar intensity at which the solar cells were originally tested.

ΔI_1 is negative and ΔV_1 is positive for reduced intensity (i.e., $S' < S$), leading to a lower short-circuit current, I_{scs}, and a slight shift toward higher voltages even though the actual cell open-voltage will decrease by

$$V_{S'} = k \log (S'/S)$$

where k depends upon the cell type. The four solar cell parameters change as follows due to a change in intensity (indicated by the additional subscript s):

$$I_{scs} = I_{scg} + \Delta I_1$$

$$I_{mps} = I_{mpg} + \Delta I_1$$

$$V_{mps} = V_{mpg} + \Delta V_1 + \Delta V_{S'}$$

$$V_{ocs} = V_{ocg} + \Delta V_1 + \Delta V_{S'}.$$

Solar Cell I-V Curve at Operating Temperature. The I-V curve is now adjusted for the actual solar cell operating temperature, T_{op}. The I-V curve is shifted in the I-V coordinate system by amounts ΔI_2 and ΔV_2, given by

$$\Delta I_2 = \beta_I I_{sc}(T_{op} - T_0)$$

$$\Delta V_2 = \beta_V (T_{op} - T_0)$$

where

β_I = temperature coefficient for current in units of $°C^{-1}$
β_V = temperature coefficient for voltage, in units of $V \cdot °C^{-1}$
I_{sc} = the cell I_{sc} before the temperature change
T_0 = reference temperature at which the solar cells were initially tested.

The values of β_I are usually positive and those of β_V are negative. Therefore, a temperature increase $(T_{op} > T_0)$ causes an increase in I_{sc} and a decrease in V_{oc}. The four cell parameters change as follows:

$$I_{sc_T} = I_{scs} + \Delta I_2$$

$$I_{mp_T} = I_{mps} + \Delta I_2$$

$$V_{mp_T} = V_{mps} + \Delta V_2$$

$$V_{oc_T} = V_{ocs} + \Delta V_2.$$

Degraded Solar Cell I-V Curve. The solar cell I-V curve is now further adjusted for the assembly and temperature cycling degradation factors, F_A and F_{TC}, respectively. Both F_A and F_{TC} usually introduce additional series resistance in the solar cell or in an assembly of cells and thereby tend to depress the cell's maximum power output without affecting the I_{sc} and V_{oc}. Therefore, it is desirable to depress both I_{mp} and V_{mp} on the I-V curve by the amounts

$$\Delta I_3 = -(F_A \cdot F_{TC})^{1/2}$$

$$\Delta V_3 = -(F_A \cdot F_{TC})^{1/2}$$

respectively, and letting I_{sc} and V_{oc} remain unchanged. The four cell parameters will therefore change as follows:

$$I_{scd} = I_{sc_T}$$

$$I_{mpd} = I_{mp_T} + \Delta I_3$$

$$V_{mpd} = V_{mp_T} + \Delta V_3$$

$$V_{ocd} = V_{oc_T}.$$

Array *I-V* Curves. The unshadowed solar cell array *I-V* curve is computed from the single cell *I-V* curves in the following sequence:

- Multiplication of the single cell current output by the number of solar cells in parallel, N_p, on a given panel or paddle
- Multiplication of the voltage output of the N_p solar cells in parallel by N_s cells in series
- Subtraction of the voltage drops, V_D and V_W, from the panel voltage output
- Summing of all panel and paddle output currents at constant voltages.

The above computations result in an array *I-V* curve at operating temperature and after environmental degradation. This process of calculation is treated mathematically in Sections 2-39 and 2-40 and results in the following four array output parameters:

$$I_{sc_A} = I_{scd}N_p$$

$$I_{mp_A} = I_{scd}N_p$$

$$V_{mp_A} = V_{mpd}N_s - (V_D + V_W)$$

$$V_{oc_A} = V_{ocd}N_s - (V_D + V_W).$$

If the solar cell array is partially shadowed, the unshadowed power output must be reduced according to the method described in Sections 2-40 through 2-42.

SHADOW ANALYSIS

2-52. Shadows

In this and the next section, methods are described by which the geometries of the shadows falling on solar cell arrays can be determined. The electrical response of the array to these shadows is discussed in Sections 2-39 through 2-42.

A *shadow* is defined as the absence of solar illumination on a solar cell array due to a blocking of the sunlight by a shadow-casting object. For example, an antenna or a boom may cast a shadow on the array at certain angles of illumination, or some solar cell panels in an array field may cast shadows on other panels at low sun elevation angles.

The naturally occurring lack of illumination on the dark side of a body-mounted space array (the so-called *eigenshadow*) is specifically excluded from the definition of the shadow because the output from these non-illuminated array areas is already computed by the array models of Section 2-49 to be zero. A second inclusion of the naturally non-illuminated areas in the shadowing factor would lead to erroneous results.

The *shadowing factor* is a term affecting the electrical performance of the array; it is defined in Section 2-42. The shapes of shadows cast on the array are known as *shadow patterns*. The effect of shadow patterns on the array electrical output depends strongly on the size and location of a shadow on each string of solar cells. Therefore, shadow patterns must be determined in relation to the *string layout* of solar cells on the array.

Techniques of determining shadow patterns may be taken from books on descriptive geometry. Also, computerized or photographic procedures may be employed. The following material[24] illustrates some simple concepts useful for studying shadows.

Figure 2-49 shows the geometry of a shadow cast by a cylindrical rod parallel to a surface (extending perpendicularly through the plane of the paper) onto that surface in the vicinity of earth, where the surface is normal to the object-sun axis. From this figure,

$$\alpha_1 = 2 \text{ arc tan } (D/2L_1)$$

$$\alpha_2 = 2 \text{ arc tan } [D/2(L + B)]$$

$$\frac{B_1}{L_1} = \frac{d}{D} \text{ and } \frac{B}{L} = \frac{d}{D}$$

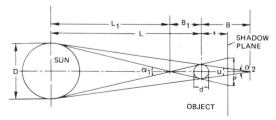

Fig. 2-49. Shadow geometry.[24]

$$\frac{L}{L_1} = \frac{L_1 + B_1}{L_1} = \frac{D+d}{D}$$

$$\frac{L+B}{L} = \frac{D+d}{D}$$

where

α = planar angle subtended by the sun's diameter

B = length of umbra

D = diameter of the sun = 0.86×10^6 miles = 1.4×10^6 km

d = width or diameter of object causing a shadow

L = distance from the object to sun at 1 AU.

Since $d \ll D$, we have $L = L_1$ and $L + B = L$. Therefore,

$$\alpha_1 \approx \alpha_2 = 2 \text{ arc tan } (D/2L) = 9.25 \times 10^{-3} \text{ rad}$$

$$B \approx B_1 = d/[2 \tan (\alpha/2)] = 108.1\,d.$$

Then, the width u of the *umbra* of the shadow becomes

$$u = \frac{d(B-s)}{B} = \frac{108.1\,d - s}{108.1} = d - \frac{s}{108.1}$$

and the width p of the *penumbra* is

$$p = \frac{d(B+s)}{B} = \frac{108.1\,d + s}{108.1} = d + \frac{s}{108.1}$$

and s is the distance from the object to the surface.

Normalized umbra and penumbra widths as a function of normalized distance are shown in Fig. 2-50.

Intensity Distribution. The light intensity in the penumbra ranges from unity at the outer edge to zero at the edge of and throughout the umbra for cases of $s < B$, and from unity to an indeterminate value for cases of $s > B$. The illumination intensity distribution within the shadow, and its average value, is a function of the shadow plane location relative to B and of the shape of the shadow-casting object.

The relative darkness at a point in the shadow can be determined by viewing the sun from that point. A portion A of the solar disc, appearing to have a radius R, will be obscured by the object. In other words, A is the projected area of the shadowing object on a circle with radius R, and R is the radius of the circle subtended by an angle α at a distance s. The relative darkness $K = A/(\pi R^2)$. The normalized illumination intensity is defined as $I = 1 - K$. Integrating K over the full shadow area and dividing by the total area gives the average darkness $\overline{K}$. The average normalized illumination intensity within the shadow is $\overline{I} = 1 - \overline{K}$.

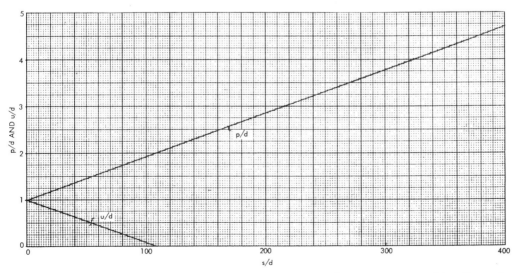

Fig. 2-50. Dimensionless representation of normalized Umbra width, u/d, and Penumbra width, p/d, as a function normalized distance to shadow casting object, s/d.[24]

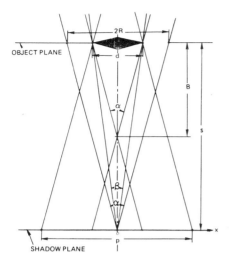

Fig. 2-51. Further shadow geometry to show relation of distance, s, to apparent solar diameter, $2R$, and object width, d.[24]

Cylinder Parallel to Shadow Plane. The case for a shadow resulting from a cylindrical rod or from a bar parallel to the shadow plane (and perpendicular to the paper), which is normal to the sun-object axis, is illustrated in Fig. 2-51. The view angle β, from distance s, of the object with width d, and the corresponding sun diameter $2R$, are related by $\beta = 2 \ \text{arc} \ \tan (d/2s)$ and by $\alpha = 2 \ \text{arc} \ \tan (R/s)$. Consequently, $d/2R = \tan (\beta/2)/\tan (\alpha/2)$ and $d/2R = B/s$. At a solar distance of 1 AU, we obtain

$$d/2R = 108/(s/d)$$

which is solved graphically in Fig. 2-52.

Observing the object of width d, as shown in Fig. 2-51, from the shadow plane at various locations along the x-axis while moving from $x = 0$ to $x = p/2$ results in images as shown in

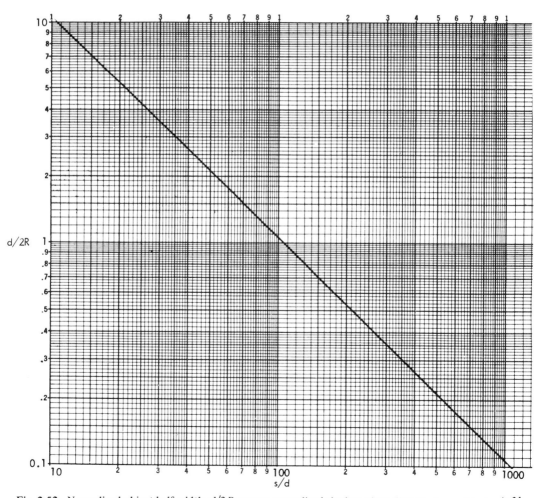

Fig. 2-52. Normalized object half-width, $d/2R$, versus normalized shadow plane distance from object, s/d.[24]

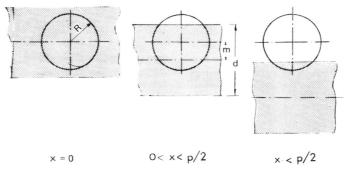

$x = 0$ $0 < x < p/2$ $x < p/2$

Fig. 2-53. View of shadow area toward sun for $s < B$, starting from sun-object centerline and moving toward edge of Penumbra (refer to text).[24]

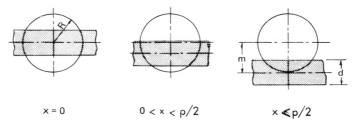

$x = 0$ $0 < x < p/2$ $x \leqslant p/2$

Fig. 2-54. View from shadow area toward sun for $s > B$, starting from sun-object centerline and moving toward edge of Penumbra.[24]

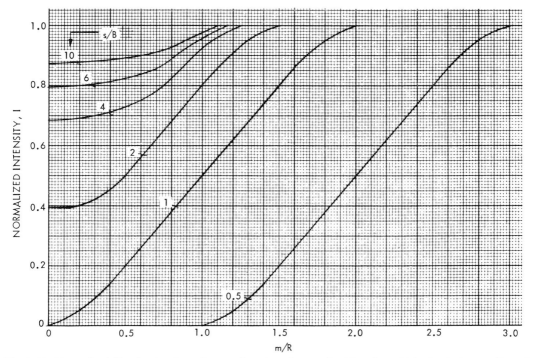

Fig. 2-55. Normalized illumination intensity as a function of normalized location within the shadow, m/R, with the normalized distance, s/b, as a parameter.[24]

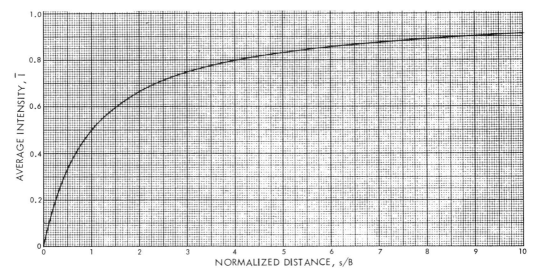

Fig. 2-56. Average light intensity, I, in a shadow from a long object parallel to the shadow plane as a function of normalized distance, s/B.[24]

Figs. 2-53 and 2-54 for the cases of $s < B$ and $s > B$, respectively.

In the case of Fig. 2-53, the moving point is in the umbra for locations of $x = 0$ to $x = u/2$; $x = u/2$ is reached when $m/R = (r/R) - 1$. (The distance between center of a circle of radius R and center of a shadow object of width d is denoted by m). While moving from $x = u/2$ to $x = p/2$, the viewing point will be located in the penumbra; $x = p/2$ is reached when $m/R = (r/R) + 1$. By inspection of Fig. 2-51, it can be seen that $u = d - 2R$ and $p = d + 2R$. For the case of Fig. 2-54, the moving point is always in the penumbra from $x = 0$ to $x = p/2$.

The normalized illumination intensity as a function of the normalized location in the shadow, m/R, is shown in Fig. 2-55 with the parameter s/B ranging from 0.5 to 10. Integrating the area under the curves in Fig. 2-55 to obtain

$$\bar{I} = \frac{1}{i} \int_0^i I \, d(m/R)$$

results in the average normalized illumination intensity as a function of s/B, shown in Fig. 2-56. Multiplying $1 - \bar{I}$ by the normalized shadow width $p/d = 1 + s/B$ results in a constant $(1 - \bar{I})p/d = 1$, which indicates that the total amount of light intensity loss in any shadow

is equivalent to the light intensity loss by an umbra-type shadow which has the same width as the object (for parallel rays of light) and has no penumbra.

Application to Solar Cell Arrays. For series parallel-connected solar cells subjected to a shadow not exceeding in width the dimension of the parallel connected cells, as shown in Fig. 2-57, an equivalent total umbra shadow of a width corresponding to a projection of the object can be used to determine the electrical out-

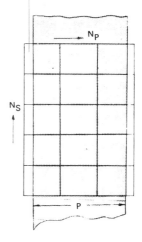

Fig. 2-57. Example of shadow across a solar cell module consisting of series-parallel connected cells.[24]

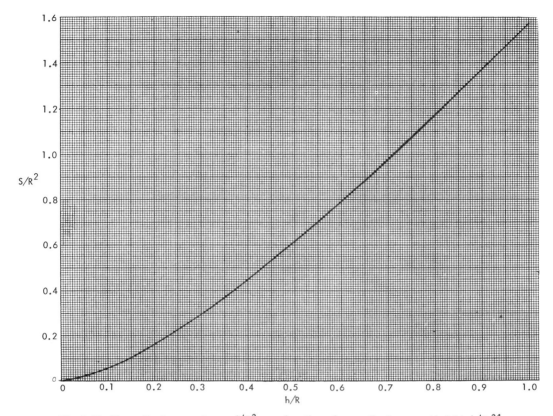

Fig. 2-58. Normalized segment area, S/R^2, as a function of normalized segment height, h/R.[24]

put reduction due to the shadow under consideration.

In the calculations used to determine the illumination intensity distribution to the penumbra, the segment area of a circle as a function of the segment height h must be known. This relationship is shown in Fig. 2-58.

THERMAL ANALYSIS

2-53. Heat Flow and Temperature

The solar cell operating efficiency, and thereby the maximum amount of power that can be extracted from a solar cell array, strongly depends upon the cell's operating temperature. Of the amount of solar energy falling onto an array, about 80 to 90% goes into heating the array, while only 10 to 20% gets converted into electricity. In operation, the incident solar energy causes the solar cell temperature to rise to such a level at which the heat outflow plus the elec-

trical output balances the solar energy inflow; this temperature level is known as the *equilibrium*, or *operating* temperature. For terrestrial arrays, the heat outflow is by heat convection and radiation, while for space arrays it is by radiation only. Usually only a negligible amount of heat is transported from the array by conduction through the array support structure. Of course, the heat generated in the solar cells must be conducted to the array outer package, from which it is then radiated or convected away.

The various components of radiative and convective heat flow that participate in a *heat flow balance* are illustrated in Figs. 2-59 and 2-60. Obviously, the accurate determination of the temperature of terrestrial arrays is more complicated and less certain than that of space arrays, partly because air and sky temperatures are highly variable.

Heat transfer calculations require knowledge of a number of material properties. Those of

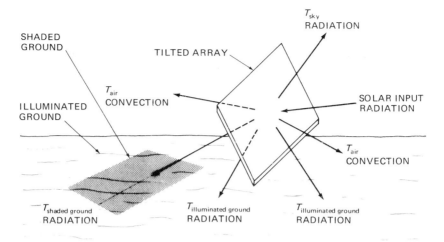

Fig. 2-59. Heat balance for terrestrial arrays.

concern in radiation heat transfer are the absorptance or absorptivity, α, the reflectance or reflectivity, ρ, the transmittance or transmissivity, τ, and the emittance or emissivity, ϵ. The material property of concern in heat conduction is the thermal conductivity, k, and the properties of concern in transient thermal analysis are the thermal conductivity, k, the mass, m, and the specific heat capacitance (at constant pressure), c_p. In general, all of these material properties are functions of temperature, their values

tending toward zero as the absolute temperature approaches zero.

The *absorptance*, α, is the ratio of the energy absorbed by a material to the energy incident on the surface of this material. The *spectral absorptance* α_λ, is the absorptance at a specific wavelength, λ. The *solar absorptance*, α_S, is the spectral absorptance integrated over the solar spectrum

$$\alpha_S = \int_0^\infty S(\lambda)\alpha_\lambda \, d\lambda \qquad (2\text{-}64)$$

where $S(\lambda)$ is the solar spectrum (see Sections 9-2 and 9-6). For surfaces composed of different materials (such as a solar cell array), an *average* or *mean solar absorptance*, $\bar{\alpha}_S$, can be defined such that

$$\bar{\alpha}_S = \frac{\sum_{i=1}^{m} \alpha_{Si} A_i}{\sum_{i=1}^{m} A_i} \qquad (2\text{-}65)$$

where

m = number of difference surface materials
α_{Si} = solar absorptance of the ith material
A_i = area of the ith material having α_{Si}.

An *effective solar absorptance*, $\bar{\alpha}_{Se}$, which includes the effect of electrical energy flowing

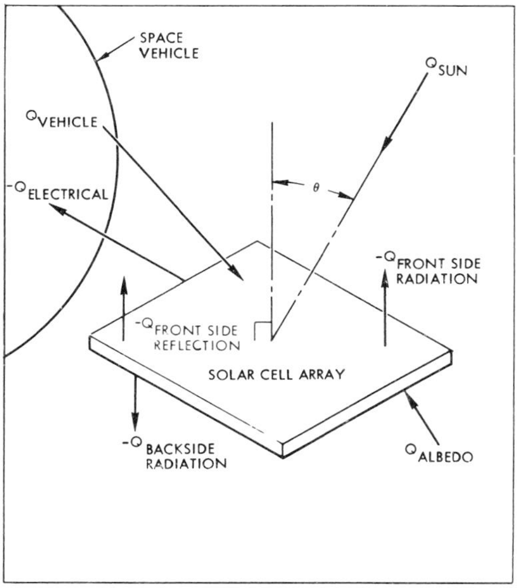

Fig. 2-60. Heat balance for space arrays.

from the solar cells and thereby reducing the heating of the cells, is defined in Eq. 2-66.

$$\bar{\alpha}_{Se} = \bar{\alpha}_S - F_p \eta_{op} \qquad (2\text{-}66)$$

where

F_p = packing factor, defined as the ratio of the total *active* solar cell area to the total substrate area for which $\bar{\alpha}_{Se}$ is to be determined

η_{op} = solar cell operating efficiency.

The *reflectance*, ρ, is defined as the ratio of the energy reflected from the surface of a material to the energy incident upon the surface of that material. The *spectral reflectance*, ρ_λ, is the reflectance at a specific wavelength, λ.

The *transmittance*, τ, is defined as the ratio of energy inside a transparent material at the exit surface to the energy at the entrance surface (excluding the front surface reflectance). Frequently, the *total transmittance*, τ_t, is defined as the ratio of the energy emanating from a transparent material to the energy incident on the front surface of that material (including both front surface and back surface reflectance). The *spectral transmittance*, τ_λ, is the reflectance at a specific wavelength, λ.

The *emittance*, ϵ, is defined as the ratio of the total emissive power of a *gray* surface to the total emissive power of a *black* surface at the same temperature. The *total emissive power* is the total radiant energy emitted (ejected) at a given temperature per unit time and per unit area of a surface. A *black surface* is the (hypothetical) surface of a (hypothetical) *black body* having the characteristic of absorbing all radiant energy striking it and reflecting or transmitting none of it (i.e., $\rho = \tau = 0$ and $\alpha = \epsilon = 1$). The *monochromatic* or *spectral emittance*, ϵ_λ, is the emittance at a specific wavelength, λ. The *directional emittance*, ϵ_D, is the emittance measured in a direction vector that makes an angle ϕ to the normal of the surface. The *normal emittance*, ϵ_N, is the directional emittance measured perpendicular to the emitting surface. The *hemispherical emittance*, ϵ_H, is the normal emittance integrated over 2π steradians (for experimental relationships between ϵ_N and ϵ_H, see Chapter 8). For a surface composed of several different materials, an *average*, or *mean*, or *effective* *hemispherical emittance*, ϵ_H, can be defined such that

$$\bar{\epsilon}_H = \frac{\sum\limits_{i=1}^{n} \epsilon_{Hi} A_i}{\sum\limits_{i=1}^{n} A_i} \qquad (2\text{-}67)$$

where

n = number of different surface materials

ϵ_{Hi} = hemispherical emittance of the ith material

A_i = area of the ith material having ϵ_{Hi}.

Radiant energy incident upon a surface may either be absorbed, reflected, or transmitted. By the principle of conservation of energy, at any instant of time and at a given temperature, Eq. 2-68 holds true.

$$\alpha + \rho + \tau = 1$$
$$\alpha_\lambda + \rho_\lambda + \tau_\lambda = 1 \qquad (2\text{-}68)$$

For opaque surfaces, $\tau = 0$, so that we have Eq. 2-69 in all its forms.

$$\alpha + \rho = 1$$
$$\alpha_\lambda + \rho_\lambda = 1$$
$$\epsilon = \alpha = 1 - \rho$$
$$\epsilon_\lambda = \alpha_\lambda = 1 - \rho_\lambda \qquad (2\text{-}69)$$

The conditions $\epsilon = \alpha$ and $\epsilon_\lambda = \alpha_\lambda$ are defined by *Kirchhoff's law*, which states that at a given temperature the total emissive power for any gray surface is equal to its absorptance multiplied by the total emissive power of a black surface at that temperature. However, it should be noted that*

$$\alpha_S \neq \epsilon, \alpha_S \neq \epsilon_D, \alpha_S \neq \epsilon_N, \alpha_S \neq \epsilon_H,$$
$$\bar{\alpha}_S \neq \bar{\epsilon}_H \text{ and } \bar{\alpha}_{Se} \neq \bar{\epsilon}_H.$$

The energy, q, emitted by a gray surface is given by Stefan-Boltzmann's law (Eq. 2-70).

$$q = \epsilon \sigma A T^4 \qquad (2\text{-}70)$$

where

ϵ = emissivity at temperature T

σ = Stefan-Boltzmann's constant

*$\neq$ means "does not equal"

A = emitting area
T = absolute temperature.

The governing physical principle in the solution of any heat transfer problem is the *conservation of energy*. For any (hypothetical) volume fully enclosed by a (hypothetical) surface:

$$\sum q_{in} + \sum q_{out} + \sum q_{stored} = 0 \quad (2\text{-}71)$$

where q_{in} and q_{out} are the rates of energy flow per unit time and per unit area through the surface, and q_{stored} is the energy stored inside the volume per unit time.

2-54. Heat Transfer by Conduction

Consider the small slab of material of area A and thickness t shown in Fig. 2-61. This slab can be assumed to be a piece of a wall separating two media that are at different temperatures, T_H and T_L. Subscripts H and L denote high and low temperature, respectively. The heat will be conducted through the wall in the direction of the arrow. The amount of heat flowing through the wall is

$$q_k = \frac{kA}{t}(T_H - T_L) \quad (2\text{-}72a)$$

where the subscript k denotes conductive heat flow. The proportionality constant k is known as the *thermal conductivity*, or *heat conductivity*, of the material through which the heat flows. Different materials have different values of thermal conductivity (see Chapter 10). In calculus notation, the heat flow is represented by the rate of energy flow, $q = dQ/dt$, in a thermally conducting medium, due to a temperature gradient dT/dx across this medium, given by Eq. 2-72b.

$$q = -kA \frac{dT}{dx} \quad (2\text{-}72b)$$

The minus sign in Eq. 2-72b indicates positive heat flow in the positive x-direction in response to a negative temperature gradient, dT/dx (i.e., decreasing temperature with increasing x).

If the conducting medium is homogeneous and is of constant cross-sectional area,

$$\frac{dT}{dx} = \frac{T_H - T_L}{s}$$

where T_H and T_L are the high and low temperatures, respectively, separated by distance s.

For heat flow through a sandwich of different materials, the same quantity of heat, q, flows through each layer of the sandwich and results in temperature gradients, $\Delta T / \Delta d$, across each layer of thickness d, whose magnitudes are inversely proportional to the thermal conductivity of the layers. Such a system, illustrated in Fig. 2-62, is defined by the set of equations (for heat flow per unit area) given in Eq. 2-73.

$$-\frac{q}{A} = k_1 \frac{\Delta T_1}{d_1} + k_2 \frac{\Delta T_2}{d_2}$$

$$T_H - T_L = \Delta T_1 + \Delta T_2 \quad (2\text{-}73)$$

For radial heat flow through a cylindrical wall, as shown in Fig. 2-63, the area through which the heat flows increases with increasing distance

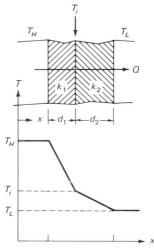

Fig. 2-62. Heat flow through sandwich (above) and corresponding temperature profile (below).

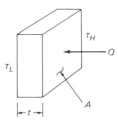

Fig. 2-61. Conductive heat transfer.

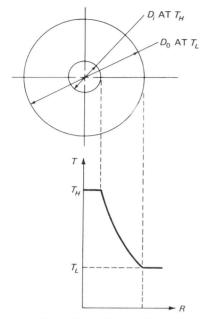

Fig. 2-63. Radial heat flow.

from the center. The solution of Eq. 2-72b, applied to this problem, shows that the effective area is given by the so-called *logarithmic-mean* area (Eq. 2-74).

$$A_{lm} = \frac{A_0 - A_i}{\ln (A_0/A_i)} = \pi l \frac{D_0 - D_i}{\ln \dfrac{D_0}{D_i}}$$

$$(2\text{-}74)$$

Otherwise, the heat flow is given by Eq. 2-72. A typical example of radial heat flow is the dissipation of I^2R losses from insulated current-conducting wires.

2-55. Heat Transfer by Convection

The process of air-cooling of solar cell modules (or liquid-cooling of concentrator solar cells) is known as *convective* cooling. The amount of heat, q_c, removed from an area A is given by

$$q_c = hA(T_S - T_A) \qquad (2\text{-}75)$$

where the subscript c indicates *convective* heat transfer, h is the convective heat transfer coefficient, also known as *surface* or *film* coefficient, and subscripts S and A on the temperature T indicate the surface and the ambient air or liquid, respectively. The ambient temperature is measured far away from the surface.

Equations 2-75 and 2-72 appear similar; however, the heat transfer coefficient h depends upon the surface material and its roughness and on the coolant's velocity, temperature, viscosity, pressure, composition, and direction of flow relative to the module surface, as illustrated in Fig. 2-64. In still air, the angle of the module relative to the horizontal and adjacent obstructions also play a role. Depending upon the conditions, the value of h may change easily over one order of magnitude, but usually never more than two orders of magnitude. The largest temperature gradient dT/dx occurs immediately adjacent to and in the first few millimeters of the module's surface.

The addition of fins, pins, or spines (Fig. 2-65) to the module's backside significantly increases the amount of heat that is removed under otherwise fixed conditions. The fins may be in the form of long ribs, short metal tabs, rods, or any other configuration. The effectiveness of the fins depends upon the air speed, the

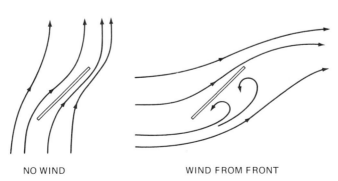

NO WIND   WIND FROM FRONT

Fig. 2-64. Air cooling of arrays.

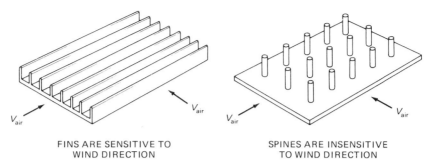

FINS ARE SENSITIVE TO   SPINES ARE INSENSITIVE
WIND DIRECTION   TO WIND DIRECTION

Fig. 2-65. Finned heat sinks.

thermal conductivity of the fins in relation to their length and cross-sectional area, and the thermal coupling of the fins to the solar cells.

Unfortunately, no simple analytical solutions to convective heat transfer problems exist, and the reader is referred to a textbook on heat transfer.

2-56. Heat Transfer by Radiation

Any surface with area A having an average hemispherical emittance $\bar{\epsilon}_H$, and being at an absolute temperature T, emits heat energy at a rate given by Eq. 2-70. The net rate of energy flow between two different, geometrically neighboring surfaces at different temperatures, T_1 and T_2, is given by Eq. 2-76.

$$q_{\text{net}} = A_1 \mathcal{F}_{12}\,\sigma(T_1^4 - T_2^4) = A_2 \mathcal{F}_{21}\,\sigma(T_1^4 - T_2^4)$$

$$(2\text{-}76)$$

$\mathcal{F}$ is a geometric factor (also known as the "script F" or view factor), defined in Eq. 2-77.

$$\mathcal{F}_{12} = \frac{\text{energy intercepted by } A_2}{\text{energy emitted by } A_1}$$

$$\mathcal{F}_{21} = \frac{\text{energy intercepted by } A_1}{\text{energy emitted by } A_2} \quad (2\text{-}77)$$

The subscripts 1 and 2 refer to the first and second surface, respectively. All other symbols are as defined earlier.

The geometric factor, $\mathcal{F}$, varies between zero and unity. In practice, $\mathcal{F}$ is determined with an optical instrument consisting of a polished, convex parabolic mirror. The mirror is subdivided into graduations that are calibrated in fractions of F where $F = \mathcal{F}$ when $\epsilon = 1$. That is, $\mathcal{F}$ includes

effects of emissivity while F is a purely geometric factor. Alternately, F may be computed (for $\epsilon = 1$) from Eq. 2-78.

$$F_{12} = \frac{1}{A_1}\frac{1}{\pi}\int_{A_1}\int_{A_2}\frac{\cos\theta_1\cos\theta_2}{s^2}\,dA_1\,dA_2$$

$$(2\text{-}78)$$

The symbols in Eq. 2-78 are defined in Fig. 2-66. Geometric factors are given in some books on heat transfer.

Radiation Heating in Space. Solar cell operating temperatures may be estimated by making the following assumptions:

- The temperature gradient throughout the solar cell stack and the substrate thickness is zero (i.e., the array is isothermal)
- There are no thermal interactions between the solar cell array and other structural elements or heat sources of the spacecraft
- The earth radiation and albedo energy inputs to the array are negligible.

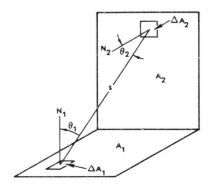

Fig. 2-66. Heat exchange by radiation between two small black surface elements.

For this simplified case, the heat balance equation per unit area is given in Eq. 2-79.

$$q_{in} - q_{electrical} = q_{out}$$

$$\overline{\alpha}_{Se} S \cos \Gamma = (\overline{\epsilon}_{HF} + \epsilon_{HB}) \sigma T^4 \quad (2\text{-}79)$$

where

$\overline{\alpha}_{Se}$ = effective solar absorptance (per Eq. 2-66)

S = value of the solar constant

Γ = the angle between the solar cell array normal and the array-sun line

$\overline{\epsilon}_{HF}$ = effective hemispherical front side emittance (per Eq. 2-67)

ϵ_{HB} = hemispherical back side emittance

σ = Stefan-Boltzmann constant

T = absolute temperature.

Rearranging Eq. 2-79 results in Eq. 2-80, with the solar cell operating temperature, T_{op}, replacing T.

$$T_{op} = \left(\frac{\overline{\alpha}_{Se}}{\overline{\epsilon}_{HF} + \epsilon_{HB}} \frac{S \cos \Gamma}{\sigma} \right)^{1/4} \quad (2\text{-}80)$$

Radiation Cooling in Space. Solar cell array eclipse exit temperatures may be estimated by making the following assumptions:

- The temperature gradient throughout the solar cell stack and the substrate thickness is zero (i.e., the array is isothermal)
- There are no thermal interactions between the solar cell array and other structural elements or heat sources of the spacecraft
- The emitting array surface areas on the front and back side are equal
- The earth radiation and albedo energy inputs to the array are negligible
- The eclipse is an instantaneous absence of solar illumination (i.e., no penumbra shadow).

For this simplified case, the heat balance equation per unit area is given in Eq. 2-81.

$$q_{out} + q_{stored} = 0$$

$$(\overline{\epsilon}_{HF} + \epsilon_{HB}) \sigma T^4 + (\overline{mc_p}) \frac{dT}{dt} = 0$$

$$(2\text{-}81)$$

This equation can be restated as Eq. 2-82.

$$aT^4 = -b \frac{dT}{dt} \quad (2\text{-}82)$$

where

$$a = (\overline{\epsilon}_{HF} + \epsilon_{HB}) \sigma$$

$$b = \overline{mc_p}.$$

The equivalent thermal mass, $\overline{mc_p}$, is defined in Eq. 2-83.

$$\overline{mc_p} = \sum_{i=1}^{n} m_i c_{pi} \quad (2\text{-}83)$$

In the above equation, m_1 is the ith mass (per unit array area) and c_{pi} is the ith specific heat capacitance of the n different materials found in that unit area of array. The other symbols are as defined previously.

Equation 2-80 can be restated as Eq. 2-84.

$$-\frac{a}{b} \int_0^{t_e} dt = \int_{T_{op}}^{T_e} T^{-4} \, dT \quad (2\text{-}84)$$

The limits of integration for time t are from the start of the eclipse ($t_e = 0$) to t_e, and the limits for temperature T are from the operating temperature T_{op} to the eclipse temperature T_e, which is reached at time t_e. The operating temperature T_{op} is the array or solar cell temperature according to Eq. 2-80, just prior to entering the eclipse. If t_e is equal to the eclipse duration, T_e is the eclipse exit temperature.

Integrating both sides of Eq. 2-84 gives the following equation.

$$-\frac{a}{b} t_e = -\frac{1}{3} (T_e^{-3} - T_{op}^{-3})$$

or

$$T_e(t_e) = T_{op} \left(1 + \frac{3a}{b} T_{op}^3 t_e \right)^{-1/3} \quad (2\text{-}85)$$

Substituting Eq. 2-82 back into Eq. 2-83 gives Eq. 2-86.

$$T_e(t_e) = T_{op} \left(1 + \frac{3(\overline{\epsilon}_{HF} + \epsilon_{HB}) \sigma T_{op}^3}{\overline{mc_p}} t_e \right)^{-1/3} \quad (2\text{-}86)$$

For most practical cases, the emittance ϵ and the specific heat capacitance c_p are functions of temperature. As a first order approximation, both ϵ and c_p may be assumed to be linear functions of absolute temperature; i.e., $\epsilon_T = ET$ and $c_{pT} = CT$. Inclusion of ϵ_T and c_{pT} in Eq. 2-81 leads to the following three cases. Their applicability should be judged from the value of the expected T_{op} and the decrease of ϵ and c_p with decreasing temperature, as shown in Chapter 10.

Emittance Variable with Temperature. The heat balance equation becomes Eq. 2-87.

$$(E_F + E_B)\sigma T^5 + (\overline{mc_p})\frac{dT}{dt} = 0 \quad (2\text{-}87)$$

The solution to Eq. 2-87 is given in Eq. 2-88.

$$T_e(t_e) = T_{op}\left(1 + \frac{4(E_F + E_B)\sigma T_{op}^4}{\overline{mc_p}}t_e\right)^{-1/4}$$

$$(2\text{-}88)$$

Specific Heat Capacitance Variable with Temperature. The heat balance equation becomes Eq. 2-89.

$$(\overline{\epsilon}_{HF} + \epsilon_{HB})\sigma T^3 + \overline{Cm}\frac{dT}{dt} = 0 \quad (2\text{-}89)$$

The solution to Eq. 2-89 is given in Eq. 2-90.

$$T_e(t_e) = T_{op}\left(1 + \frac{2(\overline{\epsilon}_{HF} + \epsilon_{HB})\sigma T_{op}^2}{\overline{Cm}}t_e\right)^{-1/2}$$

$$(2\text{-}90)$$

Both Emittance and Specific Heat Capacitance Variable with Temperature. This case is identical to that of Eq. 2-86, where both emittance

and specific heat capacitance are invariant with temperature. Hence, for most applications, Eq. 2-86 can be expected to yield the most realistic eclipse temperatures.

2-57. Electrical Heat Transfer Analogy

The flow of heat in a thermal field is phenomenologically identical to the flow of electric current in an electric field. Therefore, electrical networks can be used in the analysis of heat transfer problems. Electrical characteristics that are analogous to thermal characteristics are shown in Table 2-5. Solutions to electrical network problems are discussed in Sections 2-21 through 2-25.

For an electrical network to analogously represent a thermal heat flow problem, the governing electrical and thermal differential equations or integro-differential equations must be similar, and the boundary conditions used for solving the equations must be similar.

Conductive Heat Transfer. For a steady-state heat flow, q_{1-2}, from point "1" to point "2" in a homogeneous bar of constant cross-sectional area A and length L between the two points, the electrical analogs are as follows:

Thermal	Electrical Analog

$$q_{1-2} = \frac{kA}{L}(T_1 - T_2) \qquad I_{1-2} = \frac{1}{R_c}(V_1 - V_2)$$

where

k = thermal conductivity
T_1 = higher temperature
T_2 = lower temperature

Table 2-5. Analogous Quantities.

Electrical		Thermal	
Parameter	Unit	Parameter	Unit
Charge, Q	coulomb	Heat energy, Q	watt-second
Current, I	ampere	Heat flow rate, q	watt
Potential, V	volt	Temperature, T	kelvin
Resistance, R	ohm	Resistance, R	kelvin/watt
Conductivity, k	per (ohm · meter)	Conductivity, k	watt/(meter · °K)
Capacitance, C	coulomb/volt	Heat capacitance, mc_p	watt-second/°K)

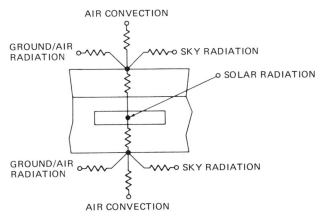

Fig. 2-67. Thermal model for terrestrial modules.

I_{1-2} = current flow from point "1" to point "2"

R_c = resistance (convective)

V_1 = higher potential

V_2 = lower potential.

Radiative Heating. For solar energy incident on the front surface of an array having reflectivity ρ, the amount of energy transmitted into the array, in both thermal and electrical analog notation, is given below.

Thermal Equation | Electrical Analog

$$q_{in} = q_s(1 - \rho) \qquad I_{in} = I_s(1 - \rho)$$

Radiative Cooling. The transient thermal equations and their respective electrical analogs appear below.

Thermal Equation

$$aT^4 + b\frac{dT}{dt} = 0$$

$$T_e(t_e) = T_{op}\left(1 + \frac{3aT_{op}^3}{b}t_e\right)^{-1/3}$$

Electrical Analog

$$\frac{1}{R_r}V^4 + C\frac{dV}{dt} = 0$$

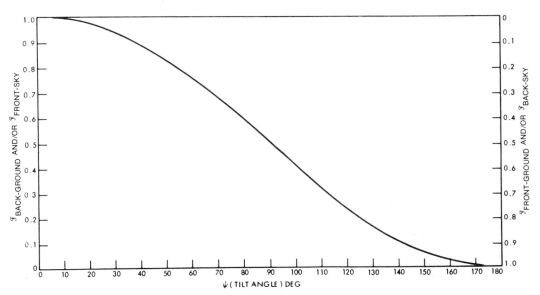

Fig. 2-68. Radiation view factors for tilted arrays.[25]

$$V_e(t_e) = V_{op} \left(1 + \frac{3V_{op}^3}{R_r C} t_e\right)^{-1/3}$$

The thermal equations correspond to Eqs. 2-82 and 2-85 and utilize the same nomenclature given for them (R_r = radiative resistance).

2-58. Terrestrial Array Operating Temperatures

It has been found that the heat transfer from terrestrial, flat plate modules is by convection as well as radiation, as shown in Fig. 2-59. For installations in moderate climate locations, the ratio of the amount of heat removed by radiation to the amount of heat removed by convection is typically in the range between 3 : 2 and 2 : 3. A simplified thermal model for terrestrial flat plate modules is illustrated in Fig. 2-67. The heat balance equation can be written in accordance with Sections 2-53 through 2-56 and Eq. 2-91.

$$q_{in} - q_e = q_{RFSG} + q_{RFIG} + q_{RFS} + q_{RBSG}$$

$$+ q_{RBIG} + q_{RBA} + q_{CBA} + q_{CFA} \quad (2\text{-}91)$$

The subscripts denote the following: e = electrical, R = radiated, C = convected, F = front, B = back, IG = illuminated ground, SG = shadowed ground, and A = air. The "script F" factor for radiation heat exchange from an inclined module is given in Fig. 2-68.[25]

RELIABILITY ANALYSIS

2-59. Reliability and Failure Rates

Solar array reliability analysis is a statistical tool with which one hopes to compute the probability that the array will, after a given length of time in service, provide a given amount of electrical output. Typical reliability analyses as executed today and reported in the literature are concerned with expected and potential random failure mechanisms, wearout phenomena, and other, naturally occurring phenomena of a statistical but macroscopic nature which may, in time and when having occurred in certain combinations or frequencies, potentially reduce the available power from the array in excess of the predicted degradation due to the reasonably well known environmental degradation factors.

What has not been included in such reliability analyses are microscopic failure mechanisms and uncertainties in environmentally-caused degradation of materials and components. Nevertheless, present-day reliability analyses can be excellent tools to aid the array designer in comparing the expected performance of alternate design approaches as well as in determining the weakest link in his chain of design elements.

The calculated *reliability*, R, of a solar cell array is equal to the calculated *probability of success*, p_s, for the array to produce a given power output at a given time, t, after deployment. The power output is that expected after the naturally occurring array output degradation due to environmentally induced mechanisms has taken place. The probability of success is related only to component, material, or assembly failures, including:

- Interconnector joint open-circuit failures
- Solar cell short-circuit and open-circuit failures
- Blocking diode short-circuit and open-circuit failures
- Wire, cable and connector short-circuit and open-circuit failures.

Each joint or component is assumed to have a certain failure rate, λ, given in units of *number of failures per operating hour* or in units of *bits*. A failure rate of *one bit* is defined as 1×10^{-9} failures per part operating hour. Alternately, the failure rate, λ, may be given in units of *number of failures per temperature cycle*, and the time, t, may be given in units of *temperature cycles*.

Components and joints are typically assumed to fail in such a fashion that the probability of success, p_s (i.e., the reliability), of each component or joint is related to the operating time, t, by

$$p_s = R = e^{-\lambda t}$$

where

e = base of the natural logarithm
λ = failure rate
t = operating time (or number of temperature cycles as appropriate).

The probability of failure, p_f, is given by

$$p_f = 1 - p_s$$

For two independent failure mechanisms operating on a system or component, the reliability can be expressed as Eq. 2-92.

$$R = e^{-[\lambda_1 d + \lambda_2 (1-d)]t} \qquad (2\text{-}92)$$

where

λ_1, λ_2 = two different failure rates
d = duty cycle factor ($0 \leqslant d \leqslant 1$).

As an example, Eq. 2-92 would be applicable for cases where one failure rate would apply for temperature-cycling-induced failures while the other failure rate would relate to operating time at the upper equilibrium temperature.

Failure Rates. Solar cell failure rates have not been well established because the failure rates are too low to be measured accurately. The orbital performance of space solar cell arrays has indicated that the most likely open-circuit failure rates in orbit are on the order of 1 bit (i.e., one solar cell fails in an open-circuit mode for every 1×10^9 solar cell operating hours), and perhaps as low as 0.01 bit.

2-60. Failure Modes and Effects

Reliability analysis deals essentially with failure modes, failure effects, and failure rates. As an illustrative example, consider a small, oriented array consisting solely of two solar cells in parallel by ten cells in series. Let each group of two paralleled cells be electrically interconnected. Let the only failure mode be solar cell open-circuit failure (cell fracture or contact strip lifting), occurring at some rate. The effect of the first cell failure is a reduction in array output by very nearly one-half. A second cell failure may cause one of two effects, depending upon where this failure occurs. If it occurs in the paralleled cell adjacent to the already failed cell, the array output drops to zero; however, if it fails anywhere else on the array, no additional output losses occur. It can be seen that if a large number of failure modes, each having its peculiar failure rate, are postulated, failure effects can become quite complex and interrelated. A large number of potential failure modes can indeed be listed and they have actually been observed in ground testing of solar cell arrays for space applications. Orbital array performance, however, seems to indicate that the failure rates of these failure mechanisms are typically orders of magnitude lower than observed in ground testing. Practically, therefore, most failures can be lumped into a single "open cell" failure mode with a very low failure rate compared with the failure rates of other components.

The predominant failure mode of solar cell circuits is the open-circuit failure of soldered or welded electrical joints. (Short-circuit failures are rare and are usually the result of correctable manufacturing deficiencies.) The effect of solar cell open-circuit failures on array output may be severe.

For this reason, circuits are generally designed with multiple strings paralleled at the cell level. In physical terms, this means that submodules, composed of two or more cells soldered or welded to a common interconnector (usually at the positive contact of n/p silicon cells), are electrically wired in series to form modules. The modules, which may consist of 10 to 20 submodules, are then connected in series to obtain the total required series dimension for the solar cell circuit.

The rationale for this practice is that if electrical connection between any two series cells is lost due to an open-circuit failure, the remaining cells of the affected submodule will each carry a portion of the current of the string containing the open-circuited cell, thereby mitigating the effect of the failure. In general, the power lost due to an open-circuit cell failure decrease as the number of parallel cells in the submodule increases. The capability of the unfailed cells of an affected submodule to carry additional current depends upon the short-circuit currents and the reverse leakage current characteristics of the unfailed cells, and the array voltage available to reverse bias the unfailed cells. (The capability may also be limited by the ability of the unfailed cells and their electrical connections to dissipate the heat produced when they are reverse biased, as discussed in Section 2-46).

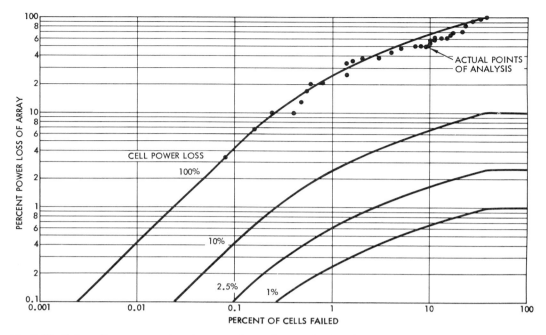

Fig. 2-69. Solar cell array power loss due to random cell open-circuit failures (100% cell power loss) or cell fractures (1%, 2.5%, 10% power loss). (Illustrative example)

Figure 2-69 shows the percentage of solar array power lost as a function of the percentage of cells failed due to random open-circuits for a circuit composed of 10 parallel strings of 42 three-cell submodules in series (1260 cells total). It is seen that even with paralleling at the submodule level, a relatively large power loss results from a relatively small number of open-circuited cells. For example, with 0.08% cells failed (one cell) the array power output is reduced by 3.3%.

The assumptions below were used in the analysis which produced the results shown in Fig. 2-69.

- A cell "open" is defined as one which exhibits an infinite impedance which results in a 100% cell power loss.
- The first cell failure in any series string (three cells in parallel) produces a one-third power output loss from the string. (This is equivalent to a one-third current loss at the constant bus voltage.)
- An additional cell failure in the same series string, but not in the same submodule, has no additional effect on power output.

- An additional cell failure in the same series string and in the same submodule produces an additional one-third power loss.
- A cell with a power loss less than 100% is defined as a cell with a corresponding short-circuit current loss but an unchanged I-V curve shape (i.e., a cell having a corner broken off).
- The general effect of a partial cell failure on power loss is to reduce power by the product of the partial percentage loss and the "one-third" factor.

The analysis consisted of the four steps outlined below.

1. Each cell was assigned a number in the range of 1 to 1260.
2. Using a random number generator, each cell was associated with a failure event.
3. As each cell was removed from the circuit, the power loss was assessed according to the assumptions stated above.
4. Figure 2-69 was plotted. Power losses of less than 3.3% were obtained by the direct ratio of 3.3% power loss per 0.08% failures.

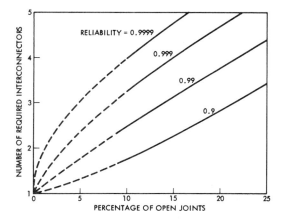

Fig. 2-70. Required number of dual path interconnectors per solar cell to meet specific string reliabilities when the end-of-life percentage of open joints is known. (Illustrative example)

Another aspect of reliability concerns the number of soldered or welded connections made to each solar cell. Figure 2-70 shows the relationship between the number of connections per cell and the percentage of open joints for cells of a string composed of single cells. From the figure it is clear that, within reasonable bounds, as the reliability goal on the joint failure rate increases, the number of joints per cell must also increase. (Additional examples of solar cell array failure modes and effects are described in Section 6-4.)

2-61. Reliability Models

Reliability models are logic block diagrams that represent hardware *systems* in terms of mission success. Let a system S be defined by one or more pieces of equipment, or parts, or elements of parts, A, B, C, ... Let the probability of success of the system be defined by P_S and that of the parts by P_A, P_B, P_C, ... The system probability of success is as given below for a number of different systems, illustrated in Fig. 2-71. The derivation of the so-called *survival equations* is based on the fact that the system's probability of success depends upon both the probability of mission success with each component operating and the probability of mission success with any component failed.[26] For example, for the second system illustrated in

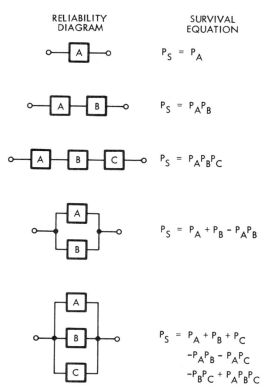

RELIABILITY DIAGRAM   SURVIVAL EQUATION

$$P_S = P_A$$

$$P_S = P_A P_B$$

$$P_S = P_A P_B P_C$$

$$P_S = P_A + P_B - P_A P_B$$

$$P_S = P_A + P_B + P_C$$
$$-P_A P_B - P_A P_C$$
$$-P_B P_C + P_A P_B P_C$$

Fig. 2-71. Reliability models for system mission probability of success, P_S.

Fig. 2-71 (two parts in series), the probability of mission success is given in Eq. 2-93a.

$$P_S = P_{SAW} P_A + P_{SAF} P_{Af} \qquad (2\text{-}93a)$$

where

P_{SAW} = probability of mission success with A working

P_{SAF} = probability of mission success with A failed

P_{Af} = probability of A failing.

Since $P_{SAW} = P_B$ and $P_{Af} = 1 - P_A$, Eq. 2-93a becomes Eq. 2-93b.

$$P_S = P_B P_A + 0(1 - P_A) = P_A P_B \quad (2\text{-}93b)$$

As another example of the derivation of the survival equation, consider the fourth reliability diagram in Fig. 2-71 (two parts in parallel). The symbols are as defined for Eq. 2-93c; however, their values are different:

$$P_S = P_{SAW} P_A + P_{SAF} P_{Af}$$

$$= 1 \, P_A + P_B(1 - P_A)$$

$$= P_A + P_B - P_A P_B \qquad (2\text{-}93\text{c})$$

Actual solar cell array models are composed of many detailed reliability diagrams and the survival equations become quite complex.[27]

ORBITAL ANALYSIS

2-62. Spacecraft Motion in Orbit

After launch, a spacecraft may be in *powered* or *unpowered* flight, depending upon whether or not a rocket propulsion system accelerates the spacecraft. The flight path of a spacecraft is known as its *orbit*. Frequently, but not universally, closed-loop flight paths are termed *orbits* while open-loop flight paths are called *trajectories*.

When under power, the spacecraft usually is on a *spiralling* type of path. When unpowered, the flight path can be described (to a first-order approximation) by a *conic section*. A conic section would describe the flight path accurately if the spacecraft would be subject only to the gravitational forces from the planet or other celestrial body, known as the *central body*, it is intended to orbit or pass. In practice, however, other celestial bodies exert gravitational forces, the sun exerts solar radiation pressure (especially on spacecraft having area-to-mass ratios greater than approximately 2.5 m²/kg), and at lower altitudes (below 475 km above the earth), aerodynamic drag exerts forces on spacecraft that *perturb* a purely conic-section orbit. Spacecraft orbits about the earth are also perturbed by the earth's non-spherical mass distribution and by electromagnetic forces (both due to interactions between the earth's magnetic field with electromagnetic fields produced by current loops on the spacecraft, and due to electrostatic charging of the spacecraft in the space plasma) in addition to the gravitational forces exerted by the sun and the moon.

A spacecraft in an elliptic orbit around a central body reaches its lowest or highest altitude at an *apsis* (the plural of apsis is *apsides*). The point nearest the central body is *periapsis* and the farthest point is *apoapsis*. A line drawn between periapsis and apoapsis, called the *line of apsides*, lies in the orbit plane and passes through the center of the central body. The apsides of an earth orbit are called *perigee* and *apogee*, those of a solar orbit are called *perihelion* and *aphelion*, and those of a lunar orbit are called *perilune* and *apolune*.

2-63. Simplified Orbit Theory

Simplified orbit theory is concerned with the description of the orbits of two bodies about each other, without consideration of perturbations of the orbits by the actions of other forces. Perturbations are of significance to satellite mission planners and attitude control system designers, but are usually negligible for solar cell array design work.[28-34]

Energy and Momentum. After launch, a space vehicle accelerates away from the earth. At some time after launch, the booster or propulsion stage will burn out or will be shut down and the spacecraft will be released from the remaining launch vehicle. After release, the spacecraft will possess kinetic energy, E_k, and potential energy, E_p, given by Eq. 2-94.

$$E = E_k + E_p = mv^2/2 - \mu m/r \qquad (2\text{-}94)$$

where

    m = spacecraft mass
    v = spacecraft velocity
    r = distance between the spacecraft and the center of earth
  $-\mu$ = gravitational parameter (the minus sign is based on the convention that the potential energy of a body is zero if it is at infinity).

The gravitational parameter is defined for the earth by Eq. 2-95.

$$\mu = G m_e \qquad (2\text{-}95)$$

where

    G = Universal Gravitational constant
    m_e = mass of the earth.

In the absence of drag forces or additional propulsion efforts (from the attitude control system, for example), the energy of the space-

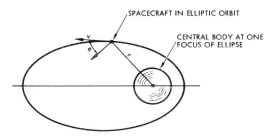

Fig. 2-72. Definitions for angular momentum.

craft will be conserved (i.e., will remain constant with time).

The moving spacecraft also possesses momentum which is conserved throughout the spacecraft's life. Linear momentum of a point mass m is defined as mv and angular momentum as $mr^2\omega$, where r is the distance of the point mass from a center and ω is the angular velocity. The tangential velocity of the rotating point mass is ωr, pointing in a direction perpendicular to r. For a satellite in an elliptic orbit about a central body (illustrated in Fig. 2-72), the angular momentum is given by

$$H = mrv \cos \phi$$

where

- m = satellite mass
- r = satellite-center of central body distance along the *local vertical*
- v = tangential satellite velocity (same as in Eq. 2-94)
- ϕ = angle between the tangential velocity vector (direction of velocity) and the normal to r, also known as the *local horizontal*.

The spacecraft energy E and angular momentum H will determine the orbit altitude (more correctly, the distance r) as a function of time. The orbital relationship is given by Kepler's first law, which, when applied to spacecraft, states that spacecraft will describe closed circular or elliptic orbits about central bodies if they are permanently associated with them (i.e., when their velocity is lower than the escape velocity for the particular central body), or they will describe open parabolic or hyperbolic orbits if they are not permanently associated with them.

Kepler's first law can be stated mathematically by the so-called *vis viva* or *energy* equation (Eq. 2-97).

$$v^2 = \mu \left(\frac{2}{r} - \frac{1}{a} \right) \qquad (2\text{-}97)$$

As defined in Fig. 2-73, a is the semimajor axis. For a circular orbit $r = a$, Eq. 2-97 reduces to Eq. 2-98.

$$v_c^2 = \mu/r \qquad (2\text{-}98)$$

v_c is known as the *circular velocity*. When the spacecraft possesses the escape velocity v_e, the orbit becomes a parabola with $a = \infty$.

$$v_e^2 = 2\mu/r \qquad (2\text{-}99)$$

The orbital parameters (illustrated in Fig. 2-73) are related to spacecraft energy and angular momentum as in Eqs. 2-100 and 2-101.

$$a = -\mu/2E \qquad (2\text{-}100)$$

$$b^2/a = H^2/\mu \qquad (2\text{-}101)$$

b is the semi-minor axis. The eccentricity of the ellipse, e, is geometrically related to a and b as shown in Eq. 2-102.

$$e^2 = 1 - b^2/a^2 \qquad (2\text{-}102)$$

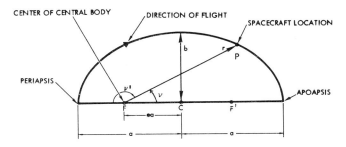

Fig. 2-73. Geometry of the ellipse (one-half of ellipse shown for illustration).

Closed Orbits. A satellite in an elliptic orbit about a central body describes a path as illustrated in Fig. 2-73 and given by Eq-2-103a. (All symbols are as defined previously and ν is the angle between apoapsis and P, known as the *true anomaly*.)

$$r = \frac{a(1 - e^2)}{1 - e \cos \nu} \qquad (2\text{-}103a)$$

If the angle is measured from periapsis, Eq. 2-103b holds true.

$$r = \frac{a(1 - e^2)}{1 + e \cos \nu} \qquad (2\text{-}103b)$$

(For analytical convenience, note that $1 - e^2 = (1 + e)(1 - e)$ and that one of these terms cancels with the denominator if $\nu = 0$ or $\nu = \pi$.)

Orbit Period. The period of a satellite in an elliptic orbit is measured by the time between successive passes of a characteristic point on the orbit (such as periapsis). From Newton's formulation of Kepler's third law, the period, T, is related to the semi-major axis by a constant, k.

$$T^2 = ka^3 \qquad (2\text{-}104)$$

where

$$k = 4\pi^2/\mu \qquad (2\text{-}105)$$

Eq. 2-104 shows that the period is independent of the orbit eccentricity.

2-64. Altitude in Elliptic Orbit

The altitude of a spacecraft (as a function of time) in an elliptic orbit may be of interest to a solar cell array designer for estimating the solar cell radiation damage (described in Section 3-32). Ordinarily, this information would be available from the orbital analyst assigned to the same project. However, in the absence of such data, the array designer may have to perform his own analysis.

The relationship between time and position in orbit is given by Kepler's second law, which states that a straight line between the centers of the two bodies orbiting each other (in any closed or open orbit) sweeps out equal areas in the orbital plane in equal intervals of time. Letting the incremental area swept out in incremental time dt be denoted by dA, we have Eq. 2-106, where r is given by Eq. 2-103.

$$\frac{dA}{dt} = \frac{r^2 d\nu}{2dt} = \text{constant} \qquad (2\text{-}106)$$

The solution of transcendental Eq. 2-106 must be obtained by numerical or graphical methods. From the solution, the altitude, h, is found from Eq. 2-107, where r is given by Eq. 2-103 and R is the mean radius of the idealized spherical earth.

$$h = r - R \qquad (2\text{-}107)$$

Eq. 2-106 can be solved numerically, for example, using the following procedure and a digital computer; the program can be written easily.

1. Divide the half-ellipse of Fig. 2-73 into n sectors of equal area, each sector having an area of A_n.

$$A_n = \pi ab/2n \qquad (2\text{-}108)$$

2. Note that the area of each sector is given by Eq. 2-109, where r is given by Eq. 2-103.

$$A_n = \int_a^b \frac{1}{2} r^2 d\nu \qquad (2\text{-}109)$$

Numerically integrate Eq. 2-109 by incrementing ν in small steps, starting from $a = 0$ to such a value of b where A_n approximately equals the value of A_n computed from Eq. 2-108. Also compute the corresponding values of r and h. Next, let $b = a$ and repeat the process until the areas and values of h for all n segments are computed. The values of b thusly determined (while ν is varied from 0 to π radians) are separated by n equal time intervals.

3. Divide the orbit period T into n equal time intervals and plot h versus successive time intervals, or tabulate the results for further use.

2-65. Location in Space

The location of a spacecraft in three-dimensional space requires both the definition of a coordinate system and the description of the spacecraft position within that coordinate system. Hence, six parameters are required to uniquely determine the location of the spacecraft.

One important property of a coordinate system is that it is *inertial* (i.e., non-rotating in time, but free to translate). For mathematical correctness, *heliocentric*, *geocentric*, or other coordinate systems are in use, their choice depending upon the problem to be solved. For orbits about the sun, a heliocentric system is the obviously preferred choice, while for earth orbits a geocentric system is preferred.

The Geocentric Coordinate System. Let us define a *celestial sphere* of infinite radius whose center coincides with the center of the earth. All celestial bodies are projected onto the surface of the celestial sphere as they appear in the sky as seen from the earth. A plane of infinite extent through the earth's equator (the equatorial plane) defines the *celestial equator* on the celestial sphere.

Let the origin of the geocentric coordinate system be located at the center of the immovable, but spinning earth (daily rotation), and let the X- and Y-axes lie in the equatorial plane. The Z-axis then is coincident with the earth's spin axis. Also, let the X-axis point toward the *first point of Aries*, a point on the celestial sphere that originally pointed to, but is now displaced by, an angle of about 30° from the constellation Aries. The first point of Aries is now defined by the line of intersection between the earth's equatorial plane with the ecliptic plane, also known as the *line of equinoxes* or the *line of nodes*. The resulting coordinate system is shown in Fig. 2-74. In this coordinate system, the sun will orbit the earth counterclockwise in the *ecliptic plane* and will cross the X-axis at the vernal equinox. The angle ϵ between the equatorial and ecliptic planes is constant.

A spacecraft in orbit about the earth moves in its orbit plane. The line of intersection between the orbit and equatorial planes is called the *line of ascending nodes*. The angle subtended by the line of ascending nodes and the X-axis, measured counter-clockwise in Fig. 2-74, is known as the *argument* (angle) of the right

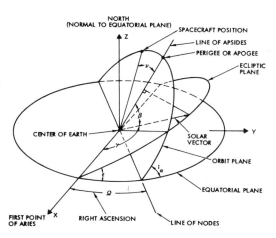

Fig. 2-74. Geocentric equatorial coordinate system.

ascension or, in short, the *right ascension*, Ω. The angle between the orbital and equatorial planes is the orbit *inclination*, i_a.

Of the many different sets of six parameters that can describe the position of a spacecraft in space, the following is a convenient set:

- Orbit inclination, i_a
- Orbit semi-major axis, a
- Orbit eccentricity, e
- Right ascension, Ω
- Epoch time, t_0
- Argument of perigee, ν.

The first and fourth parameters are defined above, and the second and third parameters are defined in Section 2-63. The *epoch* (instant of time) may be any arbitrary point in time, t_0, from which significant events are counted. Some examples of epoch are launch date and time, when passing perigee, or time when passing the ascending node.

The *argument of perigee* is the angle measured in the orbital plane from perigee to the line from the center of the earth to the spacecraft known as the *local vertical*. This angle is the same as ν in Fig. 2-73 and is related to time as shown in Section 2-64. A plane perpendicular to the local vertical is known as the *local horizontal*.

Orbit Inclination. A spacecraft launched from a launch site, located at $L°$ latitude, at an azimuth angle of $A°$ (i.e., the vehicle's heading measured clockwise from true north) will enter an orbit whose plane is inclined i_a° to the equatorial plane such that Eq. 2-110 is true.

$$\cos i_a = \cos L \sin A \qquad (2\text{-}110)$$

For Cape Kennedy, $L = 30°N$, and for Vandenberg, $L = 35°N$, approximately. For range safety reasons, however, not all values of A are permissible, so that some orbit plane inclinations must be obtained by special maneuvers.

The orbit plane inclinations determine the movement of the line of ascending nodes (known as *precession*) as shown below, when the North Pole is viewed from the star Polaris.

Inclination (deg)	Orbit Type	Precession
0	Equatorial	Counter-clockwise
$0 < i_a < 90$	Posigrade	Counter-clockwise
90	Polar	Stationary
$90 < i_a < 180$	Retrograde	Clockwise

2-66. Illumination of the Orbit Plane

The angle of incidence of the sunlight on the orbit plane is of interest to the conceptual solar cell array designers and constitutes a significant driving function for defining the array's geometric configuration and sun orientation mechanism.

The angle of sunlight incidence on the orbit plane, β, is defined as the geocentric angle between the so-called solar vector (the earth-sun line) and the local vertical (spacecraft-earth center line) in the orbit plane when the spacecraft is closest to the sun (orbit noon).[35-38] The angle β is given by Eq. 2-111.

$$\sin \beta = A(B \sin \gamma \cos \Omega - \cos \gamma \sin \Omega) - C \sin \gamma$$
$$(2\text{-}111)$$

where

$$A = \sin i_a$$
$$B = \cos \epsilon$$
$$C = \cos i_a \sin \epsilon.$$

β is positive when the sun is seen from the earth to lie above (north of) the orbit plane (see Fig. 2-74). The *sun central angle*, γ, is measured in the ecliptic plane from the X-axis to the earth-sun line, and is approximately given by Table 2-6. The rate of change of γ due to the earth's rotation about the sun (or the sun's rotation about the earth as defined in Fig. 2-73), is denoted by $d\gamma/dt$ and is given approximately by Eq. 2-112.

$$d\gamma/dt = 360/365.24 = 0.98565°/\text{day}$$
$$(2\text{-}112)$$

If γ is related to a specific angle γ_0 at time t_0 (such as the launch or equinox), γ is given at a later time t by Eq. 2-113.

$$\gamma = \gamma_0 + (t - t_0)\frac{d\gamma}{dt} \qquad (2\text{-}113)$$

The angle of the right ascension, Ω, decreases with time, mainly due to effects caused by the earth's oblateness. The time rate of change of Ω is given approximately for circular earth orbits by Eq. 2-114.

Table 2-6. Calculated Values of the Sun Central Angle.

Season (Northern Hemisphere)	Approximate Starting Date	Duration (days)	Approximate Calendar Day, t (day)	Approximate Sun Central Angle, Y (deg)	Solar Declination (deg)
Spring	21 March (Vernal Equinox)	92.77	79.4	0.0	0.0
Summer	21 June (Summer Solstice)	93.50	172.2	88.0	+23.44
Autumn	23 September (Autumnal Equinox)	89.85	265.7	183.4	0.0
Winter	22 December (Winter Solstice)	89.12	355.6	271.0	-23.44
TOTAL		365.24			

$$\frac{d\Omega}{dt} = \frac{JR^2\mu^{1/2} \cos i_a}{(R+h)^{7/2}} \qquad (2\text{-}114)$$

For elliptic earth orbits, the time rate of change of Ω is given by Eq. 2-115.

$$\frac{d\Omega}{dt} = \frac{JR^2\mu^{1/2} \cos i_a}{a^{7/2}(1-e^2)^2} \qquad (2\text{-}115)$$

where

$J = 1.624 \times 10^{-3}$, the dimensionless, general coefficient of gravitational harmonics

$\mu = 3.986 \times 10^5 \ \text{km}^3 \cdot \text{seconds}^{-2}$, the product of the universal gravitational constant and the mass of the earth.

All other symbols are as previously defined. At time t after the launch (or other epoch) time t_0, Eq. 2-116 holds true.

$$\Omega = \Omega_0 + (t - t_0)\frac{d\Omega}{dt} \qquad (2\text{-}116)$$

If in Eqs. 2-114 or 2-115 dt is replaced by the orbital period T per Eq. 2-104, the resulting angle increment $\Delta\Omega$ gives the regression in degrees longitude between successive orbits. For example, Eq. 2-115 becomes Eq. 2-117.

$$\Delta\Omega = -\frac{2\pi J \cos i_a}{(a/R)^2(1-e^2)^2} \qquad (2\text{-}117)$$

Examination of Eq. 2-111 reveals that β varies cyclically at a relatively rapid rate between limits that vary at a slower rate. The rapid rate is due to $d\Omega/dt$ and is of peak-to-peak magnitude $|\beta| = 2|i_a|$. The slower rate is due to $d\gamma/dt$ and determines the variation of the cyclical limit band for β between an upper limit of $(i_a + \epsilon)$ at summer solstice. At the vernal and autumnal equinoxes, the limit band restricts β to the range of $\beta = \pm i_a$.

The largest or smallest values of β for certain values of γ and Ω may be found by differentiating Eq. 2-111 with respect to each of these angles and setting the results equal to zero. The corresponding values of γ and Ω for which β is a maximum (or minimum), denoted by the subscript βm, can be found from Eqs. 2-118 and 2-119.

$$\tan \Omega_{\beta m} = -(B \tan \gamma)^{-1} \qquad (2\text{-}118)$$

$$\tan \gamma_{\beta m} = \frac{C - AB \cos \Omega}{A \sin \Omega} \qquad (2\text{-}119)$$

Special Cases. Equatorial synchronous and sun-synchronous orbits constitute two special cases that illustrate the variation of β during one year. For equatorial orbits,

$$i_a = 0$$

$$\beta = \sin^{-1}(\sin \epsilon \sin \gamma).$$

The variation of β during one year is from $-\epsilon$ to $+\epsilon$ or from $-23.44°$ to $+23.44°$. The variation of β during one orbit is zero. For polar orbits,

$$i_a = 90°$$

$$\beta = \sin^{-1}(\cos \epsilon \sin \gamma \cos \Omega - \cos \gamma \sin \Omega).$$

By selecting a combination of the orbital parameters a and e, one may hope to achieve $d\gamma/dt = d\Omega/dt$. (Eqs. 2-112, 2-113, and 2-114, for definition). If γ_0 and Ω_0 (Eqs. 2-113 and 2-116) could be made equal, a sun-synchronous orbit with β varying according to $\beta = \sin^{-1}(0.0413 \sin 2\gamma)$, or between $\pm 2.3°$, would result. In practice, such sun-synchronous orbits can be achieved only for relatively low-altitude circular orbits with inclinations between $92°$ and $112°$ and the variation in β being correspondingly larger. Spacecraft in sun-synchronous orbits, also known as constant sunlight orbits, may or may not be subject to eclipses due to the earth's shadow, depending upon the combinations of the orbital parameters.

2-67. The Sun Angle

The sun angle θ was defined in Section 2-49 as the angle between the spacecraft-sun line and a central axis (or spin axis) of the solar cell array, measured in a plane defined by the spacecraft-sun line and the spacecraft central axis. Once the sun angle is known, the angle of illumination (i.e., the angle between the solar vector and the outward normals to the solar cell array surfaces) can be determined by the formulas given in Section 2-49.

The sun angle θ is determined by the degrees-of-freedom of the solar cell array orientation capability. The degrees-of-freedom are determined by the number of axes about which the

Table 2-7. Solar Cell Array Degrees-of-Freedom.

Number of Spacecraft Axes	Number of Array Axes	Array Degrees-of-Freedom	Maximum Range of θ (degrees)
0	0	0	±180
1	0	1	±β
2	0	2	0 to ±β
3	0	3	0
0	1	1	±β
1	1	2	0 to ±β
2	1	3	0
0	2	2	0 to ±β
1	2	3	0
0	3	3	0

array can be rotated, as illustrated in Table 2-7. Obviously, any three degree-of-freedom orientation methods can achieve the desired condition of $\theta = 0°$.

To illustrate the relationships between θ and the orbit characteristics, consider the spacecraft with a two degrees-of-freedom array in Fig. 2-75. For convenience, let the earth-pointing spacecraft roll axis be coincident with the local vertical, and let the array articulation axis lie in the orbit plane. Let the spacecraft location be given by the position angle, τ, measured in the orbit plane in the direction of the spacecraft motion from orbit noon (the point on the orbit path which is closest to the sun). (In the special case illustrated in Fig. 2-74, orbit noon is coincident with one of the apsides and $\tau = \nu$, where ν is defined by Eq. 2-103). For this spacecraft/array configuration, the sun angle is related to the other angles by Eq. 2-120.

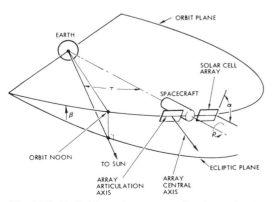

Fig. 2-75. Definition of geometry for determination of sun angle, θ, between sun line and array central axis.

$$\cos \theta = (\cos \alpha \cos \rho \sin \beta + \sin \alpha \cos \tau \cos \beta$$
$$- \cos \alpha \sin \rho \sin \tau \cos \beta) \quad (2\text{-}120)$$

where

α = array articulation angle between the array central axis (pointing away from the earth) and the local horizontal

β = illumination angle of the orbit plane, as defined in Section 2-66

ρ = spacecraft roll angle ($\rho = 0$ when the array articulation axis lies in the orbit plane, increasing counter-clockwise when viewed in the direction of the roll axis toward the earth)

τ = angle from solar noon, as described above.

Equation 2-120 degenerates into simple expressions for some frequently used array configurations and orientation methods, as illustrated below.[37-42]

For body-mounted, spinning arrays in equatorial orbits, with the spin axis perpendicular to the orbit plane and pointing northward,

$$\cos \theta = \sin \beta.$$

With the spin axis pointing toward the earth along the local vertical,

$$\cos \theta = \cos \beta \cos \tau.$$

For oriented, one degree-of-freedom arrays in equatorial orbits, the central axis is pointed into the direction of the sun (but not necessarily directly at the sun) and the tracking mechanism maintains this pointing direction. (Example: the array rotates about an axis through the spacecraft while the spacecraft orientation (pitch, roll, and yaw) is not available to aid in the array orientation.) For this case,

$$\theta = \beta.$$

2-68. Solar Eclipses

Whenever the earth moves into the spacecraft-sun line, the solar illumination of the solar cell array is interrupted. The length of time of this interruption, known as the *solar eclipse* (or *occultation*) time, depends upon the orbit altitude and the β-angle, as defined in Fig. 2-74 (discussed in Section 2-66). A fraction of sun

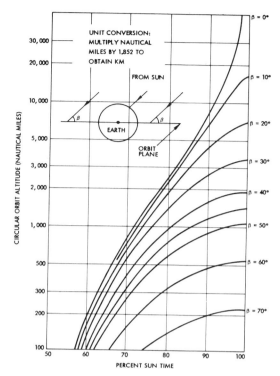

Fig. 2-76. Percent sun time as a function of altitude and sun angle for circular orbits.

time in orbit, f, is defined in Eq. 2-121, where t_i is the time of illumination and T is the orbit period, according to Eq. 2-104.

$$f = t_i/T \qquad (2\text{-}121)$$

For circular orbits, Eq. 2-122 is true, where R and a are as defined in Sections 2-63 and 2-64, and β is given by Eq. 2-111.

$$f = \frac{1}{2} + \frac{1}{\pi}\sin^{-1}\left\{\frac{[1 - (R/a)^2]^{1/2}}{\cos\beta}\right\}$$

$$(2\text{-}122)$$

Figure 2-76 shows the variation of f (expressed in percent rather than in fractional form) with orbit altitude and β.[43]

REFERENCES

1. M. Wolf and H. Rauschenbach, "Series Resistance Effects on Solar Cell Measurements," in *Advanced Energy Conversion*, Vol. 3, Pergamon Press, Elmsford, New York, 1963.
2. R. J. Stirn, "Junction Characteristics of Silicon Solar Cells, Non-illuminated Case," NASA **TM 33-557**, Jet Propulsion Laboratory, August 1972.
3. G. C. Jain and F. M. Stuber, "A Distributed Parameter Model for Solar Cells," in *Advanced Energy Conversion*, Vol. 7, Pergamon Press, Elmsford, New York, 1967.
4. R. J. Handy, "Theoretical Analysis of the Series Resistance of a Solar Cell," in *Solid State Electronics*, Vol. 10, Pergamon Press, Elmsford, New York, 1967.
5. From notes by N. Sheppard, General Electric Company.
6. W. D. Brown *et al*, "Computer Simulation of Solar Array Performance," Report No. **SSD 70135R**, Hughes Aircraft Co.
7. W. Luft, J. R. Barton, and A. A. Conn, "Multifacted Solar Array Performance Determination," TRW Systems Group, TRW, Inc., Redondo Beach, California, February 1967.
8. W. Shockley, *Holes and Electrons in Semiconductors*, Van Nostrand Reinhold Co., New York, 1950.
9. D. E. Sawyer and R. H. Rediker (p. 1122) in *Proceedings of the IRE*, Vol. **46**, 1958.
10. T. E. Hartman, "Transient Photovoltaic Response of Diffused-Junction Silicon Photodiodes," (pp. 127–133) in *Solid State Electronics*, Vol. **3**, Pergamon Press, Elmsford, New York, 1961.
11. D. W. Zerbel, "Fast Response Solar Array Simulator," Final Report for Contract **NAS 5-11581**, TRW Systems Group, TRW, Inc., 1968.
12. D. W. Zerbel and D. K. Decker, "AC Impedance of Silicon Solar Cells," in *Proceedings of the Intersociety Energy Conversion Engineering Conference*, Vol. **1**, September 1970.
13. "Nimbus-B Quarterly Technical Report No. 5, Sept-Nov 1966," *Report No.* **R-3125**, Contract **NAS 5-9668**, RCA Astro Electronics Division, 1966.
14. W. D. Brown *et al*, "Computer Simulation of Solar Cell Array Performance," Report No. **SSD 701 35 R**, Hughes Aircraft Company.
15. H. S. Rauschenbach, "Electrical Output of Shadowed Solar Arrays," in *Conference Record of the 7th Photovoltaic Specialists Conference*, IEEE, November 1968.
16. W. Luft, "Partial Shading of Silicon Solar Cell Converter Panels," in *Conference Paper* **CP 62-204**, AIEE, October 1961.
17. F. C. Treble, "Field Tests on UK3 Solar Cell Assemblies," Technical Report No. **66112**, Royal Aircraft Establishment, April 1966.
18. R. M. Sullivan, "Shadow Effects on a Series-Parallel Array of Solar Cells," Report No. **X-636-65-207**, NASA/Goddard Space Flight Center, Greenbelt, Maryland.
19. Filed patent application now pending by W. R. Baron, entitled, "A Method of Reducing the Effects of Cell Shadowing on a Series/Parallel String of Solar Cells, Photovoltaic or Other Incident

Energy Conversion Devices," and assigned to TRW, Inc.

20. W. R. Baron and P. F. Virobik, "Solar Array Shading and a Method of Reducing the Associated Power Loss," in *Proceeding of the 4th Photovoltaic Specialists Conference, Vol.* **II, PIC-SOL 209/5.1,** August 1964.

21. Internal documentation of work by P. F. Virobik, J. R. Barton, and A. A. Conn, TRW DSSG, TRW, Inc., 1964–1966.

22. W. Luft, J. Barton, and A. Conn, "Multifaceted Solar Array Performance Determination," presented at 1967 Intersociety Energy Conversion Engineering Conference, Miami Beach, Florida, August 1967.

23. H. S. Rauschenbach, "Skylab Orbital Workshop SAS Z-local Vertical Study," TRW Systems Report No. **SAS.4-3117,** *Vol.* **II,** November 1971, prepared for McDonnel Douglas Astronautics Company, Western Division, under contract **MDAC-WD-70-2-004.**

24. Internal documentation of work performed by W. Luft, TRW DSSG, TRW, Inc., 1968.

25. J. W. Stultz and L. C. Wen, "Thermal Performance Testing and Analysis of Photovoltaic Modules in Natural Sunlight," JPL Report **5101-31,** July 29, 1977.

26. *MIL-HDBK-217B, Military Standardization Handbook, Reliability Prediction of Electronic Equipment,* September 20, 1974.

27. W. A. Klein and S. N. Lehr, "Reliability of Solar Arrays," in *Second Annual Seminar on Reliability in Space Vehicles,* Los Angles, California, December 1961.

28. F. T. Geyling and H. R. Westerman, *Introduction to Orbital Mechanics,* Addison-Wesley, Reading, Massachusetts, 1971.

29. H. F. Lesh, "Determination of Interplanetary Trajectories," Technical Memorandum **33-414,** Jet Propulsion Laboratory, November 1968.

30. K. A. Ehricke, *Spaceflight, Vol.* **I,** "Environment

and Celestial Mechanics," Van Nostrand, Princeton, 1960.

31. J. M. A. Danby, *Fundamentals of Celestial Mechanics,* MacMillan, New York, 1962.

32. R. W. Wolverton (Ed), *Flight Performance Handbook for Orbital Operations,* John Wiley & Sons, New York, 1961.

33. J. Jensen *et al, Design Guide to Orbital Flight,* McGraw-Hill, 1962.

34. R. M. L. Baker, Jr. *et al, An Introduction to Astrodynamics,* Academic Press, New York, 1960.

35. *The American Ephemeris and Nautical Almanac,* Washington, D.C., published annually.

36. L. G. Stoddard, "Eclipse of Artificial Earth Satellites," in *Astronautic Sciences Review,* April–June 1961.

37. W. W. Hough and B. D. Elrod, "Solar Array Performance as a Function of Orbital Parameters and Spacecraft Attitude," in *Journal of Engineering for Industry,* February 1969.

38. W. E. Allen, "Design Analysis of Solar Cell Array Configurations for Vertically Stabilized Satellites in Near-Earth Orbits," Technical Memorandum **TG-1066,** The Johns Hopkins University (Applied Physics Laboratory), August 1969.

39. "Olsca: Orientation Linkage for a Solar Cell Array," Technical Report **AFAPL-TR-68-76,** July 1968.

40. A. L. Greensite, *Analysis and Design of Space Flight Control Systems, Vol.* **XII,** "Attitude Control in Space," NASA **CR-831,** August 1967.

41. M. B. Tamburro *et al, Guidance, Flight Mechanics and Trajectory Optimization, Vol.* **I,** "Coordinate Systems and Time Measure," NASA **CR-1000,** February 1968.

42. L. A. Pipes, *Matrix Methods for Engineering,* Prentice-Hall, Englewood Cliffs, New Jersey, 1963.

43. F. G. Cunningham, "Calculation of the Eclipse Factor for Elliptical Satellite Orbits," *ARS Journal,* December 1962.

3
Array Design

DESIGN CONCEPTS

3-1. The Design Process

The process of engineering design, in general, can be described in many ways. In the least formal sense, it is the movement from the general to the specific, from disorder to order, and from thought to matter. In the most formal sense, it consists of the identification of a set of design requirements and constraints followed by the steps of synthesis, analysis, selection, fabrication, test, and evaluation. On the one hand, the design process is logical and mathematical; on the other hand, it is intuitive and defies description. The process is affected by the kind of product to which it is applied, by the organizational environment under which it is applied, by time and fiscal constraints, and—perhaps most important—by the skills, experience, and personalities of the personnel responsible for its execution.

The design process for solar cell arrays is essentially identical to the general design process, with perhaps one major exception being the relatively large number of design constraints imposed on the design of space arrays. More than most other components on a modern spacecraft, the solar cell array has a very noticeable design impact on almost any other subsystem or system on board.

3-2. Design Phases

The design process begins with the *conceptual* design phase during which the general nature of

a new terrestrial or space system and an associated solar cell array are conceived and defined. Trade-off studies involve concepts rather than precise answers. The typical result of this phase may be the selection of a fixed or oriented array, or of a low- or a high-voltage array, having an approximate specified area.

In the following *preliminary* design phase, solar cells, covers, substrates, and other parts and materials are selected and a detailed design evolves on paper. Design optimization and trade-off studies involve more accurate analyses that are usually supported by computer modeling and exploratory testing of new components and materials.

During the *final* design phase, the solar cell layout is definitized and the final components, parts, and material selections are made. The performance and characteristics of the final design are predicted accurately.

The *product* design phase, typically concurrent with the final design phase, leads to the design of the array package and the preparation of the production drawings.

During the design *verification* phase, also known as the *qualification* phase, the new design is subjected to formal verification tests and review of the analyses to demonstrate its adequacy.

Not all projects have all these design phases; frequently, existing designs are modified with minimal effort, and their adequacy is demonstrated by similarity with existing hardware.

Even though the division of the design process into the various design phases may be of great significance within a given project organization, it is of no consequence to the treatment of technical design activities described in the remainder of this chapter.

3-3. Design Personnel

In practice, the solar cell array *designer* is a member of a design team. Furthermore, he is most likely a specialist in a particular field. During the entire array design process, many designers will have contributed to the design, each in his own right.

The early conceptual design is frequently done by a *systems specialist* whose main concern is to evolve the overall power system concept. The *solar cell array specialist* gets involved no later than during the preliminary design phase. Actually, he is more of an *"array generalist"* than a specialist, because he must now consider the many aspects and interfaces of importance in the design process. Frequently, he assumes a technical managing role as a *responsible engineer.* Especially during the intermediate and final design phases, he is a member of the *design team* which evolves the detailed design. Other members of this design team typically include specialists from the following engineering areas: product (packaging) design, structures, electrical design, materials and processes, quality assurance, testing, manufacturing engineering, thermodynamics, heat transfer, procurement, reliability, and others.

3-4. Uncertainties and Risks

Even though solar cell arrays have been successfully designed, fabricated, and deployed in space or on the ground for nearly two decades, there is no design which has been or will be carried forward with full knowledge of all the important facts pertaining to the environment, materials, or processes. For this reason, the designer must be able to cope with uncertainty to the extent that he must attempt to quantize uncertainty and use it as a design parameter. This need for quantization of uncertainty arises from the need to transmit from one engineer to another, from the array designer to the system

designer, and from the technical personnel to the manager, the risks associated with one design approach or another. In this sense, the progression from the conceptual through the final design stages can be viewed as reduction, but not elimination, of uncertainty.

3-5. Design Optimization

Design optimization is an ongoing process which is particularly important during the early (conceptual) design phase of a project. Frequently not recognized as such, design optimization is a direct result of informal design critiques that take place between interfacing design team members. Often, informal design critique leads to significant design improvement (i.e., design optimization).

Design optimization activities may also result from the findings of formal design reviews, customer redirections, improvements made in components and materials by suppliers, and new research and development efforts undertaken elsewhere. The design process typically requires reiterative selection and arrangement of components and materials and repeated design analysis.

The purpose of design optimization may be to truly optimize the overall system, or just the solar cell array, with respect to some definite criteria (such as lowest cost or lowest weight), or it may be to achieve a balance between various design objectives. It should be realized that a well optimized overall system may lead, by necessity, to a highly non-optimized solar cell array design. Therefore, it is incumbent on the array designer to interface thoroughly and frequently with the overall system designers—as well as other involved subsystem designers—to assure that the results of any array design or redesign activities meet the overall system design objectives and, only secondarily, optimize, in consonance with the overall system, the array design.

Design optimization criteria of significance to the solar array designer may include the following: power output at significant mission events (such as at maximum solar distance, worstcase off-pointing, or end-of-life), array mass, array size, array cost, development time and risk factors, and reliability.

3-6. Design Requirements, Criteria, and Interfaces

Design *requirements* are the basic technical statements that delineate the designer's task and determine the ultimate acceptability of the design by the customer. A typical list of design requirements is given in Table 3-1. These requirements come from several different sources; the power output requirements are inherently specified, but the conditions under which this power can be produced relate to the natural environment (sunshine, environmental degradation, etc.), the induced environment (operating temperature, etc.), other requirements (mechanical strengths, reliability, etc.), design interfaces (cabling, orientation system, etc.), and design criteria.

Design *criteria* are technical statements, based on value systems, that are intended to relate to success or failure. Design criteria may or may not affect array performance. Therefore, such criteria will always be surrounded by controversy. Nevertheless, they must be established and they are as "real" as any other requirements in terms of their impact on parts procurement, fabrication and rework cost, quality assurance or customer buy-off, and delivery dates. Typical examples of the more frequently encountered design criteria are given in Table 3-2. (The index facilitates finding the sections that provide more detailed discussions.) The code for the "Category" column is given below.

F = Functional; potentially affects performance, life, or reliability.

Table 3-1. Design Requirements.

Power output

Average power
Peak power
Power profile per day or per orbit
Maximum power voltage profile
Energy per day or per orbit

Conditions under which power output must be met

Illumination
Intensity (solar constant)
Spectrum (air mass)
Solar distance (season)

Table 3-1. (*Continued*)

Conditions under which power output must be met

Orientation (off-pointing)
Shadowing
Temperature
Operating range
Ambient conditions
Electrical losses
Solar cell interconnections
Wiring, connectors, circuit breakers
Slip rings
Blocking diodes
Mismatch
Reliability
Grounding (electrical)
Electromagnetic interference
Electrostatic charging
Mechanical
Size and dimensions
Weight (mass)
Center of gravity
Stiffness (rigidity)
Strength
Life
Wear-out life
End-of-mission
Environmental–space (ground)
Storage, handling, testing
Environmental–space (launch)
Pressure/altitude
Acceleration
Shock
Vibration and acoustic noise
Environmental–space (on-orbit)
Temperature cycling
Charged particle radiation
Ultraviolet radiation
Micrometeoroids
Deposits
Magnetic cleanliness
Magnetic moment
Environmental–terrestrial
Storage, handling, testing, installation
Ultraviolet radiation
Deposits and dirt accumulation
Humidity
Temperature cycling
Weathering
Miscellaneous
Transducers (temperature)
Test points
Transportability
Repairability
Transient overvoltage
Schematic diagram
Insulation resistance
Dielectric voltage breakdown strength
Identification and marking

Table 3-2. Design Criteria.

Criteria	Category	Applicability
Design-related		
Potential failure modes and effects	F	S, T
Circuit fault isolation	F	S, T
Redundancy	F	S, T
Design margin	F	S, T
Electrical	F	S, T
Mechanical	F	S, T
Thermal	F	S, T
Electrical layout	F	S, T
Insulation resistance and voltage breakdown	F	S, T
Defects induced by environmental testing	D	S, T
Cell and cover cracking	D	S, T
Interconnector and wire breakage	D	S, T
Bond separations	D	S, T
Testability (test points, connectors, etc.)	D	S, T
Handleability (handling fixtures, protective covers, etc.)	D	S, T
Protusions (snagging clothing)	D	S, T
Packing density	D	S, T
Repairability	D	S, T
Manufacturability (parts size, complexity, etc.)	D	S, T
Workmanship		
Solder fillets	D	S, T
Welding electrode imprints	D	S, T
Wire wrapping on terminals	D	S, T
Coverglass positioning over solar cell	D	S
Wire routing and lead dressing	D	S
Wire bonding to substrate (size, shape, etc.)	D	S
Cell interconnector deformations	D	S
Material and parts discolorations	D	S, T
Adhesive in cell-to-cell gaps	D	S
Cleanliness		
Solder flux residue on parts	D	S, T
Solder flux residue on coverglass	D	S
Adhesive on coverglass	D	S
Dust and dirt on coverglass	D	S
Fingerprints on coverglass	D	S
Fingerprints on thermal control paint	D	S
Imperfections		
Coverglass edge and corner chips	D	S
Cracked covers	D	S, T
Solar cell edge and corner chips	D	S, T
Cracked solar cells	D	S, T
Thermal control coating scratches	D	S
Cell interconnector deformations and discolorations	D	S, T
Pinholes in cover or cell filter coatings	C	S

D = Decisionable; either functional or cosmetic, depending upon a specific design for a specific mission.

C = Cosmetic; has no measurable or otherwise demonstrable impact on the functional performance.

In the "Applicability" column:

S applies for *space* arrays
T applies for *terrestrial* arrays.

Design *interfaces* delineate the interactions between designers that are responsible for different elements of the design (array, orientation drive, power control, etc.), as well as the physical mating requirements for mechanical and electrical elements (mounting brackets, connectors, etc.). Table 3-3 provides a checklist for the most frequently encountered interfaces.

Table 3-3. Solar Cell Array Design Interfaces.

Interfacing Design Activity	Nature of Data
Overall system	Size and configuration
	Orientation to sun
	Shadows and reflections
	Concentration
	Solar distance
Mechanical	Substrate
	Size and geometry
	String layout
	Unavailable areas
	Weight
	Structural support
	Deployment system
	Orientation drive
	Methods of mounting and structural support
Thermal	Array temperature
	Operating temperature
	Extreme low temperature
	Extreme high temperature
	Thermophysical
	Cell operating efficiency
	Absorptance, emittance
	Thermal control coatings
	Deposits (outgassing)
Electrical	Array output
	Power levels and profiles

Table 3-3. (*Continued*)

Interfacing Design Activity	Nature of Data
	Minimum, mean, maximum
	Beginning/end of life
	Maximum power voltage
	Power quality (ripple, etc.)
	Bus impedance
	Interconnections
	Cabling connectors
	Circuit arrangement
	Transducers (temperature sensors, etc.)
	Wiring and blocking diode losses
	Fault isolation and prevention
	Blocking diodes
	Redundancy
	Electromagnetic Compatibility (EMC)
	Grounding
	Electrostatic charging protection
	Twisting and shielding of wires
	Arcing and corona
Magnetic	Attitude control
	Cancellation of magnetic moments
	Experiments (spacecraft)
	Non-magnetic materials
Ground handling and test	Provisions for mounting
	Protective covers and containers
	Permanent or temporary handling facilities
	Test points and connectors
Programmatic	Cost
	Development time
	Procurement time
	Risk

3-7. Policy Constraints

Certain design practices are constrained by various policies. Applicable policies may be issued by the procuring organization (the customer), the project office, or the performing company (the contractor). Typical examples of such policies include the following:

- Military and federal specifications and similar documents for certain materials, components, and processes
- Project approved parts lists
- Company quality assurance manuals and workmanship standards
- Company drafting room manuals
- Company and project oriented procurement policies
- Company and project design review policies.

The designer's responsibility is to adhere to such applicable policies and, in case of conflict between specified requirements and restraining policy, bring such conflict to the attention of the appropriate management for proper resolution.

3-8. Design Review

Formal design reviews are typically held to examine a design in detail after a given design phase has been completed. Most projects have at least one major, formal design review that is held after completion of the major design activity and prior to fabrication of assembly tooling and operational hardware. When necessary, this major design review may be held in several separate parts to facilitate scheduling of long-lead items (items having long delivery periods).

The purpose of formal design review is to have the design critiqued by a relatively large number of senior specialists who understand the unit (component) aspects of the solar cell array as well as the system's implications. Typical, specific items of the design to be examined are given below.

- *Basic design objectives*
  Operational mission (high radiation level in space, terrestrial climate, etc.).
  Mission reliability (probability of success to meet the mission's objectives).
  Functional modes and characteristics.
  Physical characteristics (size, weight, center of gravity, etc.).
  Power output under various conditions.
  Environmental extremes (temperature, humidity, wind, radiation, etc.).
  Fail-safe.

- *Design implementation*
  Functional flow (block) diagrams.
  Array specifications.
  Test specifications.
  Fail-safe and redundancy provisions.
  Assessed reliability (as compared to apportionment).
  Drawings (structural, packaging, schematics, etc.).
  Measurements and test data.
  Parts, materials, and processes lists.
- *Supporting arguments*
  Description of alternate designs.
  Trade-off analyses.
  Interface compatibility analyses.
  Tolerance accumulation analyses.
  Use of preferred parts, materials, and processes.

Members of the design review team are instructed to follow a review plan. A typical review plan would include the guidelines below.

- *Look for:*
  Misunderstandings
  Omissions
  Errors
  Functional inadequacies
  Excessive risk.
- *Review for:*
  Use of prior state of the art
  Soundness of invention
  Accurate documentation
  Complete documentation
  Experimental proof.
- *Assess:*
  Variety of alternatives
  Depth of analysis
  Logical convergence
  Decisiveness
  Cost and value awareness.
- *Plan for:*
  Specific items of discussion by the Design Review Committee
  Specific documented "payoff" from the Design Review Meeting.

The findings of a design review are typically summarized in Design Review Minutes. As a result of the review, three types of important notices may be issued by the design review committee chairperson.

1. *Action items*—assigned (and "monitored to closeout") when additional work is necessary to resolve critical problems which inhibit approval of the design as presented.
2. *Agreements*—entered into Design Review Minutes to record important concurrences reached that are essential for approval of the design as presented.
3. *Alerts*—entered into Design Review Minutes to communicate the need for extra caution during subsequent design, test, production, or operational phases.

3-9. Producibility and Cost

The solar cell array designer can significantly influence the development, fabrication, and test costs of solar cell arrays. The influence on cost which is exerted by the array design is often not recognized because it filters into the final design through a number of different documents:

- Parts (solar cell, coverglass, etc.) specifications
- Process and material (adhesives, primers, soldering, etc.) specifications
- Solar cell layout drawings (cell spacing, wire routing, etc.)
- Solar cell interconnector design (defining manufacturing and assembly complexity) and subassembly drawings (tolerances, process control requirements, etc.)
- Workmanship criteria.

Solar cell arrays are costly, and if they are of any substantial size, they will consume a substantial fraction of the total system project cost budget. Solar cell array costs, therefore, have been of concern to both project personnel and designers since the beginning of the space program as well as for terrestrial applications.

Some of the avenues open to the designer for effecting cost reductions are discussed in the sections following. It is estimated that arrays are currently being fabricated at lower costs (based on an average cost at constant dollars) per installed solar cell than they were 15 years ago. It can probably be said that every reasonable attempt has been made by a large group of diversely skilled individuals over the past 20 years to reduce array cost. It appears, however, that no single patent and no single method has made a major cost reduction impact, but rather, that progress has been made slowly and continually by constantly improving designs, materials, and processes.

3-10. Human Engineering

Solar cell array design involves human engineering. An important consideration in terms of overall project cost and schedule are those man-hardware interfaces that occur during the fabrication, test, and system integration phases. "Accidental" damages to designs that are difficult to fabricate, awkward to handle due to size or flexibility, or difficult to test adequately are frequently not purely accidental. The array design team (array designer, fabrication, and test engineers) must consider these aspects of the overall design early in the design process; otherwise, the ability to turn a design into a tested hardware reality may be severely hampered.

PHOTOVOLTAIC SYSTEM DESIGN

3-11. Load Profile Development

Solar cell array systems may be designed for a great variety of electrical loads. Only in rare cases is the load resistive and of constant value. Converter circuits draw pulsating power of nearly constant magnitude independent of the input voltage. Motors have inductive components. User equipment does not operate at constant power during periods of sunlight, but is switched on and off and may require energy during periods when no sunlight is available. Switching operations may produce transient voltage and current conditions unlike those encountered in circuits that are connected to rotating machine type electric generators.

Rotating machines and batteries are capable of providing nearly constant bus voltage at significantly high, temporary overload conditions. Solar cells, however, have no such capability. A sudden current demand in excess of 10% of the cell's rated maximum power output current at given operating conditions may cause the temporary collapse of the cell's output voltage. Therefore, it is usually necessary to use a rechargeable energy storage battery in conjunction with the solar cell array to handle the transient loads rather than to oversize the array. The battery also serves as energy source during periods of no sunshine, and gets recharged during periods of sunshine.

The orderly presentation of the actual loads to be operated from a solar cell array system is known as the *load profile* for that system. For illustration, consider the simple terrestrial or space photovoltaic power system depicted in block diagram form in Fig. 3-1. The array output feeds through a blocking diode to the battery. The diode prevents current flow from the battery through the solar cells when they are not fully illuminated. A shunt-type regulator absorbs all excess energy from the array when the battery is fully charged and the loads are disconnected. There are *n* loads connected to the system; each may be switched on or off independently.

Illustrative Example No. 3-1

Problem: Determine the load profile for the power system shown in Fig. 3-1. Assume that the battery has nominally 25 V and the loads are as follows:

Load 1 is a constant power load transponder that draws 50 W continuously, day and night; *Load 2* is an electric motor-driven water pump that operates three times a day for one hour: once before sunrise, once near noon, and once after sunset; and draws a starting current of 20 A for 5 seconds and a running current of 4 A; and
Load 3 is a scientific experiment that operates approximately every 2 hours for 6 minutes, day and night, and draws a current of 3 A.

Solution: The current drawn by Load 1 is 50 W/25 V = 2 A. This current is plotted as function of time for a 24 hour period in Fig. 3-2. The other load currents are similarly plotted. The time phasing of Loads 2 and 3 are arbitrary, except that it must be assumed that all worst-case loads can be "on" simultaneously, resulting in a *peak current* drain from the battery (at night) of 2 + 20 + 3 = 25 A. The combined loads in Fig. 3-2 were obtained by simple addition of the current levels at each time. Loads 1 and 3 are shown to be switching independently, causing a slightly different combined load profile.

The *average* current drain, defined by the area under the curve of the combined loads (in units of ampere-hours, Ah; ampere-seconds are abbreviated as As), is calculated as shown.

Load 1
   2 A × 24 h = 48 Ah
Load 2
   3 × 20 A × 5 s = 300 As
   300 As/3600 = 0.08 Ah
   3 × 1 h × 4 A = 12 Ah
Load 3
   12 × 0.1 h × 3 A = 3.6 Ah
Combined loads
   48 + 0.08 + 12 + 3.6 = 64 Ah

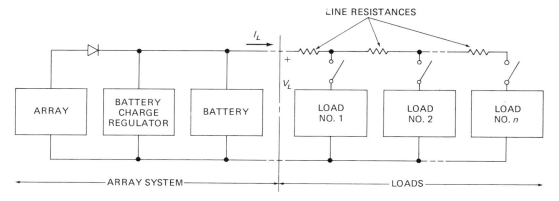

Fig. 3-1. Simple Power System.

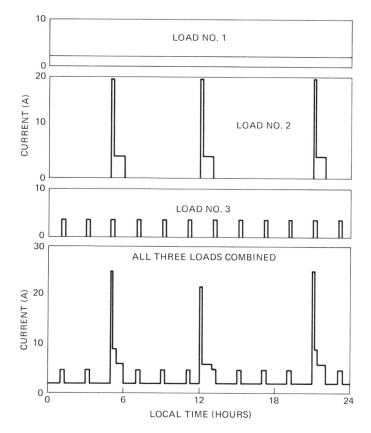

Fig. 3-2. Load profile. (Illustrative example)

Average combined load
64 Ah/24 h = 2.7 A
2.7 A × 25 V = 67 W

It is interesting to note that Load 1, having the lowest peak current drain, requires the largest amount of energy (Ah). The high starting current of the motor consumes only a negligible amount of energy, but essentially determines the ampere rating of the battery and the associated wiring and switching gear.

3-12. Illumination Profile Development

The illumination profile defines the amount of solar energy available as function of time during one orbit in space or during one day between sunrise and sunset, as well as the angular relationship between the sun line and the solar cell array. These relationships are developed for space arrays in Sections 2-49 and 2-62 through 2-67, and for terrestrial arrays in the following.

Consider a reference system centered at the surface of the earth at the site of an observer or a solar cell array installation. The site is located at $L_a°$ latitude and $L_o°$ longitude. The local *civil* time, or *local standard* time, is defined by the longitude of the standard meridian, L_{sm}. The standard meridians for time zones in the U.S. are shown in Table 3-4.

The sun reaches its highest point in the sky, known as its *zenith*, at *true solar time noon*. At that time, an observer located north of the Tropic of Cancer views the sun due south. The true solar time, H_s, is related to the local standard time, H_{ls}, by Eq. 3-1.

$$H_s = H_{ls} + E_{qt}/60 + (L_{sm} - L_{ob})/15$$

$$(3\text{-}1)$$

Table 3-4. Some Time Zones.

Zone Number	Standard Time	Longitude (° West)
0	Greenwich	0
–	U.S.	–
5	Eastern	75
6	Central	90
7	Mountain	105
8	Pacific	120
9	Eastern Alaska	135
10	Alaska and Hawaii	150

E_{qt} is the *equation of time* (in units of minutes) taken from Fig. 3-3 (the units of H_s and H_{ls} are hours). Figure 3-3 illustrates that during most of the year, the true sun time is either ahead or behind the local standard time, a fact that requires consideration when designing precise tracking equipment for concentrator arrays requiring high pointing accuracy. When viewing the sun from the site at which the aforementioned reference system is fixed, the sun rises in the east, as illustrated in Fig. 3-4, and moves across the sky according to the following equations.

$$\sin \phi_e = \cos L_a \cos \delta \cos h + \sin L_a \sin \delta$$

(3-2)

and

$$\sin \phi_a = -\cos \delta \sin h / \cos \phi_e \quad (3\text{-}3a)$$

or

$$\cos \phi_a = (\sin \delta - \sin L \sin \phi_e)/\cos L_a \cos \phi_e$$

(3-3b)

where

ϕ_a = azimuth angle of sun, measured in the horizontal plane from the north-south line

ϕ_e = sun elevation angle, measured in a perpendicular plane

L_a = latitude of site

L_o = longitude of site

δ = solar declination angle given in Fig. 3-3.

The sun hour angle h is given by Eq. 3-4 and H_s is defined by Eq. 3-1.

$$h = 15(12 - H_s) \quad (3\text{-}4)$$

The sunrise and sunset times, expressed in hours, according to the true solar time hour are approximately as given in Eqs. 3-5a and b.

$$H_{st,sr} = (1/15) \text{ arc cos } (\tan L_a \tan \delta) \quad (3\text{-}5a)$$

$$H_{st,ss} = 12 + (1/15) \text{ arc cos } (-\tan L_a \tan \delta)$$

(3-5b)

The corresponding sunrise and sunset times for local standard time are given in Eqs. 3-6a and b.

$$H_{lt,sr} = H_{st,sr} - E_{qt}/60 + (L_{ob} - L_{sm})/15$$

(3-6a)

$$H_{lt,ss} = H_{st,ss} - E_{qt}/60 + (L_{ob} - L_{sm})/15$$

(3-6b)

The hours of possible sunshine, H_p, are given in Eq. 3-7.

$$H_p = (2/15) \text{ arc cos } (-\tan L_a \tan \delta) \quad (3\text{-}7)$$

In Fig. 3-4, EAST and WEST indicate the 90° and 270° angles measured in the horizontal plane from true north. During the summer months, the sun's path encompasses a greater angle than 180° from east to west; however, not all the energy available outside the 180° arc may be usable by a fixed, flat plate array. The amount of energy that can be used depends upon the latitude, sun declination, time of year, and array tilt angle toward the south. The analytical relationship can be developed from Eq. 2-62 in Section 2-49 and Eqs. 3-2 and 3-3, by noting that the sun zenith angle $\phi_z = 90 - \phi_e$ and that ϕ_z is identical to the sun angle θ. The array tilt angle is α and the azimuth angle $\phi_a = \psi$ (see Fig. 3-5). The resulting expression for the compound angle Γ between the sun line and the normal to the flat plate array is Eq. 3-8.

$$\cos \Gamma = \cos \theta \cos \alpha + \sin \theta \sin \alpha \cos \psi$$

(3-8)

where

$\cos \theta = \sin \phi_e$ as given by Eq. 3-2

$\sin \theta = \sin$ [arc cos $(\cos L \cos \delta \cos h$ + $\sin L \sin \delta)$]

$\cos \psi = \cos \phi_a$ as given by Eq. 3-3b.

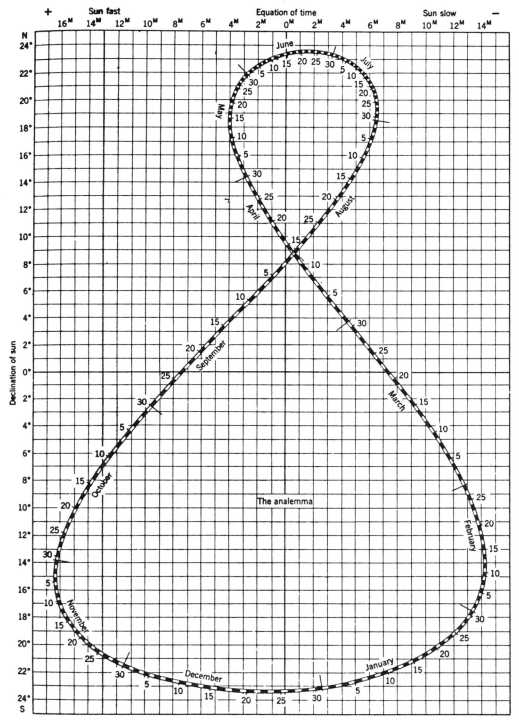

Fig. 3-3. The analemma. (From A. N. Strahler (1960), *Physical Geography*, New York, John Wiley & Sons, Reprinted with permission)

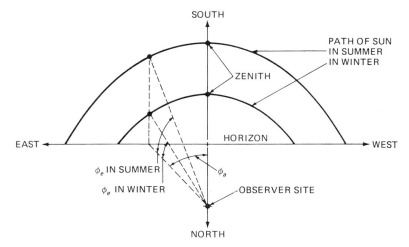

Fig. 3-4. Path of sun as seen north of Tropic of Cancer.

By plotting Γ versus H_s for different values of α and δ, the total solar intensity/time profile can be optimized. Of course, the effects of clouds must be added.

A simpler, but less accurate, approach to establishing an average daily insolation level incident on an inclined plate or on other array configurations consists of taking data from terrestrial sunshine tables (Appendix B).

Illustrative Example No. 3-2

Problem: For a fixed, tilted, flat plate solar cell array to be located in Albuquerque, New Mexico ($35°$ north, $106.5°$ west), optimize

the tilt angle and estimate the maximum available illumination profile.

Solution: From the data in Table B-3, the lowest "total tilt" and "direct normal" energy was available during November and February. During these two months, the sun declination, according to Fig. 3-3, ranged between approximately $8°$ and $22°$. The average declination is given by the averages of the cosines:

$$\cos \delta_{av} = \frac{\cos -8° + \cos -22°}{2} = \frac{0.990 + 0.927}{2}$$

$$= 0.959$$

$$\delta_{av} = -16.5°.$$

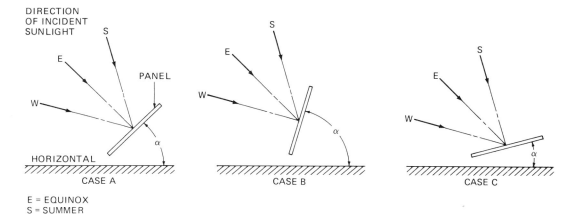

E = EQUINOX
S = SUMMER
W = WINTER

Fig. 3-5. Tilt angle definition. Angle α is optimized for vernal and antumnal equinox in Case A, for winter in Case B, and for summer in Case C.

The optimum tilt angle is $\alpha_0 = 35° + 16.5° = 51.5°$, where the tilt angle is as defined in Fig. 3-5.

The hours of possible sunshine, from Eq. 3-7, are

$$H_p = (2/15) \text{ arc cos } (-\tan 35° \tan -16.5°)$$

$$= (2/15) \text{ arc cos } (-0.700 \times -0.296)$$

$$= (2/15) \, 78.0$$

$$= 10.4 \text{ hours at } \delta = 16.5°.$$

H_p is only 9.7 hours at $\delta = 22.3°$ in December. During June, the sunshine is possibly available for 13.6 hours. During solar noon, the maximum sun elevation above the horizontal is $35° - 23.5° = 11.5°$ in winter and $35° + 23.5° = 58.5°$ in summer. The light intensity on the array, as defined by the compound angle Γ, can now be calculated according to Eq. 3-8.

3-13. Preliminary Array Sizing—Area Method

The power output capability of any terrestrial or space array, P_A, can be expressed as Eq. 3-9.

$$P_A = S \cdot \cos \Gamma \cdot \eta \cdot F \cdot A_A \qquad (3-9)$$

S is the terrestrial or space solar intensity, expressed in units of W/m^2, Γ (gamma) is the compound angle between the sun line and the array normal, η is the solar cell efficiency, F is the sum-total of all array design and degradation factors, and A_A is the array area. Solving Eq. 3-9 for A_A, we get Eq. 3-10.

$$A_A = P_A/S \cdot \cos \Gamma \cdot \eta \cdot F \qquad (3-10)$$

Equation 3-10 permits calculation of the required array area to meet the load requirements, P_A. The value of the solar constant is given in Sections 9-3 and 9-6, respectively; for more detailed design work, the illumination profile treated in Section 3-12 is used. The angle Γ is defined in Section 3-12, η in Section 4-17, and F in Section 3-16.

Illustrative Example No. 3-3

Problem: Establish the preliminary array and battery size for the array in Illustrative Example No. 3-1, assuming a terrestrial array being illuminated as discussed in Illustrative Example No. 3-2 and using $\eta = 10\%$, $F = 0.5$, and a bat-

tery charging efficiency of 60%. The full load is to be supported for 7 continuous days of cloudy weather (no sunshine), and the battery is to be fully recharged in 3 days.

Solution: The required array output is composed of the load and the battery recharge current. From Illustrative Example No. 3-1, the average load is 67 W for 24 hours, or $67 \times 24 \times 7 = 11.3$ kWh for 7 days. The battery charging requirement is $11.3/0.60 = 18.8$ kWh. To recharge the battery in 3 days, each day having 9.7 hours of sunshine in winter, the array must provide $18.8/9.7 \times 3 = 0.65$ kW for the battery recharging, plus 67 W average for the load during the 9.7 hours, plus $67(24 - 9.7)/9.7 \times 0.60 = 165$ W to carry the daily load through the night. The array output capability, therefore, must be $P_A = 650 + 67 + 165 = 882$ W $= 0.882$ kW.

From Table B-3, the lowest monthly insolance on a tilted plate is 181 kWh/m^2, or $181/9.7 \times 30 = 0.62$ kW/m^2 daily average. This quantity replaces $(S \cdot \cos \Gamma)$ in Eq. 3-9 and 3-10. The required array area is, according to Eq. 3-10:

$$A = 0.882/0.6 \times 0.10 \times 0.5 = 28.5 \text{ m}^2.$$

3-14. Preliminary Array Sizing—Cell Efficiency Method

This method is similar to that described in Section 3-13, except here the array area A_A is replaced by the total number of solar cells in the array, N_t, and the cell area, A_c.

$$P_A = S \cdot \cos \Gamma \cdot \eta \cdot F \cdot N_t \cdot A_c \qquad (3-11)$$

Solving Eq. 3-11 for N_t gives Eq. 3-12.

$$N_t = P_A/(S \cdot \cos \Gamma \cdot \eta \cdot F \cdot A_c) \qquad (3-12)$$

Illustrative Example No. 3-4

Problem: Find the number of solar cells for the array of Illustrative Example No. 3-3. Assume that each cell has a diameter of 2.25 inches.

Solution: The cell area is given by

$$A_c = \frac{d^2 \pi}{4} = \frac{(2.25 \times 2.54)^2 \pi}{4} = 25.6 \text{ cm}^2$$

$$= 25.6 \times 10^{-4} \text{ m}^2.$$

The number of cells required, according to Eq. 3-12, is

$$N_t = 0.882/0.62 \times 0.10 \times 0.5 \times 25.6 \times 10^{-4}$$

$$= 11,100.$$

3-15. Preliminary Array Sizing—Cell Power Method

In terms of the solar cell power output, P_c, the array power, P_A, is given in Eq. 3-13, where S_0 is the reference intensity at which the cell power output P_c was determined.

$$P_A = \frac{S \cdot \cos \Gamma}{S_0} \cdot F \cdot N_t \cdot P_c \qquad (3\text{-}13)$$

The required number of cells is N_t.

$$N_t = \frac{P_A \cdot S_0}{F \cdot P_c \cdot S \cdot \cos \Gamma} \qquad (3\text{-}14)$$

Illustrative Example No. 3-5

Problem: Find the number of solar cells for the array of Illustrative Example No. 3-3. Assume that each cell has an area of 25.6 cm² and a power output density of 10 mW/cm² at one solar constant intensity (1.0 kW/m²).

Solution: The cell power output is $10 \times 25.6 = 256$ mW $= 0.256 \times 10^{-3}$ kW. From Eq. 3-14.

$$N_t = 0.882/0.62 \times 0.5 \times 0.256 \times 10^{-6}$$

$$= 11,100.$$

DETAILED ARRAY DESIGN

3-16. Detailed Array Sizing

Even though most of the following sections are developed for space arrays, they are equally applicable to terrestrial arrays with a few obvious exceptions. The reason for presenting the space design concepts is that terrestrial design activities have not yet reached the stage of sophistication that the space activities have. It may be argued that for terrestrial designs, such sophistication is unwarranted; however, as lower-cost designs are sought, a deeper understanding of all design aspects may prove helpful. Of course,

not even all space arrays are analyzed at the level of detail shown; the experienced designer is able to make many simplifications without loss of accuracy or validity of the end results.

Array sizing is an analytical process by which the physical and electrical properties are established that describe a solar cell array which meets a specific performance (output) requirement at some critical mission time (usually at end-of-mission).

Sizing Procedure

Step 1. Select one or more candidate combinations of array components intended for the design-to-emerge:

  Solar cells (from Chapter 4)
  Solar cell covers (from Chapter 5)
  Other electrical components (from Chapter 6)
  Substrates (from Chapter 7).

Step 2. For each candidate configuration of Step 1, determine for the end-of-mission (or for any other mission-critical event) the glassed, degraded, maximum power output, P_C, of a single solar cell from Eq. 3-15.

$$P_C = P_0 \cdot S' \cdot F_{RAD} \cdot F_{T_{op}} \cdot F_M \cdot F_{SH}$$

$$\cdot F_{BD} \cdot F_{CONF} \qquad (3\text{-}15)$$

The terms are defined below.

P_0 = initial, unglassed and undegraded solar cell output at normal incidence at one solar constant intensity, and at a reference temperature (25° or 28°C).

S' = effective solar intensity, including the effects of cover transmission degradation, solar distance, and non-normal incidence.

F_{RAD} = solar cell radiation degradation factor, defined by either Eq. 3-16* or 3-17.**

---

*PD = percent orbital solar cell degradation.

**P_{mp} = cell maximum power output. The additional subscripts ϕ and 0 refer to the end-of-mission 1 MeV fluence, ϕ, and the initial, zero fluence condition, respectively. (The 1 MeV fluence is obtained according to the procedure described in Section 3-34.)

$$F_{RAD} = 1 - PD/100 \quad (3\text{-}16)$$

$$F_{RAD} = P_{mp\phi}/P_{mp0}$$
$$(3\text{-}17)$$

$F_{T_{op}}$ = operating temperature degradation factor defined by Eq. 3-18.*

$$F_{T_{op}} = P_{mpT_{op}}/P_{mp0}$$
$$(3\text{-}18)$$

F_M = miscellaneous assembly and degradation factors identified and discussed in Section 2-47 and not covered specifically in Eq. 3-15. For most array design cases, F_M will range between 0.95 and 1.00.

F_{SH} = shadowing factor, as defined in Section 2-42. For unshadowed arrays, $F_{SH} = 1.00$.

F_{BD} = blocking diode and wiring loss factor, prorated for a single cell and defined by Eq. 3-19, where V_D = diode voltage drop, V_W = voltage drop of the wiring between the array and the load, and V_B = array bus voltage at the spacecraft load.**

$$F_{BD} = 1 - \frac{V_D + V_W}{V_B + V_D + V_W}$$
$$(3\text{-}19)$$

F_{CONF} = configuration factor, also known as aspect ratio, as given in Section 3-17. (For flat plate arrays, $F_{CONF} = 1$. For cylindrical, spinning arrays, $F_{CONF} = 1/\pi$.)

Step 3. Determine solar cell array characteristics as shown below.

---

*The additional subscripts T_{op} and 0 refer to the operating temperature and reference temperature, respectively. $P_{mpT_{op}}$ is computed according to Section 2-51, while T_{op} is estimated according to Section 2-56. If appropriate values of F_p and η_{op} are not yet defined, one can assume as a first cut $F_p = 0.9$ and $\eta_{op} = 0.05$ for long-life high-radiation or higher-temperature orbits or $\eta_{op} = 0.1$ for low radiation or lower-temperature orbits.

**If the blocking diodes and wiring losses are not yet defined, $(V_D + V_W) = 1.4$ V is a good first-cut approximation for single silicon diodes on arrays below 1 kW size, and $(V_D + V_W) = 2.8$ V for higher power levels.

Number of solar cells:

$$N = P_A/P_C \quad (3\text{-}20)$$

where

P_A = required power output
P_C = single-cell output from Eq. 3-15.

Substrate area:

$$A_s = A_c N/F_p \quad (3\text{-}21)$$

where the packing factor, F_p, is defined below, and A_c is the overall solar cell area.

Substrate mass:

$$M = mA_s \quad (3\text{-}22)$$

where m is the mass per unit area (kg/m^2) from Sections 1-16 and 1-17.

Packing factor:

$$F_p = \frac{N \cdot A_c}{A_s} \quad (3\text{-}23)$$

where

N = total number of solar cells on a given solar cell panel or array
A_c = overall area of a solar cell
A_s = substrate area.

Different definitions for A_s are being used, depending upon how A_s is to be used in computations. A_s may define the following substrate areas or portions thereof:

- Areas under the solar cell modules and strings only
- All so-called "available" areas onto which solar cell circuits, including cabling, may be mounted
- The substrate gross area with the exception of areas reserved for hinges and similar elements and with the exception of cutouts (larger openings) in the substrate
- The entire gross, overall area without regard to solar cell circuit placement and unavailable areas.

Frequently, the applicable literature does not provide any indications as to which definition was used by the author. Practical packing factors, using the first definition above, range from around 0.85 to 0.92. Packing factors of 0.95 and greater are very difficult to achieve with flat solar cell laydown designs. Conical and trapezoidal solar cell panels may exhibit packing factors as low as 0.5 to 0.6.

Packing Density. Indicating the number of the solar cells of a given size which can be fitted into a given substrate area, the packing density, N', is related to the packing factor (Eq. 3-23) by Eq. 3-24.

$$N' = \frac{A_s F_p}{A_c} \qquad (3-24)$$

Table 3-5 provides some examples of different packing densities.

3-17. Space Array Configuration Selection

The evolution of the solar cell array configuration is strongly dependent upon the evolution of the overall spacecraft design and is primarily in response to the following interface considerations:

- Payload and communication equipment directional pointing requirements
- The range of the angles of incidence of the sunlight falling onto the spacecraft and onto the solar cell array throughout mission life
- The change in the array-to-sun distance during mission life
- The required power level and power profile of the array
- Size, volume, and mass constraints imposed by the launch vehicle and the overall spacecraft design.

Different solar cell array configurations are illustrated in Section 1-8. The use of the projected solar cell areas of the array as discussed in this section usually provides sufficient analytical accuracy for conceptual design studies. For more refined configuration studies, actual solar cell array I-V characteristics should be used rather than the projected areas. One commonly used method is to assume a hypothetical array of 100 cells in parallel by 100 cells in series and to compute the array output by the method described in Sections 2-47 through 2-51 for a number of different geometries and estimated operating temperatures. The deviations of actual array power output curves from the projected area curves may be substantial.

Different geometric shapes may be added to the array to achieve a desired power profile (power output as a function of the sun angle θ in Figs. 3-6 through 3-8.

In Fig. 3-6, the comparative power output of a number of different array configurations as a function of angle of incidence is shown. This figure will help to select the most desirable array configuration, or combination of configurations, to obtain any desired power profile as function of sun angle. Figures 3-7 and 3-8 permit the optimization of paddle angles and cone angles, respectively. The relationships between a cylindrical array and approximation of a cylindrical array by a series of flat facets is illustrated in Table 3-6.

3-18. Number of Required Solar Cells

Number of Cells in Series. A sufficient number of solar cells must be electrically connected in series to provide the bus voltage plus any voltage drops in the blocking diodes and in the wiring. The required number of cells in series, N_S, is found from

$$N_S = \frac{V_B + V_D + V_W}{V_{mp}} \qquad (3-25)$$

where

V_B = spacecraft load or battery bus voltage
V_D = array blocking diode forward voltage drop
V_W = total wiring voltage drop between the solar cells and the spacecraft load or the battery (in both the hot and return lines)
V_{mp} = solar cell end-of-mission (or other mission critical event) degraded out-

Table 3-5. Packing Densities for 2 × 2 cm and 2 × 4 cm Solar Cells.

F_p	Number of Cells (per ft²)		Number of Cells (per m²)	
	2 × 2 cm	2 × 4 cm	2 × 2 cm	2 × 4 cm
0.8	186	93	2000	1000
0.9	208	104	2250	1125
1.0	232	116	2500	1250

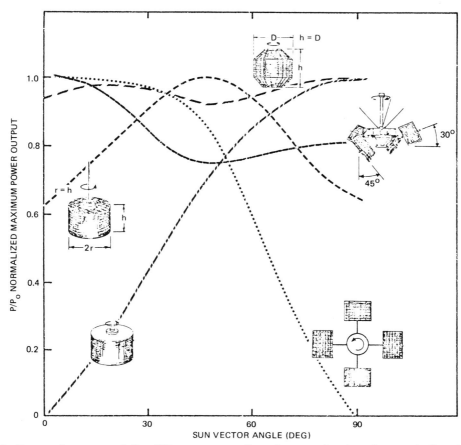

Fig. 3-6. Comparative output of five different array configurations as a function of sun angle (i.e., the angle between the solar vector and the satellite spin axis).

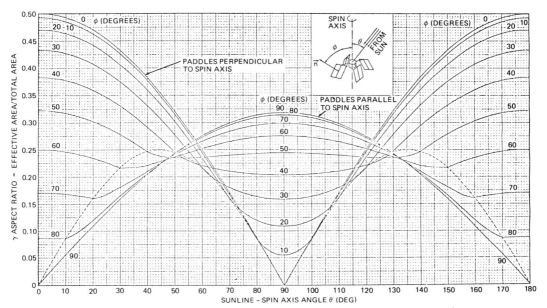

Fig. 3-7. Aspect ratios of paddle mounted arrays, shadowing effects ignored.[1]

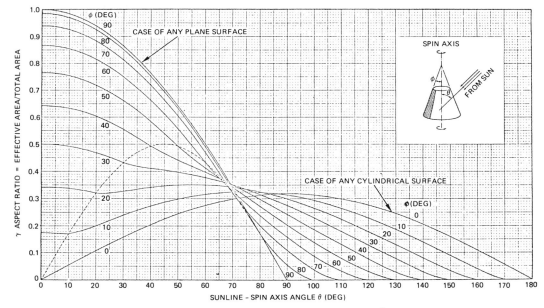

Fig. 3-8. Aspect ratios of conical solar arrays.[1]

put voltage at the cell's maximum power point and under operating temperature and intensity.

The value of V_B is usually project-peculiar and depends primarily upon the battery's electrochemical characteristics. Values for V_D are typically near 0.7 V for silicon diodes. Values for V_W are project-peculiar; however, Section 3-20 provides a procedure for selecting V_W for a minimum weight array-plus-bus wiring design. Values for V_{mp} can be determined from the following procedure: for each of the solar cell and cell cover types selected in Section 3-16 (or for the types for which a design already exists), determine for the end-of-mission (or for any other mission critical event) the glassed, degraded, maximum power voltage of a single cell from Eq. 3-26.

$$V_{mp} = V_{mp\phi} + \Delta V_{S'} + \beta_{Vp}(T_{op} - T_0)$$

$$(3\text{-}26)$$

where

$V_{mp\phi}$ = glassed solar cell maximum power output voltage at the reference temperature T_0 after irradiation with 1 MeV electrons to a level of $\phi e \cdot cm^{-2}$

$\Delta V_{S'}$ = change in the maximum power voltage due to a change in the light intensity from S to S', as described in Section 2-50 (the corresponding voltage change is determined from the solar cell data in Chapter 4 or from Section 2-51)

β_{Vp} = temperature coefficient for the maximum power voltage, as defined in Section 4-21

Table 3-6. Relative Area of Faceted Cylinders.

Number of Facets (n)	Relative Area (A_R)
∞ (cylinder)	1.000
4	0.637
6	0.827
8	0.900
10	0.936
12	0.955
16	0.974
20	0.984
24	0.988

$$A_R = A_n/A_{\text{cylinder}} \text{ and}$$
$$A_n = \tfrac{1}{2}nr^2 \sin(2\pi/n)$$

where A_n is the area of a polygon of n sides inscribed in a circle of radius r.

T_{op} = solar cell operating temperature, obtained from Section 2-56 or from Section 3-24

T_0 = solar cell standard test temperature (25°C or 28°C).

Number of Cells in Parallel. Let a group of N_s solar cells, all connected in series, be defined as a *series string*, or simply as a *string* of cells. The total solar cell array consists of N_p strings that are connected in parallel and, together, provide the required load current. N_p is found from Eq. 3-27, where I_{mpav} is the average maximum power point current output of all N_p cells in parallel after glassing and degradation, at the operating temperature, T_{op}, and under reduced illumination conditions due to cover darkening and non-normal incidence.

$$N_P = \frac{I_L}{I_{mpav}} \qquad (3\text{-}27)$$

To compute I_{mpav}, proceed as in Eq. 3-28.

$$I_{mpav} = \frac{\sum_{i=1}^{n} I_{mpi}}{n} \qquad (3\text{-}28)$$

where

$$I_{mpi} = I_{mp\phi} \cdot (S')_i \cdot [1 + \beta'_{Ip}(T_{op} - T_0)]$$
$$\cdot F_m \cdot (F_{SH})_i \qquad (3\text{-}29)$$

The terms are defined below.

$I_{mp\phi}$ = glassed (but with undegraded transmission) solar cell maximum power point output current at the reference temperature T_0 after irradiation with 1 MeV electrons to a level of $\phi e \cdot cm^{-2}$.

S'_i = effective solar intensity for the ith parallel-connected string of cells, including the effects of cover transmission degradation, solar distance and non-normal incidence (as defined in Section 2-50). S'_i is in units of "solar constants." For a flat panel array, all S_i are the same and the subscript i may be dropped.

β'_{Ip} = temperature coefficient for I_{mp}, as defined in Section 4-21, expressed in units of °C^{-1}.

T_{op} = solar cell operating temperature, obtained from Section 2-56 or from Section 3-24.

T_0 = solar cell standard test temperature (25°C or 28°C).

F_m = miscellaneous solar cell assembly and degradation factors (identified and discussed in Section 2-47); for most array designs, F_m will range from 0.95 to 1.00.

$(F_{SH})_i$ = the shadowing factor for the ith parallel-connected string of solar cells, as described in Section 2-42. For unshadowed strings, $F_{SH} = 1.00$.

Parallel Circuits. As a minimum, all series strings of cells are parallel-connected at their ends. However, it has been common practice to parallel-connect groups of cells at the cell level into strings that have two, three, or more cells connected in parallel.

The purpose of such parallel connection is to achieve higher array reliability by providing a parallel current path in case of a cell open-circuit failure due to cell fracturing, contact lifting, or interconnector failures.

In case of an open-circuit failure, adjacent parallel-connected solar cells can share a part or all of the current flow that is blocked by an open-circuited solar cell. The amount of current which can be carried by the unfailed cells depends upon the difference between the cell's operating current level before the failure occurred and the sum of the short-circuit currents of the parallel-connected unfailed cells after failure. If that current difference is less than the current which was originally carried by the cell which failed, the unfailed cells will be driven into reverse bias, as described in Section 2-45. Reverse biased solar cells can, in turn, be caused to fail by excessive overheating, as discussed in Section 2-46.

If reverse biasing of solar cells can occur on a particular design, the design practices given in Section 3-21 should be considered.

3-19. Array Layout

The solar cell array layout activity consists of arranging the series strings of parallel-connected solar cells on the available substrate area to achieve the highest possible power output per unit area while providing space for the electrical conductors from the solar cell circuits to the solar panel terminals. Also, room is provided for the blocking (isolation) and shadowing (bypass) diodes, if required.

Dimensional Analysis. The minimum gap sizes between adjacent cells, measured at room temperature, are determined primarily by the solar cell and cover assembly dimensions, the thermal expansion coefficient of the substrate, and the lowest possible temperature excursion (eclipse exit temperature). Tolerances on the assembly process, such as non-centered cell-to-substrate adhesive pads, play roles, as do the interconnector expansion loop sizes and voltage differentials between solar cells in adjacent strings.

Minimum practical gaps are 0.1 mm between adjacent cells in the parallel-connected group of cells, 0.5 mm between cells in the (electrical) series directions, and 0.5 to 1.0 mm between adjacent electrical strings. This gap size refers to the cell-to-cell gap width when undersized or "same" size covers are used, and to cover-to-cover gaps when oversized covers are used. Using the definitions given in Fig. 3-9, the required area for a group or string can be calculated from Eqs. 3-30a and b.

$$A = MC + (M - 1)H \qquad (3\text{-}30a)$$

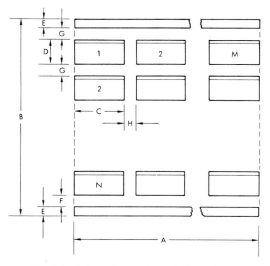

Fig. 3-9. Solar cell array layout dimensions.

$$B = ND + NG + F + 2E \qquad (3\text{-}30b)$$

where

C = solar cell width—parallel
H = cell gap—parallel
D = cell length—series
G = cell gap—series
E = end contact bar width
F = end contact/cell gap.

The dimensions C and D must be based on the maximum size of the glassed cells. (Additional information relating to intercell spacings is given in Section 6-12.)

3-20. Array Wiring

The electrical output from the solar cells is collected by solar cell interconnectors and is transmitted by cables, wires, or flat conductors to the terminals of a solar cell panel or solar cell assembly, as discussed in Chapter 6. The terminal board or connector mates with a connector or "pig tail" from the primary bus. The various types of electrical circuit components for solar cell arrays, as well as appropriate design practices, are all described in detail in Chapter 6. Electrical conductor sizing is described in the following.

Weight limitations for most spacecraft usually do not permit electrical conductors to be sized for near-zero power losses. Instead, the permissible power loss is determined by a trade-off between the weight due to increased array size.[2] For arrays having power levels in the order of 1 kW, total power losses in the spacecraft primary bus wiring in the order of 1% are common, ranging from about 0.5 to 5% for different designs.

Conductor/Array Mass Trade-off. Consider the solar cell array terminals to be separated from the load terminals by the distance L. The total resistance of a pair of conductors between the array and the load is

$$R_2 = 2\rho L/A$$

and their total mass (neglecting the insulation) is

$$m_c = 2LAd$$

where

ρ = electrical conductivity of conductors
A = cross-sectional area of conductors
d = density of conductors.

Let the required load power be P_L and the power losses in the conductor be P_R. The array must, therefore, be sized to provide $P_L + P_R$.

Let the array mass corresponding to P_L be m_L and the array mass corresponding to P_R be m_R. Then the sum-total of the masses of the array and the conductors is

$$M = m_L + m_R + m_c.$$

However,

$$m_R = m_L P_R / P_L$$

and

$$P_R = I_L^2 R_2 = I_L^2 \rho L / A$$

and

$$P_L = V_L I_L$$

where V_L is the load voltage and I_L is the load current. Thus we find Eq. 3-31.

$$M = m_L + \frac{2 m_L I_L \rho L}{A V_L} + 2LAd \quad (3\text{-}31)$$

Differentiating M with respect to A and setting the result equal to zero permits the minimum M to be found for which the cross-sectional area, denoted by A_m, is given by Eq. 3-32.

$$A_m^2 = m_L I_L \rho / V_L d \quad (3\text{-}32)$$

The value for A_m can then be used to calculate the P_R for which M results in a minimum (lowest weight) configuration.

Aluminum vs. Copper Conductors. The resistance of a single conductor is given by $R = \rho L / A$ and its mass by $M = ALd = \rho d L^2 / R$, where ρ is the electrical resistivity of conductor, L is the conductor length, and d is the conductor density. Let the mass of an aluminum conductor be denoted by M_a and that of a copper conductor by M_c. The mass ratio of two, for the same resistance R and length L is

$$\frac{M_a}{M_c} = \frac{\rho_a d_a}{\rho_c d_c}.$$

The subscripts a and c refer to aluminum and copper, respectively. For $\rho_a/\rho_c = 1.64$ (from the data in Chapter 10), $d_a = 2.70$, and $d_c = 8.89$ g · cm^{-3}, we obtain

$$M_a/M_c = 0.50.$$

Hence, aluminum conductors weigh one-half of copper conductors for the same power loss and conductor length.

3-21. Hot-spot Design Considerations

The so-called *hot-spot* phenomenon due to reverse biasing of solar cells (as described in Section 2-45) may lead to solar cell failures and associated solar cell array power losses (as described in Section 4-25).

The magnitude of the hot-spot problem, if it exists at all for a given design, depends upon both the electrical and the thermal solar cell array designs. Potentially damaging reverse voltages can occur only if the difference between the load voltage and the solar cell string open-circuit voltage is sufficiently high. Potentially damaging heating of reverse biased solar cells can occur only if the heat dissipation in the cell or cells is of sufficient duration and of sufficient magnitude relative to the quantity of heat conducted and radiated away from the cell or cells.

If a given design is suspected to be subject to a hot-spot problem, it should be analyzed according to Section 2-45. Sections 2-46, 2-54, and 2-56 permit the solar cell temperatures to be determined.

If an analysis shows that a real or a potential hot-spot problem exists, the design changes listed below should be considered to reduce the magnitude of the reverse voltage and/or heat dissipation.

- Eliminate operational short-circuiting of an array or array section (i.e., let shunt regulators shunt the array to the load voltage rather than to near short-circuit).
- Reduce the number of solar cells connected in series, or install shunt diodes across each parallel group of cells. For example, the splitting up of the array into two equal-sized, series-connected arrays, tied together

by a common bus connected to a shunt regulator, effectively reduces the number of cells in series by one-half.

- Use single cell series strings rather than parallel-connected groups of cells in the series strings.
- Increase the number of cells connected in parallel (at the cell level) until unfailed cells can carry just a little more current than a failed (open-circuited) cell originally carried. (This typically requires about ten or more cells in parallel.)
- Increase the lateral heat conduction and/or heat dissipation from solar cells and the substrate.

3-22. Designing for Reliability

Array design for reliability, as defined in Sections 2-59 through 2-61, involves two aspects: oversizing the array and providing redundancy. Oversizing of the array by one or more series strings of cells compensates for potential string failures that may occur during a mission due to statistically estimated failure rates of solar cells, interconnectors, soldered or welded joints, connectors, etc. Redundant current paths through soldered or welded joints, interconnectors, wires, connectors, etc., can significantly improve the array reliability.

3-23. High-Voltage Design

High-voltage solar cell arrays, attractive both for minimizing I^2R losses in higher-power level arrays (in excess of 10 kW), and for direct operation of ion-thrust engines, have been studied for voltage ranges between 2 and 16 kV. High-voltage effects become increasingly pronounced as the array voltage increases above 100 V and as the available array output current level decreases correspondingly (assuming a fixed power output array).[3,4]

Specific high-voltage effects on the ground and during space flight include plasma leakage currents and insulation material damage. Leakage currents of significant magnitude can be carried by the plasma or air surrounding the array (see Section 9-44 through 9-49), thereby shunting a significant portion of the solar cell array output. High-voltage stress and corona can deteriorate or destroy insulating materials (see Section 10-17).

Design Practices. Design practices presently envisioned to be required for successful high-voltage array operation include the following:

- Complete insulation of the high-voltage array solar cell circuits, including solar cells, interconnectors, and joints, from the surrounding plasma or air
- Minimization or complete avoidance of pinholes and voids in the insulating layers
- Provisions for shunt diodes to both increase the array reliability and to minimize hot-spot (reverse biasing) effects.

THERMAL DESIGN

3-24. Temperature Control in Space

Temperature control of solar cell arrays in space is by radiative heat transfer only, as described in Sections 2-53 and 2-56. From these discussions, the steady-state operating temperature is given by Eq. 3-33.

$$T_{op} = \left[\frac{(\bar{\alpha}_s - F_p \eta_{op})A_F}{(\bar{\epsilon}_{HF}A_F + \epsilon_{HB}A_B)} \frac{S \cos \Gamma}{\sigma} \right]^{1/4}$$

$$(3\text{-}33)$$

The transient eclipse temperature as a function of eclipse time, t_e, is given by Eq. 3-34.

$$T_e(t_e) = T_{op} \left[1 + \frac{3(\bar{\epsilon}_{HF}A_F + \epsilon_{HB}A_B)T_{op}^3}{\overline{m c_p}} t_e \right]^{-1/3}$$

$$(3\text{-}34)$$

The symbols (defined in the sections indicated) represent the following:

$\bar{\alpha}_s$ = average solar cell solar absorptance (Section 2-53)

F_p = solar cell packing factor (Section 2-53)

η_{op} = solar cell operating efficiency (Section 4-17)

A_F = array total front side area

A_B = array total back side area

$\bar{\epsilon}_{HF}$ = hemispherical emittance of the array front side (Section 2-53)

ϵ_{HB} = hemispherical emittance of the array back side (Section 2-53)

S = value of the solar constant (Section 9-3 or 9-6) and, in case of concentrator solar arrays, times the actual concentration ratio

σ = Stefan Boltzmann's constant (Appendix C)

$\overline{mc}_p$ = array thermal mass (Section 2-56)

Γ = angle of incidence of the sunlight on the solar cells (Section 2-49).

Common to both of the above equations are the emissivity of the array's front and back sides and the emitting areas. From this, it follows that a lowering of the operating temperature through enhanced heat emission also causes an undesirable lowering of the eclipse exit temperature. Therefore, the best approach is first to lower the array's average solar absorptance (increasing the solar cell efficiency), and then to improve the heat emission.

A low eclipse exit temperature can be raised by increasing the thermal mass of the array by either increasing the total mass of the array, or by substituting materials having higher specific heat capacitances. The metal *beryllium* has been used for this purpose because it can absorb about twice as much heat per unit mass as aluminum can absorb near room temperature. At low temperature, however, the advantage of beryllium is diminished.

The strong variation of T_{op} with solar distance according to Eq. 3-32 is illustrated in Fig. 3-10. In the equation, the cells are nonoperating ($\eta_{op} = 0$), the sun intensity S varies with distance from the sun according to Eq. 2-63, and $\Gamma = 0$. The α/ϵ ratio shown on the graph is for $\overline{\epsilon}_{HF} = \overline{\epsilon}_{HB}$ and should be divided by 2 when used in the calculation of T_{op} according to Eq. 3-33.

The variation of an oriented flat solar cell panel in earth orbit as function of altitude is illustrated in Table 3-7. The temperature rise, arising from the earth albedo and infrared radiation, diminishes with increasing distance from the earth.

3-25. Temperature Control on Earth

For thermal design purposes of terrestrial modules, it can be assumed that the amount of heat removed by radiative cooling is roughly the same as that removed by convective cooling. The thermal network given in Section 2-58 illustrates the heat flow paths. The applicable equations of Sections 2-54 through 2-56 in-

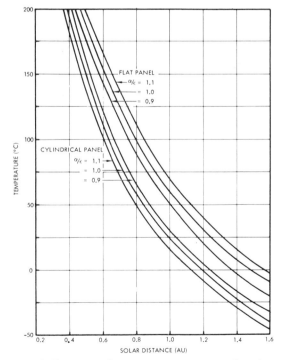

Fig. 3-10. Solar cell array temperature as a function of solar distance. (Flat panel and spin axes are perpendicular to sunlight; cylindrical arrays are spinning)

Table 3-7. Flat Solar Panel Temperature Variation as a Function of Orbit Altitude.

Circular Orbit Altitude (km)	Solar Panel Steady-State Temperature (°C)
370	67
740	65
1,110	64
1,850	62
7,410	57
14,820	55
22,240	54
35,880	53

dicate that, from strictly a thermal point of view, the module window should be made from as thin and thermally conductive and highly emitting material as can be found, and that the solar cells should be bonded to that window with as thin a bondline as practical. The substrate should preferably be metallic and carry fins for effective convective cooling and should be coated with a highly emitting paint. The bond line between the cells and the substrate, including the thickness of the cell-to-substrate dielectric, should be as thin as possible. The front (cell-mounting) side of the substrate should have low solar absorptivity.

3-26. Decreasing Absorptance

The average effective solar absorptance $\bar{\alpha}_s$, (defined in Section 2-53) of the array can be lowered by any one or combination of the following:

- Using spectrally selective reflecting filters rather than absorbing filters to reflect all sunlight that cannot be converted into electrical energy (see Section 5-9)
- Minimizing cover and cover adhesive darkening at end-of-life (see Chapter 5 and 10)
- Covering all array areas not covered by solar cell active areas with highly sunlight-reflective materials
- Maximizing the end-of-mission solar cell operating efficiency (defined in Section 4-17).

A decrease in the absorbing area A_α also reduces the operating temperature without significantly affecting the eclipse exit temperature. A decrease in the absorbing area can be achieved by any of the methods given in Section 3-29.

The sensitivity of the solar array temperature to changes in any of the parameters that affect the cell temperature can be studied by differentiation of Eq. 3-33 or 3-34 with respect to the parameter that is of interest. If the differentiated equation is divided by the original equation, the result permits evaluation of the fractional change in absolute temperature.

Illustrative Example No. 3-6

Problem: What is the change in operating temperature of a space array due to a change in the solar absorptance, $\bar{\alpha}_S$, from 1.00 to 0.95?

Solution: Eq. 3-33 can be restated as

$$T^4 = k(\bar{\alpha}_S - F_p \eta_{op})$$

where k is a constant representing all other symbols in Eq. 3-33 (k is of no further interest). Differentiating this equation, we obtain

$$4T^3 dT = k(d\bar{\alpha}_S).$$

Dividing the second equation by the first and rearranging terms,

$$\frac{dT}{T} = \frac{d\bar{\alpha}_S}{4(\bar{\alpha}_S - F_p \eta_{op})}.$$

Substituting numbers, assuming $F_p \cdot \eta_{op} = 0.1$, and letting $dT = \Delta T$ and $d\bar{\alpha}_S = \Delta\bar{\alpha}_s = \bar{\alpha}_{S2} - \bar{\alpha}_{S1}$, we obtain

$$\frac{\Delta T}{T} = \frac{0.95 - 1.00}{4(0.95 - 0.1)} = -0.0147.$$

For an operating temperature of 300°K (23°C), $\Delta T = -0.0147 \times 300 = -4.4°$K. For an operating temperature of 330°K (53°C), $\Delta T = -0.0147 \times 330 = -4.9°$K. Hence, a lowering of $\bar{\alpha}_S$ from 1.00 to 0.95 reduces the array temperature by approximately 5°K or 5°C.

3-27. Increasing Emittance

The average, effective emittance, $\bar{\epsilon}$ (defined in Section 2-53), of the array can be increased by increasing the emittance of the solar cell covers (for example, ceria-stabilized microsheet has a higher emittance than fused silica, but also a higher absorptance), by covering all frontal array areas not covered by solar cell active areas with highly emitting (but also reflecting) materials (such as white thermal control paint), and by covering the array back sides with highly emitting material (white or black paint).

A decrease in the solar cell operating temperature can also be achieved by increasing the emitting area, A_ϵ, as discussed in Section 3-29.

Illustrative Example No. 3-7

Problem: What is the change in the operating temperature of an oriented space array due to a change in the front side emittance, $\overline{\epsilon}_{HF}$, from 0.90 to 0.95? Assume $\overline{\epsilon}_{HB}$ = 0.95.

Solution: Restating Eq. 3-33 as

$$T^4 = k'(\overline{\epsilon}_{HF}A_F + \epsilon_{HB}A_B)^{-1}$$

and differentiating with respect to $\overline{\epsilon}_{HF}$ yields

$$4T^3 dT = - \frac{k'A_F d\overline{\epsilon}_{HF}}{(\overline{\epsilon}_{HF}A_F + \epsilon_{HB}A_B)^2} .$$

Dividing the second equation by the first and letting the differentials become increments results in

$$\frac{\Delta T}{T} = - \frac{A_F \Delta \overline{\epsilon}_{HF}}{4(\overline{\epsilon}_{HF}A_F + \epsilon_{HB}A_B)} .$$

For a flat plate array, $A_F = A_B$, so that

$$\frac{\Delta T}{T} = - \frac{\Delta \overline{\epsilon}_{HF}}{4(\overline{\epsilon}_{HF} + \epsilon_{HB})} .$$

Substituting numbers,

$$\frac{\Delta T}{T} = - \frac{0.95 - 0.90}{4(0.90 + 0.95)} = - 0.0068.$$

For an operating temperature of 330°K, $\Delta T = -2.2°K = -2.2°C$. Hence, increasing the front side emittance from 0.90 to 0.95 decreases the operating temperature by approximately 2°C.

3-28. Increasing Convection

Convection cooling of terrestrial modules can be accomplished either by increasing the surface areas from which heat is carried away, by increasing the flow rate of coolant, or by changing the coolant type.

For naturally cooled modules, the addition of cooling fins to the back side of the modules is helpful only for wind velocities greater than about 1 m/second. Tilting the modules and removing all possible obstructions to air flow is also helpful. This includes providing spacings between adjacent modules, as discussed in Section 7-5.

3-29. Improving the Geometry

High-temperature control problems are typically encountered on spacecraft that approach the sun or the inner planets. Reduction of the solar cell operating temperature is typically achieved by increasing the emitting areas, and the subsequently encountered low-temperature problems may have to be tolerated.[5] Solar cell operating temperatures can be reduced by any one or combination of the following:

- *Off-pointing*—non-normal angles of incidence reduce solar heating proportional to the cosine of the angle of incidence
- *Mosaic array*—highly reflecting and emitting thermal control elements are interspersed with the solar cells to decrease both $\overline{\alpha}$ and A_α and increase both $\overline{\epsilon}$ and A_ϵ
- *Partially reflective covers*—a portion of the area of each solar cell cover carries a highly reflective coating, thereby reducing both $\overline{\alpha}$ and A_α while keeping $\overline{\epsilon}_{HF}$ and A_ϵ constant
- *Semi-transparent covers*—the solar cell covers carry a partially reflecting, partially transmitting coating applied uniformly over the cover areas, thereby reducing $\overline{\alpha}$ without affecting $\overline{\epsilon}_{HF}$
- *Cooling fins*—flat or curved solar cell panels carry radiating fins, thereby increasing the emitting area on the array back side
- *Non-flat array geometry*—solar panels having conical or other shapes exhibit greater effective emitting areas than absorbing areas
- *Spinning array configurations*—the emitting array is approximately π times as great as the absorbing area.

High temperature control problems related to sunlight concentration are handled essentially similarly to flat plate temperature problems, except that, in addition, the concentrated heat must be conducted from the solar cells to radiating surfaces. For heat concentration, see Section 5-20. Heat conduction is discussed in Sections 2-54.

3-30. Minimizing Eclipse Exit Temperatures

The rate of heat transfer by radiative cooling decreases significantly at lower array temperatures (see Eq. 2-70 in Section 2-53), so that the governing parameter becomes the thermal mass of the array, mc_p, as given by Eq. 2-83 in Section 2-56. Also, in actual practice for any eclipse durations of greater than approximately 30 minutes, the eclipse exit temperature as given by Eq. 3-34 becomes rather independent of T_{op}, further illustrating the importance of $\overline{mc_p}$. Of course, the easiest solution to low temperature eclipse problems is to solve the associated thermomechanical or electrical problems so that there is no constraint on the permissible eclipse exit temperature. However, if this is not achievable, increasing the thermal mass may be required.

Illustrative Example No. 3-8

Problem: What is the change in eclipse exit temperature due to a change in $\overline{mc_p}$ by 10%?

Solution: Restating Eq. 3-34 as

$$\left(\frac{T_e}{T_{op}}\right)^{-3} = 1 + 3(\overline{\epsilon}_{HF} A_F$$

$$+ \epsilon_{HB} A_B) T_{op}^3 t_e (\overline{mc_p})^{-1}$$

and differentiating with respect to $\overline{mc_p}$ yields

$$-\frac{3}{T_{op}^{-3}} T_e^{-4} dT_e = -3(\overline{\epsilon}_{HF} A_F + \epsilon_{HB} A_B)$$

$$\cdot T_{op}^3 t_e (\overline{mc_p})^{-2} d(\overline{mc_p}).$$

Dividing the latter equation by the former and letting the differentials become increments results in

$$\frac{\Delta T_e}{T_e} = \left\{ (\overline{mc_p}) \left[3 + \frac{(\overline{mc_p})}{(\overline{\epsilon}_{HF} A_F + \epsilon_{HB} A_B) T_{op}^3 t_e} \right] \right\}^{-1}$$

$$\cdot \Delta(\overline{mc_p}).$$

For most cases, the operating temperature T_{op} is between $100°$ and $400°$K, so that the term containing T_{op} is small compared to 3. The

equation can therefore be simplified to

$$\frac{\Delta T_e}{T_e} = \frac{1}{3} \frac{\Delta(\overline{mc_p})}{\overline{mc_p}}.$$

For a 10% change in $\overline{mc_p}$, $\Delta(\overline{mc_p})/(\overline{mc_p}) = 0.10$ and $\Delta T_e/T_e = 0.10/3 = 0.0333$. For an original eclipse exit temperature of $100°$K $(-173°$C), ΔT_e would be $100 \times 0.033 = 3.3°$K or $°$C. An increase in $\overline{mc_p}$ results in an increase in T_e; for the example, T_e increases from $100°$ to $103.3°$K (from $-173°$ to $-169.7°$C).

RADIATION SHIELDING DESIGN

3-31. Solar Cell Radiation Shielding

Radiation shielding design is concerned with the protection of solar cells from the particulate radiation environment found in space. Since complete protection of the solar cells is not feasible, the typical radiation shielding design activities involve making trade-offs and finding optimum compromises between at least the following major parameters:

- Solar cell end-of-life power output
- Solar cell array mass (especially as determined by the substrate and solar cell cover masses)
- Solar cell array component and assembly cost.

The natural space radiation environment, described in Chapter 9, affects solar cell arrays (as discussed in Chapter 4, 5, and 9). Depending upon the orbit, the space radiation environment may require implementation of two distinctly different radiation shielding design approaches:

1. Shielding against radiation penetration of the solar cell cover and the solar cell beyond the cell's junction to minimize the reduction in minority carrier lifetime, as discussed in Sections 4-35 through 4-37; and

2. Shielding against low energy protons that become absorbed at or near the solar cell junction to prevent electrical shunting of the cell, as described in Section 4-38.

3-32. Damage-Equivalent Fluence in Orbit

The space radiation of significance in solar cell array design is characterized in Table 3-8. In addition, man-made radiation may exist (see Section 1-8). This space radiation may affect the array in transfer and temporary parking orbits as well as in its final, operational orbits. (The conversion of the natural environment into damage-equivalent 1 MeV fluence is discussed in Section 4-36.)

Circular Earth Orbits. The 1 MeV fluence arising from the trapped environment is given in Appendix E and illustrated in Figs. 3-11 and 3-12.

Synchronous Orbit. The 1 MeV fluence arising from the trapped environment is given in Appendix E (altitude = 3.34×10^4 km). A typical reduction in the fluence due to coverglass shielding is illustrated in Fig. 3-13 for a number of different radiation particle types.

Elliptic Earth and Transfer Orbits. The total 1 MeV fluence in elliptic and spiral (transfer) orbits, ϕ_T, can be determined from Eq. 3-35.

$$\phi_T = \int_0^T \phi(h)h(t)\,dt \qquad (3\text{-}35)$$

where

$\phi(h)$ = 1 MeV fluence at altitude h as given approximately in Appendix E

$h(t)$ = solar cell array altitude as a function of time, t

T = time at which ϕ_T is sought; typically, T = EOM (end-of-mission).

Equation 3-35 can be evaluated numerically by using one of the following two procedures.

1. *Graphical procedure.* a) prepare a graph of altitude versus time, $h(t)$; the range of t for spiral orbits is from shroud ejection ($t = 0$) to reaching the on-station orbit ($t = T$), and for elliptic orbits from any point in orbit ($t = 0$) through the same point for one period ($t = T$)— note: use Keppler's second law, described in Section 2-64; b) multiply the h values in the $h(t)$ graph from Step a with the $\phi(h)$ values for all particles [obtain $\phi(h)$ from Appendix E] to obtain a $\phi(h)h(t)$ graph; c) numerically integrate under the 1 MeV fluence/time graph and enter the resulting data in Table 3-9; d) repeat steps a through c for all front shield thicknesses of interest, assuming infinite back shielding, and for all back shield thicknesses of interest, assuming infinite front shield thickness.

2. *Tabular procedure.* Proceed as described in the graphical procedure above except instead of using a graph, prepare a table of average altitudes, $\overline{h}$, for constant time intervals, Δt; multiply the $\overline{h}$ values by the $\phi(h)$ values; and sum the $\phi(h)h(\phi t)$ tabular entries to obtain ϕ_T.

Interplanetary Trajectories. The 1 MeV fluence in interplanetary space is due to solar flare protons and potentially due to solar flare alpha particles only. (The values of the fluence components are given in Section 9-45.)

3-33. Shielding Thickness Determination

To a first-order approximation, the shielding effectiveness of a solar cell cover is proportional to the mass density of the shielding material.

Table 3-8. Earth Orbit Radiation.

Approximate Altitude Range (km)	Radiation Particles
0 to 250	Negligible
250 to 1600	Trapped electrons and protons
1600 to 50,000 (includes synchronous altitude of 35,786	Trapped electrons and solar flare protons and alpha particles
Above 50,000	Solar flare protons and alpha particles

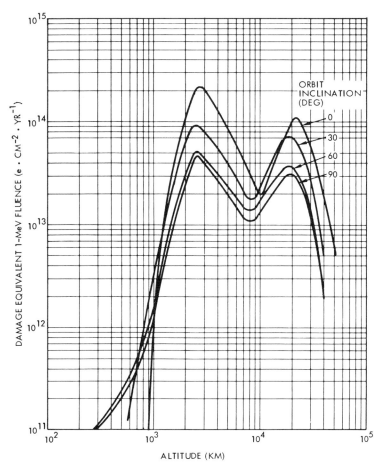

Fig. 3-11. Damage equivalent 1-MeV fluence in circular earth orbits due to trapped electrons for I_{sc} and P_{mp} of silicon cells protected by 0.15-mm thick fused silica covers and infinitely thick back shields.[6]

However, no simple relationship exists for the effect of shield thickness (Figure 3-14). Shield thickness is usually expressed in units of

(mass density) × (shield thickness)

or mass per unit area. Convenient conversion tables are given in Tables 3-10 and 3-11.

The total front and back side shield thicknesses, d_{sf} and d_{sb}, are calculated by adding the shield thickness (in g/cm^2) of all i front elements and of all j back side shield thicknesses, Eqs. 3-36 and 3-37, respectively.

$$d_{sf} = \sum_{i=1}^{n} d_{si} \qquad (3\text{-}36)$$

$$d_{sb} = \sum_{j=1}^{m} d_{sj} \qquad (3\text{-}37)$$

For substrate materials not listed in Table 3-11 and for composite substrates, the total shield thickness, d_{st}, of a multilayer sandwich structure can be found from Eq. 3-38, where d_{st} is in units of g/cm^2, the ρ_i are the material densities in g/cm^3, and the t_i are the corresponding thicknesses in cm.

$$d_{st} = \rho_1 t_1 + \rho_2 t_2 + \ldots + \rho_n t_n = \sum_{i=1}^{n} \rho_i t_i$$

$$(3\text{-}38)$$

All material must cover the same substrate areas; for honeycomb core, use the expanded core density, and for interconnectors, use an average interconnector density per total substrate area considered.

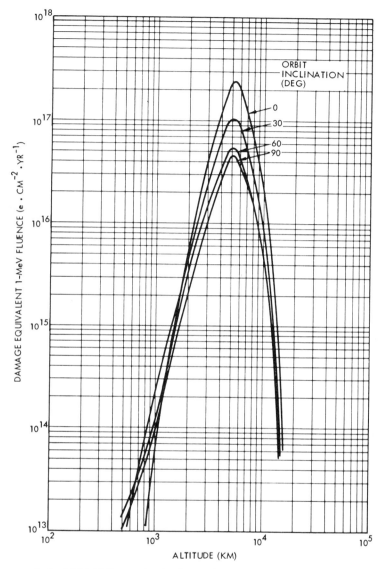

Fig. 3-12. Damage equivalent 1-MeV fluence in circular earth orbits due to trapped protons for P_{mp} of silicon cells protected by 0.15-mm thick fused silica covers and infinitely thick back shields.[6]

Balancing Front and Back Side Shielding. For minimum-weight solar cell array designs, it is important to approximately balance the quantities of the 1 MeV fluence components that damage the solar cells from the front side (through the cover) and from the back side (through the substrate). A balance of radiation damage is achieved when the shielding thicknesses of the solar cell cover and of the substrate are equal.

Shielding by the Solar Cell. Radiation incident on the solar cell back side also reduces the solar cell output. This occurs due to two mechanisms: reduction of the minority carrier lifetime by all particles, and introduction of a mild junction at the cell back contact by protons of certain energies. The exact cell degradation due to back side irradiation is presently not well established so that it may be safest to assume that back side-irradiation is not shielded at all by the

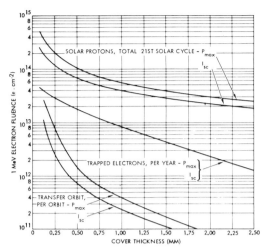

Fig. 3-13. Solar cell 1 MeV fluence after penetration of a fused silicon cover of given thickness.[6]

solar cell silicon base layer thickness. For more optimistic assessments, the shielding thicknesses of Table 3-12 have been used.

For so-called field or p^+ solar cells (described in Chapter 4), the back side radiation damage may be considerably greater than for other, non-field cells. Therefore, detailed design approaches should be based on actual test data of the solar cells contemplated for a specific mission.

3-34. Procedure For 1 MeV Fluence Analysis

The 1 MeV fluence must be determined for specific front and back shielding thicknesses because the shielding effectiveness changes with the incident radiation particle type and particle

Table 3-9. Tabulation of 1 MeV Fluence Components.

Orbit	Particles	1 MeV Flux ($e \cdot cm^{-2} \cdot yr^{-1}$)		1 MeV Fluence ($e \cdot cm^{-2}$)	
		Front	Back	Front	Back
Transfer	Trapped electrons				
	Trapped protons				
_____ orbits	Subtotal				
On-station	Trapped electrons				
	Trapped protons				
	Flare protons				
_____ years	Subtotal				
Other					
	Subtotal				
Total	Sum vertically				
Grand total	Front + back	✕		✕	✕
Shield thickness Front: _____ Back: _____					

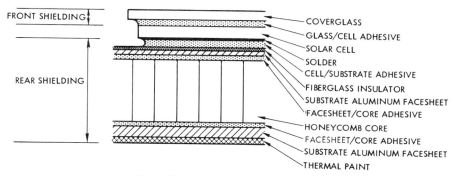

Fig. 3-14. Typical solar cell shielding.

energy, and the mix between different particles as well as their energy distributions change with orbit altitude and orbit inclination. Different 1 MeV fluence values arise for each shielding thickness from the environment. Table 3-9 provides a convenient format for recording and summing of the computed 1 MeV fluence values. For detailed design work, the same fluence components shown on Table 3-9 should also be determined for I_{sc}. (See Section 4-36 for a discussion of the different 1 MeV fluence values.)

Procedure. The general procedure for estimating the solar cell damage-equivalent 1 MeV fluence is as follows:

- Determine the required inputs (see below)
- Determine the 1 MeV fluence components as defined in Table 3-9, entering the solar cell from the front side for infinite back side shielding
- Determine the 1 MeV fluence components entering the solar cell from the back side for infinite front side shielding
- Enter all 1 MeV fluence components in Table 3-9 and sum up.

Analysis Inputs. The information required to prepare an estimate of the solar cell damaging

1 MeV fluence is typically available from the cognizant project office, from mission planners, or from satellite system designers. The minimum information required is given below.

Requirements for all missions:
- Launch date (affects solar flare proton fluence)
- Mission duration (defines end-of-mission, EOM)
- Characteristics of transfer or parking orbits
- Number of transfer or parking orbits
- Design data, as described below.

Additional requirements for earth orbits only:
- Apogee (farthest point from earth)
- Perigee (nearest point to earth)
- Inclination (angle between the orbit plane and the earth's equatorial plane).

Additional requirements for interplanetary probes only:
- Array-sun distance variation with time after leaving parking orbit.

Design data:
- An additional required input is the solar cell front and back side shield thicknesses.

Table 3-10. Variations in Fused Silica Shielding Thickness with Actual Thickness.

g/cm^2	1.68E-2	3.35E-2	6.71E-2	1.12E-1	1.68E-1	3.35E-1
g/cm^2	0.0168	0.0335	0.0671	0.112	0.168	0.335
inch	0.003	0.006	0.012	0.020	0.030	0.060
mm	0.075	0.15	0.30	0.50	0.75	1.50

Table 3-11. Variation in Shielding Thickness with Material.

Material	Density (g/cm^3)	Shielding Thickness per 25 μm (0.001 in.) Thickness (g/cm^2)*	Shielding Thickness Relative to Fused Silica
Coverglass — Fused Silica	2.20	5.59E-3	1.00
Coverglass — Microsheet	2.51	6.38E-3	1.14
Glass/Cell Adhesive	1.0 to 1.70	2.54E-3 to 4.32E-3	0.45 to 0.77
Silicon Wafer	2.4	6.1E-3	1.09
Solar Cell Back Solder	7.82	3.38E-3	0.60
Cell/Substrate Adhesive	1.10	2.79E-3	0.5
Fiberglass Insulator	1.87	4.75E-3	0.85
Substrate Al Facesheet	2.82	7.16E-3	1.28
Honeycomb Core	0.026	6.60E-5	0.0118
Thermal Control Paint	1.55	3.94E-3	0.70

*$E - 3 = 10^{-3}$, etc.

(The method for calculating the equivalent shield thickness is given in Section 3-33.)

3-35. Shielding Against Low Energy Protons

To prevent excessive power degradation due to low energy proton damage, three approaches for completely shielding the active solar cell area are possible: Approach I employs an oversized coverglass which positively protects the entire active cell area; Approach II uses a coverglass overhanging the active solar cell area in one direction only, and one adhesive fillet for protecting a gap between the cover and the contact bar; and Approach III uses a cell stack with the cover being flush with two

cell sides and adhesive fillets covering each of the two otherwise unprotected gaps. These three approaches are illustrated in Fig. 3-15 together with an undersized cover baseline design, identified as Approach IV.

Approach I. The desired low energy proton protection is obtained by installing coverglasses on the solar cells so that the entire active cell area, as well as a portion of the n-contact areas, are protected from the proton flux. In one version of this approach, the cover is installed with one edge indexed 1.00 ± 0.05 mm off the outer cell edge which runs along the n-contact strip, as shown in Fig. 3-16. In another version of this approach, a slightly larger cover than shown in this figure also overhangs the left-hand cell edge.

Table 3-12. Solar Cell Base Thickness Shielding Effectiveness for Particulate Irradiation Incident on the Cell Back Side.

Cell Thickness		Shielding Thickness	
(inches)	(mm)	(% of thickness)	(g/cm^2)
0.014	0.35	86	0.0734
0.012	0.30	83	0.0608
0.010	0.25	80	0.0488
0.008	0.20	75	0.0366

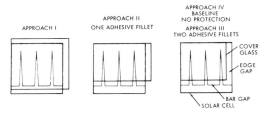

Fig. 3-15. Description of alternate approaches (gaps and glass overhangs grossly exaggerated for illustration).

The assembled cell stack always exhibits overhanging coverglass on at least two sides. For perfectly square-cut cells and covers, this overhang may range from 0.02 to 0.5 mm in the worst case, and is estimated to fall within 0.1 to 0.2 mm most of the time. This minimum overhang is required because cells may have as much as 0.15 mm run-out (covers 0.10 mm) due to non-square cutting. However, due to the center indexing in the glassing operation, only one-half of this total 0.25 mm run-out will probably cause cover overhang. The chipping problem of the overhanging glass may be minimized by allowing an adhesive fillet to form under the glass overhanging the cell.

Approach II.

In this approach, low energy proton protection, shown in Fig. 3-17, the covers are smaller than the active cell area in one dimension, but overhang the cell area in another dimension. An adhesive bead is applied over the active cell area gap between the n-contact collector bar and the edge of the coverglass.

Approach III.

In this approach, the covers are smaller than the active cell area. An adhesive bead is applied over the active cell area between the n-contact collector and the edge of the coverglass, and a natural adhesive fillet is allowed to form along the outer cell edge normal to the collector bar.

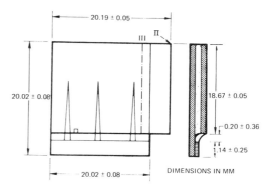

Fig. 3-17. Design for approaches II and III, Example.

Requirements for Adhesive Fillets. After glassing and soldering the cells, an adhesive bead is applied across the unprotected active area strip between the n-contact bar and the cell cover edge. The width of this strip is nominally 0.20 mm and may vary to 0.6 mm in extreme cases. The outside strip will be protected by an adhesive fillet, as shown in Fig. 3-18. Care should be taken not to overclean this edge fillet which forms somewhat naturally. A maximum fillet is desirable.

Suitable materials for coating uncovered active solar cell areas must be compatible with other materials and adhesive systems already in use on the solar panels. For example, some adhesives will not cure in the presence of other cured adhesives.

Adhesive and flexible epoxy fillets for low

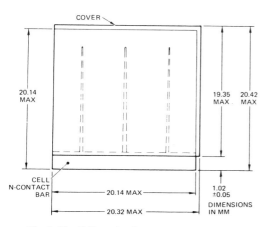

Fig. 3-16. Cell stack of approach I, Example.

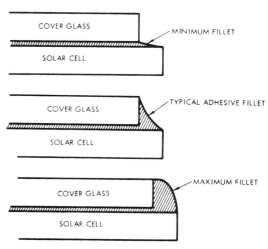

Fig. 3-18. Adhesives fillets in approach III.

energy proton protection have been used successfully by several solar cell array manufacturers. As an example, one process was adopted using Dow Corning RTV-3140 protective coating with 0.1% by weight of Calcofluor White fluorescent material added. The process required that the material be applied with an air-actuated resin dispenser (hypodermic syringe) and that visual examinations be made in a darkened room under ultraviolet light.

Most modern array designs now use fully overhanging covers because of lower in-orbit degradation and lower assembly and inspection

cost than can be achieved with the adhesive bead approach.

3-36. Absorbed Dose in Cover and Cover Adhesive

Some of the energetic radiation particles entering the solar cell covers will lose all of their energy in the covers and become absorbed, while others will penetrate the covers and exit with reduced energy. Some of these particles, in turn, will be absorbed by the cover adhesive, while others will penetrate into the solar cells.

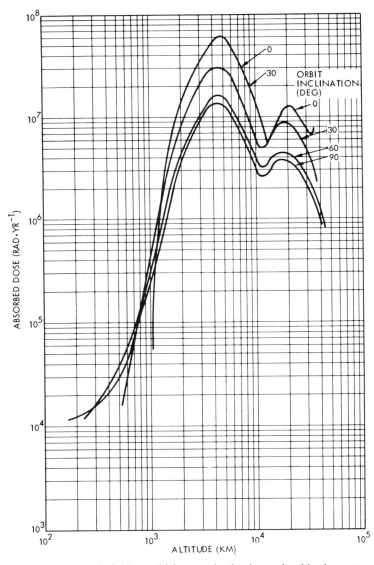

Fig. 3-19. Average absorbed dose in 0.15-mm thick covers in circular earth orbits due to trapped electrons.

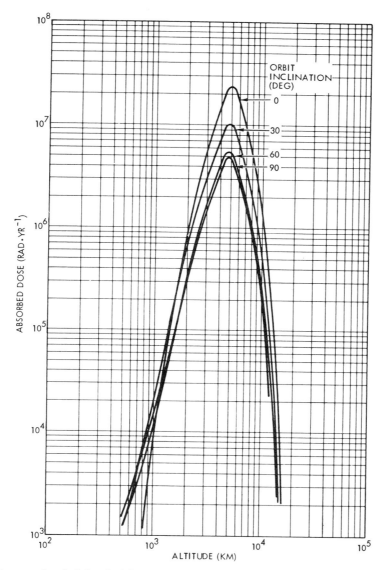

Fig. 3-20. Average absorbed dose in 0.15-mm thick covers in circular earth orbits due to trapped protons.

Since the radiation particles in space can have energies over a wide range, and the particles having lower energies tend to be more numerous, the number of particles that come to rest in a solar cell cover (i.e., the absorbed dose) is greatest near the front surface of the cover and diminishes with increasing distance from the front surface. The resultant dose-depth profile is similar to the 1 MeV fluence-depth profile illustrated in Fig. 3-13. The average dose in the cover, accumulated in circular earth orbits, is illustrated in Figs. 3-19 and 3-20.

The amount of cover and cover adhesive

darkening associated with the absorbed dose is at the present time unclear. Therefore, it is suggested that the test data in Chapter 8 and the orbital performance data in Chapters 1, 4, and 5 be consulted.

ELECTROMAGNETIC DESIGN

3-37. Electrostatic Shielding

Certain satellite experiments require that the plasma in which a satellite moves does not become disturbed in the vicinity of the satellite.

An electrically neutral satellite can be designed approximately when the entire satellite, including its solar cell array, is made *equipotential*.[7,8] This can be achieved with conductive coatings placed over all non-grounded and dielectric surfaces connected to spacecraft ground. A typical requirement for a maximum potential difference of 0.5 V between any two points on the satellite can most likely be achieved by sizing the conductive coatings for a maximum resistance of 10^5 ohms to ground. Typically, pinholes and voids up to 5 mm in diameter and expansion gaps up to 2 mm in width and of any length are permissible.

Conductive coatings over the solar cell array must reach over all solar cells, contact bars, and wiring. Two different approaches have been used. For the *Explorer 31* array, the solar cells were mounted to a transparent "superstrate" which not only carried on its outer surface the conductive coating, but also served as the mechanical holding device for the solar cells within an array frame structure. For the *Helios* array, the solar cells were mounted to a conventional substrate and were covered with individual coverglasses, each of which carried a conductive coating and coating terminal pads. The individual covers were interconnected by welding ribbons to the terminals, in a fashion similar to the interconnection of solar cells. Additional design efforts to achieve an electrostatically clean solar cell array include minimizing the array voltage and the electromagnetic fields it produces. Minimizing the voltage level of any circuit element can be achieved by the use of low bus voltage or by grounding the center of the array. Stray fields are minimized by cancellation of the electromagnetic fields by back-wiring to achieve a counterflow of currents, and by shielding all wiring and circuits electrostatically.

Candidate materials for conductive coatings are indium oxide (In_2O_3—used on Explorer 31 and GEOS), beryllium oxide (BeO), and tin oxide (SnO_2). Currently, only indium oxide has been qualification-tested and used on space flight programs. Contact reinforcements may be silver, gold, or other metals compatible with both the conductive coating and an assembly process. Special considerations must be given to the design and fabrication process

control of conductive coatings. The conductive coating must adhere to the substrate over the entire environmental range of exposure (ultraviolet and charged particle irradiation, temperature cycling) without subliming, cracking, or being eroded away. Light transmission to the solar cells should be maximized. The long wavelength emittance should be maximized and the solar absorptance minimized (an $\alpha = 0.93$ was achieved on Explorer 31 for a coating conductivity of 1 to 3×10^3 ohms per square). Metallic contact areas on the outer surface should be minimized because metals generally have low emittance and can cause significant increases in array operating temperature.

3-38. Magnetic Cleanliness

Magnetic cleanliness may describe any one of three design features of a solar cell array: 1) a solar cell circuit topography that minimizes the magnetic field about a net current loop which encompasses the entire array surface and leads to a magnetically induced *torque* on the spacecraft; 2) a solar cell circuit arrangement that minimizes the *local magnetic field* at a given position relative to the array; and 3) a solar cell circuit design that minimizes the *overall magnetic field* intensity and direction of the magnetic field vectors such that low-energy charged particles in the plasma through which the array travels are disturbed as little as possible. The first condition is of concern to the spacecraft attitude control system,[9,10] the second to the location of magnetometers on the spacecraft, and the third to the measurement of low-energy charged particles.

Magnetic cleanliness is affected both by the electrical current patterns of the array and by the presence of magnetic materials on the array. The effect of the electric current through illuminated solar cells and the associated array wiring can be assessed with reference to Fig. 3-21. The magnetic field contribution $d\mathbf{B}$ at a point (x, y, z) in a Cartesian coordinate system, due to a current I in an elemental conductor (or in an elemental solar cell) of length $d\mathbf{l}$ is given by Eq. 3-39.*

*For a definition of vectors see Appendix A.

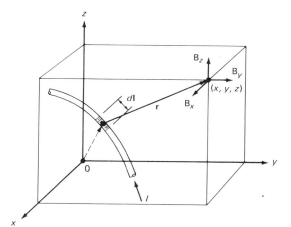

Fig. 3-21. Magnetic field due to current-carrying conductor.

$$dB = \frac{\mu_0}{4\pi} \frac{Id\mathbf{l} \times \mathbf{r}}{r^3} \qquad (3-39)$$

where μ_0 is the permeability of empty space and $\mathbf{r}$ is the vector from the current element $Id\mathbf{l}$ to the point (x, y, z). The total field $\mathbf{B}$, obtained by summing over all current elements $Id\mathbf{1}$, has three directional components, B_x, B_y, and B_z. A current-carrying conductor element produces no magnetic field component in the direction of the current. For example, a conductor element lying parallel to the y-axis produces field components B_x and B_z, but none along the y-axis (i.e., $B_y = 0$). By "mirroring" the current-carrying conductor elements of an array, certain degrees of magnetic field cancellations may be achieved, as illustrated in Fig. 3-22. Applying the principles illustrated in this figure to a hypothetical, two-wing solar cell array, the different solar cell string layout options shown in Fig. 3-23 suggest themselves (12 strings per wing were chosen arbitrarily for illustration). Figure 3-23c illustrates the most effective wiring for minimizing the array's magnetic fields.[11]

Further reductions in the magnetic field are possible by "back-wiring" the array: the return lines of the solar cell strings are routed along the substrate backside or "underneath" the solar cells such that the direction of the current in the back-wires is opposite to the direction of current in the solar cells. Figure 3-24 illustrates several back-wiring concepts.[12,13] Figure 3-24d illustrates the most effective method. If several

wires are used, they should be spaced symmetrically to the solar cell strings (the spacing is critical) and should carry the same current as the adjacent solar cells whose fields are to be cancelled. This can be aided by collecting the currents from the solar cell strings centrally rather than offset (Fig. 3-25) and otherwise balancing the currents. Open-circuit failures in the solar cell strings or in the back-wiring may cause imbalances in the current patterns and thereby cause the original magnetic cleanliness to be lost. Twisting of wires also reduces the magnetic field.[14,15]

The use of materials which may become magnetized should be avoided in design situations which require extreme magnetic cleanliness. However, under normal circumstances, the use of soft magnetic materials such as Kovar or Invar as a solar cell interconnect material may be entirely reasonable. For example, NASA-GSFC evaluated Kovar as a candidate interconnector material for the ATS-6 satellite solar array. The proposed application consisted of approximately 1.4 kg of the material distributed over a total area of 20 m² in 8000 separate connections. The ATS-6 solar panels are each 2.44 m long and are located at their nearest point about 6.40 m from a magnetometer. The results of the evaluation performed by the GSFC Magnetic Test Facility showed that by comparison with similar configurations, the maximum field at the magnetometer would be a few tenths of a gamma if the Kovar were magnetized to a fairly high level (e.g. 300 gamma at 0.46 m). However, there would be little likelihood of the Kovar becoming magnetized. Spacecraft demagnetization ("deperm") would eliminate magnetization. Furthermore, the Kovar would not distort the earth's magnetic field in the immediate vicinity of the magnetometer. Although Kovar was approved for this application, the material was not selected for the final design for other unrelated reasons.

3-39. Minimizing Magnetic Moments

The minimization of magnetic fields arising from solar cell array currents as described in Section 3-38 generally also minimizes the array's magnetic moment. However, the layout of solar cell strings may result in the formation

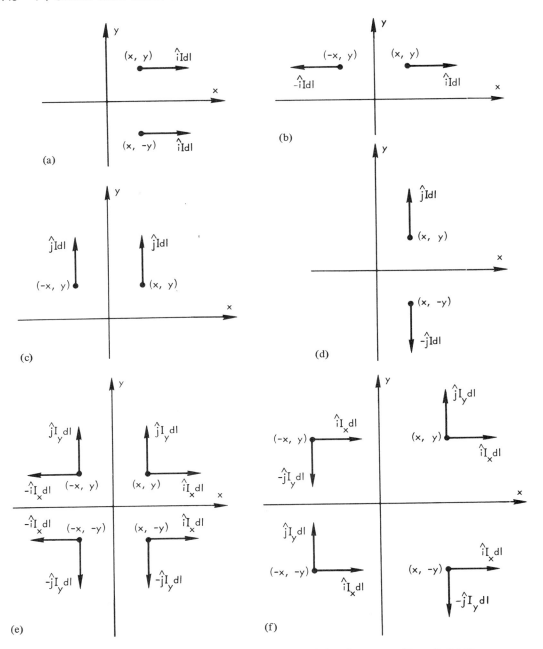

Fig. 3-22. Cancellation of magnetic field components of elemental electric currents. (From Ref. 11)

a) X-directed current elements mirrored about the $y = 0$ plane produce B_y and B_z fields, except $B_z = 0$ everywhere in the $y = 0$ plane. $B_x = 0$ everywhere. B_y may be zero somewhere, but in general $B_y \neq 0$.

b) X-directed current elements mirrored about the $x = 0$ plane produce B_y and B_z fields. $B_y = B_z = 0$ everywhere in the $x = 0$ plane. $B_x = 0$ everywhere.

c) Y-directed current elements mirrored about the $x = 0$ plane produce B_x and B_z fields. $B_z = 0$ everywhere in the $x = 0$ plane; B_x may be zero also but in general $B_x \neq 0$.

d) Y-directed elements mirrored about the $y = 0$ plane produce B_x and B_z fields, except $B_x = B_z = 0$ everywhere in the $y = 0$ plane. $B_y = 0$ everywhere.

e) X- and y-directed current elements mirrored about the $x = 0$ and $y = 0$ plane produce several planes in which $B_x = B_y = B_z = 0$.

f) X- and y-directed current elements mirrored about the $y = 0$ plane and anti-mirrored about the $x = 0$ plane also produce several planes in which $B_x = B_y = B_z = 0$.

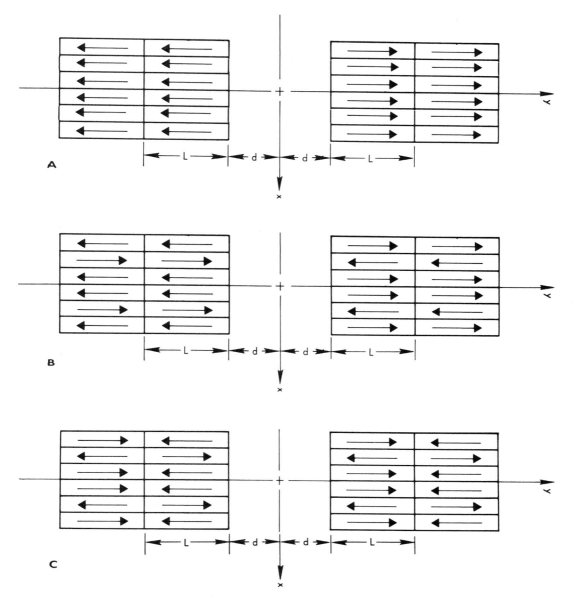

Fig. 3-23. Several solar cell string configurations for magnetic field cancellation. (From Ref. 11).

a) Mirror configuration about $x = 0$ plane produces zero magnetic field only in $y = 0$ plane. B_x and B_z field components provide both contaminant fields and interactions with planetary magnetic fields, resulting in torques on spacecraft.

b) Mirro-mirror configuration about the $x = 0$ and $y = 0$ planes and anti-mirror configuration about the $y = \pm(d + L)$ planes provides improved magnetic field cancellation over Fig. a).

c) Mirror-mirror configuration about the $x = 0$, $y = 0$ and $y = \pm(d + L)$ planes provides improved magnetic field cancellation over Fig. b).

of an uncompensated current loop along the array's perimeter, as illustrated in Fig. 3-26. To minimize the effects of such current loops, the mirror image properties discussed in Section 3-38 can be utilized advantageously, as illustrated in Fig. 3-27.

3-40. Electrostatic Charging Control

During geomagnetic substorm activity, as defined in Section 9-49, dielectric surfaces of the solar array are subject to electrostatic charging and subsequent sudden discharge effects, result-

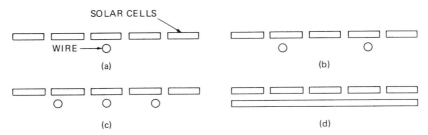

Fig. 3-24. Solar cell string back-wiring. (Strings and conductors extend into the plane of the paper)
a) One back wire.
b) Two back wires.
c) Three back wires.
d) Conductive sheet back wiring.

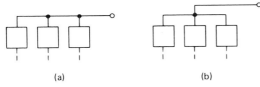

Fig. 3-25. String connections located offset (a) and central (b).

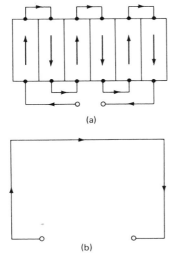

Fig. 3-26. Uncompensated current loop of folded string.

ing in electromagnetic interference (EMI) and potentially in the destruction of materials and electronic components, unless appropriate precautions are taken. Figure 3-28 illustrates an example of a solar panel made with dielectric facesheets and the appropriate electrostatic charging model. As is seen in the figure, potentials of up to 20 kV can be predicted.

Substorm countermeasures for this design consisted of application of a conductive coating on the back side facesheet, grounded to the aluminum honeycomb core, and making the honeycomb core continuously conductive over the entire array area.

Swarm tunnel tests verified the findings of others that discharges on the coverglass side (occuring during eclipses only) are neither violent nor damaging to the solar cells, apparently because of the proximity of the solar cell interconnectors that lead to low current density discharges.

Significant amounts of charge will not build up on the front Kapton facesheet because solar illumination reduces the Kapton bulk resistivity sufficiently to cause charge drainage. Under the worst case assumption that all ground points except for one have failed and that the maxi-

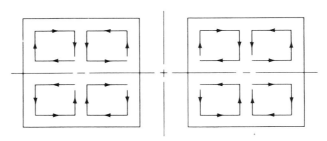

Fig. 3-27. Mirror-Mirror compensation of net current loops.

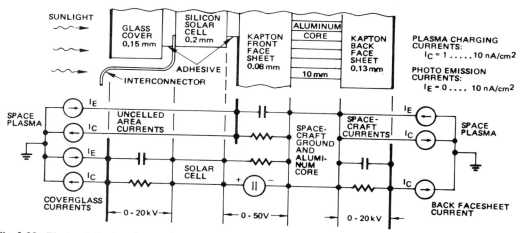

Fig. 3-28. Electrostatic charging model. Array without conductive coat. Sizes Not to scale. (Reprinted with permission of the IEEE)[16]

mum voltage differential across a facesheet shall not exceed 100 V at a plasma current density of 10 nA/cm², a maximum conductive paint sheet resistance of 10^6 ohms per square is required. The actual paint used in 0.01 to 0.04 mm thickness produced acceptable resistance values in the order of 10^3 to 10^4 ohms per square.[16]

Electrostatic charge build-up can also be expected on the glass covers and on other dielectric surfaces of terrestrial arrays, especially during high-wind and thunderstorm conditions.

REFERENCES

1. Saint-Jean, NASA **TN D-1904**, 1963.
2. J. Roger, "Optimal Bus Bars for Rectangular Solar Arrays," in *Conference Records of the 9th IEEE Photovoltaic Specialists Conference*, 1972.
3. E. Levy, Jr. *et al*, "High Voltage Solar Cell Power Generating System," in *Conference Records of the 10th IEEE Photovoltaic Specialists Conference*, 1973.
4. K. L. Kennerud, "High Voltage Solar Array Operation in the Ionosphere," in *Conference Records of the 8th IEEE Photovoltaic Specialists Conference*, 1970.
5. R. C. Ross *et al*, "Measured Performance of Silicon Solar Cell Assemblies designed for use at High Solar Intensities," **TM 33-473**, Jet Propulsion Laboratory, March 1971.
6. H. Y. Tada and J. R. Carter, Jr., "Solar Cell Radiation Handbook," JPL Publication **77-56**, November 1, 1977.
7. A. Atzei and J. Capart, "Evaluation and Reduction of the Electromagnetic Fields Associated with a Solar Array," in *Conference Records of the 9th IEEE Photovoltaic Specialists Conference*, 1972.
8. H. W. Boller *et al*, "Solar Cells and Generator Technology for the Helios Sun Probe," in *Conference Records of the 9th IEEE Photovoltaic Specialists Conference*, 1972.
9. W. M. Robbins, Jr., "Electromagnetic Forces on Space Structures," NASA **CR-476**, May 1966.
10. L. E. Wiggins, "Relative Magnitudes of the Space-Environment Torques on a Satellite," in *AIAA Journal*, Vol. 2, *No. 4*, April 1964.
11. J. M. Sellen, Jr. and H. S. Ogawa, "Contaminant Magnetic Fields from Large Area Solar Arrays," Report No. **12738-6006-R0-00**, TRW Systems Group, TRW, Inc., June 1969. (Part of Ref. 15.)
12. J. M. Sellen, Jr., "Backwire and Busbar Placement for Magnetic Cleanliness on Large Area Solar Arrays," Report No. **12738-6007-R0-00**, TRW Systems Group, TRW, Inc., June 1969. (Part of Ref. 15.)
13. J. D. Tarasuk *et al*, "Temperature and Current Distribution in an Electrically Heated Wide Metallic Foil," in *Eleventh Annual Meeting of the Society of Engineering Science, November 11–13, 1974*, Duke University, Durham, North Carolina.
14. A. Y. Alksne, "Magnetic Fields Near Twisted Wires," in *IEEE Transactions on Space Electronics and Telemetry*, December 1964.
15. R. K. Cole *et al*, "Study of Electric Propulsion Spacecraft Plasmas and Field Interactions," Report No. **12738-6016-R0-00**, TRW Systems Group, TRW, Inc., prepared under NASA Contract **NAS 7-100** for the Jet Propulsion Laboratory, California Institute of Technology, July 1970.
16. H. S. Rauschenbach *et al*. (p. 232), Record of the 13th IEEE Photovoltaic Specialists Conference, 1978.

PART II

Array Building Blocks

4
Solar Cells

PHOTOVOLTAICS

4-1. Solar Cell Devices

Solar cells are relatively small, wafer-like semiconductor devices. Also known as *solar batteries*, solar cells produce an electric power output while being exposed to sunlight. Many individual solar cells, properly electrically interconnected, constitute an *array* of solar cells, multiplying the output of an individual cell.

Semiconductor devices constitute a family of solid-state electrical components that include the well known transistors, rectifier diodes, light emitting diodes, and integrated circuits that are used in modern electronic consumer products.

Present-day solar cells may have sizes ranging from about 1 mm to over 100 mm in diameter (25.4 mm = 1.0 inch; 1 mm = 0.0394 inch). Solar cells may be round, square, rectangular, or of any desired shape. The smaller solar cells are used primarily in sensing and control circuits, while the larger cells are used primarily for producing electric power.

Because semiconductor materials are relatively costly, solar cells are made as thin as practical. The typical thickness range for the most common silicon cells is 0.2 to 0.4 mm.

The power output of solar cells arises from solar energy in the form of sunshine falling onto the solar cells. The amount of energy contained in sunlight just outside the earth's atmosphere is about 1.4 kW/m^2. Bright sunlight on a clear day on the earth's surface contains about 1.0 kW/m^2, to which about 10 to 20% is added from sunlight reflected and scattered by the upper atmosphere. In actual use, solar cells convert between 5 and 20% of the incident solar energy into electric energy, depending upon the specific solar cell construction and prevailing operating conditions.

4-2. Direct Energy Conversion

In the context of electric power generation, *direct* energy conversion processes are processes by which one form of energy is directly converted (or transformed) into electrical energy. In contrast, *indirect* energy conversion utilizes one or more intermediate energy conversion processes, as exemplified by the fossil fuel burning power plant: chemical energy (oil or coal) is first converted into thermal energy (heated steam), then into mechanical energy (rotating steam turbine shaft), and, finally, into electricity (electric generator).

Direct energy conversion processes include chemical, photochemical, thermionic, thermoelectric, photoelectric, photovoltaic, and others. In all of these processes, chemical, thermal, or light energy is converted directly into electricity.

Solar cells operate on *photovoltaic* principles. The term implies that the application of light (phot—Greek prefix, relating to light) results in the generation of a voltage, also known as *light-generated electromotive force* and *photovoltage*. In today's highly efficient solar cells, the photovoltage is capable of driving significant amounts of electric current through externally connected circuits. All practical solar cells are solid-state semiconductor devices. However, feeble photovoltaic processes have also been observed in some liquids.

Photoelectric energy converters utilize metallic or semiconductor elements of different material compositions in intimate contact with each other; these are known as *thermocouples*. Upon heating of their junctions on one side and cooling of them at the other side, an electric current is generated. Another type of photoelectric converter, known as a *thermionic diode*, utilizes a heated, electron emitting surface (cathode) in a vacuum or cesium atmosphere and an adjacent cooled electron collector (anode) instead of thermocouples.

Photochemical energy conversion is found in all living plants in which a photosynthesis process is operating. Certain chemical reactions, activated by light, may be utilized directly to deliver free electrons to electrodes, thus making electric current available to flow in an external circuit.

4-3. Discovery of the Photovoltaic Effect[1]

The recorded beginning of photovoltaic research dates back to 1839, when Becquerel published his work on photoelectric experimentation with acidic aqueous solutions and noble metal electrodes. The first work on solid-state, photovoltaic devices was reported in 1876. Both photoconductive and photovoltaic effects in selenium and at selenium/metal oxide potential barriers were investigated. Commercial exploitation, first of photoconductive and later of photovoltaic selenium cells began about 1880 and has continued through today. Even though the energy conversion efficiency of selenium cells has never been high—typically in the order of 1 to 2%—the close match of the spectral (color) sensitivity of selenium cells with that of the human eye made these cells desirable for a wide range of photometric (light measurement) applications.

Intensive research conducted on selenium, copper oxide, and many other semiconductor compound/metal oxide type barrier devices during the 1920's and 1930's provided the foundations for the theoretical understanding of photovoltaic potential barrier solar cells and their mathematical modeling.

During the late 1930's and early 1940's, intensive semiconductor material research was spurned by the World War II effort on germanium and silicon. This effort resulted in the development of the transistor and, in 1954, of the silicon solar cell essentially as we know it today.

4-4. History of Contemporary Silicon Cells[1-9]

After considerable theoretical and experimental work, started in the 1930's and carried on with great vigor during the 1940's, the Bell Telephone Laboratories produced the first practical solar cell in 1954. This cell was of the planar junction, single crystal silicon type and was the forerunner of today's solar cell. Significant technological advances which permitted the development of such solar cells were breakthroughs in purifying the silicon material, growing crystals by the so-called Czochralski method developed during the late 1940's and early 1950's, and forming p-n junctions by high-temperature vapor diffusion in 1954.

The early solar cells were of circular shape— approximately 3 cm in diameter—that was determined mainly by the grown crystal diameter. These cells were of the p-on-n, wraparound contact type and had relatively low conversion efficiencies (of up to 6%). This was mainly due to high internal series resistance, in the order of 5 to 10 ohms, and excessive material defects. The theoretical maximum efficiencies calculated at that time ranged from about 18 to 22% for a solar intensity of 1 kW/m^2 of AM1 (Air Mass 1) spectrum (see Section 9-6).

In the U.S., the original material used for solar cells was n-type silicon, while in the U.S.S.R. it was p-type material. Silicon of the p-type was used by the Russians (1956) for two reasons: 1) to scientifically contrast the U.S. work; and 2) because p-type material was cheaper in the U.S.S.R. than was n-type. It was later found that cells made from p-type silicon were more resistant to corpuscular radiation as found in space than were cells made from n-type material. Thus, after discovery of the Van Allen radiation belts, U.S. solar cell production after 1960 switched over to diffusion of n-layers into p-type silicon.

While the Bell Telephone solar cell was initially considered for terrestrial use only, the success of solar cells in space began in 1958 when rectangular 0.5×2 cm cells (still p-on-n) were selected for Vanguard, the first U.S. satellite. Later, cell sizes were increased to 1×2 cm, 2×4 cm, and larger. Contact grid lines over the active cell area were utilized to reduce cell internal resistance to between 0.1 and 1 ohm; silicon monoxide anti-reflective coatings and improved processes increased peak cell conversion efficiencies below 13% at AM0 (Air Mass Zero) conditions (by 1960), with the mean efficiency at around 10 to 11%.

Between 1961 and 1971 no major progress in silicon solar cell technology was reported. Emphasis was placed on achieving radiation resistance and weight and cost reductions. A large number of avenues to improve cell efficiency or reduce cost were attempted and abandoned. Foremost among those efforts were the developments of the dendritic cell and the lithium-doped cell, both utilizing single crystal silicon.

Dendritic solar cells are fabricated from silicon sheet which has been produced by dendritic growth, rather than by cutting and slicing of large, cylindrical crystals for conventional silicon cells. In the dendritic growth technique, two coplanar dendrites from a single crystal seed are introduced into the molten silicon. As these seeds are pulled from the melt, a silicon web freezes between them, resulting in a continuous length of silicon ribbon having the proper finished solar cell dimension in its cross-section. Major difficulties were encountered with temperature control (better than $\pm 0.02°C$ at approximately $1420°C$ is required) to achieve uniform dendritic growth. Solar cell energy conversion efficiency of such cells has been nearly as high as that obtained during the same time period from conventional cells.

The development of lithium-doped, single crystal silicon cells was initiated in the early 1960's and continued through 1974 to improve the resistance of solar cells to corpuscular radia-tion. It had been discovered that the controlled introduction of small quantities of elemental lithium would anneal radiation-induced defect centers in the silicon lattice; thereby, in orbits where radiation levels were high, solar cell electrical output would degrade less. Lithium-annealing of radiation damage was indeed achieved in cells produced in pilot line quantities.

Lithium-doping was found to be most effective in annealing the cell's electrical degradation that was caused by protons and neutrons. For annealing to occur, solar cells manufactured from oxygen-rich silicon required temperatures of at least $50°C$ to operate, while those manufactured from float-zone processed silicon required at least $30°C$. It was also found that the lithium concentration and doping profile had to be adjusted for a specific end-of-life charged-particle fluence for lithium-doped silicon solar cells to realize a net gain in power output over conventional 10 ohm $\cdot$ cm base resistivity silicon solar cells; the annealing rate (i.e., the rate of recovery of the electrical output after irradiation) was not found to be a reliable indicator of cell quality. The recently developed families of high efficiency solar cells (Section 4-11) appear to have pushed the need for further development of lithium-doped silicon cells into the background.

In 1972, the first step in solar cell efficiency improvement in ten years was announced. Efficiency was increased for space application cells by about 30% over state-of-the-art space cells. This improvement was achieved by critically examining and revising existing theories, increasing the cell blue response, decreasing the internal cell resistance to about 0.05 ohm, and improving the charge carrier collection process within the cell. The resultant—so-called "violet"—cell maintained its superior performance after electron bombardment with integrated fluences beyond 10^{16} 1 MeV e/cm^2.

Another noteworthy development announced in 1972 was the Vertical Multijunction (VMJ) solar cell device. An experimental array has been assembled from these cells and tested. The VMJ device took its name from its construction: many alternate layers of n- and p-type silicon form a multilayer stack similar to a "layer cake." By turning the "layer cake" on its side, the layers stand vertical, and sunlight impinges from above—on the "sides" of the "layers," so to speak. Each junction separates the charge carriers, and the junction voltages add up algebraically. A pair of ohmic contacts, one on each end of the stack, permit extraction of power. By its nature, the device produces high voltage at low current and has inherently a relatively low internal resistance. Also known as edge-illuminated multijunction cells, recent developments using single crystal silicon attempt to make this cell type practical for concentrator applications utilizing concentration ratios in excess of 600.

Theoretical analyses had shown that VMJ cells would exhibit a higher radiation resistance than planar cells while the initial efficiencies would be comparable, but a practical fabrication process for such cells could not be found. A design modification, however, led to the concept of the single vertical junction cells. These cells consist of silicon wafers into which deep and narrow grooves are etched. After diffusion, the junction follows the surfaces up and down the walls, along the bottom of the grooves, and over the tops of the walls. Experimental cells fabricated in 1977 exhibited 12.6% efficiency under AM0 illumination, but significantly improved radiation resistance over planar junction, hybrid cells of the same efficiency class was not observed.

Between 1972 and 1976 a variety of single crystal silicon solar cells were developed for space use and marketed under a variety of names. *Blue-shifted*, *ultra-blue*, *violet*, and *super-blue* cells appeared, indicating a shallower diffusion and, hence, an improved sensitivity to the solar energy spectrum in the wavelength range between 300 and 800 nm. *Drift field*, *field*, and p^+ cells exhibited higher output by virtue of an additional electrostatic field, built into the solar cell's back surface, that aided in the carrier collection process. Different surface treatments to minimize light reflections from the cell's front surface led to the development of *non-reflecting*, *black*, *velvet*, *textured*, and *texturized* cells. More efficient anti-reflective coatings such as titanium oxide, and, later, tantalum pentoxide, replaced silicon monoxide. Various combinations of

these cell improvements were traded as *enhanced*, *augumented*, *intermediate*, or *hybrid* high-efficiency cells, in addition to the *Comsat Violet*, *Comsat Non-reflecting*, and *Helios* type cells. To take advantage of the enhanced short-wavelength sensitivity of these high-efficiency solar cells, the cut-on wavelength of the ultraviolet rejection filter on the coverslides was lowered from the earlier used range between 400 and 435 nm to 350 nm.

During the 1976 to 1977 time period, it was realized that the cell output gains achieved by surface texturing were accompanied by relatively large increases in the solar absorptance, which, in space, caused the cells to operate at a higher temperature. The increased temperature nearly counteracted any efficiency improvement that arose from non-reflective cell surface treatment. Texturing for space cells was then mostly abandoned, but continued to offer potential advantages for terrestrial use.

Another noteworthy achievement was the so-called ultra-thin single crystal silicon solar cell. Starting in the mid-1970's, 0.050 mm thick solar cells of 2×2 cm size and larger have been developed and fabricated in pilot line quantities. In 1978, efficiencies of cells with p^+ back fields reached 12.5%. Intended for space use, such ultra-thin cells are expected to exhibit high radiation resistance at high efficiency and at low weight.

During the mid-1970's, the development of silicon solar cells for terrestrial applications was also pursued with great vigor. The prime emphasis was placed on lowering the cell fabrication costs rather than on improving cell efficiency. Attempts to replace the vacuum-deposited metallic solar cell contacts with fired metallic paints and inks were only marginally successful. The major progress toward cost reduction was made in growing larger, purer, and more stress-free silicon crystals, using new silicon cutting techniques that produced less work damage in the silicon. Advanced process controls were developed for larger through-put in production equipment. However, by 1977, it became obvious that terrestrial array systems costs could not be brought in line unless high-efficiency solar cells would be available at low cost. It also became apparent that fabricating larger and larger solar cells would not necessarily lead to lower cell cost per unit power output, because larger cells tended to exhibit lower efficiencies than smaller cells. For example, encapsulated solar cells having 4 cm² area showed 19% efficiency at AM1 illumination, while those having 25 cm² are showed only 15% average in larger production quantities. Even larger, 80 cm² cells reached only 10 to 12% in production quantities under the same conditions. The reason for this efficiency drop-off lies in material defects that play significant roles in larger devices, but can be easier eliminated by rejection of low-output devices from production lots of the smaller size cells.

One potential approach to lowering the cost of solar cell array systems is to replace the rather costly solar cells with lower cost optical elements—such as plastic Fresnel lenses—that would concentrate the sunlight falling on larger areas onto relatively smaller solar cell areas. Early trade-off studies performed during 1977 and 1978 indicate, however, that concentrator optical elements with their structural supports, and the associated electrical wiring, may offer no weight and cost advantages over non-concentrator, flat plate arrays for either space or terrestrial applications using silicon solar cells. Other approaches to reduce array costs currently being pursued are to reduce the costs of single crystal silicon cells or to utilize polycrystalline silicon. Ultimately, other types of solar cells, such as gallium arsenide cells (see Section 4-5), may perform more favorably than silicon cells because of their potentially higher energy conversion capabilities.

4-5. History of Non-Silicon Cells[1-9]

The intensive semiconductor material studies undertaken during the early 1950's were not restricted to silicon, but included germanium and many compound semiconductors. Unlike silicon, a group IV single element semiconductor, non-silicon solar cell materials belong to group III-V, group II-VI, or other compound semiconductors.* (Germanium, another group

*See Periodic Chart of Elements in Appendix C.

IV single element semiconductor, is not a suitable solar cell material.) Of the many compound semiconductor materials investigated, gallium arsenide and cadmium sulfide have achieved prominent use for solar cells.

Gallium Arsenide (GaAs) Cells. The photovoltaic effect in gallium arsenide material was first reported in 1954. In 1955, solar cell efficiencies of 1 to 4% were reported for small polycrystalline devices and of 6.5% for cadmium-diffused GaAs wafers. At that time, it was shown that GaAs has the greatest efficiency and radiation tolerance potential of all group III-V compound cells. As the starting material technology improved and single crystal GaAs ingots could be grown, 2 cm² p-on-n cells typically having 8.5% efficiency and 13 to 14% maximum were achieved in 1962. The theoretically predicted lower temperature coefficient and higher resistance to proton irradiation were confirmed. In 1962 and 1963, n-on-p cells of 13% efficiency were found to be less resistant to proton radiation than were p-on-n cells, but electron radiation degraded both cell types equally. Low energy protons, however, were found to damage GaAs cells much more than silicon cells. As a consequence of the different bandgaps, silicon cells lost red response and GaAs cells lost blue response during irradiation. In 1964, the silicon technology surpassed the gallium arsenide solar cells for space use and the GaAs work ceased in the U.S. The inherently high material costs and difficulties encountered in working with this material made GaAs attractive only for high-concentration and high operating temperatures, features that became of interest again in the mid-1970's.

After Russian workers reported in 1971 on an GaAlAs/GaAs cell structure, world-wide activities sprang up in several research centers. A thin GaAlAs layer, known as the "window," is deposited on an p-on-n GaAs cell and significantly reduces surface recombination losses. The new cell design paved the way for increased cell efficiency, exceeding 16% in 1977 at AM0 in 2 × 2 cm sizes. Efficiencies in excess of 23% under AM1 illumination for 0.25 cm² cells was claimed. Some workers showed increasing efficiency with increasing concentration ratios, but others showed the opposite effect. Similarly, some workers showed higher radiation resistance than silicon cells, others showed lower. Nevertheless, the GaAs cell type appears to become competitive with the silicon cell, especially since Ga and As material costs are decreasing rapidly. By 1990, the material costs for Si and GaAs cells will probably be equal.

Cadmium Sulfide (CdS) Cells. The photovoltaic effect in single crystal cadmium sulfide and in thin CdS films was discovered in 1954. During the late 1950's, thin layers of semiconductor materials were sought to reduce solar cell material costs and increase the power-to-weight and weight-per-unit-area ratios for space applications. Cadmium sulfide, as well as cadmium telluride (CdTe), GaAs, and other materials, were available for producing thin film semiconductor layers on glass, metal foil, or plastic film substrates. The semiconductor films were polycrystalline and promised to exhibit higher radiation resistance than silicon cells. By 1961, thin film CdS cells, having 5.2% efficiency and 0.2 cm² area, had been developed. Larger cells, having 100 cm² area, showed only 1.2% efficiency. It was found necessary to encapsulate the thin film cells completely to protect the semiconductor material from humidity. Manufacturing processes were not repeatable, frequently resulting in low efficiency and shorted cells. Self-degradation, moisture attack, and degradation in temperature cycling were significant problems. A pilot line production attempt during 1966 and 1967 to improve both efficiency and cell stability was not successful.

As a parallel effort during 1960 through 1967, cadmium telluride (CdTe) was hoped to eliminate the problems encountered with CdS. Work included first single crystal, and later thin film polycrystalline material. In 1967, 4 to 5% efficient cells of 25 cm² area had be fabricated, but the stability problem had not been solved. Gallium arsenide thin film cells, pursued between 1962 and 1967, resulted in 3.5% efficient cells.

CdS work, as well as other thin semiconductor research, was continued only on a small scale in the following years. Essentially every year, a group of workers announced the solution to the self-degradation and instability mechanisms of these cells, but by 1977, a lasting solution still had not been found. CdS cells, nevertheless, have been used successfully under controlled conditions. Protected by glass sheets and dry nitrogen gas, and electrically loaded to minimize self-degradation by internal ion migration, CdS cells have demonstrated a life capability of several years.

The maximum CdS cell efficiency measured so far is in the order of 8% at room temperature; 15% has been calculated as the theoretical limit. This limited efficiency, however, does not detract from the potential attractiveness of CdS cells, because their fabrication cost is predicted to be at least one order of magnitude lower than the cost of silicon or GaAs cells. Therefore, research on CdS cells is continuing.

SOLAR CELL TYPES

4-6. Solar Cell Classification

Solar cells may be classified into many different families or types. Even though, at present, there exists no universally agreed-upon nomenclature for most mass-produced or experimental solar cells, classification according to some important criteria, as follows, is useful (the parenthetically referenced sections provide more detailed discussions):

Cell applications (4-7)
Cell materials and processing (4-8)
Cell internal construction (4-9)
Cell optical characteristics (4-10)
Cell efficiency (4-11, 4-12, 4-17, 4-26)
Cell size and shape (4-29)
Cell thickness (4-30)
Cell contacts (4-32, 4-33)
Cell radiation resistance (4-35, 4-37).

4-7. Classification According to Application

Solar cells are intended either for terrestrial or for space use, and either for energy conversion or for electro-optical sensor applications. Any of these applications may require the solar cells to operate at low, medium, or high solar intensities, usually requiring different, specifically optimized solar cell designs.

Terrestrial Solar Cells. Presently designed, fabricated, and tested involving less rigid quality control standards than space cells, the prime feature of terrestrial solar cells is low relative cost (dollars per peak watt). The cell's spectral response is optimized for slightly longer wavelengths than for space cells, owing to the absence of most of the ultraviolet solar energy that is found in space but it absorbed by the upper regions of the earth's atmosphere.

Space Cells. Typically designed and fabricated according to rigid quality and process control standards, space cells are highly reliable devices, capable of withstanding extremes in temperature and other space environments. Since weight is usually critical for space applications, cells are designed to provide the greatest practical power output per unit weight (W/kg). The cell design is optimized for space sunlight illumination and for achieving the lowest operating temperature in orbit, frequently coupled with high radiation resistance.

1 AU Cells. Not actually designated as such, the vast majority of all space and terrestrial cells have been optimized for operation at solar intensities encountered near 1 AU (astronomical unit; see Section 9-3) distance from the sun. These cells typically would not perform well under very low or very high illumination intensities.

Low-intensity Cells. These cells are optimized for operation at relatively low intensities. They may possess larger internal series resistance values than do higher-intensity cells, but they may not have relatively low shunt resistance values. In general, operation at low light intensities is accompanied by operation at low temperatures (see also Section 4-24).

High-intensity Cells. Optimized for high solar intensity as found in close proximity to the sun or in concentrator applications, these cells are characterized by high gridline density to minimize the cell's internal series resistance. Typi-

cally, operation at high light intensities is accompanied by operation at elevated temperature (see also Section 4-23).

Concentrator Cells. These are the same type as high-intensity cells.

4-8. Classification According to Materials and Processing

Presently, solar cells can be classified (for the convenience of the array designer) according to basic semiconductor material type, as follows:

- Silicon cells
- Gallium arsenide cells
- Cadmium sulfide cells
- Other cells.

Silicon Cells. Silicon cells are divided into *single crystal* and *polycrystalline* cells. Single crystal cells are cut from silicon crystal ingots that can now be grown easily in 10 cm diameters or larger by approximately 50 cm in length or longer. Polycrystalline silicon, also known as *amorphous* silicon, is obtained by a casting process, followed by a heat treatment that causes very small individual silicon grains to combine and form larger grains having sizes of several millimeters in length and width.

The material property of interest to solar cell users is the cell's *base resistivity*. Cells are classified into typical resistivity ranges of 1 to 3 ohm $\cdot$ cm, 7 to 14 ohm $\cdot$ cm, and others. Generally, cells made from lower base resistivity silicon exhibit higher efficiency but lower radiation resistance than do cells made from higher resistivity material.

The silicon cell's spectral response is affected by the diffusion process. Classified as deep-diffused cells, having a junction depth of about 0.5 μm, these cells have little response at wavelengths below 450 nm. Shallow-diffused cells exhibit greater short-wavelength response, but also greater internal cell series resistance losses. Therefore, *shallow-diffused* cells, also known as *blue-sensitive*, or just *blue*, or *violet* cells, carry higher-density gridline patterns to minimize series resistance losses.

Silicon cells may be made by different junction formation methods. Most cells are fabricated by utilizing a diffusion process. In pilot line quantities, junctions have also been formed by ion implantation, a process by which the impurity atoms are "shot" into the semiconductor base materials with ion guns.

Lithium-doped Silicon Cells. These cells constitute a class of developmental devices that exhibit a relatively high proton and neutron radiation hardness, which is achieved by the addition of lithium to the n-base of p-on-n silicon cells. The lithium causes an apparent annealing of radiation-induced damage, and effects a partial recovery of cell output after irradiation.

N-P and N-P-P$^+$ Silicon Cells. The foregoing solar cell types are of the *single* p-n junction type. Their structure is illustrated in Fig. 4-1a (except for the lithium silicon cells, the p and n layers are reversed). A now common type, known alternately as *drift field*, *field*, p^+, and *back surface field* (*BSF*) cells, has an additional p^+ layer immediately adjacent to the cell's back contact, as illustrated in Fig. 4-1b. This field aids in the separation of photon-generated electron-hole pairs and the collection of the minority carriers. The p^+ field is subject to degradation due to space radiation effects. At radiation levels of 1×10^{15} 1 MeV electrons/

cm^2, most present BSF cell types show no greater efficiency than equivalent non-BSF cells. Solar cell device specialists differentiate between BSF and p^+ cells because of slightly different internal carrier collection mechanisms.

Gallium Arsenide (GaAs) Cells. These cells constitute a class of experimental cells that someday may displace silicon cells in both space and terrestiral applications. The presently most promising cell utilizes a GaAlAs-GaAs structure, as shown in Fig. 4-1c. This p-on-n cell type has reached AM0 efficiencies of up to 16%.

Most present-day gallium arsenide solar cells are made by epitaxial growth of the upper layers on a single crystal GaAs wafer. Since GaAs is a very expensive and relatively scarce material, ways are sought to make the entire cell by epitaxially growing all GaAs layers very thinly on low-cost substrates made of a different material.

Cadmium Sulfide (CdS) Cells. These cells belong to the class of thin film cells that are made from compound semiconductors. The most promising CdS cell type has a Cu$_x$S-CdS structure, as illustrated in Fig. 4-1d. Typically, x is approximately equal to 2 in the copper sulfide layer, but many different forms of copper-sulfur

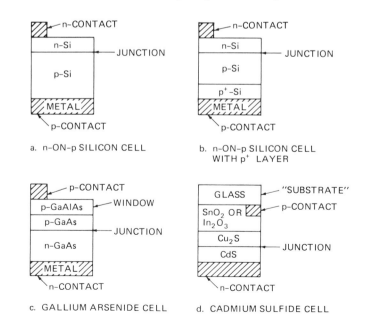

a. n-ON-p SILICON CELL

b. n-ON-p SILICON CELL WITH p$^+$ LAYER

c. GALLIUM ARSENIDE CELL

d. CADMIUM SULFIDE CELL

Fig. 4-1. Solar cell construction (cross-section not to scale).

compounds, known as chalcogenides, may actually be present.

CdS cells are made by low-cost spray or dip processes rather than by crystal growing. The semiconductor layers are very thin and, when deposited on metal foil or plastic film substrates, are highly flexible. In more recent fabrication processes, the semiconductor materials are deposited on window glass that is a much more effective humidity barrier than plastic film.

Other Cell Types. These include compound semiconductor cells as well as metal oxide cells. Practical compounds can be formed from chemical group III-V, group II-VI, and other group elements. For example, GaAs and GaAlAs are group III-V combination, Cu_2S is a group I-VI, and Cds is a group II-VI compound. Many different compounds can be formed, but most of them do not offer high theoretical efficiency potentials.

Metal-insulator-semiconductor (MIS) cells are of the Schottky barrier type, with the exception that a very thin insulating layer is placed between the metal and the oxide, yielding improved cell efficiency. In cells in which this insulating layer is an oxide, the cells are called metal-oxide-semiconductor (MOS) cells.

4-9. Classification According to Construction

Most solar cell types may be constructed in several different ways, as discussed below.

Cell Polarity. Cells may be either of the n-on-p or of the p-on-n type, also written n-p and p-n, or n/p and p/n, respectively. The first letter indicates the dominant semiconductor material type nearest to the cell's upper, light-sensitive side, and the second letter that of the bulk, or base material, except when the term "p-n junction" is used generically, no such significance is attached.

The n-material assumes the negative, and the p-material the positive, polarity of the photovoltage. The p^+ or p^{++} layers in certain cell design are synonymous with the p-layer in terms of device polarity.

Planar Junction Cells. These are of the usual, flat, wafer-like type, as illustrated in Fig. 4-2.

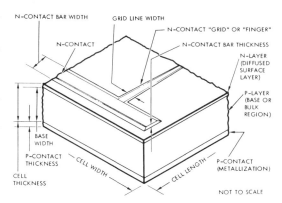

Fig. 4-2. Portion of a planar junction N-on-P silicon solar cell.

These cells may or may not utilize the so-called *planar* semiconductor device technology as developed for transistors and other components. The p-n junction is located just below the upper cell surface and extends over the entire upper cell area, including the area that is covered by the n-contact bar and the grid lines.

Modern n-on-p solar cells, as illustrated in Fig. 4-2, are fabricated by first growing single crystal p-type silicon ingots, and cutting and slicing them into thin wafers. An n-type impurity is then diffused at high temperature into the wafer surfaces, thereby forming a diode junction less than 0.5 μm from the surface. The difused layer is subsequently removed from all but one large surface, which then is referred to as the cell's *active*, or *light sensitive*, area. Next, metallic contacts are applied to both the diffused n-layer and to the p-base layer. In a final step, an anti-reflective coating is deposited over the active area. Some cell contacts are also coated with lead-tin solder.

On some cell types (known as "p^+" and "back field" cells) a p^+-region is created in the p-base region near the p-contact during an intermediate fabrication step.

p-on-n solar cells are identical in appearance to n-on-p cells, as shown in Fig. 4-2, except that all n and p polarity indicators are reversed.

Vertical Junction Cells. These cells consist of wafers into which deep and narrow grooves are etched, as shown in Fig. 4-3. After diffusion, the junction follows the wall surfaces up and down, along the tops of the walls, and along the

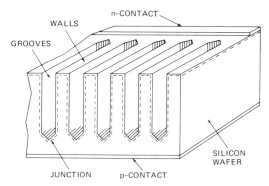

Fig. 4-3. Vertical junction silicon solar cell.

bottoms of the grooves. The junction surface area is on the order of ten times the area of a planar junction cell having the same wafer size.

Homojunctions. These are p-n or n-p junctions between like semiconductor materials, except for some minute quantities of impurities present in them. Silicon p-n junctions are an example of homojunctions.

Heterojunctions. These are p-n or n-p junctions between unlike semiconductor materials. An example of heterojunctions is the CdS/Cu_2S structure of the so-called cadmium sulfide cell.

4-10. Classification According to Optical Features

The highest cell efficiency that can be reached during the cell's actual operating conditions depends highly on 1) the amount of sunlight that penetrates into the photovoltaically active portion of the cell; and 2) the cell's operating temperature. Anti-reflective coatings on the cell's front surface promote entering of the photovoltaically useful sunlight into the solar cell, while wavelength-selective reflective coatings, either on the cell's front or back surface or on the cell's coverglass, reject portions of the sunlight spectrum that contributes only to cell heating. The following optical characteristics are available on contemporary silicon solar cells.

Polished Cells. The front surface of a polished cells is either mechanically or chemically fin-

ished and etched. The surface finish may range from a mirror-like quality to an almost matted appearance, depending upon whether acidic or sodium-hydroxide etches are used, or whether the parts are dipped in the etching solution or sprayed with it. Frequently, several different etching steps are used in sequence. The surface finish also affects the minority carrier collection process and the adhesion strength of the contacts. Polished surfaces exhibit the highest reflectivity, but permit the most precisely tailored antireflection coatings to be applied.

Matted Surface Cells. This surface, too, is achieved by chemical etching. These cells have a smooth, flat finish that reflects light more diffusely than polished cells. The majority of all silicon solar cells made before 1975 are of this type.

Non-reflecting Surface Cells. These cells are also known as rough, textured, texturized, black, velvet, or sculptured cells, and they have the lowest front surface reflectance of all cell types. The non-reflecting surface is produced by an etching process that produces a pyramide-like microstructure, as shown in Fig. 4-4.

Anti-reflective Coatings. Anti-reflective (AR) coatings are applied to the cell's front surface of any roughness to reduce light reflection losses. Conventional cells have used silicon monoxide (SiO) coatings. Modern, high-efficiency and hybrid cells use the more transparent tantalum pentoxide (Ta_2O_5) or multilayer (ML) coatings. One attractive MLAR coating is Ta_2O_5 over titanium oxide (Ti_xO_y). AR coatings are very thin, less than 1 μm thick, and are usually applied by a vacuum deposition process.

Back Surface Reflector Cells. Abbreviated BSR, these cells are provided with a highly reflective metal surface between the solar cell wafer back surface and the cell's back side contact. Any solar radiation having wavelengths greater than those absorbed by the cell for potential conversion into electrical energy (about 1150 nm in silicon) penetrate easily through the semiconductor material to the back side reflector. Upon

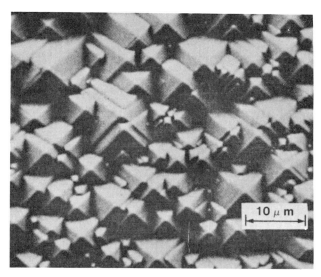

Fig. 4-4. Textured nonreflecting surface. (*Courtesy of COMSAT Corp.*)

reflection, this energy simply emanates from the cell into space. As a result of the BSR, the solar absorptance is reduced significantly over that of the more typical non-reflecting contact cells. A BSR is of limited value on non-reflecting cells because of the internal light trapping by the textured surface.

4-11. Contemporary Silicon Solar Cells for Space Use

The different types of solar cells that have been fabricated or were under development during the mid- and late-1970's are described in Table 4-1. Not all of these cells were successful in terms of long-term usage or power output per unit cell cost, and continuing developments can be expected.

The oldest of the contemporary solar cell types is the so-called *conventional* or standard cell. Produced in great quantities for space programs between 1964 and the mid-1970's, this cell type represents pre-1972 solar cell technology that was not standardized in design or in performance, and is not at all related to "standard solar cells" as discussed in Chapter 8 in conjunction with solar simulator calibration and solar cell testing. Even though no longer in production, this cell type is still of interest, since many satellites still operating in orbit, and

some satellites still in ground storage awaiting launch, carry solar cells of this type on their arrays.

Conventional cells were available in two base resisitivity ranges: 1 to 3 ohm · cm (nominally 1 or 2 ohm · cm) for low radiation environments as found in low-altitude earth orbits or in interplanetary orbits, and 7 to 14 ohm · cm (nominally 10 ohm · cm) for high radiation levels as found in the Van Allen radiation belts or in long-duration geosynchronous orbits (see also *cross-over fluence*).

4-12. Contemporary Silicon Solar Cells for Terrestrial Use

The different types of solar cells that have been fabricated for terrestrial programs since the middle of the 1970's are described in Table 4-2. The earlier terrestrial cells were of the conventional space type, as described in Table 4-1, for 2 ohm · cm base resistivity. For cost reasons, non-reflecting surface cells are used for high-performance systems, while chemically polished cells are offered as the lowest-cost cells. The greater junction depth of terrestrial cells optimizes their spectral response for AM1 to AM2 sunlight compared to shallow-junction space cells optimized for AM0 conditions.

Solar cells with printed-on contacts are a

Table 4-1. Commercial Silicon Solar Cells for Space Applications.

Cell Type	Textured	BSF or p$^+$	BSR	Base Resistivity (ohm · cm)	Junction Depth (μm)	AR Coating	Number of Grid Lines	Thickness (mm)	Efficiency 25°C AM0 (%)*	Solar Absorptance*	Radiation Factor*†
Conventional	No	No	No	1 to 3	0.3 to 0.5	SiO	6	0.2 to 0.4	10 to 11.5	0.80	0.74 to 0.78
Conventional	No	No	No	7 to 14	0.3 to 0.5	SiO	6	0.2 to 0.4	9.6 to 11.1	0.80	0.76 to 0.80
Hybrid	No	No	No	10	0.1 to 0.25	Ta_2O_5	10 to 24	0.2 to 0.3	10.5 to 11.8	0.85	0.75 to 0.80
Hybrid	No	No	Yes	10	0.1 to 0.25	Ta_2O_5	10 to 24	0.2 to 0.3	11 to 12	0.73	0.79 to 0.81
Field	No	Yes	No	20	0.15 to 0.3	Ta_2O_5	10 to 24	0.25 to 0.3	12 to 13	0.81 to 0.86	0.76
Field	No	Yes	No	10 to 20	0.15 to 0.3	Ta_2O_5	10 to 24	0.2 to 0.3	13 to 14	0.81 to 0.86	0.76
Field	No	Yes	Yes	10 to 20	0.15 to 0.25	Ta_2O_5	10 to 24	0.2 to 0.3	13.5 to 14.3	0.77	0.76
Non-reflecting	Yes	No	No	**	0.15 to 0.25	Ta_2O_5	10 to 24	0.2 to 0.3	12.1 to 13.1	0.90 to 0.94	0.74 to 0.78
Non-reflecting	Yes	No	Yes	**	0.15 to 0.25	Ta_2O_5	10 to 24	0.2 to 0.3	12.4 to 13.4	0.91	0.80
Non-reflecting	Yes	Yes	No	**	0.15 to 0.25	Ta_2O_5	10 to 24	0.2 to 0.3	13.1 to 14.0	0.88 to 0.89	0.68 to 0.73
Non-reflecting	Yes	Yes	No	**	0.1 to 0.2	Ta_2O_5	10 to 40	0.2 to 0.4	14.5 to 15.5	0.90 to 0.95	0.73 to 0.76
Non-reflecting	Yes	Yes	No	10	0.1 to 0.3	Ta_2O_5	10 to 40	0.2 to 0.4	14.5 to 15.1	0.90	0.73 to 0.76
Violet	No	No	No	**	0.1 to 0.2	Ta_2O_5	**	0.2 to 0.3	12.5 to 13.5	0.81	0.76 to 0.81
Violet	No	Yes	No	**	0.1 to 0.2	TiO/Al_2O_3	10 to 40	0.2 to 0.4	13.5 to 14.5	0.81	0.67 to 0.76
Violet	No	Yes	Yes	**	0.1 to 0.2	TiO/Al_2O_3	10 to 40	0.2 to 0.3	13.5 to 14.5	0.73 to 0.78	0.76 to 0.80

*Depends on specific cell design and processing parameters. Data is for optimally glassed cells having 3.8 cm^2 active area. For conversion of efficiency to power output, see Appendix D.

**Not disclosed.

†Radiation Factor = P_{mp} after exposure to 1×10^{15} 1 MeV electrons per cm^2/P_{mp} before exposure, both measured at 25°C and AM0.

Table 4-2. Commercial Silicon Solar Cells For Terrestrial Applications.

Geometry	Size (mm)	Thickness (mm)	Efficiency 25°C AM1 (%)*	Concentration Ratio
Circular	50 to 60	0.3 to 0.4	8 to 15	1
	75 to 100	0.3 to 0.4	8 to 13	1
Rectangular	20 × 20	0.3	10 to 17	1
	20 × 40	0.3	10 to 13	1
	20 × 60	0.3	10 to 13	1
	54 × 47	0.3	14 to 15.5	20

*Depends on specific cell design and processing parameters. For conversion of efficiency to power output, see Section 4-17.

feature presently reserved for terrestrial cells because of instabilities observed on space flight experiments using printed contacts. Similarly, most concentrator cells have vacuum-deposited contacts as used on space cells.

ELECTRICAL CHARACTERISTICS

4-13. Solar Cell Polarity

Solar cells can be fabricated as p-on-n or as n-on-p devices. The first letter denotes the semiconductor material type (see Section 4-9) of the uppermost or first layer into which the solar energy penetrates. Any solar cell's electrical behavior is related to its semiconductor material characteristics as outlined below.

- The polarity of the output voltage of an illuminated solar cell is such that the p-contact becomes positive and the n-contact becomes negative.
- An illuminated solar cell connected to a load and delivering power is said to operate in its *forward* mode.
- A solar cell, illuminated or not, is said to be biased in its *forward* direction by an external source when the positive terminal of the source is connected to the cell's p-contact and the negative terminal is connected to the n-contact.
- A solar cell, illuminated or not, is said to be biased *in reverse* by an external source when the positive terminal of the source is connected to the cell's n-contact and the negative terminal is connected to the p-contact.

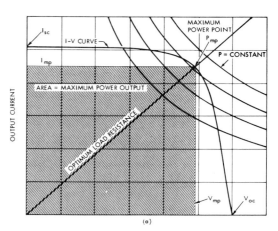

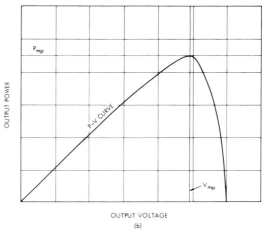

Fig. 4-5. Solar cell electrical output characteristics; (a) *I–V* Curve, and (b) *P–V* Curve.

4-14. Current-Voltage Characteristics

Current-voltage characteristics, or, in brief, *I–V* curves, describe the solar cell electrical terminal characteristics most completely. The term *I–V curve* has become customary even though the term should really be *V–I curve*, if one takes the term *X–Y coordinate system* as a reference. A solar cell *I–V* curve, illustrated in Fig. 4-5a, passes through three significant points:

1. I_{sc}, short-circuit current (cell terminal voltage is zero);
2. P_{mp}, maximum power output point, also known as the optimum power output point, P_{op}; and
3. V_{oc}, open-circuit voltage (cell terminal current is zero).

The maximum power point, P_{mp}, corresponds

to the maximum conversion efficiency, η_{max}. This point is located where the rectangle having the largest area can be drawn inside the *I-V* curve. The *I-V* curve is tangent to a constant power curve, also called an *iso-efficiency* curve at the P_{mp} point at which $dP/dV = 0$ (Fig. 4-5b). From a set of several constant efficiency curves drawn on the *I-V* curve plot, the actual cell operating efficiency can be determined when the cell is operated off the maximum power point (i.e., when the terminal voltage $V \neq V_{mp}$).

Corresponding to P_{mp} there is a maximum power (or optimum power) current, I_{mp}, and a maximum power voltage, V_{mp}. A straight line drawn from the origin through P_{mp} (Fig. 4-5a) represents the optimum load resistance, R_{Lopt}, for this cell. The slope of this line is $1/R_{Lopt} = I_{mp}/V_{mp}$.

Frequently, the values for P_{mp}, V_{mp}, and I_{mp} are to be determined from experimentally obtained *I-V* curves. As seen from Fig. 4-5a, the point of tangency of the *I-V* curve and a constant power curve is not sharply defined; as an aid to more closely defining the P_{mp} point, a *P-V* curve, as shown in Fig. 4-5b, can be constructed. *P-V* curves can be plotted during the solar cell test when *I-V* curves are taken (a signal multiplier is required, as described in Chapter 8 in connection with solar cell testing) or they can be computer-generated from *I-V* curve data.

The *I-V* curve shown in Fig. 4-5a is only the first quadrant portion of the entire *I-V* curve. In general, the *I-V* curve extends from the second quadrant through the first quadrant into the fourth quadrant, as discussed in greater detail in Section 2-33 and illustrated in Fig. 4-6.

Sometimes the *I-V* curve is shown rotated such that I is plotted on the abscissa and V on the ordinate. Such presentation is logical and correct except it is not conventional according to the solar cell theoretical model, in which output current is the dependent variable which usually is plotted on the ordinate. (Actually, the nomenclature "*I-V*" curve is reversed.)

Sometimes the photovoltaic portion of the *I-V* curve is shown "upside down" in the fourth quadrant. This presentation originated

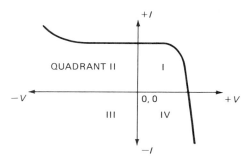

Fig. 4-6. *I-V* curve in 3 quadrants.

during the 1950's, when rectifier diode curve tracing equipment was used to study solar cells. Such equipment displays the dark diode or solar cell forward *I-V* curve on an oscilloscope screen in the first quadrant and illumination of the junction shifts the curve "downward" along the negative current axis into the fourth quadrant. As shown in Section 2-31, such representation, while logically self-consistent, is inconsistent with modern circuit analysis techniques and leads to unnecessary conceptual difficulties, such as negative power output.

Another reason (but an incorrect one) for showing the output current as negative arises from the solution of the so-called *continuity equation* (see Section 2-30) which assigns a negative sign to the cell current. This calculated cell current is an internal cell current which must flow in a certain direction to maintain the conservation of electrical charges. According to modern circuit theory (see Chapter 2), when this internal cell current flows in an outside circuit, the "sign" of it reverses and it flows identically to the conventional current, from a higher to a lower potential.

Typical averaged comparative solar cell *I-V* curves for contemporary space type silicon solar cells are shown in Fig. 4-7. The curves have been normalized to 25°C cell temperature, 4.0 cm² total cell area, and 3.8 cm² active area. Illumination is one solar constant of AM0 spectrum. Cells are glassed with fused silica covers having 350 nm cut-on wavelength.

4-15. Series Resistance

The series resistance, R_s, of a solar cell is an idealization of internal dissipative electrical

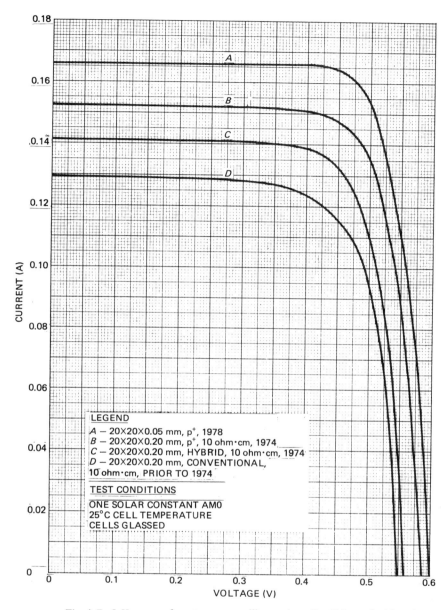

Fig. 4-7. *I-V* curves of contemporary silicon solar cells. (After refs. 10 and 11)

losses which can be deduced to occur in the cell by observing its terminal behavior. Cell series resistance represents in lumped fashion all distributed resistance elements in the semiconductor, its ohmic contacts, and the semiconductor/contact interfaces.[12] The largest contribution arises from the resistance of the diffused layer. Since R_s is a lumped quantity, it varies with practically every parameter, such as cell *I-V*

characteristics, illumination level, temperature, and radiation damage. Nevertheless, its use in engineering design and analysis is expedient and eminently practical (for measurement techniques, see Section 8-21).

Small variations of R_s can have a profound impact on the energy conversion efficiency of the cell (Fig. 4-8). Such variations are usually caused by the manufacturing process, but

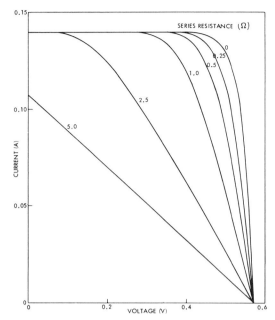

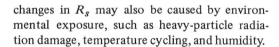

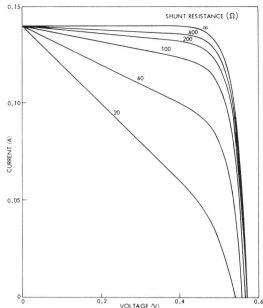

Fig. 4-8. Effect of series resistance on I-V curve shape of 2 × 2 cm solar cell. (Illustrative example)

Fig. 4-9. Effect of shunt resistance on I-V curve shape of 2 × 2 cm solar cell. (Illustrative example)

changes in R_s may also be caused by environmental exposure, such as heavy-particle radiation damage, temperature cycling, and humidity.

Effects of Series Resistance. An interesting phenomenon (applicable to spinning arrays, for example) that results from reduced illumination (less than one solar constant) is that cells having higher series resistance (i.e., "poorer" cells) show a greater absolute power output than do cells having lower series resistance (i.e., "better' cells with "sharper" I-V curves). The reason for this is that cells are normally "graded" (i.e., their performance is measured for flight acceptance) at one solar constant intensity, while at the lower, operating intensity, the I-V curve shifts toward higher voltages. Since the magnitude of this voltage shift is directly proportional to the magnitude of the series resistance, cells with higher series resistance will exhibit a greater voltage gain than will cells with lower series resistance.

4-16. Shunt Resistance

A portion of the electrical energy generated inside the solar cell is lost through internal cell leakage. Several such leakage paths have

been identified; they exist through the cell p-n junction (recombination current), along the outer cell edges (surface leakage), and through n-contact metalization shunting the junction at microscopic flaws (such as surface scratches). These leakage paths are neither uniformly distributed across the cell area nor uniform from one cell to the next. In general, they are non-linear, unstable, and not reproducible during testing. The effects of all leakage paths are conceptually combined for array design engineering in the so-called shunt resistance, R_{SH}.

The typical range of shunt resistance for 1 × 2 cm to 2 × 6 cm cells is from 10^3 to 10^5 ohm. Shunt resistance is not controlled during the manufacturing process except that at times it may be monitored for production process control purposes. The effects of shunt resistance for array design purposes are usually negligible for operation near one solar constant (Fig. 4-9), but become significant at lower light levels. (See also section 4-31).

4-17. Energy Conversion Efficiency

Efficiency, η, of a solar cell is defined in Eq. 4-1.

$$\eta = P_{\text{out}}/P_{\text{in}} = P_{\text{out}}/p_{\text{in}} \cdot A_c \qquad (4\text{-}1)$$

P_{out} is the electrical power output of the cell, P_{in} is the energy input to the cell, p_{in} is the solar illumination level per unit area or the value of the solar constant and A_c is the active solar cell area upon which the solar energy is incident. A cell operates at its *maximum* efficiency, η_{max}, when its maximum power output capability is utilized by an optimized load at a particular illumination intensity and cell operating temperature. The cell's *operating* efficiency, η_{op}, is the efficiency at which the cell is actually being utilized. For example, solar cell arrays are frequently designed such that $\eta_{op} = \eta'_{max}$ at the end of mission life after the initial maximum solar cell efficiency, η_{max}, has degraded due to environmental exposures to η'_{max}. If the load power requirement throughout mission life remains constant, the actual operating efficiency at beginning of life is equal to the end-of-life operating efficiency (i.e., $\eta_{op} = \eta'_{max}$) notwithstanding the fact that η_{max} may be considerably greater than η_{op} and may be degrading severely during mission life.

The maximum solar cell energy conversion efficiency depends mainly upon the following: the solar cell internal construction, dimension, active area, specific material properties, photovoltaic junction characteristics, anti-reflective coating, surface texture, contact and grid configuration, illumination level, cell operating temperature, particulate irradiation damage, temperature cycling, and other environmental exposure history.

Of considerable interest is the *ultimate*, or theoretically possible, efficiency. This efficiency is related to a semiconductor material property known as the band gap. Figure 4-10 illustrates the calculated efficiency for several solar cell types as a function of temperature. The theoretically superior performance of GaAs cells, especially at higher operating temperature, over silicon cells is evident.

4-18. Curve and Fill Factors

The *curve* factor is used in theoretical work associated purely with the exponential junction characteristics and deviations therefrom observed in actual solar cells. The curve factor

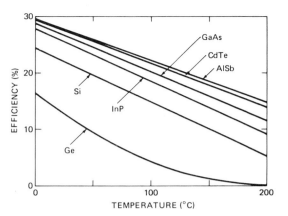

Fig. 4-10. Theoretical solar cell efficiencies. (After ref. 13)

modifies the ideal junction characteristics and appears as the "A" factor in the theoretical model as defined in Section 2-31.

The *fill* factor is a term that is used to quantitatively describe the "squareness" or "sharpness' of the I-V curve. The "squarer" such a curve is, the greater the maximum power output, P_{mp}, may be for a given I_{sc} and V_{oc}. For example, "squareness" is reduced (i.e., the I-V curve "softens") as the internal cell series resistance, R_s, is increased. Many other cell parameters also affect the fill factor. The fill factor (FF) includes the alterations of the I-V curve shape which are caused by the curve factor, and is defined in Eq. 4-2.

$$\text{FF} = \frac{V_{mp}I_{mp}}{V_{oc}I_{sc}} = \frac{P_{mp}}{V_{oc}I_{sc}} \qquad (4\text{-}2)$$

FF is always less than unity. Typical fill factors of contemporary solar cells range between 0.75 and 0.80.

The fill factor is a practical quantity to use when one wishes to compare different solar cells under the same conditions, as is required in manufacturing process control. Its use, however, may be misleading or even erroneous when one wishes to determine changes in the cell I-V curve shape due to environmental degradation, for instance. It can be shown that when the solar cell operating temperature or illumination intensity is varied over a range in which the I-V curve shape does not change, the calculated value of the fill factor will change.

Illustrative Example No. 4-1

Let a solar cell be measured at two different temperatures. Let the measured cell parameters at the first temperature be unprimed, and those at the second, higher temperature be primed. For simplicity, let only the cell output voltage change by ΔV (i.e., $I'_{sc} = I_{sc}$, $I'_{mp} = I_{mp}$, $V'_{oc} = V_{oc} + \Delta V$, and $V'_{mp} = V_{mp} + \Delta V$). For a hypothetical cell having $V_{mp} = 0.45$ V, $V_{oc} = 0.55$ V, $I_{sc} = 0.10$ A, $I_{mp} = 0.09$ A, and $\Delta V = 0.05$ V:

$$FF = \frac{0.45 \times 0.09}{0.55 \times 0.10} = 0.736$$

$$FF' = \frac{0.40 \times 0.09}{0.50 \times 0.10} = 0.720.$$

At the higher temperature, the fill factor is lower even though the curve shape has not changed; the *I-V* curve merely shifted by -0.05 V.

4-19. Effects of Solar Intensity

In practice, the solar cell operating temperature is always affected by the intensity of sunlight incident on the solar cell. Nevertheless, it is fruitful to study the changes in the cell's output characteristics while keeping the cell temperature constant. The sunlight intensity, technically known as the *radiant solar energy flux density* and measured in units of watts per square meter (W/m^2) that is directly incident on the solar cells depends upon the following:

- Angle of incidence (i.e., the angle between a normal to the solar cell array's surface and a light ray from the sun)
- Solar distance (i.e., the distance of the array from the sun; seasonal variations for terrestrial or near-earth space arrays, or variations in distance of space probes in interplanetary orbits)
- Concentration ratio of solar concentrators (mirrors, lenses, or other devices; applicable for concentrator arrays only)
- Light transmission losses in coverglasses, cover adhesive, and other optical elements
- Light transmission losses in the earth

atmosphere (applicable for terrestrial arrays only).

Additional sunlight intensity modulations are caused by solar eclipses: obscuration of space arrays by planets and of terrestrial arrays by clouds. Furthermore, shadows of objects may fall on portions of an array. Shadows and eclipses may be of the umbra (fully dark) or penumbra (not fully dark) type. (A discussion of such shadows can be found in Chapter 2.)

Changing the illumination intensity incident on the solar cells (keeping everything else constant, such as the cell's temperature and the illumination's spectral distribution) changes the cell's output characteristics, as shown in Fig. 4-11. Each point on the cell's *I-V* curve translates very nearly along the cell's series resistance (R_s) line, so that the *I-V* curve shifts toward lower current and toward higher voltage values with decreasing intensity. Even though a lowering of the intensity causes a shift toward higher voltages, the open-circuit voltage actually decreases.

For most solar cell types that were designed to operate at approximately one solar constant intensity, the *I-V* curve shape is essentially invariant with intensity over the range from approximately 0.5 to 2 solar constants. The cell's

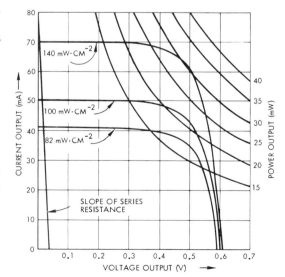

Fig. 4-11. Typical *I-V* curves of a 1 × 2 cm solar cell at three different illumination levels. (Constant spectral distribution and temperature, illustrative example)

I_{sc} is practically proportional to the intensity, V_{oc} changes logarithmically, and R_s is very nearly constant. The greater the intensity deviation from the cell's design intensity becomes, the greater will be the cell's I-V curve shape change, as described in Section 4-23.

4-20. Reversible Effects of Temperature

A change in cell temperature causes three changes in the cell I-V curve, two of which are evident in Fig. 4-12:

1. A scaling of the I-V curve along the current axis;
2. A translation (shifting) of the I-V curve along the voltage axis; and
3. A change in the I-V curve shape affecting the "roundness" of the "knee" region of the I-V curve.

An increase in the cell operating temperature causes a slight increase in the cell short-circuit current and a significant decrease in cell voltage. The increase in short-circuit current is a function of illumination level. Its value, typically less than 0.1%/°C, depends upon the spectral distribution of the illuminating light (filtered sunlight) and the spectral response

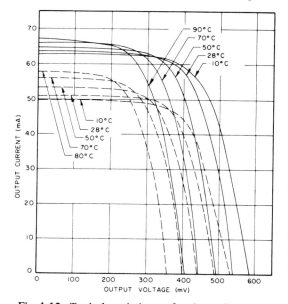

Fig. 4-12. Typical variations of solar cell current-voltage characteristics with temperature before (solid lines) and after (dashed lines) irradiation. (Illustrative example)

of the solar cells (i.e., the cell thickness, junction depth, anti-reflective coating, and state of radiation damage of the cell).

Scaling of the I-V curve along the current axis essentially corresponds to a change in the cell's energy conversion efficiency, which, in turn, is due to a change in the cell's collection efficiency with temperature (see Sections 4-27 and 4-28). Scaling of the I-V curve consists of multiplication of the value of the output current at each point on the I-V curve by a constant; for an increase in temperature, this constant is greater than unity, and for a decrease in temperature, it is less than unity.

The change in voltage with temperature is due to a change in the diode conduction characteristics. With increasing temperatures, the entire I-V curve translates toward lower voltages at a rate of approximately 2.2 to 2.3 mV/°C. This voltage change is nearly the same for all non-irradiated, thick base width solar cells (for V_{oc} and V_{mp}), as well as for general rectifier diodes made from silicon.

With increasing temperature, the "knee" region of the I-V curve tends to become more rounded. This "knee softening" can be accommodated analytically by either using separate temperature coefficients (see Section 4-21) for I_{sc}, I_{mp}, V_{mp}, and V_{oc}, by defining a temperature coefficient for R_s, or by defining a separate "curve rounding" factor. Differences between the temperature coefficients of V_{oc} and V_{mp} are usually indicative of changes in the I-V curve shape with temperature.

With increasing temperature, the cell's reverse saturation current increases in the same way the reverse current of conventional diodes increases. However, this increase in true reverse current is usually not observable because it is masked by the much larger solar cell leakage currents. Cell leakage currents do not have a well-defined temperature dependence. In the avalanche breakdown region, solar cells usually show decreasing breakdown voltages with increasing temperatures.

4-21. Temperature Coefficients

For analytical work, it is desirable, but not necessary, to express the temperature-related changes of a solar cell's *I-V* curve via the so-called temperature coefficients. The most straightforward definition of the temperature coefficient of any solar cell parameter P (where P may be I_{sc}, V_{mp}, or any other parameter) is the *instantaneous* temperature coefficient, defined by Eq. 4-3.

$$\beta'_P = \frac{dP}{dT} \qquad (4\text{-}3)$$

The *normalized instantaneous* coefficients is defined by Eq. 4-4.

$$\beta''_P = \frac{1}{P}\frac{dP}{dT} \qquad (4\text{-}4)$$

Since β'_P and β''_P are typically non-linear over all ranges of temperatures, the most practical *average* temperature coefficient is in use, defined by Eq. 4-5.

$$\beta_P = \frac{P(T) - P(T_0)}{T - T_0} \qquad (4\text{-}5)$$

where

T = temperature at which the cell output parameter P is sought

T_0 = reference temperature, usually $25°$ or $28°C$

$P(T)$ = parameter at temperature T

$P(T_0)$ = parameter at reference temperature T_0

$P = I_{sc}, I_{mp}, V_{mp}, V_{oc}, P_{mp}, R_s$.

As an example for short-circuit current, the normalized average temperature coefficient becomes β''_I (Eq. 4-6).

$$\beta''_I = \frac{I_{sc}(T) - I_{sc}(T_0)}{I_{sc}(T_0)(T - T_0)} \qquad (4\text{-}6)$$

The units of this normalized temperature coefficient are $°C^{-1}$ or, when multiplied by 100, $\%/°C$.

Average temperature coefficients for several solar cell parameters of several solar cell types of current interest are shown in Figs. 4-13 through 4-19.

Illustrative Example No. 4-2

Problem: Calculate β_P and β'_P for $P = P_{mp}$ and a solar cell having an output of $P_{mp} = 300$ mW at 28°C and 304.5 mW at 25°C.

Solution:

$$\beta_{P_{mp}} = \frac{300 - 304.5}{28 - 25} = \frac{-4.5}{3} = -1.5 \text{ mW/°C}$$

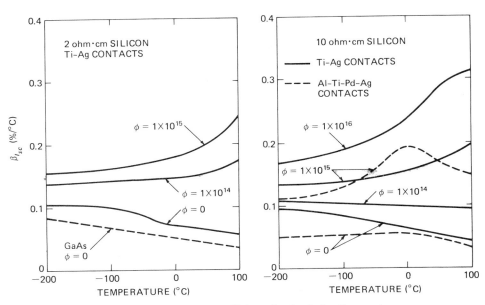

Fig. 4-13. Temperature coefficients for short-circuit current.

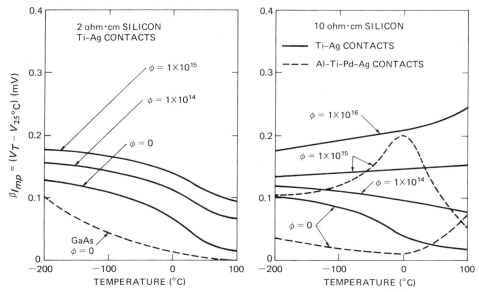

Fig. 4-14. Temperature coefficients for maximum power current.[53,54]

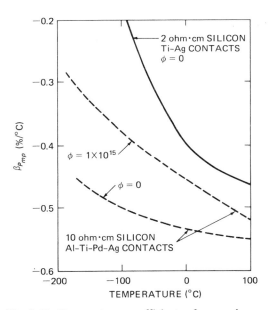

Fig. 4-15. Temperature coefficients for maximum power.[53,54]

$$\beta'_{P_{mp}} = \frac{1}{300} \times \frac{-4.5}{3} = -0.005°C^{-1}$$

$$= -0.5\%/°C.$$

The minus sign indicates that the power decreases as the temperature increases.

It is seen that the instantaneous coefficient

applies to a specific cell size only, while the normalized coefficient is valid for any cell size of the same type.

Illustrative Example No. 4-3

Problem: For a hypothetical 2 ohm · cm silicon solar cell, calculate its output parameters at 100°C when the 25°C test data is as follows: $I_{sc} = 0.25$ A, $I_{mp} = 0.20$ A, $P_{mp} = 0.10$ W, $V_{mp} = 0.50$ V, $V_{oc} = 0.60$ V.

Solution: The applicable temperature coefficient data is given in Figs. 4-13 through 4-17, respectively. The temperature coefficient values read off the graphs for $\phi = 0$ at 100°C are $\beta_{Isc} = 0.06\%/°C$, $\beta_{Imp} = 0.015\%/°C$, $\beta_{Pmp} = -0.47\%/°C$, $\beta_{Vmp} = -2.25$ mV/°C, and $\beta_{Voc} = -2.25$ mV/°C. The temperature difference $\Delta T = T - T_0 = 100 - 25 = 75°C$. At 100°C,

$$I_{sc} = 0.25 (1 + 0.0006 \times 75) = 0.261 \text{ A}$$

$$I_{mp} = 0.20 (1 + 0.00015 \times 75) = 0.202 \text{ A}$$

$$P_{mp} = 0.10 (1 - 0.0047 \times 75) = 0.065 \text{ W}$$

$$V_{mp} = 0.50 - (0.0025 \times 75) = 0.313 \text{ V}$$

$$V_{oc} = 0.60 - (0.0025 \times 75) = 0.413 \text{ V}.$$

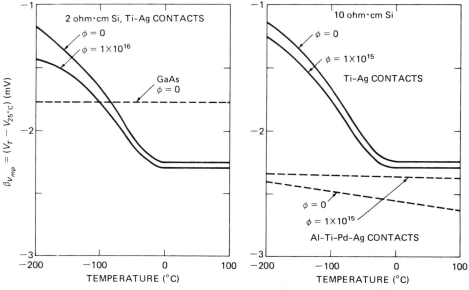

Fig. 4-16. Temperature coefficients for maximum power voltage.[53,54]

Temperature Coefficients for Planetary Missions. For planetary missions where large temperature variations are accompanied by large intensity changes, the current-voltage characteristic can be transformed from a reference temperature and intensity (T_0, H_0) to a new temperature and intensity (T_i, H_i) using the following equations; for short circuit, I_{sc}, and open-circuit voltage, V_{oc},

$$I_{sc}(T_i, H_i) = I_{sc}(T_0, H_0)\left(\frac{H_i}{H_0}\right) + \overline{\alpha}_{H_i}(T_i - T_0)$$

$$V_{oc}(T_i, H_i) = V_{oc}(T_0, H_0) + \overline{\beta}_{H_i}(T_i - T_0)$$

$$- \Delta I_{sc} R_s$$

$$\Delta I_{sc} = I_{sc}(T_i, H_i) - I_{sc}(T_0, H_0)$$

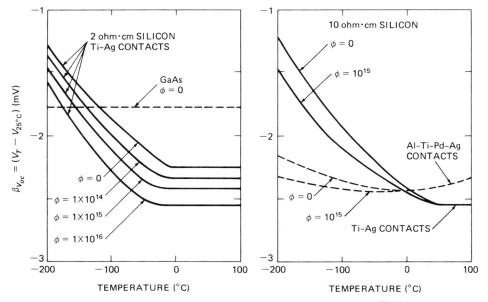

Fig. 4-17. Temperature coefficients for open-circuit voltage.[53,54]

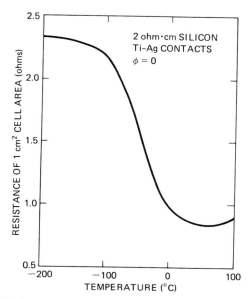

Fig. 4-18. Temperature variation of series resistance.[54]

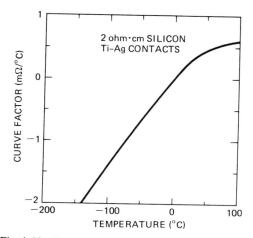

Fig. 4-19. Temperature coefficients for curvature factor.[54]

or

$$\Delta I_{sc} = I_{sc}(T_0, H_0)\left(\frac{H_i}{H_0} - 1\right) + \bar{\alpha}_{H_i}(T_i - T_0).$$

From these equations, expressions for any voltage (V) and current (I) along the I-V curve have been developed:

$$I(T_i, H_i) = I(T_0, H_0)\left(\frac{H_i}{H_0}\right) + \bar{\alpha}_{H_i}(T_i - T_0)$$

$$\Delta I = I(T_i, H_i) - I(T_0, H_0)$$

$$= I(T_0, H_0)\left(\frac{H_i}{H_0} - 1\right) + \bar{\alpha}_{H_i}(T_i - T_0)$$

$$V(T_i, H_i) = V(T_0, H_0) + \bar{\beta}_{H_i}(T_i - T_0) - \Delta I_{sc} R_s$$
$$- K_{H_i} I(T_i, H_i)(T_i - T_0)$$

where

$\bar{\alpha}_{H_i}$ = average short-circuit current temperature coefficient from T_0 to T_i at intensity H_i

$\bar{\beta}_{H_i}$ = average open-circuit voltage temperature coefficient from T_0 to T_i at intensity H_i

R_s = internal cell series resistance

K_{H_i} = average curvature correction factor from T_0 to T_i at intensity H_i (this factor is strictly a "geometric" correc-

tion factor to change the I-V curve shape, and has nothing to do with the curve factor or the fill factor of Section 4-18).

$$\Delta P_m = P_m(T_i, H_i) - P_m(T_0, H_0)$$

$$K_{H_i} = \Delta P_m / [I_m^2(T_i, H_i)(T_i - T_0)]$$

where

$P_m(T_0, H_0)$ = maximum power at reference condition T_0, H_0

$P_m(T_i, H_i)$ = maximum power for translated current-voltage characteristics from $T_i H_i$ to T_0, H_0

I_m = current at maximum power, T_i, H_i.

The value of K is positive for a softening of curvature (increasing radius of curvature) with increasing temperature. The product $K_{H_i} I(T_i, H_i)$ is the voltage change per unit temperature change resulting from changes in the I-V curve shape. Knowing K, the change in power output ΔP_m associated with the change in the I-V curve shape can be calculated from the last equation.[55]

Polynomial Coefficients. Another approach for expressing the solar cell parameter changes as functions of temperature and intensity changes utilizes fifth-order polynomials which have been curve-fitted to the experimental data. The functions which describe the cell parameters as functions of temperature T and solar intensity H are as follows:

$$I_{sc}(T,H) = C(T)H$$

where

$$C(T) = c_0 + c_1 T + c_2 T^2 + c_3 T^3 \\ + c_4 T^4 + c_5 T^5$$

and, similarly, for voltage:

$$V_{oc}(T,H) = A(T) + B(T) \log_{10} H$$

where

$$A(T) = a_0 + a_1 T + a_2 T^2 + a_3 T^3 \\ + a_4 T^4 + a_5 T^5 \\ B(T) = b_0 + b_1 T + b_2 T^2 + b_3 T^3 \\ + b_4 T^4 + b_5 T^5.$$

The numerical values for all of the coefficients a_i, b_i, and c_i were determined with computerized curve-fitting techniques from the experimental data for intensity/temperature ranges from 0.036 solar constants and $-160°C$ cell temperature up to six solar constants and $160°C$ cell temperature.[56]

Alternate Approach. The use of temperature coefficients is not mandatory to find the values of solar cell parameters at other temperatures: such data can be obtained by direct interpolation or extrapolation on a set of I-V curves measured at different temperatures, as illustrated in Fig. 4-12.

4-22. Irreversible Effects of Temperature

Exposure of solar cells to elevated temperature may, under certain conditions, lead to permanent electrical and mechanical damage to the solar cell contacts. In solder-covered silver-containing contacts, solution of the silver occurs in the solder at temperatures above the solder melting point, potentially resulting in a reduction of contact pull strength and in electrical output. Another potential degradation mechanism is corrosion of unprotected, non-passivated Ti-Ag contact solar cells in the presence of high humidity for extended periods of time (see Section 9-9), potentially resulting in a reduction of contact pull strength and electrical output.

Exposure of solar cells to low temperature may cause mechanical failures (such as silicon spalling) that are induced by thermomechanical stress (see detailed discussion in Sections 6-4 and 6-9). Failures of solar cells assembled into an array may occur when the array temperature is below approximately $-100°C$; when thick solder coatings on cells in excess of 25 to 50 μm are used; when thick layers of adhesive having a relatively large mismatch of coefficient of linear expansion relative to those of silicon and glass are utilized; or when cover-slide and cell-to-substrate adhesives, having relatively high glass transition temperatures, are selected.

4-23. High-Intensity, High-Temperature Operation

Most solar cells are efficiency-optimized for operation at approximately one solar constant and 30°C. Such cells perform poorly at very high illumination levels and even worse at the accompanying higher operating temperatures. High-intensity, high-temperature operation is of interest both for solar probes ("inbound" missions) and for solar energy concentrators. For example, the solar intensity at Mercury is 6.67 solar constants; potentially practical solar concentration ratios of up to 3:1 have been studied for space use, and ratios exceeding 1000:1 for terrestrial use. Such high-intensity operation requires special solar cell design.

The major electrical loss in the solar cell, especially at higher intensities, is in the diffused layer and contact resistances. Therefore, high-intensity solar cells have dense grid line patterns that are optimized for a specific concentration ratio and cell operating temperature. Figure 4-20 illustrates how the I-V curves of silicon cells with 5 grid lines have become softer at an intensity of 20 solar constants, while the curves of cells with 13 grid lines remained sharp. If any of these cells would have been optimized for a different intensity, their I-V curve changes would, of course, have shown a different trend. A cell's maximum power output capability and efficiency is highest at the design intensity, as illustrated in Fig. 4-21.

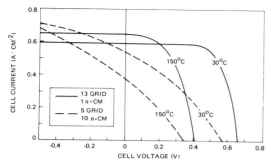

Fig. 4-20. *I–V* curves at high solar intensities (conventional 2 × 2 cm silicon cells at 20 solar constants.[14] (Reprinted with permission of the IEEE).

4-24. Low-Intensity, Low-Temperature Operation

Many solar cell types perform inadequately at low solar intensity and low temperature, such as would be encountered, for example, during a Jupiter mission (as low as 0.03 solar constant and −120° to −170°C). This inadequate solar cell performance is due to the fact that only some cells behave as they are predicted to behave, while other cells exhibit one or more of the following anomalies (Fig. 4-22): a "rectifying contact" (Schottky barrier); a low shunt resistance; and a "double slope" or "double break" *I–V* curve.

All three of these anomalies are related to the design, construction, and fabrication technology of the cells.[16] Attempts to screen from conventional cells those cells which would operate satisfactorily at low-intensity, low-

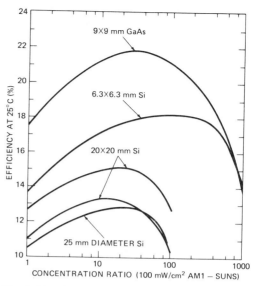

Fig. 4-21. Efficiencies of concentrator solar cells.[15]

temperature conditions have not been successful.[17] Therefore, if solar cells were to be used for such missions effectively, special solar cells would need to be developed and fabricated, with the appropriate controls.

4-25. Reverse Characteristics

When compared with other silicon p-n junction devices, such as rectifiers, silicon solar cells generally exhibit large reverse leakage currents per unit junction area, even at relatively low voltages. Under test, the reverse current-voltage characteristics are frequently unstable and not

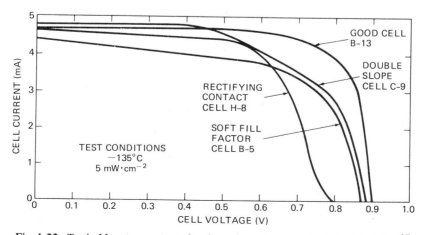

Fig. 4-22. Typical low-temperature, low-intensity solar cell output characteristics.[17]

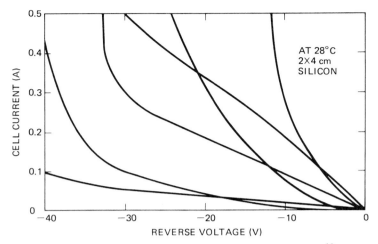

Fig. 4-23. Typical range of solar cell reverse characteristics.[19]

repeatable for reverse voltages exceeding about 5 V (see Fig. 4-23). The reverse characteristics of gallium arsenide cells are presently not known.

The solar cell reverse characteristics are typically not controlled during the cell manufacturing process except that they are occasionally monitored for certain process control activities. The design of contemporary silicon solar cells is such that the exposed p-n junction area around the perimeter of the cell is totally unprotected and subject to surface contamination, ion migration, moisture accumulation, and other surface effects. The close proximity of the metallic n-contact to the junction adds another source for potential contamination.

When connected into an array, solar cells may become reverse biased (see Section 2-45). Depending on the circumstances and the magnitude of the reverse bias, the reverse biased cells may experience excessive heating, a slight, permanent loss in power output, or permanent short-circuit failure.[18]

Cell Output Loss. A slight amount of cell power output (less than 1%) may be lost permanently as a result of subjecting solar cells to reverse voltages exceeding 15 V for 12 minutes or more.

Permanent Short-Circuit Failure. Some silicon solar cells may permanently short when exposed to a combination of high temperature, high reverse bias, and high power dissipation.

Test results of conventional n-p, 2 ohm · cm cells of 2 × 4 cm size and 0.36 mm thickness having SiO anti-reflective coating and soldered Ti-Ag contacts, believed to be applicable to all currently available planar silicon solar cell types, have shown that for cell currents greater than 0.2 A and cell temperatures above −120°C, the probability of a cell shorting is given by the product of the two probability values taken from Figs. 4-24 and 4-25. The actual reverse voltage that may develop across a solar cell depends, of course, not only on the cell's reverse characteristics, but also on a number of operating conditions, as discussed in Section 2-45.

Similar test results to those described above have been obtained on 1977 vintage shallow diffused 10 ohm · cm hybrid cells of 2 × 4 cm size, 0.2 mm thickness, having Ta_2O_5 coating and solderless Ti-Pd-Ag contacts over an aluminum back surface reflector.

OPTICAL CHARACTERISTICS

4-26. Effects of Optical Characteristics on Cell Efficiency

The solar cell's optical characteristics play two distinctly different roles in optimizing operating efficiency. One role is related to maximizing the amount of sunlight that reaches the cell's active region; the other is related to minimizing the solar heating of the cell. Cell characteristics

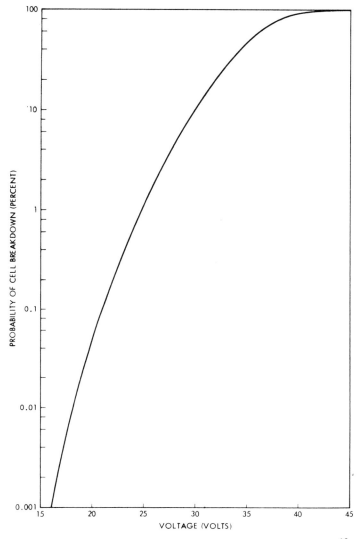

Fig. 4-24. Probability of cell shorting as a function of reverse voltage.[19]

that affect cell-junction illumination include the following: front surface finish (see Section 4-10); anti-reflection coating; spectral response of cell; spectral distribution of sunlight (related to air mass) and wavelength-selective filters placed in front of the cell; and cell energy conversion efficiency. Cell characteristics that affect cell heating include the following: spectral response of cell; spectral distribution of sunlight; spectral reflectivity of glassed cell; cell efficiency; and back surface contact reflective characteristics.

The details of the impact of the solar cell's optical characteristics on array design are given in Chapters 2 and 3. The optical characteristics of covers and filters are discussed in Chapter 5.

4-27. Spectral Response Defined

Solar cell spectral response curves appear in various forms in the literature. The cell output may be shown relative to either the energy falling onto the cell (constant energy input versus wavelength), or the number of photons incident on the cell (constant number of photons versus wavelength).

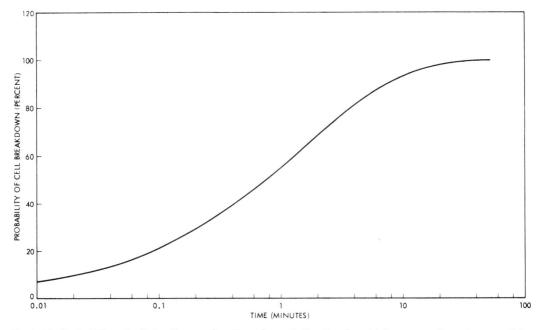

Fig. 4-25. Probability of cell shorting as a function of cumulative time for which reverse voltage stress condition exists.[19]

The cell output may be shown as a function of wavelength, (λ), light frequency (f or $\omega = 2\pi f$), wave number ($N = \lambda^{-1}$ or $2\pi \cdot \lambda^{-1}$), or photon energy.

The spectral response curve of interest to array design engineers is the cell output relative to constant energy input at all wavelengths. The cell output measured in an experimental set-up is typically the I_{sc}, while the energy input is measured with a radiometer-type of instrument. Radiometers (such as thermocouples or thermopiles) measure the product of the incident number of photons per unit of time and per unit area, and the energy of the incident photons. The solar cell I_{sc} output (in amperes) represents the number of minority carriers per unit time collected from the cell area.

A spectral response curve relative to constant numbers of incident photons for all wavelengths is of special interest in solar cell *device* development. Such spectral response curves are frequently called *quantum efficiency* or *collection efficiency* curves. The nomenclature used by different authors is not uniform; however, the tendency is as follows: *quantum efficiency* denotes the number of electron-hole pairs or minority carriers created per photon (having an energy greater than 1.1 eV for silicon cells) incident on the cell or per photon absorbed in the silicon; and *collection efficiency* denotes the number of minority carriers collected by the junction per photon incident on the cell, per photon absorbed in the silicon, or per photon absorbed in a specified region in the cell.

The conversion of constant-number-of-photon spectral response curves into constant-energy curves is illustrated in Fig. 4-26. This figure shows highly idealized spectral response curves of a silicon cell covered with a filter having 0.4 μm cut-on wavelength. To convert the curve of Fig. 4-26a into that of Fig. 4-26b, the value of the cell output at each wavelength is simply divided by the photon energy corresponding to that wavelength. Thereafter, the newly obtained curve is scaled to some convenient vertical scale. (Usually, the peak of the response curve is normalized to 100%.) The relationship between photon energy, wavelength, and wave number is given in Appendix D.

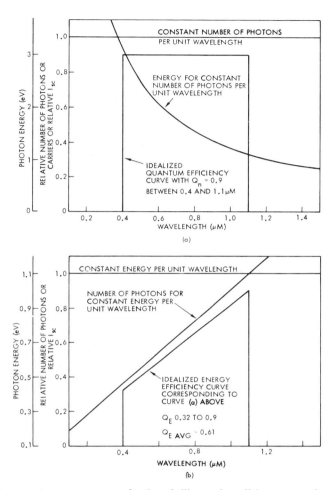

Fig. 4-26. Idealized spectral response curves of a glassed silicon solar cell (cut-on wavelength 0.4 μm; energy gap 1.1 eV corresponding to 1.1 μm wavelength) for (a) constant number of photons per unit wavelength input and (b) constant energy per unit wavelength input).

4-28. Spectral Response of Solar Cells

The sensitivity of single-crystal planar junction silicon solar cells ranges from approximately 0.3 to 1.2 μm. In general, solar cell spectral response characteristics depend heavily on solar cell design, construction, material properties, junction depth, and optical coatings (see Fig. 4-27). Solar cells are practically never used without any filters or covers which further modify the cell response. The solar cell spectral response changes with both temperature and radiation damage. With increasing temperature, the red response of silicon cells increases while the blue response remains approximately con-

stant. This increase in red response is due to both a shift in the "absorption edge" of the silicon around 1.1 μm toward longer wavelengths (below 1.0 μm wavelength, the silicon is absorbent; above 1.2 μm, the silicon is transparent) and an increase in the minority carrier lifetime. The increase in red response results in the observed increase in I_{sc} with increasing temperature (see Fig. 4-28a).

Corpuscular radiation degrades the red response of cells (Fig. 4-28b). The extent of degradation depends upon the particle species and energy. This phenomenon is related to the defect centers introduced into the crystal lattice by the radiation, which, in turn, lowers

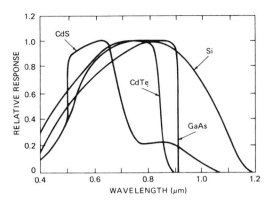

Fig. 4-27. Spectral response of several solar cell types.[20]

the mean diffusion length of the minority carriers. As a consequence of this, the electron-hole pairs created by "red light" photons farther away from the junction than the diffusion length are no longer collected.

Similarly, red response of silicon cells is lost when the cell base width (i.e., cell thickness) is made equal to or smaller than the mean dif-

fusion length (Fig. 4-28c). However, after appreciable corpuscular radiation damage, when the degraded diffusion length is less than the base width, thick and thin cells have the same output (everything else being equal).

Changes in the spectral response of gallium arsenide cells with radiation damage are seen primarily in the blue response of deeper junctions, but in the red response of shallower junctions (Fig. 4-29). Shallower junctions also generally exhibit greater radiation resistance.[24]

MECHANICAL CHARACTERISTICS

4-29. Solar Cell Sizes and Shapes

Space Cells. Solar cells for space use have been square or rectangular in shape to maximize the number of cells that can be packed on a solar panel. The smaller 2×1 cm sizes gave way to 2×2 cm cells in the mid-1960's. In the early 1970's, 2×4 cm and 2×6 cm cells became available. Most larger solar cell arrays today utilize 2×4 cm cells; however, 2×2 cm and

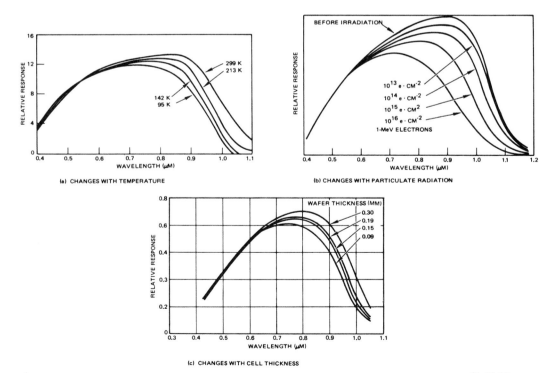

Fig. 4-28. Changes in the spectral response characteristics of silicon cells; illustrative examples.[21,22,23] (Fig. b reprinted with permission of the Pergamon Press.)

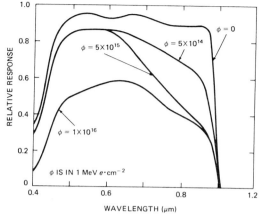

Fig. 4-29. Changes in the spectral response characteristics of gallium arsenide cells with 1 MeV electron irradiation.[24]

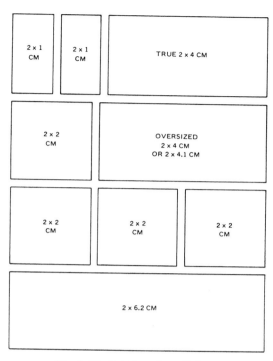

Fig. 4-30. Relative solar cell sizes.

2 × 6 cm cells are also used. Sizes up to 10 × 10 cm have been made experimentally. Smaller quantities of 1 × 1 cm, 2 × 3 cm, and 3 × 3 cm also have been produced; 2 × 6 cm is the largest currently practical size. Frequently, "nominally" 2 × 4 cm and 2 × 6 cm size cells are actually cut to 2 × 4.1 cm and 2 × 6.2 cm size. This "oversizing" in the long direction (i.e., electrically in the parallel direction) permits the interchangeable use of either a larger number of smaller cells or a smaller number of larger cells connected in parallel for a particular solar cell layout drawing without having to change the drawing. The "oversized" cells either may be equivalent to the output of the number of 2 × 2 cm cells which they can replace, or it may be greater by the ratio of the increased active cell area (typically 2 to 4% greater). Some relative solar cell sizes are illustrated in Fig. 4-30.

Terrestrial Cells. Solar cells for terrestrial use are shaped square, rectangular, circular, quarter-circular, hexagonal, and circular with flats. Most terrestrial cells used today are either of the rectangular or of the circular shape, but apparently dimensions have not been standardized. Rectangular cells, built in quantities, measure 50 × 38 mm and 20 × 20 mm. Round cells built in quantity are typically 25, 51, 54, 57, and 76 mm in diameter.

Solar cells in the larger sizes tend to be lower in cost per unit cell area, but also lower in efficiency. In the larger cells, material defects, leading to internal power losses, appear to play a greater role than in smaller cells; at least smaller cells permit more economical culling out the low-performance end of the manufacturing distribution.

4-30. Cell Thicknesses

Earlier space and terrestrial silicon cells were made as thick as 0.5 mm (0.02 inch). During the 1970's, most space cells ranged in thickness between 0.20 and 0.30 mm (0.008 to 0.012 inch). Most current terrestrial cells range between 0.2 and 0.5 mm. Recently, silicon cells of nominally 0.050 mm (0.002 inch) have been developed and produced in pilot line quantities.

As silicon cells are made thinner and thinner, power output and material costs decrease while handling costs and breakage increase. The lowest cost space cells having the highest power-to-weight ratio are approximately 0.25 mm thick. The decrease in power output is illustrated in Figs. 4-31 and 4-32. This reduction in output arises primarily from a reduction in the cell's

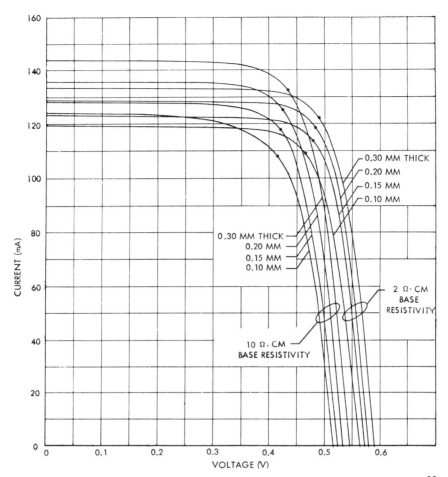

Fig. 4-31. *I–V* curves of thin non-field silicon solar cells at one solar constant AM0 and 28°C.[25] (Reprinted with permission of the IEEE.)

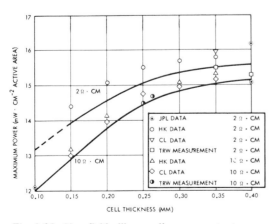

Fig. 4-32. Non-field silicon cell power output versus base thickness (one solar constant AM0 intensity and 28°C cell temperature.[25,26]

red response (see Section 4-28), but can be compensated for by introducing a p$^+$ field at the cell's back side.

Charged particle irradiation of solar cells decreases their minority carrier lifetime. Hence, the cell thickness at which the effect on power output becomes noticeable moves toward lower values of cell thickness with increasing radiation dosage, as shown in Fig. 4-33.

4-31. Active Area

The active area, A_c (or light-sensitive area), of a solar cell is always smaller than the junction area of a planar cell. Some of the junction area, by necessity, is covered with electrical contacts and so-called *grid lines* or *fingers*, which aid in

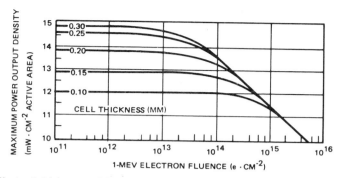

Fig. 4-33. Effects of thickness and fluence on conventional non-p$^+$ silicon solar cell performance.[26]

the electrical power collection from the illuminated active cell area. The quoted efficiency of solar cells is not a unique number, in that sometimes it is calculated based on the total overall cell area (4 cm^2 for a 2 × 2 cm cell), while at other times it is based on only the net active, non-contact-bearing solar cell front area (3.7 cm^2 for a 2 × 2 cm cell). In most cases, however, it is based on the so-called "active" area, including the grid lines but excluding the n-contact bar (3.8 cm^2 for a 2 × 2 cm cell). To avoid such ambiguity, solar cell output should be quoted in terms of actual output power at a given cell temperature, light intensity, and spectrum, such as "50 mW at 28°C, one solar constant, AM0 (Air Mass Zero)," for example.

The output of solar cells changes as both the active and the total area are changed. The parameters I_{sc}, P_{mp}, and I_{mp} increase very nearly proportionately with an increase in active area, while V_{mp} and V_{oc} remain very nearly constant. Small deviations from true proportionality occur because the active solar cell area is in practice shunted by two electrical paths: a non-illuminated forward biased diode path under the cell contact areas on the front (active) side, and a leakage path through the shunt resistance.

CONTACTS

4-32. Solar Cell Contact Types

Solar cell contacts are metallizations on the solar cell p- and n-type semiconductor surfaces which permit the making of low-resistance electrical connections to the cell, typically by sol-

dering or welding of solar cell interconnectors (see Chapter 5) to the cell contacts.

To minimize internal electrical losses in the cell, the electrical resistance of the cell contacts should be low, the electrical resistance of the semiconductor-to-contact interface should be low, and the semiconductor-to-contact interface should not form a junction (known as a Schottky barrier). Contacts that are free of Schottky barriers have the same linear current-voltage characteristics in either direction of current flow; i.e., they are *purely ohmic*. On most cells, Schottky barriers become noticeable only at low temperatures causing non-linear temperature coefficients of voltage and power.

The term *ohmic contact* or simply *ohmic*, is frequently used to describe the upper contact bar (but not the grid lines) of "gridded" solar cells. Sometimes, but less frequently, the back contact is also referred to as an *ohmic*. In this usage connotation, there exists no relationship to the electrical properties discussed above.

Electroless Nickel Contacts. During the 1950's, the predominant contact application technique was electroless nickel plating of unmasked portions of the otherwise finished silicon solar cell wafer and immersion of the plated cells in soldering flux and liquid solder baths.

Space Cell Contacts. The contacts currently in use on silicon solar cells for space use are vacuum-deposited titanium/silver layers. The titanium, deposited first on the well cleaned silicon surface, is typically 0.1 μm thick. The following silver layer is typically 3 to 5 μm thick. Since the titanium/silver contacts are sensitive to humidity, a thin—typically 20 to 50 nm thick—palladium interlayer between the silver and the titanium is frequently used. This palladium layer has been found to passivate the contacts and grid lines. A thin, soft solder coating of at least 2 μm thickness also protects the contacts and grid lines from humidity, while solar cell anti-reflective coatings such as SiO_x do not provide significant protection from humidity.

Concentrator Cell Contacts. Contacts for terrestrial silicon solar cells to be used in conjunction with concentrators are usually of the chromium-palladium-silver type. These contacts are also applied to the cells by a vacuum deposition process.

Printed Contacts. Contacts for non-concentrator, low-cost terrestrial silicon cells are frequently made by a printing process. A conductive ink or paint, typically containing silver particles, is printed onto wafers and fired into silicon at some elevated temperature. The heating process drives the silver particles through the natural oxide layer on the silicon to establish a good ohmic contact. Experimental attempts to utilize printed-on contacts for space cells showed that such contacts were not stable in the space environment, leading to early and anomalous cell output degradation.

Other Contact Systems. Many other contact systems of interest have been developed, but have not been used on as large a scale as the electroless nickel and titatnium-silver contact systems described above. Except for evaporated and sintered aluminum contacts, all other systems used in the U.S. or in Europe use less economically attractive schemes, and provide only marginally superior contact adhesion and electrical conductivity over the titanium-silver system. The humidity resistance of the titanium-silver system with either palladium passivation or protection by solder is more than adequate for space use, except that solder may impose an undesirable weight penalty.

Soldered Contacts. Cell contacts are delivered either solder-free or solder-covered. Solder-covered contacts may be *dipped* or *pressed*. Dipped solder is typically 75 μm thick. It forms a meniscus when molten, and freezes, with the solder thickness peaking at about 150 μm. Machine or hand pressing of the solder-covered contacts at temperatures above solder melting squeezes out solder. Different solder thicknesses can be obtained, but thickness control is difficult. A clean-up process to remove solder flash may also be required. (Solder thickness control may be required for low-temperature operation, low-energy proton protection, and assembly convenience.)

Weldable Contacts. Certain solderless solar cell interconnector joining operations require a certain smoothness of the contact metallization, the underlying silicon surface, the interconnector material, and the interconnector plating (if a plating is used). The degree of the required smoothness depends upon the following (not in order of importance): stiffness of the cell interconnector, *footprint* area of the joining tool, joining method, joining schedule (joining parameters), and amount of soft metal available to fill crevices in the parts to be bonded.

Various solderless interconnector joining techniques are discussed in Chapter 8. The surface finish currently believed to be required for parallel-gap resistance welding of Ti-Ag and Ti-Pd-Ag contacts is 0.4 μm rms or better, both on the cell and on the interconnector.

4-33. Contact Configurations

Solar cell contact geometries differ from type to type and from one cell manufacturer to another. Each contact type provides advantages and disadvantages during the array assembly. Full-area contacts extend to the cell edge, while *picture frame* contacts are slightly smaller than the cell area and expose active cell area all around the contact bar. *Wrap-around* contact cells have both the p- and n-contacts on their back sides to maximize the active cell area, or on their front sides to ease assembly. Figure 4-34 shows some typical contact configurations.

The original circular Bell Telephone cell had wrap-around contacts; that is, both the n- and p-contacts were on the same solar cell side, the

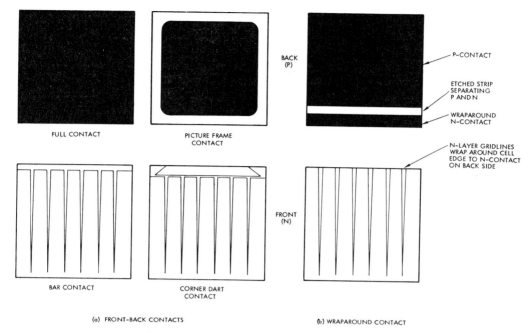

FULL CONTACT

PICTURE FRAME
CONTACT

BACK
(P)

P-CONTACT

ETCHED STRIP
SEPARATING
P AND N

WRAPAROUND
N-CONTACT

N-LAYER GRIDLINES
WRAP AROUND CELL
EDGE TO N-CONTACT
ON BACK SIDE

BAR CONTACT

CORNER DART
CONTACT

FRONT
(N)

(a) FRONT-BACK CONTACTS

(b) WRAPAROUND CONTACT

Fig. 4-34. Some solar cell contact configurations.

back side. By 1958, space applications forced cell shapes to be rectangular or square for enhanced packing density, and cell internal resistance forced the contacts to be placed on each of the respective cell sides; i.e., the n-contact on the cell n-side, the p-contact on the p-side. By 1964, wrap-around contacts had reappeared, but this time for the purpose of utilizing more active cell area for energy conversion for the rectangular and square cells. However, significantly increased cell efficiency did not materialize from wrap-around contact cells, because internal losses increased at nearly the same rate at which the active cell area was increased. For ultralightweight solar cell arrays, wrap-around contacts on the front side appear to offer advantages in controlling weight and speeding assembly.

4-34. Contact Strength

Contact strength is the capability of metallizations to adhere to the solar cell semiconductor material. The purpose of the metallic contacts is two-fold: to establish permanent, low-electrical loss interfaces between metallic circuit conductors and the semiconductor material,

and to provide convenient areas to which solar cell interconnectors can be attached.

High mechanical contact strength is not necessarily synonymous with good electrical properties of the contact, but, in most cases, tests of contact strengths permit assessment of potential solar cell problems, which, in turn, can negatively influence the solar cell array assembly processes and the array performance. For this reason, solar cell contact pull-strength tests have become one of the most important tests (next to electrical output testing) for monitoring and assuring adequate solar cell and array quality.

Contact strength is measured in two ways: 1) during the cell manufacturing cycle, vacuum-deposited metallizations are tape-peel tested; and 2) after the cell manufacture has been completed, pull-strength tests are performed. For pull-strength testing, wires or ribbons are soldered or welded to the cell contacts and a force is applied to separate the wires or ribbons from the cell. The direction of application of this pull-force relative to the cell surface ranges from 0° (shear loading) to 90° (peel loading for thin wires and ribbons, or tensile loading for thick wires and ribbons). A 45° pull test is believed by some to cause the most realistic mixture of shear and peel loading by soldered joints, simulating actual stresses of interconnectors on solar cells in service. At any rate, a good correlation between the actual stresses on the cell contacts when assembled in a solar cell array and the stresses imposed by pull test methods has not been reported. The practice has been to maximize the solar cell contact strength during the solar cell manufacturing process and, for array assembly quality assurance purposes, to establish certain minimum strength requirements using specific test methods and procedures. These test methods usually have meaning only in the context for which they were established. As a consequence, most pull test data are presented in the literature in units of force rather than force per unit area, and the size of the bond area is usually not stated. This is justifiable, since in most practical tests, a reasonable uniform contact loading cannot be achieved. The factors which can affect the contact pull strength are presented in Table 4-3.

The true contact strength of solderless *welded* joints is very difficult to measure, in that even small bending moments applied by the test equipment via the interconnector to the typically very small weld nugget in many cases caused the tensile strength of the silicon to be exceeded and the silicon to spall during the test. For this reason, shear loading of the contacts leads to more realistic contact integrity assessment.

Effects of Temperature. The contact test pull-strength varies with temperature. This phenomenon is of interest because most solar cell arrays operate at temperatures other than room temperature, and the stresses and material properties under actual operating conditions may be quite different from those observed in near room temperature pull-strength testing. It was found[27] that the 90° pull-strength is greatest between 0° and –100°C and falls off rapidly below –100°C and above 0°C (Fig. 4-35). The fall-off at higher temperatures is expected due to a reduction in the strength of solder. The fall-off at lower temperatures is also expected, but is due to an increase in the strength of solder and associated prestressing of the silicon.

Table 4-3. Factors Influencing Contact Pull Strength.

Soldered Joints	Welded Joints
Solder joint area	Weld nugget area
Solder thickness on contact	Metallization thickness on contact weld nugget area
Solder fillet cross section	Ribbon thickness, ductility, and stiffness
Wire or ribbon thickness and stiffness	Ribbon surface roughness and plating thickness
Angle and rate of pull force	Angle and rate of pull force
	Surface roughness of silicon wafer underneath weld area

This thermally induced prestress reduces the silicon's capability to support external tensile loads and leads predominantly to silicon spalling during pull testing at low temperature.

RADIATION EFFECTS

4-35. Solar Cell Radiation Damage

Solar cells, like all semiconductor devices, are subject to permanent electrical degradation when exposed to *particulate* radiation, also known as *corpuscular* radiation. Of interest to space array designers are the effects of electrons and protons, and, to a lesser extent, of gamma rays and neutrons. Electrons and protons are also called *charged particles*. The comparative damage, expressed as degradation of short-circuit current density (short-circuit current per unit active cell area), is shown in Fig. 4-36. While this graph shows data for conventional 10 ohm · cm cells, measured under simulated one AM0 solar constant intensity, it can be taken as generally applicable for all contemporary n/p non-field and non-p$^+$ silicon cells of 0.2 to 0.3 mm thickness.

Effects of Electrons, Gamma Rays, and X-Rays. Solar cells and other materials subject to electron, gamma, or X-ray radiation experience an atomic process known as *ionization*. The incident particles or photons collide with atoms in the crystal lattice and liberate otherwise bound electrons from them (see Section 2-27). Thus, the irradiation of solar cells by the above radia-

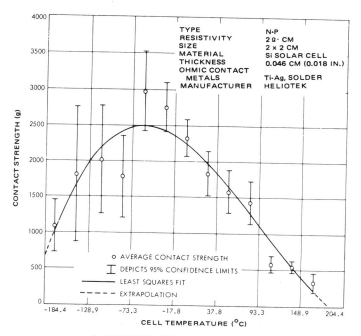

(a) N-CONTACT STRENGTH (90-DEGREE PULL)

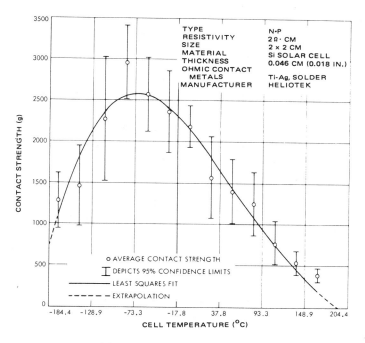

(b) P-CONTACT STRENGTH (90-DEGREE PULL)

Fig. 4-35. Contact pull strength of solder-coated titanium-silver contact, n-on-p solar cells as a function of temperature.[27]

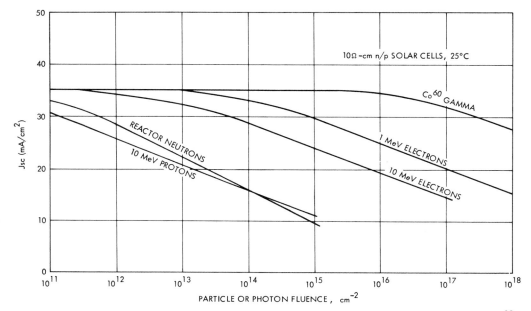

Fig. 4-36. Variation of silicon solar cell short-circuit current density with fluence for various radiations.[28]

tion species gives rise to a photocurrent that is, like the light-generated current, proportional to the number of incident particles or photons. The excess energy of the radiation species is so great, however, that their energy is not only converted into heat, but may dislodge atoms from their regular position in the crystal lattice, causing *displacement damage*. In silicon, the displaced atoms undergo some other atomic processes that proceed at a rate depending upon the cell's temperature until, after some time, measured in hours or days, equilibrium is established. The displacement sites are electrically active, causing a reduction in the minority carrier diffusion lengths and lifetimes in the cell's base region, manifested by a reduction in the cell's output current, voltage, and power.

In organic material, the ionization process causes destruction of molecular bonds, resulting in the darkening (discoloration) of clear materials and generally a deterioration of the mechanical properties of the material. Coverglass materials darken similarly.

Effects of Protons. Protons produce similar effects as electrons, except that the displacement damage they produce is several orders of magnitude larger than that produced by electrons. Furthermore, as the protons lose their energy inside a material by collision with its atoms and finally come to rest, they produce the largest damage just before they reach the end of their travel.

Effects of Neutrons. In silicon, neutrons do most of their damage upon entering the material. Neutrons are of interest only in connection with warfare in space.

Radiation Resistance. This is also known as *radiation tolerance* or *hardness*. The terms are frequently used in radiation studies of semiconductors. Most often, these terms denote a value of particle fluence at which a device parameter has degraded to a specific fraction (usually 75%) of its original value. This fluence is also known as the *critical fluence*. These terms are of little interest to solar cell array designers because the relative degradation (or lack thereof) is not important. Rather, the absolute values of the solar cell performance parameters, after the cell has received a specific value of particle fluence, are important.

4-36. Damage-Equivalent 1 MeV Fluence

For analytical and test convenience, the concept of damage-equivalent, normally-incident, mono-energetic 1 MeV fluence, or, in brief, *1 MeV fluence*, has been developed. The actual damage produced in silicon solar cells by electrons of various energies is related to the damage produced by 1 MeV electrons by the so-called *damage coefficients for electrons*.

Similarly, the damage produced by protons of various energies is related to the damage produced by 10 MeV protons by the *damage coefficients for protons*. The damage produced by 10 MeV protons is, in turn, related to the damage produced by 1 MeV electrons by a single damage conversion factor. One 10 MeV proton does approximately the same damage as 3000 electrons of 1 MeV energy. Conversion factors ranging from 2000 to 7000 have been used for various silicon cell types by different investigators; however, the value of 3000 was recently verified for high-efficiency hybrid cells.

Electrons damage solar cells such that a single value of equivalent 1 MeV fluence can be used to describe the degradation of cell currents and voltages.

Typical solar cell *I–V* curves before and after exposure to a heavy dose (approximately 10^{15} $e \cdot cm^{-2}$) of 1 MeV electrons are illustrated in Fig. 4-12. This figure also illustrates an increase in the temperature coefficient for I_{sc} and no change in the temperature coefficients for V_{oc} and V_{mp} with radiation.

Protons damage solar cells such that two different values of equivalent 1 MeV fluence must be used; one value is used to describe the degradation of cell currents and another value is used to describe the degradation of cell voltages.

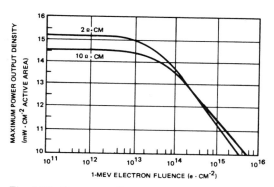

Fig. 4-37. Cross-over fluence of conventional, 0.25 mm thick solar cells with SiO coating.[26]

At the cross-over fluence (Fig. 4-37), both 2 and 10 ohm · cm cells have the same power output (cell area and thickness being assumed to be the same). The cross-over point generally falls within a fluence range between 1×10^{14} and 1×10^{16} $e \cdot cm^{-2}$ of 1 MeV energy and depends heavily on the initial output (efficiency) of the cells being compared.

An optimum base resistivity can be defined at which the absolute cell output is greatest after a given radiation dose.[29] Figure 4-38 shows that absolute power output after irradiation is a mild function of base resistivity. Therefore, optimizing base resistivity is of little engineering significance, and rather broad tolerances of the base resistivity are permissible. Typical tolerance ranges are shown below.

Nominal	Range
1 or 2 ohm · cm	1 to 3 ohm · cm
10 ohm · cm	7 to 14 ohm · cm

4-37. Effects of Base Resistivity

Choice of the solar cell material base resistivity affects both the pre-irradiation energy conversion efficiency (see Fig. 4-32) and the cell radiation resistance of non-field silicon cells. An increase in the base resistivity lowers the efficiency while it increases the radiation resistance. A consequence of this cell behavior is that for low-fluence missions, low-base resistivity (1 to 3 ohm · cm) cells provide the largest output; while for high-fluence missions, high-base resistivity (7 to 14 ohm · cm) cells provide the highest output at end-of-life.

4-38. Low-Energy Proton Damage

Low-energy proton damage to solar cells causes shunting of the p-n junction, independent of minority carrier lifetime considerations. Low-energy proton damage can occur in one of two ways: from medium- or higher-energy protons having sufficient energy to just penetrate the solar cell covers or contact metallizations, or from lower-energy protons incident directly on the solar cells in small gap areas that are not protected by the solar cell covers or contacts.

The number of protons that can be expected to penetrate solar cell covers are usually of no

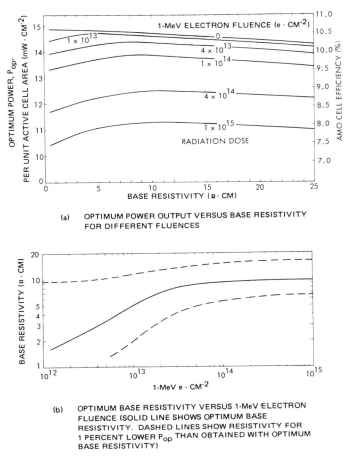

(a)   OPTIMUM POWER OUTPUT VERSUS BASE RESISTIVITY
FOR DIFFERENT FLUENCES

(b)   OPTIMUM BASE RESISTIVITY VERSUS 1-MeV ELECTRON
FLUENCE (SOLID LINE SHOWS OPTIMUM BASE
RESISTIVITY. DASHED LINES SHOW RESISTIVITY FOR
1 PERCENT LOWER P_{op} THAN OBTAINED WITH OPTIMUM
BASE RESISTIVITY)

Fig. 4-38. Effects of varying base resistivity on power output.[29] (*Reprinted with permission of the IEEE.*)

significance in most orbits except in those which are in the radiation belts. However, the number of low-energy protons that can potentially damage solar cells directly are available in great abundance not only in the radiation belts, but also above them and at synchronous altitude. The proton energy levels of concern are in the 100 to 500 keV range when incident on the silicon front surface, and up to approximately 5 MeV when incident on the front of coverglasses.

Protons which come to rest (i.e. lose all their energy) near the solar cell p-n junction introduce shunt paths across the junction. These shunts cause the cell output to degrade significantly more than the ratio of the damaged cell area to the total cell area may indicate. The shunt defect induced by low-energy protons has a diode-like current-voltage characteristic

which leads to a relatively small loss in I_{sc} and to progressively larger losses toward P_{mp} and V_{oc}.[30] This is indicated by the *loss function* of Fig. 4-39.

The low-energy proton damage mechanism was discovered on several satellites in synchronous orbit, and was verified by extensive ground testing. Excessive orbital degradation due to low-energy proton damage had been as large as approximately 20%.

The results of numerous investigations with regard to low-energy proton damage in geosynchronous orbit have shown the following:

- Even small, unprotected areas (in the order of 1%) can lead to excessive output degradation (in the order of 10% at P_{mp})
- Small, unprotected strips of cell area parallel to the n-contact collector bar are several

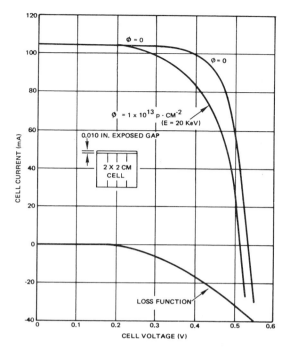

Fig. 4-39. Solar cell current loss function curve.[39]

times more damaging than unprotected strips away from the n-contact.

- The entire active cell area not covered by metallic contacts should be protected by the coverglass.

(For design implementation of full cell coverage by covers, see Chapter 3.)

4-39. Radiation Damage Annealing and Output Instabilities

In general, the crystalline damage and associated electrical degradation sustained by a solar cell during exposure to corpuscular radiation is not totally stable. Two phenomena have been observed on irradiated cells: damage annealing and further degradation during exposure to sunlight.[31, 32]

Damage annealing occurs only at temperatures above approximately 20°C, and tends to be more significant for proton and neutron irradiated cells than for electron irradiated cells. The observed magnitude in recovery of the solar cell power output after 1 MeV electron irradiation ranges from zero to a few percent (typically less than 5%). Higher annealing

temperatures (up to approximately 100°C) accelerate the annealing process, but do not appear to change the amount of possible recovery.

Damage annealing was found to occur only in solar cells made from crucible-grown silicon, the typical process used in the U.S. for producing solar cell material.

Analysis of orbital flight data (Chapter 1) has verified that a part of the solar cell output lost due to solar flare proton events is regained after some time.

Photon Effects. Solar cells that have experienced electrical degradation during irradiation with charged particles may either degrade further or recover during subsequent long-term illumination (photon irradiation). A further electrical degradation can be expected in all solar cells fabricated from float-zone refined silicon that was typically used in Europe during the 1960's and early 1970's. Typical contemporary solar cells can be expected to exhibit some small instability problems, both in unirradiated and irradiated solar cells. This may have an inpact on the ultimate solar cell calibration accuracy that can be achieved, especially with 1 ohm · cm, crucible-grown silicon cells, which may be unstable, and should therefore not be used as standard solar cells.

The light (photon) induced degradation in the output of 1 ohm · cm and 10 ohm · cm float-zone silicon and of 10 ohm · cm crucible-grown silicon cells (before particle irradiation) is typically less than 1%, causing a loss in both the minority carrier lifetime and the cell's red response. This leads to the conclusion that lifetime is not a constant material property as heretofore assumed, but rather depends strongly on thermal and light exposure history of the material. Photon irradiation immediately after 1 MeV electron irradiation to a fluence of 1×10^{15} $e \cdot cm^{-2}$ resulted in the further degradation of 10 ohm · cm float-zone and 1 ohm · cm crucible grown silicon cells, but led to recovery of the 10 ohm · cm crucible-grown and 1 ohm · cm float-zone silicon cells.[31]

Recent tests of crucible-grown 10 ohm · cm silicon, n/p, shallow-diffused hybrid cells, made by OCLI and Spectrolab, have shown between 0 and 5% recovery of power output after 48 hours exposure to light following exposure to 1×10^{15} $e \cdot cm^{-2}$ of 1 MeV energy.[33]

PRACTICAL CONSIDERATIONS

4-40. Glassed Cell Output

The power output from, or the efficiency of, solar cells measured in the unglassed condition becomes meaningful only when related to the *glassed* condition. For space arrays, glassing consists of the application of a coverslip. For terrestrial arrays, "glassing" consists of encapsulating the solar cell in the entire optically transparent package. To assess the effect of glassing, the so-called *glassing factor*, F_G, has been defined as

$$F_G = \frac{I_{sc} \text{ (glassed)}}{I_{sc} \text{ (unglassed)}} .$$

(Numerical values for F_G are given in Chapter 5.)

4-41. Distribution of Parameters

The solar cell performance data shown in this chapter is *averaged* data. Actually, in any lot of solar cells that is manufactured, some cells show lower-than-average, others high-than-average performance. This variation is known as the *statistical distribution* of parameters (see also *mismatch losses*).

4-42. Handling Precautions

Silicon solar cells of 0.2 mm thickness or greater, up to 2×4 cm in size, are relatively rugged devices; however, they require some care in handling. Silicon is a brittle material and breaks approximately as readily as glass. The most damage-sensitive portions are the peripheral edge of planar junction cells where the junction is exposed. Even small scratches can reduce the fill factor and thereby degrade the cell output.

Textured ("black") and vertical junction cells are more easily damaged than are planar junction cells and require extra care in handling and assembly, especially in parallel-gap welding. Even minor scratches can cause major power output degradation.

Generally, soldering of silicon solar cell contacts is easily and safely accomplished as long as the heat application process is controlled. (For potential contact damage from soldering or welding, see Chapter 8.)

4-43. Storage

Solar cells may require storage precautions. Silicon solar cells can be stored indefinitely under almost any storage conditions except for precautions that must be taken to protect the solar cell contacts. The two potential problems with presently manufactured solar cell contact systems are 1) corrosion in high-humidity, elevated temperature environments; and 2) silver tarnishing of solderless contacts prior to assembly. Corrosion protection for ten years or longer periods consists of desiccated containers or plastic bags that are limited to 50% relative humidity accumulation and storage at normal air-conditioned room temperatures (typically 25°C maximum). Silver tarnishing is prevented by packing susceptible solar cells in sulfide absorbing materials such as "Silver Saver" paper.

SOLAR CELL PERFORMANCE DATA

4-44. Solar Cell Space Flight Experiments

A number of spacecraft carried flight experiments to study the environmental degradation of solar cells in space and compare it with degradation observed in laboratory testing. A summary of the results obtained in the flight experiments follows.

Nimbus-2.[34] This spacecraft was launched on May 15, 1966, into a near-circular, 1111 km, high-noon, sun-synchronous orbit. The solar cell radiation experiment consisted of two equally illuminated coplanar panels, each having 30 series-connected solar cells bonded to an aluminum honeycomb substrate. The cells on the panel were provided with 0.15 mm thick fused silica covers; the other cells had 2.54 mm thick fused silica covers. The covers were bonded to the cells with Furane 15E adhesive. Each solar cell was loaded with a 1.46 ohm resistance near the short circuit. Solar cells were

1 ohm · cm, n-on-p silicon cells, manufactured for the Nimbus-2 solar array by RCA.

Figure 4-40 shows that for the orbital degradation of the cells with 0.15 mm covers follows the predicted curve reasonably well. For the 2.54 mm covers, the orbital degradation is significantly above the prediction. Because slightly undersized 2.54 mm thick covers were used, this excessive degradation was attributed to low-energy proton damage. Neither the 0.15 mm experiment, the 2.54 mm experiment, nor the satellite's solar cell array (also having 0.15 mm thick covers) showed the expected 3 or 4% decrease in current during the first 100 hours of sunlight exposure due to ultraviolet degradation of the coverglass-filter-adhesive solar cell combination.

ATS-1.[35, 36] The ATS-1 spacecraft was launched on December 7, 1966. The spacecraft executed one and one-half transfer ellipses (perigee: 185 km; apogee: 42, 600 km; period: 15 hours) before entering its final circular, near-synchronous equatorial orbit at 41, 190 km altitude. The final station was over the Pacific equator at 157° west longitude. The spacecraft was spin stabilized at about 100 rpm.

The solar cells of the experiment were all nominally 1 X 2 cm, conventional, 0.30 mm thick, silicon, boron-doped, n-on-p, SiO coated, and of nominally 10 ohm · cm base resistivity. Pairs of cells were fitted with 0, 0.025, 0.15, 0.38, 0.76 and 1.76, and 1.52 mm thick shields. Except for the 0.025 mm thick "integral" type (7740 glass powder melted to cover the cells), all shields were Corning type 7940 fused silica, attached with Dow-Corning XR-6-3488 adhesive. These shields had blue rejection filters with a 400 nm cut-on wavelength.

The experimental data is shown in Table 4-4, averaged over the two cells in each pair. The initial values were read 0.064 days after lift-off and were assumed to be undegraded. Figure 4-41 illustrates the rapid degradation of Cell No. 25 compared to the typical degradation of Cell No. 5, shown in Fig. 4-42. Degradation of Cell No. 20, shown in Fig. 4-43, was relatively high for its shield thickness. Figs. 4-44 and 4-45 illustrate the observed data trends. The experimenter made the conclusions below.

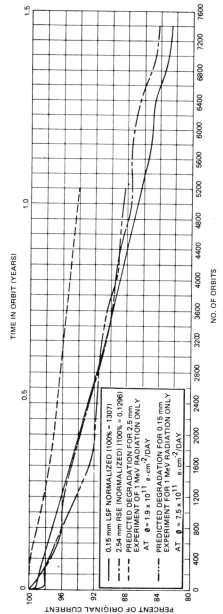

Fig. 4-40. Normalized current loss versus orbit for two Nimbus-2 solar cell experiments.[20]

Table 4-4. ATS-1 Flight Experiments Solar Cell Performance.

(Reprinted with permission of the IEEE).[36]

1	2	3	4	5	6	7	8	9	10	11
Cell No.	Shield Material	Shield Thickness (mm)	Time After Lift-Off (days)	I_{sc} (mA)	V_{oc} (mV)	P_{mp} (mW)	Fill Factor	$\frac{I_{sc}}{I_{sc0}}$ (%)	$\frac{V_{oc}}{V_{oc0}}$ (%)	$\frac{P_{mp}}{P_{mp0}}$ (%)
25, 26	None	0.0	0.064	70.3	548.3	26.7	0.694	100.0	100.0	100.0
		0.0	3.28	61.5	425.8	16.9	0.644	87.6	77.7	63.0
		0.0	20.3	(55.0)	330.6	10.3	(0.566)	(78.3)	60.3	38.5
		0.0	100.7	(44.5)	311.9	6.3	(0.458)	(63.4)	56.9	23.8
		0.0	270.4	(34.5)	305.1	4.0	(0.383)	(49.2)	55.7	15.0
		0.0	416.8	(29.0)	301.6	3.1	(0.349)	(41.4)	55.0	11.4
15, 16	7740 Glass	0.025	0.064	62.4	544.0	24.5	0.722	100.0	100.0	100.0
		0.025	3.28	61.6	540.0	24.4	0.735	98.7	99.3	97.6
		0.025	20.3	60.8	538.7	23.8	0.729	97.4	99.0	97.4
		0.025	100.7	59.0	536.8	22.0	0.694	94.5	98.7	89.6
		0.025	270.4	57.2	531.8	21.4	0.702	91.7	97.8	87.4
		0.025	416.8	56.2	528.8	20.8	0.699	90.1	97.2	84.9
5, 6	7940 Fused Silica	0.15	0.064	67.9	558.7	27.5	0.724	100.0	100.0	100.0
		0.15	3.28	67.0	560.3	28.1	0.749	98.6	100.3	102.1
		0.15	20.3	65.9	559.5	27.3	0.743	97.0	100.2	97.7
		0.15	100.7	64.9	555.4	26.2	0.727	95.6	99.4	95.5
		0.15	270.4	63.2	552.5	25.6	0.736	93.0	98.9	93.5
		0.15	416.8	62.2	552.4	25.4	0.739	91.7	98.9	92.5
23, 24	7940 Fused Silica	0.38	0.064	67.7	560.0	27.1	0.714	100.0	100.0	100.0
		0.38	3.28	67.9	563.0	28.1	0.736	100.4	100.2	103.5
		0.38	20.3	66.4	560.3	26.3	0.707	98.2	99.7	96.9
		0.38	100.7	65.4	557.6	25.9	0.709	96.7	99.3	95.2
		0.38	270.4	63.8	555.6	25.0	0.704	94.4	98.9	91.9
		0.38	416.8	62.7	554.6	24.1	0.692	92.7	98.7	88.7
21, 22	7940 Fused Silica	0.76	0.064	69.6	558.8	28.0	0.719	100.0	100.0	100.0
		0.76	3.28	69.1	561.2	28.2	0.729	99.3	100.5	101.1
		0.76	20.3	67.6	555.7	26.9	0.715	97.2	99.5	96.1
		0.76	100.7	66.5	554.1	25.9	0.704	95.6	99.2	92.7
		0.76	270.4	65.6	554.0	25.2	0.695	94.4	99.2	90.3
		0.76	416.8	64.5	551.3	24.3	0.683	92.6	98.7	86.9
20	7940 Fused Silica	1.52	0.064	69.2	563.1	28.4	0.729	100.0	100.0	100.0
		1.52	3.28	68.6	564.0	28.2	0.729	99.1	100.2	99.3
		1.52	20.3	68.2	560.1	27.0	0.707	98.6	99.5	95.1
		1.52	100.7	66.9	557.5	25.4	0.681	96.7	99.0	89.4
		1.52	270.4	66.1	559.4	24.4	0.660	95.5	99.3	85.9
		1.52	416.8	65.0	553.5	23.8	0.660	93.9	98.3	83.5

NOTE: Data normalized to 1.00 AU solar distance, 24.4°C, operating temperature, and perpendicular sunlight incidence.

1. The solar cell degradation was greater than that expected from the particle environment.
2. Unprotected solar cells degraded significantly during three passages through the radiation belts during the launch procedure.
3. The degradation in power of the more heavily shielded cells was relatively large compared to degradation in short-circuit current or open-circuit voltage.
4. The above conclusion points to a damage mechanism (among others) in which series resistance developed within the cell, possibly at the unshielded areas near contacts, by some action not ordinarily considered in radiation damage studies.
5. Cells bearing 6 mil shields degraded, in power, less than cells bearing either thicker or thinner shields.
6. Thicker shields were effective in protecting the cells against degradation in short-circuit current.
7. Short-circuit current was not a valid indicator of solar cell damage under the conditions of this experiment.
8. To qualitatively account for the shape of the various voltage-current curves, it is necessary to postulate various combinations of a) illumination decrease; b) par-

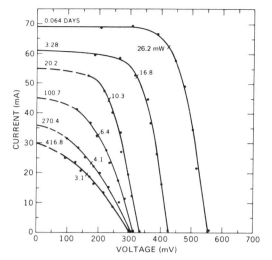

Fig. 4-41. A voltage-current family for Unshielded Cell No. 25.[36] (*Reprinted with permission of the IEEE.*)

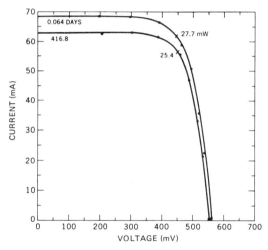

Fig. 4-42. Voltage-current curves for Cell 5, with a 0.15 mm silica (7940) shield.[36] (*Reprinted with permission of the IEEE.*)

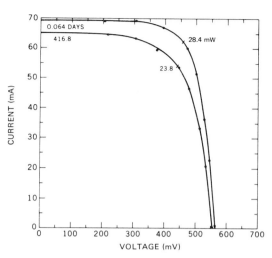

Fig. 4-43. Voltage-current curves for Cell 20, with a 1.52 mm silica (7940) shield.[36] (*Reprinted with permission of the IEEE.*)

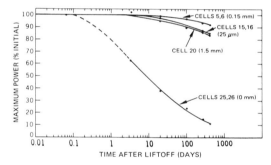

Fig. 4-44. Maximum power versus time for several cells with various shields.[36] (*Reprinted with permission of the IEEE.*)

ticle radiation damage; and c) a mechanism introducing large power losses, in the maximum power region, for heavily shielded cells.

LES-6.[37,40] The sixth Lincoln Laboratory Experimental Satellite (LES-6) was launched into a synchronous orbit on September 26, 1968. Through 1975, I-V characteristics were measured on 30 experimental solar cells, none of which are currently available from their manufacturers. Further research and development on these cell types has been in progress for many years. For this reason, the flight data are not reproduced here.

ATS-5.[41,42] The ATS-5 satellite was launched into synchronous orbit on August 12, 1969. The experiment consisted of 65 solar cells whose I-V curves could be measured. Some of the cells were mounted on a rigid honeycomb substrate and others on a flexible Kapton/glass cloth film substrate that was exposed to radiation from both sides. The satellite failed to achieve its intended gravity stabilized mode and, thereby, reduced the accuracy of the flight

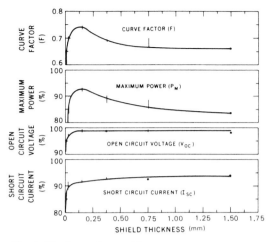

Fig. 4-45. Curve factor (F), maximum power (P_{mp}), open-circuit voltage (V_{oc}), and short-circuit current (I_{sc}) versus shield thickness, at 416 days after lift-off.[36] (*Reprinted with permission of the IEEE.*)

data. A large solar flare, 82 days after launch, caused significant solar cell degradation before a baseline output measurement could be made in orbit, causing an additional uncertainty in the orbital data. Failure of an on-board signal processor within the first month in orbit caused one-half of the solar cell data to be lost. Nevertheless, significant amounts of data could be gathered with only slightly impaired accuracy.

The solar cells were conventional, production type single crystal, n-on-p, boron-doped silicon, representing 1967 technology. Junction depth was about 0.5 μm. The cells were SiO coated and had Ti-Ag contacts. Some contacts were solderless, others solder-dipped. Cells of 2 ohm · cm base resistivity were 0.20 mm thick

and were covered by 0.15 mm thick fused silica. Cells of 10 ohm · cm base resistivity were 0.30 mm thick and were covered by 0.15, 0.30, 0.51, or 1.52 mm thick fused silica. All covers carried anti-reflective coatings and ultraviolet filters having 410 nm cut-on wavelength. Cover adhesive was RTV-602. Some of the 10 ohm · cm cells with 0.30 mm thick covers purposely had an 0.38 mm wide strip along the n-contact bar left unprotected by the coverglass.

The cells mounted to the rigid substrate were essentially shielded from all radiation incident from the back side. The cells on the flexible substrate received radiation through the back side after having penetrated an 0.025 mm thick Kapton H-film, which was bonded to an 0.025 mm thick type 108 fiberglass scrimcloth.

For comparison, unglassed solar cells of the same type were irradiated in the laboratory with unidirectional 1 MeV electrons. After annealing for 5 minutes at 100°C, the cell output was as depicted in Fig. 4-46. The equivalent 1 MeV fluence in synchronous orbit was calculated to be as shown in Table 4-5, using the AE-4 trapped electron and AP-5 trapped proton environments (see Section 9-48). Low-energy proton tests of glassed 10 ohm · cm cells with 0.43 mm wide bar contact gaps, simulating the AP-5 environment, showed the results given in Table 4-6.

After 6.5 years of orbital data gathering, data reduction, and comparison with predictions based on ground test data (Fig. 4-47), the following conclusions were made.

1. The solar cells on the rigid substrate de-

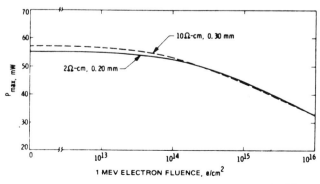

Fig. 4-46. Results of laboratory radiation tests at one solar constant AM0, 25°C.[42] (*Reprinted with permission of the IEEE.*)

Table 4-5. Equivalent 1 MeV Fluence Components for Trapped and Solar Flare Radiation in Synchronous Orbit.*

(Reprinted with permission of the IEEE.)[42]

	Coverslide Thickness (mm)					
	0	0.025	0.15	0.30	0.51	1.52
Trapped electrons from AE4 ($e \cdot cm^{-2} \cdot$ year)	4.9 E + 13	4.4 E + 13	2.98 E + 13	2.14 E + 13	1.48 E + 13	3.58 E + 12
Trapped protons from (AP5) ($e \cdot cm^{-2} \cdot$ year)	1.43 E + 25		5.31 E + 02	9.15 E – 02	0	0
8/4/72 Flare ($e \cdot cm^{-2}$)	2.6 E + 14	1.35 E + 14	6.6 E + 13	4.8 E + 13	3.7 E + 13	2.3 E + 13

*The notation E + 13 means 10^{13}, etc.

Table 4-6. Solar Cell Degradation Due to Irradiation of Partially Exposed Active Areas with Low-Energy Protons.

(Reprinted with permission of the IEEE).[42]

Gap = 0.011 mm near busbar

Radiation Level (years)	I_{sc}	$\frac{I_{sc}}{I_{sc0}}$	V_{oc}	$\frac{V_{oc}}{V_{oc0}}$	P_{mp}	$\frac{P_{mp}}{P_{mp0}}$
0	138.6	1	566.8	1	56.6	1
0.5	136.3	0.983	560.4	0.989	54.6	0.964
1.0	134.3	0.968	566.1	0.981	52.1	0.921
7.0	133.4	0.964	559.2	0.987	52.2	0.926

graded approximately as predicted, except V_{oc} degraded somewhat less, I_{sc} and P_{mp} somewhat more than predicted.

2. The solar cells on the flexible substrate degraded much faster than predicted. This was attributed to either deposition of a contaminant on the solar cell covers or proton damage on the solar cell back sides or edges.

3. Thicker covers provided greater shielding than did thinner covers, as predicted.

4. The cells with the exposed bar gap degraded faster than fully protected cells in consonance with low-energy proton ground test experience.

5. No differences in degradation rates were discernible between solderless and solder-dipped n-contacts.

6. The rigid panel temperature increased at approximately 1°C/year, while the flexible panel temperature remained constant.

ATS-6.[43,44] The ATS-6 satellite was launched on May 30, 1974 into synchronous orbit and carried a solar cell flight experiment. I–V curves from 16 different solar cover assembly configurations (shown in Table 4-7) were obtained from the three axis stabilized spacecraft. Sixty-five of the solar cells were mounted on a rigid, 6.3 mm thick aluminum honeycomb substrate and 15 of them were mounted on a flexible substrate. The flexible substrate consisted of a 25 μm thick fiberglass cloth and a 25 μm thick Kapton sheet and received space radiation from both sides. The cells on the rigid panel were essentially shielded from all radiation through the back side.

The solar cells had thin solder-coated Ti-Ag contacts. The covers were installed without leaving unprotected cell areas, and the n-constant bars were covered with a coating after assembly to provide additional low-energy proton protection. Even though the experiment package

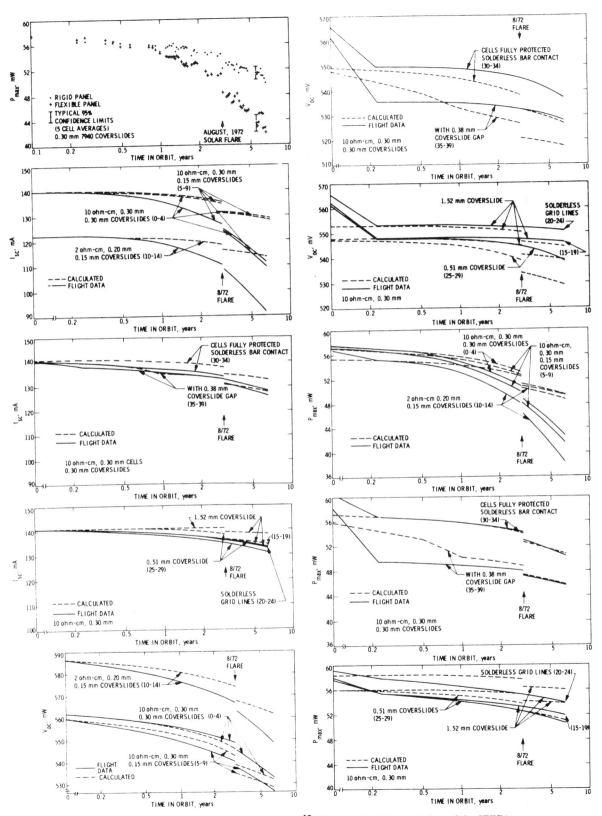

Fig. 4-47. Results of ATS-5 flight experiments.[42] (*Reprinted with permission of the IEEE.*)

ut. SOLAR CELLS 203

Table 4-7. ATS-6 Solar Cell Flight Experiments.
(Reprinted with permission of the IEEE).[43]

Configu-ration	Resistivity, (ohm · cm)	Cell Thick-ness, (cm)	Cover Glass Thickness, (cm)	Remarks	Location
1	10	0.030	0.0076	–	Rigid
2	10	0.030	0.015	–	Rigid
3	10	0.030	0.030	–	Rigid
4	10	0.030	0.076	–	Rigid
5	10	0.030	0.0076	Plain 7940 fused silica cover; no filter or coatings on cover	Rigid
6	10	0.030	0.0038	7940 integral cover	Rigid
7	10	0.030	0.0076	7070 integral cover	Rigid
8	2	0.030	0.015	–	Rigid
9	2	0.020	0.015	–	Rigid
10	10	0.030	0.015	Cover without UV filter; cover adhesive of 0.005 cm FEP	Rigid
11	10	0.020	0.015	–	Rigid
12	1	0.025	0.015	COMSAT violet cell; cerium doped micro-sheet cover without UV filter	Rigid
13	10	0.030	0.013	FEP cover without added adhesive	Rigid
14	10	0.020	0.015	–	Flexible
15	2	0.020	0.015	–	Flexible
16	2	0.030	0.015	–	Flexible

developed several problems. some significant data could be obtained. The orbital data was corrected using ground test data of temperature coefficients (Fig. 4-48) and angle of incidence effects. The angle of incidence data showed deviations from the cosine law that were related to cover thickness and the presence or absence of an anti-reflection (AR) coating on the cover (see Fig. 4-49).

After two years of orbital operation and data reduction, the following conclusions were drawn (the data are shown in Table 4-8 and Figs. 4-50 and 4-51).

1. The higher cell I_{sc} output at beginning-of-life output observed in space, compared to the preflight laboratory measurements (Table 4-8) was attributed to a calibration error in the flight experiment equipment, rather than to an error in the solar simulator calibration. Voltage errors of vari-

able magnitude affected the results from the cells on the flexible panel; therefore, only the data for the rigid panel were presented.

2. The violet solar cells exhibited about 26% greater output than the conventional 2 ohm · cm cells initially, but a greater rate of degradation.

3. Cells with covers having no MgF AR coating (Configurations 5, 6, and 7) had about 3% to 9% lower I_{sc} than those with AR coating.

4. The average percentage I_{sc} degradation due to ultraviolet radiation induced optical transmission losses was assessed as shown in Table 4-9. The statistically pooled data indicated that the ultraviolet radiation induced I_{sc} degradation for all discrete covers with AR coating was about 2%; that for discrete covers without AR coating, the degradation was about

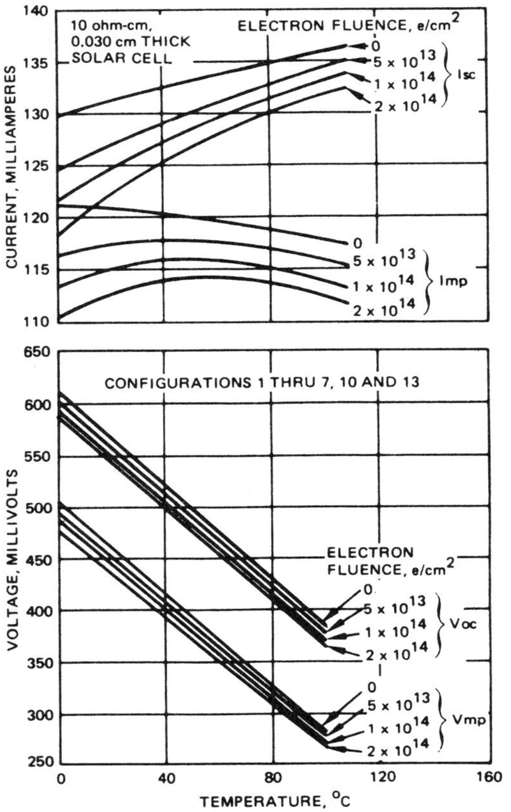

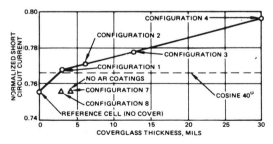

Fig. 4-48. Cell parameter variation with temperature and fluence.[44] (*Reprinted with permission of the IEEE.*)

Fig. 4-49. Normalized I_{sc} at 40° angle as a function of coverglass thickness.[44] (*Reprinted with permission of the IEEE.*)

3%; and that for integral covers, the degradation was about 1%.

5. The degradation of FEP-Teflon, used as a cover-to-cell adhesive, was approximately the same as the degradation of Sylgard 182, both under fused silica covers without ultraviolet filters.

6. The current and power degradation observed on both the flight experiment and on the satellite main array were greater than predicted based on ground testing and 1 MeV electron irradiation and greater than observed on other arrays made by the same manufacturer with similar solar cells. The main array used 0.34 mm thick 2 ohm · cm cells with Corning 0211 microsheet covers. Its north wing had degraded by 20% and its south wing by 22% after two years. The corresponding experiment degradation is given in Table 4-10.

NTS-1.[45] The Navigation Technology Satellite (NTS-1) was launched on July 14, 1974 into a 13,529 km circular orbit with an inclination of 125°. The orbit intersected regions of intense trapped radiation, causing solar cell degradation in one year that was equivalent to 4×10^{14} 1 MeV electrons. The number of thermal cycles was 1250/year. The highest solar cell temperatures were 70°C, peaking at 98°C for a period of four months due to satellite instabilities. The solar cell flight experiment carried the solar cells and covers given in Table 4-11. The cells of Exp. Nos. 1 through 8 were mounted to rigid honeycomb panels. Even though the experiment package developed several problems, some significant data could be obtained.

The orbital data were corrected for temperature using the coefficients given in Table 4-12. The equivalent 1 MeV fluence was calculated for the cells of the main array, shielded by 0.30 mm thick fused silica, to be 3.6×10^{14} $e \cdot cm^{-2}/$ year. This fluence was composed of 2.6×10^{14} $e \cdot cm^{-2}/$year due to trapped electrons of the AE-5 environment, and 1.0×10^{14} $e \cdot cm^{-2}/$ year due to trapped protons of the AP-6 environment (see Section 9-47).

After two years of orbital operation and data reduction, the conclusions below were drawn.

1. The current output and power degradation was much greater than predicted, and a satisfactory explanation for this phenomenon could not be found. The flight data are shown in Table 4-13 and in Fig. 4-52.

2. The performance of the Helios (K-6) and

Table 4-8. Laboratory and Flight Data Comparison.
(Reprinted with permission of the IEEE).[44]

Configuration	Cell	Pulsed Xenon Simulator I_{sc} (mA)	V_{oc} (mV)	P_{mp} (mW)	Curve Factor	Space Data — 2 to 7 Days in Orbit I_{sc} (mA)	V_{oc} (mV)	P_{mp} (mW)	Curve Factor	50 Days in Orbit I_{sc} (mA)	V_{oc} (mV)	P_{mp} (mW)	Curve Factor	765 Days in Orbit I_{sc} (mA)	V_{oc} (mV)	P_{mp} (mW)	Curve Factor
1	10	140	558	56.3	0.724	149	554	59.1	0.718	145	552	57.3	0.714	127	542	49.2	0.715
	15	140	553	57.7	0.744	149	550	60.2	0.734	148	549	59.7	0.733	130	543	51.9	0.738
	22	138	553	57.2	0.752	147	556	60.6	0.744	144	556	59.4	0.740	122	544	49.6	0.743
2	25	141	560	57.9	0.734	149	550	59.1	0.721	148	549	58.0	0.716	130	542	50.2	0.716
	38	139	554	57.4	0.744	149	554	60.2	0.731	146	552	58.6	0.728	122	540	48.2	0.728
3	8	138	550	56.7	0.745	144	544	57.5	0.733	141	543	56.0	0.729	125	537	48.9	0.731
	16	140	550	57.5	0.746	146	548	59.0	0.738	146	548	58.6	0.734	129	543	51.2	0.732
4	19	141	559	58.0	0.723	146	552	58.0	0.719	143	551	56.6	0.719	124	544	48.0	0.712
	35	139	549	56.7	0.744	144	559	59.5	0.742	142	557	58.0	0.735	122	549	49.4	0.734
	37	141	551	57.4	0.740	146	549	58.4	0.729	144	549	57.6	0.729	127	545	50.4	0.728
5	28	139	562	58.7	0.751	144	557	59.2	0.741	139	554	56.7	0.737	119	545	48.0	0.740
	30	139	561	58.8	0.755	145	564	60.5	0.739	141	560	57.3	0.727	120	549	47.8	0.726
6	6	127	553	52.6	0.747	136	548	54.3	0.727	136	545	52.8	0.715	120	534	45.6	0.713
	24	127	549	51.8	0.744	136	541	53.7	0.733	135	539	53.1	0.727	120	532	46.5	0.729
	31	128	559	53.4	0.749	138	554	55.8	0.730	136	551	54.1	0.723	117	540	46.1	0.729
7	9	131	550	53.3	0.749	141	544	56.4	0.736	138	542	54.7	0.732	120	536	47.5	0.737
	14	131	557	54.8	0.754	138	540	54.5	0.731	138	539	54.2	0.729	122	534	48.1	0.735
8	11	131	589	59.0	0.764	140	576	60.1	0.743	136	575	57.4	0.735	117	560	48.6	0.742
	23	132	592	60.2	0.771	140	589	62.1	0.754	137	589	60.6	0.751	117	573	50.8	0.759
	27	131	591	59.8	0.773	138	584	60.9	0.757	136	583	59.6	0.753	117	570	50.7	0.760
9	20	126	575	56.7	0.782	135	569	58.6	0.762	133	568	57.2	0.759	114	558	48.0	0.756
	36	126	578	56.6	0.778	135	564	58.0	0.759	134	564	57.0	0.754	116	555	48.6	0.754
10	21	142	561	56.6	0.711	146	556	58.8	0.724	143	556	57.8	0.725	120	546	48.5	0.736
	29	142	561	59.9	0.753	147	554	60.3	0.739	145	553	58.8	0.734	124	544	49.6	0.739
11	39	140	551	56.5	0.735	146	547	58.8	0.728	143	545	56.7	0.728	—	—	—	—
	7	131	549	54.1	0.751	140	542	56.1	0.741	137	541	54.8	0.740	—	—	—	—
	17	133	547	54.2	0.746	141	536	55.6	0.736	141	536	55.3	0.734	124	532	48.5	0.736
	32	134	542	54.7	0.753	140	544	56.9	0.749	137	542	55.4	0.747	118	535	47.4	0.752
12	26	166	601	78.0	0.784	176	598	81.8	0.776	173	595	79.5	0.772	143	574	62.9	0.767
	33	167	598	78.0	0.779	179	598	83.1	0.776	174	594	80.0	0.773	141	573	61.8	0.764
13	18	146	558	59.8	0.735	151	553	60.1	0.720	149	549	58.4	0.714	125	470	35.0	0.595
	34	144	558	60.4	0.749	150	560	62.6	0.747	147	558	61.1	0.743	120	468	33.9	0.606
14	0	133	548	53.6	0.735	144	483	48.2	0.695	142	486	47.8	0.694	125	495	43.3	0.702
	3	134	548	53.3	0.726	146	494	49.8	0.689	144	496	49.3	0.689	128	503	44.6	0.696
	12	130	541	53.7	0.760	142	488	48.6	0.703	140	491	48.5	0.705	125	498	44.2	0.709
15	1	126	576	54.9	0.753	139	512	49.9	0.701	137	515	49.4	0.699	121	518	43.6	0.699
	4	125	575	54.9	0.768	135	522	51.4	0.729	134	524	50.9	0.727	117	524	44.6	0.729
	13	125	580	55.4	0.765	137	516	50.8	0.718	136	518	50.2	0.715	120	521	44.6	0.716
16	2	130	586	58.1	0.763	140	524	52.7	0.715	138	526	51.8	0.710	119	525	45.0	0.722
	5	131	594	59.0	0.755	142	536	53.8	0.706	140	538	53.0	0.703	122	535	46.5	0.714

violet cell types was superior to that of all other cells.

3. The lithium-diffused cells, having aluminum contacts, degraded severely due to an unknown mechanism.

NTS-2.[46,48] The second Navigation Technology Satellite (NTS-2) was launched on June 23, 1977 into a 20,192 km circular orbit having 63° inclination, with an orbit period of 12 hours. The flight experiment consisted of 15 solar cell experiments, including one involving gallium arsenide cells, as described in Table 4-14. The 20 × 20 mm solar cells were mounted

to aluminum honeycomb panels and connected into series strings of 5 cells each.

During orbital operations, the temperatures of the two body-mounted solar cell panels which carried the experiments increased as shown in Fig. 4-53. On day 69, the string of experimental low-cost space cells of Exp. No. 8 failed in open-circuit mode. After day 170, the output of the string of experimental vertical junction cells began to degrade rapidly (Fig. 4-54). A number of possible failure mechanisms have been postulated, but none has yet been verified. The peak solar cell temperature, having increased from 71.5°C to 101.4°C on day 233, and the

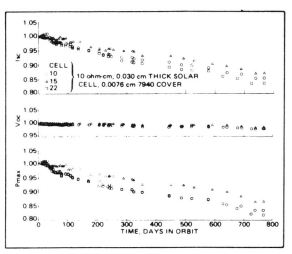

a) CONFIGURATION 1

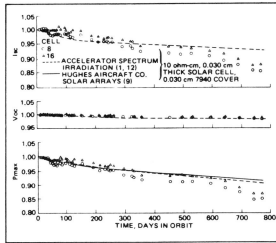

c) CONFIGURATION 3

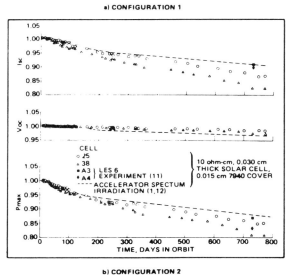

b) CONFIGURATION 2

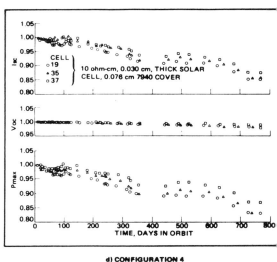

d) CONFIGURATION 4

Fig. 4-50. Normalized results of ATS-6 experiments.[44] (*Reprinted with permission of the IEEE.*)

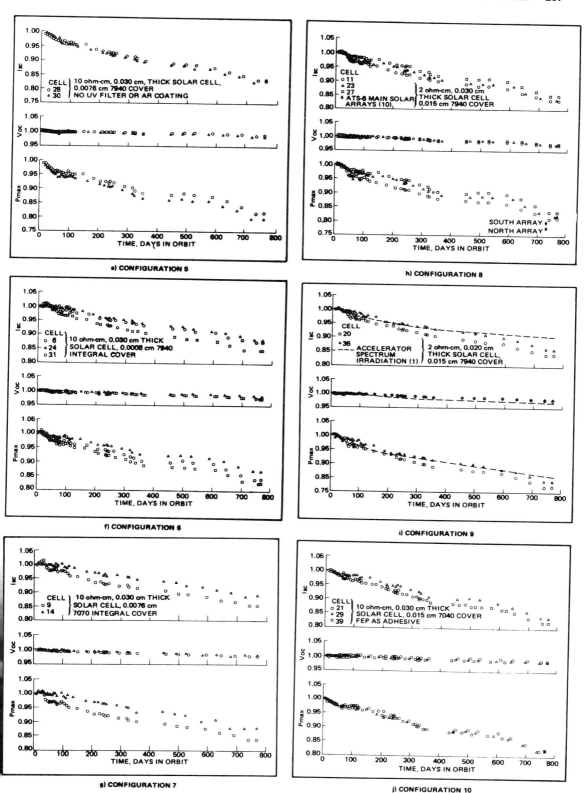

e) CONFIGURATION 5

h) CONFIGURATION 8

f) CONFIGURATION 6

i) CONFIGURATION 9

g) CONFIGURATION 7

j) CONFIGURATION 10

Fig. 4-50. (Continued)

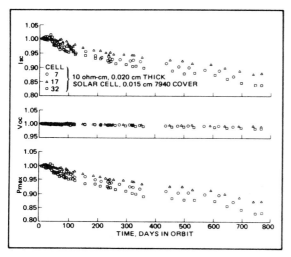

k) CONFIGURATION 11

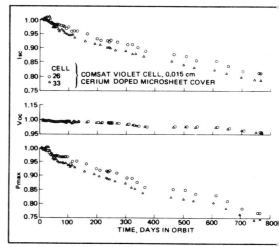

l) CONFIGURATION 12

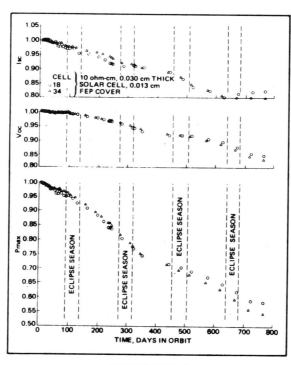

m) CONFIGURATION 13

Fig. 4-50. *(Continued)*

frequent temperature cycles, may have played a contributory role in the cell failures. After 233 days in orbit and after orbital data reduction, these four conclusions were drawn.

1. The silicon solar cell degradation was greater than predicted, based on the calculated equivalent 1 MeV fluence (see NTS-1, above). The orbital data are shown in Table 4-15. If non-anomalous cell degradation were to be assumed, the actual fluence would be as given in Table 4-16,

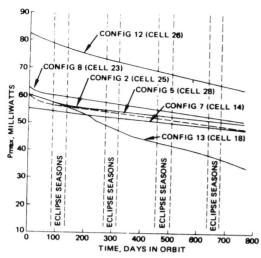

Fig. 4-51. Maximum power performance of six configurations.[44] (*Reprinted with permission of the IEEE.*)

Table 4-9. Ultraviolet Induced Percentage Degradation of I_{sc}.[44]

Configuration	After 50 days	After 2 years
1, 2, 3, 4, 8, 9, 11	1.6 ± 0.7	—
5	3.3 ± 0.1	6.3
6, 7	0.8 ± 1.1	—
10, 13	1.8 ± 0.1	4.8
12	2.3 ± 0.9	5.3

Table 4-10. ATS-6 Solar Cell Degradation in Two Years.
(Reprinted with permission of the IEEE).[44]

Configuration	Average Percentage Loss		
	I_{sc}	V_{oc}	P_{mp}
1	14.7 ± 2.0	1.8 ± 0.5	16.3 ± 2.6
2	15.3 ± 3.9	2.0 ± 0.9	17.4 ± 4.3
3	12.7 ± 1.7	1.1 ± 0.4	14.1 ± 1.6
4	14.2 ± 1.3	1.3 ± 0.6	15.3 ± 2.2
5	17.2 ± 0.4	2.4 ± 0.5	20.0 ± 1.9
6	13.0 ± 2.2	2.2 ± 0.5	15.6 ± 2.3
7	12.8 ± 2.8	1.4 ± 0.4	13.7 ± 3.5
8	16.1 ± 1.0	2.6 ± 0.8	18.0 ± 1.4
9	15.0 ± 1.5	1.9 ± 0.3	17.1 ± 1.7
10	16.8 ± 1.3	1.8 ± 0.3	17.6 ± 0.2
11	14.0 ± 3.2	1.1 ± 0.7	14.7 ± 3.5
12	19.4 ± 2.0	4.2 ± 0.1	24.4 ± 2.2
13	18.6 ± 2.4	15.7 ± 1.4	43.2 ± 3.5

approximately twice to three times as large as the prediction. The degradation rate for Exp. Nos. 1, 2, and 10 are illustrated in Fig. 4-55.

2. The experiments with fused silica covers, having no ultraviolet (UV) reflection filter, showed degradation comparable with that of the same covers with UV filters, except for the COMSAT CNR (Exp. No. 5) cell, which degraded severely (Fig. 4-56).

3. FEP Teflon cover adhesive degraded approximately as the RTV adhesives did.

4. The lithium-doped cells annealed well after severe electron damage. The high cell temperature may have aided in the annealing process.

4-45. Laboratory Test Data for Space Cells

The electrical characteristics at different temperatures and sunlight intensities for a number of unirradiated solar cell types of current interest are presented below.

Conventional 2 ohm · cm.[49] Fabricated for the Mariner '71 program in 1968 to 1969 by Heliotek from crucible-grown, boron-doped p-type silicon, they were phosphorous-diffused cells approximately 0.3 μm deep. Cell size was 20 × 20 × 0.46 mm; AR coating was SiO_x. Contacts

were Ti-Ag, solder dipped, with six grid lines. The data for a sample of seven unglassed cells are shown in Fig. 4-57.

OCLI Violet.[50] Manufactured from 1976 to 1978 by OCLI from crucible-grown, boron-doped p-type silicon of nominally 2 ohm · cm base resistivity, they were 20 × 20 × 0.25 mm in size and generally available for space use. AR coating was Ta_2O_5. The top contact was solderless Cr-Au-Ag with a 3 × 19 finger grid pattern. Cells were glassed with 0.38 mm thick 7940 fused silica covers having a UV reflective coating with 350 nm cut-on wavelength. Cover adhesive was Dow Corning 182. The data for a sample of 14 glassed cells are shown in Fig. 4-58.

Table 4-11. NTS-1 Solar Cell Flight Experiments.
(Reprinted with permission of the IEEE).[45]

Exp. No.	Cell Type	Cell Size (cm)	Coverslip (cm)	Coverslip Cement	Module Size	Interconnect
1	CEN Radial Grid n/p, 10 ohm-cm	2 × 2 × .01	Fused silica .030	R63-489	5 series cells	Tinned Kovar
2	CEN Violet n/p	2 × 2 × .03	Fused silica .030	R63-489	5 series cells	.025 cm silver-plated molybdenum
3	HEL p/n, Al contact	2 × 2 × .02	Fused silica .030	R63-489	5 series cells	.025 cm aluminum
4	CEN Lithium p/n, Al contact	2 × 2 × .02	Fused silica .030	R63-489	5 series cells	.025 cm aluminum
5	CEN Violet n/p	2 × 2 × .03	Fused silica .030	R63-489	47 series cells	silver-plated molybdenum
6	HEL Helios n/p	2 × 2 × .03	Fused silica .030	R63-489	48 series cells	.050 cm silver-plated copper
7	CEN 2 ohm-cm n/p	2 × 4 × .03	Fused silica .030	R63-489	23 series cells	silver-plated molybdenum
8	Comsat Violet	2 × 2 × .028	Ceria glass .015	Sylgard 182	5 series cells	.025 cm silver and silver mesh
9A	Ferranti, FZ n/p, 10 ohm-cm	2 × 2 × .0125	Ceria glass .010	RTV 602		
9B	Ferranti, CZ n/p, 10 ohm-cm	2 × 2 × .0125	Ceria glass .010	RTV 602	2 parallel, 2 series for V_{oc}	.025 cm silver-plated molybdenum
9C	Ferranti, FZ n/p, 1 ohm-cm	2 × 2 × .0125	Ceria glass .010	RTV 602	3 parallel, 2 series for I_{sc} and I_{mp}	
9D	Ferranti, FZ n/p, 10 ohm-cm	2 × 2 × .0125	Sputtered 7070 glass .025 − .050	RTV 602		

Table 4-12. Voltage- and Current-Temperature Coefficients for NTS-1 Solar Cell Experiments.
(Reprinted with permission of the IEEE).[45]

Exp. No.	$\dfrac{dV_{oc}}{dT}$ (mV/°C)		$\dfrac{dI_{sc}}{dT}$ (mA/°C/4 cm²)	
	Ground Measurement	Space Measurement	Ground Measurement	Space Measurement
1	2.114	2.139 ± .178	.045	.197 ± .064
2	2.082	2.144 ± .113	.058	.213 ± .137
4	1.941	1.871 ± .149	.096	.271 ± .093
5	2.191	2.098 ± .117	.046	.139 ± .047
6	2.082	1.989 ± .140	.058	.170 ± .041
7	1.973	2.089 ± .149	.076	.231 ± .055
8	2.082	2.098 ± .127	.058	.225 ± .061

Solarex 50 μm.[51] Presently under development, these are early data on 20 × 20 × 0.050 mm cells fabricated from crucible-grown p-type silicon of nominal resistivity of 2 ohm · cm. An aluminum alloy p⁺ back surface field was diffused through the phosphorus-diffused layer on the back side. AR coating was Ta_2O_5. Front contacts were a 3 × 10 finger grid pattern. The data for a sample of unglassed cells are given in Fig. 4-59.

OCLI Hybrid MLAR.[52] Manufactured by OCLI and generally available for space applications, the cells were made from crucible-grown boron-

Table 4-13. Output and Percentage Loss After Two Years in Orbit.[45]

Exp. No.	Initial Output*		Percentage Loss**	
	I_{sc} (mA)	P_{mp} (mW)	I_{sc} (%)	P_{mp} (%)
1	149	59	24.8	33.9
2	176	74	26.1	32.4
3	144	65	†	†
4	146	61	19.8	47.5
5	172	73	23.8	35.6
6	168	71	25.0	38.0
7	143	64	28.7	39.1
8	187	84	32.6	41.7

*Measured at day 9. Output is for 20 × 20 mm cells.
**Between day 753 and day 9.
†Solar cell string failed in open-circuit mode after day 261.

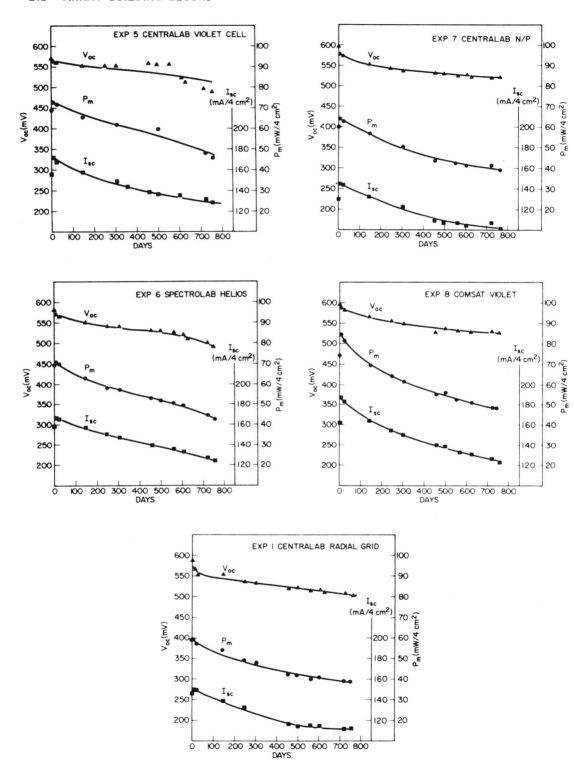

Fig. 4-52. Results of NTS-1 flight experiments, normalized to 25°C.[45] (*Reprinted with permission of the IEEE.*)

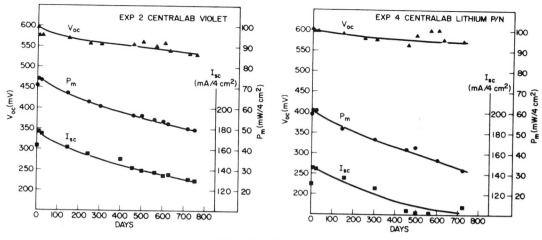

Fig. 4-52. (*Continued*)

Table 4-14. NTS-2 Solar Cell Experiments.
(Reprinted with permission © 1978 Society of Automotive Engineers).[48]

Exp. No.	Cell Type	Thick- ness (cm)	Coverslip (cm)	Coverslip Bond (cm)	Interconnect	Efficiency 28°C (%)
1	OCLI Conventional, 2 ohm-cm	0.025	Corning 7940, AR and UV, (0.030)	R63-489	Cu/Ag	10.7
2	Spectrolab "Helios" p⁺ 15-45 ohm-cm	0.0228	Ceria microsheet w/o AR, (0.025)	DC 93-500	Moly/Ag (.0025)	11.5
3	Spectrolab Hybrid Sculptured 7-14 ohm-cm	0.020	Corning 7940, AR and UV, (0.0152)	DC 93-500	Moly/Ag (.0025)	10.5
4	Spectrolab Hybrid Sculptured 7-14 ohm-cm	0.020	Corning 7940, w/o AR or UV, (0.0152)	FEP Teflon (0.0051)	Moly/Ag (.0025)	11.1
5	Comsat Non-Reflecting, p⁺ Textured, 1.8 ohm-cm	0.025	Corning 7940, AR, w/o UV (.030)	R63-489	Ag; thermo- compression bonding	14.5
6	Comsat Non-Reflecting, p⁺ Textured, 1.8 ohm-cm	0.025	Corning 7940, AR and UV (.030)	R63-489	Ag; thermo- compression bonding	14.6
7	Solarex Vertical Junction, p⁺, 1.5 ohm-cm	0.030	Ceria microsheet w/o AR (.0152)	Sylgard 182	Ag mesh	13.0
8	Solarex Space Cell, p⁺ 2 ohm-cm	0.025	Ceria microsheet w/o AR (0.0152)	Sylgard 182	Ag mesh	12.8
9	Spectrolab "Helios" p⁺ Sculptured, BSR, 10 ohm-cm	0.030	Corning 7940 (.030) w/o AR or UV	FEP teflon (.003)	Ag mesh (.003)	14.2
10	OCLI Violet, 2 ohm-cm	0.025	Corning 7940 (.030) AR and UV	R63-489	Cu/Ag	13.5
11	Spectrolab P/N Li-doped 15-30 ohm-cm, Al contacts	0.020	Corning 7940, AR and UV, (0.015)	Silicone	Aluminum (.0025) Ultra- sonic welding	10.8
12	Spectrolab Planar Diode in series with Exp. 11	NA	NA	NA	NA	NA
13	OCLI Conventional, 2 ohm-cm	0.025	Corning 7070 (.028)	Electrostatic bonding	Cu/Ag	10.2
14	Spectrolab HESP, no p⁺, Sculptured, 2 ohm-cm	0.030	Corning 7940, AR and UV (0.0305)	R63-489	Moly/Ag (.0025)	13.6
15	Hughes Gallium-Aluminum Arsenide	0.0305	Corning 7940, AR and UV, (0.0305)	DC 93-500	Aluminum GPD (.0025), epoxy	13.6

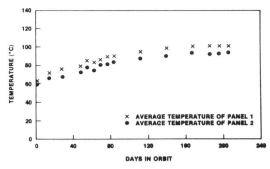

Fig. 4-53. Average temperature of NTS-2 solar cell experiments.[46] (*Reprinted with permission of the IEEE.*)

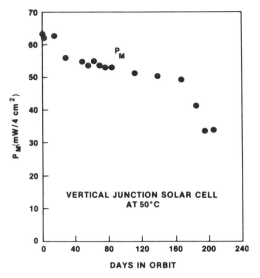

Fig. 4-54. Power degradation of Experiment No. 7.[46] (*Reprinted with permission of the IEEE.*)

doped silicon of 10 ohm · cm nominal resistivity. Cells were 20 × 20 × 0.25 mm and carried a multilayer anti-reflective (MLAR) coating. Front contacts were Ti-Pd-Ag with 8 grid lines. The back contact was Ti-Pd-Ag with picture frame. Cells were glassed with 0.15 mm thick 7940 fused silica covers, having a 350 nm cut-on wavelength. Adhesive was Dow Corning 182. The cell data for a sample of 14 cells are shown in Fig. 4-60.

Hughes GaAs.[24] Currently under development by several organizations, the Hughes Aircraft

Company cell data are shown as one example of the performance of GaAlAs-GaAs solar cell types. These cells were designed for 1 to 20 × concentration ratio space applications and were 20 × 20 mm in size and had 24 grid lines. The GaAlAs window had thicknesses between 0.5 μm and 2 μm, with the thicker ones required

Table 4-15. Solar Cell Parameters and Degradation at 25°C from Day 1 Through Day 223.[46,48]

Exp. No.	Short-Circuit Current			Open-Circuit Voltage			Maximum Power		
	X-25 (mA)	Day 1 (mA)	Day 223 (% Loss)	X-25 (mV)	Day 1 (mV)	Day 223 (% Loss)	X-25 (mW)	Day (mW)	Day 223 (% Loss)
1	135.4	136.5	10.4	533	549	0.9	53.1	56.3	13.9
2	154.5	155.5	6.6	527	546	3.3	57.9	60.0	12.7
3	155.6	154.0	7.0	491	508	1.4	52.4	53.5	11.0
4	151.0	149.6	4.5	491	505	1.4	54.6	55.4	8.8
5	184.8	180.4	30.6	533	555	3.4	72.8	74.7	33.6
6	180.8	178.7	8.1	533	549	1.6	70.1	72.0	12.2
7	158.4	160.5	16.8	528	521	18.4	63.1	62.2	46.5
8	155.9	158.8	100	535	541	100	60.6	63.1	100
9	174.3	175.8	7.1	550	545	3.5	66.0	70.0	13.6
10	165.1	164.3	10.0	550	552	1.6	67.5	66.6	13.5
11	136.2	132.6	10.0	552	559	2.5	53.2	55.8	15.8
12	134.5	132.4	9.9	523	523	2.3	42.0	42.1	16.2
13	147.3	146.1	6.6	488	490	3.9	47.0	46.8	13.9
14	166.2	165.8	7.4	533	528	5.1	63.3	63.8	15.5
15	102.9	100.6	12.3	914	895	1.2	70.0	61.4	4.6

Table 4-16. Equivalent 1 MeV Electron Fluence for NTS-2.
(Reprinted with permission of the IEEE).[46]

	BOL	Fluence at 200 Days	Fluence at 1 Year	Fluence at 3 Years
\multicolumn{5}{c}{OCLI Conventional 2 Ω-cm, 10 mil cell, 12 mil FS Coverslip}
I_{sc}	136.0 mA	1.5×10^{14}	2.7×10^{14}	8.2×10^{14}
V_{oc}	548 mV	3×10^{13}	5.5×10^{13}	1.6×10^{14}
P_{mp}	56.5 mW/4 cm²	1.3×10^{14}	2.4×10^{14}	7.1×10^{14}
\multicolumn{5}{c}{Spectrolab Helios, 10 Ω-cm, 9 mil cell, 10 mil Ceria Coverslip}
I_{sc}	154 mA	1.3×10^{14}	2.4×10^{14}	7.1×10^{14}
V_{oc}	545 mV	1×10^{13}	1.8×10^{13}	5.5×10^{13}
P_{mp}	60.5 mW/4 cm²	9×10^{13}	1.6×10^{14}	4.9×10^{14}
\multicolumn{5}{c}{Spectrolab Textured Hybrid, 8 mil cell, 6 mil FS Coverslip}
I_{sc}	156 mA	5.0×10^{14}	9.1×10^{14}	2.7×10^{15}
V_{oc}	522 mV	5.0×10^{14}	9.1×10^{14}	2.7×10^{15}
P_{mp}	53.8 mW/4 cm²	3.3×10^{14}	6.0×10^{14}	1.8×10^{15}
\multicolumn{5}{c}{OCLI Violet}
I_{sc}	166 mA	1×10^{13}	1.8×10^{14}	5.5×10^{14}
V_{oc}	552 mV	2×10^{13}	3.7×10^{13}	1.1×10^{14}
P_{mp}	67.5 mW/4 cm²	7.5×10^{13}	1.4×10^{14}	4.1×10^{14}

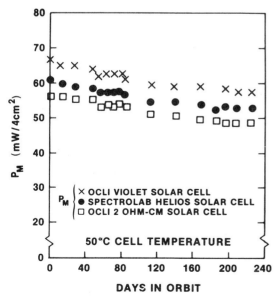

Fig. 4-55. Comparison of power degradation of three cell types on NTS-2 experiment.[48] (*Reprinted with permission © 1978 Society of Automotive Engineers.*)

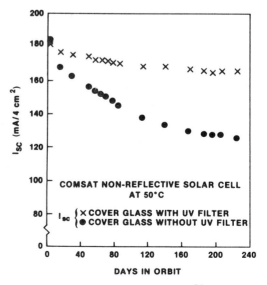

Fig. 4-56. Degradation of CNR cell.[46] (*Reprinted with permission of the IEEE.*)

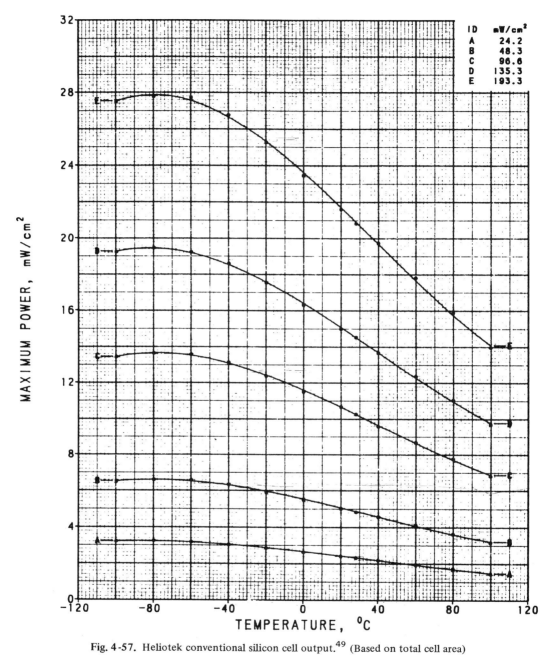

Fig. 4-57. Heliotek conventional silicon cell output.[49] (Based on total cell area)

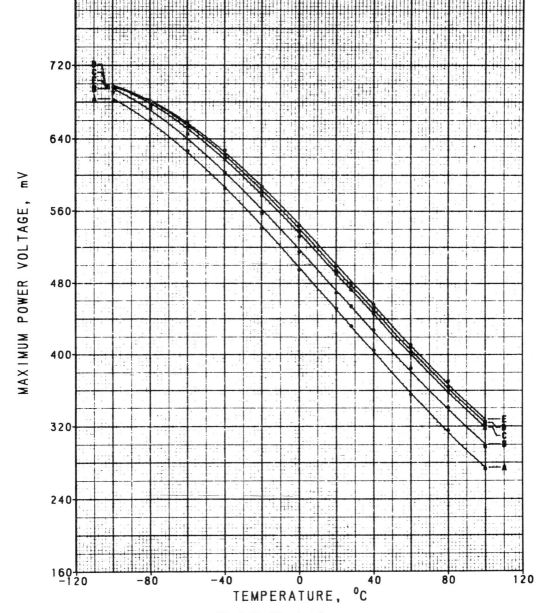

Fig. 4-57. (*Continued*)

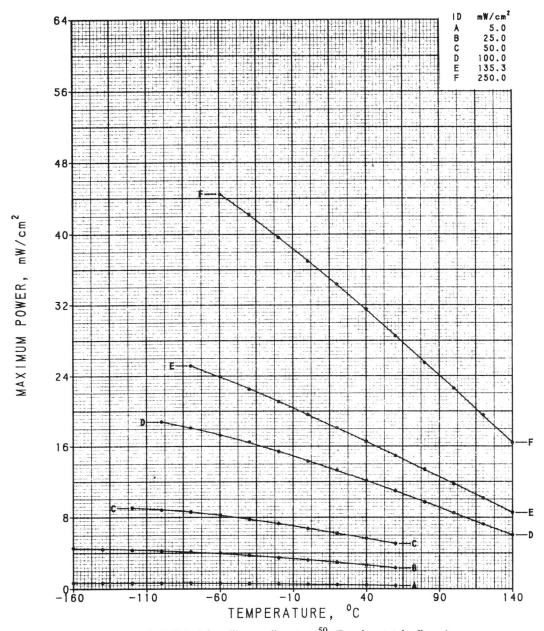

ID	mW/cm^2
A	5.0
B	25.0
C	50.0
D	100.0
E	135.3
F	250.0

Fig. 4-58. OCLI violet silicon cell output.[50] (Based on total cell area)

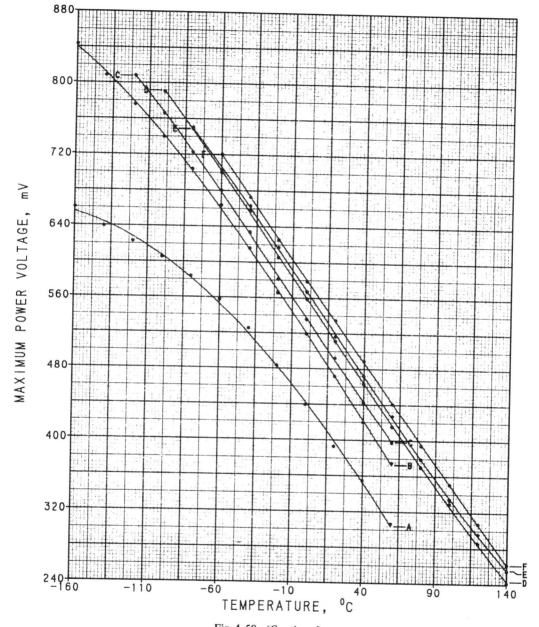

Fig. 4-58. (*Continued*)

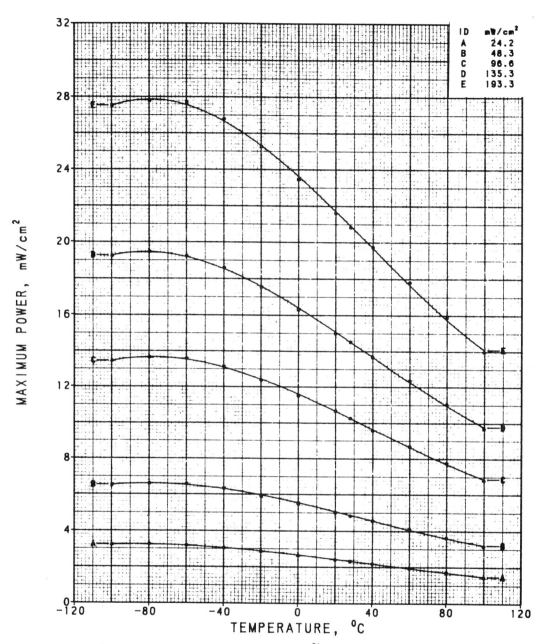

Fig. 4-59. Solarex 50 μm silicon cell output.[51] (Based on total cell area)

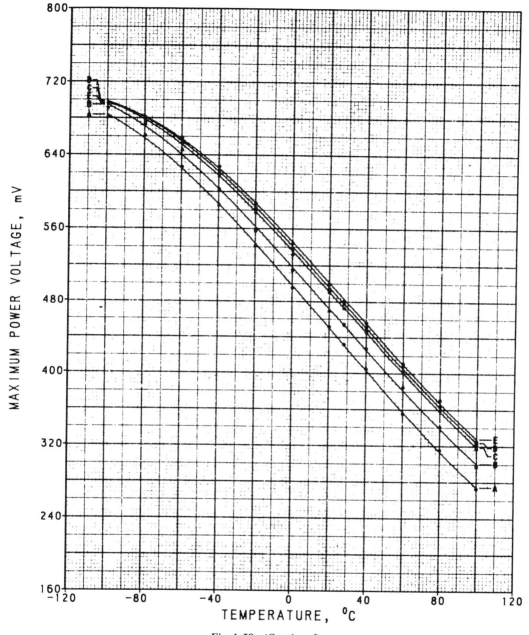

Fig. 4-59. (*Continued*)

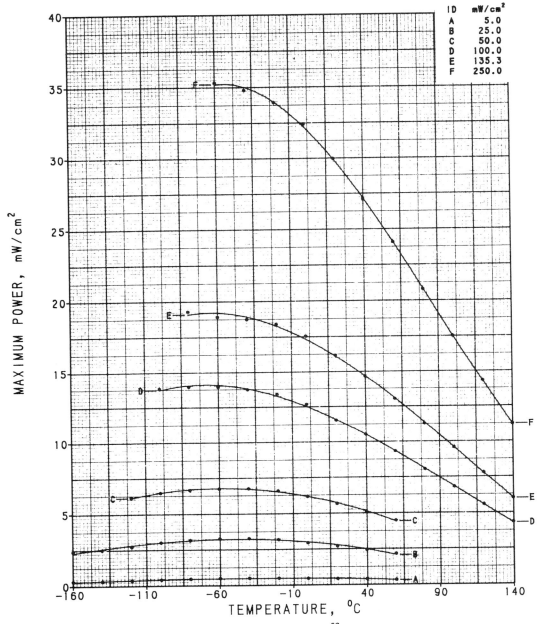

Fig. 4-60. OCLI silicon hybrid MLAR cell output.[52] (Based on total cell area)

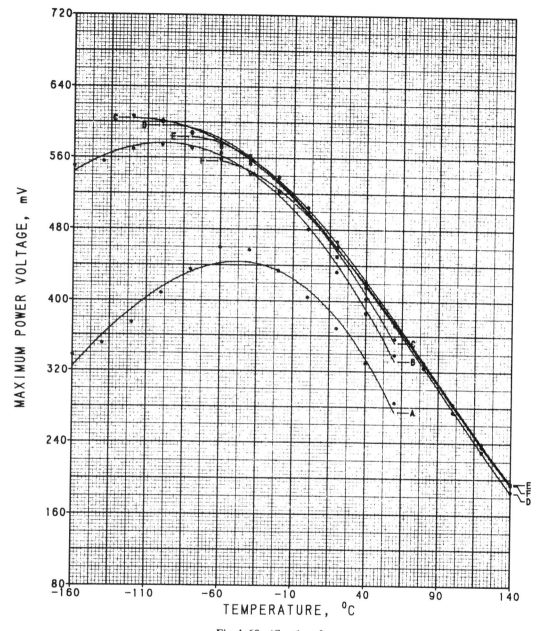

Fig. 4-60. (*Continued*)

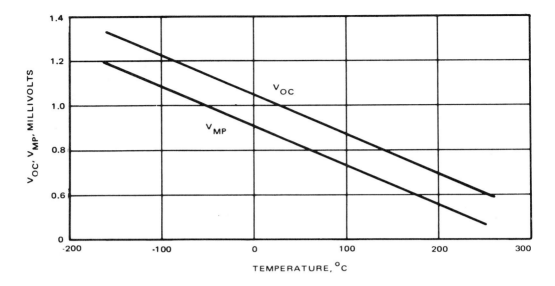

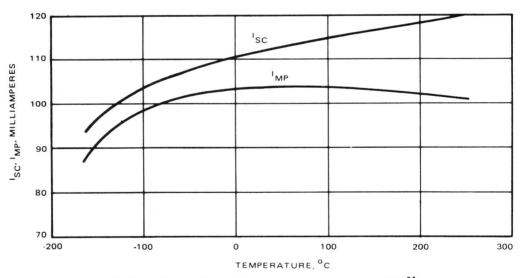

Fig. 4-61. Hughes GaAs cell output at one solar constant AM0.[24]

for higher concentration ratios. Average data for unglassed cells are shown in Fig. 4-61.

4-46. Radiation Test Data for Space Cells

Data are shown for a variety of currently available experimental and production cells (Fig. 4-62). Data with an asterisk is lower than should be expected in the future. The actual output available from specific production lots may differ significantly from the data shown here. Nevertheless, the trends may be used for extrapolation prior to the availability of new test data. The data trends due to irradiation with 1 MeV electrons shown here may not be paralleled by data due to proton irradiation. However, very little proton degradation data for the newer solar cell types presently exists. In Figures 4-63 through 4-73, typical data for cell types of current interest are given. Test conditions

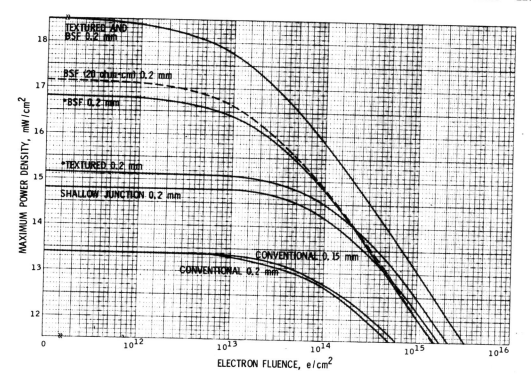

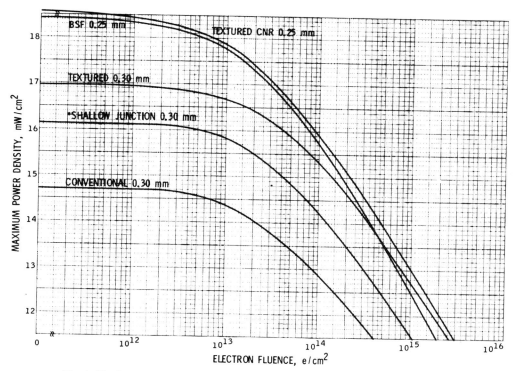

Fig. 4-62. Comparative degradation of a number of different silicon solar cells.[28]

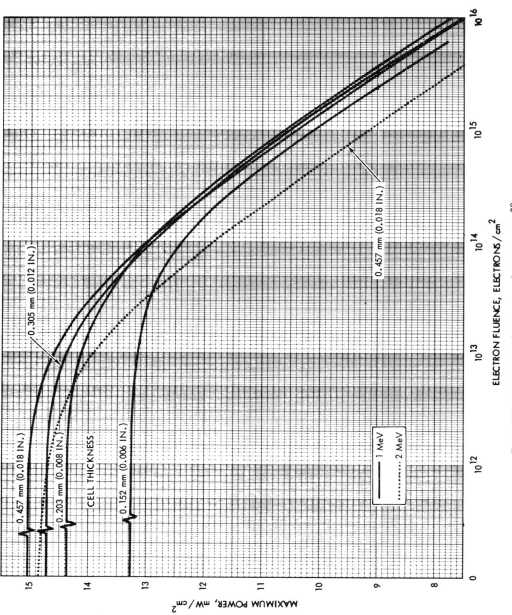

Fig. 4-63. Conventional 2-ohm · cm n/p silicon cells.[28]

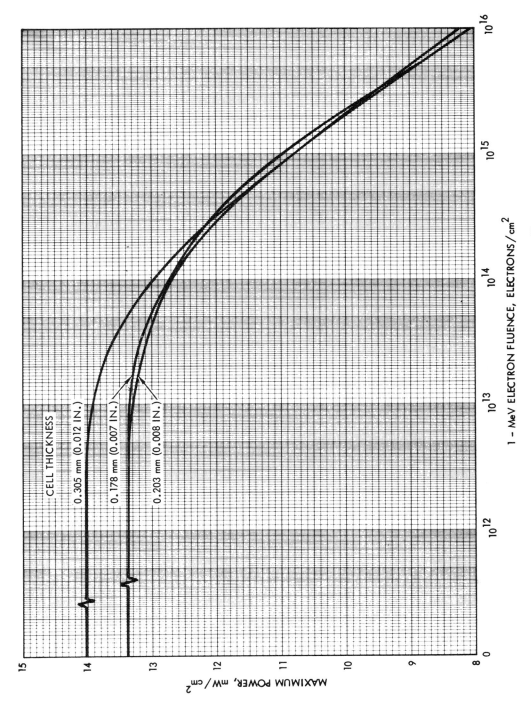

Fig. 4-64. Conventional 10-ohm · cm n/p silicon cells.[28]

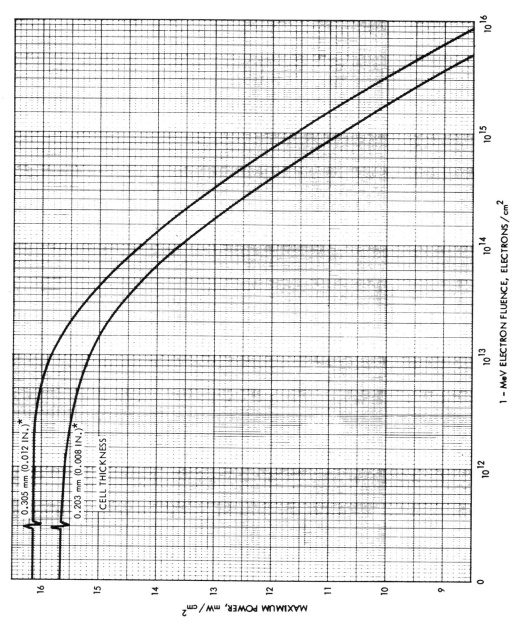

Fig. 4-65. Shallow junction hybrid 2 ohm · cm n/p silicon cells.[28]

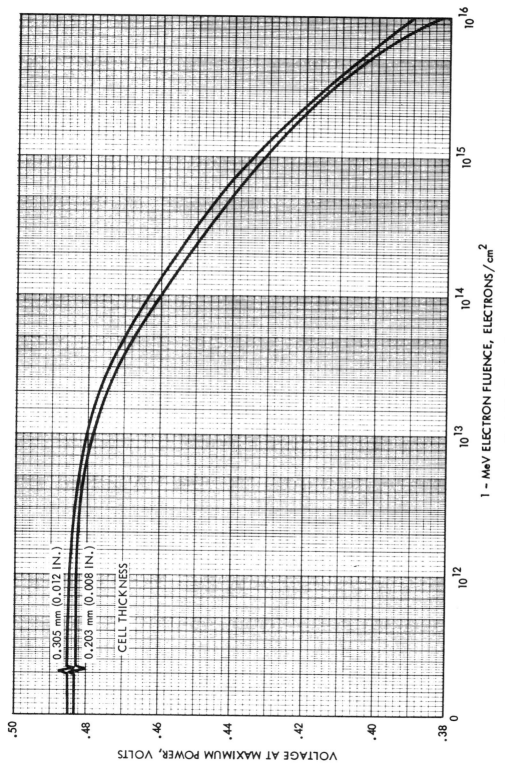

Fig. 4-65. (Continued)

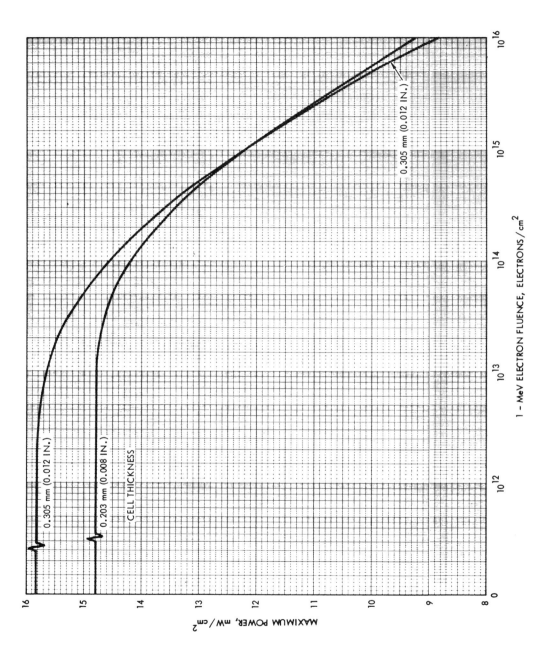

Fig. 4-66. Shallow junction hybrid 10 ohm · cm n/p silicon cells.[28]

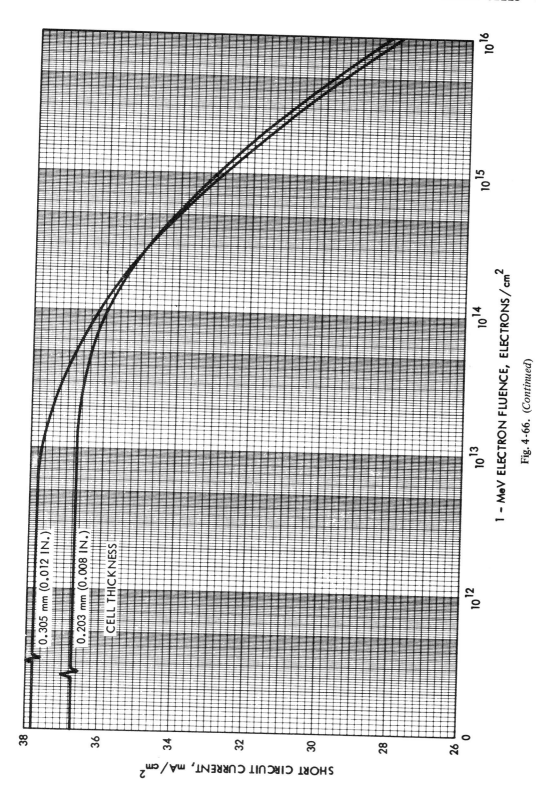

1 – MeV ELECTRON FLUENCE, ELECTRONS / cm²

Fig. 4-66. (*Continued*)

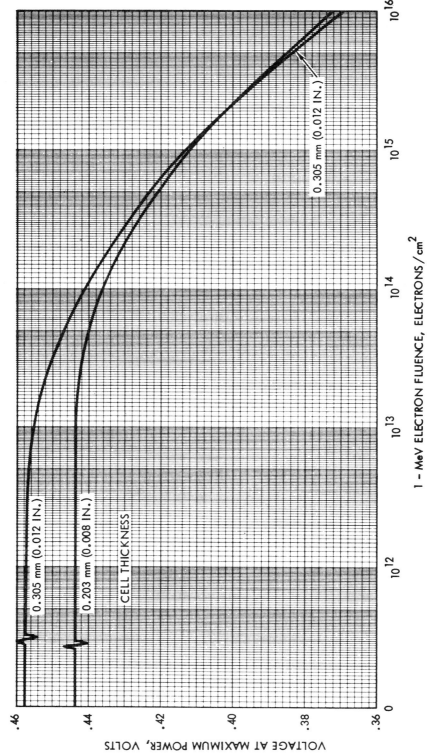

Fig. 4-66. (*Continued*)

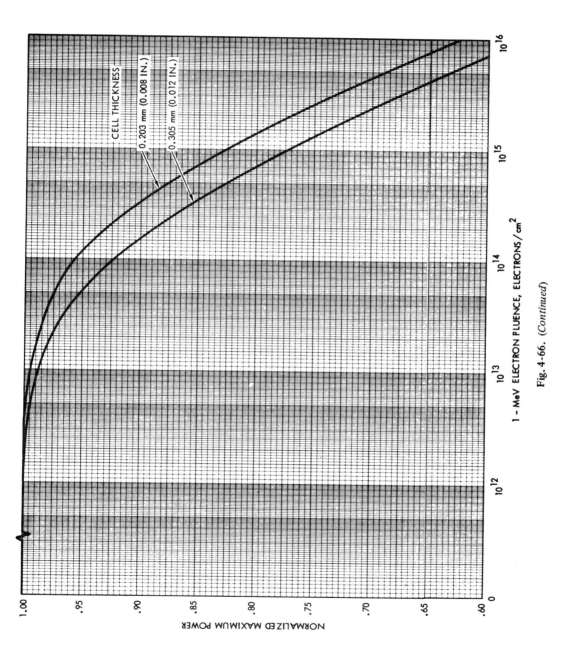

Fig. 4-66. (*Continued*)

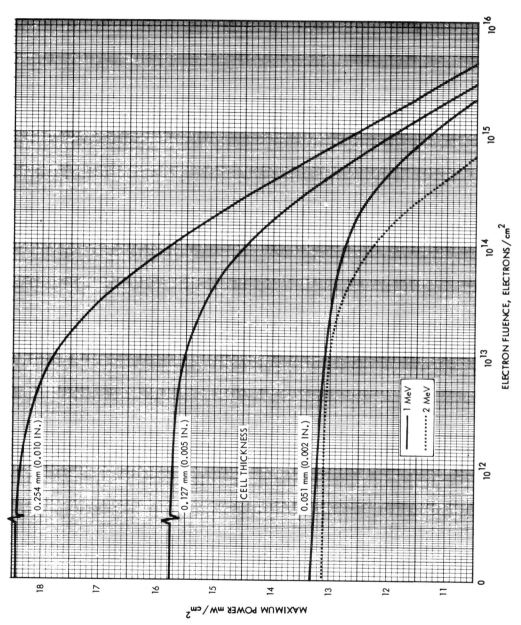

Fig. 4-67. Hybrid back surface field 2 ohm · cm n/p silicon cells.[28]

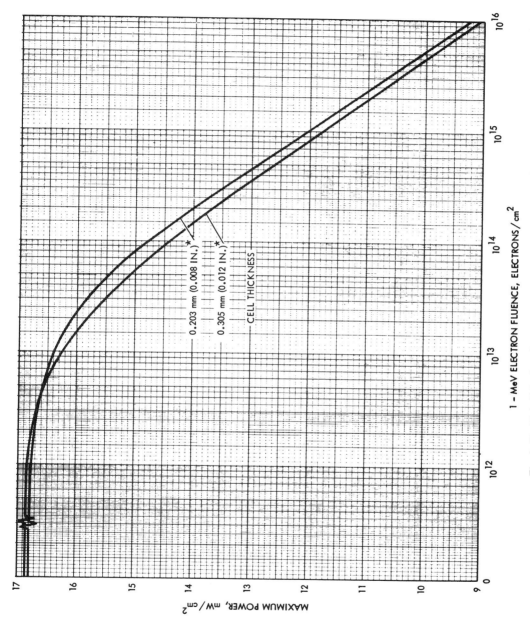

Fig. 4-68. Hybrid back surface field 10 ohm · cm n/p silicon cells.[28]

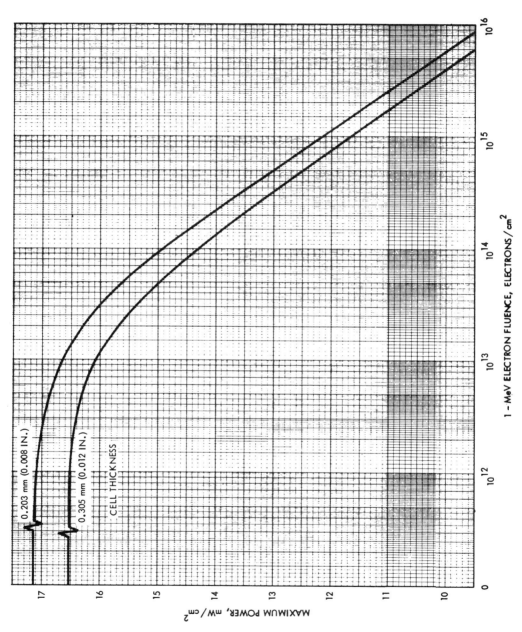

Fig. 4-69. Hybrid back surface field 20 ohm · cm n/p silicon cells.[28]

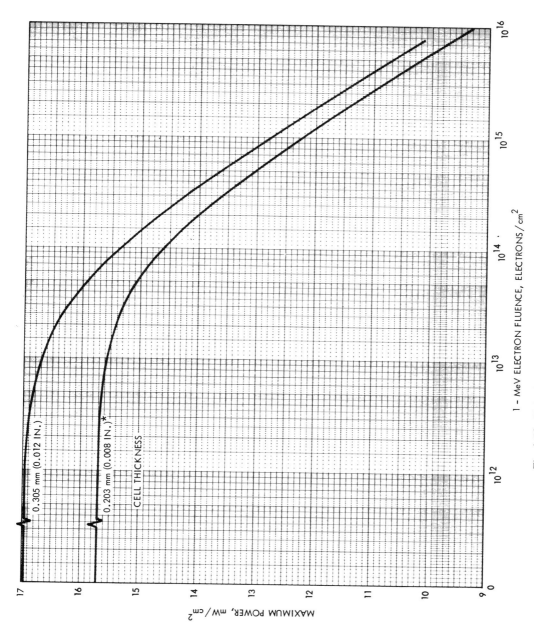

Fig. 4-70. Hybrid textured 2 ohm · cm n/p silicon cells.[28]

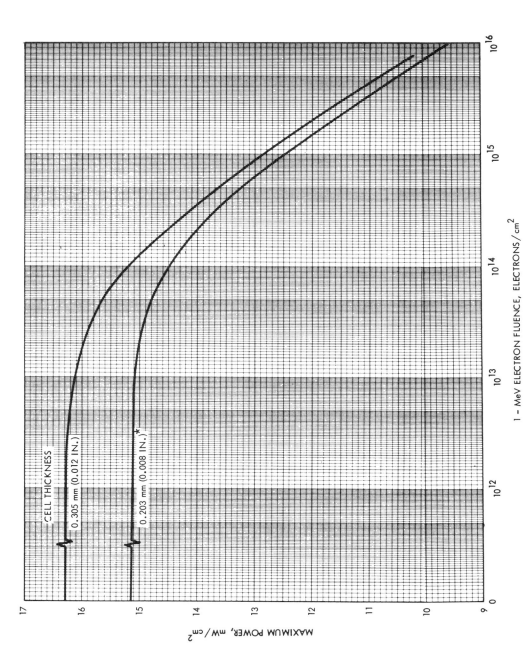

Fig. 4-71. Hybrid textured 10 ohm · cm n/p silicon cells.[28]

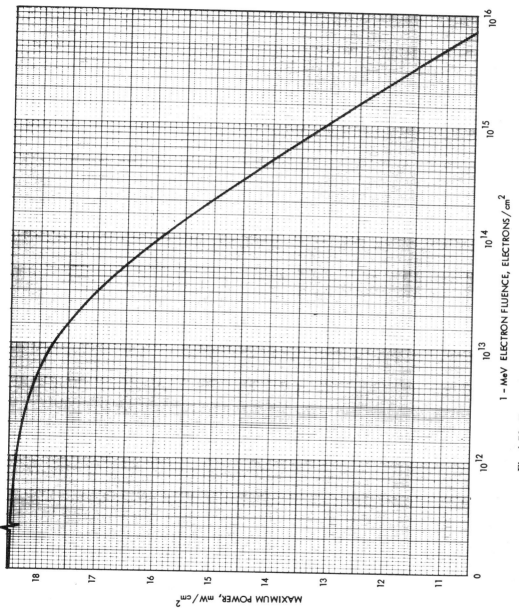

Fig. 4-72. Textured back surface field 10 ohm · cm n/p silicon cells.[28]

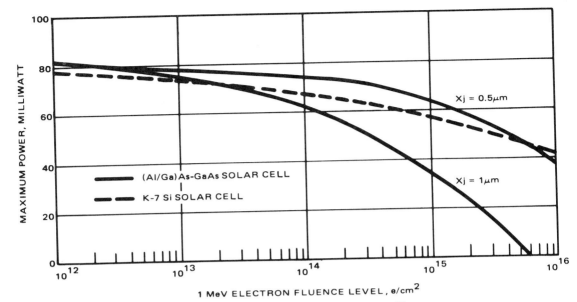

Fig. 4-73. Experimental gallium arsenide cells.[24]

were one solar constant AM0 and 28°C. Current and power densities were based on total cell area.

REFERENCES

1. P. A. Crossley, G. T. Noel, and M. Wolf, "Review and Evaluation of Past Solar Cell Development Efforts," Final Report, RCA Astro-Electronics Division, Princeton, New Jersey, June 1968.
2. *Conference Records of the 6th IEEE Photovoltaic Specialists Conference*, March 1967.
3. *Conference Records of 9th IEEE Photovoltaic Specialists Conference*, May 1972.
4. *Conference Records of the 10th IEEE Photovoltaic Specialists Conference*, November 1973.
5. *Conference Records of the 11th IEEE Photovoltaic Specialists Conference*, May 1975.
6. *Conference Records of the 12th IEEE Photovoltaic Specialists Conference*, November 1976.
7. *Conference Records of the 13th IEEE Photovoltaic Specialists Conference*, June 1978.
8. *Records of International Conference, Photovoltaic Power Generation*, Hamburg, Germany, September 1974.
9. *Records of International Conference, Evaluation of Space Environment on Materials*, Toulouse, France, June 1974.
10. E. L. Ralph and J. Scott-Monck in *Records of International Conference, Photovoltaic Power Generation*, Hamburg, Germany, September 1974.
11. W. Luft in *Records of International Conference, Evaluation of Space Environment on Materials*, Toulouse, France, June 1974.
12. M. Wolf and H. Rauschenbach, "Series Resistance Effects on Solar Cell Measurements," (pp. 455–479) in *Advanced Energy Conversion*, *Vol. 3*, Pergamon Press, Elmsford, New York, 1963.
13. J. J. Loferski (p. 1) in *Conference Records of the 10th IEEE Photovoltaic Specialists Conference*, November 1973.
14. W. Luft, "Silicon Solar Cell Performance at High Intensities," in *IEEE Transactions on Aerospace and Electronics*, *Vol.* **AES-6**, *No. 6*, November 1970.
15. T. T. Rule *et al* (p. 744) in *Conference Records of the 12th IEEE Photovoltaic Specialists Conference*, November 1976.
16. A. R. Kirkpatrick, "Silicon Solar Cell Development and Radiation Effects Study for Low Temperature and Low Illumination Intensity Operation," Report N72-26033, NASA **CR 114429**, Ion Physics Corporation, Burlington, Massachusetts, January 1972.
17. W. Luft, "Silicon Solar Cells at Low Temperature," in *IEEE Transactions on Aerospace and Electronic Systems*, *Vol.* **AES-7**, *No. 2*, March 1971.
18. H. S. Rauschenbach and E. E. Maiden (p. 217) in *Conference Records of the 9th IEEE Photovoltaic Specialists Conference*, May 1972.
19. H. S. Rauschenbach, "Skylab Orbital Workshop Solar Array System, Z-Local Vertical Study," TRW Report No. **SAS 4-3117**, Contract **MDAC-WD-70-2-004**, TRW, Inc., November 1971.

20. Yasui *et al*, Jet Propulsion Laboratory, Pasadena, California.

21. H. W. Brandhorst, Jr. and R. E. Hart, Jr., "Spectral Responses of Silicon Solar Cells at Low Temperature," **TMX 52870,** NASA, 1970.

22. W. Luft, "Effects of Electron Irradiation on n-on-p Silicon Cells," (pp. 21–41) in *Advanced Energy Conversion, Vol.* **5,** Pergamon Press, Elmsford, New York, 1965.

23. J. H. Martin *et al*, "Radiation Damage to Thin Silicon Solar Cells," Intersociety Energy Conversion Engineering Conference, Miami Beach, Florida, August 1967.

24. S. Kamath *et al*, "GaAs Concentrator Photovoltaic Power System Feasibility Investigation," **AFAPL-TR-77-80,** December 1977.

25. E. L. Ralph (p. 98) in *Conference Records of the 6th IEEE Photovoltaic Specialists Conference,* March 1967.

26. Unpublished data measured by TRW, Inc., during 1968 (solar cells were SiO-coated, 2 × 2 cm, unglassed, 2 ohm · cm Heliotek, 10 ohm · cm Centralab).

27. R. K. Yasui and P. A. Berman, "Solar Cell Contact Pull Strength as a Function of Pull Test Temperature," NASA **TR 32-1563,** Jet Propulsion Laboratory, Pasadena, California.

28. H. Y. Tada and J. R. Carter, Jr., "Solar Cell Radiation Handbook," JPL Publication **77-56,** November 1977.

29. W. Luft and H. Rauschenbach (p. 75) in *Conference Records of the 6th IEEE Photovoltaic Specialists Conference, Vol.* **III,** March 1967.

30. "ATS Power Subsystem Radiation Effects Study, Phase I/Final Report," Report No. **SSD 80089R,** Hughes Aircraft Company, February 1968.

31. R. L. Crabb (p. 329) in *Conference Records of the 9th IEEE Photovoltaic Specialists Conference,* May 1972.

32. H. Fischer and W. Pschunder (p. 403) in *Conference Records of the 10th IEEE Photovoltaic Specialists Conference,* November 1973.

33. Unpublished data measured by TRW DSSG, TRW, Inc., during 1977.

34. Based on Data Collected and Provided by Jet Propulsion Laboratory.

35. R. C. Waddel, "Solar Cell Radiation Damage on Synchronous Satellites ATS-1," pp. 195–205 in *Proceedings of the 7th IEEE Photovoltaic Specialists Conference,* 1968.

36. R. C. Waddel, "Radiation Damage Shielding of Solar Cells on a Synchronous Spacecraft," (pp. 122–137) in *Proceedings of the 1968 Intersociety Energy Conversion Engineering Conference, Vol.* **1.**

37. F. W. Sarles, Jr., A. G. Stanley, and C. Burrowes, "Solar Cell Calibration Experiments on LES-6," in *Proceedings of the 7th IEEE Photovoltaic Specialists Conference,* 1968.

38. F. W. Sarles, Jr. and A. G. Stanley, "Observed Degradation on the LES-6 Synchronous Solar Cell Experiment," in *Proceedings of the 8th IEEE Photovoltaic Specialists Conference,* 1970.

39. F. W. Sarles, Jr. and A. G. Stanley (p. 331) in *Conference Records of the 9th IEEE Photovoltaic Specialists Conference,* May 1972.

40. F. W. Sarles, Jr. (p. 199) in *Conference Records of the 11th IEEE Photovoltaic Specialists Conference,* May 1975.

41. B. E. Anspaugh (p. 308) in *Conference Records of the 9th IEEE Photovoltaic Specialists Conference,* May 1972.

42. B. E. Anspaugh (p. 191) in *Conference Records of the 12th IEEE Photovoltaic Specialists Conference,* November 1976.

43. L. J. Goldhammer and J. P. Corrigan (p. 194) in *Conference Records of the 11th IEEE Specialists Conference,* May 1975.

44. L. J. Goldhammer and L. W. Slifer, Jr. (p. 199) in *Conference Records of the 12th IEEE Specialists Conference,* November 1976.

45. R. L. Statler *et al* (p. 208) in *Conference Records of the 12th IEEE Photovoltaic Specialists Conference,* November 1976.

46. D. H. Walker *et al* (p. 100) in *Conference Records of the 13th IEEE Photovoltaic Specialists Conference,* June 1978.

47. *Proceedings of the 13th Intersociety Energy Conversion Engineering Conference,* August 1978.

48. R. L. Statler and D. N. Walker (p. 97) in *Proceedings of the 13th Intersociety Energy Conversion Engineering Conference, Vol.* **I,** August 1978.

49. P. S. Berman *et al*, JPL Publication **77-27,** *Rev.* **1,** August 1977.

50. T. A. Casad *et al*, JPL Publication **78-15,** *Vol.* **I,** March 1978.

51. R. G. Downing *et al*, JPL Publication **78-15,** *Vol.* **II,** August 1978.

52. R. G. Downing and R. S. Weiss, JPL Publication **78-15,** *Vol.* **III,** September 1978.

53. Based on previously unpublished measurements made by TRW.

54. J. Bruno, "Sunlight Checkout Tests for SAS," Final Report, Volumes I, II, and III, Report No. **MCR-71-320,** Martin-Marietta Corporation, March 1972.

55. J. D. Sandstrom, "A Method for Predicting Solar Cell Current-Voltage Curve Characteristics as a Function of Incident Solar Intensity and Cell Temperature," *Records of the 6th IEEE Photovoltaic Specialists Conference,* 1967.

56. R. E. Patterson and R. K. Yasui, "Parametric Performance Characteristics and Treatment of Temperature Coefficients of Silicon Solar Cells for Space Applications," NASA **TM 32-1582,** Jet Propulsion Laboratory, May 1973.

5
Optical Elements

FUNCTIONS OF OPTICAL ELEMENTS

5-1. Flat Plate Optics

Non-concentrator type solar cell arrays, commonly referred to as planar or *flat plate* arrays, utilize transparent covers and thin coatings for three reasons: 1) to protect the solar cells and their associated wiring from deleterious environmental influences; 2) to enhance the amount of sunlight reaching the active portions of solar cells; and 3) to aid in the heat rejection from the solar cells to reduce the cell operating temperature and thereby achieve a higher cell operating efficiency.

The development of silicon solar cells in the 1950's was accompanied by great optimism that such cells would last indefinitely, because silicon is one of the hardest and environmentally most stable materials. In practice, however, the metallic contacts of solar cells are subject to corrosion in the terrestrial environment. Therefore, solar cell modules for terrestrial applications must be fully encapsulated and hermetically sealed to prevent the entry of moisture into the module package. The package's front window fulfills a triple function, providing a hermetic seal, low-loss sunlight transmission, and efficient heat rejection. The window material may be glass or plastic. Anti-reflective coatings can improve their light transmission characteristics and improve the scratch resistance of plastics. Wavelength-selective reflection coatings may be used to reflect all energy having wavelengths outside the solar cell's range of sensitivity, thereby reducing the heat input to the solar cells. Window materials having higher long-wavelength infrared emission characteristics and higher thermal conductivities will provide for a more efficient solar cell cooling. However, most window materials and some coatings exhibit degradation of their optical characteristics with time that is caused primarily by the solar ultraviolet radiation.

Covers and coatings are also required on solar cells for space applications. While hermetic sealing of solar cell modules is not required, the space radiation environment requires full-area protection of the solar cells by coverglasses. The intense ultraviolet radiation in space quickly darkens most transparent glasses and all transparent plastics. The covers are usually cemented to the solar cells, requiring ultraviolet light protection of the cement. Either ultraviolet reflecting or absorbing filters may be used for this purpose.

5-2. Concentrator Optics

The artificial increase in the solar intensity incident on solar cells by means of some optical or other device is called *sunlight concentration* or *solar concentration*. Optical concentration devices may consist of mirrors (reflectors), lenses (refractors), or a combination of both. Concentrators not only increase the amount of sunlight that is usable by the solar cells, but also increase the amount of heat that raises the cell's operating temperature. Therefore, wavelength-selective coatings play a greater role in photo-voltaic concentrator design than in flat plate module design. Both refractive and reflective optical concentrator elements are subject to deterioration from terrestrial or space environmental causes. Because of their physical size, concentrators usually do not aid, but rather hinder, in the solar cell cooling process.

5-3. Historical Developments

The early terrestrial use of selenium and other photovoltaic devices had shown that such cells were not stable in the terrestrial environment. While most cells were either not protected at all or were just varnish coated, cells used as calibration standards were contained in hermetically sealed, evacuated or dry nitrogen-filled packages with soldered-in glass windows. Since their development in the mid-1950's, early silicon solar cells were used unprotected or with inadequate protection. This practice led to premature cell and system failures. Encapsulation by clear plastic was somewhat more successful, but reasonable weatherability required a relatively thick layer of encapsulant. In the late 1950's, emphasis of solar cell encapsulation shifted toward the space program, but returned during the mid-1970's to terrestrial applications.

Since the beginning of solar cell use in space, it has been recognized that in practical applications solar cells must be used in conjunction with other optical elements. Initially, transparent solar cell covers were employed for temperature control only, but by 1960 it was generally recognized that covers were also required to protect the solar cells from charged particle radiation found in space above a 400 km altitude. Therefore, since 1960, solar cell array designers considered both thermal control and shielding from corpuscular radiation. A third consideration, also investigated since the late 1950's, has been micrometeoroid erosion of uncovered solar cell surfaces and, later in this period, of both the solar cell covers and their filters. However, losses due to micrometeoroids have never been observed clearly. Estimates have put potential losses in the 0 to 2% range for 10 year missions.

Solar cell protection was attempted in the late 1950's with silicon oxides applied by various methods directly to the cells. These directly applied covers, now called *integral* covers, potentially offered weight and cost advantages over discrete covers that were fabricated separately and glued to the solar cells. Adequate infrared emittance, comparable to that of discrete covers, could be achieved with integral covers only when their thicknesses were so great that they would either not adhere properly to the solar cell or not possess sufficient transparency.

Numerous efforts have been attempted to develop a successful method of applying the integral glass cover directly to the silicon solar cell. However, as of this writing, success has not been achieved in the sense that fully developed and tested integral covers could be purchased in large quantities and used for operational hardware with a high degree of confidence of mission success. Below, some of these efforts are described.

Fused Glass.[1] A limited amount of success was achieved with coatings which were applied in glass-slurry form and fused to the cell at a temperature between 850° and 950°C. The solar cell diffusion and contact application procedures had to be modified to prevent this high-temperature fusing cycle from drastically degrading the cells.

Thermal Decomposition.[1] The thermal decomposition process involves passing of an inert gas, as a carrying vapor, from a deposition agent over heated solar cells. The decomposing vapor deposits a film on the cells. A large number of silanes have been used with deposition temperatures in the range of 400° to 900°C. The high deposition temperature led to severe cell degradation and relatively poor film quality for depositions thicker than 1 μm.

Reactive Sputtering.[1] SiO_2 films in excess of 25 μm thickness have been deposited on silicon by reactive sputtering. Silicon was used as the cathode in this process and the sputtering operation in an oxygen-rich atmosphere deposits SiO_2 on the substrate. Reactively sputtered

SiO_2 can produce a thick film which is exceptionally smooth; however, the sputtering rate must be kept below 0.02 μm/minute and the substrate temperature must be kept above 500°C. At this temperature, however, severe cell degradation occurs. At higher deposition rates or lower substrate temperatures, this process produced unsatisfactory films.

Electron Beam Deposition. SiO_2 films in excess of 0.125 mm have been deposited by focused electron beam techniques using quartz as the source material. A major advantage of this technique is the substrate's relatively low temperature during deposition. Normally, the substrate temperature may be below 50°C during the deposition to minimize thermal stress problems. A disadvantage of this technique is the degree of control required to maintain a low evaporation rate in order to keep large particles of quartz from being evaporated. Highly strained films, which readily strip from the silicon, are commonly deposited with this technique unless a very low deposition rate (normally less than 0.03 μm/minute) is utilized. Integral covers capable of withstanding typical space thermal cycling environments have not been produced.[1]

With a similar process, called *electron beam evaporation*, Corning Glass No. 1720 (an aluminosilicate glass) was deposited onto TiO_x-coated silicon solar cells. Integral cover coatings of up to 0.15 mm thickness were produced, but only coatings of 0.05 mm thickness had sufficiently low internal stress to withstand limited space qualification testing. These coatings exhibited relatively low light transmission below 0.5 μm wavelength, but radiation induced darkening was only slight. These covers would not be suitable for modern, blue-sensitive, high-efficiency solar cells.[2]

High-Vacuum Sputtering.[1] This technique has reportedly yielded films with excellent optical and mechanical characteristics; however, the rate at which the films are deposited is very low. An average SiO_2 deposition rate is 0.01 μm/minute. No flight quality covers have been produced.

Radio Frequency Sputtering. It has been demonstrated that complex thin films, such as certain glasses and Pyrex (Corning 7740), deposited by radio frequency (RF) sputtering may have physical and chemical properties basically identical with the parent bulk material. The RF sputtering process has the advantage of high deposition rates (greater than 1 μm/minute for SiO_2) and low substrate temperatures (less than 200°C). RF-deposited integral quartz films of 25 to 50 μm thickness have successfully passed five thermal shock cycles from -196° to +100°C with no mechanical or physical deterioration or delamination from the solar cell. Again, acceptable coatings for space applications have not been produced.[1]

A more recently developed RF sputtering process of Dow Corning Glass No. 7070 (borosilicate glass) onto TiO_x-coated silicon solar cells has produced relatively low stresses. The light transmission loss in 0.12 mm thick covers occurred below 0.4 μm and fell to 95% at 0.35 μm, making this cover useful for modern, blue-sensitive, high-efficiency solar cells. In a thickness of 50 μm, the sputtered 7070 glass showed a 1% broad-band transmission loss after irradiation with 10^{15} $e \cdot cm^{-2}$ of 1 MeV energy.[3]

Electrostatic Bonding.[4] The most recent and most successful method of preparing integrally covered silicon solar cells utilizes an electrostatic field to bond (without adhesive) discrete covers to solar cells. The bonding operation, known also as *electrostatic field-assisted glass-to-metal sealing technique*, is performed at approximately 400°C and requires the presence of a strong electric field for several minutes. The bond is permanent and the bond strength is greater than the ultimate strength of silicon. The cover material, Corning Glass No. 7070 (a borosilicate glass), can be bonded to SiO_x and Ta_2O_5 solar cell coatings. Covers of 0.15 to 3.0 mm thickness have been bonded. At the 400°C bonding temperature, the solar cells degrade unacceptably.

Environmental tests conducted on 0.15 to 0.30 mm thick covers showed that the radiation induced darkening of Corning 7070 glass is similar to that of Corning 0211 microsheet glass and not significantly worse than that of Corning 7940 fused silica, adhesive mounted to the cells with Sylgard 182 RTV and the corresponding Sylgard Primer. Ultraviolet radiation was found to almost completely bleach the charged particle induced darkening of 7070 and 0211 glass.

Discrete Covers. The lack of success that had been had with the development of integral covers led to the early adoption and continued use through today of the economically less desirable method of mounting a separate cover-slide to the solar cells. Glass provides excellent emissivity and has high transmission for solar radiation.

The two types of covers most frequently used between 1960 and 1974 were fused silica and microsheet. Fused silica was used in a thickness ranging from 75 μm (0.003 inch) to 1.5 mm (0.060 inch), with the three most common thicknesses being 150, 300, and 500 μm. Microsheet was used only in a 150 μm thickness.

To affect efficient heat transfer from the cells to space, the glass covers had to be cemented directly to the cells. This created a new problem: all cements darkened under the strong ultraviolet radiation present in space, thus reducing the solar illumination reaching the cells. To reduce adhesive darkening, ultraviolet reflecting coatings were developed to keep the damaging ultraviolet radiation away from the cement.

The protection of the coverglass adhesive was obtained through the incorporation of ultra-violet reflective coatings having cut-on wave-lengths of 450 nm initially. (The cut-on wave-length is defined as the wavelength where the transmittance has reached its 50% value.) The good results obtained with these covers and filters, together with the more radiation tolerant silicone adhesives which became available, led to a gradual lowering of the cut-on wavelength to first 430 and then 400 nm. Recent developments of more and more blue-sensitive solar cells pushed the cut-on wavelength to even lower values. Present "super blue" or "violet" sensitive cells require approximately a 350 nm cut-on wavelength to fully realize their improved energy conversion capability.

To optimize the solar cell cover and filter design and at the same time protect the ultraviolet reflective coating from possible degrada-tion by low energy, heavy particles in space, the ultraviolet reflective coating was placed inside the solar cell/cover stack, while the outside surface of the cover was coated with an anti-reflective coating. This outer anti-reflective cover coating, vacuum-deposited magnesium fluoride (MgF_2), reduced reflection losses on the first surface from approximately 4% to approximately 2%.

Inside the cell/cover stack, provisions were required to match the optical impedance of the cover to those of the cover adhesive and the silicon. Choice of a transparent silicone adhesive, instead of the originally used epoxy, and application of a silicon monoxide (SiO) coating to the silicon accomplished these objectives. The silicon monoxide anti-reflective coating on the solar cell was used beginning in the early 1960's, and throughout 1975. With this coating, cell output degraded in glassing by approximately 2 to 5% due to mismatches of the indices of refraction between the cover-glass, the adhesive, and the silicon monoxide. Work was started in Europe in the late 1960's to reduce such *glassing losses* by better matching of the indices of refraction. Solar cell anti-reflective coatings using TiO_x, Ta_2O_5, and others have improved glassed cell performance. Considerable development effort was required, however, before a repeatable process and optimized electrical performance was obtained. Since late 1974, high-efficiency production cells have used a Ta_2O_5 coating almost exclusively. New coatings are presently under development to further improve glassed cell performance for both space and terrestrial applications.

OPTICAL ENERGY TRANSFER

5-4. The Optical System

Sunlight penetrates a number of optical media before it reaches the photovoltaically active region of a solar cell. At each surface, the penetrating sunlight experiences reflection losses, and in each medium, it experiences absorption losses. Typically, reflection and absorption losses are not uniform over all wavelengths and over all angles of incidence. Hence, all the optical media that are applicable to solar cell arrays constitute an *optical system* that requires careful consideration in design and analysis. For non-concentrator arrays, the optical system has the following components (in the order of penetration by the sunlight):

- Space and/or planetary air
- Anti-reflective layer on the cover (if used)
- Cover bulk material
- Ultraviolet-reflective layer on the cover (used only when the cover bulk material transmits ultraviolet radiation)
- Cover adhesive (if used)
- Anti-reflective layer on the active solar cell surface
- Solar cell photovoltaically active region
- Solar cell bulk material
- Reflective, absorptive, or transmissive solar cell back surface contact.

In the case of concentrator solar cell arrays, refractive or reflective components may increase the optical system's complexity.

The radiant solar energy flux (sunlight) incident on the solar cell array front surface is partly reflected from that surface, partly absorbed by it, and partly transmitted into deeper layers of the array (through the solar cell covers into the solar cells). When the incident flux is reflected from a smooth, polished surface, the reflected beam is referred to as *specular* reflection. Reflections from rough surfaces are termed *diffuse*. The ratio of the reflected radiant flux to the incident radiant flux is the *reflectance*. The same ratio for a specific wavelength of the flux is the *spectral reflectance*. The ratio of the reflected radiant flux to the radiant flux incident upon a specific surface is called the *reflectivity* of that surface. In practice, the terms reflectance and reflectivity are used interchangeably.

The ratio of the transmitted radiant flux (at some distance measured from the front surface of the transmitting media) to the flux that entered the media is called the *transmittance* or *internal transmittance*. Frequently, the front-surface reflectance is not subtracted from the transmittance. Transmission of flux may be specular or diffuse; in the latter case it is called *scattered*. The ratio of the transmitted to the entered flux at a specific wavelength is termed

spectral transmittance. Transmittance at normal incidence through a flat plate is defined as *transmissivity* or *percent transmission*. In practice, the terms transmittance and transmissivity are used interchangeably. The term *electrical transmittance* is sometimes used to denote changes in the cover transmittance as determined by solar cell short-circuit current output.

The ratio of the absorbed radiant flux to the incident flux is called the *absorptance*. The same ratio at a specific wavelength is the *spectral absorptance*. In practice, the terms *absorptance* and *absorptivity* are used interchangeably. The common logarithm (base 10) of the absorptance is termed the *absorbance* (or *spectral absorbance*, respectively). The absorptance in homogeneous media increases with thickness according to Eq. 5-1.

$$I = I_0 e^{-at} \qquad (5\text{-}1)$$

I is the flux density at a distance t from the front surface at which the density of the entered flux is I_0. The constant e is equal to $2.718\ldots$ and a is the *absorption coefficient* (a is a function of wavelength). The wavelength at which the absorptance changes abruptly (in silicon at about 1.2 μm) is referred to as the *absorption edge*.

The absorptance, α, reflectance, ρ, and transmittance, τ, are related such that at any point in a material under thermodynamic equilibrium and at any wavelength or in any wavelength band, Eq. 5-2 is true.

$$\alpha + \rho + \tau = 1 \qquad (5\text{-}2)$$

For normally incident light, traversing the interface between two optical media having different indices of refraction, the reflected portion is given by Eq. 5-3.

$$\rho = \frac{(n_2 - n_1)^2}{(n_2 + n_1)^2} \qquad (5\text{-}3)$$

n is the index of refraction of an optical medium, subscript 1 refers to the medium from which the light is approaching the interface, and subscript 2 refers to the medium into which the light is entering. For the special case of solar cell covers in air or in space, the index of refraction of $n_1 = 1$ and that of the cover, n_2, is a material property. The value of ρ

Table 5-1. Indices of Refraction and First-Surface Reflection Losses at Normal Incidence from Several Solar Cell Cover Materials.[5-13]

Material	Wavelength $\lambda(\mu m)$	Index of Refraction n	Reflectance (%)
Empty space	0 to ∞	1	0
Fused silica	0.5 to 0.7	1.46	3.5
(Corning 7940)	1.0	1.45	3.4
Microsheet (Corning 0211)	–	1.531	4.4
Ceria-doped microsheet	–	1.537	4.5
FEP-Teflon	–	1.341 to 1.347	2.2
R63-489	–	1.43	3.1
adhesive	–	1.41	–
SiO	0.4 to 1.1	1.8 to 2.0	9.6
TiO_x	–	2.2	14.0
Silicon	0.5	4.1	37.0
	1.0	3.5	31.0
Sapphire	0.4 to 1.1	1.71	6.7
Natural quartz	0.4 to 1.1	1.53 to 1.57	4.7
MgF_2	0.4 to 1.1	1.37 to 1.39	2.6
Ta_2O_5	0.4 to 1.1	2.15	13.3

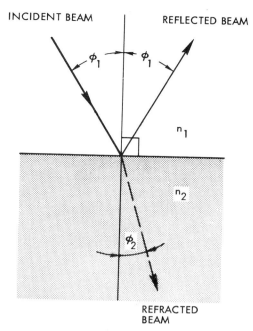

Fig. 5-1. Light beam incident on interface between two different optical media.

indicates the portion of light lost and not available for conversion into electrical energy by the solar cell. Typical values of n are listed in Table 5-1 together with the corresponding calculated values of ρ.

For non-normal angles of incidence (i.e., when the incident beams make an angle ϕ_1 with the normal to the cell covers—see Fig. 5-1), ρ is given by Fresnel's formula (Eq. 5-4).

$$\rho = \frac{1}{2}\frac{\tan^2(\phi_1 - \phi_2)}{\tan^2(\phi_1 + \phi_2)} + \frac{1}{2}\frac{\sin^2(\phi_1 - \phi_2)}{\sin^2(\phi_1 + \phi_2)}$$

$$(5-4)$$

The angle of the refracted beam with the normal, ϕ_2, is related to ϕ_1, by Snell's law (Eq. 5-5).

$$n_1 \sin \phi_1 = n_2 \sin \phi_2 \qquad (5-5)$$

The reflectance, according to Eq. 5-4, increases with increasing angles of incidence, ϕ_1 (for normal incidence, $\phi_1 = \phi_2 = 0$), and is one of the reasons for the deviation of the solar cell output from the *cosine law*.

The reflectance at any surface (interface between two optical media having different indices of refraction) is given by Fresnel's formula (Eq. 5-3). This formula was evaluated

for fused silica covers without any coatings and resulted in Fig. 5-2. This figure shows both the fraction of incident light reflected from the cover front surface and the fraction transmitted into the cover. A significant deviation from the cosine law at the larger angles is evident. The presence of an anti-reflective coating on the cover front surface modifies the front surface reflectance, reducing the reflectance at the smaller angles and usually accentuating the increase in reflectance at the larger angles.

5-5. The Air (or Space)-to-Cover Interface

To minimize reflection losses at the front surface, so-called *anti-reflection* or *anti-reflective* coatings have been developed. Such coatings are typically very thin and are made of vacuum-deposited magnesium fluoride, MgF. The anti-reflective coatings are one or several quarter-wavelengths thick (typically at the solar cell peak spectral response under sunlight illumination, namely, approximately at 0.6 μm wavelength). In addition to their natural index of refraction, they utilize optical interference phenomena to provide an *effective* index of

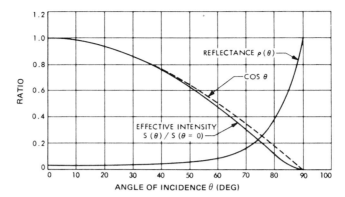

Fig. 5-2. First-surface reflection for fused silica and effective intensity that would reach the cell in the absence of additional reflection and absorbtion losses versus angle of incidence.[15]

refraction, n_e. Minimum reflection losses occur (at a single wavelength) when Eq. 5-6 holds true.

$$n_e^2 = n_1 \cdot n_2 \qquad (5\text{-}6)$$

Replacement of a single quarter-wavelength layer by two or more such layers, each having a slightly different effective index of refraction, causes the minimum reflectance wavelength to broaden into a wavelength band. In actuality, it is not practical to fabricate homogeneous quarter-wavelength layers so that a broadening of the minimum reflectance band occurs naturally.

The theoretical aspects of refraction and reflection are treated in most of the more comprehensive books on physics or optics.

5-6. The Cover-To-Cell Interface

The cover-to-cell interface contains two optical transition regions: from the cover bulk through the ultraviolet reflective interference filter (if such a filter is used) into the cover adhesive, and from the cover adhesive through the solar cell anti-reflective coating into the cell semiconductor material.

The reflection and refraction equations given in Sections 5-4 and 5-5 apply also for the cases discussed in this section, except that the anti-reflective coating on the solar cell also acts as a (multiple) quarter-wavelength thick interference filter. The cover adhesive is typically thicker than 20 μm and, therefore, classified as *optically thick* (that is, interference phenomena are not induced by it).

The primary objective of the optical design of the cover/cell interface is to minimize losses at the interfaces between optical media having differing indices of refraction and to minimize absorption losses in the wavelength region in which the solar cell is responsive.

A secondary objective is to minimize the solar absorptance and maximize the emittance of the covered cell assembly, thereby minimizing the solar cell operating temperature and maximizing the solar cell efficiency during operation.

Minimization of the reflection losses can be achieved by selecting materials having indices of refraction that (according to Eq. 5-6) result in minimum reflection losses.

In a practical sense, the indices of refraction of the silicon, adhesive, or coverslides cannot be altered. Instead, anti-reflective (AR) coatings must be used to provide an optical "impedance match" between the different media in contact with each other in accordance with Eq. 5-6. The UV reflective coating on the coverslide also serves as an AR coating between the cover and the cover adhesive while another AR coating is applied to the solar cell. The AR coating on the cell also relies partly on optical interference effects and partly on the natural index of refraction of the coating material. The theoretically expected reflection losses, ρ, arising from the differences in the indices in refraction only, are given in Table 5-2. This table also gives the desired index of refraction, n_e, which, according to Eq. 5-6, yields the lowest reflectance.[9,10]

If a minimum reflection is desired at a specific wavelength of light, the *optical thickness* of the

Table 5-2. Indices of Refraction and Reflection Losses at Interfaces between Two Optical Media.

Material Interface	n_1/n_2	r (%)	n_e
Air/silicon	1.0/3.4 to 4.1	33.5	1.94
Fused silica/adhesive	1.46/1.43	0.01	1.445
Microsheet/adhesive	1.53/1.43	0.11	1.48

NOTES:

r —reflectance without AR coating

n_e —effective index of refraction of an ideal AR coating which would give a minimum reflectance at the interface

coating must be one quarter-wavelength. The optical thickness is defined as the product of the physical thickness and the index of refraction. Since a single layer AR coating typically has constant reflection properties over a fairly large wavelength range, it is possible to achieve a coating designed for minimum reflection at a specific wavelength (such as about 0.6 μm for space-type solar cells) while good AR properties over most of the solar cell response range can be maintained at a given angle of incidence. In general, the coating thickness on cells intended for operation near normal angles of incidence should be greater than that on cells intended for spinning satellites.

5-7. Glassing Factors

Installation of a cover on a solar cell, commonly called *glassing*, decreases or increases the amount of light energy reaching the solar cell. Therefore, the solar cell output parameters change due to glassing as described in Section 4-19 (effect of illumination).

The properties and characteristics of AR solar cell coatings can be adjusted such that any of the following three parameters are maximized: 1) the *bare* (unglassed) cell output; 2) the cell output *increase* due to glassing; or 3) the glassed cell output.

Obviously, only the last parameter (absolute cell output after glassing) is of significance. Ta_2O_5 coatings, for example, can be "adjusted" to provide approximately from -2 to $+6\%$ output gain due to glassing; however, coatings with about 1% gain yield the highest absolute power output after glassing (using fused silica covers with 0.35 μm cut-on wavelength and DC 93-500 adhesive).

The glassing factor is expressed as Eq. 5-7.

$$F_g = \frac{I_{sc} \text{ (glassed)}}{I_{sc} \text{ (unglassed)}} \qquad (5\text{-}7)$$

I_{sc} is the solar cell's short-circuit current. A numerical value of F_g greater than unity indicates a greater cell output after cover installation (i.e., a glassing gain), while a value smaller than unity indicates a glassing loss.

Typical glassing factors for various AR coatings are shown in Table 5-3.

5-8. Angle of Incidence Effects

At an oblique angle of solar illumination (i.e., when the angle of incidence of the illumination

Table 5-3. Typical Measured Solar Cell Output Changes Due to Installation of Covers.

Solar Cell Characteristics		Cover Characteristics			I_{sc} Output Change (%)*		
Type	Anti-reflection Coating	Material	Cut-on Wavelength (m)	Adhesive	Typical	Minimal	Maximal**
n/p	SiO	Fused Silica	0.41	R63-489	-2.5	-1	-4
n/p	Ta_2O_5	Fused Silica	0.35	DC 93-500	$+1.5$	-2	$+6$

*A positive change denotes output increase.

**For controlled processes only; for uncontrolled processes the range may be significantly greater toward the low cell output side.

deviates from 0°−normal incidence), the power output capability of the solar cells will be reduced. The solar cell short-circuit current will fall off approximately according to the cosine of the angle of incidence, while the maximum available power will fall off faster than the cosine indicates. Deviations from the cosine law generally are of no consequence for off-point angles of about 30° or less, but are important in the design of cylindrical or paddle-wheel arrays. The deviations may be due to optical effects relating to apparent changes in the optical thickness of coatings and filters, thereby causing apparent changes in the spectral transmittance and reflectance values. Edge effects may cause refraction, scattering, and additional light collection by solar cells and covers, especially by thicker covers. Shadowing of solar cells by solar cell cover edges, solar cell interconnectors, wires, and other relatively small array components may also cause power losses.

Increasing angles of incidence on the solar cell cover front surface also cause varying reflection and transmission losses in the cover, cover adhesive, and solar cell and at the cover/adhesive and adhesive/cell interfaces. These effects arise because at larger angles, the AR coatings on the solar cells increase their apparent optical thickness, the apparent spectral response of the solar cell changes (the cell appears to be more deeply diffused), multi-layer blue-reflecting coatings on the covers tend to shift their apparent cut-on wavelengths toward shorter wavelengths, and absorbing filters (such as ceria-doped microsheet) increase their apparent thickness and thereby shift the cut-on wavelengths toward longer wavelengths.

Curved and Cylindrical Arrays. On cylindrical solar cell arrays, the angle of incidence of the solar illumination on the solar cells ranges from 90° (grazing incidence) to 0° (normal incidence). An *equivalent angle of incidence* can be postulated for a hypothetical flat array that would contain the same number of solar cells as the illuminated side of a cylindrical array and would produce the same power output (assuming the same cell temperature). For an angle of 90° between the solar vector and the array spin axis, the equivalent angle of incidence is between approximately 60 and 70°. The precise

equivalent angle depends strongly on all the characteristics discussed previously. The conclusion to be drawn from these effects is that solar cells and covers that were design-optimized for normal angle of incidence illumination may not perform optimally on cylindrical arrays. A considerable power output increase (in excess of 5%) can possibly be gained by optimizing the solar cell AR coating thickness in conjunction with the coating's index of refraction, the cell's spectral response and the cover cut-on wavelength, the cover AR coating thickness, and the intercell spacing (actually the cover-to-cover spacing) in conjunction with the cover size (relative to the cell size) and the cover thickness.[14]

Other angle of incidence effects include increased cover adhesive darkening due to the sunlight striking the adhesive layer on the side of the cell stack and the adhesive. The entire adhesive area will be nearly uniformly illuminated because the adhesive layer will act as a "light pipe," trapping the sunlight by internal reflection.

5-9. Thermal Control

The overall objective of solar cell array temperature control is to maximize the solar cell's power output under actual operating temperature conditions. This objective is reached by the design and the selection of materials for optical elements and coatings that 1) minimize the array's solar absorptance; 2) maximize its infrared emittance; and 3) maximize the broad-band transmittance of the optical elements.

Ultraviolet Filters. The primary purpose of ultraviolet reflecting filters on space arrays is to keep the cover adhesive from darkening due to ultraviolet radiation. However, this filter may also be utilized to minimize the solar energy input to the solar cells which is not convertible into electrical energy, but rather only raises the cell operating temperature. For illustration, consider the solar cell spectral output curves in Fig. 5-3. The curve shape of each of the four curves (arbitrarily normalized such that the peaks of their responses coincide) can be described functionally by Eq. 5-8.

$$I(\lambda) = k \cdot S(\lambda) \cdot R(\lambda, \phi) \cdot \tau(\lambda, \phi) \quad (5\text{-}8)$$

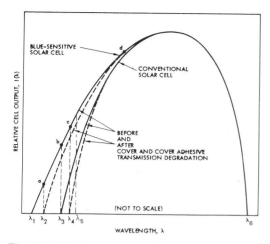

Fig. 5-3. Relative output as a function of wavelength of covered solar cells in sunlight (illustrative example).

where

$I(\lambda)$ = solar cell output current at wavelength λ

k = scaling factors to normalize the curves to equal height

$S(\lambda)$ = sunlight spectral distribution

$R(\lambda)$ = solar cell spectral response

$\tau(\lambda, \phi)$ = combined cover and cover adhesive spectral transmission characteristics

λ = wavelength

ϕ = combined ultraviolet and charged particle radiation flux that causes over darkening (solar cell damage occurs also, but is assessed separately).

Equation 5-8 describes the solar cell output as a function of wavelength when the covered cells are illuminated by sunlight. Hence, the curves in Fig. 5-3 differ from the spectral response curves given in Section 4-28 by having been multiplied by the solar spectrum, $S(\lambda)$.

The solar cell short-circuit current or maximum power outputs are proportional to the areas under the curves of Fig. 5-3 (See Eq. 5-9).

$$pI_{sc} = qP_{mp} = k \int_{0.3 \,\mu m}^{1.2 \,\mu m} S(\lambda) \cdot R(\lambda, \phi)$$

$$\cdot \tau(\lambda, \phi) d\lambda \qquad (5-9)$$

p and q are proportionality constants relating to the solar cell energy conversion efficiency at a given cell temperature.

Inspection of Fig. 5-3 reveals that installation of a cover on a blue-sensitive solar cell, having a cut-on wavelength at λ_2, would reduce the cell output even before the cover and cover adhesive have darkened. The amount of output loss is given by the ratio of the area bounded by λ_1, λ_2, and a to the total area under the curve. A darkened cover and cover adhesive with a cut-on wavelength at λ_2 would not affect the cell output over and above the light transmission loss which is caused by darkening (as given by the ratio of the area bounded by λ_2, d, and a to the total area under the curve). A similar argument applies to the conventional cell illustrated in the figure.

In practice, the cut-on wavelength for conventional cells is not set to λ_3 or λ_4, but rather to λ_5. The reason for this is that the solar energy in the wavelength range below λ_5 causes more cell heating and associated cell output power loss than could be obtained from a cell with the cut-on set to λ_4. A similar argument applies also to blue-sensitive cells except that the cut-on wavelength must be moved toward much shorter wavelengths in order to keep the cell output losses to a minimum. However, as the cut-on wavelength is moved toward shorter wavelengths, the degree of darkening of the cover adhesive may increase, thereby setting a practical lower limit on the cut-on wavelength. Increased darkening results in less light transmission to the cell and increased light absorption, and hence in higher cell operating temperatures.

Practical cut-on wavelengths have been 450 nm for earlier conventional cells, 400 nm for more recent conventional cells, and 350 nm for modern high-efficiency and blue-sensitive cells.

Infrared Filters. The purpose of infrared reflecting filters is to minimize solar cell heating. Therefore, such filters are also called *hot mirrors*, reflecting the "hot" (long) but transmitting the "cold" (short) wavelengths. A similar type, known as *cold mirror*, reflects the "cold" and transmits the "hot" wavelengths. Cold mirrors are used in medical operating lamps, film projectors, and sunlight concentrators for photovoltaic energy conversion. Hot and cold mirrors belong to the class of *dichroic* mirrors or *beam splitters*.

Blue-Red Filters. The ultraviolet and infrared reflecting properties can be combined into so-called blue-red filters. The combination involves broad-band transmission compromises that, so far, have stood in the way of large-scale exploitation.

Partial Mirrors. Partial mirrors may belong to one of two types: 1) partially transmitting and partially reflecting; or 2) nearly fully reflecting over some areas and nearly fully transmitting over other adjacent areas. The former type is also known as the *semi-transparent* type, and the latter type is often referred to as a *mosaic* or as *striped* or *half-mirrored*. Partial mirrors are primarily of concern to the designers of arrays for solar probes, spacecraft that approach the sun very closely.[15]

COVERS FOR SPACE APPLICATIONS

5-10. Classification of Covers and Coatings

Solar cell covers for use on current space type solar cell arrays are coated, transparent plates of inorganic materials which have approximately the same dimensions as the solar cells. Solar cell covers are also known as *coverslides*, *coverslips*, or *coverglasses*. The material from which the plates are made is referred to as the cover *substrate* material.

Solar cell covers with reflecting filters are typically coated on both sides. The "outer" or exposed side of the cover has a single layer AR coating which is designed to enhance the transmission of light energy through the cover and into the solar cell. The other or "inner" side of the cover has a UV energy reflective coating.

Solar cell covers made of absorbing filter materials are typically coated on their outer sides only with an AR filter. The cover bulk material absorbs ultraviolet radiation and thereby protects the cover adhesive. Solar cell covers may be classified by the parameters shown below.

- Substrate (or bulk) material
  Inorganic (glasses)
  Organic (plastics)
- Method of attachment to solar cell
  Discrete (adhesive-mounted)
  Integral

- Type of optical filter
  Filterless
  Reflecting
  Absorbing

The classification of covers by substrate material is associated primarily with the cover's resistance to darkening under UV and corpuscular radiation. In general, more radiation resistant materials are also higher in cost than lower radiation resistant materials. Inorganic covers exhibit much higher radiation resistance than do organic covers.

Practically all solar cell covers used for space programs (not counting flight experiments) have been of the inorganic, discrete type. With few exceptions, these covers have been adhesive-mounted to each individual solar cell.

Optical coatings on solar cell covers can be classified as follows:

- Anti-reflective (AR)
- Index-of-refraction matching
- Adhesive protection
- Thermal control
- Conductive.

Most solar cell covers used for space programs carried first-surface magnesium-fluoride AR coatings and second-surface UV reflecting filters. Since about 1971, the use of absorbing UV filters (ceria-doped glasses) has been spreading.

Special solar cell covers, such as those using conductive coatings, have been used successfully, but only occasionally, to satisfy specific space mission requirements.

5-11. Cover Materials

Solar cell cover material properties of interest for space application include charged particle and UV radiation resistance, density, optical transparency in the wavelength range between approximately 300 and 1200 nm, infrared emissivity, coefficient of linear thermal expansion, brittleness (relating to manufacturability), and, for certain applications, electrical conductivity.

Covers have been fabricated from fused silica (Corning Glass 7940), microsheet (Corning Glass 0211), ceria-doped glass (Pilkington Perkin-Elmer), and sapphire. Industrial grade fused silica has probably been used most widely, in

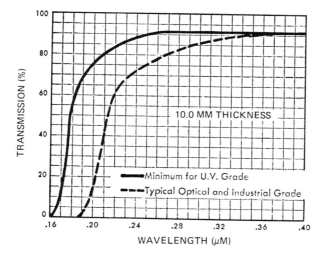

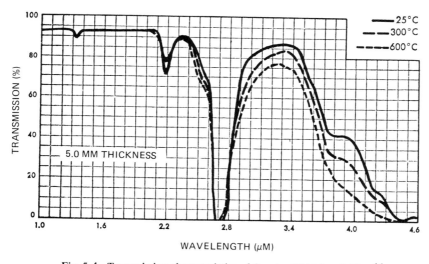

Fig. 5-4. Transmission characteristics of Corning 7940 fused silica.[16]

thicknesses ranging from 0.15 mm (0.006 inch) to 1.5 mm (0.060 inch). Microsheet has also been used extensively, but typically only in a 0.15 mm thickness to limit radiation induced darkening.

Fused Silica. Fused silica, also called fused quartz, is a synthetic, colorless, and highly transparent silicon dioxide glass. Typical transmission characteristics are shown in Fig. 5-4. In contrast to natural quartz, industrial grade fused silica is nearly—and ultraviolet-grade fused silica is completely—free of impurities that result in transmission-impairing color centers during UV or charged particle radiation. Like other glasses, fused silica is a supercooled

liquid, exhibiting a softening at elevated temperatures (above 1000°C) rather than a well defined melting point. Due to its low coefficient of thermal expansion, it can endure severe thermal shock without shattering.

Fused silica must be cut with a diamond saw and polished. The material is brittle but can withstand severe thermal shock treatments.

Fused silica has excellent resistance to ordinary weathering. It also has the typically high resistance of silica to attack by nearly all chemical reagents. Rapid attack occurs only on exposure to hydrofluoric acid or concentrated alkaline solutions, the rate of attack being increased at elevated temperatures.

When exposed to weathering (corrosion by

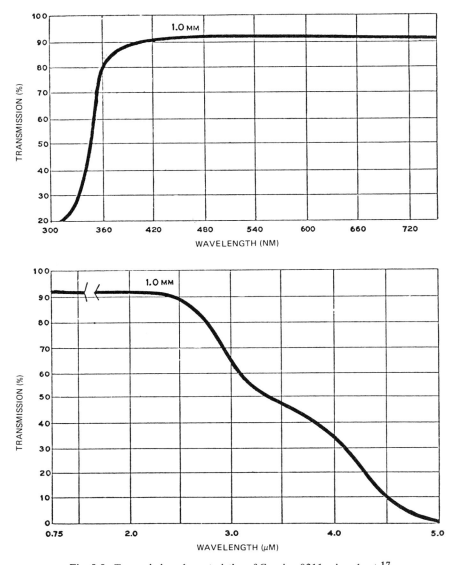

Fig. 5-5. Transmission characteristics of Corning 0211 microsheet.[17]

atmospheric gases; i.e., CO_2, H_2O), fused silica shows virtually no clouding of the surface or electrical surface leakage.

Microsheet. Microsheet is thin, optical-quality glass sheet with a flame-polished surface finish. Its transmission characteristics are shown in Fig. 5-5. It is made in several thickness ranges, from 50 to 610 μm. Microsheet is cut to size with a diamond saw, but could potentially be scribed and broken.

Microsheet is available in cut rectangles, squares, circles, and in standard stock sheets, which measure about 33 $\times$ 35 cm. Stock thicknesses are as follows: Gage No. 00: 50 to 84 μm; Gage No. 0: 84 to 130 μm; Gage No. 1: 130 to 160 μm; Gage No. 1$\frac{1}{2}$: 160 to 190 μm; Gage No. 2: 190 to 250 μm.

Ceria-doped Microsheet. The addition of a small percentage of cerium oxide to some glasses has been found to prevent the formation of color centers in these glasses during exposure to UV and charged particle radiation.

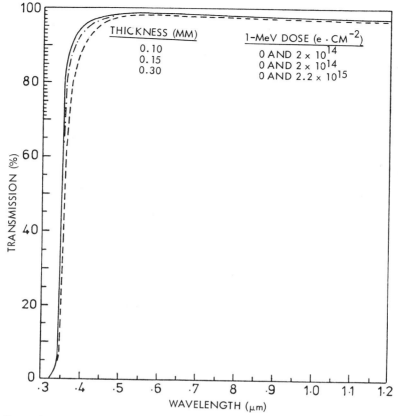

Fig. 5-6. Transmission characteristics of ceria-doped glass. (*Reprinted with permission of the IEEE.*[18])

Ceria-doped microsheet, in 0.1 mm thickness, exhibits a natural, sharp, cut-on wavelength at approximately 0.35 μm (about 0.36 μm for 0.3 mm thickness) and thus does not require the application of a blue-reflecting coating, as illustrated in Fig. 5-6.

5-12. Coatings and Filters

Filters on solar cell covers block certain wavelength bands and transmit others. Cover filters may be of the absorbing or reflecting type. Examples of absorbing filters are the ceria-doped glass filters; they absorb the UV radiation which may damage the cover adhesive. Examples of reflecting filters are the so-called *blue* and *blue-red* reflecting, multilayer, interference-type filters. The reflecting filters are located on the "inner" surface of the (mounted) solar cell cover to be protected from environmental damage.

Figures 5-7 and 5-8 illustrate the nomenclature for the commonly used blue-reflecting filter and a blue-red-reflecting filter which was developed for solar probes.

The transmission characteristics shown in these figures are obtained when the cover is surrounded on both sides by air or vacuum. However, when the cover is cemented to a cell, its transmission characteristic changes because of the change in the index of refraction of the optical media (i.e., cover adhesive) on the light exit side. Such a typical change is illustrated in Fig. 5-9.

5-13. Mechanical Characteristics

Cover Sizes. Discrete solar cell covers are frequently referred to as *undersize, same-size.* or *oversize* covers. These designations describe the cover size relative to the cell size. Prior to 1968, most covers were undersized by approxi-

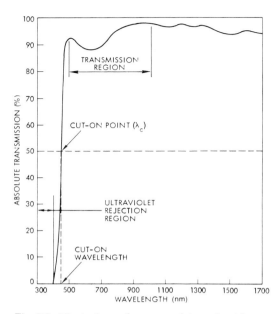

Fig. 5-7. Illustration of nonmenclature for blue-reflecting solar cell covers.[19]

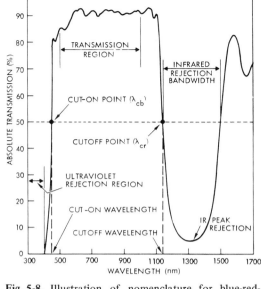

Fig. 5-8. Illustration of nomenclature for blue-red-reflecting solar cell covers.[19]

mately 50 to 500 μm for assembly tooling reasons. After the discovery of low-energy proton damage during 1967 and 1968, oversized solar cell covers began to be utilized for orbits through the radiation belts and at synchronous altitude.

Same-size covers are somewhat of a misnomer, in that in actual practice, solar cells and covers—even when fabricated to the same dimensional and tolerance specifications—will not be of exactly the same size, owing to size and angularity variations that occur normally in the cutting and solar cell etching operations. With same-size covers, low energy proton damage is possible.

For lower altitude orbits, where low-energy

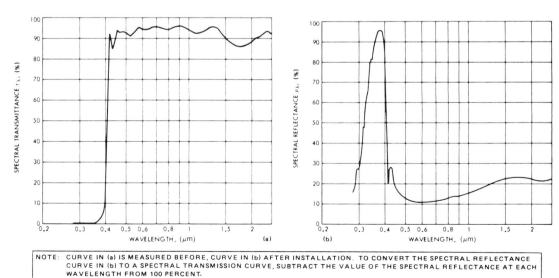

NOTE: CURVE IN (a) IS MEASURED BEFORE, CURVE IN (b) AFTER INSTALLATION. TO CONVERT THE SPECTRAL REFLECTANCE CURVE IN (b) TO A SPECTRAL TRANSMISSION CURVE, SUBTRACT THE VALUE OF THE SPECTRAL REFLECTANCE AT EACH WAVELENGTH FROM 100 PERCENT.

Fig. 5-9. Change of transmission characteristics of blue-reflecting filter (0.41 μm cut-on) due to installation on SiO-coated 2 ohm · cm silicon solar cell.[15]

protons are absent, undersize or same-size covers are acceptable.

Oversize covers typically *overhang* the solar cells on three or all four sides by between 0 and 1 mm.

Cover Tolerances. Typical cover tolerances are given below.

Length and width	$\pm 50 \ \mu m$
Thickness	± 25 to $\pm 50 \ \mu m$
Parallelism of edges	$\pm 50 \ \mu m$
Perpendicularity	$\pm 30'$

Nonfunctional Defects. The workmanship-type defects that are typically permitted are described below.

Edge chips	0.25 mm maximum projecting into the cover
Corner chips	0.25 to 0.50 mm maximum in any direction

Bubbles

Cover Thickness (mm)	Maximum Bubble Size (mm)
Less than 0.18	0.08
Up to 0.38	0.13
Up to 0.63	0.25
Greater than 0.63	0.38

Orientation. Cell covers can be purchased with different coating orientation markings, as shown in Fig. 5-10. The markings assure that the UV reflective coating is facing down and is protected from the space environment, while the different marking types permit flexibilities in the glass/cell stack design and in assembly process automation.

The light transmitting surfaces of solar cell covers, except for flame-polished microsheet covers, are typically cut from synthetic crystals and mechanically polished. The cover sides perpendicular to the light transmitting surfaces are rough cut only.

5-14. Conductive Coatings

Conductive coatings are thin (about 10 μm thick) transparent, electrically conductive films that are deposited on the outer surface of solar cell covers and other optical elements to achieve equipotential outer surfaces of a spacecraft. Conductive coatings have been used only on a

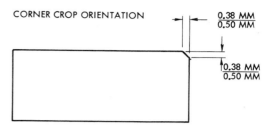

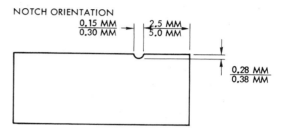

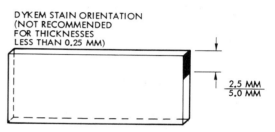

Fig. 5-10. Solar cell cover orientation markings (shown in the positions in which they are to be bonded to the cells; UV-coating is down.)[19]

small number of spacecraft, but for certain missions they are essential.

Conductive coatings are metal oxides such as tin oxide or indium oxide. To date, only indium oxide (InO) has been used for space hardware. Neither the chemical composition nor the electrical conduction mechanism of indium oxide are known exactly.[20] However, the conduction properties of InO are primarily similar to those of a metal and secondarily similar to those of n-type semiconductors having a carrier density of 10^{19} cm^{-3} and a Hall mobility of 100 cm$^2 \cdot$ V$^{-1} \cdot$ seconds^{-1}. The temperature coefficient of electrical resistance is about 5×10^{-4} °K^{-1} (0.05% K^{-1}).

Design Requirements. The actually required surface conductivity is strongly mission and design dependent; however, as a general guideline, the resistance from any point on the solar cell array (or the spacecraft) to spacecraft ground may not need to be lower than 10^4 ohms and may possibly be higher than 10^6 ohms.[21] The maximum permissible resistance must be calculated based on the maximum permissible voltage (electrostatic potential) gradient on the spacecraft/solar cell array, the maximum space plasma-induced current flow, and the potential erosion of the conductive coating by charged particle and UV radiation that may be expected during mission life. Depending upon the length of the current path through the conductive coatings of a specific solar cell array design, the actually required surface resistance of the coating, in units of ohms per square, is then calculated.

An increase in the electrical conductivity is achieved by an increased thickness of the conductive coating. At the same time, however, the optical transmittance of the coating decreases. A compromise between electrical conductivity and optical transparency is required. The emittance of the cover also diminishes as the conductive coating thickness is increased.

Solar Cell Substrate Covers for Explorer 31. Fused silica panels (Corning Glass No. 7940) of 250 mm length, 76 mm width, and 1.5 mm thickness served in a dual function as solar cell covers and as structural support members for the solar cells. The sheet resistance of the transparent conductive layer on the outer side was specified to be no greater than 1000 ohms per square. A second, highly conductive, non-transparent coating along the edge of the face of each panel served as current collector and facilitated electrical grounding.[22]

On their inner sides, the panels carried a blue-reflecting filter with 0.41 μm cut-on wavelength. The overall (blue filter and conductive coating) average transmission characteristics (in air) were specified to be at least 85% in the wavelength band between 0.45 μm and 1.10 μm, 85% between 0.60 μm and 0.80 μm, and 76% between 0.50 μm and 0.60 μm. The typically achieved transmittance was about 95% between 0.45 μm and 1.10 μm.

Second-surface Mirrors. A number of second-surface mirrors, carrying conductive coatings on their first surface, were tested for the combined effects of temperature, UV radiation,

and proton radiation expected during a near-sun mission. The test was conducted in vacuum at a pressure of 10^{-5} N $\cdot$ m^{-2} or less. The sample temperature was $174 \pm 5°C$. Illumination was provided by 16 solar constants intensity in the 0.25 μm to 0.40 μm wavelength band. The proton energy was 10 keV, the proton flux was 10^{10} $p \cdot$ cm^{-2} seconds^{-1}, and the proton fluence 3×10^{16} $p \cdot$ cm^{-2}. The test continued for 13,000 equivalent UV sun hours.

The test results showed that the resistance of parts, having an initial value of less than 25,000 ohms per quare, increased by factors of between 1.5 and 5 for UV only, protons only, or UV and protons combined. The solar absorptance showed an increase of less than 0.05 after 812 hours of exposure.[21]

Solar Cell Covers for HELIOS and GEOS. The solar cell covers were oversized fused silica covers of 0.15 mm thickness, and carried InO conductive and 0.35 μm cut-on wavelength, blue-reflecting coatings. The InO coatings were electrically terminated in pairs of Ti-Pd-Ag contact pads located on two opposite cover edges. The contact pads were sized to 1.05 mm $\times$ 1.80 mm $\times$ 10 μm. The covers were electrically interconnected in series and connected to spacecraft ground. Cover interconnectors, utilizing silver-plated molybdenum, were parallel-gap resistance welded to the cover contact pads.[20, 23]

The required sheet resistance for HELIOS was 10^4 ohms per square maximum; actually achieved values were 900 ± 50 ohms. The light transmission loss in the conductive coating caused a 2.5% loss in the solar cell I_{sc} output. An additional 1% power loss was caused by shadowing of the solar cells by the cover interconnect contact pads. The conductive coating was found undegraded after exposures to 95% relative humidity at 20°C for 200 hours, 95% relative humidity for three 24 hour cycles between $\leqslant$37°C and 52°C with two hours dwell at the upper limit, and ten temperature cycles between $-193°C$ and $+177°C$ with a rate of change of about 400°C/minute.

5-15. Cover Adhesives

Discrete solar cell covers are permanently attached to solar cells using so-called *cover ad-*

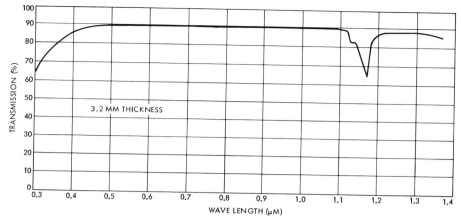

Fig. 5-11. Transmission of DC R6-3488 and DC R6-3489.[24]

hesives. Cover adhesives must possess high light transmission in the 0.35 to 1.2 μm wavelength band; a low degree of darkening from UV and particulate radiation; resistance to thermomechanically induced stresses (lack of debonding, crazing, etc.), especially stresses occurring at low temperature and during temperature cycling; and low outgassing characteristics. Transmission characteristics for a widely used cover adhesive are shown in Fig.

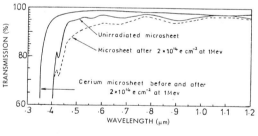

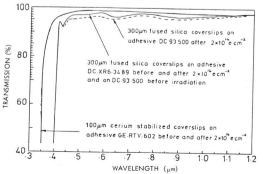

Fig. 5-12. Transmission of filtered ordinary microsheet, ceria-doped microsheet, and filtered fused silica solar cell covers.[18] (*Reprinted with permission of the IEEE.*)

5-11. The effects of space environmental exposures are illustrated in Fig. 5-12.

5-16. Integral Organic Covers

Between the late 1950's and late 1970's, considerable effort went into the development of spray-on and heat-laminated plastic covers. Promising considerable cost savings, such plastic covers would replace the conventional coverglass and its adhesive. A prime candidate for such coatings is FEP-Teflon, having good transmission characteristics, as shown in Fig. 5-13. Both spray-on and heat-laminating processes have been perfected; however, the material loses about 10% of its broad-band transmission after 5000 equivalent sun hours of solar UV radiation, and embrittles and delaminates from the solar cells during solar eclipses.[26-30] Nevertheless, organic covers are of continued interest for larger, lightweight, and low-cost solar cell arrays, or for use as thermoplastic cover adhesives for conventional coverglasses.

WINDOWS FOR TERRESTRIAL APPLICATIONS

5-17. Window Construction

Solar cell covers for terrestrial solar cell arrays cover entire modules, rather than only single cells (as on space arrays). Terrestrial solar cell covers constitute windows in a hermetically

a. 0.1 to 2.6 μM

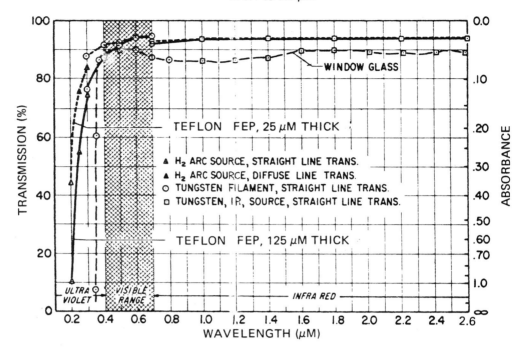

*Du Pont's registered trademark

b. 2.5 TO 15 μM

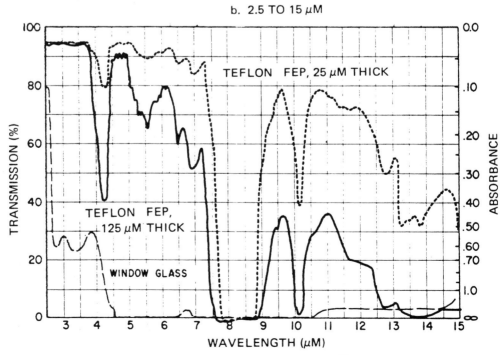

Fig. 5-13. Transmission of FEP-Teflon.[25]

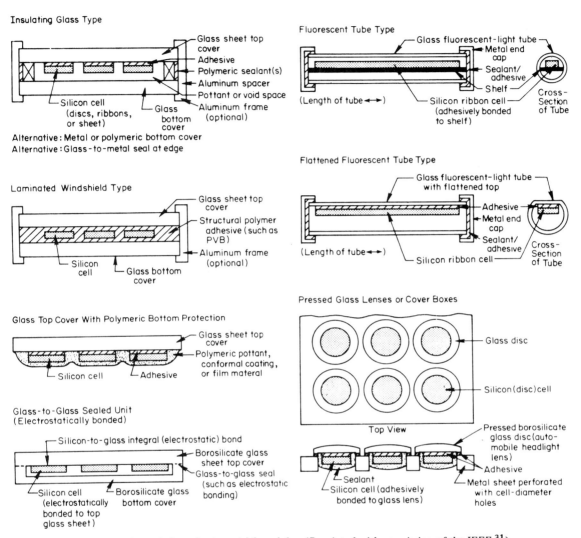

Insulating Glass Type

- Glass sheet top cover
- Adhesive
- Polymeric sealant(s)
- Aluminum spacer
- Pottant or void space
- Aluminum frame (optional)
- Silicon cell (discs, ribbons, or sheet)
- Glass bottom cover

Alternative: Metal or polymeric bottom cover
Alternative: Glass-to-metal seal at edge

Laminated Windshield Type

- Glass sheet top cover
- Structural polymer adhesive (such as PVB)
- Aluminum frame (optional)
- Silicon cell
- Glass bottom cover

Glass Top Cover With Polymeric Bottom Protection

- Glass sheet top cover
- Polymeric pottant, conformal coating, or film material
- Silicon cell
- Adhesive

Glass-to-Glass Sealed Unit (Electrostatically bonded)

- Silicon-to-glass integral (electrostatic) bond
- Borosilicate glass sheet top cover
- Glass-to-glass seal (such as electrostatic bonding)
- Silicon cell (electrostatically bonded to top glass sheet)
- Borosilicate glass bottom cover

Fluorescent Tube Type

- Glass fluorescent-light tube
- Metal end cap
- Sealant/adhesive
- Shelf
- Silicon ribbon cell (adhesively bonded to shelf)
- (Length of tube ←→)
- Cross-Section of Tube

Flattened Fluorescent Tube Type

- Glass fluorescent-light tube with flattened top
- Adhesive
- Metal end cap
- Sealant/adhesive
- Silicon ribbon cell
- (Length of tube ←→)
- Cross-Section of Tube

Pressed Glass Lenses or Cover Boxes

- Glass disc
- Silicon(disc)cell
- Top View
- Pressed borosilicate glass disc(automobile headlight lens)
- Adhesive
- Metal sheet perforated with cell-diameter holes
- Sealant
- Silicon cell (adhesively bonded to glass lens)

Fig. 5-14. Glass windows for terrestrial modules. (*Reprinted with permission of the IEEE.[31]*)

sealed package, keeping moisture away from the solar cells.

At its simplest the window is formed by a transparent potting compound or encapsulant that is poured over the interconnected solar cells. A more durable construction method uses a casting process by which the interconnected solar cells are encapsulated in a rather hard plastic. Another way to protect modules embedded in relatively soft plastic is to put a harder plastic or glass window right over the soft material.

The use of hard windows over soft encapsulants suggests an upside-down module construction: the interconnected solar cells are first mounted facedown to the window; then the solar cell back sides are potted and an optional substrate material is placed over them. The substrate may be transparent or opaque, and may be made from glass, plastic, or metal.

Windows made from glass and substrates made from glass or metal provide the greatest resistance to moisture permeation. However, adequate edge sealing is also required. Figures 5-14 and 5-15 illustrate a number of different approaches.

The moisture permeability of plastic materials can be minimized by using multiple layers of

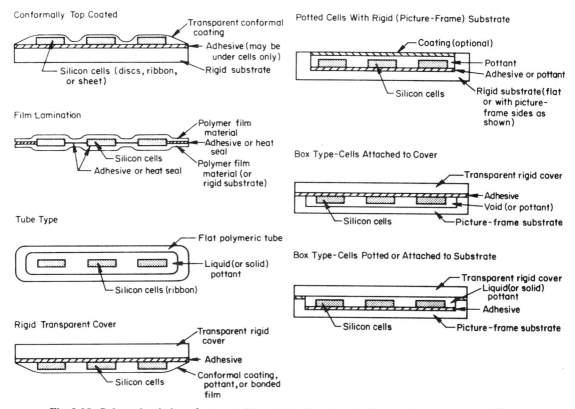

Fig. 5-15. Polymeric windows for terrestrial modules. (*Reprinted with permission of the IEEE.*[31])

different materials. Multilayer module construction can also provide greater impact strength of the window material and less impact transmission to the solar cells.

5-18. Window Requirements

The windows of terrestrial solar cell modules are exposed to a variety of environments. At the present time, it is not totally clear how these environments interact with window materials, or precisely which material properties are required to provide sufficient protection. Material characteristics of interest are discussed below.

Weatherability. A general material characteristic, this is an indication of the relative resistance of different materials to general outdoor exposure. Typical material deterioration includes such phenomena as discoloration, loss of gloss, surface crazing, chalking, erosion, corrosion, cracking, embrittlement, loss of strength,

and loss of flexibility. In severe cases, the material turns into a grainy or powdery mass and crumbles away entirely. Atmospheric oxygen, moisture, and light, especially UV radiation from the sun, aid in the destructive process. Local concentrations of ozone and industrial effluxes, as well as heat, usually add to the deleterious effects (see also Chapter 9).

Transparency. This is the wide-band optical transmittance as required by the spectral response of the solar cells, and includes both the effects of discoloration (darkening) of the material and surface deterioration.

Index of Refraction. An optical material property, this determines the light losses in the module by surface reflection (see Sections 5-5 and 5-6 for details).

Moisture Permeability. This characteristic is a measure of the rate at which water vapor penetrates the encapsulation. All plastics and some glasses are permeable to some degree. Moisture penetrating to the solar cells and cell interconnectors may cause internal module corrosion and power loss.

Fungus Resistance. This is an indication of a material's ability to retard or inhibit the growth of fungus. Usually, plasticizers, lubricants, stabilizers, and other additives provide most of the nutrients for fungus growth. Surface attack by fungi results in surface etching and light transmission loss.

Soil Accumulation. This measures a material's ability to attract and hold air-borne dust and dirt.

Tensile Properties. These are required to calculate the design stresses in the module, including the modulus of elasticity, the yield strength, the ultimate strength, and the elongation (see Sections 10-7 through 10-12 for definitions).

Coefficient of Linear Thermal Expansion. This characteristic may be of importance in certain module designs because it is responsible for relative motions in the package seals and their ultimate wear-out.

Impact Resistance. The amount of stress/strain energy a material can absorb before fracturing is measured by this characteristic. Impacts can arise from transportation, installation, and vandalistic loads. Some plastics can withstand large impact loads. Some glasses can be treated to have greater impact strength than ordinary glass.

Abrasion Resistance. This is an indication of the relative resistance to surface marring and scratching by abrasives such as wind-blown sand. A small amount of scratching usually does not impair the light transmission characteristics, but heavy abrasion does. Plastic windows can be protected by hard, scratch-resistant coatings.

Insulation Resistance. The insulation resistance of covers is not of great importance for low-voltage systems, but becomes significant for higher-voltage systems. The voltage between the solar cells and the substrate or window frame may cause electrolytic corrosion or shunt excessive amounts of electric energy to ground. On the other hand, some finite (but high) resistance may be desirable for draining off static electric charges from the window, thereby reducing the soil accumulation problem.

Flammability. This indicates a material's ability to ignite at some high temperature, to sustain a flame, or to burn at a certain rate. Flammability is usually related to the material's shape and thickness. Almost all plastic materials are classified as flammable.

Thermal Conductivity. This characteristic describes a material's suitability for effective heat transfer (see Section 2-54).

5-19. Window Materials

Window materials may be glass or plastic. Some glasses have better weather resistance than others. The best plastics have a higher weather resistance than the worst glasses. The most resistant plastics found so far are polytetrafluoroethylene and polymethyl methacrylate plastic materials. Polyethylene terephthalate and polycarbonate compounds have medium weather resistance. Polyethylene, polyvinyl chloride, cellulose, polystyrene, natural rubber, and nylon generally have low weather resistance. However, many materials can be modified by the addition of anti-ozonants, UV stabilizers, and other additives that can significantly improve their weather resistance.[31]

The most useful classes of materials for windows are the fluorocarbons, silicones, and acrylics, all of which are on the higher material cost end of the scale. Kel-F, PFA, CR-39, and various Plexiglass formulations generally weather well, while Tedlar, C-4 polycarbonate, and Tenite 479 weather poorly. Soil accumulation on hard surfaces is usually slight, resulting in broad-band transmission loss. Soft materials such as RTV 615, Sylgard 184, and Viton AHV accumulate large amounts of soil, resulting in 20 to 60% transmission loss. In actual practice, soft materials should be protected by harder ones.

SUNLIGHT CONCENTRATORS

5-20. Principles of Sunlight Concentration

The intensity of the sunlight falling onto a solar cell can be increased over its naturally occuring value by the use of *sunlight* or *solar concentrators*. A concentrator possesses a larger *entrance apperture* area, A_a, and a smaller *exit apperture*, or *target* area, A_t. A *geometric concentration ratio*, C_g, is defined in Eq. 5-9.

$$C_g = A_a/A_t \qquad (5\text{-}9)$$

Because of unavoidable imperfections of, and losses in, optical elements, the actually achievable concentration ratio, C_a, is always less than the geometric ratio. The degree of perfection of an optical system is given by its *optical efficiency*, η_0, such that the actual concentration ratio is as shown in Eq. 5-10.

$$C_a = \eta_0 C_g \qquad (5\text{-}10)$$

The actual concentration ratio, as determined from the entrance apperture and target planes, can also be defined as the ratio of the solar intensity indicent on the entrance apperture, S_i, to the intensity at the target plane, S_t (Eq. 5-11).

$$C_a = S_t/S_i \qquad (5\text{-}11)$$

The concentration ratio calculated from Eqs. 5-10 and 5-11 is, of course, identical. In practice, however, the accurate determination of C_a is quite difficult. A simpler efficiency to determine is the overall concentrator/array system efficiency, defined in Eq. 5-12.

$$\eta_a = \frac{P_\text{out}}{S_a A_a} \qquad (5\text{-}12)$$

P_out is the electrical output (in units of W) from the array (or a cell); S_a is the solar intensity at the entrance apperture (in units of W/m^2); and A_a is the entrance apperture area, measured (in m^2) perpendicular to the principle optical axis of the system. The system efficiency defined by Eq. 5-12 implies that the solar cells operate at their equilibrium

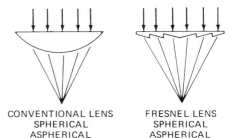

CONVENTIONAL LENS	FRESNEL LENS
SPHERICAL	SPHERICAL
ASPHERICAL	ASPHERICAL

Fig. 5-16. Refractive concentrators (illustrative examples).

temperature, and that energy requirements for cooling purposes are included (apportioned per cell or optical unit) or are stated separately.

5-21. Concentrator Types

Sunlight can be concentrated by refraction, reflection, wavelength conversion, diffraction, and laser action. *Refraction* is accomplished by lenses and *reflection* by mirrors. Lenses may be of the planoconvex, biconvex, or Fresnel type (see Fig. 5-16). The lens surfaces may be spherical or aspherical. A variety of practical reflector types are illustrated in Fig. 5-17.

Either refractive or reflective concentrators may be of the *imaging* or *non-imaging* type. Imaging elements project a reduced view of the sun onto the imaging plane (i.e., the focal plane) in accordance with the laws of geometrical optics. Non-imaging elements simply "bundle" the sun's rays together onto a small spot without forming an image of the sun.

Reflective or refractive components may be of the *point-focusing* or *line-focusing* type (whether they are imaging or not), as illustrated in Fig. 5-18. Point-focusing concentrators are also called *axial*, *coaxial*, or *three-dimensional* concentrators. Line-focusing concentrators also known as *troughs*, *linear*, or *two-dimensional* concentrators.

Point-focusing concentrators may be of the fully axi-symmetric (circular) or of a polygonal type. The four-sided type, illustrated in Fig. 5-18, is frequently used for conveniently fitting a number of Fresnel lenses or mirrors into square or rectangular frames.

Concentrators may also be classified according to the number of concentration *stages* they

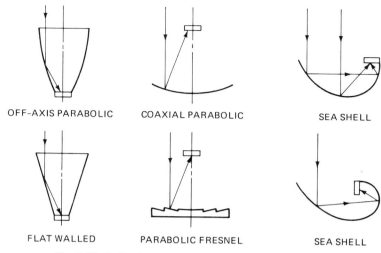

OFF-AXIS PARABOLIC   COAXIAL PARABOLIC   SEA SHELL

FLAT WALLED   PARABOLIC FRESNEL   SEA SHELL

Fig. 5-17. Reflective concentrators (illustrative examples).

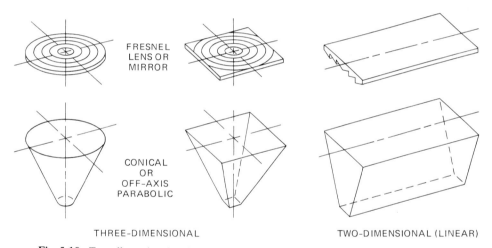

FRESNEL LENS OR MIRROR

CONICAL OR OFF-AXIS PARABOLIC

THREE-DIMENSIONAL   TWO-DIMENSIONAL (LINEAR)

Fig. 5-18. Two-dimensional and three-dimensional concentrators (illustrative examples).

utilize. Figure 5-19 illustrates two concentrators, both of which are two-stage. One, also known as a Cassegrainian system (named after the telescope of similar design) uses two mirrors to concentrate the light. A third reflector, not counted as a concentration stage, serves to "catch" beams reflected from imperfect portions of the optical surfaces and when the system's optical axis is imperfectly pointed toward the sun. The other two-stage system uses one *external* surface and one *internal* surface for reflection. Internal reflection, also known as *total* reflection, occurs when the light beam in a medium of higher index of refraction tries to leave into a medium of

lower index of refraction and when the angle of incidence on the boundary between the two media is sufficiently large.

In sunlight concentration by *wavelength conversion*, the solar energy in the entire solar wavelength spectrum is "concentrated" into a single wavelength at which the solar cell exhibits its highest energy conversion efficiency. This wavelength corresponds to the cell's bandgap energy (see Sections 4-17 and 4-27). Wavelength conversion can be achieved, for example, by incandescent bodies or by photoluminescent dyes. In the incandescent types, an element that is coated with wavelength-selective emitting material is heated by optical concentrators,

CASSEGRANIAN TYPE

WINSTON TYPE

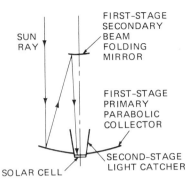
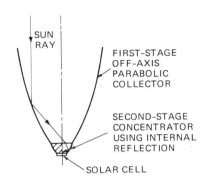

Fig. 5-19. Two-stage concentrators (illustrative examples).

while the element radiates energy in a narrow photon energy (i.e., wavelength) band at or near the cell's bandgap.

Photo-luminescent sunlight concentration (LSC) is also known as flat plate or *planar* concentration (PSC). Sunlight falling onto a flat plate that contains luminescent or fluorescent dyes is absorbed by the dyes. In this absorption process, the incident photons excite the dye molecules such as to cause them to reradiate their acquired energy at the specific wavelengths that are characteristic of the dye composition. The reradiated energy is trapped inside the flat plate by total internal reflections and falls, after multiple reflections, onto solar cells mounted to the circumferencial edges of the plate.[32,33]

Sunlight concentration by diffraction and by laser principles has not been demonstrated yet.

REFERENCES

1. Anon, "Survey and Study for an Improved Solar Cell Module, STOD Task No. 43," JPL Document No. **900-270**, August 1969.
2. H. Somberg *et al*, "Manufacturing Methods for Silicon Solar Cells with Integral Coverslips," Technical Report **AFML-TR-72-81**, Air Force Materials Laboratory, Air Force Systems Command, Wright Patterson Air Force Base, Ohio, July 1972.
3. G. Brackley *et al*, "Integral Covers for Silicon Solar Cells," in *Conference Records of the 9th IEEE Photovoltaic Specialists Conference*, Silver Springs, Maryland, May 1972.
4. A. R. Kirkpatrick, "Stress Free Application of Glass Covers for Radiation Hardened Solar Cells and Arrays," Technical Report **AFAPL-TR-75-54**, Air Force Aeropropulsion Laboratory, Air Force Systems Command, Wright Patterson Air Force Base, Ohio, August 1975.
5. "Corning Glass Works," Product Data Sheet.
6. "Solar Cell Coverslips," Product Data Sheet, Pilkington Perkin-Elmer.
7. "Teflon-FEP," Technical Information Bulletin, Dupont.
8. "Dow Corning," Product Data Sheet.
9. G. Seibert, "Increased Solar Cell Output by Improved Optical Matching, Part I: Theoretical Considerations," **ESRO TN-90** (ESTEC), March 1969.
10. G. Seibert, "Increased Solar Cell Output by Improved Optical Matching, Part II: Experimental Results," **ESRO TN-91** (ESTEC), April 1969.
11. W. Luft, "Status of TiO_x Antireflective Coating in the U.S.," in *IEEE Transactions on Aerospace and Electronic Systems, Vol.* **AES 10**, *No. 2*, March 1974.
12. M. Neuberger and S. J. Welles, "Silicon," Report **DS-162** for Air Force Materials Laboratory under Contract **F33615-68-C-1225**, October 1968.
13. E. L. Ralph and J. Scott-Monck, "Development and Space Qualification of New High-Efficiency Silicon Solar Cells," in *Records of International Conference, Photovoltaic Power Generation*, Hamburg, Germany, September 1974.
14. R. W. Objorden, "Solar Cell Optical Design Considerations," in *Conference Records of the 9th IEEE Photovoltaic Specialists Conference*, Silver Springs, Maryland, May 1972.
15. R. G. Ross *et al*, "Measured Performance of Silicon Solar Cell Assemblies Designed for Use at High Solar Intensities," Jet Propulsion Laboratory, Technical Memorandum **33-473**, March 1971.
16. Corning Glass Works Product Information Sheet on Fused Silica Code 7940.
17. Corning Glass Works Product Information Sheet **IC-31**, July 14, 1961.
18. R. L. Crabb, "Evaluation of Cerium Stabilized Microsheet Coverslips for Higher Solar Cell Outputs," in *Conference Records of the 9th IEEE*

Photovoltaic Specialists Conference, Silver Springs, Maryland, 1972.

19. "Solar Cell Cover," Product Specification No. **6024000,** Optical Coating Laboratory, Inc., July 1971.

20. H. Gochermann, "Vorlaeufiger Schlussbericht, Entwicklung und Qualifikation einer Conductive-Coating-Technik, Vertrags-Nr. **RVI 1-07/16/70 Z,**" Allgemeine Electricitaets-Gesellschaft, AEG-Telefunken, Wedel, Germany, October 1971.

21. Private Communication with I. Sachs, Optical Coatings Laboratory, Inc., Santa Rosa, California, 1975.

22. "Specification **SSE-4-S-74,** Fused Silica Panels," The Johns Hopkins University, Applied Physics Laboratory, Silver Springs, Maryland, July 27, 1974.

23. G. Pohl and H. Braasch, "The GEOS Solar Generator," in *Conference Records of the 11th IEEE Photovoltaic Specialists Conference*, Catalog No. **75CH0948-OED,** 1975.

24. New Product Information Sheet, **XR-63-488** and **XR-63-489** Resin, Dow Corning Corporation, Midland, Michigan, November 15, 1970.

25. DuPont Technical Information Bulletin **T-5,** "Teflon FEP, Optical."

26. A. F. Forestieri, J. Broder, and D. T. Bernatowicz, "Silicon Solar Cell Array Patent Application," NASA Case **LEW-11, 069-1** Patent Application No. **83,816,** October 1970.

27. A. F. Forestieri and J. Broder, "Improvements in Silicon Solar Cell Cover Glass Assembly and Packaging Using FEP-Teflon," NASA **TMX-52875,** July 1970.

28. S. A. Greenberg, M. McCargo, and W. L. Palmer, "Investigation of FEP-Teflon as a Cover for Silicon Solar Cells," Report No. NASA **CR-72970, LMSC-D243070,** Lockheed Palo Alto Research Laboratory, August 1971.

29. J. D. Broder and G. A. Mazaris, "The Use of FEP-Teflon in Solar Cell Cover Technology," NASA **TMX-71485,** NASA Lewis Research Center, Cleveland, Ohio.

30. H. S. Rauschenbach *et al*, "FEP-Teflon Encapsulated Solar Cell Modules—Further Progress," in *Conference Records of the 11th IEEE Photovoltaic Specialists Conference*, Catalog No. **75CH0948-OED,** 1975.

31. D. C. Carmichael *et al*, (p. 317) in *Conference Records of the 12th IEEE Photovoltaic Specialists Conference*, 1976.

32. C. F. Rapp and N. L. Boling, (p. 690) in *Conference Records of the 13th IEEE Photovoltaic Specialists Conference*, 1978.

33. J. R. Wood and J. F. Long, (p. 1158) in *Conference Records of the 13th IEEE Photovoltaic Specialists Conference*, 1978.

34. *Conference Records of the 13th IEEE Photovoltaic Specialists Conference*, 1978.

6
Electrical Elements

SOLAR CELL INTERCONNECTORS

6-1. Interconnector Terminology

The electrical energy generated by the hundreds or thousands of solar cells on an array must be collected and conducted to the load and, frequently, to an energy storage battery. Solar cell interconnectors conduct the electrical current from one cell to the next and—at the end of a series string of solar cells—to a terminal or tie point. From these tie points, current conductors (wires) lead to other terminals or tie points, connecting increasing numbers of solar cell strings in parallel and—sometimes—in series.

The terminology for solar cell array subassemblies and the various electrical circuit interconnecting elements used by the many workers in this field is quite diverse. The following nomenclature is based on what appears to be the most frequent usage throughout the industry.

Solar cell *interconnectors*, also known as *interconnects*, are conductive elements that electrically connect individual solar cells in series and/or parallel arrangements. Interconnectors may simply consist of wires, but more typically, they consist of metallic mesh or shaped metal ribbons.

Frequently, solar cells are pre-assembled (usually for manufacturing convenience) into modules consisting of between 2 and usually less than 100 cells. After installation of the modules on the solar cell panel or array substrate, the modules are electrically interconnected via *module interconnectors* (or module

interconnects). Module interconnectors may be identical to solar cell interconnectors or may be quite different in design.

An "electrical string" of solar cells, also called a group or a circuit, consists of a number of solar cells connected in parallel and series that provides power output at a bus voltage (a system may have several buses: shunt bus, primary power bus, battery charging bus, etc.). At each end of the electrical string, the solar cells are connected to a power collecting conductor, called the bus, via so-called string terminations. Bus conductors are typically insulated round conductors, stranded wires, or flat cables.

"Electrical strings" are often physically longer than the solar cell array substrate dimension. In those cases, the electrical string must be "turned around" by 90° or in hairpin fashion by 180° so that two "physical strings" may be required to accommodate one electrical string on a substrate.

Interconnectors used for U-turns or turn-arounds may be similar to module interconnectors or string terminations, or they may be of a different design.

Connectors are cable termination assemblies designed for quick connecting and disconnecting, usually referred to as *mating* and *demating*, respectively. The conductive portions of the connectors are referred to as *contacts*. Contacts may be *male* or *female*. Connectors with female contacts are also called *receptacles* and *sockets*. Connectors are available to be fitted to the ends of round cables or flat cables.

Terminals are electrical elements, fastened to insulating terminal strips, terminal boards, or barrier strips, that permit repeated joining and unjoining of two or more wires from different circuits. For space applications, the joints are usually soldered.

Wires may be round (circular or cylindrical) or flat (ribbon) conductors that may be used insulated or bare. A number of wires bundled together is called a *cable*. A number of flat conductors contained within sheet-like insulators is called a *flat cable* or a *printed circuit cable*.

6-2. Interconnector Types

Solar cell interconnectors may be divided into different types according to Fig. 6-1. The printed circuit types on rigid boards were used primarily during the 1960's, while those on flexible substrates (Kapton) have just been coming into use during the late 1970's. Most interconnectors used during the 1960's and 1970's were of the discrete mesh type, with formed piece parts following closely. The formed types, when made from low-expansion metals, have achieved the longest temperature-cycling life capabilities when low temperature limits were involved. Aside from printed circuit types, mesh interconnectors are easiest to manufacture; they may be either etched from foil or die-cut in closed form, expanded into mesh, and rolled

flat. Etching is a practical process only if a single metal is involved or if the etching rates of each metal of multi-metal interconnectors can be properly adjusted. Multi-metal interconnectors must be made such as to avoid bimetallic bending of interconnectors during thermal cycling, to reduce external stresses acting on soldered or welded joints.

Out-of-plane expansion loops deform during temperature cycling by changing their bend radii. In-plane expansion loops actually deform very little in-plane, but primarily warp out-of-plane in the areas where high bending stresses occur. In-plane mesh interconnectors deform easily into one direction only if they are not restrained from deforming into the perpendicular direction; the deformation is also accompanied by out-of-plane warpage.

6-3. Solar Cell Interconnector Design Requirements

The purpose of solar cell interconnectors is to conduct electrical energy from the individual solar cells to the power collection wire harness throughout the defined life of the solar cell array. To fulfill this purpose, the interconnectors must meet the following general requirements:

- Electrical conductivity
- Temperature cycling endurance

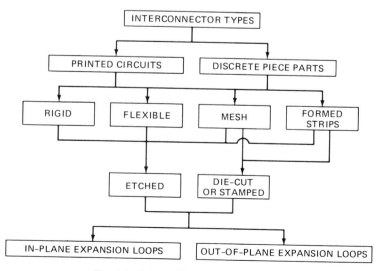

Fig. 6-1. Solar cell interconnector types.

- Manufacturability and repairability
- For certain space array designs, consist of non-magnetic or low-atomic number metals
- For certain roll-up or fold-up arrays, possess rollability or foldability
- Vibration (transportation or launch into space) endurance
- For certain array designs, fulfill other functions, such as:
    Heat transfer from the cell
    Solar cell junction low energy proton and radiation shielding (for space only)
- Reliability.

Reliability considerations usually determine the required number of parallel-redundant current paths and interconnector-to-cell joints, and their location on the cell to permit maximum output utilization from accidentally fractured solar cells.

For modern space arrays and terrestrial concentrator arrays requiring long life, temperature cycling endurance is one of the more difficult requirements to meet (see Section 6-4). Figure 6-2 provides typical temperature cycling requirements for space missions. Temperature excursions on earth are, by comparison, considerably less severe.

6-4. Solar Cell and Interconnector Failure Modes

Silicon solar cell arrays for space use are subject to a number of temperature-related, mechanical failure mechanisms, as illustrated in Fig. 6-3, which, in time, may cause the electrical output from the solar cell array to degrade. Open-cir-

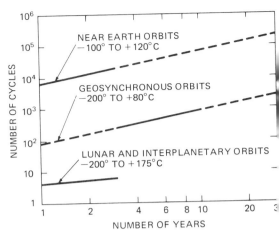

Fig. 6-2. Temperature cycling requirements for space (worst case limits.)[1]

cuit failures of soldered joints on the array can be caused by creep at higher temperatures, typically in excess of 100°C, and by silicon fracture at lower temperatures, typically below −100°C. Under less severe upper and lower temperature limits, large numbers of alternating stresses, caused by cyclic temperature variations of solar cell arrays, can lead to fatigue cracking of solar cell interconnectors and interconnector solder joints. Imbedded interconnectors may fail when the strength of the surrounding dielectric material approaches or becomes greater than the strength of the interconnector conductor (see Fig. 6-4).

Failure Definition. In the ideal case, any component or assembly of components should survive its intended mission without any failure or

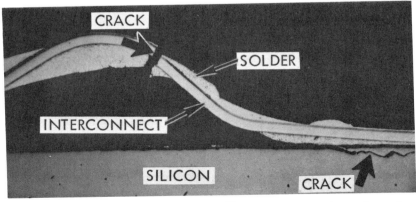

Fig. 6-3. Typical failure modes at very low temperatures.[23] (*7th Intersociety Energy Conversion Engineering Conference 1972.*)

Fig. 6-4. Fatigue fracture of imbedded in-plane expansion loops.[2]

deterioration. In actuality, however, the properties and characteristics of presently known materials require that the overall design accommodate deterioration and certain types of "failures." In a practical sense, then, a solar cell array "failure" must be defined. A typical definition of "failure" is the degradation of array power output below a certain specified limit. In the context of solar cell interconnector and joint fatigue life, the array degradation is assessed (independent of other degradation mechanisms such as charged particle radiation) statistically, using joint and loop failure rates established by ground testing. While loop failures are usually clearly observable open-circuit failures, joint failures are usually not easily defined because some workers believe that the onset of cracking is a failure, while others hold that any highly stressed solder joint will, in time, develop cracks so that only complete joint fracture may be a more realistic failure criteria.[3,4,5,6]

In a functional sense, only a completely fractured joint constitutes mechanical joint failure, but not necessarily an electrical open-circuit failure.

Joints, when located on the solar cell back side (bottom) contacts, when imbedded in adhesive, or when physically not separable from the cell contact during inspection by probing, cannot positively be identified either as being completely fractured and still making pressure contact, or as being only partially fractured.

The criterion for what constitutes a "failed" joint must, therefore, be defined in the light of reliability and other considerations for each specific design case and project requirement.

6-5. Historical Developments of Solar Cell Interconnectors

Until the end of 1960, many solar cell arrays were arrangements of parallel and series-connected modules, each consisting of a small number of cells connected in series, generally about five cells of 1×2 cm size. These five-cell modules were assembled by directly soldering the front contact strip of each cell to the bottom contact of the opposite side of the adjacent cell, forming a rigid "shingled" subassembly, as shown in Fig. 6-5.

The geometry of such configurations created high stress points, especially at the intercell solder joints. Such assemblies have led to frequent problems, in many cases as the result of repetitive thermal cycling. The most frequent failure mode was separation of solar cell contact metallization (electroless nickel plating at that time) from the silicon wafer.

The next generation of cell interconnectors consisted of solid or stranded wires that in snake-like fashion connected positive and negative cell contacts. This wire implementation made a first attempt to reduce mechanically or thermally induced stress. A significant improvement in interconnector flexibility was achieved by utilizing formed and shaped metallic "piece parts."

The flexible metal foil interconnector system shown in Fig. 6-6 was introduced at the beginning of 1961. This technique is based upon the use of parallel bussed submodules. In this arrangement, cells are connected into small parallel groups, using a "tab strip" soldered along the bottom of the cells. The series interconnecting tabs extend out and up from the edge of the bus, and are stress relieved before connection with the next succeeding series group, as shown in Fig. 6-6 for an early version of the design. Redundancy is achieved by use of the multiple tabs and solder joint connections.[8]

To further reduce the possibility of interconnection failure, a more recent design incorporates a bus bar with extended interconnectors or tabs on the underside of the cell so as to

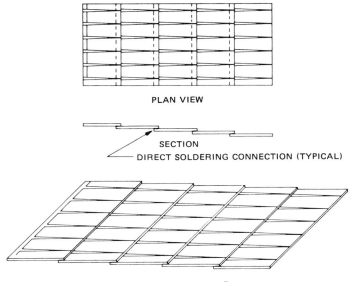

PLAN VIEW

SECTION
DIRECT SOLDERING CONNECTION (TYPICAL)

Fig. 6-5. Rigid shingle.[7]

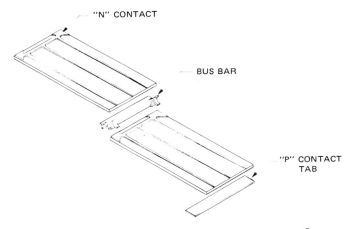

"N" CONTACT

BUS BAR

"P" CONTACT
TAB

Fig. 6-6. Early bus bar/tab approach for 1 × 2 cm cells.[7]

locate the positive and negative connections in close proximity on opposite faces of the cell, as shown in Fig. 6-7.

Two additional, similar configurations were used for interconnecting 2 × 2 cm cells and large area 2 × 6 and 2 × 7.15 cm cells, as used on the Skylab Apollo Telescope Mount solar array. However, these designs exhibited performance limitations as mission requirements became more severe and solar cell sizes became larger. Therefore, a two-metal interconnect system for 2 × 6 cm cells was developed by 1968 (Fig. 6-8).

A different approach used a combination of expanded metallic mesh on the cell back contacts and wires on the front contacts.[9] Thereafter, the wire portion of the cell interconnectors was eliminated and the expanded metallic mesh was used to connect cells both in parallel and in series.[10] Expanded metallic mesh interconnects have since been used widely in a variety of sizes and materials, mainly because of their low fabrication cost and ease of installation during solar cell module and array fabrication. The most popular mesh has been from 50 to 125 μm thick soft silver, made by die-cutting,

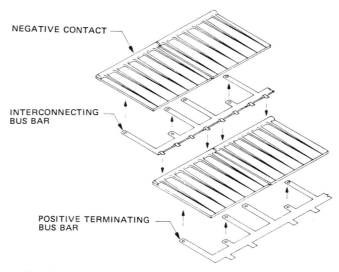

Fig. 6-7. Advanced bus bar/tab approach for 2 × 2 cm cells.[7]

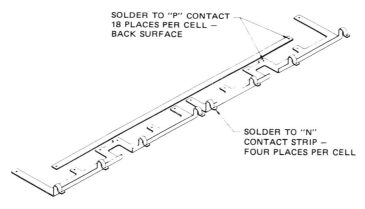

SOLDER TO "P" CONTACT 18 PLACES PER CELL — BACK SURFACE

SOLDER TO "N" CONTACT STRIP — FOUR PLACES PER CELL

Fig. 6-8. Two-part interconnect design for two 2 × 6 cm cells with zero parallel stress. (*Reprinted with permission of the IEEE.*[3])

expansion, rolling flat, and annealing. Copper mesh, made by the same process, has been a close second. Occasionally, mesh interconnectors have been produced by chemical etching.

The drawback of metallic mesh interconnectors is that the mesh loses its flexibility when it is either imbedded in adhesive or covered with solder. Under such conditions, mesh performs not much better than a solid sheet of the same material. Furthermore, the fine metal strands caused handling problems during soldering, and were subject to early fatigue life failure in thermal cycling.

To improve the cell interconnecting technique, several workers used formed metal strip

interconnectors that were usually made from copper, beryllium-copper, or Kovar, and occasionally also from molybdenum. Kovar and molybdenum, having expansion coefficients close to that of silicon, permit lower operating temperatures and larger numbers of temperature cycles than do copper or copper alloys. Some of the interconnector types which have been in use are shown in Fig. 6-9.

6-6. Soldered or Welded Joints?

A long-debated question, whether soldered or welded joints will ultimately exhibit longer temperature cycling fatigue life capability, has

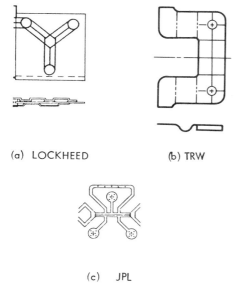

(a) LOCKHEED   (b) TRW

(c)   JPL

Fig. 6-9. Interconnect configuration varieties.[7,9,11,12]

still not been answered. Figure 6-10 illustrates the fatigue life improvements that have been made over the years. Decreasing temperature was plotted upwards in this figure because it corresponds to increasing strain, as discussed in Sections 6-20 and 6-21, and permits correlation of interconnector temperature cycling test data with general fatigue life test data and with fatigue life theory.

THE INTERCONNECTOR DESIGN PROBLEM

6-7. Interconnector Material Selection

The design of solar cell interconnectors calls for a material that possesses both high electrical conductivity and low thermal expansion, a material that does not exist. Therefore, engineering compromises must be made to at least approach the properties of the ideal material. Thermomechanically imposed design requirements call for thin, flat ribbons made from low-expansion (high electrical resistivity) alloys, while electrical design requirements call for thick conductors made from low electrical resistivity (high thermal expansion) materials.

From the many available materials, the following metals and platings have been found most suitable for long life or severe temperature cycling requirements (not in order):

- Copper, annealed, oxygen-free high-conductivity (OFHC), unplated or silver plated
- Silver, annealed, high-fine
- Kovar, annealed, nickel/copper/solder or silver plated
- Invar, annealed, silver plated
- Aluminum, 1100 pure, annealed, unplated or silver plated
- Molybdenum, annealed, silver plated

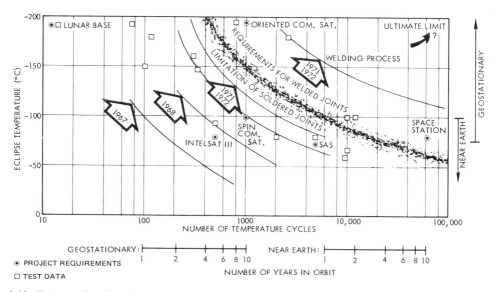

Fig. 6-10. Fatigue life of soldered and welded solar cell interconnecting systems, estimated in 1972.[11] (The project identifications are of no significance to this presentation.)

• Beryllium-copper, annealed, silver or solder plated.

For each of these materials, it may be important to specify the chemical purity, temper, thickness tolerances, and surface finish. .

6-8. Interconnector Electrical Design

The interconnector electrical design must be performed in conjunction with the mechanical design because the thermomechanically imposed design requirements tend to be in opposition to the design requirements for good electrical performance.

Design Criteria. The adequacy of the electrical interconnector design is judged on the basis of electrical losses in the interconnector system. Losses may be expressed in terms of voltage drops or power ($I^2 R$) losses. The values of these two losses, when expressed as fractions, are the same. A convenient expression is "percent cell output loss," because this quantity has approximately the same value when based on single cell or on total array output capability.

After an interconnector material is selected for thermomechanical reasons and after the interconnector shape is defined, the interconnector material may have to be plated to achieve the desired electrical conductivity. If the basic interconnector material is a low-expansion alloy (Kovar, Invar, etc.), the electrical conductivity of this material can usually be ignored and only the highly conductive plating (copper, silver, etc.) needs to be considered.

The effect on electrical conductivity due to over-plating with solder should be considered with caution because extensive thermal cycling tends to destroy the continuity of smooth solder coatings and causes their electrical resistance to increase.

Interconnector Sizing. The total electrical resistance, R, between two series-connected solar cells is

$$R = \rho L / AN$$

where ρ is the resistivity, L is the current path length (between solder joints), A is the cross-sectional area of each interconnector "leg," and

N is the number of interconnector "legs" per cell.

For a design criterion which specifies a maximum voltage drop of D,

$$D = IR = I\rho L / AN$$

where I is the nominal cell output current and the other symbols are defined above. Replacing the cross-sectional area, A, with w for the width and d for the thickness of a commonly used rectangular cross-sectional area of interconnectors,

$$D = \rho IL / Nwd.$$

A graph of D versus w for copper is shown in Fig. 6-11 for conveniently estimating interconnector electrical performance characteristics.

Plating Thickness Sizing. A conductor of length L, resistivity ρ_0, with rectangular cross-sections having width w, and thickness d, has a resistance of

$$R_0 = \frac{\rho_0 L}{wd}.$$

A conductive plating of such a conductor, hav-

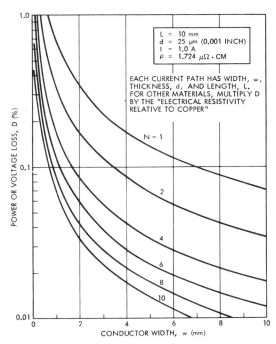

Fig. 6-11. Power or voltage loss in cell-to-cell copper interconnector having N current paths between cells.

ing a resistivity ρ_p and a plating thickness d_p, has a resistance of

$$R_p = \frac{\rho_p L}{2d_p(w + d + 2d_p)}.$$

The combined plated conductor resistance is

$$R = \frac{\rho_0 \rho_p L}{\rho_p wd + 2d_p \rho_0(w + d + 2d_p)}.$$

For high-resistivity, low-expansion alloys such as Kovar or Invar, $R_0 \gg R_p$, so that the plated conductor resistance can be simplified to $R = R_p$. A further simplification is possible when the plating thickness is much less than the interconnector base material thickness $(d \gg d_p)$, so that

$$R \approx \frac{\rho L}{2d_p(w + d)}$$

and, for multiple cell-to-cell conductors,

$$D = \rho I L / Nwd'$$

where $d' = 2(d_p + d_p d/w)$ and N is the number of conducting "legs" in parallel.

For practical interconnector cases, $(d_p d/w) \gg d_p$, so that approximately

$$d' = 2d_p$$

and

$$D = \rho_p I L / Nw(2d_p).$$

For $d' = 25~\mu m$, Fig. 6-11 can be used for selecting w for a given D, or, conversely, for given w and D, select the plating thickness, d_p.

6-9. Minimizing Thermomechanical Stress

The solar cell interconnector design activity essentially comprises the selection of materials and the conceiving of a configuration such that the combination of both reduces stresses in the interconnector/solar cell joints and in the interconnector expansion loops to permissible values. The permissible stress levels vary, depending upon specific mission requirements and solar cell array design characteristics.

Stresses of greatest significance to the designer are typically induced in the joints and in the interconnector expansion loops by two separate mechanisms.

1. Differences in the coefficients of linear thermal expansion of materials in intimate contact; or
2. By externally applied forces and moments that may arise from handling during fabrication and assembly or small but significant dimensional changes in the solar cell layout and interconnector geometry (during operation) when the array temperature changes.

The total stresses in joints and loops caused by temperature variations and by external forces can be found by superposition of the stresses from the different mechanisms discussed separately in the following sections.

6-10. Thermomechanical Stress in Rigid Joints

Rigid joints (or bonds) are found in the metallic contact layers on silicon solar cells, in the plating layers on solar cell interconnectors, in interconnector-to-solar cell soldered or welded joints, and in adhesive layers (cover-to-cell and cell-to-substrate) at lower temperatures, typically below $-100°C$.

For illustration of stresses in rigid joints, consider two long strips of different materials bonded to each other in intimate permanent contact, as shown in Fig. 6-12. Each material is characterized by its elastic modulus, E; linear coefficient of thermal expansion, α; Poisson's ratio, ν; and thickness, t. (For definitions of these items, see Chapter 10.) As the temperature T changes by an amount ΔT from the equilibrium temperature T_0, so that $\Delta T = T - T_0$, the two materials tend to expand or contract at different rates. But since they are physically joined together, the changes in length (or strains) in each material must be equal at their interface. If the strips are long compared to their thickness, then away from their edges it can be assumed that the stress conditions across

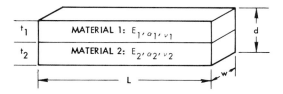

Fig. 6-12. Two-strip model (rigid bond).

their thickness are uniform. If, in addition, the strips are narrow compared to the length and thickness, the stresses in the lateral (i.e., width) direction can be neglected, and if the strips are restrained from curving (i.e., they remain flat), the strains are given by Eq. 6-1.

$$\epsilon_1 = \alpha_1 \Delta T + \frac{\sigma_1}{E_1} = \epsilon_2 = \alpha_2 \Delta T + \frac{\sigma_2}{E_2}$$
(6-1)

The subscripts 1 and 2 refer to the first and second material, respectively. Since no net axial load is applied to the two strips, we have an equilibrium equation (Eq. 6-2).

$$\sigma_1 t_1 + \sigma_2 t_2 = 0 \quad \text{or} \quad \sigma_2 = -\sigma_1 \frac{t_1}{t_2}$$
(6-2)

Substituting Eq. 6-2 for σ_2 into Eq. 6-1 gives Eq. 6-3.

$$\sigma_1 = -\frac{E_1 \Delta\alpha\Delta T}{1 + mn}, \qquad \sigma_2 = \frac{E_2 \Delta\alpha\Delta T}{1 + \frac{1}{mn}}$$
(6-3)

where

$$\Delta\alpha = |\alpha_1 - \alpha_1| \quad \text{and} \quad m = \frac{t_1}{t_2}$$

and

$$n = \frac{E_1}{E_2}.$$

For each case, in Eq. 6-3, the numerator is the stress in one element which would result if the other element were infinitely rigid, while the denominator gives the reduction in stress due to the actual flexibility of the second element.

For several layers rigidly fastened together, the stress in the ith layer can be determined by Eq. 6-4.

$$\sigma_i = E_i(\bar{\epsilon} - \alpha_i \Delta T)$$
(6-4)

where

$$\bar{\epsilon} = \frac{\sum t_i E_i \alpha_i \Delta T}{\sum t_i E_i}$$

is the value of the longitudinal strain.

For the common case in solar cell arrays where the joined layers are not narrow strips but wide plates, the stresses in all directions in the plane of the layers are equal. Therefore, due to the effect of Poisson's ratio, the values of E_i in the above equations have to be replaced by their effective values $E_i' = E_i/1 - \nu$. Thus, for bonded two-dimensional layers, the thermal stresses can be significantly higher than for one-dimensional strips. In many cases, geometric discontinuities may lead to so-called stress riser effects that may increase the stress in certain localized areas even more.

When the layers are allowed to bend, the stresses away from the edges of the layers vary linearly through the thickness with the maximum stresses occurring at the interface between the layers[13,14] (see Fig. 6-13), causing the strips to bend into a radius ρ or curvature $1/\rho$ (Eq. 6-5a,b).

$$\frac{1}{\rho} = \frac{-6\Delta\alpha\Delta T(1 + m)^2}{(t_1 + t_2)[3(1 + m)^2 + (1 + mn)(m^2 + 1/mn)]}$$
(6-5a)

$$(\sigma_1)_{max} = \frac{2}{\rho}\left[\frac{E_1 I_1 + E_2 I_2}{t_1(t_1 + t_2)} + \frac{t_1 E_1}{4}\right]$$
(6-5b)

For the special case where the two strips have the same elastic modulus and the same thickness (i.e., $m = n = 1$), the maximum stresses in the two strips are equal to their values without bending, as given by Eq. 6-3. If, as is the case of solder plating on solar cells, the first

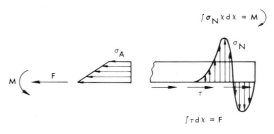

Fig. 6-13. Force and moment equilibrium between interior stresses and edge shear and normal stresses.

layer is much thinner than the second layer (i.e., $m \ll 0$), then Eq. 6-5 can be simplified (by neglecting m^2), giving Eq. 6-6.

$$\sigma_1 = \frac{E_1 \Delta\alpha\Delta T}{1 + 4mn} \qquad (6\text{-}6)$$

By comparing Eq. 6-6 with Eq. 6-3, it is seen that when the effect of curvature is included, the reduction in the stress in layer 1 due to the flexibility of layer 2 is increased by a factor of 4.

The stresses discussed so far exist in portions of the bonded strips which are remote from the edges. However, it is obvious that near the edges, additional stresses must exist, since the boundary condition at the edges is that the axial stress is zero. The edge problem has been investigated analytically[15] and by a finite element numerical analysis,[16] showing that the stresses given by Eq. 6-5 persist almost unchanged up to a distance of approximately one total thickness $d = t_1 + t_2$ from the edge. Closer to the edge, normal and shear stresses develop, and increase rapidly as the edge is approached. The shear stress balances the axial forces in the members (Fig. 6-13); that is, the integral of the shear stress equals the axial force in each member and is essentially independent of the values of m and n. The normal (or prying) stress balances the bending moments in the layers. Thus, the normal stresses are very sensitive to the values of the thickness and stiffness ratios m and n. For the particular case where $m = 1$, the normal forces are zero. Figures 6-14 and 6-15 show typical variations of the interface shear and normal forces near the edge of a joint, while Fig. 6-16 shows the variation of the axial stress through the thickness of the layers at various distances near the end. Notice that for the thicker member, the axial stress variation through the thickness is quite non-linear and that the maximum value of the axial stress occurs very near the edge.

Thus, the maximum stresses in the joint occur locally, near the ends. If the material is ductile, and if there are only a few load cycles, then these local peak stresses are of little concern, since the material will simply yield and relieve the stress. Failure will only occur if the fracture strain capability of the material is exceeded. However, for a brittle material,

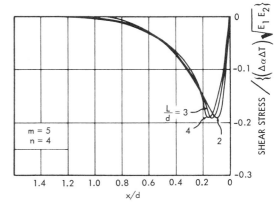

Fig. 6-14. Influence of variation in half-length/thickness ratio on shear stress at interface.[16] (*Reprinted with permission of the ASCE.*)

such as silicon, these high stresses can cause failures which involve pulling out small chunks of silicon called divots. If a brittle failure occurs near the edge, it will transfer the undiminished load to the next—as yet unfailed—section of material, so that propagation of the fracture to complete failure ensues. If the load application is repeated many times, then failure can occur by fatigue at lower stresses than required for

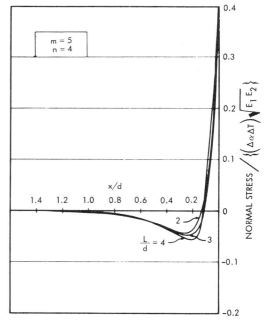

Fig. 6-15. Influence of variation in half-length/thickness ratio on normal stress at interface.[16] (*Reprinted with permission of the ASCE.*)

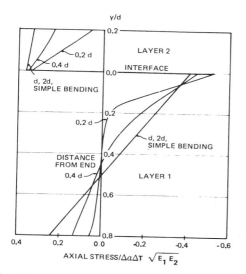

Fig. 6-16. Longitudinal stress in strip at various distance d from end of strip.[16] (*Reprinted with permission of the ASCE.*)

failure at the first application of the load. (This will be discussed further in Sections 6-19 through 6-22.)

If the length of the joined strips is less than twice the total thickness, d (such as would be the case for an interconnector joint to a silicon cell), then the axial loads in the layers do not reach the value for a long joint, since the edge effects overlap.[15] However, in this case, the cross-sectional stress distribution is not linear, as shown in Fig. 6-16, and thus the maximum stress in the thicker element could be significantly higher than the stresses computed by Eq. 6-15. This was actually noticed in experiments where silicon fracture occurred in joints for which the calculated stresses were less than the strength of the silicon.[17] The experimental results were used to determine a stress concentration factor for this condition.

Illustrative Example No. 6-1

To obtain some numerical insight of typical thermal stresses, assume that a 0.35 mm thick silicon cell with a 25 μm thick layer of solder, initially stress-free at 20°C, is subjected to various temperatures. Actually, since the solder was applied at a higher temperature than 20°C, the solder will be initially under some stress, but this will be ignored for the present. Modifying Eq. 6-6 for the biaxial condition, and using

subscripts "so" for solder and "si" for silicon, we get Eq. 6-7.

$$\sigma_{so} = \frac{E_{so}(\alpha_{so} - \alpha_{si})(T - 20)}{(1 - \nu_{so})\left(1 + 4\dfrac{(1 - \nu_{si})E_{so}t_{so}}{(1 - \nu_{so})E_{si}t_{si}}\right)}$$

(6-7)

Using material property values for 62/36/2 solder and silicon from Chapter 10, the solder stresses were computed and are shown in Fig. 6-17 together with the values of the solder yield stress. Since the stresses in all directions in the plane of the solder are equal, while the stress normal to the surface and the shear stress are zero, $\sigma_1 = \sigma_2 = \sigma_s$, $\sigma_3 = 0$, and the effective stress $\bar{\sigma} = \sigma_s$. Thus, the solder yields when σ_s exceeds σ_y. It is seen from Fig. 6-17 that the solder will yield when subjected to temperatures lower than -45°C or greater than 50°C.

Once the solder yields, Eq. 6-7 has to be modified to account for the reduced plastic modulus. This can be obtained from the plastic stress strain curve, but to do this it is necessary to know the effective plastic strain, $\bar{\epsilon}$. The strain in all directions in the plane of the solder equals ϵ_a, while the strain normal to the surface equals ϵ_n.

$$\epsilon_n = -\frac{2\nu\epsilon_a}{(1 - \nu)}$$

(6-8a)

$$\epsilon_1 = \epsilon_2 = \epsilon_a, \quad \epsilon_3 = \frac{-2\nu}{1 - \nu}\epsilon_a$$

(6-8b)

$$\bar{\epsilon} = \frac{1}{1 - \nu}\epsilon_a$$

(6-8c)

In the above, $\nu \to 0.5$ for large plastic strains. Thus the effective strain, $\bar{\epsilon}$, is approximately twice the direct strain, ϵ_a, in the plane of the solder. With the decrease in the solder modulus, this strain rapidly approaches the strain which would result if the silicon were rigid, i.e., $\Delta\alpha\Delta T$.

6-11. Stresses in Joints Due to External Forces

Changes in the intercell gap width with temperature cause expansion loops to deform. This

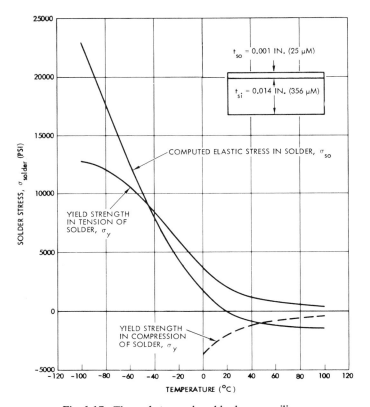

Fig. 6-17. Thermal stresses in solder layer on silicon.

deformation, in turn, causes three types of forces to be transmitted to the soldered or welded joints: shear forces, attempting to slide the interconnector attachment areas along the solar cell contacts; moments, attempting to pry the interconnector attachment areas away from the solar cells; and torques, attempting to "twist" interconnectors out of their joints.[18,19,20,21,22]

An idealization of an out-of-plane stress relief loop in the series-direction between two typical "flat mounted" solar cells is illustrated in Fig. 6-18a. When the interconnector loop is removed from both cell contacts, its free-body diagram is as illustrated in Fig. 6-18b. The shear forces are denoted by P and the prying moments by M.

The stress distributions in bonded joints due to external forces and moments are similar to those with the shear stress distributions resulting from thermal contraction of the interconnectors. For the assumed thickness ratio, the maximum shear stress due to a bending moment occurs at the loaded interconnector end, while the maximum shear stress due to an axial load occurs at the opposite end. In actual practice, this peak will be minimized due to the gradual taper of the solder at that end. Due to the assymmetry of the shear stress distribution, the algebraic signs of the applied axial load and moment will influence the stress distributions. For the load directions pictured in Fig. 6-19, the bending moment adds to the shear stress at the critically loaded end of the interconnector, while the axial load subtracts. For the opposite loading directions, the reverse stress effects would occur. Since both the thermal stresses and the applied loads are functions of the temperature, their relative directions are unchanged during thermal cycling and are a function only of the configuration. The original magnitude and direction (i.e., sign) depend upon the interconnector configuration, the material choices for the interconnector, cell adhesive and substrate, and the intercell gap width.

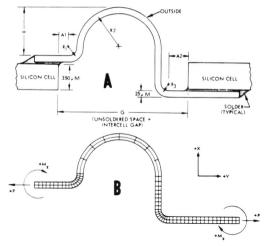

Fig. 6-18. Typical interconnector loop model for soldered joints (a) and its free-body diagram and finite element representation (b).[23] (*7th Intersociety Energy Conversion Engineering Conference 1972.*)

Stresses Due to Contact Pull and Peel Testing. The strength of joints (joint strength or bond strength) between solar cell interconnectors and solar cell contacts is evaluated by pull or peel testing. The stresses and test failure modes created by such tests are strongly dependent upon the interconnector stiffness and the test

method (especially upon the angle of the applied pull force) and may or may not reflect the actual loading of the joints or their response to this loading. Stress conditions created by the test include tensile stresses in the interconnector, joint, cell contact, and silicon surface, and shear and peel stresses in the joint and cell contact.

Stresses Due to Torques (Rotational Forces). For illustration, consider two solar cells that are parallel-connected by a bus bar, as illustrated in Fig. 6-20. Assume that at room temperature the assembly is stress free (a). Exposure to low temperature will cause all components to contract, each by a different amount. A bus bar made from copper would contract approximately by the same amount as the aluminum substrate, but considerably more than the silicon solar cells (b). If the tabs extending from the bus bars are relatively short and stiff, rotational forces on the soldered or welded joints are unavoidable. The use of a low-expansion bus bar (Kovar) would also cause rotational forces, but in a different way (c).

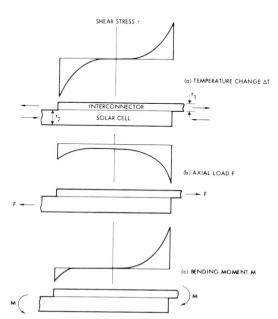

Fig. 6-19. Illustration of interface shear stress distribution in an interconnector/solar cell joint ($m = t_1/t_2 \ll 1$) for the three loading conditions.

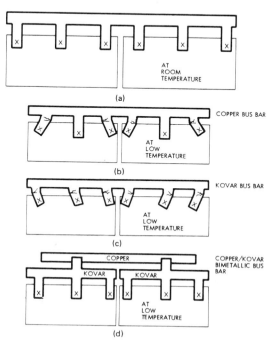

Fig. 6-20. Bimetallic bus bar eliminates rotational forces on solder joints (highly accentuated for illustration for aluminum substrate).

The design solution to eliminate rotational forces consists of utilizing a "bimetallic" bus bar, as shown in (d). Ideally, the parts of the bus bar which are attached to the solar cells have a coefficient of linear thermal expansion identical to that of the solar cells, while the remaining parts have an expansion coefficient identical to that of the substrate. For practical design cases, a combination of Kovar or Invar and copper for the bus bar may be more than adequate for aluminum substrates. Such "bimetallic," or two-part, bus bars actually have been implemented[3] (see Section 6-6).

6-12. Changes in the Intercell Gap Width

Consider the schematically illustrated cross-section of an assembly of two solar cells (without interconnectors) mounted to a substrate shown in Fig. 6-21. The top sketch (Case 0) shows the array in equilibrium and stress-free at a reference temperature T_0. The center-to-center distance between solar cells is D_0, the cell length is L_0, the intercell gap width is W_0 and the cell indexing distance is I_0. From the geometry of the assembly, we find Eqs. 6-9 and 6-10.

$$W_0 = D_0 - L_0 \qquad (6\text{-}9)$$

$$I_0 = L_0 + W_0/2 \qquad (6\text{-}10)$$

Now let the temperature of this assembly be lowered to T_L and equilibrium be established

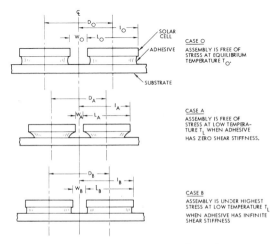

Fig. 6-21. Changes in cell spacings due to low temperature.

again. The assembly may now be either stress-free (Case A) or under stress (Case B), depending upon the stiffness of the cell-to-substrate adhesive.

Case A. In Case A (Fig. 6-21), the hypothetical zero-stiffness adhesive permitted undisturbed contraction of the solar cells and the substrate in accordance with their respective thermal expansion coefficients due to the decrease in temperature $\Delta T = T_L - T_0$ (ΔT is a negative quantity for this example), so that we get Eqs. 6-11 and 6-12, where α_c and α_s are the linear thermal expansion coefficients for the cell and the substrate, respectively.

$$L_A = L_0(1 + \alpha_c \Delta T) \qquad (6\text{-}11)$$

$$D_A = D_0(1 + \alpha_s \Delta T) \qquad (6\text{-}12)$$

We also get Eq. 6-13.

$$W_A = D_A - L_A = W_0 + W_0 \alpha_s \Delta T$$
$$+ L_0(\alpha_s - \alpha_c)\Delta T \qquad (6\text{-}13)$$

Since, for practical purposes, $W_0 \ll L_0$, Eq. 6-13 reduces to Eq. 6-14.

$$W_A = W_0 + L_0(\alpha_s - \alpha_c)\Delta T \qquad (6\text{-}14)$$

The change in gap width is represented by Eq. 6-15.

$$\Delta W_A = W_A - W_0 = L_0(\alpha_s - \alpha_c)\Delta T$$
$$(6\text{-}15)$$

Similarly, the indexing distance is given by Eq. 6-16.

$$I_A = I_0 + I_0 \alpha_s \Delta T \qquad (6\text{-}16)$$

And the change in the indexing distance is ΔI_A (Eq. 6-17).

$$\Delta I_A = I_A - I_0 = I_0 \alpha_s \Delta T \qquad (6\text{-}17)$$

Equation 6-15 confirms the intuitive suspicion that the change in the cell gap width, ΔW_A, from W_0 to W_A, is proportional to the cell length, L_0, the differential expansion coefficient $(\alpha_s - \alpha_c)$, and the temperature excursion, ΔT. Equation 6-17 indicates that the change in the cell indexing distance, ΔI_A, is identical to the change in the substrate length (cell center-to-center distance) $\Delta D_A = D_0 - D_A$.

Practical cases of nearly zero-stiffness adhesives are found when using RTV adhesives above approximately −100°C or adhesive spot bonds rather than full area bonds placed at the center lines of the solar cells.

Case B. In Case B (Fig. 6-21), a hypothetically "stiff" adhesive in the shear direction is used between the solar cells and the substrate such that the cell and substrate on either side of the adhesive interface contract or expand at identical rates (assuming further that the elastic modulus of the adhesive is negligibly small). As a consequence of this stiff coupling between cell and substrate, the cells become stressed in compression, and the substrate (over the extent of the bond area) becomes stressed in tension, resulting in a greater amount of contraction of the solar cell length, but in a lesser amount of contraction of the substrate as compared to Case A. The degree to which the cells and the substrate deform depends upon the ratio of the lateral stiffness of the solar cells to that of the substrate. The lateral stiffness in this example is the product of the elastic modulus times the cross-sectional area (of either the solar cells or the substrate) in the direction parallel to the substrate.

The effect of a stiff coupling between the solar cells and the substrate of Case B is a lesser change in the gap width than was observed in Case A, giving Eqs. 6-18 and 6-19.

$$W_B < W_A \qquad (6\text{-}18)$$

$$\Delta W_B < \Delta W_A \qquad (6\text{-}19)$$

Practical cases of stiff coupling between solar cells and the substrate arise from the use of certain epoxy type adhesives, thin bond lines, and lower temperatures than approximately −120°C.

6-13. Loop Deformation

For illustration, consider the interconnector between the two series-connected solar cells in Fig. 6-22a and the corresponding free-body diagram in Fig. 6-22b. From this figure, it is seen that Eq. 6-18—where R is the required deformation of the expansion loop, since points X and Y are actually coincident and permanently fastened together—is true.

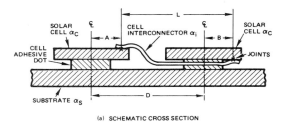

(a) SCHEMATIC CROSS SECTION

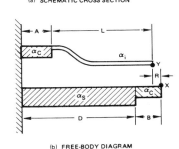

(b) FREE-BODY DIAGRAM

Fig. 6-22. Required loop deformation, R, with points, x, y coincident and temperature variable.

$$A + L + R = D + B \qquad (6\text{-}18)$$

A change in temperature, ΔT, will change all dimensions as described in Eq. 6-19 (after rearranging the terms).

$$\Delta R = D\alpha_s \Delta T + (B - A)\alpha_c \Delta T - L\alpha_i \Delta T$$

$$(6\text{-}19)$$

The α's are the average coefficients of linear thermal expansion, and the subscripts s, c, and i refer to the substrate, cell, and interconnector, respectively. Rearranging the terms again, we obtain Eq. 6-20.

$$\frac{\Delta R}{\Delta T} = D\alpha_s + (B - A)\alpha_c - L\alpha_i \qquad (6\text{-}20)$$

This equation is plotted parametrically in Fig. 6-23 for a range of values for α_s and α_i covering most practical design cases. The condition where $B = 10$ mm represents the usual interconnector loop designs depicted in Fig. 6-26 (a and b).

6-14. Stresses in Interconnector Expansion Loops

Stresses of significance to solar cell interconnector and wire stress relief loops (also called "service loops") include tensile, compressive, shear, and bending stresses. Bending

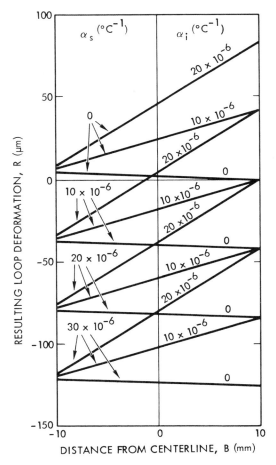

Fig. 6-23. Loop deformation resulting from different choices of substrate materials (α_s), interconnector materials (α_i), and interconnector attachment distances (B), according to Eq. 6-12 for $A = 10$ mm, $D = 21$ mm, $T = 175°C$.

stresses in interconnectors and wire arise from different changes in length of different components on the solar cell array with changes in temperature.

In unplated interconnectors, the internal stresses in the expansion loops are largely due to forces (displacements) applied externally at the ends of the loops. In plated interconnectors, additional, internally created stress components arise from differences in the coefficients of linear thermal expansion of the base material and the platings. The stresses in plated interconnectors, especially in areas where the maximum bending takes place, may readily exceed the yield strength of the plating material

and cause cracks to develop in the plating that may propagate into the base material and lead to unsuspected, premature fatigue failure of the expansion loops.

For illustration, consider the simplified expansion loop of a solar cell interconnector shown in Fig. 6-18. In general, the interconnector is subjected to the separating force, F, and the moments M_L and M_R, at the left- and right-hand edges, respectively. It is assumed that the height, D, is fixed by the thickness of the cell and that only the dimensions, H, L, and t are available to be changed. In practice, the length, L, is limited by the desire to pack the cells as close together as possible, and the height, H, is limited by the desire to minimize the projection above the coverslide. Applying strength-of-materials theory, the force and moments can be expressed in terms of the deflection, δ, as in Eq. 6-21.

$$F = f\frac{EI\delta}{D^3} \ , \quad M_L = m_L\frac{EI\delta}{D^2} \ , \quad M_R = m_R\frac{EI\delta}{D^2}$$

$$(6\text{-}21)$$

where

$$f = \left[-1/6h^3 + 1/3(1 - 1/2\,h)(1 + h)^2 \right.$$
$$\left. + (1/2 + h + h^2)\frac{h^2 + hs - 1/2}{2h + s + 1} \right]^{1/2}$$

$$(6\text{-}22a)$$

$$m_L = \frac{h^2 + hs - 1/2}{2h + s + 1}f \qquad (6\text{-}22b)$$

$$m_R = m_L + f \qquad (6\text{-}22c)$$

and

$$\alpha = \frac{H}{D}, \quad \beta = \frac{L}{D} \ .$$

The moment, M at the top of the interconnector is given by Eq. 6-23.

$$M_T = M_L - FH \qquad (6\text{-}23)$$

The values of the non-dimensional coefficients f, m_L, and m_R are shown in Figs. 6-24 and 6-25 as functions of the shape parameters h and s. It is seen that both the forces and moments decrease rapidly as h and s are increased, but for values of h and s greater than

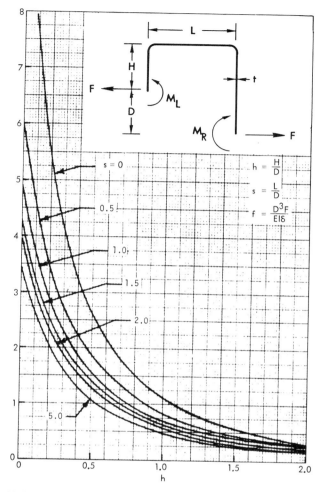

Fig. 6-24. Variation of non-dimensional force coefficient f with geometric ratios h and s.

unity, the decrease is small. For values of h greater than 0.6, there is negligible change in m_L, but m_R and f continue to decrease as the height ratio h is increased.

For a given interconnector geometry, h, s, and D, Eq. 6-21 indicates that the force, F, and moments, M_L and M_R, are proportional to the moment of intertia, EI, of the interconnector cross-section, or t^3 for a given material and interconnector width, b. This is in contrast to the case for a simple interconnector without a stress relief loop, where the force is proportional to EA, or t for a given material and width (A is the cross-sectional area). Through the use of an interconnector loop of practical dimensions, the axial force between solder joints can be reduced by orders of magnitude compared

to the value obtained with a straight interconnector. The main problem then becomes the bending stresses in the interconnector and the bending moments applied to the joints.

The maximum stress in the interconnector itself is given by Eq. 6-24.

$$\sigma_m = \frac{F}{A} \pm \frac{Mt}{2I} \qquad (6\text{-}24)$$

M is the maximum of M_R, M_L, or M_T. For an interconnector made of a single material, Eq. 6-25 holds true.

$$I = \frac{1}{12} bt^3 \qquad (6\text{-}25)$$

Since b is the interconnector width, this gives us Eq. 6-26.

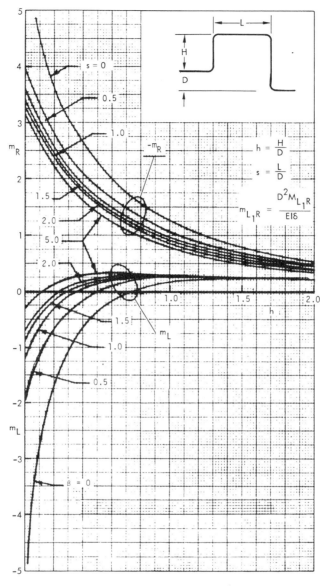

Fig. 6-25. Variation of non-dimensional moment coefficients m_{1_L} and m_{2_R} with geometric ratios h and s.

$$\sigma_m = \left[\frac{1}{12}f\left(\frac{t}{D}\right)^2 + m\left(\frac{t}{D}\right)\right]\frac{E\delta}{D} \quad (6\text{-}26)$$

Thus, the stress in the interconnector itself due to a given displacement, δ, is also reduced by decreasing the thickness of the interconnector. To maintain a given electrical resistance, an improved design interconnector loop, both with respect to the forces and moments applied to the interconnector joint and to stresses in the interconnector itself, can be achieved by re-

ducing the interconnector thickness and increasing its width correspondingly.

6-15. Stress-free Interconnector Loops

With reference to Fig. 6-22, if $R = 0$ at $T = T_0$, the interconnector is stress-free at T_0. For the interconnector to remain stress-free at any temperature, the condition $\Delta R/\Delta T = 0$ is required for the temperature range between T_0 and T. The conditions under which the interconnector remains stress-free are found by setting Eq. 24 equal to zero, giving Eq. 6-27.

$$D\alpha_s + (B - A)\alpha_c = L\alpha_i \qquad (6\text{-}27)$$

Practical solutions to Eq. 6-27 show that the interconnector remains stress-free ($\Delta R = 0$) at any temperature if the expansion coefficients of the substrate and interconnector materials are alike ($\alpha_s = \alpha_i$) and if the interconnector is attached to the lower contact directly below the upper contact ($B = A$ in Fig. 6-22). Furthermore, if α_s and α_i are different, Eq. 6-27 can be solved by substituting Eq. 6-18 with $R = 0$ to find the interconnector length, L, for which the interconnector remains stress-free at any temperature (Eq. 6-28).

$$L = \left(\frac{\alpha_c - \alpha_s}{\alpha_c - \alpha_i}\right) D \qquad (6\text{-}28)$$

In a practical sense, a purely stress-free interconnector design cannot be achieved, because the coefficients of linear thermal expansion of different materials are uniquely non-linear with temperature. Nevertheless, significant stress reductions and fatigue life extensions can be achieved by this method.

6-16. Stresses in Imbedded Interconnectors and Conductors

Imbedded interconnectors include such elements as conductors in flat cables, conductors bonded to substrates, and solar cell interconnectors encased by adhesive or other dielectric material.

Stresses in imbedded interconnectors include tensile, compressive, shear, and bending stresses. These stresses arise from the differences in the coefficients of linear thermal expansion of the different materials in intimate contact with each other. The stress magnitude increases mainly at lower temperatures, where the strength and stiffness of most insulating materials used on solar cell arrays increase significantly. Excessively high stresses can occur, particularly at low temperatures, where they may cause open-circuit failure of conductors (see Fig. 6-4).

The probability of conductor failure in-

creases with a decrease in array temperature and with increases in the insulator/conductor cross-sectional area ratio and the insulator/conductor material strength ratio.

6-17. Practical Interconnector Design Considerations

The analysis of solar cell stack and interconnector stresses is informative and essential. However, the interactions between the many different solar cell stack and substrate components, especially in view of deviations of a mass-produced design from its ideal, and the highly non-linear mechanical material properties with both temperature and stress level, pose limitations to what can be designed on paper only. In practice, many interconnector design aspects require attention as indicated below, starting with the solar cell interface.

Contact pads on the solar cell should be designed as small as possible to maximize the cell's active area, but sufficiently large that stresses are not too highly concentrated. The solar cell pad sizes and tolerances should also be compatible with the interconnector pad size and the positioning accuracy of the joining equipment to be used. Sharp corners and abrupt changes in dimensions act as stress risers and should be avoided.

Solderable pads should facilitate the formation of a solder fillet around the interconnector circumference. The practice of using solder reflow inspection holes in the pads is controversial. Some workers believe that the existence of such holes lead to earlier joint fatigue failures while others favor the opposite viewpoint. Therefore, it is suggested that a decision for or against solder reflow inspection holes be based on experimental data obtained for each specific design. The surface of the pad (or its plating) should promote solder wetting. A precoating of the pad with solder is desirable.

Weldable pads, or those intended for thermocompression or ultrasonic joining, require precise control of the solar cell wafer surface roughness and the metallization thickness. Similar surface roughness and plating thickness requirements exist for the interconnectors. Not all metals can be joined with the same ease

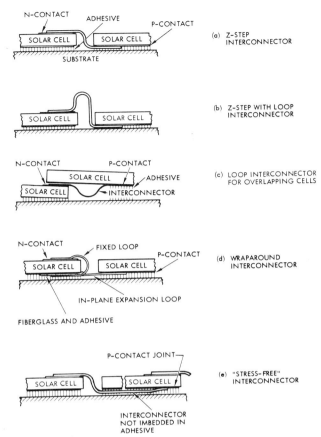

Fig. 6-26. Alternate cross-sectional interconnector configurations for conventional contact solar cells.[24]

or with any joining process. Surface oxidation (tarnishing) may impede joining.

Expansion loops should be made as short as possible to minimize electrical resistance and enhance handleability, but they should be sufficiently long to prevent thermal expansion loops from transmitting significant stresses into the joints. The interconnector configuration should be designed symmetrically about the joints so as to cause no rotating forces to act on the joints (see Section 6-9).[25] Conductors should be redundant for both reliability and electrical conductivity reasons, and should possess adequate strength (material yield strength and cross-sectional area) to withstand fabrication, handling, assembly, and operational forces arising from imbedment.

Out-of-plane expansion loops for conventional *front-back* solar cell contacts connect the contact on the top of one cell to the con-

tact on the bottom of the next cell. The available alternate interconnector configurations are illustrated in Fig. 6-26.

The choice of the cross-sectional expansion loop configuration from those shown is nearly independent of the plane-view geometry of the interconnectors. The dimensions of the expansion loops depend strongly upon the magnitude and frequency of the intercell gap width variation throughout mission life. Other significant design considerations include manufacturability and potential interference with the solar cell cover.

The fatigue (flex) life of the expansion loop configurations in Fig. 6-26a, b and c can be increased by reducing the interconnector thickness, by increasing the expansion loop height, and by increasing the distance (and thereby the interconnector length) between attachments to the cells, measured across the intercell gap.

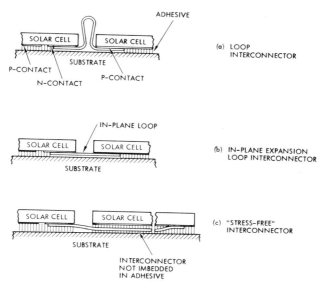

Fig. 6-27. Alternate cross-sectional interconnector configurations for wrap-around contact solar cells.

Modification of the dimension of the interconnector loop in the direction in Fig. 6-26 which is perpendicular to the plane of the paper such that the maximum bending moment no longer concentrates at a single point on the loop, may also help. Solder filling (wicking) and adhesive overflow should be prevented because they may cause stiffening of the expansion loops.

Out-of-plane expansion loops for *wrap-around* contact solar cells connect the solar cell p and n contacts on the same cell side and in the same plane. The available alternate interconnector configurations (in cross-section) are illustrated in Fig. 6-27. The loop configuration in Fig. 6-27a is generally impractical because of interference of the loop with the solar cell covers, leading to a poor cell packing density.

In-plane expansion loops deform by true in-plane bending of portions of the interconnectors in the "hard-to-deform" direction (about the Z-axis shown in Fig. 6-28) and by out-of-plane warping of portions of the interconnectors and bending in the "easy-to-deform" direction (about the X-axis).

To assure adequate fatigue life, the in-plane expansion loops must be able to endure the same deformations as the out-of-plane expansion loops, and rotational forces at the interconnector joints must equally be prevented.

For interconnectors imbedded in adhesive or other dielectric material (discussed in Section 6-16), the interconnectors must be made significantly stronger than the surrounding dielectric material (strength = yield strength × cross-sectional area). The imbedded, effective interconnector stiffness (caused by the conductor and the surrounding dielectric) should be reduced by bringing the expansion loops as close to the joints as possible. The expansion loops should be designed such that they can locally slice through the dielectric and develop small cavities in which they can more freely deform. Mesh interconnectors display excel-

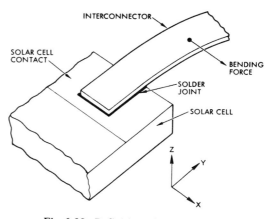

Fig. 6-28. Definition of bending axes.

lent flexibility when unrestrained; however, this flexibility depends upon the freedom of a piece of mesh to contract in one direction when elongated into a perpendicular direction. After soldering or welding to solar cells and attaching the cells to a substrate, the flexibility of the mesh is largely lost. Imbedment of the mesh in adhesive further reduces its flexibility.

Expanded and flattened mesh may be more flexible than etched or stamped mesh if some of the original warping is retained by the expanded mesh after flattening.

Solar cells, even at room temperature, are not free of internal stress. The internal stress arises from cell manufacturing processes. The p and n layers have different atomic densities due to the effects of doping, and hence they have slightly different dimensions. The cell contacts are sintered at elevated temperature and contract at a greater rate than does the semiconductor material during cooling. While these stress levels are sufficiently high to mechanically distort only very thin cells, they are also present in thicker cells and add to other stresses that are caused externally or environmentally.

Cell-to-cover adhesive can be expected to add to the stresses in the solar cell, the cover, and the front contact joints. In general, stresses are minimized by minimizing the adhesive layer thickness. However, some adhesives do not cure properly when their thickness is less than about 25 μm.

Cell-to-substrate adhesive contributes to the stress at low temperatures in the lower surface of the solar cell wafer. The stress level generally increases with increasing adhesive thickness, but adhesive layer thicknesses of less than 25 μm may prohibit proper curing of certain adhesives. Below the brittle point (glass transition region) the adhesive may cause additional, significant stress components in the interconnector joints due to tensile, compressive, or shear loading of the interconnectors.

Substrate rigidity or flexibility may also contribute to stresses in the silicon at the solar cell/ substrate interface. Insufficiently flat substrate surfaces ("dimples" in thin-face sheet honeycomb panels) may lead to irregular adhesive layer thickness and stress riser effects, potentially cracking solar cells.

Insulating layers on conductive substrate facesheets may become debonded from the substrate by excessive forces exerted by the cell-to-substrate adhesive.

6-18. Stresses in Flexible Bonded Layers

Flexible bonds are found in the cover-to-cell adhesive and in the cell-to-substrate adhesive layers at temperatures above approximately $-100°$C, and in solder at elevated temperatures. For flexible bonds, it is possible to neglect the axial stiffness of the adhesive layer compared to the other two layers and just consider its shear stiffness.[18] To illustrate, consider the lap joint of length L shown in Fig. 6-29. This is similar to the previously analyzed joints except for the addition of the third bonding material with thickness t_3 and shear modulus G_3. The basic equilibrium equations equate the change in axial stress, σ_i, in each of the outer layers to the shear stress, τ, in the bond layer, where x is the distance from the center of the joint, the subscripts 1, 2, and 3 refer to the respective layers, and σ_1, σ_2, and τ are as defined in Eq. 6-30.

$$t_1 \frac{d\sigma_1}{dx} + \tau = 0, \quad t_2 \frac{d\sigma_2}{dx} - \tau = 0$$

$$(6\text{-}29)$$

$$\sigma_1 = E_1 \left(\frac{du_1}{dx} - \alpha_1 \Delta T \right)$$

$$\sigma_2 = E_2 \left(\frac{du_2}{dx} - \alpha_2 \Delta T \right) \quad (6\text{-}30)$$

$$\tau = \frac{G_3}{t_3} (u_2 - u_1)$$

The displacements in the axial (x) direction in layers 1 and 2, respectively, are u_1 and u_2.

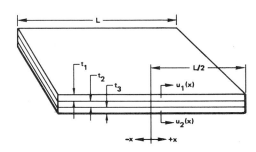

Fig. 6-29. Model of three laminated layers.

The solution to Eq. 6-29 can be obtained in terms of hyperbolic functions, and, after some manipulation, expressed as shown below.

$$\sigma_1 = -\frac{E_1 \Delta\alpha\Delta T}{1 + mn} \left(1 - \frac{\cosh 2\beta x}{\cosh \beta L}\right)$$

$$(6\text{-}31a)$$

$$\sigma_2 = -m\sigma_1 \qquad (6\text{-}31b)$$

$$\tau = \frac{2E_1 t_1 \Delta\alpha\Delta T}{L(1 + mn)} \frac{\beta L \sinh 2\beta x}{\cosh \beta L}$$

$$(6\text{-}32)$$

$$\Delta u = u_2 - u_1 = \frac{t_3}{G_3}\tau$$

$$= \frac{1}{2}\Delta\alpha\Delta TL \frac{\sinh 2\beta x}{\beta \cosh \beta L} \qquad (6\text{-}33)$$

$$\Delta u\left[x = \frac{L}{2}\right] = \frac{1}{2}\Delta\alpha\Delta TL \frac{\tanh \beta L}{\beta L} \qquad (6\text{-}34)$$

where

$$\beta^2 = \frac{1}{4}\frac{G_3}{t_3}\left(\frac{1}{E_1 t_1} + \frac{1}{E_2 t_2}\right) \qquad (6\text{-}35)$$

The parameter βL is a measure of the relative stiffness of the strips and the adhesive.

It is seen that Eq. 6-31a for σ_1 is identical to that for the rigidly joined long strips, Eq. 6-3, except for the addition of the bracketed term, which acts as a correction term, increasing the stress as the edge is approached. Figure 6-30 shows the variation of the axial and shear stresses with distance from the edge for three values of the stiffness parameter, βL. For a large value of βL, the axial load reaches its limiting value only a short distance from the end of the joint, and thereby causes a sharp local peak in the shear stress. This sharp, local stress concentration approximates the previous results for the rigid bond of two strips and is typical of an unyielded solder joint. For low values of βL, the axial load increases more slowly and the shear stress varies approximately linearly with distance from the center of the strip. Both the maximum values of the axial stress and shear stress are considerably reduced as the stiffness G/t_2 of the adhesive layer is decreased.

Figure 6-31 shows the relative axial displacement $\Delta u(x = L/2)$ between the two strips at

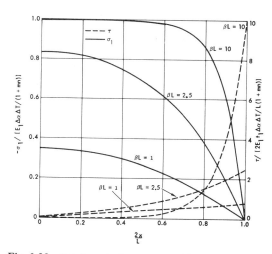

Fig. 6-30. Axial and shear stress distribution in a bonded joint for different values of the stiffness parameters βL.

their ends. The normalized value is the relative thermal displacement between the two strips without any connection between them. This relative displacement is of interest in determining the displacements required of interconnectors joining successive cells which are bonded to the same substrate.

Illustrative Example No. 6-2

Consider a 10 mil $\times$ 0.8 inch square (0.25 mm thick, 2 $\times$ 2 cm) silicon cell which is bonded to a 5 mil (0.125 mm) thick aluminum substrate

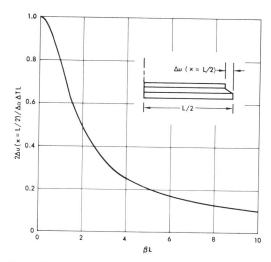

Fig. 6-31. Variation of the relative edge displacement of a bonded joint with the stiffness parameters βL.

with 4 mils (0.1 mm) of a silicone adhesive having a shear modulus of 500 psi (3.45 MN/m²); then

$$\beta L = \frac{0.8}{2}\sqrt{\frac{500}{0.004}\left[\frac{1}{10\times27\times10^3}+\frac{1}{5\times10\times10^3}\right]}$$

$$= 0.69.$$

Thus, the stress distribution approximates the lower curves ($\beta L = 1$) in Fig. 6-30. However, at temperatures below $-100°C$, the stiffness of silicone adhesives increases to values as high as 3.45 GN/m² (500 ksi). Assuming a value of 0.7 GN/m² (100 ksi) for G_3, then

$$\beta L = 9.75$$

so that the stress distribution corresponds to the upper ($\beta L = 10$) curves in Fig. 6-30. The result of this adhesive stiffening below $-100°C$ is an increase in the axial stress by a factor of 3 for the same value of $\Delta\alpha\Delta T$ and an increase in the shear stress by a factor of 10.

The foregoing analysis suggests that the selection of an adhesive with the lowest possible stiffness (shear modulus) at the required low temperature limit is desirable. This is synonymous with selecting an adhesive with the lowest possible glass transition (brittle point) temperature.

INTERCONNECTOR FATIGUE

6-19. Static and Dynamic Material Stress

Failures of materials by fracturing may occur in response to two distinctly different methods of loading, also called stressing.

1. By exceeding the ultimate strength of the material in a single application of the load, the material fails under a *static load*.
2. By cyclically loading a material such that the stress alternates between positive and negative values (viz., tension and compression) but with the peak stress never approaching or exceeding the ultimate strength of the material, the material fails by *fatigue*.

In general engineering practice, fatigue failures

of parts are avoided by designing them such that the stress levels in the parts are sufficiently low even though there are cases where this is not always possible.

Many solar cell array interconnector design problems, however, cannot be solved by reducing stress levels to values that would result in a very long or infinite fatigue life. Rather, the design effort must be directed toward extending an *a priori* limited fatigue life to a minimum acceptable number of thermal cycles.

The first step of a fatigue analysis actually is a thermomechanical stress analysis, as described in Sections 6-9 through 6-18. The stress analysis is an excellent tool to aid the solar cell array designer in selecting materials and altering configurations until the lowest possible stress in the various array materials for a given temperature cycling range has been found.[22] Ultimate failure of a part by fatigue, however, is not so much related to the stress level, but rather to the material's behavior when it undergoes plastic deformation (i.e., when it yields). The capability of a material to withstand alternating plastic deformations is related to the material's microscopic and metallurgical properties that are macroscopically reflected in such terms as ductility, elongation, reduction in area, crack formation, crack propagation, work hardening, work softening, and others.

For many solar cell arrays, the cyclically alternating plastic material deformations of solar cell contacts and solar cell/interconnector soldered and welded joints cannot be prevented by design or material selection efforts. A linear-elastic stress analysis will simply indicate that yielding has occurred, while an elastic-plastic stress analysis will indicate the degree to which yielding will take place. The next step, then (since plastic deformation cannot be eliminated), is to make further design and material selection changes that will prolong either the onset of fatigue cracking or the completion of crack propagation through the interconnectors or interconnector joints. The theoretical investigations of these mechanisms are called fatigue or wear-out analyses. Fatigue failures due to repeated mechanical load cycles are a well known phenomenon which has been extensively investigated.[26,27,28] However, there are still many unknown factors, and considerable scatter is found in test results.

The fatigue life of parts has been found to be proportional to a high power of the stress. Therefore, the approach to obtaining a required fatigue life is to increase the amount of material so that the stress is reduced below the level which causes failure. For life requirements in the millions of cycles, maximum working stress levels considerably below the yield strength are required. However, for thermally loaded structures which are subjected to strain rather than stress, this approach does not necessarily lead to a solution. As one element of the structure is reinforced, it will only cause the load to be transferred to the other elements of the structure. Thus, in many cases where the differential thermal expansions cannot be avoided, it may be necessary to live with material yielding and to include its effect in the fatigue analysis.

6-20. Stress and Strain Loading

Structural members are said to be loaded by *stress* (applied force per unit area) or by *strain* (deformation). An example of stress loading is a coil spring of an automobile suspension system that supports a part of the automobile's weight. An example of strain loading is the thin silver contact layer on a silicon solar cell which is strained (stretched or compressed) by the much stronger and stiffer silicon when the tem-

perature is varied. Strain loading due to changes in temperature is also referred to as *thermal loading*.

Stress and strain loading is illustrated by the two simplified examples shown in Fig. 6-32. In Fig. 6-32a, a bar is stress loaded by a force. The stress in the bar is unaffected by yielding. In Fig. 6-32b, the same bar is rigidly clamped at its ends and is subjected to an increase in temperature, ΔT. If the bar were unrestrained, it would increase in length by $\alpha \Delta T L_0$, where α is the thermal coefficient of expansion. The rigid clamping, however, causes a stress, σ, to be developed, which would cause a mechanical compression of the unrestrained bar to its restrained length, L_0. From Eq. 6-1, $\sigma/E = -\alpha \Delta T$ or $\sigma = -E\alpha\Delta T$. As the temperature increases to a value where the thermally induced stress exceeds the elastic strength of the bar, the bar begins to yield. This yielding tends to limit the stress in the bar so that failure does not occur even if the computed stress (using an elastic stress analysis) equals or exceeds the bar's ultimate strength.

While Fig. 6-32 illustrates that a member in a mechanically loaded structure is subjected to a given force while a member in a thermally loaded structure is subjected to a given deformation or strain, in actual solar cell and array applications, a combination of stress and strain loading exists. Nevertheless, solder coatings, solar cell contacts, and solar cell/interconnector

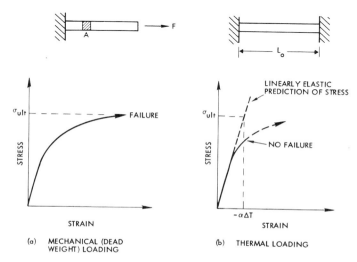

Fig. 6-32. Comparison of mechanical and thermal loading with plasticity.

joints, even when designed properly, are predominantly loaded by thermally induced strain. Additional stress loading may occur in improperly designed arrays.

6-21. Fatigue of Materials

In recent years, there has been an increasing number of design cases in which fatigue lives in the thousands rather than the millions of cycles must be accepted, and in which some yielding is required to be endured by the structure. Soldered and welded joints on silicon solar cells operating in geosynchronous orbit are examples where yielding occurs during part of the time. Other applications in which some yielding cannot be avoided have placed greatly increased emphasis on "low cycle" fatigue or fatigue with relatively large strains and plasticity. For these cases, it has been found that the critical parameter which determines the fatigue life is the *strain range*, rather than the *stress* or *load* range. Thus, the fatigue life can be expressed implicitly by the empirical formula given in Eq. 6-36.[29,30]

$$\Delta\epsilon = D^{0.6} N_f^{-0.6} + 3.5 \frac{\sigma_u}{E} N_f^{-0.12} \quad (6\text{-}36)$$

where

$\Delta\epsilon$ = total strain range (double amplitude)
N_f = number of cycles to failure
σ_u = material ultimate strength
E = Young's modulus

D = ductility or true fracture strain
    $[= \ln 1/(1 - R)]$
R = reduction in area.

The first term in the equation represents the contribution of the plastic strain (D being the failure strain for a single cycle) and is the predominant factor for short lives and large strains, while the second term represents the contribution of the elastic strain (σ_u/E being the "elastic" failure strain) and is predominant for large values of N_f. Notice that this equation indicates that a single material may perform differently at the two ends of the fatigue scale. For a good fatigue life at low strain levels, a high value of ultimate strength is required, while for a high fatigue life at large strains, a large value of ductility or ultimate plastic strain is required.

Extensive experimental results reported on a wide variety of materials have indicated surprisingly good correlation with this equation.[31] Typical results shown for silver in Fig. 6-33 indicate that the plastic strain predominates for fatigue lives of less than 1000 cycles, while the elastic strain predominates for fatigue lives greater than 20,000 cycles—with the cross-over point occurring at about 10,000 cycles. This is typical of most materials. Thus, the plastic strain component predominates for most fatigue lives of interest in solar cell array analysis.

Figure 6-34 shows the fatigue of 36/62/2 solder computed for 20° and −180°C (using Eq. 6-36). Also shown are room temperature experimental fatigue results obtained for 5Sn/95Pb solder. The room temperature values for

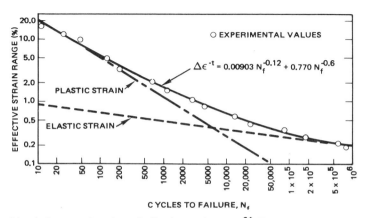

Fig. 6-33. Fatigue life of silver as a function of effective strain range.[31] (*Reprinted with permission of the IEEE.*)

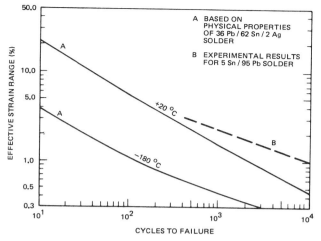

Fig. 6-34. Fatigue life of solder predicted by the method of universal slopes (mechanically cycled at constant temperature); Curve *A* after Ref. 32, Curve *B* after Ref. 33.

solder are essentially identical with the results for silver (Fig. 6-33). The computed results for the fatigue life at −180°C show a major reduction due to the decreased value of solder ductility at this low temperature. The fatigue life of silver at −180°C would not be similarly affected, since its ductility remains unchanged as the temperature is reduced. The reduction of the fatigue life of solder joints cycled to −180°C would not be expected to be as great as shown by the lower curve of Fig. 6-34, since only a portion of the cycles would occur at that temperature.

These experimental results were obtained with uniaxial loading, where $\Delta\epsilon$ refers to the strain in the loading direction. For the case of multiaxial loading such as occurs in solder joints, it has been suggested that, by analogy with the use of effective stresses and strains for plastic stress analyses, the *axial strain range*, $\Delta\epsilon$, be replaced by the effective strain range $\Delta\bar{\epsilon}$ (Eq. 6-37), where $\Delta\epsilon_i$ are the three principal strains.[29] Several investigations have obtained good experimental confirmation of this proposal.[34,35]

$$\Delta\bar{\epsilon} = \frac{1}{\sqrt{2}(1+v)}$$
$$\cdot\sqrt{(\Delta\epsilon_1-\Delta\epsilon_2)^2+(\Delta\epsilon_2-\Delta\epsilon_3)^2+(\Delta\epsilon_3-\Delta\epsilon_1)^2}$$
$$(6\text{-}37)$$

The results discussed above were obtained by mechanically loading the specimens; that is,

applying external forces to the specimens. This leaves the question as to whether these results are applicable to structures subjected to thermal loading. It was found that the mechanically obtained data could be used to compute the fatigue life of a thermally loaded structure when the mechanical properties over the temperature range were similar to those for the mechanical tests.[36,37] In making this calculation, the computed mechanical strains (strains due to stresses) were used in the calculations. Thermal strains alone do not have an influence on the fatigue life of a chemically stable material.

A second major result of the low-cycle, high-strain fatigue was the finding that the initial stress-strain behavior of the material is modified by strain cycling. It is well known that materials can be strain hardened by loading beyond the yield stress in one direction. However, due to the so-called Bauschinger effect, the yield stress for loading in the reverse direction is generally reduced. After continued cycling, though, the material develops a symmetrical stress-strain behavior which may either be softer or harder than the initial condition. Typically, materials in the hardened condition are softened, and materials in the annealed condition are hardened. Thus, it would be expected that solder would be hardened by strain cycling; however, what would happen due to a combination of strain and thermal cycling is unknown. It has been suggested that strain cycled properties obtained

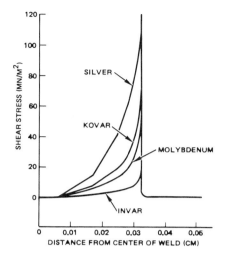

Fig. 6-35. Comparison of shear stresses for various interconnector materials.[38] (*Reprinted with permission of the IEEE.*)

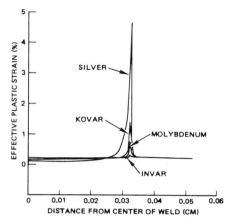

Fig. 6-36. Comparison of effective plastic strains for various interconnector materials.[38] (*Reprinted with permission of the IEEE.*)

at the mean of the temperature range be used.[29] Therefore, for a thermal cycle between +100° and -180°C, the values at -40°C would be used. Although this is a reasonable assumption for materials whose properties do not vary over the temperature range of interest, it appears questionable for a material such as solder, whose properties vary quite radically with temperature.

6-22. Fatigue Life of Interconnectors

Fatigue analyses using the procedures of Section 6-21 were made for welded joints between various silver plated interconnector materials and silver contacts on silicon solar cells.[38,39] The interconnectors were 25 μm thick with 5

μm of silver plating on each side. The silicon was 254 μm thick with a single side 3 μm thick plating of silver. The results are shown in Figs. 6-35 through 6-37. Figure 6-35 shows the variation of the shear stress in the silver across the joint for the various materials for a temperature range of 100° to -196°C. For this temperature range, the silver plating on the silicon has yielded so that the effective stiffness of the silver in the joint area is equal to the plastic modulus of the silver rather than to its elastic modulus. This accounts for the fairly wide distribution of the shear stress which would not have resulted from a purely elastic analysis, as indicated in Section 6-10. The effective plastic strain distribution is shown in Fig. 6-36, and Fig. 6-37 shows the computed values for the

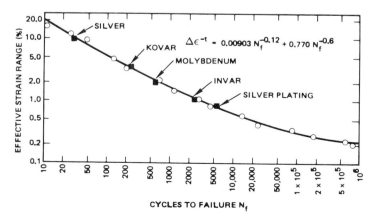

$$\Delta \epsilon^{-t} = 0.00903 \, N_f^{-0.12} + 0.770 \, N_f^{-0.6}$$

Fig. 6-37. Computed fatigue lives for various interconnector materials superimposed on experimental data.[38] (*Reprinted with permission of the IEEE.*)

fatigue life of the interconnector joints and of the silver plating itself. These results show the considerable fatigue life improvements for Invar and molybdenum interconnectors, compared to silver and, to a lesser extent, Kovar, which are brought about from the better match between their thermal coefficients of expansion and that of silicon. Silver weld joints are quite sensitive to the thermal match because of the relative thinness of the silver plating compared to the interconnector. Similar results for soldered joints with the same interconnector thickness indicate decreased sensitivity to the interconnector material and more dependence on the solder properties due to the increase in the proportion of solder thickness to the interconnector thickness.

Temperature cycling test results of solar cell array assemblies have shown that the observed fatigue life of soldered and welded joints is significantly greater than the computed fatigue life. One of the reasons for this may be that deposited thin layers of metals may possess different material properties than rolled stock. Another reason may be that the fatigue test results obtained for fatigue test specimens at constant temperature are most likely not directly related to fatigue failures induced by large temperature excursions during which the material properties may vary considerably. Furthermore, the test atmosphere may have influenced the test results. The empirical fatigue data upon which the analyses were based was obtained by mechanical cycling in a standard atmosphere, while solar cell thermal cycling testing was performed in a nitrogen-rich atmosphere. There are indications that the presence of oxygen causes a significant reduction in the fatigue strengths of copper and lead. Other atmospheric constituents may also play roles.[40,41]

DIODES

6-23. Diode Applications

Solar cell arrays utilize diodes in three different major applications: as blocking, shunt, and Zener diodes.

Blocking diodes, also called *isolation* diodes, are permanently inserted between electrical strings of solar cells and a power bus such that they will conduct electrical current from illuminated solar cells to the bus, but will block current flow from the bus through the solar cell strings when, for whatever reason, the string output voltage is less than the bus voltage.

Shunt diodes, also called *bypass* diodes or *shadow* diodes, are connected in parallel with solar cells or submodules (groups) of solar cells such that when the solar cells are illuminated, the shunt diodes are biased in reverse. During periods when some of the solar cells in a string of cells become shadowed, fractured, or fail in an open-circuit mode, the shunt diodes automatically become forward biased and thereby permit power to flow from the remaining illuminated solar cells of the string to the power bus. Shunt diodes also eliminate the so-called hot spot problem discussed in Section 2-45.

Zener diodes, also called *voltage limiting diodes*, are connected in parallel with the array output terminals to limit the maximum array output voltage at low load or at low array operating temperature conditions to protect voltage-sensitive circuit components such as input transistors in power regulators or converters.

6-24. Blocking Diodes for Energy Conservation

A non-illuminated array, or a portion thereof, behaves as a string of series-connected rectifier diodes that is connected in the forward conduction mode across the power bus. The amount of current that could be drained by a non-illuminated array or string of cells without isolation diodes depends upon the bus voltage and the steepness of the solar cell or string I-V curve between the maximum power point and open-circuit voltage, as illustrated in Fig. 6-38.

Blocking diodes conserve energy not only when solar cells become non-illuminated, but whenever the solar cell string output capability falls below the bus voltage (more precisely, when the string's V_{oc} falls below the sum of the voltage and the diode forward drops). The blocking diodes, however, cause a voltage drop that subtracts from the solar cell output voltage and thereby causes an energy loss when the solar cells produce energy. For example, for

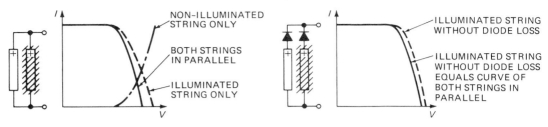

Fig. 6-38. Current loss in non-illuminated array portion.

a typical 30 V array and an 0.6 V diode voltage drop, 2% of the energy generated by the solar cells is lost in the form of heat in the blocking diodes.

A decision for using or not using blocking diodes can, in part, be based on the trade-off between energy losses by non-illuminated cells (described in detail in Section 2-39) and energy losses in the blocking diodes. This trade-off may be affected by the percentage of non-illuminated strings of solar cells and the fractional time of non-illumination. For terrestrial and body-mounted space arrays, blocking diodes are essential. Bus voltage variations in relation to the changes of the solar cell I–V curves with temperature and degradation throughout mission life are highly important.

6-25. Blocking Diodes for Fault Isolation

When properly placed, blocking diodes may prevent serious or even catastrophic power subsystem failures when primary power bus short-circuit faults occur. Such faults can occur in cables, in connectors, at terminals, between adjacent strings of solar cells, and between solar cell circuits and metallic structural elements such as a metallic substrate.

Faults can be initiated by inadequate design considerations, improper handling, misuse, and/or operational effects. Operational effects in space include installation, launch and deployment stresses, thermal expansion and contraction, high-temperature creep (punch-through) of insulation materials, and micrometeoroid impacts. Similar operational effects also occur in terrestrial installations.

Four of several possible locations for blocking diodes near a solar cell array/spacecraft interface are illustrated in Fig. 6-39. The shaded areas in the figure illustrate areas where the

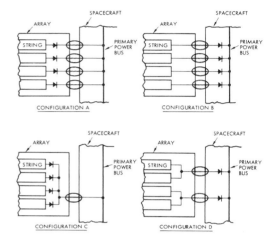

Fig. 6-39. Some possible blocking diode locations and potential electrical failure areas (shaded).

susceptibility of wires to damage is relatively high. Table 6-1 illustrates the impacts of diode and wire faults on the power subsystem performance capability of a simple, hypothetical system. Actually, this system could equally well be a terrestrial system.

A failure mode and effects analysis similar to that described in the (Table 6-1) example above can and should be performed for each solar cell array design to determine the optimum location of the blocking diodes. Such analysis could also demonstrate the need for blocking diodes in the first place.

Another likely and catastrophic short-circuit failure mode could occur even on non-conductive substrates, as illustrated in Fig. 6-40. At low temperatures (in an eclipse), adjacent solar cell strings could touch each other and cause a primary bus near-short-circuit fault. A similar fault could exist in a single string which is turned in hairpin fashion by 180° such that the positive and negative string ends are adjacent to each other.

Table 6-1. Illustration of Impact on Power Subsystem Performance when a Single-Point Failure on the Array/Structure Interface Occurs. (Hypothetical solar cell array consists of four strings without redundancy.)

| Configu-ration | Subsystem Power Loss (Percent) | | | |
| | Failure of One Diode | | Failure of One Wire | |
	Short	Open	Short to Ground	Open
A	~0	25	100	25
B	~0	25	25	25
C	~0	100	100	100
D	~0	50	50	50

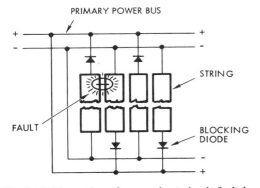

Fig. 6-40. Illustration of a near-short-circuit fault between adjacent strings of solar cells (blocking diodes prevent a catastrophic primary bus failure).

6-26. Blocking Diode Characteristics

Typical isolation diodes are conventional, high-reliability rectifier diodes with suitable current ratings. Since these diodes are operated in the space vacuum environment with a very limited amount of conduction and/or radiation cooling, they must be appropriately derated from their terrestrial current-carrying capability. On the other hand, higher diode operating temperatures result in desirable, lower forward voltage drops.

Blocking diodes have been developed that have the physical properties of solar cells and the electrical properties of conventional rectifier diodes.[42] Such blocking diodes are espe-cially useful for flexible solar cell array blankets. These diodes require coverslides and have the characteristics shown below (only sample quantities have been produced).

Size (including cover)	10 × 20 × 0.38 mm
Weight	0.258 g max
Forward voltage drop (20°C)	0.8 V max at 0.3 A 1.2 V max at 3.0 A
Reverse leakage current (20°C)	0.1 mA max at 80 V 1.0 mA max at 140 V
Coverslide	Fused silica, Corning Glass 7940 Second surface aluminized
Cover adhesive	RTV 3144 or other
Thermo-optical characteristics (glassed)	$\alpha_S = 0.10 \pm 0.01$ $\epsilon_H = 0.81$

Corpuscular radiation damages the junction characteristics of isolation diodes, resulting in lower forward voltage drops and increased reverse leakage current. Normally, however, even a several order of magnitude increase in the reverse leakage current from microamperes to milliamperes is inconsequential for most applications.

Some isolation diodes of the axial lead, glass-envelope type are sensitive to light falling approximately perpendicular to the axial direction onto the silicon diode wafer. Illumination of the rectifier diode causes changes in the diode conduction characteristics similar to those caused by illumination of solar cells. The effects of illuminating a blocking diode are an undesirable, increased forward voltage drop and an inconsequential, high-current flow in the reverse directions, as compared to the dark reverse leakage, depending on the amount of light incident on the diode junction.

Blocking diode specifications may vary, depending upon whether the diodes are located on the solar cell array or in the spacecraft interior. However, in general, blocking diodes are selected according to the criteria given below.

- Lowest possible forward voltage drop at the nominal current level and at the actual diode operating temperature (frequently, this current level is the average or peak current at end of life).

- Sufficient peak-inverse voltage rating, based on post-irradiation worst diode temperature, highest bus voltage with superimposed transient voltage spikes, and assumed solar cell string short-circuit failure conditions.
- Reliability and preferred failure mode (the preferred failure mode should be "open-circuit," so that a high array reliability can be obtained by the use of parallel-redundant diodes).
- Capability to withstand temperature cycling throughout mission life without mechanical or electrical failure.
- Highest possible permissible steady state operating temperature.

6-27. Shunt Diode Use

Shunt diodes, also known as bypass diodes, are used to minimize output losses and for protecting solar cells.

On partially shadowed solar cell arrays, the array power output may decrease by a greater fraction than what may be deduced from the amount of array area that is shadowed. This mechanism and how shunt diodes can improve the array power output capability is discussed in detail in Chapter 2 (Array Circuit Models).

The power output capability of a fully illuminated array may also be limited by fractured (broken) solar cells. This can occur when parts of the fractured cells become electrically disconnected from their remainders. The effects of fractured cells in an array are similar to those of a partial shadow on the array.

Shunt diodes are connected across single cells, rows of parallel-connected solar cells (submodules), or across modules (several submodules connected in series). The connection is such that the shunt diodes are reverse biased when all solar cells are fully illuminated. When the current flow through any solar cell submodule becomes limited, it may be due to shadowing or cell fracture. This "affected" submodule automatically becomes reverse biased; hence, the parallel-connected shunt diode becomes forward biased and conducts, and the full current can flow in this shunt diode-equipped submodule. However, the voltage output capability of a string of solar cells containing

such an affected submodule is reduced by the voltage drop that appears across the shunt diode.

Solar cells in arrays that are subject to shadowing may become permanently damaged from high reverse voltages and power dissipations so that permanent cell short-circuit failures may occur (see Section 4-25).

The high damaging reverse bias can be limited by the installation of shunt diodes as well.

6-28. Shunt Diode Characteristics

Essentially three different types of shunt diodes have been used: conventional diodes, packaged rectifier diodes, unpackaged diode wafers, and shunt diodes that are integral with the solar cells (so-called "integral shunt diodes").

The major criteria in selecting shunt diodes is their physical size and eventual location on the solar cell array. The only practical way to install shunt diodes is in the immediate vicinity of the solar cells or the submodules they are to protect.

The use of conventional rectifiers as shunt diodes can severely lower the solar cell packing density because the diodes and their leads take up a considerable amount of space (see Fig. 6-41). On relatively small solar cell panels, or when only few submodules require shunt diode protection, the space (surface area) requirements by conventional rectifiers may be tolerable; however, on relatively large panels with many cells to be protected, their profuse use may become impractical.

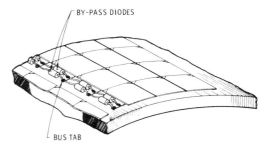

Fig. 6-41. Illustration of the use of conventional rectifier type diodes as shunt diodes. (*Reprinted with permission of Gordon & Breach, Science Publishers, Ltd.*[43])

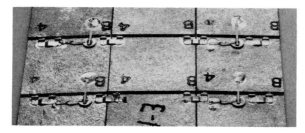

Fig. 6-42. Use of unencapsulated rectifier wafers on the back side of flexible, overlapping solar cell module.[44]

For the protection of large numbers of solar cells on a densely packed array, the best location of shunt diodes is underneath the solar cells. Figure 6-42 illustrates one possible approach of using unpackaged rectifier wafers in a flexible, overlapping solar cell module. A redundant pair of diodes protects each three-cell submodule of 2×2 cm cells. After installation on the substrate, neither the diodes nor the solar cell interconnector expansion loops were imbedded in adhesive. Both the solar cell interconnectors and the diode leads were made from Kovar ribbons that were plated with copper and solder. The diode wafers were touching the solar cells but they were not attached to the cells. This design was qualified for temperature cycling between $-160°$ and $+80°C$ for 300 cycles. The diodes were made to special order at the time.

A significant improvement in the use of shunt diodes, especially on cells installed "flat" on a substrate (by the "flat laydown" technique) can potentially be achieved when solar cells with integral shunt diodes are used. Figure 6-43 illustrates the solar cell and interconnector design. Figure 6-44 shows the solar

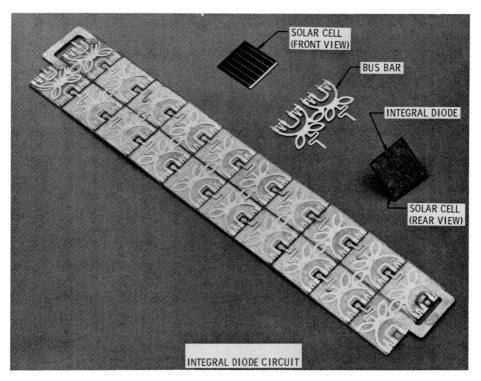

Fig. 6-43. Solar cell module, solar cell with integral shunt diode, and interconnector design. (*Reprinted with permission of Gordon & Breach, Science Publishers, Ltd.*[43])

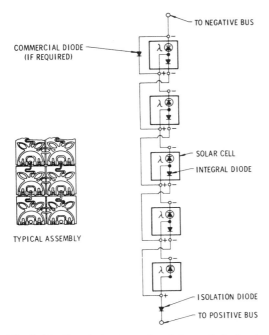

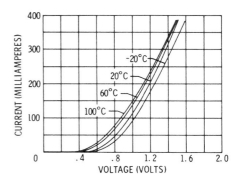

Fig. 6-45. Integral diode forward I-V characteristics. (*Reprinted with permission of Gordon & Breach, Science Publishers, Ltd.*[43])

Fig. 6-44. Electrical schematic of integral diode circuit. (*Reprinted with permission of Gordon & Breach, Science Publishers, Ltd.*[43])

cell interconnector design for use in conjunction with such solar cells schematically. Figure 6-45 indicates relatively high forward voltage drops that would be inadequate for low-voltage arrays (less than 100 V), but that could be adequate for high-voltage arrays (over 1 kV). Negligible leakage currents were observed with reverse voltages up to 30 V.

Solar cells with integral Schottky barrier diodes have been reported to have lower forward voltage drops than the diffused diodes exhibit.[45] Schottky barriers (metal-semiconductor junctions transporting majority carriers) have been fabricated, using Ti-Pd-Ag contacts that, for the diode to form, were rendered non-ohmic by a temperature treatment. These diodes did not

require large areas for voltage drops to be low, but instead required long junction periphery. Diode drops of 1.2 V for 10 ohm · cm cells and 0.8 V for 1 ohm · cm cells at 0.15 A and at room temperature have been reported.

The incorporation of Schottky diodes (as well as diffused diodes) on the cell back sides reduces solar cell power output by several mechanisms: increased cell series resistance in the base region; leakage current through the integral shunt diode; a photovoltaic current produced by the shunt diode junction and flowing such that it subtracts from the cell output current; and a transistor effect, causing a current flow which also subtracts from the cell output current.[44] For these losses to be small, the solar cells with integral diodes must be designed carefully and their fabrication processes must be controlled very closely.

6-29. Zener Diodes

Zener diodes, also known as *breakdown* diodes, limit the maximum voltage that can develop across a string of solar cells, as illustrated in Fig. 6-46. As long as the voltage output from

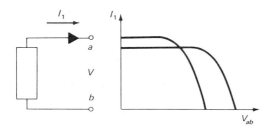

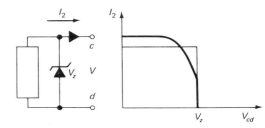

Fig. 6-46. Zener diodes as voltage limiters.

the string is less than the Zener voltage, or breakdown voltage, V_z, the Zener diode does not conduct. However, if the string output voltage tends to become greater than V_z, the Zener diode *clamps* the string voltage to V_z.

Zener diodes dissipate power of magnitude $P_z = V_z I_z$. Since this power can be quite large and the heat dissipation by radiation in space is not very efficient, several Zener diodes are usually connected in series and physically mounted over a larger area. Mounting to relatively heavy—preferably metallic—structural elements provides the best heat sinking. Typically used stud-mounted diode packages must be installed using insulating washers having sufficient voltage breakdown and temperature ratings.

WIRING AND CABLING

6-30. Wires and Cables

Wires, or, more correctly, *electrical wires*, are designed and manufactured to 1) conduct electricity optimally, and 2) confine the electric current to specific circuits. Optimum conduction is assured by the proper selection and trade-off of the following parameters: electrical conductivity (or resistivity), cross-sectional area, length, temperature coefficient of resistance, weight, cost, resistance to fracture due to bending and flexing in assembly and service, and practicality of termination. For non-flexing applications, *solid* wires are appropriate. For flexing applications, *stranded* wires are required.

Confinement of the electrical current to specific circuits is assured by proper dc insulation and, for certain circuits, by ac shielding. Insulation is provided by one or more layers, or sheaths, of appropriate dielectric material surrounding the conductor. The dielectric materials are chosen primarily to withstand one or more of the following service environments: heat, moisture, space radiation, and voltage breakdown. For terrestrial application, certain wires and cables may require additional mechanical protection over the outside dielectric layer, known as *armour*.

Shielded wires are sometimes used for sensitive transducer circuits. Usually, however, *twisted* wire pairs are adequate to cancel out unwanted ac signals. Occasionally, twisted wires are used to minimize electromagnetic interference that is generated by switching regulators or power converters and radiated by the array wiring.

Wires are tied together into wire *bundles* or *cables*. Subassemblies consisting of a number of wires and usually one or more attached connectors are known as wire *harnesses*. Flat cables may be made of round or flat conductors.

Wires are rated according to their conductor material, conductor size (cross-section's area), insulation stand-off voltage capability, and insulation service temperature limitations. The most widely used conductor material is copper. The use of aluminum is spreading slowly because termination is somewhat more involved than with other metals (see Section 6-36).

6-31. Methods of Wiring

The general method for solar cell array wiring for power collection wiring is similar to the general method for power distribution wiring, except that the electric current is in the opposite direction. It is as important to be able to disconnect faulted solar cell circuits from a large power collection network as it is to disconnect faulted loads from a large power distribution network. Automatic fault isolation on a large solar cell array, however, may not be quite as simple as fault isolation on a power distribution system, because of internal impedance differences between solar cell circuits and electric loads under fault conditions.

For initial test and later maintenance reasons, it is desirable to be able to separate relatively low-power solar cell strings from the power collection wiring. Figure 6-47 illustrates a generally used method for larger space arrays: strings of cells are bussed first at the panel to minimize the number of connector pins, and to maximize the electrical output test resolution. Increasing numbers of circuits are then connected together to minimize overall wire weight and cost. As shown in the figure, the wire size increases toward the load.

Electrical grounding is important for both space and terrestrial arrays. Space arrays must be grounded primarily for electromagnetic

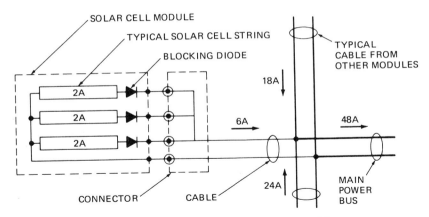

Fig. 6-47. Power collection (illustrative example).

interference (EMI) reasons, while terrestrial arrays must be grounded primarily for safety reasons. The array or panel structural ground should always (for terrestrial as well as space applications) be carried along separately from the solar cell circuit common bus (negative or return bus).

The electrical currents on space arrays may form current loops that exert undesirable magnetic forces on the spacecraft. Therefore, it may be necessary to lay out all solar cell circuits and wiring such that the magnetic forces cancel each other (see Section 3-38).

Minimum wire sizes, redundancy, and insulation voltage ratings are typically mission and project peculiar. Resistance values for various gage conductors are shown in Table 6-2.

Wire routing and installation on solar cell arrays should be performed carefully and should follow the guidelines listed below.

- Wires routing over sharp edges should be avoided. The edges may cut through the insulation and potentially cause short circuits. The wire insulation should have good cut-through resistance.
- Thermal expansion loops should be provided. Copper expands and contracts with temperature at a different rate than aluminum, fiberglass-epoxy, Kapton, or other materials, causing relative motion between interconnected parts.
- A sufficient quantity and quality of wire tie-down places (spot bonds, cable clamps, etc.) should be provided to prevent wire damage during launch on space arrays or

flexing (wind, vibration, etc.) on terrestrial arrays.
- The insulating materials should be compatible with:

  1. The ultraviolet and charged particle radiation dose expected during life;
  2. The temperature range, both operating and non-operating, that the array will be exposed to, considering the rise in wire temperature due to current flow; and
  3. The humidity and other environments.

- The inner wires in cable bundles will operate at a higher temperature. Therefore, the wire size should be determined based on proper derating.
- The bend radius of a single wire should be at least several times its outside diameter. The bend radius of a wire bundle should be not less than ten times its outside diameter.
- Current feed and return wires of the same circuits should be twisted if practical.
- Signal wires (from temperature transducers, etc.) should be kept separate and away from power wires as much as practicable.
- Stranded wires possess greater flex life than do solid wires.
- Wires or wire bundles passing over flexible interfaces, hinged joints, etc., should be made from stranded wire and looped around their joints, such that a minimum of wire twisting, rather than a large amount of bending, occurs when the joint articulates.

Table 6-2. Wire Tables for Solid Annealed Copper.[49]

AWG	Diameter		Cross-Section			Resistance at 20°C*		Weight	
	mm	mils	mm²	Circular mills	inch²	ohm/1000 ft	ohm/km	lb/1000 ft	kg/km
0000	11.684	460.0	107.23	211600	0.1662	0.04901	0.1608	640.5	953.2
000	10.404	409.6	85.03	167800	0.1318	0.06180	0.2028	507.9	755.8
00	9.266	364.8	67.42	133100	0.1045	0.07793	0.2557	402.8	599.4
0	8.252	324.9	53.48	105500	0.08289	0.09827	0.3224	319.5	475.5
1	7.348	289.3	42.41	83690	0.06573	0.1239	0.4065	253.3	377.0
2	6.544	257.6	33.63	66370	0.05213	0.1563	0.5128	200.9	299.0
4	5.189	204.3	21.18	41740	0.03278	0.2485	0.8153	126.4	188.1
6	4.116	162.0	13.30	26250	0.02062	0.3951	1.296	79.46	118.2
8	3.264	128.5	8.366	16510	0.01297	0.6282	2.061	49.98	74.38
10	2.588	101.9	5.261	10380	0.008155	0.9989	3.277	31.43	46.77
12	2.053	80.81	3.309	6530	0.005129	1.588	5.210	19.77	29.42
14	1.628	64.08	2.081	4107	0.003225	2.525	8.284	12.43	18.50
16	1.291	50.82	1.309	2583	0.002028	4.016	13.18	7.818	11.63
18	1.024	40.30	0.8231	1624	0.001276	6.385	20.95	4.917	7.317
20	0.8118	31.96	0.5176	1022	0.0008023	10.15	33.30	3.092	4.601
22	0.6439	25.35	0.3255	642.4	0.0005046	16.14	53.81	1.945	2.894
24	0.5105	20.10	0.2047	404.0	0.0003173	25.67	84.22	1.223	1.820
26	0.4049	15.94	0.1288	254.1	0.0001996	40.81	133.9	0.7692	1.145
28	0.3211	12.64	0.08097	159.8	0.0001255	64.90	212.9	0.4837	0.7198
30	0.2548	10.03	0.05093	100.5	0.00007894	103.2	338.6	0.3042	0.4527

*For temperature coefficients see Section 10-16.

6-32. Wiring for Terrestrial Arrays

Wiring practices, codes, and standards for terrestrial photovoltaic systems have not yet been officially formulated. However, it can be assumed for practical reasons that the various established national and local codes and standards developed for utility power distribution will be applicable to a large extent for solar cell arrays as well. For the U.S. the National Electrical Code (NEC) establishes the minimum standards for wiring, primarily to protect the public from life and fire hazards. Over 600 municipal electrical wiring ordinances establish additional requirements. Wiring design and installation practices that assure an adequate or efficient system are established by national and local standards. For systems interfacing with the public utility grid, additional rules are established by the various power companies.

Many of the codes and standards are concerned with fire and electrical shock hazards and, therefore, apply also to low-voltage systems and to systems that are not connected to the public utility network.

Even though terrestrial solar cell systems are still mostly experimental, adherence to the existing applicable portions of electrical design codes, practices, and standards is highly recommended. A local library, a municipal licensing office or engineering department, or a local electrical contractor may be contacted to obtain the appropriate documents.

6-33. Wiring of Space Arrays

Wiring of space arrays is similar to wiring of terrestrial arrays except that the electrical codes and standards guiding the design are replaced by appropriate military specifications, NASA (National Aeronautics and Space Administration) documents, and various design practices and standards of the aerospace industry. In addition, in space, the radiation environment dominates, while for terrestrial applications, weatherability is a prime consideration.

For space arrays, weight is a critical design parameter. On small arrays (less than about 1 kW), the minimum wire gage (AWG #28) is defined by handleability and reliability criteria, and on larger arrays, the power losses must be traded off against the wiring weight. For arrays in the 0.5 to 2 kW range, power losses in the wiring between 1% and 4% have usually resulted in minimum weight power subsystems.[46]

6-34. Wire Insulation Properties

The properties of the more common wire insulating materials for terrestrial considerations are given in Table 6-3. The exact upper

Table 6-3. Wire Insulation—Terrestrial.[50,51]

Insulation Material Type	Typical Temperature Limits	Application
Rubber, heat resistant	75° to 90°C	Dry only
Rubber, moisture resistant, heat and moisture resistant	60° to 75°C	Dry and wet
Thermoplastic, heat resistant	60° to 90°C	Dry only
Thermoplastic, moisture resistant, heat and moisture resistant	60° to 75°C	Dry and wet
Silicone—asbestos	90° to 125°C	Dry only
FEP (fluorinated ethylene propylene)	90° to 200°C	Specialized
Kapton	200° to 350°C	Specialized
Asbestos and varnished cambric	85° to 110°C	Dry and wet

Table 6-4. Wire Insulation—Space and Terrestrial.[51, 52, 53]

Property	Kapton Polyimide	Teflon TFE	Teflon FEP	PTFE	Tefzel ETFE	Kynar PVF$_2$
Upper temperature rating, °C	200	260	200	–	150	150
Lower temperature rating, °C	–273	–273	–273	–273	–	–65
Short-time temperature limit, °C	500	325	280	327	–	300
Tensile strength, MN/m^2	170	28	20	–	–	17 to 34
Elongation, %	70	300	250 to 330	200 to 300	200	150 to 300
Cut-through resistance	Excellent	Fair	Fair	High	High	High
Ionizing radiation resistance	Excellent	Fair	Fair	$>10^8$ rads	Excellent	$>10^8$ rads
Density, g/cm^3	1.42	2.15	2.14 to 2.17	2.13 to 2.20	1.7	1.3 to 1.76

service temperature limits and permissible applications depend upon the specific insulator material formulations. The appropriate manufacturer's data should be consulted. Insulation materials for external applications in space must be tolerant to the charged particle and ultraviolet radiation environment, and must possess low outgassing characteristics. The materials given in Table 6-4 have been used widely.

Kapton insulation, not subject to melting or cut-through by cold flow, is the material with the highest practical service temperature of near 250°C. Above 350°C, Kapton decomposes. Kapton wire insulation is finding increasing use in aircraft and spacecraft.

6-35. Current Carrying Capability

The maximum amount of current a wire can carry, also known as its *ampacity*, is determined 1) by the ability of its insulation to withstand the heat that is generated in the conductor by I^2R heating, and 2) by the heat transfer afforded by the wire's surroundings. Single wires of bare conductors in ambient air can carry the most amount of current, while insulated wires in the middle of thick bundles in the space vacuum can carry the least amount of current through a given conductor cross-section for a given upper temperature limit. The ampacity, based on general design practices, is illustrated in Fig. 6-48.

TERMINALS AND CONNECTORS

6-36. Wire Terminations

Wires must be terminated to become useful. After removal of the insulation, the wire end is terminated by soldering or by mechanical pressure. Soldered terminations include soldering to other wires, lugs, circuit boards, stand-off terminals, connector pins, connector receptacles, and other devices. Mechanical pressure termination includes clamping, crimping, and wire wrapping. Clamping may be by springs, clamps, crews and washers, and other devices.

The selection of a specific termination method depends primarily upon the environment to which the termination is exposed, the current level, and the ease with which the termination needs to be made initially and taken apart later for maintenance and check-out purposes.

Most important for terrestrial installations, but by no means negligible for space applications, is to avoid bringing dissimilar metals in close contact with each other. Dissimilar metals are defined as those occupying relatively widely separated positions on the electrogalvanic scale (see Chapter 10). In humid environments, especially in the presence of ionic compounds (finger prints, salt, industrial atmospheres, dust, etc.), electrolytic corrosion takes place (see Chapter 9).

Aluminum conductors must be terminated with aluminum terminals. The transition from aluminum to copper requires special care. Typi-

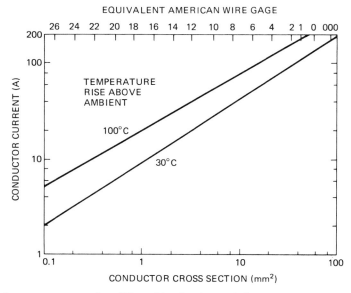

Fig. 6-48. Approximate current-carrying ability of insulated annealed copper wires (up to three conductors in a bundle for terrestrial applications).[50,51]

cally, the aluminum is plated with one or several interlayers before copper contact is made. Some metals, such as chromium, provide no protection because of their porosity.

Soldered connections have not been found to be as reliable as crimped connections in low-current (0.1 to 10 A) space applications and in high-current (10 to 1000 A) terrestrial applications, especially when large temperature excursions are present.

The implementation of any termination method should be in compliance with the wire and termination device manufacturer's recommendations. To assure adequate fatigue life in vibration or flexing applications (due to thermal expansion), conductors should not be nicked, and adequate mechanical stress relief and stress relief loops should be provided.

6-37. Connectors and Terminals for Space Arrays

Connectors permit quick connection and disconnection of solar cell panels to and from the array power collection cabling, respectively, while the use of terminals requires soldering operations to be performed.

The decision to use either connectors or terminals on solar cell arrays, as well as the selec-tion of the types of connectors or terminals, is generally project peculiar. Some organizations prefer one type of connector or terminal over another, depending upon what their past successes or failures were with specific connector or terminal designs. Many firms have developed very specific process and assembly procedures and techniques for certain types of connectors which virtually assure their successful flight, even though other organizations may have been less successful with that same type.

For weight reasons and sometimes due to packing density restraints, usually the smallest and lightest connectors or terminals are selected. Manufacturing ease and workmanship considerations also play important roles in the selection. It is usually advantageous to specify a size that has a few more contacts than actually required during an early design stage. Frequently, during the later design stages, additional circuits must be accommodated that may or may not be related to the solar cell array layout. If no such additional requirements arise, the unused contacts can always be used in parallel with others to improve the connector reliability.

Connector Reliability. In general, connectors are less reliable than hard-wired connections between terminals. The advantage of connectors, however, is that they permit greater freedom during the post-fabrication test and systems integration checkout phases, especially on more complex spacecraft electrical systems.

Connectors become less reliable with the number of times they are mated and demated because of wearing away (wiping) of usually soft contact metals such as gold. To minimize the deleterious effects due to repeated mating, so-called "connector savers" are used. Connector savers are short, male/female adapters of identical types to the flight connectors. The connector savers are mated with the flight connector only once on one side, while all repeated connections for test and checkout purposes are made on the other side. The connector savers are removed after all spacecraft systems have been successfully checked out.

The disadvantage of hardwiring to terminals is that wires may be soldered and unsoldered reliably only a limited number of times, since during each heating cycle, the possibility of scavenging of terminal plating by the molten solder and weakening of the terminal/insulating material interface exists and usually occurs to some degree.

6-38. Connectors and Terminals for Terrestrial Use

Connectors permit rapid and safe connection and disconnection of solar cell panels from the power collection network, simply by "plugging in" and "unplugging." Terminals, lower-cost devices than connectors, usually require some labor to make or break the connections. For higher voltage systems (in excess of about 30 V), work on "hot" terminals is not safe, and disconnect switches, removable fuses, or circuit breakers are required as well.

6-39. Termination Design Practices

Termination Sizing. There are two alternate approaches to terminating solar cell circuits and connecting them to a power collection network: to bring many low-current level conductors out from each solar cell panel and route them across the mechanical panel interface to a power bus terminal or connector, or to bring

only a few high-current level conductors across. The criteria for the selection of the best approach must be established for each specific design and application. Important considerations include the check-out feasibility of individual circuits (strings); location of the blocking diodes (see Section 6-25); size and flexibility constraints on the cables that cross the mechanical interfaces; potential damage to wires (chafing, pinching, cutting, etc.) from handling, assembly, launch, and deployment; array orientation; and reliability estimates for the various elements involved.

General Design Practices. The general design practices outlined below are usually followed.

- High-vapor pressure alloys and metallic coatings, such as brass, zinc, and cadmium, should be avoided, as these materials may vaporize and condense on cooler spacecraft surfaces and cause thermal or optical problems. (For sublimation rates of metals in vacuum, see Section 9-34.)
- Insulating, bonding, and potting materials should have low outgassing rates in vacuum, or these materials should be pre-outgassed prior to assembly on the spacecraft. (For outgassing properties of materials, see Section 10-33.)
- Insulating, bonding, and potting materials should be compatible with the ultraviolet and charged particle radiation environment. Charged particles impinge on all sides of the solar cell array from all directions (i.e., are omnidirectional) and may penetrate metallic shields. (For radiation effects on materials, see Section 9-34.)
- Adequate derating factors should be used for the current carrying capability of contacts (i.e., pins and sockets) and terminals.
- Adequate voltage ratings of insulators for wires, terminal boards, and terminal blocks should be used. Insulators should not be stressed to levels where corona discharge may start. (Some materials, such as Teflon, are more subject to damage by corona than are others.) Also, it should be considered that the arc-over voltage rating decreases significantly for several minutes during ascent of the space vehicle.

REFERENCES

1. W. Luft, "Solar Cell Interconnector Design," in *IEEE Transactions on Aerospace and Electronic Systems*, Vol. **AES-7**, *No. 5*, September 1971.
2. "FEP-Teflon Encapsulated Solar Cell Module Development," Final Report, Work Performed by TRW for the NASA Lewis Research Center, Cleveland, Ohio, under Contract **NAS 3-16742**, 1976.
3. J. D. Gum *et al*, "Solar Arrays Utilizing Large Area Silicon Solar Cells," in *Conference Records of the 7th IEEE Photovoltaic Specialists Conference*, November 1968.
4. W. Luft and E. Maiden, "Temperature Cycling Effects on Solar Cell Panels," in *IEEE Transactions on Aerospace and Electronic Systems*, Vol. **AES-5**, *No. 6*, November 1969.
5. "Development of Highly Reliable Soldered Joints for Printed Circuit Boards," Final Report No. **8402A**, Westinghouse Defense and Space Center, Aerospace Division, Baltimore, Maryland, August 1968.
6. D. J. Curtin and W. T. Billerbeck in *Proceedings of the Section "The Photovoltaic Power and its Application in Space and on Earth,"* International Congress, "The Sun in the Service of Mankind," Paris, France, July 1973.
7. "Survey and Study for an Improved Solar Cell Module," Document No. **900-270**, Jet Propulsion Laboratory, August 1969.
8. A. E. Mann *et al*, "Solar Cell Array," U.S. Patent No. **3,094,439**, June 1963.
9. R. F. Julius, "Solar Cell Array," U.S. Patent No. **3,375,141**, March 1968 (filed July 1963).
10. J. G. Haynos, "Interconnection of Solar Cells," U.S. Patent No. **3,459,391**, August 1969 (filed February 1964).
11. From TRW's mostly previously unpublished work on solar cell assemblies.
12. W. R. Baron, "Solar Cells with Flexible Overlapping Bifurcated Connector," U.S. Patent No. **3,459,597**, TRW, Inc., August 1969; and U.S. Patent No. **3,837,924**, "Solar Array," TRW, Inc., September 24, 1974.
13. S. Timoshenko, "Analysis of Bi-Metal Thermostats," (pp. 223–255) in *Journal of the Optical Society of America*, Vol. **2**, September 1925.
14. U. U. Savolainen and R. M. Sears, "Thermostat Metals," (Ch. 10) in *Composite Engineering Laminates*, A. G. H. Dietz (ed.), MIT Press, 1969.
15. Milton S. Hess, "The End Problem for a Laminated Electric Strip—II. Differential Expansion Stresses," (pp. 630–641) in *Journal of Composite Materials*, Vol. **3**, October 1969.
16. A. C. Agerwal and M. W. Haggers, "Differential Expansion in Elastic Laminates," (pp. 655–633) in *ASCE Journal of the Structural Division*, April 1973.
17. E. L. Ralph and J. Roger in *Solar Cells, Proceedings of the International Colloquium Organized by the European Cooperation Space Environment Committee (ECOSEC), July 1970, Toulouse, France*, Gordon and Breach Science Publishers, New York, 1971.
18. L. W. Butterworth and R. K. Yasui, "Structural Analysis of Silicon Solar Arrays," Report No. **32-1528**, Jet Propulsion Laboratory, May 1971.
19. J. J. Bikerman, *The Science of Adhesive Joints*, Academic Press, New York, 1968.
20. L. J. Hart-Smith, "Adhesive-Bonded Lap Joints," NASA CR **112236**, Douglas Aircraft Co., McDonnel Douglas Corp., January 1973.
21. W. J. Renton and J. R. Vinson, "The Analysis and Design of Composite Material Bonded Joints under Static and Fatigue Loadings," **AFOSR-TR-73-1627**, Department of Mechanical and Aerospace Engineering, University of Delaware, August 1973.
22. M. A. Salama, R. M. Rowe, and R. K. Yasui, "Thermoelastic Analysis of Solar Cell Arrays and their Mechanical Properties," **TM 33-626**, Jet Propulsion Laboratory, September 1973.
23. H. S. Rauschenbach and P. S. Gaylard, "Prediction of Fatigue Failures in Solar Arrays," in *Proceedings of the 7th Intersociety Energy Conversion Engineering Conference 1972*, published by the American Chemical Society, pages 666 and 670.
24. E. L. Ralph and R. K. Tasui, "Silicon Solar Cell Lightweight Integrated Array," in *Conference Records of the 8th IEEE Photovoltaic Specialists Conference*, Seattle, Washington, 1970.
25. E. L. Ralph and J. Roger in *Solar Cells, Proceedings of the International Colloquium Organized by the European Cooperation Space Environment Committee (ECOSEC), July 1970, Toulouse, France*, Gordon and Breach Science Publishers, New York, 1971.
26. H. J. Grover, "Fatigue of Aircraft Structures," **NAVAIR 01-1A-13**, 1966.
27. P. J. E. Forsyth, *The Physical Basis of Metal Fatigue*, American Elsevier, New York, 1969.
28. S. S. Manson, "Fatigue a Complex Subject—Some Simple Approximations," (pp. 193–226) in *Experimental Mechanics*, July 1965.
29. S. S. Manson, *Thermal Stresses and Low Cycle Fatigue*, McGraw-Hill, New York, 1966.
30. L. F. Coffin, "Design Aspects of High Temperature Fatigue with Particular Reference to Thermal Stresses," (pp. 527–532) in *Transactions ASME*, April 1956.
31. R. W. Smith, M. A. Hirschberg, and S. S. Manson, "Fatigue of Materials under Strain Cycling in Low and Intermediate Life Range," **TN D-1574**, NASA, April 1963.
32. D. J. Curtin and W. U. Billerbeck, "Development of Advanced Interconnectors for Solar Cells," (pp. 53–68) in *Comsat Technical Review*, Vol. **4**, *No. 1*, 1964.
33. H. S. Rathose, R. C. Yeh, and A. R. Edenfeld, "Fatigue Behavior of Solders used in Flip-Chip

Technology," (pp. 170–178) in *ASTM Journal of Testing and Evaluation*, *Vol. 1*, March 1973.

34. J. L. Mattavi, "Low Cycle Fatigue Behavior under Biaxial Strain Distribution," (pp. 23–31) in *ASME Journal of Basic Engineering*, March 1969.

35. S. Y. Zamrick and J. Goto, "The Use of Octahedral Shear Strain Theory in Biaxial Low Cycle Fatigue," (pp. 551–562) in *Proceedings of the International American Conference on Materials Technology*, San Antonio, Texas, Sponsored by Southwest Research Institute and ASME.

36. S. S. Manson, "Behavior of Materials under Conditions of Thermal Stress," NACA Rep. **1170**, 1954.

37. L. F. Coffin, Jr., "A Study of the Effects of Cyclic Thermal Stresses on a Ductile Metal," (pp. 931–950) in *Transactions ASME*, *Vol. 76*, *No. 6*, August 1954.

38. A. Kaplan, "Fatigue Analysis of Solar Cell Welds," (pp. 281–286) in *Proceedings of the 10th IEEE Photovoltaic Specialists Conference*, November 1973.

39. J. G. Crose and R. M. Jones, "SAAS III Finite Element Stress Analysis of Axisymmetric and Plane Solids with Different, Orthotropic Temperature Dependent Material Properties in Tension and Compression," **SAMSO-TR-71-103**, June 1971.

40. N. J. Wadsworth and J. Hutchings," "The Effects of Atmosphere Corrosion on Metal Fatigue," (pp. 1154–1155) in *Philosophical Magazine*, *Vol. 3*, 1964.

41. K. U. Snowdon, "The Effect of Atmosphere on the Fatigue of Lead," (pp. 295–303) in *ACTA Metallurgica*, *Vol. 12*, March 1964.

42. E. Levy, Jr. and R. J. McGrath, "Reverse Current Blocking Diodes for Flexible Solar Array Protection," Technical Report **AFAPL-TR-75-23**, Air Force Aeropropulsion Laboratory, Air Force

Systems Command, Wright-Patterson Air Force Base, Ohio, April 1975.

43. R. M. Diamond and E. D. Steele in *Solar Cells*, *Proceedings of the International Colloqium Organized by the European Cooperation Space Environment Committee (ECOSEC)*, *July 1970*, *Toulouse, France*, Gordon and Breach Science Publishers, New York, 1971.

44. W. Luft, "1967 Technology Report on Photovoltaic Conversion," Report No. **99900-6414-5000**, TRW Systems Group, TRW, Inc., December 1967.

45. H. Fischer and W. Pschunder in *Proceedings of the Section "The Photovoltaic Power and its Application in Space and on Earth,"* International Congress, "The Sun in the Service of Mankind," Paris, France, July 1973.

46. J. Roger, "Optimal Bus Bars for Rectangular Solar Arrays," in *Records of the 9th IEEE Photovoltaic Specialists Conference*, Silver Spring, Maryland, May 1972.

47. *Proceedings of the Section "The Photovoltaic Power and its Application in Space and on Earth,"* International Congress, "The Sun in the Service of Mankind," Paris, France, July 1973.

48. *Solar Cells, Proceedings of the International Colloquium Organized by the European Cooperation Space Environment Committee (ECOSEC)*, *July 1970, Toulouse, France*, Gordon and Breach Science Publishers, New York, 1971.

49. *Reference Data for Radio Engineers*, Fourth Edition, International Telephone and Telegraph Corporation, 1956.

50. *Standard Handbook for Electrical Engineers*, Tenth Edition, D. G. Fink, (ed.), McGraw-Hill, New York, 1969.

51. *Insulation/Circuits Desk Manual*, 1977, Lake Publishing Co.

52. Raychem Corporation, Wire and Cable Division.

53. DuPont de Nemours and Co.

7
Mechanical Elements

ARRAY MECHANICAL CHARACTERISTICS

7-1. Array Design Options

Solar cell arrays may be classified, according to their mechanical construction (as shown in Fig. 7-1), into two broad categories: arrays for terrestrial applications and arrays for space applications. Significant differences in array design and construction between terrestrial and space arrays result primarily from the differences in the environments that these two classes of arrays must endure. In addition, space arrays usually must meet severe weight requirements.

Both terrestrial and space arrays may or may not utilize solar cell concentration devices to increase the amount of power generated from a given number of solar cells having a given size. For example, if it were possible to focus (i.e., *concentrate*) onto a cell the sunlight falling onto an area 100 times as large as the solar cell area without also increasing the heat input to the solar cells, 100 times the amount of solar energy could be converted by the same number of cells. This is equivalent to reducing the solar cell cost for a given array power rating to one-hundredth, or to 1%. Sunlight concentration, however, creates thermal problems that limit the amount of concentration that can be practically utilized.

Non-concentrator arrays, also called *flat plate* arrays, are used both in terrestrial and space applications and both in a fixed position and a tracking mode. Not all non-concentrator arrays are of the flat plate type; they may be curved, canted (V-shaped or A-shaped), or any other desired shape or configuration, either for terrestrial or for space use.

Except for body-mounted arrays, *space* arrays are of the deployable type. The array panels are folded up or rolled up in some fashion for launch, and are deployed (i.e., unfolded or erected and locked in place) once a desired orbital position has been reached.

Non-concentrator *terrestrial* arrays consist of one or more interconnected solar cell modules, also known as *solar modules* for short. Each module is a self-contained package of solar cells that are well protected from the environment.

Solar cell space panels or terrestrial modules are attached to each other and to a mechanical *support structure*. In the case of fixed arrays, the support structure is either attached to a vehicle (spacecraft, truck, etc.) or to the ground (the earth, the moon, etc.). For tracking type arrays, the support structure is attached to an orientation mechanism and the orientation mechanism is, in turn, mounted to the vehicle or to the ground.

Arrays may be constructed of rigid, semi-rigid, or flexible solar cell panels or modules. Rigid panels have been used most frequently in the past for both space and terrestrial applications. Semi-rigid panels rely on a network of supporting beams to which a somewhat flexible substrate, module, or solar cell blanket is fastened. Typically, the substrate is stretched like a membrane. Other designs utilize non-stretched (limb) substrates that are supported by some type of mechanical support.

Flexible substrates, also known as solar cell

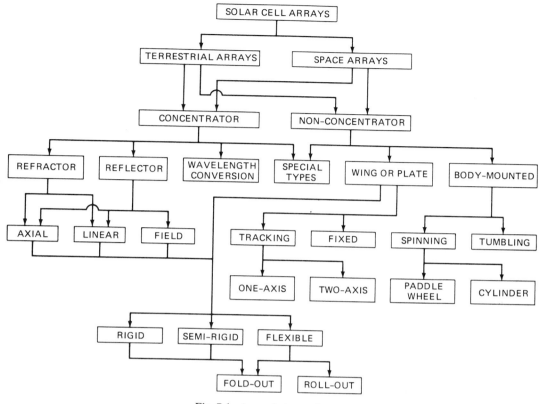

Fig. 7-1. Array design options.

blankets, are used in space only as a membrane between rigid support frames or as a non-supported sheet. The support frames necessitate fold-out deployment. Non-supported sheets may be folded up into a flat-pack or rolled up on a drum for stowage, but require a deployable element that draws the blanket outward and away from the stowage mechanism.

7-2. Array Mechanical Elements

The mechanical construction of most solar cell arrays may be generalized and subdivided into a number of distinct parts, as shown in Fig. 7-2.

Terrestrial arrays are typically assembled from so-called *solar cell modules*. Modules are self-contained, packaged, and hermetically sealed assemblies that contain a group of interconnected solar cells. The modules may be of the non-concentrator types, also called *flat plate modules*, or of the concentrator types, in which case they are called *concentrator modules*.

The module package may or may not provide all of the required mechanical support. For example, in a package consisting primarily of an aluminum extrusion and a plastic lens in front of the solar cells, the aluminum member provides essentially all of the solar cell support. However, in a package consisting primarily of a glass plate to which solar cells are attached with their active areas, and a potting compound is applied over the cell's back sides, the glass plate "superstrate" provides all of the mechanical support and strength.

Space arrays, not requiring hermetic sealing of the solar cells, consist of so-called solar cell *panels*, also called *modules*. By long-established industry convention, space panels are subdivided into electrical and mechanical parts. The electrical part consists of the solar cells, coverglasses, interconnectors, wiring, cabling, electrical connectors, diodes, cover and cell adhesives, and other materials and components that are added to the substrate during the course of the panel

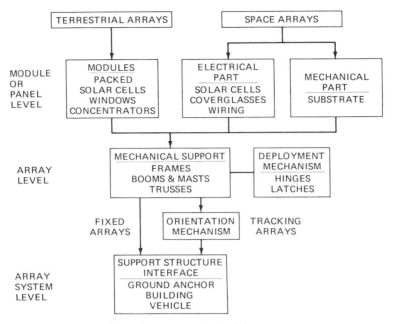

Fig. 7-2. Array mechanical elements.

assembly process. The electrical part is quite independent of the mechanical part, in that different solar cell and coverglass types can readily be installed on any of a number of different substrate types.

Substrates are the structural elements that mechanically support and hold in place the solar cells, cell interconnectors, and the associated wiring. Substrates are plate-like or sheet-like elements that may be flat or curved, rigid or flexible, and may carry solar cells on one or both surfaces. Functioning as true substrates, they may be located behind the solar cell's back sides, or, functioning as *superstrates*, they may be located in front of the solar cell's active areas. Superstrates, of course, must be optically transparent.

Mechanical support members hold the terrestrial modules or space panels of an array in fixed positions relative to each other and to a support structure interface or to an orientation mechanism. The support structure may consist of concrete blocks, a building, or a vehicle such as a buoy, a truck, or a spacecraft.

An orientation mechanism consists of one or more moveable elements that permit sun-tracking of the array. An orientation drive unit supplies the mechanical energy to move the array.

Sun-tracking may be done only approximately or very precisely, depending upon the system design. Both terrestrial and space arrays may utilize one-axis or two-axis tracking schemes. At the end of one day, or in space at the end of one orbit, the array must either be able to continue rotating or must reset or "unwind" itself. Continuous rotation requires the use of slip rings and brushes to facilitate electric power transfer, while resetting arrays can utilize lower-cost flexible wire loops. Orientation drives may be composed of a variety of bearings, hinges, linkages, gear or screw drives, hydraulic elements, electric motors, wheels on guide rails, or other elements.

Deployment mechanisms are used on vehicular terrestrial arrays and on space arrays. During launch, relatively large solar cell arrays are folded up or rolled up (*stowed*) so they will fit into a relatively confined volume. Upon arrival at a destination or in space, the array is deployed and oriented toward the sun.

TERRESTRIAL FLAT PLATE ARRAYS

7-3. Flat Plate Modules

Flat plate solar cell modules for terrestrial applications are characterized by intercon-

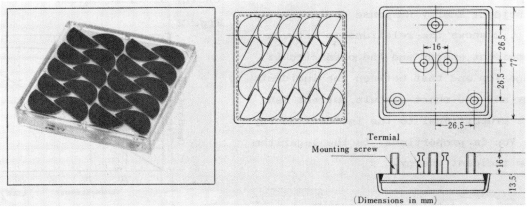

Fig. 7-3. Early terrestrial module. (*Courtesy of Sharp Corp.*[1])

Terminal
Mounting screw
←16→
26.5
26.5
77
←26.5→
16
13.5
(Dimensions in mm)

nected strings of solar cells which are hermetically sealed and durably packaged.

A commercial module available since about 1960 in Japan is illustrated in Fig. 7-3. The n-on-p silicon solar cells (10% efficient) are soldered to a printed circuit board and completely enclosed by a heat-resistant alkaline acrylic resin. The 20 semi-circular solar cells are interconnected into two series strings, producing 0.36 W at 4.2 V minimum at 100 mW/cm^2 intensity and 25°C cell temperature. The module weight is 100 g.[1]

Six of the higher-powered solar cell modules fabricated in the U.S. during the mid-1970's are illustrated in Figs. 7-4 and 7-5. The corresponding cross-sectional views are given in Fig. 7-6. Table 7-1 summarizes the construction characteristics. Tests performed on these modules and others of similar construction have shown that epoxy/glass board does not withstand ultraviolet radiation for long periods of time; it decomposes and, after some time, admits moisture into the package.

Modules of Type E and F utilized a clear substrate, permitting the incident solar radiation which was not intercepted by the solar cells to penetrate the module with little absorbtion. The hoped-for reduction in cell operating temperature did not materialize, however, because the transparent substrate's relatively low

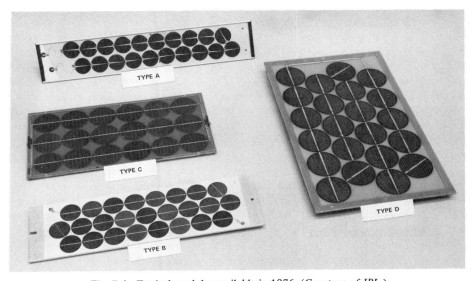

Fig. 7-4. Typical modules available in 1976. (*Courtesy of JPL.*)

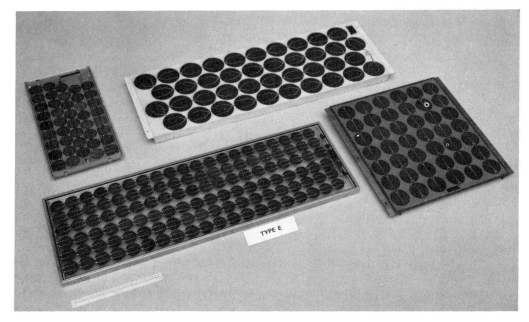

Fig. 7-5. Typical improved module, 1976/77. (*Courtesy of JPL.*)

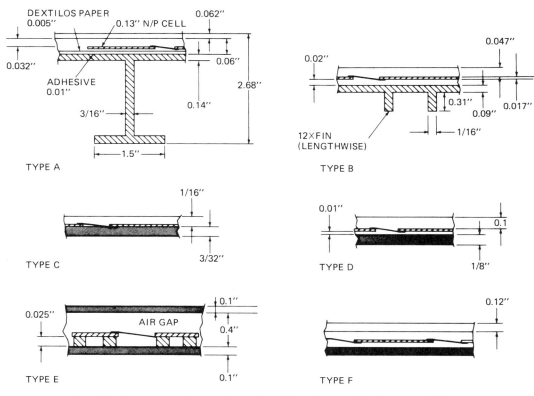

Fig. 7-6. Cross-sectional views of modules of Figs. 7-4 and 7-5. (*Courtesy of JPL.*)

Table 7-1. Module Characteristics.[2]

Component	Module Designation					
	Type A	Type B	Type C	Type D	Type E	Type F
Module dimensions (mm)	124 × 648	165 × 572	244 × 482	330 × 572	320 × 413	381 × 122
Cover material	Tempered glass	Sylgard	Sylgard	Sylgard	Plexiglass	Glass
Encapsulant	Sylgard	Sylgard	Sylgard	Sylgard	Air	Plastic
Solar cell diameter (mm)	54.0	50.8	76.2	86.4	76.2	50.8
Number of cells	20	25	18	22	12	120
Cell area/module area	0.57	0.54	0.70	0.68	0.41	0.55
Substrate	Aluminum	Aluminum	G10 board	G10 board	Plexiglass	Polyester film
Number of fins	1	12	0	0	0	0

thermal conductance relative to that of metal substrates caused a cell temperature increase. For installations over roofs or close to the ground, the transparent substrates caused a "green-house" (or "hot-house") effect, making them actually perform at a lower power level than similarly installed modules having opaque substrates. The air gap in module Type E created a similar green-house effect, causing the cell temperature to be more than 10°C higher than if the gap had been filled with a transparent compound.

The experience gained from the fabrication, test, and operation of the earlier modules has led to further module design improvements. There are now many companies in the business of fabricating terrestrial solar cell modules. Three of these are illustrated in Figs. 7-7 through 7-10; their characteristics are summarized in Table 7-2. These products are not specifically endorsed; they simply serve to illustrate the typical design features of many similar currently available products.

Many module designs now utilize white epoxy paint or an equivalent material over the exposed substrate area to reflect sunlight. Part of this light is trapped inside the module by total reflection, and adds to power output.

7-4. Open Frame Supports

Most terrestrial solar cell modules are installed in open frames, which, in turn, are mounted to a support frame or truss. The modules are oriented to face the equator and are tilted by an angle that is typically equal to the local latitude.

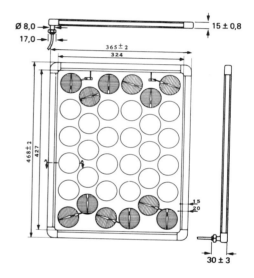

Dimensions in mm

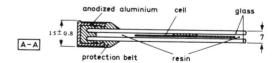

Fig. 7-7. Module Type G. (*Courtesy of North American Philips Co.*)

However, other angles, within a plus or minus 11° range of the local latitude, are sometimes used to optimize the module output during the most cloudy season (see Chapter 3). Figure 7-11 illustrates typical module supports of the fixed and adjustable type.

Open frame installations provide the best possible cooling of the modules by wind or self-induced convection air currents, especially

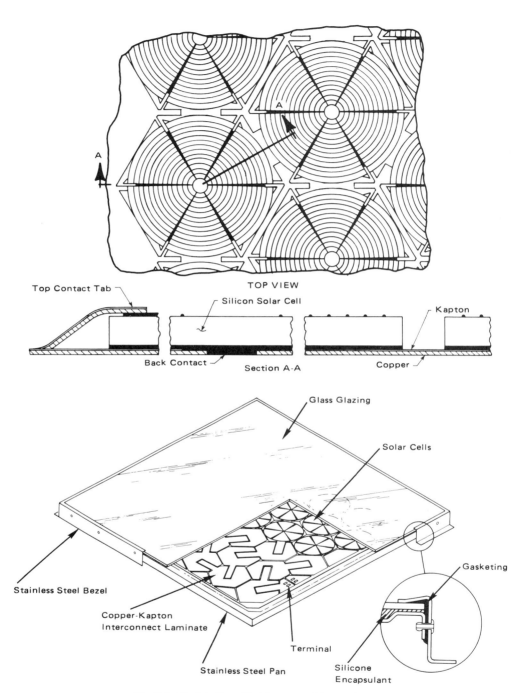

Fig. 7-8. Module Type H. (*Courtesy of Motorola, Inc.*)

Fig. 7-9. Module Type I. (*Courtesy of Solarex Corp.*)

Fig. 7-10. Module Type J. (*Courtesy of Solarex Corp.*)

when the modules are mounted more than one meter above ground. Several typical installations are depicted in Fig. 7-12.

7-5. Roof Supports

The installation of solar cell modules on roofs of buildings is illustrated schematically in Fig. 7-13. Most roofs do not aid in the transfer of heat from the modules. Since they behave essentially like thermal insulators, roofs are said to be *adiabatic*. The degree of module cooling that can be achieved depends upon the following factors: the spacing of the modules above the roof (g), the spacing of adjacent modules (s), the module height (h), and the total length of the roof array (l). Ambient air is drafted into the gap, g, and moves upward, by the chimney effect. As the air moves upward, its temper-

Table 7-2. Module Characteristics.[3]

Component	Type G	Type H	Type I	Type J
Module dimensions (mm)	365 × 468	490 × 579	533 × 581	533 × 533
Weight	2.4 kg	4.2 kg	5.2 kg	5.4 kg
Cover material	Glass	Glass	Glass	Glass
Encapsulant	Transparent resin	Silicone	Silicone	Silicone
Solar cell size (mm)	57	76.2	76.2	63.3 × 63.3
Number of cells	34	36	36	64
Cell area/module area	0.51	0.58	0.53	0.88
Substrate	Glass	Silicone	Silicone	Silicone
Power Output at 100 mW/cm^2 and 25°C	11 W	21 W	22 W	35 W
Maximum power voltage at 25°C	15.5 V	16.1 V	16.2 V	14 V

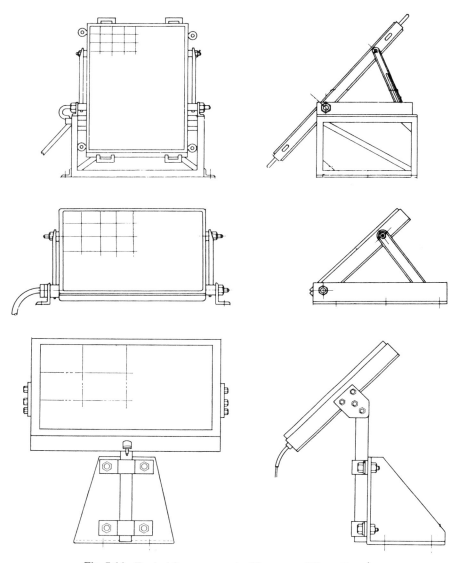

Fig. 7-11. Typical frame supports. (*Courtesy of Sharp Corp.*[1])

ature continues to rise. As the gap, g, is made larger, a greater *infiltration* of air can be expected. Also, if the spacing between adjacent modules, s, is increased, some of the hot air can escape while some cooler ambient air can be drawn in.

For the modules depicted in Figs. 7-4 through 7-6, mounted 76 mm above a simulated roof, at a low air infiltration level of 10 volumes/hour, cell temperature rises above the ambient air temperature ranged from 40° to 70°C for Types A, B, C, D, and F, and 150°C for Type E. At a

nominally expected infiltration level of 200 volumes/hour, the temperature rises ranged from 30° to 60°C for Types A, B, C, D, and F, and 80°C for Type E. The manufacturer of Module Type G (Table 7-2) does not recommend installation of his glass substrate module over hot roofs; this recommendation may also apply to other, similar module designs of different manufacturers.

For Types A through F, power losses due to high temperatures caused by roof installation, as compared to open air frame-mounting, ranged

Fig. 7-12. Typical frame-mounted module installations. (*Courtesy of Solarex Corp., JPL, and NASA Lewis Research Center.*)

from 7 to 34% for the bottom row of modules and from 13 to 40% for the top row of modules, at an air infiltration level of 200 volumes/hour.

7-6. Flat Plate Orientation Mechanisms

Flat plate solar cell arrays are typically mounted in a fixed position. Some installations utilize an adjustable tilt angle mount similar to that depicted in Fig. 7-11, requiring operator attendance. The amount of power that can be gained by using a tracking mechanism is usually likely to be offset by the tracking drive power requirements and the resultant degradation in the reliability of the system. However, installations requiring large amounts of power and having

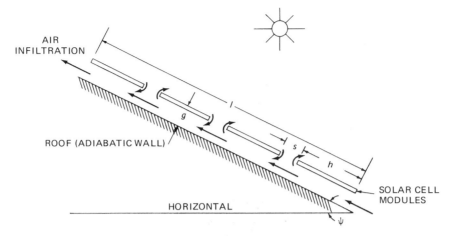

Fig. 7-13. Rooftop installation of modules (cross-sectional view).

available personnel for maintenance, may bene-fit from an orientation system. Concepts include larger central shaft systems (similar to rotating advertising sign designs), large circular railroad track systems, and systems using many small, articulated mechanisms.

TERRESTRIAL CONCENTRATOR ARRAYS

7-7. Linear Concentrator Modules

Linear concentrators, also known as *trough* or *two-dimensional* concentrators, focus the sun-light only in one plane rather than in two (as is done by *axial*—or *three-dimensional*—concentrators). The advantage of linear concentration is that tracking is required only in one direction. The axis of rotation of linear concentrators may be placed either horizontally in an east-west or north-south direction to permit seasonal or daily tracking, respectively. To increase the module output, the axis may also be inclined at an angle equal to the local latitude and in a north-south direction for daily tracking, a method known as *polar axis tracking*. However, increased structural and ground space require-ments, the latter to prevent shadowing of modules by other, adjacent modules, may not result in a W/m² performance improvement.

A small, non-tracking, low-concentration ratio array is illustrated in Fig. 7-14. The six modules are electrically connected in series to produce 112 W peak power at 48 V at 25°C and 100 mW/cm² solar intensity at normal inci-

Fig. 7-14. Linear trough concentrator array. (*Courtesy of Solarex Corp.*)

dence. Each module is comprised of 17 nearly square solar cells having 37 cm² area each, an anodized aluminum heat sink, and two plastic sheet reflectors. The solar cells are attached to the heat sink with, and are protected by, a layer of silicone rubber encapsulant. The geometric concentration ratio is 2, and the concentrator efficiency is 0.80. The array is installed facing the equator. The tilt angle must be adjusted seasonally, otherwise the performance degrades to that of a flat plate array having the same number of solar cells.

Another linear concentrator module concept

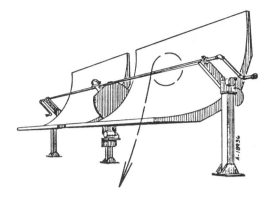

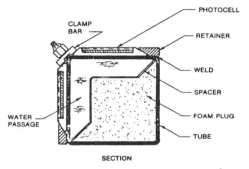

PHOTOCELL

CLAMP
BAR

RETAINER

WELD

SPACER

WATER
PASSAGE

FOAM PLUG

TUBE

SECTION

Fig. 7-15. Line-focused hybrid system.[4]

is shown in Fig. 7-15. The linear parabolic reflector has a geometric concentration ratio of 36. The square solar cells, mounted along two sides of a square tube, are water-cooled. A similar concept is currently being implemented in

what is believed will become the world's largest photovoltaic system by 1979. To be located in Arkansas, the 360 kW peak electrical output from 600 modules will charge a 2400 kWh battery bank and operate, with computer control, an entire community college (Fig. 7-16). Each module is comprised of an extruded aluminum channel to which 100 glassed-faced solar cells are bonded (Fig. 7-17). A liquid cooling system is to maintain the cells at approximately 55°C while operating at a concentration ratio of 20 at an energy conversion efficiency of 14%.

A different linear reflector concept is shown in Fig. 7-18. The entire 10 kW peak output array is mounted on a carousel truss structure that rotates about a central pivot. Wheels riding on a circular track of a steel rail stabilize the structure. The modules are also linked for elevation tracking. Each of the 40 modules is comprised of 78 cells of 53 mm by 31.7 mm size, an extruded, finned aluminum heat sink, and three linear reflectors. As shown in Fig. 7-19, the primary reflector, located at the bottom of the module, reflects light upward into the entrance apperture of an off-axis, assymetric parabolic trough. The cells are passively cooled and, at a geometric concentration ratio of 25, are expected to operate below 74°C. The cell assembly is illustrated in Fig. 7-20. By mounting the solar cells facing downward, dust accumulation and rain penetration problems are

Fig. 7-16. Planned Mississippi County Community College (MC³) installation. (*Courtesy of Solarex Corp.*)

Fig. 7-17. Concentrator hybrid module. (*Courtesy of Solarex Corp.*)

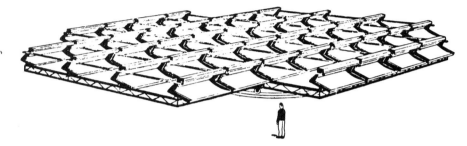

Fig. 7-18. Steerable line-focused concentrator array.[4]

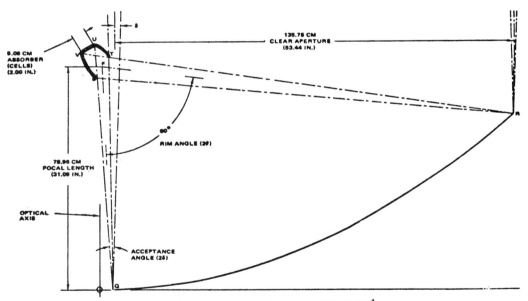

Fig. 7-19. Optical system for array of Fig. 7-18.[4]

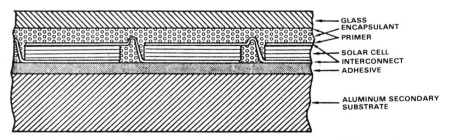

Fig. 7-20. Cell-mounting and encapsulation for system shown in Fig. 7-19.

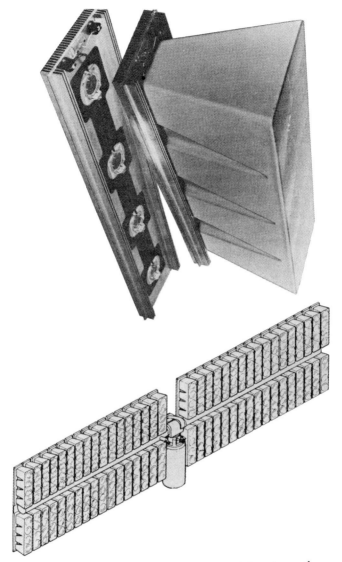

Fig. 7-21. Fresnel lens concentrator module and array.[4]

minimized. However, dust accumulation on the heat sink fins may nullify these advantages.

7-8. Axial Concentrator Modules

Axial concentrators, also known as *coaxial*, *axisymmetric*, or *three-dimensional* concentrators, are designed such that the concentrating lens or mirror is positioned on the same optical axis as the solar cell. A concentrator module consists of one or several such rigid concentrating device/solar cell assemblies. One such module assembly (or a number of them) is then attached

to a two-axis orientation drive. Lens type concentrators are usually of the Fresnel type, while reflectors are of the parabolic type.

One concentrator array, depicted in Fig. 7-21, is made up of two wings having 34 modules each, mounted to a support tube. The array produces a total of approximately 2.3 kW at 115 V at 30°C and 100 mW/cm² intensity. The 272 solar cells on the array are wired as a single series string. The overall array dimensions are 12.8 m in length by 2.75 m in height. The array weighs 1720 kg, including the centrally located drive mechanism and control and tracking electronics. The array mounts to a cylindrical reinforced concrete pier foundation of approximately 1.5 m height above ground.[4]

Each module contains eight circular solar cells (without glass cover), mounted to a substrate and a load-bearing finned aluminum extrusion for passive cooling by the ambient air. Injection-molded plastic housings, together with glued-on cast-acrylic Fresnel lenses, hermetically seal groups of four solar cells. The lenses, mounted with their grooves pointing inward, have 85% light transmission and a concentration ratio of about 40. The enclosure formed by the housing and the lens prevents the concentrated light beam from burning personnel or igniting wind-blown inflammables.

A typical *parabolic* concentrator module is illustrated in Fig. 7-22. This Cassegrain type design exhibits a shorter overall mechanical length than an equivalent, ordinary parabolic reflector design would have for the same focal length-to-entrance apperture diameter (f/D) ratio. The beam is reflected twice, permitting the use of wavelength selective reflectors to remove non-usable solar energy before it heats the solar cell. Cooling fins on the reflectors as well as on the cell support aid in reducing the cell's operating temperature. Application of a highly reflective and emissive paint on the fins

of the secondary mirror heat sink, facing the sun, is necessary. The glass dome, sealed against all metal parts with silicone O-rings, provides hermetically sealed protection of the solar cell and the mirror surfaces.

In contrast to the foregoing, rather heavy design, the lightweight concept depicted in Fig. 7-23 utilizes a thin, aluminized plastic sheet reflector, fabricated from a number of gores, and shaped by a low air pressure that holds the sheet against a parabolic cavity. The surrounding bubble, an inflated, transparent dome, provides environmental protection and takes all wind loading. The concentrator is presently being designed for concentration ratios of 100 to 200 with an f/D ratio of approximately 0.5.

A different axial concentrator approach is illustrated in Fig. 7-24. The array depicted consists of nine modules mounted three each to a subassembly, as shown in Fig. 7-25. The array utilizes polar axis tracking and produces 300 W. Each module uses a 6 × 6 array of lenses having 100 cm² area each and a geometric concentration ratio of 400. Both plano-convex and Fresnel lenses were investigated; the Fresnel lenses showed superior optical performance. Also, two types of heat sinks were investigated, as shown in Fig. 7-26. The solar cells are small, measuring only 5.6 mm.

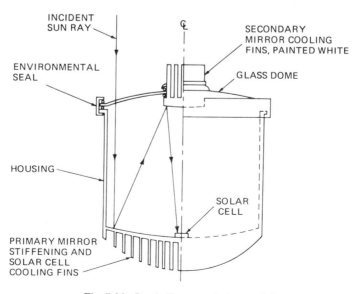

Fig. 7-22. Parabolic concentrator module.

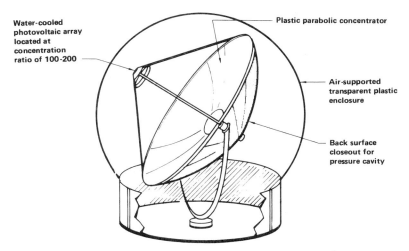

Water-cooled
photovoltaic array
located at
concentration
ratio of 100-200

Plastic parabolic concentrator

Air-supported
transparent plastic
enclosure

Back surface
closeout for
pressure cavity

Fig. 7-23. Lightweight parabolic concentrator module.[4].

Fig. 7-24. 300 W Fresnel lens concentrator unit.[4]

7-9. Mirror Field Systems

Mirror fields are primarily used in concentrator designs for solar thermal systems and large solar furnaces. However, photovoltaic applications are possible when active cooling is used. One such system is made up of a number of 3.3 kW modules, depicted in Fig. 7-27. Each such module uses 16 parabolic mirrors to focus the sunlight at a concentration ratio of 200 onto a water-cooled receiver, as shown in Fig. 7-28.

The square solar cells are series-connected in a densely packed array. The mirrors, approximately 1.0×1.5 m in size, are mounted four to a frame, as shown in Fig. 7-29, for Y-axis control. Each of the four mirrors is, in turn, pivoted and connected to a linkage for X-axis control.

A necessary requirement for such high-concentration ratio systems is the installation of a fail-safe device that prevents solar cell damage in case of a coolant system malfunction. Such a device should be triggered by a temperature-sensitive actuator and either misorient the mirrors or place a light shield in the incident beam. The light shield must, of course, possess adequate heat dissipation capability and must not itself heat the solar cells excessively.

SPACE ARRAYS

7-10. Space Array Overview

During the 1970's, the power consumption of satellites has been increasing to levels that require the use of deployable solar cell arrays. For launch, the arrays are stowed into compact packages that are attached to the spacecraft. Once they have reached their orbital paths, they are unfurled and become appendages to the spacecraft.

A variety of concepts have been conceived to create the largest possible solar cell array areas with structural elements that exhibit the

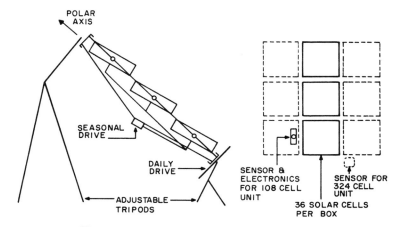

Fig. 7-25. Schematic of system shown in Fig. 7-24.

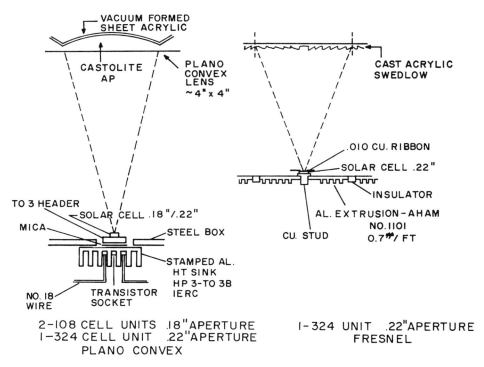

Fig. 7-26. Alternate cell-mounting designs for system shown in Fig. 7-24.

lowest weight, highest deployment reliability, and highest possible natural bending frequency (i.e., the highest possible bending stiffness). In practice, solutions to these individual design parameters are in opposition to each other, so that the practical array designs that have evolved are the results of trade studies to optimize each array for a specific mission.

Specific array performance, expressed in W/kg, is primarily related to the total array mass, and only secondarily related to small differences in solar cell packing densities and array thermal design (assuming that solar cells having the same efficiency are installed on different array designs.) The total array mass is primarily composed of the structural, solar cell,

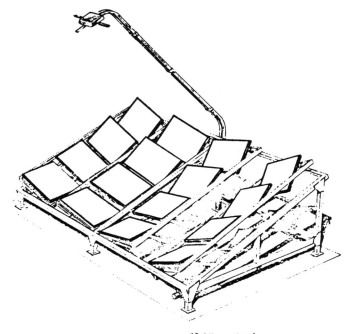

16-Mirror 200/1 Module

Fig. 7-27. 3.3 kW hybrid system.[4]

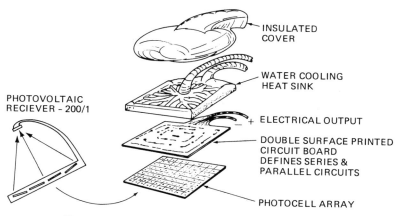

PHOTOVOLTAIC
RECIEVER - 200/1

INSULATED
COVER

WATER COOLING
HEAT SINK

+ ELECTRICAL OUTPUT

DOUBLE SURFACE PRINTED
CIRCUIT BOARD
DEFINES SERIES &
PARALLEL CIRCUITS

PHOTOCELL ARRAY

Fig. 7-28. Solar cell array of system depicted in Fig. 7-27.

and coverglass masses. Hence, the structural efficiency, expressed in deployed array stiffness—or natural bending frequency—per unit mass is of paramount importance. Presently, natural bending frequencies in the order of 0.1 Hz are required by attitude control systems. However, work has been in progress for some time to facilitate precise spacecraft attitude control of satellites with large, flexible appendages having much lower natural frequencies than 0.1 Hz.

Most of the larger, more recently developed arrays are designed for a range of power output. However, it is not possible for such arrays to have the same specific (W/kg) performance at all power levels within the design range. For some design concepts, the W/kg performance always decreases with increasing size; for others, it increases; and for others yet, it first increases and then decreases. A typical example of the effects of varying the array size on the specific

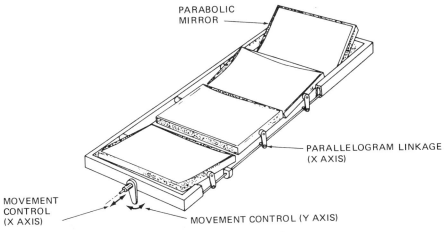

PARABOLIC MIRROR

PARALLELOGRAM LINKAGE (X AXIS)

MOVEMENT CONTROL (X AXIS)

MOVEMENT CONTROL (Y AXIS)

Fig. 7-29. Mirror control.[4]

performance and natural bending frequency is given in Figs. 7-30 and 7-31.

Details of some of the space array designs of current interest are given in Sections 7-11 through 7-17. The major characteristics of these arrays are summarized in Table 7-3.

7-11. Rigid Honeycomb Panels

A honeycomb sandwich structure is a panel made up of two facesheets that are glued to a honeycomb core. The hexagonal cells space the two facesheets apart. Their approximately cylindrical walls possess high buckling strength even though they are very thin (usually made from approximately 0.02 mm thick aluminum). The facesheets can carry high tensile and compressive stresses. The honeycomb cells stabilize the facesheet that is loaded in compression. The entire honeycomb panel is very stiff and strong, yet relatively light.

Most spaceflight solar cell arrays built through the 1970's utilized some kind of honeycomb structure. Honeycomb panels have been fabricated in spherical, conical, cylindrical, paraboloidal, and flat configurations, using metal or reinforced plastic cores and facesheets. The more typical substrates have used aluminum core and aluminum facesheet. A second choice has been aluminum core with glass/epoxy facesheets. During the past few years, graphite/plastic structures have come into more use. Some examples of each are given below.

NASA's Skylab spacecraft, illustrated in Fig. 7-32, was a manned vehicle which carried two separate solar cell array systems: the Apollo Telescope Mount (ATM) array and Orbital Workshop (OWS) array. During launch, both arrays were stowed in folded-up positions. The ATM array was stowed coaxially above the OWS and protected by a nose cone. The two

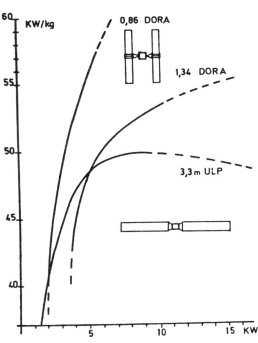

Fig. 7-30. Variation of specific performance with array size. (*Reprinted with permission of the IEEE.*[40])

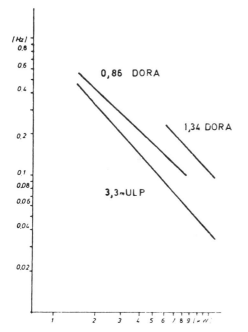

Fig. 7-31. Variation of first bending resonance frequency with array size. (*Reprinted with permission of the IEEE*.[40])

wings of the OWS array were stowed on the sides of the OWS and protected during launch by a beam fairing. Because of high dynamic forces that occured during launch, the OWS array was made relatively strong and, therefore, heavy. The ATS array was of a somewhat lighter-weight design.

OWS. The OWS array consisted of two wing assemblies, as shown in Fig. 7-33, each of which contained a forward fairing, a beam fairing, and three wing sections. The wing assemblies were permanently attached to the OWS cylindrical structure through the forward fairing assemblies. Machined, hinged fittings attached the beam fairings to the forward fairing assemblies. During launch, they were also attached to the OWS structure by six explosive attachment fittings, distributed along the length of the beam fairings.

After Skylab was inserted into orbit, spring-loaded deployment actuator-dampers released the beam fairings and drove them outward to pivot about their hinges. Following this,

Table 7-3. Solar Cell Array Characteristics.

Described in Section	Project	Type	Deployment	Power BOL (kW)	Specific Performance* BOL (W/kg)	Specific Performance* EOL** (W/kg)	Deployed Natural Frequency (Hz)	Status
7-11	Skylab	Rigid	Fold-out	13	5.6	5.3	NG	Flight
7-12	FLTSATCOM	Rigid	Fold-out	1.8	18.2	13.7	0.32	Flight
7-12	MATRA	Rigid	Fold-out	1.3	32.6	25.1	NG	Development
7-12	TDRSS	Rigid	Fold-out	3.1	24.9	17.6	0.5	Near flight
7-12	Intelsat V	Rigid	Fold-out	1.7	26.6	21.2	0.36	Near flight
7-13	ULP	Rigid	Fold-out	1.6	42.6	30.4	0.3	Development
7-13	ULP	Rigid	Fold-out	7.1	55.0	39.3	0.048	Development
7-13	Aerospatiale	Rigid	Fold-out	1.1	31.8	22.6	0.28	NG
7-14	CTS	Flexible	Fold-out	1.3	22.2	16	0.32	Flight
7-14	SEPS	Flexible	Fold-out	25	66	47	0.04	Flight
7-15	FRUSA	Flexible	Roll-out	1.3	47.4	34	0.25	Flight
7-15	DORA	Flexible	Roll-out	9.0	50	36	0.17	Development
7-15	Space Telescope	Flexible	Roll-out	4.5	24.8	20.3	NG	Near flight
7-16	ESA-LHSA	Rigid/flexible	Fold-out	6.3	35.1	25	NG	Development
7-16	SPAR-MPDHSA	Rigid/flexible	Fold-out	2.1	41	29	0.10	Development
7-16	SPAR-MPDHSA	Rigid/flexible	Fold-out	3.7	47	34	0.16	Development

*Vernal equinox.
**As given in text.
NOTE: NG = not given.

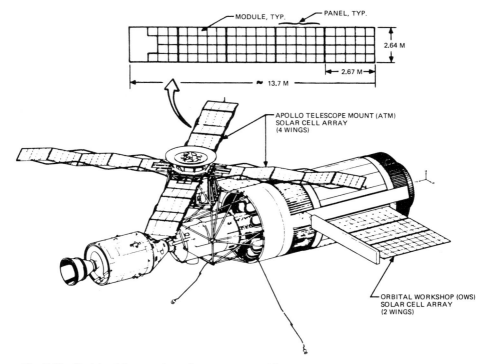

Fig. 7-32. Skylab with two solar cell array systems. (*Courtesy of Marshall Space Flight Center.*)

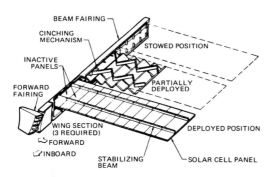

Fig. 7-33. OWS solar cell array wing assembly. (*Reprinted with permission of the IEEE.[8]*)

twelve panels (ten active and two inactive) in each of the six wing sections unfolded in the aft direction from the beam fairings until the stabilizer beams retained them in an extended position.[8,9]

Each solar cell panel consisted of a 9.7 mm thick aluminum honeycomb substrate approximately 3.31 m long by 0.74 m wide. The facesheets were 0.2 mm aluminum. The solar cells were 2×4 cm in size and 0.36 mm thick, of the conventional 2 ohm · cm, n-on-p type,

and covered with 0.15 mm microsheet coverglasses. The cells were bonded with an RTV rubber directly to the aluminum substrate through two 13 mm diameter holes per cell in a 50 μm thick, insulating Kapton sheet. In orbit, the cells operated at 76°C at normal incidence, producing 204 W per panel after 8 months in low altitude earth orbit.

The end-of-life (8 months in 435 km orbit) array power output was greater than 12.24 kW at 55 V. The initial ground test output of the 2464 cells per panel was 282 W at 71.7 V at 29°C. The total array system mass, including the aerodynamic shrouds, was 2313 kg. The mass of each finished active panel was 10.66 kg. The total system specific performance was 5.6 W/kg, beginning-of-life, and 5.3 W/kg, end-of-life.

7-12. Honeycomb Panels with Stiffeners

One approach to reducing the structural array mass has been to decrease the stiffness of the honeycomb panels to levels where they no longer were structurally adequate by themselves, and to reinforce them by tubular frames.

For the honeycomb panels, the aluminum core cell sizes were enlarged and their wall thickness reduced to the minimum practical. Aluminum facesheets were made thinner in low stress areas by chemical milling, and replaced by glass fiber and graphite fiber composites or by Kapton sheets. The solar cell operating temperature as well as the substrate weight were reduced by perforating dielectric rear facesheets. A number of representative design solutions are described in the following.

FLTSATCOM. The U.S. Navy's Fleet Satellite Communications System carried the solar array system shown in Fig. 7-34. The array consisted of two paddles on opposite sides of the satellite that were stowed wrapped around the spacecraft and deployed as shown. Each paddle was made up of three panels of nearly identical configuration; the three panels were attached together by spring hinges; the center panels were connected through deployment booms to the spacecraft.

Each panel was 2.82 m long by 1.28 m wide and consisted of a sandwich substrate supported by a frame around the perimeter. Also included as part of the frame was a cross-member 1.31 m from the bottom of the panel. Figure 7-35 illustrates a typical cross-section of the frame and sandwich substrate. The substrate consisted of 0.13 mm aluminum facesheets bonded with film adhesive to 16 mm thick aluminum honeycomb core. The frame was mechanically attached to the substrate by screws driven into inserts in the substrate. The deployment boom was a square, cross-sectional aluminum element with hinge assemblies that were controlled by a pulley and cable system. The fundamental natural frequencies were 25 Hz, stowed, and 0.32 Hz, deployed. The solar cells were conventional 10 ohm · cm n-on-p silicon cells of 2 × 4 cm size and 0.20 mm thickness, covered with 0.15 mm thick fused silica coverglasses. The array vernal equinox output was 1800 W, beginning-of-life, and greater than 1350 W after five years in synchronous orbit. The array's total mass of 90.0 kg was composed of 70.0 kg structural elements and 20.0 kg electrical components, not counting the long booms between the arrays and the spacecraft. The

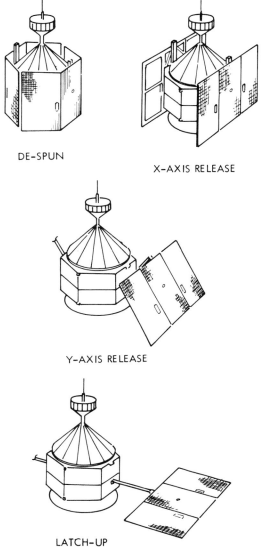

DE-SPUN

X-AXIS RELEASE

Y-AXIS RELEASE

LATCH-UP

Fig. 7-34. FLTSATCOM satellite and solar cell array configuration. (*Courtesy of TRW, Inc.*[9])

corresponding array specific performance was 20.0 W/kg and 15.0 W/kg, respectively.[9] Inclusion of the deployment boom reduced these performance numbers by a factor of 0.91.

MATRA. A combination of metallic and glass fiber composites was used by MATRA Engines for the development of a rigid, fold-up array.[11] The array consisted of five hinged panels and a deployment yoke. The panels and yoke were flat-packed against one another and were

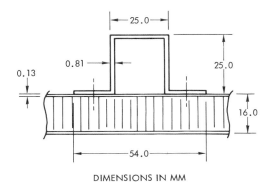

DIMENSIONS IN MM

Fig. 7-35. Cross-section of substrate and frame.[9]

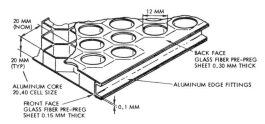

Fig. 7-36. MATRA array substrate design. (After 43)

prestressed against the spacecraft sidewall at six points, with a mechanical spacing of 5.1 mm between panels to ensure no panel-to-panel contact during the launch phase. The stowed array panel had a natural frequency of 34 Hz. Deployment was achieved through a pulley and cable system.

The array was approximately 1.0 m long by 1.5 m wide. (The substrate design is shown in Fig. 7-36.) It consisted of a 0.15 mm thick fiberglass epoxy front facesheet, a 20 mm thick aluminum honeycomb core, and a perforated 0.30 mm back facesheet. Each 12 mm diameter perforation coincided with each cell of the honeycomb structure, and aided significantly in the thermal control of the solar cells. Two

methods were used to fabricate the sandwich substrate: 1) a prepreg (i.e., preimpregnated with epoxy adhesive) facesheet was used without any additional adhesive layer; and 2) the core was edge-coated with adhesive, with the epoxy used in the facesheets. The edges of the substrate were equipped with channel-shaped, 0.1 mm thick aluminum close-out elements to provide additional stiffness and attachment points for the hinge fittings. There were two spring hinge fittings on each hinge line.

For 0.20 mm thick solar cells with 0.10 mm thick covers, the array, at a 1 kW end-of-life power level, achieved a 25.1 W/kg performance.

TDRSS. The solar array configuration (shown in Fig. 7-37) was stowed around the spacecraft in a manner similar to the FLTSATCOM con-

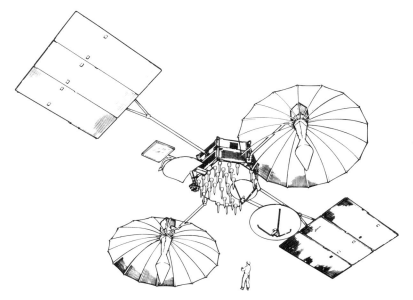

Fig. 7-37. Tracking and data relay satellite (man shown to scale). (*Reprinted with permission of the IEEE.*[13])

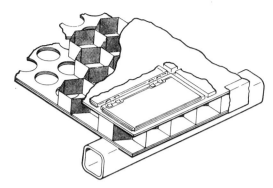

Fig. 7-38. TDRSS array substrate design. (*Reprinted with permission of the IEEE.*[13])

figuration; however, the array was larger and constructed differently. The substrate front facesheets were 0.075 mm thick Kapton; the rear facesheets were 0.13 mm thick Kapton and had 51% of their surface area perforated with circular holes spaced on an equilateral triangle pattern, permitting heat from the front facesheet to radiate through the back to space. The holes were not aligned with the hex cells. An additional 75 μm thick layer of perforated Kapton was bonded to the facesheets in the areas where the substrates were attached to the frames. The honeycomb core was 10 mm thick 5052 aluminum, having a density of 2.6 g/cm^3. The substrate was supported by graphite fiber-reinforced plastic (GFRP) box beam frames that were adhesive-bonded to the rear facesheets (Fig. 7-38). The mass of the outer substrates was 0.724 kg/m^2 and that of the center panels was 0.735 kg/m^2. The masses of the GFRP frames were 3.810 and 7.484 kg, respectively.[9,13,15]

The 31062 solar cells per spacecraft were 20.0 × 40.0 × 0.20 mm, 10 ohm · cm n/p hybrid with back surface reflector (BSR). The contacts were Ti-Pd-Ag with localized solder coverage. Covers were 0.15 mm thick uncoated ceria glass. The predicted cell operating temperature during equinox is 45°C, beginning-of-life, and 57°C after ten years in synchronous orbit. The corresponding calculated array power outputs at equinox were 3127 W and 2206 W, respectively. For a total array mass (without the long booms) of 86.1 kg, the equinox specific performance was 36.0 W/kg, beginning-of-life, and 25.5 W/kg after ten years (1.1 × 10^{15} 1 MeV $e \cdot cm^{-2}$.) Inclusion of the long deployment boom decreased these performance numbers by a factor of 0.692.

Intelsat V. The solar cell arrays for the Intelsat V series of three-axis stabilized, geosynchronous orbit communication satellites consisted of three panels and an open-frame yoke, hinged together for folding up and storage against the sides of the rectangular body of the spacecraft of 1.65 × 2.01 × 1.77 m size. Each panel measured 1.6 m in width by 2 m in length. The panel substrates were made from open-weave graphite fiber composite facesheets and aluminum honeycomb core. The substrates were reinforced at their perimeters with carbon fiber composite beams. The solar cells were insulated from the substrate by a Kapton sheet. The panels were deployed upon activation of a central release mechanism, freeing the six hold-down points per wing, due to forces supplied by spiral springs in the hinges. A closed cable loop and pulley system synchronized the panel deployment on each wing. No dampers were used. The natural frequency was 34 Hz, undeployed, and 0.36 Hz, deployed. The total array mass of 64.1 kg was composed of 22.8 kg electrical, 37.4 kg mechanical, and 3.9 kg hold-down components.

A total of 17380 solar cells were mounted to the 18.12 m^2 substrate area. The 10 ohm · cm, silicon n/p AEG-Telefunken cells were 20.95 × 40.35 × 0.25 mm in size and were TiO$_x$ coated. Contacts were solderless Ti-Pd-Ag, to which rolled mesh silver interconnectors were welded. Ceria-doped microsheet covers, 0.15 mm thick, attached with DC 93-500 adhesive, protected the entire solar cell areas. The glassed cell output was specified at 25°C, and AM0 (Air-Mass Zero) conditions as 0.2966 A at 0.450 V minimum. The cell series resistance was measured to be between 0.077 and 0.113 ohms, with an average of 0.092 ohms. The cell solar absorptance ranged between 0.807 and 0.836, 0.82 average, and the emissivity between 0.842 and 0.847, with an average of 0.84. The calculated array output, at the PCU input, beginning-of-life, was 1708 W at equinox and 1564 W at summer solstice. The corresponding values for seven years in orbit were 1358 W and 1288 W.

The degradation factors used in the analysis were -1% for temperature cycling (-190° to +80°C for 700 cycles), -12.7% for I_{sc} and -7.4% for V_{oc} for 1 MeV electron radiation (based on 1×10^{15} $e \cdot cm^{-2}$ test followed by annealing), and -1.8% for ultraviolet degradation (based on 1500 ESH Test). The specific performance values for equinox were 26.6 W/kg and 21.2 W/kg at beginning-of-life and end-of-life, respectively.[16,17]

7-13. Flexible Substrates with Rigid Frames

For arrays having power levels of 2 to 15 kW, Messerschmitt-Bölkow-Blohm (MBB) developed the ULP (ultralightweight panel) array technology, utilizing pretensioned, panel size membrane substrates, supported by rigid frames. In contrast, Aerospatiale/Cannes developed a similar concept for a 3 to 4 kW array, using small-sized membrane substrates without significant pretensioning. On both array concepts, the solar cells on the outermost panel faced outward, producing electric power during the transfer phase.

ULP. The array consisted of two identical wings, each made up of a yoke, an empty panel frame, and between 2 and 25 panels per wing for array power levels of 1 to 13 kW

(Fig. 7-39.) Each panel measured approximately 3.3 (in the wing width direction) X 1.15 m. The areas enclosed by the yokes and the empty frames were subject to shadowing; therefore, no solar cells were placed there. Each of the identical panels consisted to a carbon fiber composite, hollow tube (rectangular cross-section) framework. Solar cells were mounted to a reinforced flexible Kapton substrate, pretensioned in the direction parallel to the 3 m wing width only. The panel frame was subdivided by six pairs of small, hollow, rectangular, carbon fiber composite rods, preventing the substrate from reaching large vibrational amplitudes. In addition, the un-clamped edges of the substrate were restrained by guide wires that were stretched between the panel frame members. The panels, each 25 mm thick, folded accordion-fashion flat against each other (Fig. 7-40) and against the spacecraft side walls. Thin metal bands held each array wing in place at six tie-down points. After release, the panels deployed by the force of helical hinge springs. No deployment dampers were used. The panel angular deployment was controlled via closed loop pulley and cable systems. The array natural frequencies were about 24 Hz, stowed, and 0.3 Hz, deployed, for a 1.58 kW array; 0.048 Hz for a 7.12 kW array.[20]

Each panel carried 3600 AEG-Telefunken 10 ohm · cm solar cells of 20 X 40 X 0.20 mm size, covered by 0.10 mm thick ceria-stabilized microsheet. The cell output at 25°C, after irradiation with 2×10^{15} 1 MeV $e \cdot cm^{-2}$, was 95.7 mW. After seven years in synchronous orbit, each panel produced 268 W at 58°C during equinox. For these conditions, the array specific end-of-life performance was 30.4 W/kg for the 1.58 kW system and 39.3 W/kg for the 7.12 kW system.

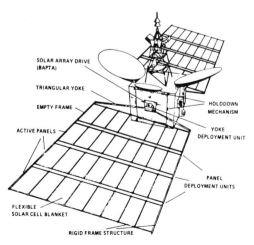

Fig. 7-39. ULP 2 kW array on ARIANE test platform. (*Reprinted with permission of the IEEE.*[41])

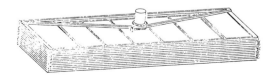

Fig. 7-40. Stowed ULP array. (*Reprinted with permission of the IEEE.*[41])

Aerospatiale. The array consisted of two wings with three panels and one open-frame yoke each. Hold-down to the spacecraft body was at six points. Helical springs at the hinges deployed the panels upon release. A closed loop cable and pulley system assured uniform panel unfolding and latch-up. The deployment rate was governed by centrifugal speed brakes.

Each solar cell panel measured 1.216 m by 1.614 m. The outside tubular frame was subdivided into four bays by three tubular transverse beams. Each bay carried 28 ribs having omega cross-section which supported a semiflexible substrate, and 476 cells were installed on each subpanel substrate prior to its mounting in the panel bays. The substrate was made from a closely woven graphite fiber composite with 12 μm thick Kapton insulation. The weave was cut on the bias to provide shear stiffening of the frames. The substrates were located in the centers of the frame to minimize vibrational deflections beyond the frame dimensions. The natural frequency was 46 Hz, stowed, and 0.28 Hz, deployed.

The AEG-Telefunken solar cells were $20 \times 40 \times 0.20$ mm with 0.10 mm thick ceria-stabilized microsheet covers. Welded-on interconnectors of two types, silver mesh and silver plated molybdenum, are being investigated.

The mass breakdown for the development model was as follows: panel, 4.27 kg, composed of 2.35 kg structural and 1.88 kg electrical components; yoke, 1.38 kg; power harness, 0.53 kg; total per wing, 17.43 kg. The array output was 1110 W at equinox and 982 W at summer solstice, beginning-of-life, and 789 W and 752 W, respectively, after seven years (2.10×10^{15} 1 MeV $e \cdot$ cm^{-2}.) The corresponding specific array performance was 31.8 W/kg or 31.4 kg/kW at equinox, beginning-of-life, and 22.6 W/kg or 44.2 kg/kW after seven years.[21]

7-14. Flexible Fold-Up Blankets

Flexible fold-up blanket type arrays consist of blankets that are folded up, accordion-fashion, during stowage, and unfurled in space by an also deployable boom or mast. Some form of cushioning is used between adjacent layers of solar cells to prevent coverglass and solar cell damage. The following examples include one smaller, non-rectractable design and one larger, rectractable design.

CTS. The solar cell array on the Canadian Technology satellite, also known as Hermes, was believed to be the first operational flexible, fold-up array. The satellite, launched on January 17, 1976, into a geosynchronous orbit, carried a fixed body-mounted array and a deployable array. The body-mounted array provided about 100 W during a 15 day spinning phase and was jettisoned thereafter. The deployable array, used in the satellite's three-axis stabilized mode, consisted of two wings, each 6.53 m long by 1.30 m wide, and was comprised of 30 foldable panels, 26 of which were solar cell covered (Fig. 7-41.) Polyurethane foam interleaf material was inserted between folds to protect the solar cells and interconnects. The packaged array was stowed within a jettisonable cover on which the body-mounted solar cells were mounted to provide power during transfer orbit. Deployment was achieved with a motorized, single element, 0.18 mm thick stainless steel, 34 mm diameter BI-STEM boom located behind (on the shadowed side of) the blanket. The boom was extended to produce a 27 N tension on the blanket.[22, 23]

The blanket consisted of a laminate of 25 μm Kapton and 35 μm fiberglass. The total thickness of the composite was 67 μm, accounting for the polyester adhesive layer. The blanket was cut into four panel assemblies. Piano type hinges for mechanical interconnection of adjacent panels were attached at both ends of each assembly. Intermediate folds were achieved by creasing the substrate. Solar cells were 20×20 mm, bonded directly to the substrate. The solar cell stack consisted of 0.2 mm thick cells with 0.1 mm thick ceria-doped microsheet covers. The solar cell interconnectors were 25 μm thick silver mesh, welded to the cells. There were 2430 cells for housekeeping and 10,206 cells for the experiments on each wing, producing a total array power of 1330 W, beginning-of-life. In addition, one blanket

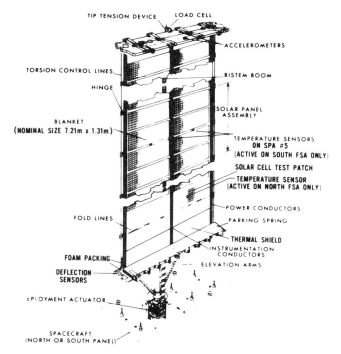

Fig. 7-41. CTS deployable array wing. (*Reprinted with permission of the IEEE.*[22])

carried a 27-cell test patch. The array experienced an eclipse temperature of −188°C followed by a heating rate of 75°C/minute. Solar cell operating temperatures ranged between 47°C and 51.5°C.

The total mass of each blanket was 6.97 kg. The mass of each wing was 30 kg, resulting in a specific beginning-of-life performance of 22.2 W/kg.

SEPS. Generally known as "a family of solar cell arrays representing SEPS (Solar Electric Propulsion Stage) technology," these arrays are being developed by the Lockheed Missile and Space Company for a variety of NASA applications requiring 10 to 100 kW during the 1980's. At present, the array furthest along in development is part of the Shuttle's power extension package (PEP).[25, 26]

The current PEP array design consists of two identical wings. Each wing (Fig. 7-42) consists of 41 folding panels that are deployed by a coilable lattice, continuous longeron mast (Fig. 7-43). Each panel measures 3.8 (in the wing width direction) × 0.76 m, folding in the middle as to create a stowed package of

0.38 × 3.8 m area and approximately 0.12 m thick. A panel consists of two layers of 0.012 mm thick Kapton, encasing printed-circuit type, copper solar cell interconnectors. Holes are laser-skived into the Kapton to permit welding electrodes to make contact with the interconnectors. The 3060 solar cells per panel are 20 × 40 × 0.20 mm with wrap-around contacts. Covers are 0.15 mm fused silica. No adhesive is used between the cells and the substrate. To facilitate retraction of the array, each panel-half is stiffened by graphite fiber composite frames (Fig. 7-44). Foam strips, mounted in the intercell gaps, provide for cell cushioning. The stowed, folded-up array blanket is contained in an aluminum or graphite fiber composite containment box having flat floor and cover panels. The cover panel is attached to the end of the mast which also carries a clamping and cinching mechanism. The latter engages during orbital restowage and preloads the array blanket for safe return to earth. While deployed, the array blanket is constrained by guide wires.

The mass of each 12.5 kW wing is composed of 113.6 kg for the blanket, 32.0 kg for the

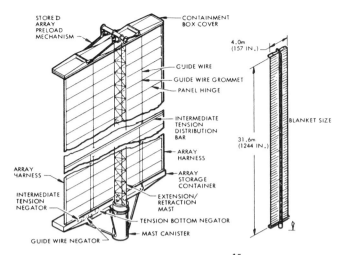

Fig. 7-42. SEP array wing.[45]

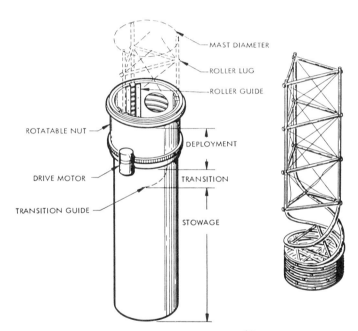

Fig. 7-43. Deployable mast.[45]

mast, 5.6 kg for the array harness, 26.8 kg for the remaining hardware, and 6 kg for contingency. The corresponding beginning-of-life specific performance is 66 W/kg.

7-15. Flexible Roll-Up Blankets

Flexible roll-up arrays consist of one or two solar cell blankets that are stowed on a cylindrical drum. For deployment, an also deployable boom or mast draws the blanket from the drum against a retracting force that keeps the blanket stretched flat. Three of the more developed designs are discussed below.

FRUSA. Hughes Aircraft Corporation, under contract to the U.S. Air Force, developed a flexible roll-up solar cell array (FRUSA). The system was launched as a flight experiment in 1971 aboard on Agena spacecraft into a

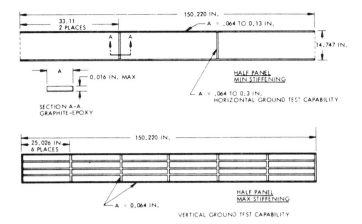

Fig. 7-44. SEP panel stiffeners.

low-earth orbit and performed satisfactorily. In-orbit blanket retraction capability was demonstrated.[27]

The roll-up array, depicted in Fig. 7-45, used two solar cell blankets 4.9 m long by 1.7 m wide, rolled up on a single 20 cm diameter drum. An embossed 50 μm thick Kapton cushion protected the solar cells in the stowed configuration during launch. During extension, this cushion was rolled up on an auxiliary take-up roller. The blankets were deployed from the common drum by a pair of extendible BISTEM steel booms, 22 mm in diameter and held under a nominal 14 N tension. The deployed natural frequency was 0.25 Hz.

The solar cell blankets were continuous laminates of Kapton and fiberglass. The 34,500 conventional silicon solar cells of 0.18 mm thickness were covered with 0.15 mm thick microsheet. The beginning-of-life power was

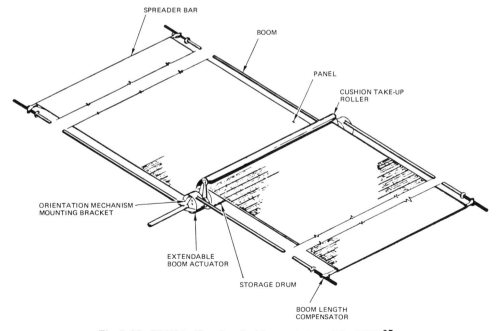

Fig. 7-45. FRUSA. (*Reprinted with permission of the IEEE.*[27])

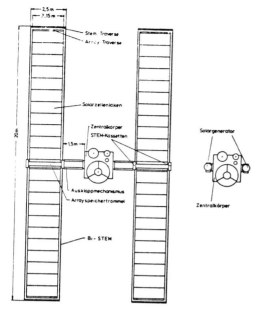

Fig. 7-46. DORA. *(Reprinted with permission of the IEEE.*[6]*)*

approximately 1500 W. The total system mass of 31.7 kg consisted of 16.2 kg for the drum mechanism, 13.1 kg for the solar cells and covers, and 2.4 kg for the blankets alone, resulting in a beginning-of-life specific performance of 47.4 W/kg.

DORA. Under development since 1974 by AEG-Telefunken, the DORA (double roll-out array) is intended for missions requiring between 9 kW and over 20 kW of power. The present 9 kW array qualification model utilizes two drums and four blankets (Fig. 7-46), known as an H-Configuration. The overall length of each wing (two blankets) is 20.6 m. Each Kapton blanket is deployed by a pair of BI-STEM booms of 34 mm diameter. A multi-element negator spring assembly inside the 15 cm diameter drum provides a blanket tension of 30 N/m. A foam layer of 1.5 mm thickness, placed between the solar cells and facing each other, is rolled up onto separate cushioning storage drums. Most structural parts of the drum mechanism, as well as the traverses, are made from graphite fiber composites.[28]

Each wing is subdivided into 11 panels of

2.15 (in the wing width direction) $\times$ 0.84 m in size, interconnected by "piano-hinges." Each panel carries 2080 solar cells of 20 $\times$ 40 mm size, interconnected on the rear side for an operating voltage of 100 V. With 0.20 mm thick solar cells and 0.10 mm thick covers, the panels weigh 1.07 kg/m². With 11.5% efficient cells (126 mW) at 25°C, AMO conditions, the array produces 9 kW beginning-of-life and 7.8 kW after five years (1.0×15^{15} 1 MeV $e \cdot cm^{-2}$) at summer solstice in synchronous orbit. The total array mass of 171 kg is composed of 80 kg for the blankets, 0.7 kg for wiring, 77.8 kg for the mechanical parts, and 12.5 kg for the hold-down and swing-out mechanisms. The deployed natural bending frequency is 0.17 Hz. The resulting array specific performance is 53 W/kg or 19 kg/kW, beginning-of-life, and 46 W/kg or 22 kg/kW after five years at summer solstice (approximately 50 W/kg at equinox.)

Space Telescope. The DORA concept was selected to power NASA's Space Telescope, to be launched in 1984. The array, a derivative of the FRUSA concept, will be built by a number of European firms. Designed for a five year mission in circular earth orbit between 398 and 593 km, the array will encounter 5600 solar eclipses per year. After five years, the array blankets will be restowed for return to earth.[29]

The array consists of two identical wings (Fig. 7-47) having an overall length of 11.82 m. The panel width is 2.83 m. The total blanket area of 47.9 m² is covered with 47,960 solar cells. The AEG-Telefunken cells are 20.95 $\times$ 40.35 $\times$ 0.25 mm in size, of 1 ohm · cm base resistivity, TiO_x-coated, n/p silicon, and produce 0.145 W output at 25°C, AMO conditions. Covers are 0.15 mm thick ceria-doped microsheet, MgF-coated, and are attached with DC 93-500 adhesive. Interconnectors are welded silver mesh with out-of-plane expansion loops, selected over more costly silver plated molybdenum. The interconnector design life is 30,000 cycles over the range from −100° to +100°C.

Each of the four blankets is made from glass fiber-reinforced Kapton. An embossed Kapton sheet serves as a cushion between the solar cell covered blankets. The total array mass, includ-

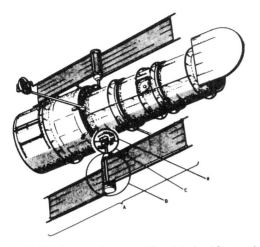

Fig. 7-47. Space telescope. (*Reprinted with permission of the IEEE*[29])

ing the solar array drive assembly, is 182.3 kg. The global modal natural frequency is 0.08 Hz, deployed. The array performance is 4.52 kW at 34 V and at 70°C, beginning-of-life, and 3.70 kW after five years. The corresponding specific performance values are 24.8 W/kg or 40.3 kg/kW and 20.3 W/kg or 49.3 kg/kW, respectively.

7-16. Hybrid Arrays

Most modern satellites designed for geosynchronous orbit operation require some amount of power during their transfer orbits prior to final orbital station acquisition and prior to deployment of larger solar cell arrays. However, most lightweight, flat-pack, fold-up or roll-up array designs are not capable of providing power output when fully stowed, and are not capable of withstanding the levels of acceleration in the transfer orbit when partially or fully deployed. To provide the necessary power, rigid solar cell panels are used in addition to the flexible, deployable arrays. In the case of CTS, a body-mounted panel was jettisoned after orbit insertion. In the case of the ESA-LHSA, a deployable, flexible flat-pack array is stowed along the outboard edge of a rigid inboard solar cell panel. In the case of the SPAR-MPDHSA, a rigid panel is mounted to the outboard end of a deployable, flat-pack array.

ESA-LHSA. The European Space Agency's lightweight hybrid solar array (ESA-LHSA), under development by the British Aerospace Dynamics Group, is also a two-wing concept for a range of multikilowatt, geosynchronous orbit missions (Fig. 7-48). Each wing consists of a yoke, a rigid solar cell panel, and a deployable, flexible, flat-pack solar cell blanket. During launch and high-thrust transfer orbits, the entire array assembly remains stowed against the satellite side walls (Fig. 7-49a). The outward facing solar cells on each of the two rigid panels (one on each of two opposite sides) produce up to 200 W. For low thrust transfer orbits, only the rigid panels are deployed (Fig. 7-49b and c). In the final orbit, the fold-out arrays are deployed from boxes located at the outer edges of the rigid panels (Fig. 7-49d). Deployment is by gas-driven aluminum telescoping masts.[30]

The yoke is made from aluminum tubing, but could be made using graphite fiber plastics to minimize thermally induced bending. Torsion springs with centrifugal dampers constitute the primary solar panel deployment mechanism. Pulley and cable systems provide controlled angular deployment of the yoke and the rigid panel. The rigid solar cell panels are made from monocurved aluminum honeycomb core with fiber-reinforced plastic face sheets. The flexible, fold-up solar cell panels are folded 16 times and held in the stowed configuration by a Kapton wrap. Solar cells are 10 ohm · cm, 20 × 40 × 0.20 mm, covered with 0.10 mm glass. The projected performance characteristics for the two-wing configuration is 3.14 kW output at end-of-life per wing. For a wing mass of 89.34 kg, the specific performance is 35.1 W/kg.

SPAR-MPDHSA. Spar Aerospace Products, under contract to the Canadian Communications Research Centre, is developing a 2.13 kW and a 3.73 kW beginning-of-life medium power hybrid solar array (MPDHSA) for geosynchronous operation. On both arrays, the rigid panels act as "body-mounted" arrays to provide power prior to array deployment. After deployment of the flexible, flat-pack arrays, the rigid panels are tilted to become plane-parallel with the flexible panels (see Fig. 7-50). Deployment of

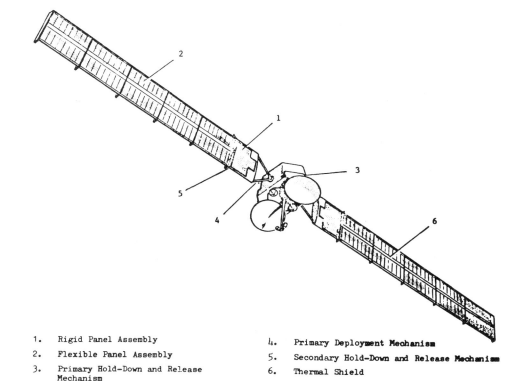

1. Rigid Panel Assembly
2. Flexible Panel Assembly
3. Primary Hold-Down and Release Mechanism

4. Primary Deployment Mechanism
5. Secondary Hold-Down and Release Mechanism
6. Thermal Shield

Fig. 7-48. ESA lightweight hybrid array deployed. (*Reprinted with permission of the IEEE.*[30])

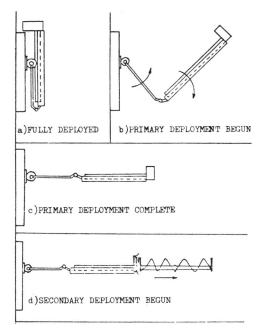

a) FULLY DEPLOYED   b) PRIMARY DEPLOYMENT BEGUN

c) PRIMARY DEPLOYMENT COMPLETE

d) SECONDARY DEPLOYMENT BEGUN

Fig. 7-49. LHSA deployment sequence. (*Reprinted with permission of the IEEE.*[30])

the blanket is via a BISTEM boom. The mass is 53 kg for the smaller array and 80 kg for the larger, resulting in specific performance numbers of 41 W/kg and 47 W/kg, respectively. The natural bending frequencies are 0.10 and 0.16 Hz, respectively.[31]

7-17. Other Developments

From the large number of developments that were undertaken to improve the array W/kg performance or to reduce fabrication cost, a few examples are cited that may be of interest again in the future.

Open Tape Substrate. Boeing, under contract to JPL in the late 1960's, and TRW, under contract to COMSAT in the mid-1970's, investigated the potential of an open weave or tape concept for a lightweight substrate design. Figure 7-51 illustrates the basic concept.[33]

The substrate consisted of fiberglass-reinforced Kapton strips. The cells were connected

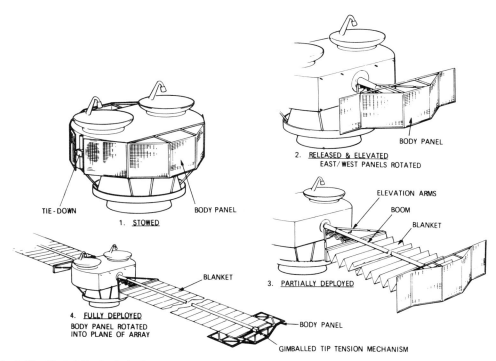

Fig. 7-50. SPAR-MPDHAS deployment sequence (2.1 kW array). (*Reprinted with permission © 1978 Society of Automotive Engineers.*[31])

directly to the substrate through spot-bond adhesive. The back surface could be painted (epoxy) for both thermal control and low energy proton protection.

As compared to a continuous, full substrate, open weave design concepts have the advantages of greatly simplified repair procedures and, because the emittance of the epoxy paint is

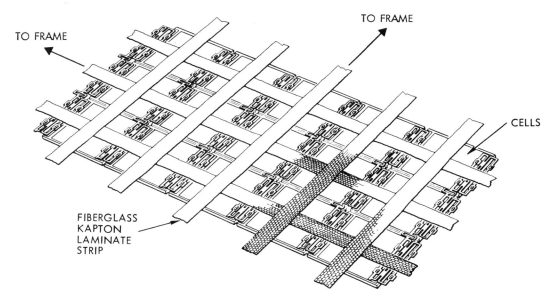

Fig. 7-51. Open weave substrate (back side shown). (*Courtesy of TRW, Inc.*)

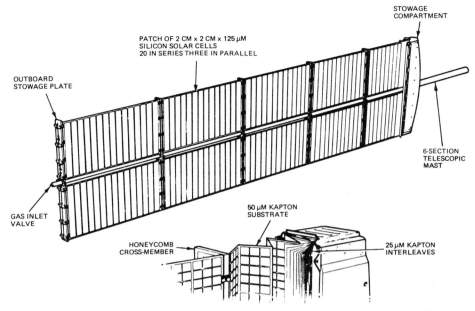

STOWAGE
COMPARTMENT

PATCH OF 2 CM x 2 CM x 125 μM
SILICON SOLAR CELLS
20 IN SERIES THREE IN PARALLEL

OUTBOARD
STOWAGE PLATE

6-SECTION
TELESCOPIC
MAST

GAS INLET
VALVE

50 μM KAPTON
SUBSTRATE

HONEYCOMB
CROSS-MEMBER

25 μM KAPTON
INTERLEAVES

Fig. 7-52. RAE lightweight array wing. (*Reprinted with permission of the IEEE.*[35])

greater than that of FEP Teflon or Kapton, improved performance.

The substrate was attached to a support frame. In the Boeing design, the substrate was sandwiched between beryllium frames to form an integral panel.[34] These panels could then be hinged together to form an array. The Boeing substrate only had a mass of 0.894 kg/m²; an entire 102 m² panel was 2.4 kg/m².

RAE. During the early- and mid-1970's the British Royal Aircraft Establishment (RAE) was involved with the development of a flat-pack, deployable, flexible substrate solar cell array which was deployed by telescoping tubes. The design principles were space-demonstrated on a small version of the larger development array on the British X4 meteorological satellite.[35,37]

Figure 7-52 shows the solar array configuration. The array blanket, 4.21 m long by 0.90 m wide, was supported and divided into subpanels by aluminum honeycomb cross-members extending from an aluminum telescopic mast. For launch, the panels were folded between cell patches into a honeycomb stowage compartment and were interleaved with sheets of corrugated, 25 μm Kapton, which remained behind

in the compartment when the paddles were deployed. The solar cell array was deployed pneumatically through a six-section aluminum telescopic mast, using nitrogen gas at 0.33 MN/m² (48 psi). When fully deployed, each section was mechanically latched, tensioning the panels to about 9 N, and the gas was allowed to leak away.

The substrate shown in Fig. 7-53 consisted of a perforated, 50 μm thick Kapton sheet. The windows in the Kapton were actually triangular as opposed to the circular shape shown, exposing 54% of the cell area. Interconnectors were 25 μm, silver plated molybdenum. The cells were interconnected and mounted on the substrate by a solderthrough, cementless technique. The back side of the array was finished with a high-emittance coating. Solar cells were Ferranti, 125 μm thick, wrap-around contact cells, covered with 0.1 mm thick, Pilkington Perkin-Elmer ceria-stabilized glass.

JPL/GE 200 W/kg. A conceptual design study for 10 kW arrays, having specific performance of 200 W/kg, beginning-of-life, at 55°C, and utilizing either a fold-up or a roll-up design, has shown the feasibility that such systems could be developed. Solar cells are 0.050 mm thick

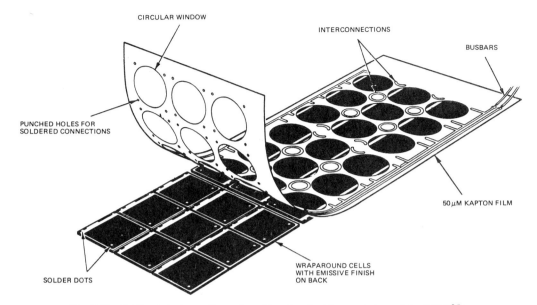

CIRCULAR WINDOW

INTERCONNECTIONS

BUSBARS

PUNCHED HOLES FOR
SOLDERED CONNECTIONS

50 μM KAPTON FILM

SOLDER DOTS

WRAPAROUND CELLS
WITH EMISSIVE FINISH
ON BACK

Fig. 7-53. RAE substrate configuration. (*Reprinted with permission of the IEEE.*[35])

cells having 13.5% efficiency at 25°C. The 160,000 cells on an array are covered by a 0.075 mm thick plastic encapsulant. Harness power losses were assumed at 2 to 3%. No blocking diodes are on the array. Design life is three years in interplanetary space. The temperature cycling range is specified to be 1000 cycles between −190°C and +140°C.

Both the non-retractable fold-out design and the retractable roll-out design are based on a V-stiffened approach (Fig. 7-54). The mast is of the coilable lattice, continuous longeron type, made from a glass fiber composite. The other structural elements utilize graphite fiber composites. The substrate is 0.025 mm thick Kapton. Solar cell interconnectors are welded-on, silver plated Invar, with in-plane stress relief loops. The array electrical weights are 31.34 kg for the roll-out array and 28.14 kg for the fold-out. The 2.86 kg difference arises from the need for slip rings by the roll-out design. The mechanical weights are 13.83 kg and 15.76 kg, respectively, the 1.93 kg difference arising partially (1.64 kg) from the use of a padding between the solar cells on the fold-out design, but no padding on the roll-out design. The corresponding array beginning-of-life specific performance is 201 W/kg for the roll-out and 211 W/kg for the fold-out design.[39]

DEPLOYMENT MECHANISMS

7-18. Deployable Booms

The central mechanical component of any packaged flexible solar array system is the deployment boom which erects and/or retracts the flexible substrate. Because it comprises a sizable portion of the total system weight, careful attention to selection and design of the proper approach is important.

The desirable features of a deployable boom include low weight, small package size, reliable performance, sufficient bending and torsional stiffness and strength, low thermally induced distortion, and good positioning accuracy. Typically, a boom does not possess all these features simultaneously. Most often a compromise has to be made in order to choose a design.

Basic Structural Forms. Table 7-4 shows the basic common forms of beams and beam members in use. Each member has advantages, and the selection of one over another involves tradeoff by weight, strength, cost, availability, and fabricability.

Table 7-5 shows beams and beam member cross-sectional variations. The form variations are generally the result of a functional consideration and are not purely structural. By example,

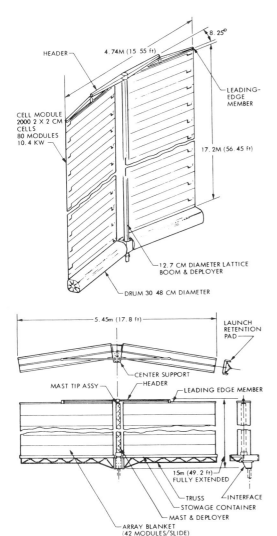

HEADER

4.74M (15.55 ft)

8.25°

LEADING-EDGE MEMBER

CELL MODULE 2000 2 X 2 CM CELLS 80 MODULES 10.4 KW

17.2M (56.45 ft)

12.7 CM DIAMETER LATTICE BOOM & DEPLOYER

DRUM 30.48 CM DIAMETER

5.45m (17.8 ft)

LAUNCH RETENTION PAD

CENTER SUPPORT

MAST TIP ASSY

HEADER

LEADING EDGE MEMBER

15m (49.2 ft) FULLY EXTENDED

TRUSS

INTERFACE

STOWAGE CONTAINER

MAST & DEPLOYER

ARRAY BLANKET (42 MODULES/SLIDE)

Fig. 7-54. Ultra-lightweight roll-out (top) and fold-out (bottom) arrays. (*Reprinted with permission of the IEEE.*[39])

the thin tubular form results from the requirement that the member be flattened for stowage.

Most solid or tubular beams become inefficient as load carrying members when the length approaches 15 m. A substitute for the solid form is the truss structure. Truss-configured beams are the most efficient structures in terms of stiffness and weight for large dimensional applications.

Stowage/Deployment Techniques. Table 7-6 illustrates the basic stowage methods and their

variations. Folding is the method most used for stowing beams and beam members. It is mechanically the simplest and most versatile stowage method. Folding is used as a basic method for stowing beams with hinges and without hinges (i.e., inflatable, lenticular tubes, curved tapes). Combined folding methods can be used to form multiple beam element booms.

Rolling beams on drums is a popular technique. The beam occupies little volume, in relation to its extended size, when stowed. It can be used for stowing beams of a variety of cross-sections. The technique stresses the material so that the beam thickness is such that the yield strain is not exceeded; this limits the beam strength. Coiling can be considered a variation of rolling.

Telescoping beams for stowage is also a relatively common method. Their stowage efficiency ratio of stowed to extended height is relatively low; however, this can be improved by combining folding with telescoping.

Table 7-7 shows the extension/retraction prime movers, which, when combined with the beam section and stowage technique, create a mechanism that can be used to operate the erection of the solar array. The prime movers can be interchanged, depending on the design constraints.

Element Types. Table 7-8 presents a brief description of 20 unique linear element extendible structures that incorporate combinations of the basic structural forms. Stowage techniques and deployment techniques were given in the previous tables.

While several boom types have been designed and developed as indicated, only a few have been used in actual developmental or operational solar array systems. Table 7-9 identifies those designs along with the specific solar array design or satellite program. The preferred designs include the following with reference to Table 7-8:

- Extendible reel stored (Type 16)
- Articulated or coiled lattice mast (Type (8/9)
- Telescoping cylinders (Type 2)
- Folding beam solid cross-section (Type 3)

Table 7-4. Basic Beam Cross-Section Forms.[42]

STRUCTURE	FORM	STRUCTURAL CHARACTERISTICS	COMMENTS
SOLID		GOOD TENSION MEMBER, MOMENT OF INERTIA CHANGES IN ORTHOGONAL DIRECTIONS	ECONOMICAL MATERIAL SECTION, FLAT SURFACES FACILITATE FABRICATION OF TRUSS STRUCTURES
		FAT SECTION SUITABLE FOR HIGH SHEAR LOADS	PRIMARILY USED IN MECHANISMS; HOWEVER USEFUL FOR SHORT BEAMS OR STRUTS
		FAT SECTION SUITABLE FOR HIGH SHEAR LOADS, CONSTANT MOMENT OF INERTIA	ECONOMICAL MAT'L SECTION, BEAM END FITTINGS FABRICATED WITH SIMPLE DRILLED HOLES
		MOMENT OF INERTIA CHANGES IN ORTHOGONAL DIRECTIONS	USUALLY A FORGED SHAPE; USED EXTENSIVELY AS A SIMPLE BEAM
TUBES		TORSIONALLY GOOD, PROVIDES DIFFERENT MOMENT OF INERTIA IN ORTHOGONAL AXIS	WIDELY USED IN ANTENNA STRUCTURES WHEREIN WAVEGUIDE SERVES ITS NORMAL MICROWAVE FUNCTION AS WELL AS STRUCTURAL SUPPORT
		TORSIONALLY GOOD, PROVIDES EQUAL MOMENT OF INERTIA IN ORTHOGONAL AXIS	USED IN STRUCTURES WHERE FLAT SURFACES FOR MOUNTING OR FABRICATION ARE DESIRED
		TORSIONALLY STIFFEST TO WEIGHT FORM AVAILABLE, CONSTANT MOMENT OF INERTIA	ECONOMICAL, WIDELY USED FORM COMMERCIALLY AVAILABE IN A BROAD SELECTION OF MATERIALS AND ALLOYS
		TORSIONALLY GOOD, PROVIDES DIFFERENT MOMENT OF INERTIA IN ORTHOGONAL AXIS	USUALLY PRODUCED IN FABRICATION SHOP BY FLATTENING A ROUND TUBE
TRUSS BEAMS		TORSIONALLY GOOD, PROVIDES DIFFERENT MOMENT OF INERTIA IN ORTHOGONAL AXIS	COMMONLY USED IN BRIDGE TRUSSES OR ANY TRUSS WITH UNSYMMETRICAL LOADING
		TORSIONALLY GOOD, PROVIDES EQUAL MOMENT OF INERTIA IN ORTHOGONAL AXIS	COMMONLY USED WHERE LOADS ARE SYMMETRICAL SUCH AS RADIO TOWERS
		TORSIONALLY GOOD, MOMENT OF INERTIA MAY BE VARIED IN ANY OF THREE DIRECTIONS	GENERALLY USED FOR SYMMETRICAL LOADS, HOWEVER CAN BE MADE ASYMMETRICAL FOR SPECIAL CONDITIONS

Table 7-5. Beam and Beam Member Cross-Section Variations.[42]

BEAM FORM	VARIATION	COMMENTS
OPEN SECTIONS		LOW OUT OF PLANE STIFFNESS LIMIT THIS TO LOW BENDING AND TORSIONAL LOAD APPLICATIONS.
		LOW TORSIONAL STIFFNESS, HIGH DYNAMIC DAMPING, EVEN WHEN MADE TO OVERLAP. WIDELY USED AS SMALL DIAME.ER, LONG MEMBERS FOR ELECTROMAGNETIC ANTENNA. SEVERE THERMAL BENDING PROBLEMS.
		BROAD RANGE OF SIZES AND MATERIALS AVAILABLE. SUITABLE FOR STIFFENERS OR COMPONENT PARTS OF A BUILT-UP BEAM OR COLUMN.
		SIMILAR TO ABOVE WITH SLIGHTLY IMPROVED BENDING STRENGTH.
		WIDELY USED AS STRUCTURAL BEAMS. IDEAL FOR HIGH BENDING LOADS ABOUT THE MAJOR PRINCIPAL AXIS
		AS ABOVE EXCEPT HIGHER FLANGE BUCKLING HAZARD. SHEAR CENTER NOT COINCIDENT WITH C.G.
ROUND TUBE		APPROACHES THE STRUCTURAL CHARACTERISTICS OF A THIN WALLED TUBE. EXACT MECHANICAL PROPERTIES DEPEND UPON INDIVIDUAL DESIGN. USUALLY <6 IN DIA AND WITH APPROX 250:1 DIAMETER TO THICKNESS RATIO. CRITICAL REVIEW OR APPLICATIONS ARE REQUIRED TO MINIMIZE THERMAL BENDING PROBLEMS.
FLATTENED TUBE		USUALLY IN THIN WALLED SECTIONS. BENDING LOAD CAPACITY VARIES WITH LATERAL CURVATURES. TEST DATA LIMITED, ANALYSIS METHOD NOT DEVELOP FOR BEAM WITH SEALED EDGES. CENTER PIECE HELPS STABILIZE SHAPE, HENCE INCREASES STRENGTH AND STIFFNESS. HOWEVER INCREASED DRUM WEIGHT SHOULD BE STUDIED IN A TRADE-OFF.
TUBULAR DELTA		USUALLY IN THIN WALLED SECTIONS AND LIMITED IN SIZE TO 6 INCHES PER SIDE.

Table 7-6. Extension/Retraction Methods.[42]

PRIME MOVER	STOWAGE METHOD	BEAM SECTION FORM	CHARACTERISTICS
ELECTRIC MOTOR	REEL STORED		REMOTE ACTUATION, CAPABLE OF MULTIPLE EXTENSIONS AND RETRACTIONS. SOME MODELS INCORPORATE TWO STORAGE REELS THAT ARE INTERCONNECTED AND DRIVEN BY A COMMON MOTOR.
			REMOTE ACTUATION, CAPABLE OF MULTIPLE EXTENSIONS AND RETRACTIONS. USES THREE STORAGE REELS INTERCONNECTED AND DRIVEN BY A COMMON MOTOR.
			REMOTE ACTUATION, CAPABLE OF MULTIPLE EXTENSIONS AND RETRACTIONS. A SINGLE STORAGE REEL IS DRIVEN BY THE MOTOR.
			WIRE TRUSS IS FOLDED AND ROLLED UP ON A SINGLE, MOTOR DRIVEN REEL.
	TELESCOPING		REMOTE EXTENSION MAY BE ACCOMPLISHED BY MOTOR DRIVEN WINCH ACTION OR A MOTOR DRIVEN HYDRAULIC SYSTEM. BEAM SECTIONS MAY BE SOLID OR TRUSS.
	FOLDING	VARIOUS	REMOTE EXTENSION MAY BE ACCOMPLISHED BY MOTOR DRIVEN WINCH ACTION OR BY A MOTOR DRIVEN SCREW JACK (USUALLY IN CONJUNCTION WITH MECHANICAL SPRINGS).
MECHANICAL SPRINGS	REEL STORED	SAME BEAM SECTION USED AS ELECT. MOTOR CONFIG.	SPRING MOTOR POWERS EXTENSION ONLY, MANUAL RETRACTION REWINDS MOTOR.
	TELESCOPING		SPRINGS OR SPRING MOTOR POWERS EXTENSION ONLY, REQUIRES MANUAL RETRACTION. GENERALLY USED WITH A DAMPER TO CONTROL EXTENSION DYNAMICS.
	FOLDING	VARIOUS	SPRINGS AT EACH JOINT EXTEND STRUCTURE, MANUAL RETRACTION REQD. MAY BE USED IN CONJUNCTION WITH AN ELECTRICAL MOTOR THAT WILL ASSIST IN EXTENSION AND CONTROL EXTENSION DYNAMICS.
PNEUMATIC (STORED GAS)	TELESCOPING		SLIDING SEALS MAKE TELESCOPIC MAST GAS TIGHT, GAS PRESSURE EXTENDS CYLINDERS. MANUAL RETRACTION REQD.
	FOLDING	VARIOUS	SEALED TUBES INFLATED WITH GAS PRESSURE, MANUAL RETRACTION REQD PNEUMATIC ACTUATORS MAY BE EMPLOYED TO ERECT HINGED JOINTS, AGAIN MUST BE RETRACTED MANUALLY.

- Simple pantograph (version of Type 5)
- Lazy tongs (Type 4).

Of those identified above, the Bistem (Type 16) is used with great frequency on moderate-sized, deployable, flexible substrate arrays. For very large arrays, the Astromast (Type 8 or 9) is preferred because of its structural efficiency.

Blanket/Boom Arrangements. Regardless of the blanket stowage method (i.e., roll-up or

Table 7-7. Basic Stowage Methods and Variations.[42]

METHOD	VARIATIONS	CHARACTERISTICS	COMMENTS
FOLDED		STOWS BY DISPLACEMENT ONLY, STOW VOLUME IS APPROX. EQUAL TO EXTENDED VOLUME.	SIMPLE, EFFECTIVE, AND WIDELY USED, LIGHT WEIGHT FOR MORE HEAVILY LOADED SYSTEMS.
		STOWS VERY COMPACTLY, REQUIRES LATCHES TO DEVELOP RIGIDITY. EXCELLENT DEPLOYMENT DEVICE	MULTIPLE HINGE JOINTS REQUIRE PRUDENT DESIGN TO MINIMIZE LOOSENESS. USUALLY SPRING LOADED AGAINST A DAMPER MECHANISM.
		STOWAGE CAPABILITY DEPENDS UPON THE MATERIAL ALLOWABLE STRESS AND THICKNESS. INFLATABLES USING METAL FOILS STOW VERY COMPACTLY	NO JOINTS OR LATCHES REQUIRED TO PROVIDE A RIGID STRUCTURE. COLUMN STRENGTH IS LIMITED BY MATERIAL THICKNESS, STOWED CONFIGURATION, AND ALLOWABLE STRESS. NO REMOTE RETRACTION.
ROLLED		BEAM IS WRAPPED AROUND A REEL AND ITSELF. REQUIRES A SECTION OF THE BEAM REMAIN EXTENDED BUT STOWS COMPACTLY. CAN BE SELF EXTENDING BUT USUALLY MOTOR DRIVEN	USUALLY CAPABLE OF MANY EXTENSIONS AND RETRACTIONS WITHOUT DEGRADING PERFORMANCE, DEVELOPS FULL STRENGTH AT PARTIAL EXTENSION. COLUMN STRENGTH IS LIMITED BY MAT'L THICKNESS STOW CONFIG. & STRESS
		USUALLY SELF EXTENDING BY STORED SPRING ENERGY, ALTHOUGH SOME MOTOR DRIVEN MODELS HAVE BEEN USED	CAPABLE OF MANY EXTENSIONS OR RETRACTIONS WITHOUT DEGRADING PERFORMANCE. COLUMN STRENGTH IS VERY LIMITED.
TELESCOPED		STOWED VOLUME FROM 20 TO 50 PERCENT OF EXTENDED VOLUME. DESIGNS READILY ADAPT TO DEVELOP ALL USABLE STRENGTH ON INDIVIDUAL MEMBERS	SIMPLE, FEW PARTS, MAKE DESIGN VERY RELIABLE. MAY BE TRUSSES, TUBES OR COMBINATIONS OF THE TWO

Table 7-8. Extendible Structures.[42]

NO. & NAME OF EXTENDIBLE STRUCTURE	ILLUSTRATION	DESCRIPTION & OPERATION OF STRUCTURE & MECHANISM (RETRACTION CAPABILITIES)	FLIGHT EXPERIENCE
1 TELESCOPING TRIANGULAR TRUSS		CONCENTRIC TRIANGULAR TRUSS SECTIONS SUPPORTED BY ROLLERS. SECTIONS ARE EXTENDED AND LATCH IN THE FULL EXTENDED POSITION. CAN BE UNLATCHED AND RETRACTED	FLIGHT EXPERIENCE: NONE
2 TELESCOPING CYLINDERS		CONCENTRIC SOLID TUBES IN GRADUATED DIAMETERS. SECTIONS ARE EXTENDED AND LATCH IN THE FULL EXTENDED POSITION. CAN BE UNLATCHED AND RETRACTED	FLIGHT EXPERIENCE: UNKNOWN

FLIGHT EXPERIENCE UNKNOWN

FLIGHT EXPERIENCE: NONE |
| 3 FOLDING BEAM | | SECTIONS MAY BE TRUSS, TUBULAR, OR SOLID: HINGES ON EITHER END AND LATCHES AT FULL EXTENSION. USUALLY DEPLOYED BY A TENSION CABLE SYSTEM WITH PULLEYS AT EACH JOINT. CAN BE UNLATCHED AND RETRACTED. | USED FREQUENTLY IN SPACE FLIGHT!, USUALLY AS RELATIVELY SHORT MEMBERS. (LESS THAN 30 FT.) |
| 4 LAZY TONG | | STRUCTURAL PANELS HINGED TOGETHER AND STABILIZED ATTACHMENT TO HINGED BEAMS AT THE EDGES. THE HINGED BEAMS ARE SOMEWHAT LONGER FROM PIVOT TO PIVOT THAN THE STRUCTURAL PANELS. THE PANELS ALIGN TO ACCEPT COLUMN LOADS. MAY BE LATCHED AT FULL EXTENSION, USUALLY NOT RETRACTABLE ONCE LATCHED. USUALLY SPRING-LOADED; MAY HAVE SCREW JACK ASSISTANCE. COULD USE A TENSION CABLE SYSTEM AS IN NO. 3 BUT THE NUMBER OF JOINTS IS USUALLY HIGH. | THIS CONFIGURATION USED EXTENSIVELY BY LOCKHEED TO DEPLOY SOLAR PANELS.

THE PEGASUS SPACECRAFT DEPLOYED FLAT-PANELS 14 BY 48 FT (EACH WING) AS METEROID DETECTORS USING THIS SYSTEM. |
| 5 TRI AXIS PANTOGRAPH | | THREE LAZY TONGS TIED AT THE NODES WITH U-SHAPED CLIPS. MAY BE LATCHED AT FULL EXTENSION. AS IN NO. 4, MOSTLY USED AS A SPRING-LOADED, NON-RETRACTING DEVICE INVOLVING ONLY LIGHT COLUMN LOADS. MAY USE A SCREW JACK ASSIST WHICH WILL CONTROL DEPLOYMENT. | FLIGHT EXPERIENCE: NONE |

flat-pack), either two booms or a single boom can be used, as illustrated in Fig. 7-55. The single boom should be near the center line of the blanket, whereas in the two-boom scheme, the booms should be near either edge of the blanket. A two-boom scheme provides greater torsional rigidity than does the single-boom design. A single-boom scheme can be obtained in two ways—one with an offset boom and the other with a split blanket. In the offset design, the blanket is one piece and the boom is offset from the blanket plane. In the case of the split design, the blanket is split in two halves and the boom is placed in the plane of the blanket in between the two halves. A split configuration requires a longer blanket (and boom) than does the offset configuration for an array width to obtain an equal blanket area. Table 7-10 summarizes blanket/boom arrangements for some developmental flight programs.

7-19. Spring/Actuator Deployment Concepts

Unlike the multitude of concepts and configurations associated with deployment booms discussed in Section 7-18, spring/actuator systems are more straightforward. Typical components include torsion or compression springs at the hinge lines, dampers, a closed-loop cable system to kinematically constrain and couple the deployment between panels, and a latch-up system. In the following, brief descriptions are given of spring/actuator systems for a few operational arrays.

SOURCE	DEVELOPMENT WORK	GENERAL DESIGN COMMENTS
TRI-EX TOWER CORP., VISALIA, CALIFORNIA	USED EXTENSIVELY IN EARTH APPLICATIONS SUCH AS PORTABLE ANTENNA TOWERS. SIMPLE CONSTRUCTION IS QUITE ADAPTABLE TO SPACE USAGE	TRIANGULAR SHAPE PROVIDES EXCELLENT STIFFNESS-TO-WEIGHT CHARACTERISTICS. MEMBERS MAY BE SIZED-UP ACCORDING TO LOAD REQUIREMENTS AND PACKAGING ENVELOPE. VERY SIMPLE DESIGN ANALYSIS. AN EXTREMELY EFFICIENT BEAM IF THREE OR LESS TELESCOPIC SECTIONS ARE USED. LOOSENESS IN THE JOINTS WILL YIELD A NON-LINEAR SYSTEM AND MUST BE AVOIDED OR MINIMIZED. AN IDEAL BEAM FOR THERMAL BENDING WHEN USED WITH A CONSTANT SUN ANGLE, AS EXPOSURE TO SUNLIGHT CAN BE NEARLY EQUAL ON ALL LONGITUDIONAL MEMBERS. UNEVEN SIDE HEATING COULD PRODUCE DEFORMATION AND RESULT IN RETRACTION PROBLEMS.
SANDERS ASSOC. INC., NASHAU, N.H.	TELESCOPING MAST WITH INCREMENTAL EXTENSION; LATCHING AND RETRACTION UNLATCHING. TWO MODELS, 21 FEET AND 30 FEET, HAVE BEEN BUILT AND TESTED. VERY INTERESTING ACTUATOR/LATCH MECHANISM.	COLUMN LOADED THIN WALL TUBES ARE BEST USED FOR INTERMEDIATE LENGTH BEAMS (LESS THAN 50 FT.). INCREASES IN LENGTH REQUIRE AN INCREASE IN TUBE DIAMETER TO MAINTAIN A MINIMUM SLENDERNESS RATIO. SIMULTANEOUSLY THE TUBE WALL THICKNESS MUST BE INCREASED TO MAINTAIN A LOW R/T RATIO TO AVOID LOCAL BUCKLING. CONSIDERABLE OVERLAP IS REQUIRED TO AVOID ROTATIONAL LOOSENESS. NONUNIFORM TEMPERATURES WILL CAUSE BENDING. CROSS-SECTION WILL NOT REMAIN CIRCULAR AND MUST BE ANALYZED FOR BINDING DURING RETRACTION. THERMAL CONTROL SURFACE MUST WITHSTAND SLIDING ABRASION DURING EXTENSION AND RETRACTION.
ROYAL AIRCRAFT ESTABLISHMENT, FARNSBOROUGH, U.K.	TWO MODELS OF PNEUMATIC OPERATED 17-FT LONG TELESCOPING MAST	
TRI-EX TOWER CORP., VISALIA, CALIFORNIA	USED EXTENSIVELY IN GROUND APPLICATIONS UP TO 100 FT, "SKY NEEDLE TOWERS". USES MOTORIZED WINCH AND CABLES SYSTEM FOR EXTENSION	
BOEING CO., SEATTLE, WASHINGTON	BOEING DID DEVELOPMENT WORK ON A 63-FT LONG SOLAR ARRAY THAT DEPLOYED IN THIS MANNER.	CHARACTERISTICS ARE THOSE OF THE BASIC SECTION SELECTED; MAY BE VERY EFFICIENT, DEPENDING UPON THE DETAIL DESIGN. LOOSENESS IN THE JOINTS WILL RESULT IN A DYNAMICALLY NON-LINEAR SYSTEM AND MUST BE MINIMIZED. THERMAL BINDING IS UNLIKELY. ALL OTHER THINGS EQUAL, THIS BEAM GENERALLY REQUIRES MORE STORAGE SPACE THAN A TELESCOPING BEAM.
FAIRCHILD HILLER CORP., GERMANTOWN, MD.	FAIRCHILD HILLER BUILT A WORKING MODEL 36-FT LONG	
MOBILE AERIAL TOWERS INC., FT. WAYNE, IND.	MANUFACTURE FOR GROUND USE A LINE OF MOBILE AERIAL TOWERS TO ELEVATE MEN AND EQUIPMENT AS HIGH AS 130 FT. SIMPLE CONSTRUCTION IS QUITE ADAPTABLE TO SPACE USAGES.	
LOCKHEED MISSILES & SPACE COMPANY, SUNNYVALE, CALIFORNIA		VERY COMPACT STOWAGE. THIS BEAM IS AN EFFECTIVE DEPLOYMENT DEVICE. PROPER LOCKING OF PANELS IS REQUIRED TO CHANGE THE DEVICE INTO A STRUCTURE. THE LARGE NUMBER OF JOINTS WILL PROBABLY LEAD TO A NONLINEAR STRUCTURE, WHICH MAKES MEANINGFUL DYNAMIC ANALYSIS DIFFICULT.
FAIRCHILD HILLER CORP., GERMANTOWN, MD.	A WORKING MODEL 8-1/2-FT LONG OF ONLY THE LAZY TONG (NO FLAT PANELS) WAS BUILT AND TESTED BY FAIRCHILD HILLER	
LOCKHEED MISSILES & SPACE COMPANY, SUNNYVALE, CALIFORNIA	A SMALL 5-FT LONG DEMONSTRATION MODEL HAS BEEN BUILT BY LOCKHEED.	THIS IS A GOOD DEPLOYMENT DEVICE BUT A VERY POOR STRUCTURE, INHERENTLY NON-LINEAR WITH LOW LATERAL AND TORSIONAL STIFFNESS. COLUMN STRENGTH IS LIMITED BY THE EXTENSION MECHANISM; OR EVEN IF LATCHED IN THE EXTENDED POSITION, ALL OF THE STRUCTURAL MEMBERS ARE LOADED IN BENDING. THERMAL BENDING WILL BE SMALL IF BEAM SELF SHADING IS HELD TO A LOW VALUE. VERY COMPACT STOWAGE.

Table 7-8. (*Continued*)

NO. & NAME OF EXTENDIBLE STRUCTURE	ILLUSTRATION	DESCRIPTION & OPERATION OF STRUCTURE & MECHANISM (RETRACTION CAPABILITIES)	FLIGHT EXPERIENCE
6 EXTENSIBLE TRUSS (PROPOSAL BASELINE)		TWO LAZY TONGS CONNECTED WITH PANELS TO PRODUCE A RECTANGULAR TRUSS BEAM WHEN EXTENDED; PANELS ALIGN TO ACCEPT COLUMN LOADS. MAY BE LATCHED AT FULL EXTENSION: USUALLY NOT RETRACTABLE ONCE LATCHED. MAY USE A SCREW JACK ASSIST WHICH WILL CONTROL DEPLOYMENT.	FLIGHT EXPERIENCE: UNKNOWN
7 BOX BELLOWS (JACK-IN-THE BOX)		FLAT RECTANGULAR PANELS JOINED LONGITUDINALLY BY HINGES, INCORPORATING TORSION SPRINGS AND SUPPORTED BY FLANGES. HINGES OPEN INWARD AND OUTWARD ON ALTERNATE PANELS. MAY BE LATCHED AT FULL EXTENSION, USUALLY NOT RETRACTABLE.	FLIGHT EXPERIENCE: UNKNOWN
8 ASTROMAST ARTICULATED LATTICE		TRIANGULAR SECTIONS ARE RIGID: THE LONGITUDINAL LINKS PIVOT AT EACH BAY. FOLDING IS ACHIEVED BY LOOSENING ONE TENSION MEMBER (WIRE ROPE) IN EACH BAY: THE TENSION MEMBERS ARE LOCKED AS EACH BAY IS EXTENDED. RETRACTABLE.	FLIGHT EXPERIENCE: UNKNOWN
9 ASTROMAST COILABLE LATTICE		FIBERGLASS CONSTRUCTION WITH WIRE ROPE TENSION MEMBERS. LONGITUDINAL SECTIONS ARE CONTINUOUS; THE TRIANGULAR BAY SECTIONS ARE RIGID AND PIVOTED ON THE LONGITUDINAL MEMBERS. RETRACTABLE. FIBERGLASS BATTENS (SIDES OF TRIANGULAR SECTION) ARE BUCKLED TO BEGIN COILING OPERATION.	FLIGHT EXPERIENCE: UNKNOWN
10 TRI EXTENDER LMSC		TRIANGULAR BOOM, PANTOGRAPH LINKS CONNECT THE LONGITUDINAL MEMBERS. EACH LONGITUDINAL MEMBER HAS A LENTICULAR SECTION BETWEEN THE LAZY TONG NODES SIMILAR TO EXT. STRUCTURE NO. 12. THE LENTICULAR SECTIONS ARE FLATTENED THEN BUCKLED ALTERNATELY INWARD/OUTWARD TO STOW. NOT RETRACTABLE	FLIGHT EXPERIENCE: NONE
11 TRIANGULAR WIRE		SOLID SPRING WIRE CONSTRUCTION. TRIANGULAR SECTIONS WELDED TO LONGERONS. ONE LEG OF THE TRIANGULAR SECTION IS MADE TO FLEX (OR HINGED) SO THAT THE REMAINING 2 SIDES CAN BE BROUGHT TOGETHER. THE FOLDED BEAM CAN THEN BE ROLLED UP ON A REEL. REEL ROTATED BY ELECT. MOTOR & GEAR TRAIN, RETRACTION ACCOMPLISHED BY REVERSING MOTOR. IF RETRACTION IS NOT REQD; SPRING FORCE (OR MOTOR) MAY BE USED FOR EXTENSION.	FLIGHT EXPERIENCE UNKNOWN
12 LENTICULAR WELDED BEAM		TWO PIECES OF SPRING TAPES ARE PRE-FORMED TO APPROXIMATE A HAT SECTION. THE TWO TAPES ARE WELDED TOGETHER AT THE FLANGES. THE SECTION IS FLATTENED AND ROLLED UP ON A REEL FOR STOWAGE OR CAN BE LOCALLY FLATTENED AND BENT IN A FIRE HOSE FOLD. THE MOTOR DRIVEN REEL WOULD BE RETRACTABLE; THE FIRE HOSE FOLD WOULD NOT BE RETRACTABLE.	FLIGHT EXPERIENCE UNKNOWN
13 TRIBEAM (LMSC)		BEAM COMPOSED OF 3 SPRING TAPES WITH EDGE FLANGES CONTAINING VELCRO TAPE AND SNAP FASTENERS. TAPES ROLL-UP ON REELS ARRANGED ABOUT THE BEAM CENTERLINE. REELS ARE INTERCONNECTED & ROTATED BY ELECT. MOTOR & GEAR TRAIN, RETRACTION ACCOMPLISHED BY REVERSING MOTOR.	NO FLIGHT EXPERIENCE
14 INSTARECT (SANDERS)		3 PIECE BEAM, TWO OUTER PRE-FORMED SPRING TAPES ARE FLATTENED & ROLLED-UP ON REELS. THE CENTER (FLAT) SPRING TAPE WITH EDGE INDEX HOLES & SLOTS IS ALSO STORED ON A REEL. THE EDGES OF THE 3 TAPES INTERLOCK AS THE BEAM EXTENDS. REELS ARE INTERCONNECTED & ROTATED BY AN ELECT. MOTOR & GEAR TRAIN. RETRACTION ACCOMPLISHED BY REVERSING MOTOR.	FLIGHT EXPERIENCE UNKNOWN
15 INTERLOCKING EXTENDIBLE REEL STORED		2 PIECES OF PRE-FORMED SPRING TAPES ARE FLATTENED & ROLLED-UP ON REELS. THE EDGES OF THE TAPES INTERLOCK AS THE BEAM EXTENDS. REELS ARE INTERCONNECTED & ROTATED BY AN ELECT. MOTOR & GEAR TRAIN. RETRACTION ACCOMPLISHED BY REVERSING MOTOR.	SIX UNITS (60 TO 120 FT LONG) WERE FLOWN ON NRL GRADIENT EXPERIMENT SATELLITES. FOUR (750 FT LONG) EDGELOCK TEES WERE USED ON RAE, 38 FT LONG HINGELOCK USED ON OGO AND FRENCH SATELLITE FR-2 EDLE.

SOURCE	DEVELOPMENT WORK	GENERAL DESIGN COMMENTS
FAIRCHILD HILLER, SPACE AND ELECTRONICS SYSTEMS DIVISION, GERMANTOWN, MD.	A SMALL DEMONSTRATION MODEL HAS BEEN BUILT BY FAIRCHILD HILLER, SPACE AND ELECTRONICS SYSTEMS DIVISION. THIS CONFIGURATION IS AN EXTENSION OF THE PRINCIPLES USED TO DEPLOY THE SOLAR ARRAY IN THE PEGASUS SPACECRAFT.	VERY COMPACT STOWAGE. PRUDENT LATCH DESIGN WILL MAKE THIS A REASONABLY STIFF STRUCTURE. HOWEVER IT WILL INHERIT SOME LESS DESIREABLE STRUCTURAL QUALITIES SUCH AS NOW LINEARITY AND LOW TORSIONAL STIFFNESS. LATCHES MAKE RETRACTION MORE DIFFICULT, LESS RELIABLE. SELF SHADING MAY PRODUCE EXCESSIVE THERMAL BENDING AND MAY INDUCE BINDING IF RETRACTION IS ATTEMPTED. BEAM IS NOT RIGID UNLESS FULLY EXTENDED.
LOCKHEED MISSILES & SPACE COMPANY, SUNNYVALE, CALIFORNIA / FAIRCHILD HILLER, SPACE & ELECTRONICS SYSTEMS DIVISION, GERMANTOWN, MD.	SMALL DEMONSTRATION MODELS HAVE BEEN BUILT BY LOCKHEED AND FAIRCHILD HILLER. LOCKHEED'S MODEL COMPLETED A 90° TURN WHEN DEPLOYED, YET FOLDS COMPACTLY.	VERY COMPACT STOWAGE. BASIC DESIGN PROVIDES GOOD TORSIONAL STIFFNESS. HOWEVER, THE HIGH L/B (SLENDERNESS RATIO) AND THE LOW B/T (LOCAL STIFFNESS) REQUIREMENT MAKE THIS STRUCTURE VERY INEFFICIENT FOR LONG BEAMS. HOLES, AT LEAST ON THE SUN SIDE, ARE PROBABLY REQUIRED TO MINIMIZE TEMPERATURE DIFFERENCES. EFFECT OF NONUNIFORM TEMPERATURES ON ABILITY TO REFOLD WOULD HAVE TO BE EVALUATED. BEAM IS NOT RIGID UNLESS FULLY EXTENDED.
ASTRO RESEARCH CORP., SANTA BARBARA, CALIFORNIA	MANY APPLICATIONS ON EARTH FROM 30 TO 100 FT LONG; BOTH CIVIL AND MILITARY. EXCEPT FOR ONE CASE THE BOOMS ARE MANUALLY ERECTED AND RETRACTED. A DEVELOPMENTAL UNIT OF A 30-FT HIGH, REMOTELY ACTUATED (ERECTING AND RETRACTION) MODEL HAS BEEN DELIVERED TO THE US ARMY. ALUMINUM OR STAINLESS STEEL IS USED FOR THE RIGID MEMBERS AND STAINLESS STELL WIRE ROPE FOR THE TENSION MEMBERS.	COMPACT STOWAGE. THIS BEAM CAN BE MADE AS EFFICIENT AS THE BASIC TRIANGULAR TRUSS, WITH HIGH STIFFNESS TO WEIGHT RATIO. BEAM IS AT FULL STRENGTH AT ALL TIMES DURING DEPLOYMENT. REMOTE (AUTOMATIC) DEPLOYMENT MAY BE MORE COMPLICATED THAN REQUIRED FOR OTHER DEPLOYABLE STRUCTURES. UNIFORM SOLAR ILLUMINATION IS BEST ACHIEVED IN A TRIANGULAR OPEN TRUSS BEAM.
ASTRO RESEARCH CORP., SANTA BARBARA, CALIFORNIA	ONE FLIGHT UNIT OF A 10 INCH BY 100 FT MAST WAS DELIVERED TO NASA, HOUSTON FOR USE IN A LUNAR EXPERIMENT AS PART OF THE APOLLO PROGRAM (EXPERIMENT CANCELLED) A 6 INCH BY 13 FOOT COILABLE MAST WILL BE DELIVERED TO GOODYEAR AEROSPACE CORP. AS PART OF A SCALE MODEL OF THE LOFT (LOW FREQUENCY RADIO TELESCOPE)	COMPACT STOWAGE, LINEAR SYSTEM, HIGH STIFFNESS TO MASS RATIO. BEAM IS AT FULL STRENGTH AT ALL TIMES DURING DEPLOYMENT. HOWEVER, THIS BEAM IS LIMITED TO LOW LOAD APPLICATIONS. AS THE LOAD INCREASES, THE REQUIRED DIAMETER OF THE LONGERON INCREASES AND QUICKLY BECOMES TOO STIFF TO COIL IN A REASONABLE STORAGE AREA. LOW TEMPERATURE BENDING CHARACTERISTICS MAY BE A PROBLEM. THE LOW THERMAL CONDUCTIVITY OF FIBERGLASS WILL ACCENTUATE TEMPERATURE NON-UNIFORMITY. PLASTIC WILL REQUIRE A PROTECTIVE THERMAL COATING TO RESIST U.V. ETC. DAMAGE.
LOCKHEED MISSILES & SPACE COMPANY, SUNNYVALE, CALIFORNIA	TWO MODELS BUILT, THE FIRST WITH 5-INCH BAYS (5 BAYS HIGH) USED LUFKINS TAPES (SEMI-LENTICULAR CROSS-SECTION) AS THE LONGITUDINAL MEMBERS. THE SECOND MODEL HAS 40-INCH SQUARE BAYS WHEN EXTENDED (3 BAYS OR 10-FEET TALL) AND IS MADE ENTIRELY OF ALUMINUM. DEVELOPMENTAL WORK IS UNDERWAY TO REPLACE SOME OF THE ALUMINUM LAZY TONG MEMBERS WITH A GRAPHITE-EPOXY COMPOSITE.	COMPACT STOWAGE, LINEAR SYSTEM. AN EXCELLENT STIFFNESS TO MASS RATIO IS ACHIEVED WITHOUT THE COMPLICATION OF LATCHES. THE LONGERONS BEND TO STOW BUT THE SECTION TO BE BENT IS FIRST FLATTENED WHICH LOWERS THE STRESSES SIGNIFICANTLY. HOWEVER, THE BENDING WILL LIMIT THE COLUMN LOADING SOMEWHAT. BROAD LENTICULAR SECTIONS MAY CAUSE MORE SELF SHADING THAN CIRCULAR SECTIONS. THE BEAM IS NOT RIGID UNLESS FULLY EXTENDED. NO REASONABLE RETRACTION SYSTEM HAS BEEN PROPOSED FOR THIS BEAM.
MARTIN MARIETTA DENVER, COLO.	SOME DEVELOPMENT WORK DONE, EXACT STATUS UNKNOWN	REQUIRES DIAGONAL MEMBERS TO ACHIEVE REASONABLE TORSIONAL STIFFNESS. BENDING STRESSES IN LONGERONS DURING STOWAGE WILL LIMIT THEIR SIZE AND CONSEQUENT COLUMN LOADING CAPACITY. ANY THERMAL CONTROL SURFACES MUST RESIST ROLLING ABRASION AND FLEXING; HOWEVER, THIS IS AN EXCELLENT DESIGN TO MINIMIZE THERMAL DEFLECTIONS. MINIMUM DEPLOYMENT/RETRACTION PROBLEMS ARE ANTICIPATED. LINEAR DYNAMIC SYSTEM, FULL-BEAM STRENGTH COULD BE DEVELOPED AS THE BEAM EXTENDS. VERY COMPACT STOWAGE.
BOEING CO., KENT, WASH / ASTRO RESEARCH CORP. SANTA BARBARA, CALIFORNIA	TRADE NAME MAST; DEVELOPMENTAL MODEL 20-FT LONG; FABRICATED AND TESTED BY BOEING. A DEVELOPMENTAL MODEL (20-FT LONG 2.3 IN. DIA) HAS BEEN DELIVERED TO MARTIN MARIETTA FOR EVALUATION. RYAN AERONAUTICAL CO. NO LONGER MANUFACTURES THIS BOOM AND MUCH OF THE RYAN TECHNOLOGY HAS BEEN ASSUMED BY THE ASTRO RESEARCH CORP.	LINEAR DYNAMIC SYSTEM, VERY COMPACT STOWAGE, BOOM, DEVELOPS FULL STRENGTH AS IT IS DEPLOYED. THIS BEAM IS GOOD FOR MEDIUM LENGTH APPLICATIONS (LESS THAN 50 FT). AS LENGTH INCREASES THE BEAM BECOMES INEFFICIENT FOR COLUMN LOADS. THE MOMENT OF INERTIA OF THE BEAM SECTION MAY BE INCREASED IN ONE DIRECTION WITH VERYLITTLE EFFECT ON STOWAGE VOLUME OR STRESSES. WELDED JOINTS SIMPLIFY THERMAL ANALYSIS. HOLE PATTERN PROBABLY REQUIRED, THERMAL COATINGS MUST WITHSTAND ROLLING ABRASION. THIS AND SIMILAR BEAMS COULD HAVE A THERMAL COMPENSATING CURVE BUILT IN.
LOCKHEED MISSILES & SPACE COMPANY, SUNNYVALE, CALIFORNIA	TWO GENERATIONS OF ENGINEERING MODELS HAVE BEEN BUILT AND DEMONSTRATED. SEVERAL BEAM SECTIONS HAVE BEEN FABRICATED AND SUBJECTED TO STRUCTURAL AND THERMAL TESTS.	HIGH DYNAMIC DAMPING, FAIRLY COMPACT STOWAGE. FOR MEDIUM LENGTH THIS IS A GOOD SELECTION. AS THE LENGTH APPROACHES 50 FT THE TRIBEAM BECOMES INEFFICIENT FOR SIGNIFICANT COLUMN LOADS. REQUIRES HOLES TO MINIMIZE THERMAL DEFLECTION. INSIDE AND OUTSIDE REQUIRE ROLLING ABRASION RESISTANT THERMAL COATINGS. POOR THERMAL CONDUCTION THROUGH THE VELCRO TAPES SHOULD CAUSE NO MAJOR PROBLEMS, IF ADEQUATE HOLE PATTERN IS USED, ESPECIALLY WHEN USED WITH A CONSTANT SUN ANGLE.
SANDERS ASSOCIATES INC. NOSHAU, N.H.	TWO GENERATIONS OF ENGINEERING MODELS HAVE BEEN BUILT, TESTED AND DEMONSTRATED. BEAM MATERIAL FULL HARD 302 STAINLESS STEEL, 40 FT LONG BY APPROX. 3 BY 4 INCHES CROSS SECTION.	LINEAR DYNAMIC SYSTEM, FAIRLY COMPACT STOWAGE. AGAIN A MEDIUM-LENGTH BEAM CANDIDATE. HIGH R/T RATIOS IN THE CURVED SHEETS AND HIGH B/T RATIO ON FLAT SHEET LIMIT THE COLUMN LOAD CAPACI. NOT LIKELY EFFICIENT IN LENGTHS GREATER THAN 50 FT. THE BEAM MOMENT OF INERTIA CAN BE INCREASED IN ONE DIRECTION WITH LITTLE EFFECT ON STOWAGE VOLUME OR STRESSES. SUBJECT TO LARGE THERMAL DEFLECTIONS IF CENTER IS SOLID. TEMPERATURE GRADIENTS DIFFICULT TO PREDICT BECAUSE OF UNCERTAINTY IN EDGE CONTACTS AND COMPLEX INNER STRUCTURE. HOLES MAY BE REQUIRED IN ALL THREE TAPES.
SPAR AEROSPAGE PRODUCTS LTD. ONTARIO, CANADA / FAIRCHILD HILLER, GERMANTOWN, MD.	TRADE NAME INTERLOCKED BI STEM. TWO INCH DIA MODEL COMPLETED AND DEMONSTRATED. STUDIES IN MATERIAL AND LARGER DIA MODELS. TRADE NAMES, EDGELOCK AND HINGELOCK TE. A SIX INCH DIA MODEL COMPLETED AND DEMONSTRATED. A TWO INCH MODEL IN NON-MAGNETIC STAINLESS STEEL COMPLETED FOR NASA, GODDARD CONTAINS 22 CONDUCTORS.	LINEAR DYNAMIC SYSTEM, VERY COMPACT STOWAGE. THIS BEAM (CONSIDERED AS A SOLID TUBE) IS GOOD FOR SHORT TO MEDIUM LENGTH APPLICATIONS (LESS THAN 50 FT). AS LENGTH INCREASES THE BEAM BECOMES INEFFICIENT FOR COLUMN LOADS. TEMPERATURE PREDICTION UNCERTAINTY IS INCREASED IF THE SUN DOES NOT SHINE SYMMETRICALLY ON THE INTERLOCKING LINE. HOLE PATTERN MAY BE REQUIRED TO OBTAIN REASONABLE THERMAL DEFLECTIONS. ROLL ABRASION RESISTANT THERMAL COATINGS ARE REQUIRED.

Table 7-8. (*Continued*)

NO. & NAME OF EXTENDIBLE STRUCTURE	ILLUSTRATION	DESCRIPTION & OPERATION OF STRUCTURE & MECHANISM (RETRACTION CAPABILITIES)	FLIGHT EXPERIENCE
16 EXTENDIBLE REEL STORED		PRE-FORMED SPRING TAPE (OR TAPES) ARE FLATTENED AND ROLLED UP ON A REEL FOR STOWAGE. THESE ARE THE SIMPLEST OF THE REEL STORED BEAMS. THE REEL IS ROTATED BY AN ELECT. MOTOR & GEAR TRAIN. RETRACTION IS ACCOMPLISHED BY REVERSING MOTOR.	USED AS ANTENNA, GRAVITY GRADIENT BOOMS, ACTUATORS, ETC. APOLLO, ATS, DODGE, MARINER AND MANY MORE SPACECRAFT APPLICATIONS. USED AS ANTENNAS, GRAVITY GRADIENT BOOMS ETC. ON RAE, OGO, NIMBUS & OTHERS. UNKNOWN. UNKNOWN. UNKNOWN.
17 SPRING HELIX		TUBE IS FORMED BY A HELICALLY PRE-STRESSED SPRING TAPE WHOSE OVERLAPPING COILS FORM A RIGID TUBE WHEN EXTENDED. MAY BE SELF-EXTENDING OR MOTOR DRIVEN. THE MOTOR DRIVE CONTROLS DEPLOYMENT SPEED AND PERMITS REMOTE RETRACTION.	USED TO ERECT FOIL SUNSHIELD OF CENTRAL CONTROL STATION ON APOLLO LUNAR SURFACE EXPERIMENTS PACKAGE.
18 INFLATABLES		GAS TIGHT TUBES (MYLAR, FOIL, MYLAR) ARE FLATTENED AND FOLDED FOR STORAGE; AN EXTERNAL GAS SUPPLY INFLATES AND ERECTS (AND REMOVES THE WRINKLES) THE TUBES. THE ALUM. FOIL SANDWICHED IN MYLAR THEN IS A THIN-WALLED TUBE AND LENDS ITSELF TO ANALYSIS. GAS PRESSURE IS RELIEVED WHEN THE SYSTEM REACHES EQUILIBRIUM. MAY BE USED AS A MULTIPLE-TUBE SYSTEM STIFFENED BY SPACERS AND GUY WIRES. ARE USUALLY NOT RETRACTABLE.	SEVERAL LOOP ANTENNAS, 6 TO 9 FT DIA, WERE FLOWN ON THE OGO SERIES (STANFORD UNIVERSITY EXPERIMENTS). ALL WERE SINGLE TUBES 1 TO 2 IN. DIA. A MECHANISM CONTAINING A COLUMN OF MULTIPLE TUBES 10 FT LONG WAS SUCCESSFULLY DEMONSTRATED ON CLASSIFIED MISSIONS.
19 RIGIDIZED INFLATABLES		TWO SYSTEMS ARE SHOWN: (A) A SOLID CORE OF RIGID FOAM IS FORMED INSIDE A FABRIC FORM WHILE RESTRAINED BY A DIE. THE PRESSURE OF THE FOAM FEEDS IN THE FABRIC FORM AS THE RIGID FOAM IS FORCED OUT THE OPPOSITE END; (B) PRE-TREATED GELATINE-GLASS FIBER LAMINATED TUBES MADE FLEXIBLE WITH A SOFTENING AGENT. THE TUBES ARE GAS-INFLATED IN SPACE AND THE SOFTENING AGENT EVAPORATES, LEAVING THE TUBES STIFF. COMPLETE RIGIDITY IS ACHIEVED IN 10 TO 20 HOURS. IS NOT RETRACTABLE.	FLIGHT EXPERIENCE UNKNOWN FLIGHT EXPERIENCE UNKNOWN FLIGHT EXPERIENCE UNKNOWN
20 FLEXIBLE TETHER		CYLINDRICAL SECTIONS WITH SPHERICAL SEATS ON EACH END, ALTERNATE WITH BALLS; ENTIRE ASSEMBLY HAS CENTER HOLE TO ACCEPT FLEXIBLE TENSION MEMBER. THE TENSION MEMBER IS FIXED TO ONE END; TENSION REACTED AGAINST THE OPPOSITE END CAUSES THE LOOSE PARTS TO ALIGN AND FORM A STRAIGHT COLUMN (THE SHORTEST LENGTH OF CABLE).	FLIGHT EXPERIENCE UNKNOWN FLIGHT EXPERIENCE UNKNOWN

Table 7-9. Most Favored Boom Types.

Boom Type	Solar Array/ Satellite Program	Array Type	Notes
Extendible reel storage	• CRC/CTS	Foldout flexible	
	• Hughes/FRUSA	Rollup flexible	
	• AEG/ROSA	Rollup flexible	Bistem
	• AEG/DORA	Rollup flexible	
	• GE/JPL 30 W/LB	Rollup flexible	
Articulated lattice mast	• LMSC Space Station	Foldout flexible	
	• GE/JPL 50 W/LB	Foldout flexible	Astromast
Telescoping cylinder	• RAE	Foldout flexible	
	• X4 Satellite	Foldout flexible	
Folding beam	• Skylab, Orbital Workshop	Foldout rigid	
Lazy tongs	• Skylab, Apollo Telescope Mount	Foldout rigid	
Pantograph	• SNIAS	Foldout flexible	

SOURCE	DEVELOPMENT WORK	GENERAL DESIGN COMMENTS
SPAR AEROSPACE PRODUCTS LTD. ONTARIO, CANADA	TRADE NAME STEM AND BI STEM (STORABLE TUBULAR EXTENDIBLE MEMBER). SELF–ERECTING MODEL THAT IS STOWED BY COILING INSIDE A CYLINDER IS CALLED "JACK–IN–THE–BOX".	LINEAR DYNAMIC SYSTEM, VERY COMPACT STOWAGE, LOW TORSIONAL STIFF-NESS. AS ABOVE, INEFFICIENT IN LONGER LENGTHS. TEMPERATURE PREDICTION IS MORE DIFFICULT BECAUSE THE JOINT THERMAL CONDUCTANCE IS UNLIKELY TO BE REPEATABLE. HOLE PATTERN MAY BE REQUIRED TO OBTAIN REASONABLE THERMAL DEFLECTIONS. ROLL ABRASION RESISTANT THERMAL COATINGS REQUIRED.
FAIRCHILD HILLER GERMANTOWN, MD.	TRADE NAME TEE (TUBULAR EXTENDIBLE ELEMENTS) A DOUBLE MODEL WITH A CROSS-SECTION RESEMBLING THE FIGURE 8 FABRICATED AND DEMONSTRATED.	
GENERAL ELECTRIC CORP. MSD, VALLEY FORGE, PA.	TRADE NAME MOLY ROD	
GENERAL DYNAMICS/CONVAIR DIV., SAN DIEGO, CA WESTINGHOUSE DEFENSE & SPACE CENTER, AEROSPACE DIV. BALTIMORE, MD.	TRADE NAME SCREEN BOOM	
AMETEK/HUNTER SPRING CO. HATFIELD PA.	TRADE NAME STACER, TWIN MOTOR-DRIVEN STACERS WERE USED TO EXTEND A NASA EXPERIMENTAL SOLAR ARRAY APPROX. 9 FT.	VERY COMPACT STOWAGE, VERY LOW AXIAL AND TORSIONAL STIFFNESS, COLUMN LOAD CAPACITY, LATERAL AND TORSIONAL STIFFNESS DEPEND ON FRICTIONAL FORCES EXISTING BETWEEN OVERLAPPING LAYERS. NO RELIABLE METHOD OF ANALYSIS HAS BEEN ESTABLISHED. STIFFNESS WILL BE DERIVED MAINLY BY TESTS. ROLL ABRASION–RESISTANT THERMAL COATINGS REQUIRED. MATERIAL CONTINUITY AND THE RESULTING SPIRAL THERMAL CONDUCTANCE PROBABLY RESULTS IN LOWER THERMAL DEFLECTIONS THAN A NON CONTINUOUS TUBE SECTION.
LOCKHEED M.S.C. SUNNYVALE, CALIFORNIA		HIGH DAMPING; PROBABLY A NON-LINEAR SYSTEM; VERY COMPACT STOWAGE. STRENGTH AND STIFFNESS VARY GREATLY AS THE STRUCTURE IS FOLDED MORE OR LESS, I.E., THE WRINKLED CONDITION OF THE FOIL. EMPIRICAL RESOLUTION MUST BE USED TO ESTABLISH FOLDING TECHNIQUES AND LIMITS. MYLAR DE-GRADES WHEN EXPOSED TO U.V., SO A PROTECTIVE COATING MUST BE USED. LARGE FRONT-TO-BACK TEMP. GRADIENTS ARE LIKELY, PARTICULARLY IF MULTI-PLE TUBE SYSTEM IS USED. ADHESION OF THERMAL CONTROL SURFACE TO THE MYLAR MAY BE DIFFICULT TO ACHIEVE.
GOODYEAR AEROSPACE CORP. AKRON, OHIO	DEVELOPED A SERIES OF INFLATABLE RIGIDIZED STRUCTURES FOR AERO PROPULSION LAB. USING DACRON FABRIC RIGI-DIZED BY EXPOSING A URETHANE RESIN TO MOISTURE IN THE INFLATING SYSTEM.	HIGH DAMPING, LINEAR SYSTEM, CONVENIENT STOWAGE SYSTEM. FOAM MATERIALS HAVE A VERY LOW YOUNG'S MODULUS. TO MAKE UP THAT DEFICIENCY, A LARGE AMOUNT OF FOAM MUST BE PROVIDED, THEREIN DEFEAT-ING THE ADVANTAGE OF USING A LOW DENSITY MATERIAL. LARGE FRONT-TO-BACK THERMAL GRADIENTS ARE LIKELY. THERMAL CONTROL SURFACE APPLICA-TION MAY BE A PROBLEM.
LOCKHEED M.S.C. SUNNYVALE, CALIFORNIA	DEVELOPED FOR NASA AN ORBITAL ESCAPE DEVICE USING IMPREGNATED FIBERGLASS THAT HARDENED BY APPLICATION OF HEAT OR VACUUM.	
MESSERSCHMITT–BOLKOW–BLOHM GMBH, MUNICH, GERMANY	DEVELOPED A RIGIDIZED STRUCTURE TO SUPPORT A 215 SQ FT SOLAR ARRAY. USES GELETINE-GLASS TUBES AND INFLATION SYSTEM EVAPORATES THE SOFTENING AGENT.	
GENERAL ELECTRIC MSD VALLEY FORGE, PA.	WORKING MODELS HAVE BEEN DEMONSTRATED ON THE GROUND AND UNDER WATER WITHOUT ANY REPORTED PROBLEMS.	POOR STORAGE CHARACTERISTICS (THE STOWED VOLUME IS EQUAL TO THE EX-TENDED VOLUME). THE TETHER REQUIRES THE CONCENTRATION OF MASS TO BE NEAR THE CENTER OF THE BEAM, RESULTING IN A POOR STRUCTURE FOR STIFF-NESS. THERMAL DEFLECTIONS ARE DEPENDENT UPON MATERIAL AND THICKNESS OF STRUCTURE.
ILLINOIS INSTITUTE OF TECHNOLOGY, MECHANICAL ENGINEERING DIV. CHICAGO, ILL.	DEVELOPED A COLLAPSIBLE CANE THAT WORKS ON THIS PRINCIPLE.	

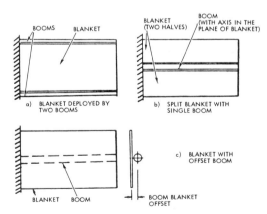

Fig. 7-55. Different arrangements for deployable solar cell arrays.

FLTSATCOM Array. This solar array structure was described in Section 7-11. The array consisted of two deployable wings attached to the spacecraft through a hinged boom. Each wing consisted of three panels. In the launch configuration, the six panels were folded around the six sides of the spacecraft. Pyrotechnic devices were used to secure the panels during the launch and release them upon command. Hinge fittings were incorporated at three locations for each panel.

The array deployment sequence was composed of two discrete events. (See Fig. 7-32 from Section 7-11). Outer panel release was accomplished by actuation of four sets of redundant bolt cutters. Deployment springs at each panel hinge actuated the outer panels to deploy 60° to form a plane with the center panel of each wing. Spring latches were incorporated at the hinges to provide structural latch-up of the panels (see Fig. 7-56). When the outer panels were latched, the two wings were released to deploy by the force from actuator compression springs that were incorporated at the boom hinges, located at both ends of the boom (one at the base of the array wing, the other at the solar cell array drive/spacecraft sidewall interface, as shown in Fig. 7-57). The boom and array panels of each wing were

Table 7-10. Blanket/Boom Arrangement in Developmental Arrays or Satellite Programs.

Program	Blanket Type	Boom Type (no. per wing)	Blanket/Boom Arrangement
CRC/CTS	Foldout	Bistem (1)	Single/Offset
Hughes/FRUSA	Rollout	Bistem (2)	Single/In-plane
AEG/ROSA	Rollout	Bistem (2)	Single/In-plane
AEG/DORA	Rollout	Bistem (2)	Single/In-plane
GE/JPL 30 W/LB	Rollout	Bistem (1)	Split/In-plane
LMSC/Space Station	Foldout	Astromast (1)	Split/In-plane
GE/JPL 50 W/LB	Foldout	Astromast (1)	Split/In-plane
RAE	Foldout	Telescoping (1)	Split/In-plane
X4 Satellite	Foldout	Telescoping (1)	Split/In-plane
Skylab ATM	Foldout	Lazy Tong (2)	Single/In-plane
Skylab OWS	Foldout	Folding Beam (2)	Single/Offset
SNIAS	Foldout	Pantograph (1)	Single/Offset

kinematically constrained to deploy symmetrically through the use of a constraining cable and pulley mechanism that passed along the length of the boom.

Matra Array. This solar cell array design, described in Section 7-13, consisted of four rigid substrate panels and a yoke that were flat-packed and prestressed against the spacecraft wall by a spring-loaded rod (see Fig. 7-58).

Two hinges on each hinge line carried the pulley of the deployment linkage constraint mechanism. Also located along the hinge edge

of the panels (but separate from the hinges) were two torsion spring fittings, as shown in Figs. 7-59 and 7-60. Upon activation of the array hold-down system, the panels deployed outward through the stored energy in the spring fittings.

The deployment was controlled through the use of a direct linkage between the relative motions of each hinge line, thus reducing the deployment to a one-degree-of-freedom process (see Figs. 7-60 and 7-61). The linkage system, comprised of a pulley and a belt, was attached along alternate sides of adjacent panels. A spring

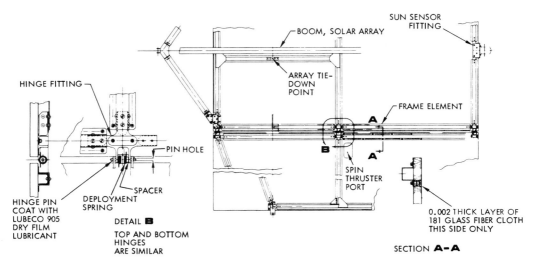

Fig. 7-56. FLTSATCOM spring hinge configuration. (*Courtesy of TRW, Inc.*)

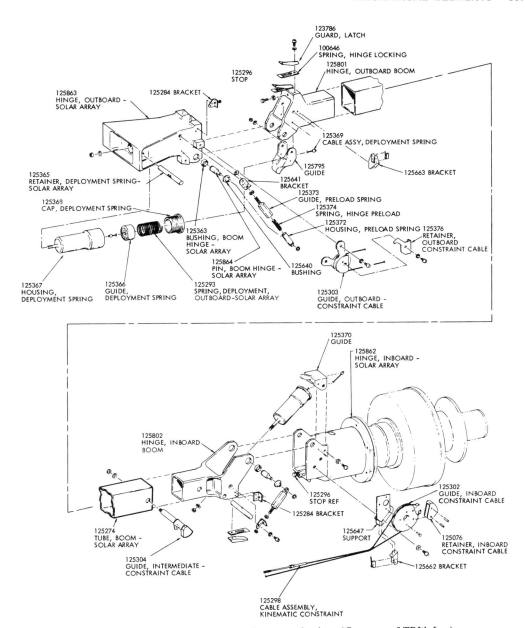

123786
GUARD, LATCH

100646
SPRING, HINGE LOCKING

125801
HINGE, OUTBOARD BOOM

125296
STOP

125284 BRACKET

125863
HINGE, OUTBOARD -
SOLAR ARRAY

125369
CABLE ASSY, DEPLOYMENT SPRING

125795
GUIDE

125663 BRACKET

125641
BRACKET

125373
GUIDE, PRELOAD SPRING

125374
SPRING, HINGE PRELOAD

125372
HOUSING, PRELOAD SPRING

125376
RETAINER,
OUTBOARD
CONSTRAINT CABLE

125365
RETAINER, DEPLOYMENT SPRING-
SOLAR ARRAY

125368
CAP, DEPLOYMENT SPRING

125363
BUSHING, BOOM
HINGE -
SOLAR ARRAY

125864
PIN, BOOM HINGE -
SOLAR ARRAY

125640
BUSHING

125367
HOUSING,
DEPLOYMENT SPRING

125366
GUIDE,
DEPLOYMENT SPRING

125293
SPRING, DEPLOYMENT,
OUTBOARD-SOLAR ARRAY

125303
GUIDE, OUTBOARD -
CONSTRAINT CABLE

125370
GUIDE

125862
HINGE, INBOARD -
SOLAR ARRAY

125802
HINGE, INBOARD
BOOM

125296
STOP REF

125284 BRACKET

125302
GUIDE, INBOARD
CONSTRAINT CABLE

125274
TUBE, BOOM -
SOLAR ARRAY

125647
SUPPORT

125076
RETAINER, INBOARD
CONSTRAINT CABLE

125304
GUIDE, INTERMEDIATE -
CONSTRAINT CABLE

125662 BRACKET

125298
CABLE ASSEMBLY,
KINEMATIC CONSTRAINT

Fig. 7-57. FLTSATCOM deployment boom mechanism. (*Courtesy of TRW, Inc.*)

with a tension adjustor was included in the linkage system to compensate for thermal expansion effects.

ICS and ULP Arrays. These arrays are similar in configuration to the Matra array. The deployment mechanisms are also similar. The deployment energy was provided by small spiral springs located at each hinge. The springs were integral parts of the hinges. The deployment was force controlled by a closed cable loop system to provide directional control and redundancy. The cable loop system prevented backlash of the interhinged panels and collision with the spacecraft. This forced control reduced the complex multiple panel array

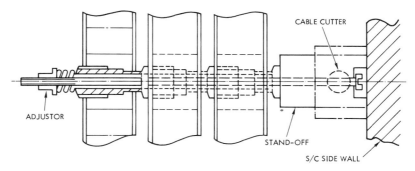

Fig. 7-58. MATRA hold-down system. (*Reprinted with permission of the Centre National d'Etudes Spatiales.*[43])

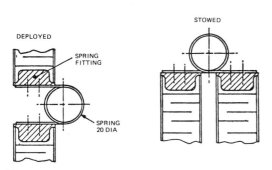

Fig. 7-59. MATRA deployment springs and fittings. (*Reprinted with permission of the Centre National d'Etudes Spatiales.*[43])

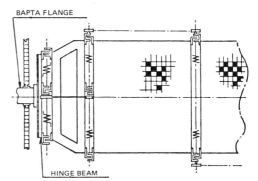

Fig. 7-60. MATRA deployment mechanisms. (*Reprinted with permission of the Centre National d'Etudes Spatiales.*[43])

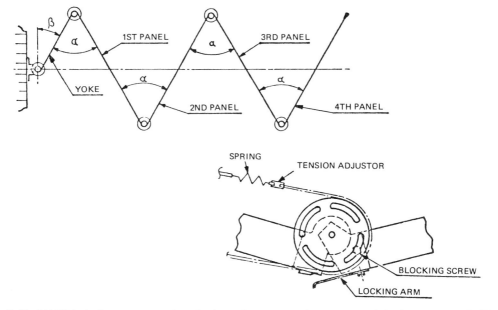

Fig. 7-61. MATRA deployment control mechanism. (*Reprinted with permission of the Centre National d'Etudes Spatiales.*[43])

to a one-degree-of-freedom system. Upon full deployment, the panels latched up through a leaf spring/cam arrangement at each hinge location. No damping devices were required because the final latch-up shock could be absorbed by the array structure.

ORIENTATION DRIVES

7-20. Orientation Mechanisms

To achieve a sun-tracking capability, an electromechanical subsystem is required to continuously keep the solar array properly oriented with the sun line and to transfer the electrical power generated by the arrays to the satellite power conditioning subsystem. Thus, it is comprised of two distinct components that are integral with one another—a motorized drive system and an electrical power transfer system. As a structural system, it must also provide the mechanical interface and structural support for the solar arrays and for the various components, such as bearings, slip rings, gears, motor, etc.

A solar cell array drive assembly is also known as a SADA. An orientation drive and power transfer mechanism is known as an ODAPT. ODAPT/SADA's have been designed with and without a sun sensor as part of the control loop. In the former, a signal from the sun sensor causes the drive system to be activated. In the latter design, once the array is initially locked onto the sun, the rotation is controlled by a clock/stepper motor arrangement which rotates the array automatically a finite increment over a finite time interval.

Solar Cell Array Drive Systems. A drive system is defined as a unit having a motor to supply rotational power, slip rings, or power transfer cables for taking electrical power across the rotating joint, and several sets of bearings to maintain proper alignment of the various mechanical parts.

A variety of drive systems have been employed in existing satellite designs. Most systems are between 5 cm and 15 cm in diameter and are designed in such a way that the satellite structure is wrapped around the drive system. Approximately 50% of the systems developed

provide full rotation, while the remaining provide limited rotation from $0°$ to $360°$.

Most of the motors used have been brushless motors, either ac servo, dc stepper, or dc torque. Brush motors have also been used (i.e., OSO and TACSAT). Motors for other programs drive through gears which produce overall gear ratios for their respective drive systems ranging from $1:1$ to $10^6:1$.

Either deep groove radial and/or preloaded angular contact ball bearings have been the preferred choice for bearings. Roller bearings usually require more torque to drive than do ball bearings because they make line contact. Roller bearings are also more susceptible to skewing loads caused by built-in misalignments which increase the torque losses and reduce bearing life. Most ball bearings are constructed from 440C stainless steel rings and balls. In most of the previously flown satellites, lubrication is self-contained within the bearings.

Power Transfer Assemblies. The design of the power transfer system and the selection of materials will be influenced by the current/voltage ratio used by the satellite. Dielectric properties of the electrical insulation will be more important for the high voltage system, but the high current system will require heavier conductors and larger contacts (and more power will be consumed in overcoming the greater frictional drag). Electrical heating due to contact resistance in brushes and conductors will result in power loss and cause brushes to run hotter. The higher operating temperature in the brushes will affect the choice of lubricant.

Almost all satellites that require continuous rotation arrays use slip rings, while flex cables are used where limited rotation is acceptable. Other devices considered include rotary transformers, rolling contacts, and liquid metal slip rings. A variety of slip ring configurations have been used, including V-groove rings, U-groove rings, and drum rings with wire brushes, and drum rings and disk rings with button brushes.

The ring is silver or gold plated copper or other suitable base material. Button type brushes are made from a composite material containing silver, copper, and graphite, with a suitable lubricant such as molybdenum disulfide

(MoS$_2$). Wire brushes are made from some precious metal. Factors critical in brush design include current density, temperature, and acceptable wear rates.

Lubrication. Lubrication is required in two areas: for bearings, gears, and other mechanical devices; and for electrical brushes and contacts. The absence of oxygen and water vapor requires that lubricants be specifically incorporated into brush compositions to prevent rapid brush wear; and the hard vacuum of space limits the selection of bearing and gear lubricants to low volatility oils and greases and to solid films and self-lubricating solids.

GE Versilube and BBRC Vac Kote oils and greases have been widely used in satellite bearing designs. Solid films have been successfully used when limited to slow speed or intermittently operated mechanisms. Oil lubricants must be provided with reservoirs for application to long-term vacuum. The purpose is to maintain the atmosphere of oil molecules in the vicinity of the parts so that the net loss of lubricant to space vacuum is from the reservoirs rather than from the impregnated materials. Oil type lubricants mean potential contamination problems due to evaporation and thus more complex sealing designs must be employed with them than with solid lubricants.

In terms of solid lubricants, molybdenum disulfide (MoS$_2$) or niobium diselenide (NbSe$_2$) are used. The latter has the advantage of also being a good conductor. Graphite, normally used in atmospheric applications, loses its lubricating qualities in a space vacuum. Evaporation loss from solid lubricants is negligible, and therefore, no reservoir system is required.

7-21. Stepping Drive Example

This design example of a solar array drive assembly (SADA) is related to the FLTSATCOM array described earlier. Figure 7-62 shows the layout. The assembly consists of two identical drive units which are connected in tandem for redundant operation. Each drive unit consists of a 1.8°/step stepper motor (four-phase, permanent magnet, inductor-type), which is coupled to the input of a harmonic drive reducer. The harmonic drive ratio is 100:1, which results in an output step size of 0.018°/step. The motor is operated by sequential energization of one phase at a time, and at normal speed, the excitation has a pulse width of 100 milliseconds, occurring every 4.32 seconds. The drive unit on the spacecraft side is the primary drive. Its housing is mounted to the spacecraft and is non-rotating. The housing of the secondary drive is the output

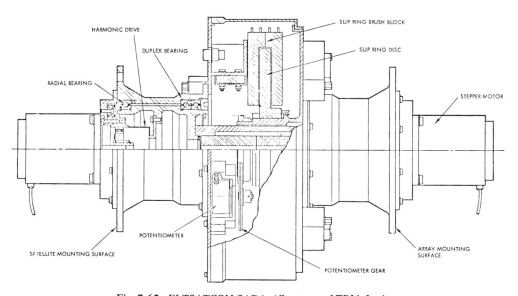

Fig. 7-62. FLTSATCOM SADA. (*Courtesy of TRW, Inc.*)

member and rotates with respect to the primary drive housing, whether driven by the primary or secondary motor.

In normal operation, the primary drive is used and its harmonic drive is used in the conventional manner; i.e., wave generator input, circular spline stationary, and flexspline output. The primary drive flexspline output drives into the flexspline of the secondary drive via a connecting shaft. In effect, the secondary drive is back-driven by the primary drive, but the rotating interface between the shaft (flexspline) and housing (circular spline) of the secondary drive is held against rotation by the detent torque of the motor. Thus, in normal operation, the secondary drive is carried on the output shaft of the primary drive and revolves as a unit.

When the secondary drive operates, its harmonic drive is used with the wave generator as the input, the flexspline stationary, and the circular spline as the output. The flexspline is held stationary by the detent holding capability of the primary drive. Thus, in secondary drive operation, its shaft (flexspline), the connecting shaft, and the primary drive shaft (flexspline) are held stationary with the primary drive housing, and only the housing of the secondary drive rotates.

The drive unit shaft is supported in the housing with a duplex pair of ball bearings at one end and a single radial bearing at the other end. The duplex pair is clamped axially in the housing and on the shaft while the radial bearing is unconstrained axially in the housing to accommodate axial thermal expansion. The duplex pair is in back-to-back arrangement for maximum moment rigidity. The shafts and housings are made from titanium alloy to minimize the differential expansion between them and the steel bearings (440C), so that changes in internal fit-up due to temperature excursion and subsequent internal loads in the bearings and friction torques will be minimized.

Other structural parts, specifically the cylindrical enclosure for the slip ring assembly in the middle of the drive, are made of 2024 aluminum alloy. The external surface of the SADA is painted black for high thermal emissive property.

Rolling and sliding parts of the electromechanical parts are lubricated with NPT-4. Lubri-cant loss through the running gap of the slip ring enclosure is replenished from Nylasint reservoirs impregnated with NPT-4 oil. These are mounted in several locations throughout the assembly. The internal surfaces of the assembly are lightly coated with NPT-4 during the assembly process to provide an additional source of lubricant. Also, all the bearings—the main support bearings and those within the rotating components—have phenolic laminate retainers which are vacuum impregnated with NPT-4 oil.

A disk type of slip ring assembly is mounted between the rotating interface of the two drive housings. The brush block assembly is mounted on the primary drive housing, and the slip ring disk is on the secondary drive housing. The slip ring assembly contains 36 signal rings (18 on each face of the disk) and two power rings (one on each face) which are equivalent to four power rings, each capable of carrying 30 A. All circuits have redundant brushes. The signal circuits consist of precious metal wire brushes riding in V-groove rings. The base material of the rings is copper, nickel plated, and covered by a thin layer of hard gold.

Two single-turn potentiometers are mounted on the stationary side of the slip ring enclosure. Anti-backlash gears on the potentiometer shafts are geared off the slip ring shaft with a 1:1 ratio. The potentiometers contain a conductive plastic resistive element, which is lightly coated with NPT-4 lubricant.

The SADA weighs 6.8 kg and is capable of transferring approximately 1.1 kW of power from the solar cell array to the power conditioning unit.

7-22. Continuous Drive Example

The Nimbus II SADA is shown in Fig. 7-63. The assembly consists of a motor gearhead unit, a potentiometer unit, and a subassembly unit containing a clutch, output shaft, and gearing. The motor of the motor gearhead unit is a Size 11, two-phase, 26 V, 400 Hz ac servo motor; it drives a 12,121:1 gear ratio, seven pass straight spur gear train in the gearhead section. All bearings and gear meshes of the motor gearhead are lubricated at assembly with G-300

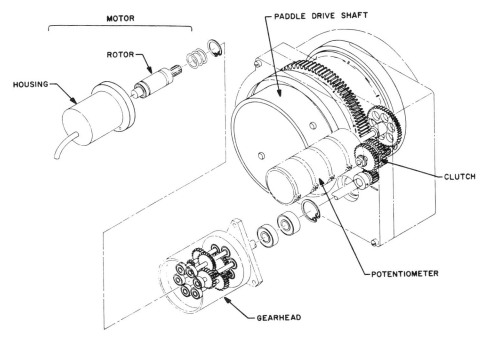

Fig. 7-63. Nimbus II SADA. (*Courtesy of JPL.*)

silicone grease. A Nylasint reservoir in the motor cover is impregnated at assembly with F50 silicone oil. The output gear of the motor gearhead drives a 7:1 spur gear reduction train in the housing subassembly unit and is connected to the output shaft. A ball-detent face clutch is provided in this gear train to protect the motor gearhead from injury by back-driving from the shaft end. Four stacked Belleville-Washer type springs load the ball detent faces. The nominal clutch slip torque is 123 cm · N. All parts in this subassembly are lubricated with G-300 silicone grease and a Nylasint reservoir is impregnated with F50 silicone oil. The potentiometer unit is mounted to the housing subassembly and contains four wire-wound potentiometer cups. It is driven by a 1:1 gear train from the output shaft independent of the clutch. The potentiometer bearings are also lubricated with G-300 grease; the wiper and windings are unlubricated noble metals. The assembly, weighing approximately 2.3 kg, has an overall gear ratio of 84,847:1. The nominal output torque is 367 cm · N—over five times greater than the anticipated required torque of 64 cm · N (90 inch · ounces). All ball bearings, of R2, R3, and R4 size, utilize 440C stainless steel balls and races in ribbon retainers.

REFERENCES

1. Technical Information on Sharp Solar Battery Power Supply System, Sharp Corp., Osaka, Japan.
2. J. W. Stultz and L. C. Wen, "Thermal Performance Testing and Analysis of Photovoltaic Modules in Natural Sunlight," JPL Report **5101-31,** July 1977.
3. *Proceedings of the ERDA Semiannual Solar Photovoltaic Program Review Meeting,* Silicon Technology Programs Branch, January 1977, **CONF-770112,** California University, San Diego, California.
4. *Records of the "First Project Integration Meeting, Photovoltaic Concentrator Technology Development Project,"* Denver, Colorado, March 1978, Sandia Laboratory Report No. **SAND 78-0374.**
5. *Records of the 12th IEEE Photovoltaic Specialists Conference,* November 1976.
6. W. Alsbach and H. Lösch (p. 430) in *Records of the 12th IEEE Photovoltaic Specialists Conference,* November 1976.
7. *Conference Records of the 9th IEEE Photovoltaic Specialists Conference,* 1972.
8. N. B. North and D. F. Baker (p. 263) in *Conference Records of the 9th IEEE Photovoltaic Specialists Conference,* 1972.
9. Based on Miscellaneous and Previously Unpublished Data from TRW DSSG, TRW Inc.
10. *Proceedings of the Section "The Photovoltaic Power and its Applications in Space and on Earth,"* International Congress, "The Sun in the Service of Mankind," Paris, France, July 1973.

11. H. Larsson (p. 261) and W. Palz (p. 45) in *Proceedings of the Section "The Photovoltaic Power and its Applications in Space and on Earth,"* International Congress, "The Sun in the Service of Mankind," Paris, France, July 1973.

12. *Records of the 13th IEEE Photovoltaic Specialists Conference*, June 1978.

13. H. S. Rauschenbach *et al* (p. 232) in *Proceedings of the 13th IEEE Photovoltaic Specialists Conference*, June 1978.

14. *Proceedings of the 13th Intersociety Energy Conversion Engineering Conference*, August 1978.

15. F. G. Kelly *et al* (p. 118) in *Proceedings of the 13th Intersociety Energy Conversion Engineering Conference*, August 1978.

16. H. N. McKinney and D. C. Briggs (p. 4) in *Proceedings of the 13th Intersociety Energy Conversion Engineering Conference*, August 1978.

17. D. C. Briggs *et al* (p. 110) in *Proceedings of the 13th Intersociety Energy Conversion Engineering Conference*, August 1978.

18. *AIAA/CASI 6th Communications Satellite Systems Conference*, Montreal, Canada, April 1976.

19. D. E. Koelle and H. von Bassewitz in *AIAA/CASI 6th Communications Satellite Systems Conference*, Montreal, Canada, April 1976.

20. H. von Bassewitz and K. Schneider (p. 2131) in *Proceedings of the 13th Intersociety Energy Conversion Engineering Conference*, August 1978.

21. G. Barkats and M. Calvy (p. 124) in *Proceedings of the 13th Intersociety Energy Conversion Engineering Conference*, August 1978.

22. J. V. Gore and S. Bay (p. 449) in *Proceedings of the 12th IEEE Photovoltaic Specialists Conference*, November 1976.

23. T. D. Harrison *et al* (p. 1387) in *Proceedings of the 11th Intersociety Energy Conversion Engineering Conference*, September 1976.

24. *Proceedings of the 11th Intersociety Energy Conversion Engineering Conference*, September 1976.

25. R. V. Elms, Jr. (p. 208) in *Proceedings of the 13th IEEE Photovoltaic Specialists Conference*, June 1978.

26. R. V. Elms, Jr. and L. E. Young (p. 1372) in *Proceedings of the 11th Intersociety Energy Conversion Engineering Conference*, September 1976.

27. E. O. Felkel, G. Wolff, *et al.* "Flexible Rolled-up Solar Array," AFALPL-TR-72-61, June 30, 1972.

28. H. Bebermeier *et al* (p. 418) in *Proceedings of the 12th IEEE Photovoltaic Specialists Conference*, November 1976.

29. I. V. Franklin and C. J. H. Williams (p. 221) in *Records of the 13th IEEE Photovoltaic Specialists Conference*, June 1978.

30. C. J. H. Williams and I. V. Franklin (p. 226) in *Proceedings of the 13th IEEE Photovoltaic Specialists Conference*, June 1978.

31. H. Borduas *et al* (p. 137) in *Proceedings of the 13th Intersociety Energy Conversion Engineering Conference*, August 1978.

32. *Proceedings, Photovoltaic Power Generation Conference*, Hamburg, Germany, 1974.

33. W. Luft in *Proceedings, Photovoltaic Power Generation Conference*, Hamburg, Germany, 1974.

34. J. A. Carlson, "Development of Lightweight Panels, "NASA **CR 66832.**

35. F. C. Treble in *Conference Records of the 9th IEEE Photovoltaic Specialists Conference*, 1972; *Proceedings of the Section "The Photovoltaic Power and its Applications in Space and on Earth,"* International Congress, "The Sun in the Service of Mankind," Paris, July 1973; and *Conference Records of the 8th IEEE Photovoltaic Specialists Conference*, 1970.

36. *Conference Records of the 8th IEEE Photovoltaic Specialists Conference*, 1970.

37. B. Collins in *Proceedings, Photovoltaic Power Generation Conference*, Hamburg, Germany, 1974.

38. F. C. Treble in *Conference Records of the 8th IEEE Photovoltaic Specialists Conference*, 1970.

39. E. N. Costogue and G. Rayl (p. 200) in *Proceedings of the 13th IEEE Photovoltaic Specialists Conference*, June 1978.

40. W. Alsbach (p. 430) in *Proceedings of the 12th IEEE Photovoltaic Specialists Conference*, November 1976.

41. H. V. Bassewitz and J. Lydorf (p. 435 in *Proceedings of the 12th IEEE Photovoltaic Specialists Conference*, November 1976.

42. "Evaluation of Space Station Solar Array Technology," First Topical Report, No. **LMSC-A981486,** 1970 and 1972.

43. H. Larsson in *Proceedings of the Section "The Photovoltaic Power and its Applications in Space and on Earth,"* International Congress, "The Sun in the Service of Mankind," Paris, France, July 1973.

44. "Space Station Solar Array Technology Evaluation Program," Second Topical Report, No. **LMSC-A99S719,** 1971.

45. "Solar Array Technology Development for SEP," Final Report **NAS 8-31352,** Lockheed Missiles and Space Company, **LMSC-D573740,** July 29, 1977.

PART III

Support Data

8
Fabrication and Test

8-1. Soldering

One of the significant subassembly cost elements is the electrical interconnection of solar cells. Most solar cells have been interconnected by soldering the interconnectors to the cells. Solder has typically been of the 36% lead, 62% tin, 2% silver composition. Various methods of soldering have been tried, including soldering irons, parallel-gap resistance soldering, resistance wire machine (peg-tip) soldering, tunnel oven and hot oil bath soldering, and others. Each of these processes has advantages and disadvantages which depend in part on the array design; in part on the production organization, customer preferences, available tooling, previous qualification status, and many other factors. However, solder exhibits some characteristics which limit its use for some solar cell array designs. The limitations of solder are its low strength at elevated temperature, decreasing to zero at approximately 170°C, and its limited fatigue life (see Chapter 6). For solar probes or any other high-temperature solar cell arrays, solder becomes unacceptable. Solderless solar cell interconnector-to-cell joining or bonding processes of interest are parallel-gap resistance welding, ultrasonic bonding, thermocompression bonding, laser welding, electron-beam welding, and similar processes discussed in the following sections. The first three of these are the simplest processes from a production point of view.

Resistance Soldering. This process is also known as reflow soldering. Heat is produced by passing an electrical current through either the parts that are to be soldered or through a high resistance soldering tip. The amount of heat produced and the force applied at the soldering tip are controlled by the equipment being used. The solder required at the joint is applied in controlled amounts in the form of solder paste or solder preforms, or by reflowing the solder that is present on the solar cell contacts or on the interconnectors. Usually a flux is required to produce acceptable joints.[1]

The advantages of the use of controlled resistance soldering processes are close control of heat amplitude, heating time, force applied to parts, and amount of solder applied to the joint. The two basic types of controlled resistance soldering are the single-point, or peg tip, and parallel-gap processes. Both have been widely used in solar cell assembly work.

Single-point Controlled Resistance Soldering. This is a versatile process that can be used in a wide variety of "one-side" applications. The process is also used extensively in joining various types of electronic components to printed circuit boards or thin films.[1]

Single-point soldering tips resemble the electrodes used in split-tip resistance welding (Fig. 8-1). The single-point tip, however, is joined at one end to form a continuous, or "single-point" resistance element which heats up from the electric current passing through. The heat is

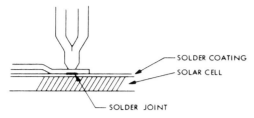

Fig. 8-1. Single-point soldering.[2]

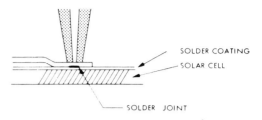

Fig. 8-2. Parallel-gap soldering.[2]

typically applied to the joint in a short pulse of less than one second duration, often with a controlled rise and fall time. Tips with thermocouples to control the upper temperature limit are also available. The tips remain in contact with the workpiece until the solder has solidified. The tip force, or pressure, is adjusted to be just sufficient to hold the parts together during soldering. Excessive tip forces will crack the solar cells. Typically, a force of 0.5 N is sufficient for an interconnector thickness of 25 μm, whereas 9 to 15 N might be required for a 250 μm thickness.

Parallel-Gap Soldering. This process is almost identical in principle to parallel-gap resistance welding. Two soldering tips approach the workpiece from one side and contact the interconnect at two points (Fig. 8-2). The heat required for making the solder joint is derived from passing an electrical current pulse from one electrode through the materials being soldered and back to the other electrode. Heat is produced by the resistance of the parts themselves. Only one soldered joint is made between and under the two tips. The size of the solder joint depends upon the tip sizes and the gap width. The force applied by each tip is the same.[1]

With separately suspended or "loaded" tips, the process is well suited for soldering uneven or bent interconnectors, except that excessively deformed interconnectors tend to burn rather than lay down flat. Normally, best soldering results are obtained when both leads and base materials are tinned or have a coating of solder. Solder preforms also can be used between the interconnect and the solar cell.

Since heat is produced by the resistance of the parts being soldered, the resistivity of the materials must be taken into account. Care must

be exercised when flux is used, as it may interfere with electric conductivity and the resulting heat produced.

Tunnel Oven Soldering. A conveyorized soldering system consisting of three process zones is utilized for this process: a preheat zone, a hot (or soldering) zone, and a cooling zone. The temperature in both the preheat and the hot zones are independently controlled. The conveyor speed is adjustable.[1]

The parts comprising a solar cell submodule are assembled and held together in a holding fixture called a *solder boat*. The soldering is performed by passing the solder boat through the tunnel oven, where it proceeds through the preheat zone, the soldering zone, and then the cooling zone. Since prolonged exposure to high temperature will deteriorate the contact strengths and the output of solar cells, it is preferred to subject them to soldering temperatures for a minimum amount of time. By varying both the temperatures in the tunnel oven and the conveyor speed, it is possible to obtain different soldering temperature-time profiles. The variation of the solder boat/submodule temperature with time as the solder boat proceeds through the tunnel oven is shown in Fig. 8-3. The various curves in this figure show the effect of varying the temperature in the heat zone of the tunnel oven and the speed of the conveyor through the oven for three modifications of the tunnel oven temperature profile, as used for the subassembly of solar cells for the Surveyor and Mariner series of spacecraft.

Soldering by Infrared Heating. For this method, tungsten or tungsten-iodine filament lamps are typically utilized for heating the workpiece. The operating temperature of the lamp is 3400°K

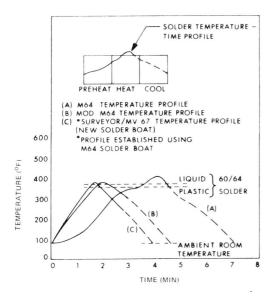

Fig. 8-3. Tunnel oven temperature-time profiles.[1]

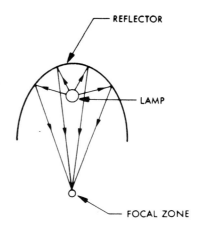

Fig. 8-4. Focused radiant heating system.[1]

shunt out too much of the available energy so that it may be better to use the RF to heat up secondary conductive elements which, in turn, heat up the joints to be soldered.

8-2. Welding

Parallel-gap Resistance Welding. This is the only practical welding process for solar cells. It derives its name from the way it is being performed: a pair of closely spaced, parallel electrodes make contact with the workpiece (solar cell interconnector), an electric current flows through the electrodes and the portion of the workpiece that is underneath and between the two electrodes, and the heat generated in the resistance offered by the workpiece raises the workpiece temperature to or above welding (fusion) temperature (Fig. 8-6). The pressure exerted by the electrodes on the workpiece facilitates making the joint.

It has been argued that the appearance of joints between interconnectors and solar cell

maximum, and its spectral output ranges approximately from 0.375 to 4.2 μm. The quartz-iodine lamp produces the maximum possible specific energy available in practical types of lamps. Arc and plasma sources produce more power for a given size, but they are more expensive and less flexible in their operation. The radiative energy from the lamp is collected by reflectors and directed onto the workpiece either in a single spot or in a line. The workpiece, located in the focal zone (Fig. 8-4), heats up at a rate and to an upper limit that is controlled by its absorptivity. In practice, relatively small variations in surface roughness and degree of oxidation (tarnishing) cause relatively large variations in the absorptivity. Therefore, infrared heating has not found widespread use.[1]

Soldering by Induction Heating. This is a promising approach for low-cost, large-scale solar cell assembly. The workpiece is inserted into a coil which is connected to a high-power radio frequency (RF) generator (Fig. 8-5). During the soldering operation, the RF energy causes eddy currents to flow in the surfaces of the workpiece, in turn causing the workpiece to heat up by I^2R heating. For solar cell array assembly work, the solar cells themselves may

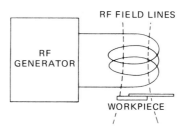

Fig. 8-5. RF soldering.

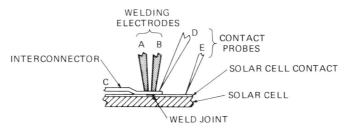

Fig. 8-6. Parallel-gap resistance welding.

contacts in microsection analysis indicates that the joints are not actually welded, but rather are fused, alloyed, thermocompression bonded, or otherwise metallurgically joined. While this may be of great concern to metallurgists, such arguments will be avoided here, as they are not overly important to array designers, fabricators, and process controllers. What is important is that metallurgically sound (or at times faulty) joints have been made in great quantity by the parallel-gap resistance welding technique.

Parallel-gap welding of solar cells was pioneered in Europe in 1968 by AEG-Telefunken. This firm ceased to produce soldered solar cell arrays at the end of 1971, and since that time has produced only welded arrays. By mid-1975, about 1.2 million welded joints had been used for five flight projects.[3] With silver plated molybdenum interconnectors welded to Ti-Pd-Ag solar cell contacts, solar cell assemblies have been qualified for temperature excursions between −200° and +200°C (Helios) and for temperature cycling for 1100 cycles between −180° and +80°C (International Ultraviolet Explorer; IUE).

Most U.S. solar cell array manufacturers now possess a solar cell welding capability.[4,5,6,7,8] However, by 1979, only one flight program is said to have used welded joints.

The following interconnector materials have been welded to silver solar cell contacts:

- Copper (unplated)
- Pure silver
- Silver plated copper
- Silver plated Kovar
- Silver plated Invar
- Silver plated molybdenum.

Welding schedules must be developed care-fully to assure adequate joint quality. In general, the following welding parameters must be considered and controlled:

- Electrode footprint size and electrode spacing
- Electrode pressure and dressing (flatness and state of oxidation)
- Electrode length (for constant voltage and capacity discharge welders)
- Solar cell heat sinking
- Weld voltage, current, and power
- Weld pulse rise and dwell and fall times
- Interconnector stiffness and electrical and thermal conductivity (related to plating thickness)
- Solar cell and interconnector surface roughness, cleanliness, and state of oxidation (tarnishing).

Inadequate welding parameters may affect the joint strength and/or solar cell electrical performance as follows:

- Inadequate weld power—low joint strength
- Excessive weld power—low joint strength
- Excessive weld power—burned interconnectors
- Excessive weld power—cell power degradation (see Section 8-5)
- Excessive weld power—silicon spalling
- Correct weld power but amplitude too high and dwell time too short—silicon spalling.

Figure 8-7 illustrates for a particular interconnector design the wide range over which joints having high pull strength can be made.[4] However, not all of the weld schedules produced joints that endured severe thermal cycling-testing. The point marked "Schedule for Test Specimens" indicates the weld schedule that was

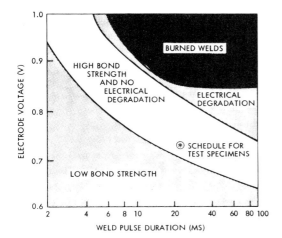

Fig. 8-7. Parallel-gap weld schedule development using 50 μm thick silver interconnects. (*Reprinted with Permission of the IEEE.*[4])

chosen for long temperature cycling life. This schedule is a compromise between high bond strength and negligible electrical degradation.

8-3. Thermocompression Joining

The joining of metals by thermocompression techniques involves the forming of a metallurgical bond at elevated temperature and under pressure. The characteristic that differentiates thermocompression joining from welding is that in thermocompression joining, the fusion temperature is below the melting or eutetic temperature of each metal or an alloy of the joining metals. In addition, the joining pressure is much greater and the joining time tends to be longer than in welding.

Thermocompression joining is potentially attractive, from a mass production point of view, in that electrical contact resistances are not important, precise electrode positioning is not required, and many joints can be made simultaneously.

Successful thermocompression joining of interconnectors to solar cells has been reported rather sparsely. In general, an increase in the joining temperature and in the joining stylus pressure (electrode force) increases the bond strength. The limiting condition on temperature is rapid oxidation of the cell contact and the interconnector surfaces when the joining is done in air. The limit on stylus pressure is set by the relatively low ultimate strength of semiconductor materials.

Solar cell and interconnector surface roughness and interconnector stiffness apparently play greater roles in thermocompression joining than in parallel-gap welding. Smoother surfaces and more compliant interconnectors, conforming to each other more readily, tend to increase the strength of joints made at a given temperature and under a given pressure.

The only solar cell interconnector materials reported as joinable are soft silver or silver plated soft metals. Stiff materials such as Kovar require large joining pressures that tend to fracture the solar cells.

Thermocompression joints having pull strength values comparable to those made by parallel-gap resistance welding were obtained with both 25 and 50 μm thick pure silver interconnectors. Schedules that resulted in good joints ranged from 9 N for 1200 seconds to 27 N for 1 second at 300°C. Joints made at 400°C exhibited higher pull strength than those made at 300°C. Below 275°C, no bonds were obtained.[4]

8-4. Ultrasonic Joining

Ultrasonic joining occurs under the influence of elevated temperature, pressure, and high-frequency acoustic vibration. The temperature rise is usually due to dissipation of the acoustic energy in the joint area; however, supplemental solar cell heating has been employed. For ultrasonic joints to exhibit high strength, the following parameters are critical: the acoustic energy coupling into the joint area; "grabbing" of the interconnector by the stylus; holding of the solar cell immovably without damping; and the acoustic energy level, dwell time, and stylus pressure. The coupling of the acoustic energy into the workpiece is accomplished by a mechanical force/amplitude transformer between the ultrasonic transducer and the bonding stylus, and excitation of the bonding stylus at a location on the stylus such that the least energy input to the joint makes the strongest bond.

The proper transformer ratio and stylus excitation location is, in practice, difficult to achieve, because different interconnectors and cells offer differing mechanical impedance values to the mechanical/acoustic circuit.

"Grabbing" of the interconnector by the joining stylus depends upon its tip configuration, shape, surface smoothness, and material composition in relation to the interconnector material properties. For a good joint to occur, the stylus normally first bonds itself to the interconnector, then the interconnector joins with the solar cell contact. If the acoustic excitation is continued, the interconnector/cell joint will reach a maximum strength and thereafter will be destroyed. The stylus typically "sticks" to the interconnector after a maximum strength joint has been made. In an ideal setup, the stylus/interconnector bond should break at the very moment in which the interconnector/cell joint reaches its maximum strength.

Ultrasonic joining of aluminum interconnectors to hundreds of titanium-silver contact and aluminum contact solar cells for nuclear-hardened solar cell arrays has been reported.[4,7,8]

Solar cell and interconnector materials that can be joined ultrasonically and exhibit high joint strength include aluminum parts to aluminum or silver contacts and silver parts to silver contacts.

8-5. Electrical Degradation Due to Joining

Parallel-gap resistance welding on the contact on the diffused side of solar cells (i.e., the n-contact on n-on-p cells) may cause electrical output degradation of the cells. The shallower diffused and textured surface solar cell types are more susceptible to this degradation than are the deeper diffused types. The output degradation manifests itself primarily in the maximum power region and is apparently caused by contact metal being driven into the junction area underneath the weld joints, thereby electrically shunting the solar cell. By making more weld joints on the same cell, the cell output continues to degrade; breaking the welded tabs from the cell (by pulling silicon divots out of the cell) very nearly restores the original cell power output. This phenomenon, illustrated in

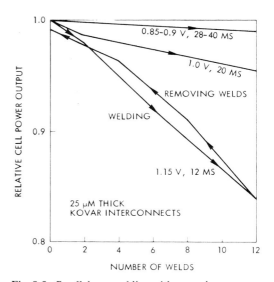

Fig. 8-8. Parallel-gap welding with excessive energy on n-contact causes electrical degradation which increases with the number of welds made. (*Reprinted with permission of the IEEE.*[4])

Fig. 8-8, was observed with both silver plated Kovar and pure silver interconnectors but at different weld voltage levels.[4]

Electrical degradation has not been observed after thermocompression joining (at 400°C) and after ultrasonic joining (at room temperature), but it does occur after soldering at excessively high temperatures or for excessively long heat cycles. The damage mechanism during soldering consists primarily of dissolution of solar cell contact metals in the liquid solder and an attendant degradation of adhesive strength of the metallization on the semiconductor material and/or electrical output degradation. The electrical degradation usually manifests itself as a deterioration of the fill factor and sometimes a change in the temperature coefficients at low temperatures.

8-6. Adhesive Bonding

One of the most important solar cell array assembly process techniques consists of the bonding together of parts using an adhesive. Examples of adhesive bonding include the following:

- Substrate fabrication (bonding of honeycomb core to face sheets, solar cell blankets to each other, etc.)

- Bonding of solar cell covers to solar cells
- Bonding of solar cells to substrates
- Bonding and spot-bonding of electrical conductors to the substrate.

The general steps common to most bonding operations are:

1. Verification that shelf life has not expired
2. Surface preparation, cleaning, and pre-treatment (priming)
3. Adhesive preparation (mixing, de-airing, etc.)
4. Adhesive application (metering, depositing, etc.)
5. Parts locating (clamping, holding, etc.)
6. Monitoring of pot life and skin-over time
7. Curing (time, temperature, pressure, relative humidity)
8. Clean-up (removing overflow and flash, trimming, etc.).

Typical adhesive types in use include the following:

- RTV (room temperature vulcanizing) rubbers, also known as silicon adhesives, sealants, and elastomers
- Epoxies
- Thermoplastic adhesives
- Thermosetting adhesives.

The appropriate specific bonding techniques are highly dependent upon each specific adhesive. The manufacturers process specifications should be followed closely and carefully.

ASSEMBLY PROCESS CONTROL

8-7. Metal Joining Control

It is known that "properly" made joints exhibit high strength and long fatigue life in temperature cycling, whether they were made by soldering, welding, or any other method. Not known is exactly what needs to be done to make joints "properly". Figure 6-10 in Section 6-6 illustrates how the fatigue life of soldered joints has increased over the years. Presumably, all of these joints had been made "properly," as evidenced by contact pull-test data (see Chapter 4). It has been found that the fatigue life of well-made soldered and welded joints is not related to the ultimate strength of joints measured by peel- or pull-testing under quasi-static loading conditions, except, of course, for poorly made joints. Cross-sectioning and metallurgical examinations under high magnification of "long-life" and "short-life" joints, chemical analysis of the solder alloy composition, and other attempts to understand the underlying phenomena, have not been successful yet. Therefore, the development of welding or soldering schedules for the assembly of long-temperature cycling arrays must not only be accompanied by visual inspection and pull- or peel-testing, but also by extended temperature cycling. The thusly obtained optimum schedule should then be maintained and controlled.

8-8. Non-destructive-testing (NDT)

Solar array assembly by welding instead of soldering poses a new set of manufacturing process control and quality assurance problems. While, on soldered joints, the amount of solder flow and solder filleting is readily inspectable, no such indicators of joint quality are evident in welding. Just as with soldered joints, not all welded joints made are "good," even if the weld schedule, electrodes, and surface properties of the parts are apparently the same for all welds attempted; therefore, some means of identifying unacceptable welds is needed.

Non-destructive-tests (NDT) rely on one or a number of non-destructively measurable or observable attributes which can be correlated to destructively determined weld quality (i.e., pull- or peel-tests and temperature cycling-tests). They may be classified according to the time of their execution into prejoining, in-process, and post-joining NDT methods.[11,12,13,14,15]

Early work on NDT methods indicated that there would be no single method which would definitely determine joint quality, but that a combination of methods could, perhaps, do so. Several organizations developed NDT systems that evaluate a number of parameters and often make weld quality accept/reject decisions by majority voting. Most of these systems utilize some form of preweld resistance measurement, welding monitoring, and post-welding inspection, as described in the following.

Prejoining Methods.

Electrical resistance measurement. Since the amount of electrical energy in the weld joint determines the weld quality, it seems reasonable to measure the electrical properties of the electrodes and materials to be welded before the actual weld pulse is applied. If the pre-weld resistance is too high or too low, an inadequate weld may be expected. All possible resistance paths in Fig. 8-6 have been measured: *A-B, A-C, A-D, A-E, C-D,* and *D-E.*

In-process Methods.

Weld pulse monitoring. Assuming that a proper welding schedule has been developed and implemented, an individual weld may still be inadequate for a number of reasons. An interconnector may be bent, contaminated, or improperly plated, or a solar cell may have an improper contact thickness, or the welder may temporarily malfunction. By measuring the current through, and the voltage across, the weld joint, and comparing them with pre-established norms for good joints, inference can be made that a joint may be good or will be a reject.

Dark-forward voltage drop. Instantaneous reversible changes in the solar cell dark-forward current-voltage characteristics during the welding cycle can potentially be used as indicators of the temperature reached during welding. The cell may be biased with either a constant voltage source or a constant current source; the signal is picked up as a change in cell terminal current or voltage, respectively.

Infrared emission. The infrared radiation emitted by the weld joint while it is being made has been used to measure the weld joint temperature or temperature/time profile. In practice, problems arise from variations in the emissivities of different interconnectors and the electrodes. Also, the electrodes, as well as the joint, emit infrared energy. As the electrodes warm up during mass production, their heat output overpowers that of the joint. A successful infrared technique would have to utilize an infrared sensor that has both a narrow field of view—trained on the joint—and a narrow spectral response characteristic that is able to reject undesired wavelengths.

Acoustic emission. Acoustic emission (noise) is caused by the melting, freezing, and stressing of a material. Acoustic emission-testing was originally developed for larger objects, but was applied to solar cell joints. Acoustic emission melt and cooldown signals were detected with piezoelectric crystals, amplified and displayed on an oscilloscope screen. Partial success with this method for unglassed solar cells was obtained, but further development would be required to implement it on a production basis.

Electrode setdown. A commonly used criteria for judging weld quality in fields other than solar cell arrays is the amount of electrode setdown occurring during the welding operation. Electrode setdown, also known as electrode *sinking*, occurs as the workpiece deforms at elevated temperature under the applied electrode pressure. The degree of electrode setdown is normally evaluated visually, frequently under a magnifying instrument. When the actual value of electrode displacement is measured during welding, this value is known as *dynamic electrode setdown*.

Electrode setdown for solar cell applications has not been found to be measurable criterion because of its extremely low magnitude, but it has been used in visual observations.

Post-joining Methods.

Visual inspection of the quality of a solar cell weld joint is restricted to observation of the electrode imprint on the cell interconnector. Typically, 20 to 60 power stereo microscopes are used. Inspection criteria may include lower and upper limits on the edge definition, depth appearance of the electrode imprint in the upper surface of the interconnector, and evidence of burned (darkened or discolored) areas of the interconnector, especially between the adjacent electrode footprints.

Infrared microscope (augmented visual). The "augmented visual" inspection of welded joints utilizes two different approaches: 1) inspection of the weld footprint size and its "visual" appearance (after image conversion to visible light); and 2) determination of welding induced stresses in the semiconductor, using crossed polarized infrared light filters.

With the infrared inspection techniques, infrared light is being utilized to which silicon (and other semiconductor materials) is transparent. The joints are inspected through the silicon wafer, requiring small metal-free silicon surface areas on the wafer side directly opposite the weld joints. The inspection technique with the infrared microscope is similar to direct visual inspection, except that an image convertor between the microscope exit and the observing eye converts the infrared light to visible light. Microscope magnification and depth-of-field relationships are nearly the same as with optical microscopes.

Other Methods. A large variety of NDT methods exist for non-solar cell applications. Most of these methods have been applied to solar cell weld joints at one time or another, with generally inadequate results. This is not to say that some innovative application could not be successful in the future. Among the methods investigated are the following. In *infrared videography*, the solar cell is heated uniformly and the joint area is scanned with an infrared detector. Temperature profiles over the cell area are displayed on the screen of a cathode ray tube. Unjoined or poorly joined interconnectors are expected to be recorded as being cooler (due to convection cooling) than properly joined interconnectors.

Holographic techniques were expected to show up imperfections in weld joints. Neither an acoustical immersion technique, which used ultrasonic frequencies between 1 MHz and 7 MHz and display of the resulting signals on a television screen, nor a laser beam and optical holography, with the results recorded on photographic film, were able to give an indication of joint quality.

Measurement of the *high-frequency impedance* of welded joints, or the magnitude of *eddy currents* induced in the weld joint areas, were expected to indicate the number and size of impurities and non-welded areas. *Acoustic signatures*—that is, the acoustic transmission and modification of an applied acoustic stimulus by the weld joint—was measured unsuccessfully. The quality of weld joints was expected to influence the reflection of high-frequency ultrasonic waves. Using an immersion technique and

frequencies from 5 to 25 MHz, it was found that only non-welded joints could be discerned.

With a microfocus *X-ray* method, magnified X-ray images of small areas can be obtained. However, definite joint interface displays could not be found. Simple *dc resistance* measurements, similar to those described under the pre-joining methods above, but performed after welding, were expected to provide indications as to the joint areas.

8-9. Adhesive Bonding Control

Adequate (or the highest practical, if required) adhesive strength can be achieved only in a production environment if proper process control is exercised. Process control, however, is not sufficient alone, because the adhesive itself may "have a problem," It is a standard practice to prepare small, representative test samples, frequently known as *cupons*, at the same time the actual hardware is fabricated, using the same processes and materials. The test samples are then subjected to destructive analysis (peel-, pull- or sheer-testing) to verify the adequacy of the adhesive bond of the hardware.

8-10. Visual Inspection

The most important process control instrument is visual inspection. Inspections may be performed with the unaided eye or with optical instruments. Stereo microscopes having 5 to 40 times magnification are in frequent use. Cracked solar cells and covers are usually best seen with the unaided eye. Soldered and welded joints, cover nicks and chips, and interconnector deformations are best observed under 10 to 20 times magnification.

8-11. Workmanship Criteria

Workmanship of a solar cell array reflects the externally visible quality that has been built into it. Workmanship criteria are stipulated conditions which make a product acceptable or not. They can be separated into two groups: functional and cosmetic. *Functional* criteria affect (or potentially may affect) the array's performance, life, or reliability;*cosmetic* criteria do not. The dividing line between these two groups generally depends upon an analysis of a specific array design and the specific set of environmental conditions associated with a particular mission. The following can be used to establish workmanship inspection criteria for each specific case.

Broken Solar Cells. Cracks are purely cosmetic if a crack has severed both p and n contact areas but each portion of the fractured cell remains electrically connected with adequate redundancy. All other cracks are functional to varying degrees. The electrical performance is not impaired by certain cracks. However, cracks in the semiconductor can be expected to propagate through contact areas during mechanical stressing and temperature cycling, and may affect the electrical performance at a later time.

Broken Covers (Applicable for Space Arrays). Cracks which are such that no active cell area can potentially be exposed are purely cosmetic. All other cracks are functional. Radiation protection and thermal properties are not impaired by cracks. If radiation protection is less than complete, degradation of a single cell stack may cause a similar degradation of the entire string of cells.

Broken Covers (Applicable for Terrestrial Arrays). Covers that provide a humidity barrier or mechanical support are functional.

Chipped Cells and Covers (Applicable for Space Arrays). A small percentage is permissible for synchronous orbits, a larger percentage for low altitude orbits, depending upon power margin and the possibility of low-energy proton damage. No cover defects are permissible for flights through the radiation belts except when the power margin is large. A single cell stack defect may cause degradation of an entire string.

Discolorations. Solar cells and covers showing different colors, especially when viewed at an oblique angle, are purely cosmetic.

Debonds. Partially debonded covers and cells, and bubbles and voids in cover adhesive fall into this category. A small percentage is permissible, depending upon power margin, severity of mechanical stress environment, and temperature cycling extremes. Debonds raise the cell operating temperature slightly. Further debonding may occur during the service life.

Adhesive Thickness. Variations in the cell and cover adhesive thickness may be functional, relating to thermomechanical stress, ability to cure, and light transmission loss near end-of-life. Small variations in thickness may be cosmetic only.

Overflow Adhesive. Overflow adhesive in the cell gaps and interconnector expansion loops is cosmetic only as long as the adhesive remains sufficiently flexible throughout the array's temperature range (operating or non-operating). At other temperatures, typically below $-100°C$, adhesives become hard and brittle, causing cells, covers, and interconnector expansion loops to fracture.

Overflowed adhesive on the front surface of the cover is subject to darkening due to ultraviolet radiation. Small areas are inconsequential, but larger areas will lead to output losses.

PHOTOVOLTAIC TESTING

8-12. History of Solar Cell-testing

Since the development of the solar cell in the 1950's, solar cell measurement techniques have progressed from an initial volt-ohmmeter-test in "fair weather" to high-altitude and space flight experiments, sunlight simulators, accurate spectroradiometric apparatus, and analog and digital data acquisition systems.

Originally, solar cells and solar cell assemblies for use on space vehicles were evaluated in the laboratory by measurement under incandescent illumination. Tungsten lamps with color temperatures of the order of 2700° to 3400°K, compared to the approximately 6000°K effective color temperature of the Air-Mass-Zero (AM0) sun, were used to illuminate the cells. In some cases, water filters were used to reduce the infrared spectral content of the incandescent lamps. Because of the necessity of periodically making measurements during solar cell panel fabrication, such equipment was used for in-process measurements at the sacrifice of accuracy and cell matching capability. The change of the water absorption wavelength with temperature, and the formation of bubbles and algae growth, caused such instabilities that most water filters were abandoned quickly.

The major light source for volume solar cell-testing through the mid-1960's was the tungsten lamp. The stability and reliability of tungsten lamps outweighed the disadvantage of their spectral irradiance being so drastically different from that of sunlight. In the 1950's, it was already realized that measurements were not repeatable in tungsten light unless the filament voltage—and hence, the color temperature of the lamp—was closely controlled and the solar cell temperature was held within close tolerances. The light intensity was adjusted with usually unencapsulated solar cells which were calibrated in natural sunlight against a pyrheliometer, a thermopile specifically designed for measuring solar flux. Solar cells were thus tested under so-called "Standard Tungsten Test Conditions" (unfiltered tungsten light of $2800°$ $±50°K$, equivalent to 100 mW/cm^2 solar radiation at $28°C$ cell temperature).

This level was set based upon the effect of natural sunlight on solar cells in normal outdoor conditions at an intensity level of 1 kw/m^2 (100 mW/cm^2). While the 1 kW/m^2 level was arbitrary, it was actually observed frequently on clear days near sea level. Thus, "standard" solar cells were taken into natural sunlight and their measured output at any intensity was then extrapolated to 1 kW/m^2. The natural sunlight intensity was measured using normal meteorological equipment, particularly the pyrheliometer. Early pyrheliometers were of the $180°$ type, but, in an attempt to improve accuracy of eliminating the effects of sky background, these were later replaced with the normal incidence type.

When precision was required, the solar cells were measured in essentially collimated sunlight; in other cases, the sky background was accounted for by applying a correction based upon the ratio of short-circuit currents of a cell measured in uncollimated light to that measured in collimated light. Having calibrated several such cells, these "standards" were then used to adjust the intensity of the tunsten lamps. By adjusting the distance from the lamp or by inserting neutral density filters in the form of wire mesh, the intensity was changed until the short-circuit current of the standard cell reached the same value as that obtained at the 1 kW/m^2 natural sunlight condition.

Immediately, several problems occurred with this procedure. First of all, natural sunlight conditions at local test sites varied significantly in both intensity and spectral content, so that correlation from one day to the next was erratic. To resolve this problem, standard cell calibration began to be performed at Table Mountain, California (then the site of the Smithsonian Institute Solar Observatory, where data on sunlight conditions and spectra had been obtained for almost 25 years).

Table Mountain is approximately 75 to 100 miles from Los Angeles (depending upon route), accessible by good highways, and generally enjoyed relatively stable atmospheric conditions through the late 1960's. The altitude of the test site is 7516 feet. The mountain is located in the extreme northerly portion of the San Bernardino mountain range immediately adjacent to the Mojave desert. This location is primarily responsible for atmospheric conditions which are generally characterized by relatively clear skies and low humidity.

By thus calibrating solar cells under sunlight conditions which were more nearly reproducible, and by maintaining control of the incandescent illumination, it was felt that sufficient accuracy could be achieved to permit adequate extrapolation of outputs to AM0. However, in 1961, it was discovered that in the attempts to improve solar cell efficiencies, the spectral response had been so significantly shifted toward the red as to introduce errors of as much as 15 to 20%. Thus, cells and panels made at that time were being measured under sources calibrated against standard cells of different spectral response, such that the cell and panel outputs appeared to be approximately 15% more efficient in space than was actually the case. As a result of this, considerable attention was focused by industry and government on the test methods.

The first milestone was an industry-wide

AIEE-IEEE joint meeting on solar cell standard-ization in 1959, in which many existing problem areas were defined and others solved. In par-ticular, a standard solar cell encapsulation package with quartz window and liquid tem-perature control facility was standardized, four-terminal solar cell measurements were specified, and collimation angles for pyrheliometers and solar cells and minimum atmospheric conditions for calibrating solar cells against the pyrheliom-eter were defined. The AIEE shortly afterward established a committee which prepared a speci-fication for measurement of solar cells using simulated solar radiation.

The prime source of error in solar cell cali-bration work at that time was the pyrheliometer. Not only did the actual pyrheliometer calibra-tion seem less accurate than ±3.5%, as had been verified by comparing different units simul-taneously in sunlight, but the great difference in spectral response between the pyrheliometer (0.2 to 3.5 μm) and the solar cell (0.4 to 1.2 μm) caused great errors.

Attempts were made in the early 1960's to eliminate the pyrheliometer as much as possible in cell calibration procedures, at least for mea-surements made in the lower atmosphere. With airplane, balloon, and satellite flights, the ulti-mate in accuracy was hoped to be achievable, but still fell short of the goal. Balloon flown standards, however, achieved the highest cali-bration accuracy and an increasing number of contracts were written around the "Balloon Standard" as a definitive light intensity stan-dard. This practice is continuing today for calibrating solar cells for space use.

During the following years, the development of solar radiation simulators was pursued vigor-ously, with the hope of finding the ultimate answer to all solar cell measurement problems. Yet spacecraft experiments cast doubt on John-son's data on the solar constant which had been the "spectral standard" for simulator perfor-mance.[16] Spectroradiometric equipment to measure the simulator performance accurately was nonexistent in 1965, and standard solar cells with "space calibrations" to verify simu-lator performance were not yet available. There-fore, solar simulators were calibrated by a combination of various methods that were generally trustworthy but lacked a solid back-ing of "space calibrated" standard cells or correlation with other valid and "traceable" means.

Small solar simulators covering up to approx-imately a 5 cm^2 area and essentially conform-ing to the AIEE recommendations were con-structed. These instruments proved very useful in providing better measurements of individual cells. However, because of limited size, such equipment could not be used for solar cell ar-rays. The solar cell array manufacturer and spacecraft manager were still unable to properly evaluate the completed arrays by 1965. Al-though tools were available for examining in-dividual cells, because of the difficulty in corre-lation between the individual cell tester and the completed arrays, even such small equipment failed to contribute to the solution of the prob-lem, although research programs had benefited substantially. Thus, the use of Table Mountain for measurement of arrays became increasingly relied upon for final acceptance-testing and for evaluation of environmental test performance, whereas for fabrication, incandescent illumina-tion remained the only available source.

With an increasing reliance on Table Moun-tain, California, for measurements, facilities needed to be prepared. Considerable differences existed between organizations wanting to per-form the necessary tests. Some improvement in this situation was accomplished during 1962, when the NASA Jet Propulsion Laboratory (JPL) acquired a test facility on Table Mountain that had previously been operated by the Smithsonian Institute.

On the other hand, technical problems in measurements at Table Mountain occurred fre-quently. The most significant difficulty was related to the availability of suitable weather. To make precise measurements, it was desirable to establish very select atmospheric conditions. Such specifications related to 1) minimum in-tensity, which could range–depending upon specific programs–from 90 to 100 mW/cm^2; 2) horizontal visibility, which generally ranged from 5 to 10 miles; and 3) sky radiation (which, for various purposes, had been specified for as little as 6 to 10% of direct sunlight—i.e., approximately 6 to 10 mW/cm^2). In some cases, measurements were permitted with sky radiations as high as 12%. There were almost always limitations on allowable time periods before and after solar noon, such that, generally on a good day, only three to four hours of test time were available.

Particularly when extended poor weather prevailed, there was increasing pressure for alternate test sites. Several such locations were considered and used, including Palm Springs, Bishop, and White Mountain, California; Kitt Peak, Arizona; Sacramento Peak, New Mexico; and, on a few occasions, locations in the eastern part of the United States. Unfortunately, most of these locations were not so readily accessible and the costs associated with such alternate test sites, particularly for the measurement of large or numerous arrays, were prohibitive.

During the mid-1960's, significant progress was made in simulating solar energy in the laboratory. Most of this equipment was not simply directed toward solar cell-testing but was also used widely for materials-testing and determination of solar absorptivities and thermal balance on the subsystems and complete satellite systems. During 1964, the capabilities of such equipment advanced to a point that arrays of solar cells could be properly tested. The most widely used solar simulators for solar cell- and array-testing since the late 1960's were the X-25 or X-25L solar simulators developed by Spectrolab Division of Textron Electronics (at that time), now a subsidiary of the Hughes Aircraft company.

The solar simulators developed in the 1960's, such as the Spectrolab X-25, used high-power, high-pressure xenon arc lamps which operated continuously and illuminated, reasonably uniformly, an area up to nearly 0.07 m^2 with a closely matched (when appropriately filtered) AM0 spectrum.[17] A need for illuminating much larger areas and entire arrays, however, continued to exist until the so-called pulsed xenon arc solar simulators became available during the late 1960's. The pulsed solar simulators permit energy densities to be reached in the lamps which can be maintained only for a few milli-

seconds to prevent lamp destruction. These simulators can thereby provide illumination over an area of 5 m in diameter at one solar constant intensity.[18,19]

In the mid-1970's, a mushrooming interest in terrestrial photovoltaic applications saw a renewal in the interest of the effects atmospheric conditions have on solar cells. A sunshine data monitoring network was established, and the atmospheric effects on solar cells were investigated more rigorously.[20,21,22]

8-13. Standard Solar Cells

Standard solar cells are used for two purposes; 1) to determine the absolute value of the solar constant over the spectral response region of solar cells, and 2) to accurately establish the light intensity of solar simulators.

Standard Solar Cells for Space Applications. Calibration data is obtained for the standard solar cells on high-altitude balloon flights conducted regularly by JPL.[23] The standard solar cell assemblies are mounted on a tracking mechanism that maintains sun orientation within ±2°. A light baffle shields the solar cells from unwanted reflections. The sun-tracker is mounted on the balloon apex, as shown in Fig. 8-9. The helium-filled balloons are typically launched to reach float altitude two hours before solar noon and to remain at the altitude until two hours after solar noon. Temperature and electrical output data for each standard cell is transmitted to a ground station during the float period. The balloon is commanded to descend by opening a valve and allowing the gas to escape at a controlled rate. The solar cell payload, solar tracker, and other reusable equipment are recovered by a ground crew.

Solar cells flown on previous flights have been reflown on several subsequent flights for correlation purposes. One cell in particular, flown over 16 times, has shown a repeatability of within ±1%, thereby indicating that balloon flight standard solar cells not only are rugged and reliable but also that the calibration accuracy obtained exceeds, on an absolute basis, the accuracy of all previous solar intensity and

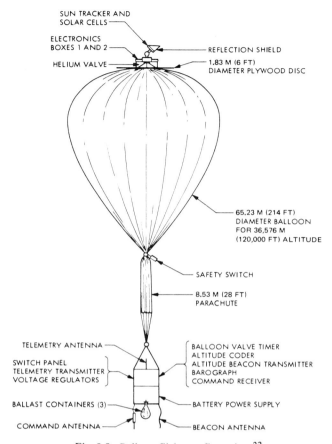

Fig. 8-9. Balloon flight configuration.[23]

solar cell calibration measurement techniques (Table 8-1).[23,24]

The altitude selected for balloon flights in 1970 and later was 36,600 m (120,000 ft). This higher altitude (24,000 m previously) was selected to eliminate, as much as possible, the effects of solar energy absorption by the earth's atmosphere. Solar cell measurements made on the 1970 flights were within 0.5% of AM0, as determined by the ratio of the atmospheric pressure at 36,600 m to that at sea level. When the spectral response of a solar cell (0.35 to 1.2 μm) is taken into consideration, the solar irradiation at that altitude is essentially that of space sunlight (see also Chapter 9).

The solar cells, which have been assembled into modular form in accordance with JPL Procedure No. EP504443A, are mounted on the face of the sun-tracker. Dow Corning No. 340 silicone heat sink compound is applied at the interface of the solar cell module and the sun-tracker mounting plate to minimize thermal gradients between these surfaces and to ensure the best possible uniform temperature on all solar cells comprising the payload. Wires soldered to the terminals of the solar cell modules electrically connect the solar cells to a 36 position stepping switch.

During the period that the sun-tracker is locked on the sun, solar cell voltages, interspersed with reference voltages and thermistor voltages, are fed into a voltage controlled oscillator (VCO). The voltages are converted to frequencies and are transmitted to a ground station with a 5 W FM transmitter modified to operate at an assigned frequency of 217.5 MHz. At the ground station, the data are recorded in digital form on printed paper tape and in analog

**Table 8-1. Repeatibility of Standard Solar Cell BFS-17A
for 29 Flights Over a 15 Year Period.[23]**

Flight date	Output, MV	Flight date	Output, MV
9/5/63	60.07	8/5/70	60.32
8/3/64	60.43	4/5/74	60.37
8/8/64	60.17	4/23/74	60.37
7/28/65	59.90	5/8/74	60.36
8/9/65	59.90	10/12/74	60.80
8/13/65	59.93	10/24/74	60.56
7/29/65	60.67	6/6/75	60.20
8/4/66	60.25	6/27/75	60.21
8/12/66	60.15	6/10/77	60.35
8/26/66	60.02	8/11/77	60.46
7/14/67	60.06		
7/25/67	60.02	Total	1746.89
8/4/67	59.83		
8/10/67	60.02	Average	60.24
7/19/68	60.31		
7/29/68	60.20	Low 59.83	−0.676%
8/26/69	60.37		
9/8/69	60.17	High 60.80	+0.935%
7/28/70	60.42		

Average $\bar{x}$ = 60.24

Maximum deviation from $\bar{x}$ = 0.935%
Each data point is an average of 20 to 30 points per flight for period
9/5/63 to 8/5/70.

For flights on 4/5/74 through 7/1/75 each data point is an average of
100 or more flight data points.

For flights starting in September 1975, each data point is an average
of 200 data points.

form on a strip chart recorder. The data are later transferred from the printed tape to punch cards compatible with a JPL computer program.

The overall accuracy of the balloon flight system has been given as ±0.5%. However, the correlations between test results obtained in the solar simulators of the different organizations and in the JPL solar simulator have generally been within ±2.0%. Solar cells other than silicon, or silicon solar cells covered with special band-pass filters, have exhibited differences as high as 13.7% (Table 8-2). These differences are attributed to the use of different light sources, different standard solar cells used to set the intensity of the light sources, and measurement error. JPL employs a Spectrolab X-25L solar simulator (see Section 8-14).

JPL corrects the balloon flight data for sun-earth distance and cell temperature. Load resistors are permanently attached to standard cells and load the solar cells near their short-circuit current points. The load resistor value is usually 1 ohm, but can be lower or higher, depending upon the cell size and filter cover used. Since the voltage drop across the load resistor is actually measured, the cell output is given in millivolts and the temperature coefficient is in millivolts per Kelvin.

Standard Solar Cells for Terrestrial Applications.
Standardization and calibration methodologies are presently in the process of being defined.[20,21,22]

Table 8-2. Correlations between Solar Simulators of Different Organizations.[24]

Module Number	Cell Type	Manufacturer[*]	Agency	Agency Source	Agency Calib	JPL[**] Calib	Deviation from JPL Calib, (%)
GSF-701	N-P	HEK	Goddard	X-25	69.6	70.4	-1.14
GSF-702	N-P	HEK	Goddard	X-25	68.7	69.5	-1.15
GSF-703	N-P	HEK	Goddard	X-25	71.2	72.7	-2.06
GSF-704	N-P	HEK	Goddard	X-25	66.9	67.7	-1.18
GSF-705	N-P	SIE	Goddard	X-25	71.1	71.4	-0.42
GSF-706	N-P	AEG	Goddard	X-25	71.0	71.2	-0.28
LRC-003A	N-P	HEK	Langley	X-25	67.16	67.4	-0.36
LRC-003B	N-P	HEK	Langley	X-25	66.50	66.6	-0.15
LRC-004A	N-P	CRL	Langley	X-25	69.20	69.3	-0.14
LRC-004B	N-P	CRL	Langley	X-25	68.87	68.7	+0.25
IPC-701	N-P	IPC	AFAPL	X-25L	67.0	66.1	+1.36
IPC-703	N-P	IPC	AFAPL	X-25L	66.0	65.5	+0.76
IPC-704	N-P	IPC	AFAPL	X-25L	66.0	65.6	+0.61
MSF-8003	N-P	CRL	Marshall	X-25	59.21	58.0	+2.09
MSF-8004	N-P	CRL	Marshall	X-25	60.97	59.2	+2.99
APL-I[***]	N-P	HEK	APL	OCLI-31	88.0	80.5	+9.32
APL-II[***]	N-P	HEK	APL	OCLI-31	80.0	82.6	-3.15
APL-III[***]	N-P	HEK	APL	OCLI-31	71.6	83.0	-13.73
APL-IV[***]	N-P	HEK	APL	OCLI-31	72.9	72.8	+0.14
APL-V[***]	N-P	HEK	APL	OCLI-31	81.1	83.5	-2.87

[*] HEK = Heliotek, SIE = Siemens Aktiengesellschaft, AEG = AEG-Telefunken, CRL = Centralab, IPC = Ion Physics Corporation.

[**] JPL calibration using Spectrosun X-25L Solar Simulator, 1-AU sunlight equivalent, 301°K (28°C).

[***] Set of solar cells each covered with a different band-pass filter.

Use of Standard Solar Cells. Standard solar cells are maintained for current and advanced development programs. The standards can be used in either of two ways:

1. When used with artificial light sources, the standard cell is placed in the light beam and the intensity is adjusted until the output of the standard cell is equivalent to the calibrated value or to any desired ratio of the calibrated value. The temperature of the standard cell is held constant at the standard temperature of 301°K (28°C). Once the intensity of the artificial light source has been set, test solar cells can be placed in the light beam and their parameters measured. *Or,*

2. When used in terrestrial sunlight, the standard cell is placed in the same field of view as the solar cell or solar cell array being measured. Provisions should be made to maintain the standard cell at the standard temperature. If this is not practical, then the temperature of the standard must be measured and the output value corrected through application of the temperature coefficient. The output value of the standard solar cell is used to determine, by direct ratio, the incident solar radiation on the photovoltaic devices under test.

8-14. Light Sources for Solar Cell-testing

Satisfactory solar cell and array measurement results can be obtained only when the measurements are performed in a solar simulator that utilizes light from a high-pressure xenon arc lamp for at least part of the spectrum in which the solar cells are responsive. A second best choice is natural sunlight under ideal weather conditions. Mercury arc and tungsten filament lamps are the poorest choices, even though they have been used widely. Mercury arcs lack output at longer wavelengths (between 0.6 and 1.0 μm), while tungsten lamps lack output at shorter wavelengths (below 0.5 μm).

Tungsten filament lamps used for solar cell measurements are either evacuated or gas filled. In use are standard types of various manufacturers, ranging from 1 V, 0.2 W, to 125 V, 1000 W types. The lamps are operated at voltages to produce color temperatures between 1800° and 3400°K and intensities up to 100 kW/m². Variations in glass thickness of lamp envelopes have little effect in the wavelength range in which solar cells are responsive.

Excessive blackening of the inside of the lamp changes the spectral output slightly and should be avoided. Most lamps with a power consumption of 100 W or more must be forced-air-cooled to prevent early lamp deterioration. While lamps are operated with direct current for critical calibration work, precision-regulated alternating current is used for routine measurements. Alternating current is preferable because it prolongs the filament life and the calibration value of the lamps used as luminosity standards.

The color temperature of tungsten filament lamps must be controlled, and it is measured with a color temperature meter, which is calibrated against a standard lamp. The most widely used color temperature for measurements and calibration work has been 2800°K. The intensity may be measured with a footcandle meter, having a spectral response closely matched to the spectral response of the human eye (Standard Luminosity Curve, 1924, CIE); however, severe intensity measurement errors may result (illustrated in Table 8-3) from the different spectral response characteristics of silicon and selenium cells and the different spectral distributions of radiant energy from various light sources. As illustrated in Fig. 8-10, the corrected footcandle meter is responsive only in the low-output region of a tungsten lamp, while the silicon cell is most sensitive near the peak output of the tungsten lamp. A variation in color temperature changes the "blue" to "red" ratio

Table 8-3. Variation in Solar Cell Short-Circuit Current Output with Color Temperature of the Incident Light for Constant Light Intensity as Measured With a Corrected Footcandle Meter.[25]

Color Temperature* (°K)	Light Intensity** (footcandles)	Relative Solar Cell Output† (%)
1800	1000	1182
2000	1000	750
2200	1000	545
2400	1000	432
2600	1000	345
2800	1000	286
3000	1000	241
3200	1000	205
3400	1000	182
6000	1000	100

*1800° through 3400°K are obtained with tungsten filament lamp; 6000°K is terrestrial sunlight on a cloudless day.
**Corrected footcandle meter spectral response.
†Silicon cell spectral response is for a deep-diffused, conventional solar cell.

of the light, and thus the silicon cell gets a proportionately different amount of energy than the footcandle meter.

Table 8-3, together with Fig. 8-10, also shows that various solar cells may put out different amounts of electrical energy with respect to one another when the spectral distribution of the light source is altered. For example, two solar cells may put out a short-circuit current of 20 mA each at 1000 footcandles of 2000°K; but when tested at 1000 footcandles of 2800°K, their output may be 5 to 7 mA. In natural sunlight near noon at sea level on a cloudless day, the solar intensity of 100 mW/cm² corresponds to a light level of 10,000 footcandles.

8-15. Solar Simulators

The solar radiation (or illumination) simulators available today fall into two classes: *continuous* output and *pulsed* output. The former type is limited in its use to the testing of relatively

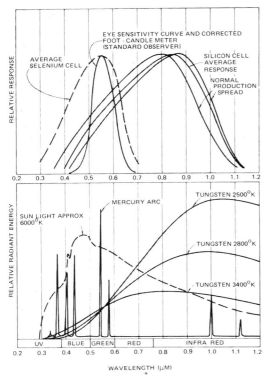

Fig. 8-10. Spectral response of some detectors (top) and spectral distributions of some sources (bottom).[25]

small panels. The latter type generally allows accurate testing of large panels and even entire arrays.

In the following, examples are given of instruments of each type that are currently in use and commercially available.

Spectrolab Model X-25 Solar Simulator.[17] The X-25 optical system, shown in Fig. 8-11, collects and distributes the radiation from a 2500 W xenon short-arc lamp to illuminate a projected area with a collimated beam. The source collecting mirror is mounted with its focus coincident with the arc of the lamp. The optical contour of the collector mirror surface is an aconic section that optimizes the energy transfer from the arc of the lamp to the image plane of the projection or collimation system to provide uniformity of the output beam with minimum filtering corrections. The field/projection lens system magnifies and projects this image either onto a projection plane for illuminating planar targets, or onto the plane of a collimating element, which, in turn, converts the radiation into a parallel beam. Various options of projected and collimated beams of varying projection distance and/or collimated beam diameters are offered by various field/projection and collimating lens system accessories.

The spectral distribution of the radiation from the Spectrosum Model X-25 solar simulator approximates the sun's emission spectrum to varying degrees, depending upon customer requirements and specification (Fig. 8-12). The

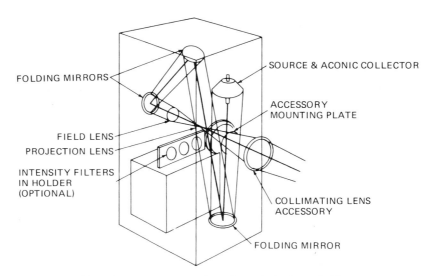

Fig. 8-11. Spectrosun Model X-25 optical schematic.[17]

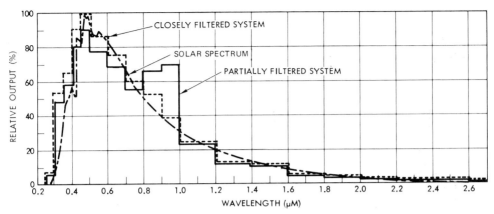

Fig. 8-12. Spectrosun Model X-25 spectral distribution.[17]

manufacturer claims the performance characteristics given below.

- Beam diameter and intensity: 1.0 to 1.6 kW/m² for 30 cm diameter filtered beam. Higher intensities available at smaller beam diameters.
- Uniformity of beam intensity: standard ±10% with 2.5 × 2.5 cm monitor; ±5% and ±2% available with uniformity-adjusting accessory.
- Collimation (or projection) angle: standard basic projection console (output) beam cone angle is ±14°. Alternate projection cone angle of ±7° is available. Collimated system collimation angles are ±1.2° for 30 cm diameter systems and ±2.4° for 15 cm diameter systems.
- Spectral match: 0.25 to .27 μm high-pressure xenon spectrum, as modified by filters and optics.
- Lamp life: Rated at 1500 hours; typically 800 to 1000 hours when used for at least 20 minutes per ignition.

TRW LAPSS III Solar Simulator.[19] The TRW Defense and Space Systems Group (TRW DSSG) Large Area Pulsed Solar Simulator (LAPSS), now available also from Spectrolab, utilizes a pulsed linear xenon arc flashtube. Upon ignition of the lamp, the light output rises to a flat-top pulse of approximately one solar constant intensity at 9 m for 1.7 milliseconds duration. During the central 1 millisecond interval, gated integrating circuits measure the short-circuit current of a standard solar cell and the test specimen output. The specimen output data is automatically adjusted to one solar constant intensity and 28°C standard test conditions. Both the corrected and uncorrected data may be printed out on a digital printer or plotted in the form of dots with an X-Y recorder.

The flux uniformity is typically better than ±2% over a 2.1 × 2.1 m area, 9 m from lamp, at 2.5 kV power supply voltage, measured with a 4 cm² solar cell in non-reflective surroundings. The intensity repeats typically within ±3%; however, the data control console corrects the intensity variations automatically to within 0.5% overall. The light intensity is maintained constant for a 1 millisecond interval by means of a five-stage delay line composed of high-voltage capacitors and a tapped inductor. This pulse duration is sufficiently long to prevent RC time constant effects to falsify the output measurements, but is short enough to prevent heating of the test specimens.

The instrumentation associated with the flashlamp is based on the use of gated integrators, which are activated during the 1 millisecond constant-intensity interval, as illustrated in Fig. 8-13. During each flash, one point on the I-V curve is measured. An automatic sequencer biases the test specimen to the next load point and refires the lamp.

The simulator has been used to calibrate Intelsat, Pioneer, and many other solar cell arrays. The accuracy and reproducibility are nominally ±1% or better in a production setting, and ±0.2% under research control.

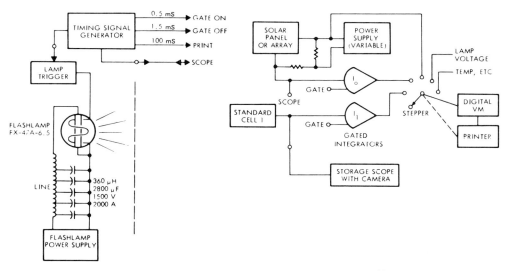

Fig. 8-13. Schematic of flashlamp and readout circuit.[18]

The effective black-body temperature of xenon flashlamps is a reproducible function of current density in the discharge volume, as shown in Fig. 8-14. The strong xenon emission lines in the red (800 to 1000 nm) are self-absorbed at increasing current density. This effect eliminates the red content characteristic of xenon lamps operated in the continuous mode.

The source-to-panel distance is determined by panel size and the acceptable variation of intensity over the panel. For an illuminated spherical surface segment of radius S,

$$\Delta M/M \cong S^2/D^2$$

where

D = source-panel distance
S = radius of illumination
M = panel illumination.

For $\Delta M/M = 0.02$ (a variation of intensity of ±1%), $D/S = 7.07$.

The plasma resistivity of linear xenon flashlamps is a function of the current density within the lamp. Similarly, the lamp resistance and lamp current are functions of the current density and lamp geometrical properties. To control color temperature, it is necessary to control current density. When this is done, both power and voltage are uniquely determined by the length and bore of the lamp. At high current densities, lamp efficiencies of 65 to 75% are obtained.

Table 8-4 summarizes the electrical properties of three pulsed xenon flashlamps commercially available. They cost under $100.00 each (1975). The data shown is for a current density of 1600 A/cm^2, which is the selected design value for the LAPSS III simulator.

The intensity of illumination at a distance D from the flashlamp is

$$M = \mu P_e/(4\pi D^2)$$

where

μ = lamp efficiency
P_e = lamp electrical power.

For $M = 1400$ W/m^2 (corresponding to sunlight) and for a lamp efficiency of 65%,

$$P_e = 2.7(10^4)D^2$$

in electrical watts.

Assuming that all of the radiant energy is absorbed in a silicon layer 0.25 mm thick, the temperature rise, θ, is given by

$$\theta = MT/(C_p dm) = 7 \times 10^{-3} \; ^\circ C$$

where

T = flash duration (2 milliseconds)
M = illumination (1400 W/m^2)
C_p = specific heat of silicon (735 J/kg $^\circ$C)

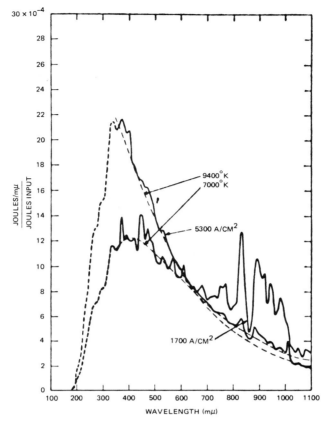

Fig. 8-14. Spectral emission from FX-47A flash tube at two current densities compared with relative spectral emittance of black bodies at 7000° and 9400°K.[18]

d = density of silicon (2.33×10^3 kg/m^3)
m = cell thickness (0.25 mm).

8-16. Solar Cell Output Measurements

Solar cells are tested for their ability to produce a specified amount of power under certain conditions of illumination and at a certain cell

operating temperature. A solar cell test setup consists primarily of a light source, a load connected across the cell's terminals, and electrical current and voltage measuring equipment.

Figure 8-15 shows the equivalent circuit of a solar cell and the basic circuit for measuring the electrical output of the cell. If the load resistor, R_L, is very small, then the voltage across the

**Table 8-4. Electrical Properties Based on Current Density of
1600 A/cm^2.**

EGMG Lamp Type	Arc Length, L (cm)	Bore Area, A (cm^2)	Resistance, R (ohms)	Maximum Power, P (MW)	Maximum Energy per Flash (joules)
FX-47C-3	7.6	1.32	0.16	0.72	2250
FX-47C-6.5	16.5	1.32	0.35	1.48	4000
FX-47C-12	30.4	1.32	0.65	2.9	9200

SOLAR CELL   MEASURING CIRCUIT

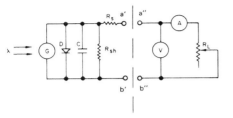

λ = INCOMING RADIATION
G = CONSTANT CURRENT GENERATOR
D = DIODE BEHAVIOR OF JUNCTION, BIASED
    IN FORWARD DIRECTION
C = JUNCTION CAPACITANCE
R_s = SERIES RESISTANCE
R_{sh} = SHUNT RESISTANCE
A = LOW IMPEDANCE MILLIAMPERE METER
V = HIGH IMPEDANCE VOLTMETER
R_L = VARIABLE LOAD RESISTANCE

Fig. 8-15. Schematic diagram of solar cell under test (left) and output measuring circuit (right).

cell is also very small and the current through R_L is considered to be the "short-circuit current," or I_{sc}. As R_L is made larger and larger, less current will flow through R_L and more voltage will appear across the cell, until a point is reached where $R_L = \infty$ and $I = 0$. This point is called "open-circuit voltage," or V_{oc}. If all the points of voltage and current of the cell are plotted, the so-called "I–V curve" is obtained (see Chapter 4). This curve can be directly plotted with an X-Y recorder. However, for routine measurements, a less costly procedure is employed.

The shape and magnitude of the I–V curve depends on the junction characteristics, shunt resistance, and series resistance (D, R_{sh}, and R_s, respectively, in Fig. 8-15), and on the total radiant energy converted into electrical energy, regardless of wavelength composition. For instance, if a certain radiation with a wavelength of 0.4 to 0.7 μm produces a certain I_{sc}, it will also produce a certain I–V curve. Another quantity of radiation between 0.8 and 1.0 μm falling onto the same cell with an intensity that will produce the same I_{sc} as before will also produce the same I–V curve, as long as the temperature remains constant. The amount of ripple in the light level, however, may produce different effects in the readout equipment. For example, xenon lamps operated from ac or un-

filtered dc supplies often produce a depressed knee in the I–V curve, as compared to the I–V curve obtained with filtered dc.

Since solar cells have a low impedance at high light levels, current meters in the measuring circuit should also have a very low impedance to prevent measuring errors. For instance, to measure short-circuit current, the internal meter resistance should be 0.1 ohm or less. At low light levels, the cell impedance becomes high and voltage measurements become more difficult. For instance, at 0.01 solar constant, the input impedance of a voltmeter should be 10 megohms or more in order to correctly measure open-circuit voltage.

8-17. Array Output Measurements

Array measurements are, in principle, conducted like single cell measurements. The major differences are that the light source must uniformly cover a larger area and that the readout circuitry must be capable of handling higher power levels.

Most array output measurements in the past were performed in natural, terrestrial sunlight, as discussed in Section 8-12. However, solar simulators are now available that permit testing of relatively large arrays (see Section 8-15). Of considerable concern is the lead resistance between the panel under test and the test equipment (as described in Section 8-19). A special type of simulated array output-testing is discussed in Section 8-22.

8-18. Standard Test Conditions

Solar cells, modules, panels, and arrays are tested under so-called *Standard Test Conditions*, as shown in Table 8-5.

Table 8-5. Standard Test Conditions.

Light Intensity		Light	Cell	Cell
mW/cm²	W/m²	Spectrum	Temperature	Type
135.3	1353	AM0	28°C or 25°C	Space
100.0	1000	AM1	25°C	Terrestrial
80.0	800	AM2	25°C	Terrestrial

8-19. Effects of Lead and Contact Resistances

Two important factors in cell and array measurements are 1) the resistance in the cable leading from the solar cell to the resistive load, and 2) the resistance resulting from poor electrical contact to the cell with metal probes. Both of these may be causing a substantial error in the measurements, in effect adding series resistance to the cell and depressing the knee of the I–V curve. For example, in Fig. 8-15, the measuring circuit is connected with only two wires to the solar cell between point a' and a'', and b' and b'', respectively; these wires and their respective metal probes to the solar cell cause voltage losses, as indicated in Fig. 8-16 for four different cases. Curve A could result from using a pair of No. 20 copper wires 3 m in length to connect the cell to the load (0.2 ohm) and at the same time have a slight amount of corrosion on the cell ohmic contact and the metal probes (0.3 ohm). Corrosion-free contacts and probes would still result in a plot resembling Curve B. If the total contact and lead resistance were reduced to 0.005 ohm by using a pair of No. 12 copper wires 1 m in length, the result would be similar to Curve C, but only if the contacts and probes remained free of any resistance. Curve D is the true cell output for comparison.

The solution to this problem lies in the so-

called four-point termination of the cell or array. Figure 8-17 shows the circuit used to eliminate the effects of lead and contact resistance. This circuit incorporates the use of two separate pairs of wires leading from four separate probes that make contact with the cell or the array terminals and the current and voltage measuring equipment.

The I–V curve resulting from the use of two pairs of leads for cell output measurements is the same as Curve D in Fig. 8-16. The I–V curve is now independent of the circuit resistance with only one exception: a larger value of contact or wiring resistance causes a gap in the curve portion near the short-circuit current. The resistance in the load circuit, however, no longer has an effect upon the shape or accuracy of the solar cell curve. This holds true for cell—as well as array—measurements.

A simple solution to extending the solar cell I–V curve to true short-circuit current or even to negative voltages is the addition of a so-called "back bias," as illustrated in Fig. 8-18.

8-20. Three Types of Solar Cell I–V Curves

Different solar cell I–V characteristics can be obtained by three different test methods.

Method A. Photovoltaic Curve. The cell is fully illuminated and a load resistance across its ter-

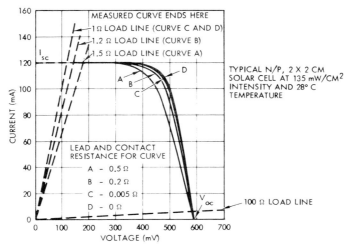

Fig. 8-16. Effect of lead and contact resistance on the current-voltage relationship of a solar cell when using two-point cell pickoff.

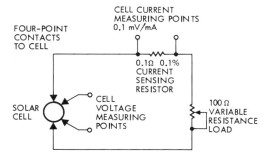

Fig. 8-17. Four-point solar cell load circuit.

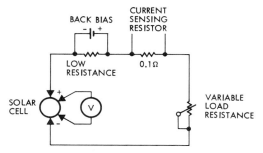

Fig. 8-18. Back bias circuit to measure true I_{sc} when large lead resistances are present.

minal is varied between 0 and ∞, as described in Section 8-16.

Method B. Diode Curve. The cell is not illuminated (dark) and an external source forward biases the cell. As the cell terminal voltage is varied between 0 and approximately 0.6 V, the corresponding values of input current are recorded.

Method C. n-p Junction Characteristics. The cell is illuminated with a variable intensity, invariant spectral distribution source. As the intensity is varied stepwise from 0 to approximately two solar constants, sets of I_{sc} and V_{oc} data points are recorded.

Corresponding Equations for Methods A, B, and C. The $I\text{-}V$ curves shown previously (in Chapter 4) were obtained with Method A. The non-illuminated cell curves discussed in conjunction with shadowed cell and array performance (Chapter 2) and with "dark forward"

testing (Section 8-22) were obtained by Method B. Method C is of interest only in solar cell research.

Neglecting the cell's shunt resistance and using the magnitude of I only (i.e., $I = |I|$), the three different curves are represented by these solar cell equations:

Method A:

$$I = I_L - I_0 \left\{ \exp\left[\frac{q}{AkT}(V + IR_S)\right] - 1 \right\}$$

Method B:

$$I = I_0 \left\{ \exp\left[\frac{q}{AkT}(V - IR_S)\right] - 1 \right\}$$

Method C:

$$I_{sc} = I_0 \left[\exp\left(\frac{q}{AkT}V_{oc}\right) - 1 \right]$$

where the symbols are as defined in Section 2-31.

8-21. Measurement of Solar Cell Series Resistance

Solar cell as well as array series resistance (defined in Section 4-15) can be measured reasonably accurately by the procedure given below.[26]

- Determine the two or more light levels at which series resistance measurements are to be made. These light levels should approximately correspond to those for which precise performance predictions are to be made.
- Determine the temperature difference between the cell test fixture and each cell to be tested at each light level. If possible, bond cells to a heat sink with solder or adhesive.
- Plot the $I\text{-}V$ curves obtained at the different light levels on separate sheets of semitransparent graph paper; then slide the curves over each other until a best match of the $I\text{-}V$ curves is obtained. Determine ΔI_{sc} and ΔV_{oc} by the offset of the graph paper rulings.
- Correct ΔI_{sc} and ΔV_{oc} for possible tem-

perature variations, and calculate R_S from

$$R_S = \frac{\Delta V_{oc}}{\Delta I_{sc}}.$$

The above method can lead to significant and intolerably high errors in the values of series resistance if the measurement techniques are not tightly controlled. Measurement errors typically arise from mechanical, electrical, or thermal sources. Mechanical backlash, friction, inadequate gain, excessive hysteresis, slight miscalibration, or zero-offset in the X–Y recorder used can lead to imprecise I–V curves. Instabilities in the light levels during the tests can lead to "wavy" and imprecise I–V curves. Excessive thermal impedance between the solar cell and the heat sink of the test fixture can result in distinctly different cell operating temperatures at the different light levels at which the I–V curves are plotted.

8-22. Dark Forward-testing

The testing of the dark (i.e. non-illuminated) solar cell array forward characteristics has received considerable attention for two reasons: 1) solar simulators which illuminate very large areas or volumes sufficiently uniformly so that arrays mounted to spacecraft can be meaningfully tested may not be available, and 2) large, articulated, oriented arrays, already integrated to a spacecraft and mounted in a stowed condition, cannot always be readily unfolded for testing. The so-called dark forward-test method

is the only presently known method which is applicable for these cases.

Dark forward-testing consists of connecting an external dc bias source to the terminals of a non-illuminated solar cell array such that the array becomes forward biased. During the test, the dark forward characteristics of the solar cell "diode" matrix are measured while the bus voltage is varied. Typically, the array current and bias voltage are recorded automatically by an electromechanical X–Y plotter.

The forward bias current level is not critical, but best results are obtained when the maximum forward bias current exceeds 50% of the short-circuit current which would be obtained under one solar constant illumination.

The accuracy of this test method depends to a large degree upon the accuracy with which the temperature of the array under test can be measured, and upon the temperature uniformity that can be achieved over the entire array. During the test, the forward bias causes a temperature rise of the array under test, and this, under most practical circumstances, leads to an undesirable error. Therefore, pulsed bias applications (up to 10 seconds dwell time) have been employed.

The dark forward-test method was effectively used during the prelaunch checkout phases of the solar cell arrays on Skylab.[27] The relationships between the photovoltaic output characteristics and the dark forward characteristics are illustrated in Fig. 8-19. The series resistance of illuminated solar cells (2 × 2 cm, 0.35 mm

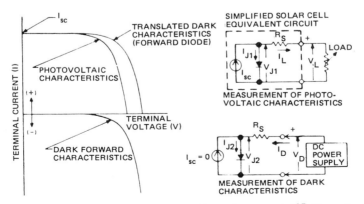

Fig. 8-19. Photovoltaic and dark forward characteristics (illustrative example.)[27] (*Reproduction granted by the American Nuclear Society.*)

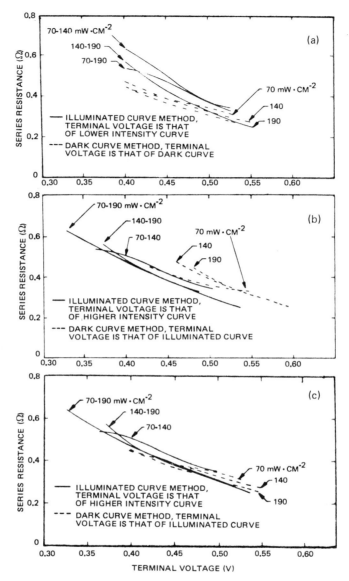

Fig. 8-20. Series resistance versus voltage obtained using illuminated and dark curve methods for Centralab 2 × 2 cm cells.[27] (*Reproduction granted by the American Nuclear Society.*)

thick, 2 ohm · cm base resistivity) was found to be a function of both illumination level and cell voltage, as shown in Fig. 8-20. The values of series resistance were used in the computation of the photovoltaic *I–V* curve based on dark forward measurements. The method was found to be sensitive to temperature, as shown in Fig. 8-21.

Figure 8-22 presents dark *I–V* curves for various modules in parallel. In Fig. 8-23 is a cross-plot of Fig. 8-22, showing the relationship be-

tween the dark terminal voltage and the number of parallel modules at several currents. These plots indicate that the dark *I–V* characteristics cannot be used to adequately determine the number of modules connected in the circuit, except for major discrepancies. For instance, in Fig. 8-23, the change in the dark terminal voltage from 20 to 19 modules is only 0.1 V, but from 20 to 16 modules, this difference is about 0.7 V.

The temperature coefficient of the dark ter-

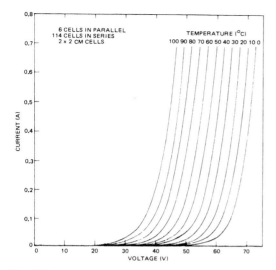

Fig. 8-21. Dark *I–V* curves at various temperatures for an ATM solar cell module.[27] (*Reproduction granted by the American Nuclear Society.*)

minal voltage at an applied current of 800 mA was found to be about – 0.26 V/°C. In view of this high sensitivity of voltage to temperature, the temperature of the cells must be accurately determined. For large solar panels, thermal gradients across the panels must also be considered.

8-23. Insulation Resistance and Voltage Breakdown

The equipment used for the measurement of the leakage resistance and the breakdown voltage of insulating sheets between solar cell circuits and a metallic substrate is of the conventional type and, therefore, is not described here.

Measurements are best performed by shorting all positive and negative solar cell circuit terminals together, and then measuring the resistance between the solar cell circuits and the substrate. Care should be exercised to prevent solar cell or blocking diode potentials from exceeding safe limits in case a low-resistance path or arc-over suddenly occurs. Solar cells generally are less sensitive to excessive reverse bias voltages than are rectifier diodes because 1) the solar cells have rather large reverse leakage currents at low voltages, and 2) the current flow from insulation resistance measuring equipment is usually limited to a few milliamperes, preventing a large voltage build-up across the solar cells.

Prior to installation of solar cells on a metallic substrate, the insulation quality is frequently

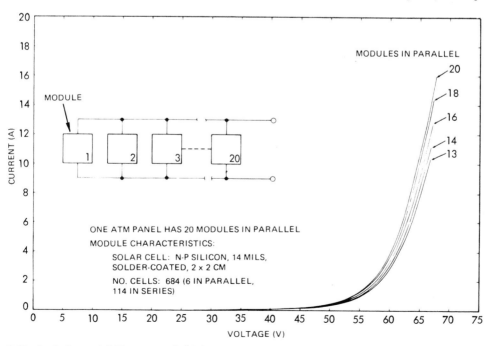

Fig. 8.22. Dark forward *I–V* curves at 25°C for an ATM panel with various numbers of modules in parallel.[27] (*Reproduction granted by the American Nuclear Society.*)

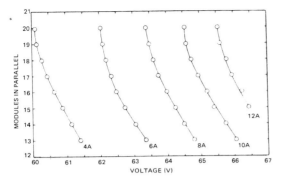

Fig. 8-23. ATM panel dark forward terminal voltage at 25°C for various numbers of modules in parallel, applied current as a parameter.[27] (*Reproduction granted by the American Nuclear Society.*)

determined by a "wet-sponge" test. Experience, however, has shown that for cell-to-substrate voltages below 100 V dc, pin-holes in the insulating sheet may be of no consequence to array operation, even though the insulating sheets may not pass the wet-sponge test.

THERMO-OPTICAL MEASUREMENTS

8-24. Measurement of Spectral Distribution and Spectral Response

The spectral distribution of light sources is measured with the aid of a spectroradiometer. Many different types of spectroradiometers are in use, ranging from relatively simple "filter wheel" devices to sophisticated, continuously recording instruments. In general, very similar or even identical instruments are being utilized for measuring the spectral response of solar cells.[28,29,30]

The use of a filter-wheel spectroradiometer for measuring the reflectance of solar cells is illustrated in Fig. 8-24. The band-pass filter indicated in this figure is actually one of 13 filters that cover the wavelength range over which solar cells are responsive. The filters are mounted on a disk ("wheel") and rotated into the optical path as shown.

8-25. Determination of the Solar Absorptance

The solar absorptance of opaque materials (glassed solar cells, etc.) is generally determined as follows:

1. Measurement of the spectral reflectance, ρ_λ (see Section 8-27).
2. Calculation of the (average) solar reflectance, ρ_S, by integrating over the solar spectrum, S_λ (see Section 9-3):

$$\rho_S = \frac{\int_a^b \rho_\lambda S_\lambda d\lambda}{\int_a^b S_\lambda d\lambda}$$

where the limits of integration, a and b, are determined by the wavelength range over which ρ_λ was measured (usually $a = 0.28\ \mu m$ and $b = 2.5\ \mu m$).

3. Calculation of the solar absorptance, α_S, from

$$\alpha_S = 1 - \rho_S.$$

8-26. Determination of the Hemispherical Emittance

The hemispherical emittance is generally determined by one of the two methods described below.

Spectral Emittance Method. The spectral emittance method consists of four steps.

1. Measurement of the spectral reflectance, ρ_λ (see Section 8-27).
2. Calculation of the average reflectance, $\bar{\rho}$, by integrating over the Planckian blackbody spectral emission spectrum, $P_{T\lambda}$, for a given absolute specimen temperature:

$$\bar{\rho} = \frac{\int_c^d \rho_\lambda P_{T\lambda} d\lambda}{\int_c^d P_{T\lambda} d\lambda}.$$

3. Calculation of the average normal emittance, $\bar{\epsilon}_N$, from

$$\bar{\epsilon}_N = 1 - \bar{\rho}.$$

4. Calculation of the average hemispherical emittance, $\bar{\epsilon}_H$, from

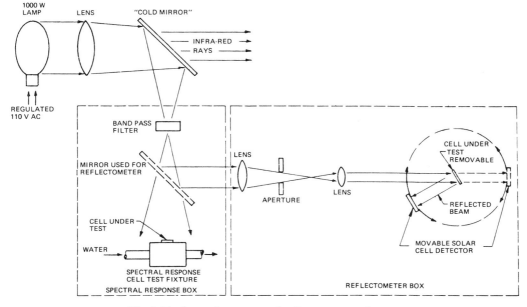

Fig. 8-24. Spectral response and reflectometer equipment.

$$\bar{\epsilon}_H = \left(\frac{\epsilon}{\epsilon_n}\right)\bar{\epsilon}_N$$

where the ratio ϵ/ϵ_n is a correction factor which is based on experimentally verified electromagnetic theory. The values of ϵ/ϵ_n are given in Fig. 8-25.

Total Emittance Method. The emittance of a sample can be determined more rapidly by the total emittance method than by the spectral emittance method. The total emittance method steps are outlined here.

1. Measurement of the total reflectance, $\bar{\rho}$ (see Section 8-28).

2. Calculation of the total normal emittance, $\bar{\epsilon}_N$, from

$$\bar{\epsilon}_N = 1 - \bar{\rho}.$$

3. Calculation of the average hemispherical emittance from

$$\bar{\epsilon}_H = \left(\frac{\epsilon}{\epsilon_n}\right)\bar{\epsilon}_N$$

where ϵ/ϵ_n is given in Fig. 8-25 (see the discussion of ϵ/ϵ_n above).

8-27. Measurement of the Spectral Reflectance

Measurement of the spectral reflectance typically utilizes either an integrating sphere or a heated cavity that is attached to a spectrophotometer. Each of these methods measures the normal spectral emittance, $\epsilon_{N\lambda}$.

Integrating Sphere Method. The test equipment typically consists of an Edwards type integrat-

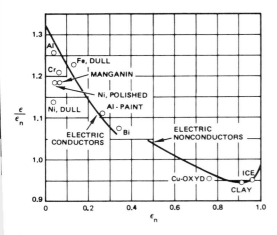

Fig. 8-25. Theoretical and experimental values for the ratio of hemispherical to normal emissivity.[31] (*Reprinted with permission of the Verein Deutscher Ingenieure Verlag.*)

ing sphere reflectometer attachment and a Beckman DK2A Spectrophotometer.[32] The Beckman DK2A is a double-beam ratio-recording spectrophotometer which automatically scans through the wavelength region of interest (from 0.28 to 2.5 microns for glassed solar cells) and records the ratio of the signal from the sample beam and the signal from the reference beam.

The inside surface of the Edwards integrating sphere is coated with Eastman 6080 white paint. This paint is highly reflecting and highly diffusing. Some relatively small openings in the sphere permit the two beams to enter and lead-sulfide and photomultiplier tube detectors to be mounted. Light sources for the equipment are a hydrogen lamp for the shorter wavelength region and a tungsten filament lamp for the longer wavelengths.

The Edwards sphere also contains a sample holder that places the specimen at the geometric center of the integrating sphere such that none of the energy reflected from the specimen can reach the wall-mounted detector without first being reflected from the sphere wall at least once. This optical design eliminates some large potential errors and permits absolute (in contrast to relative) spectral reflectance measurements to be made.

During operation of the reflectometer, the reference and sample beams are directed into the sphere through a small entrance port. The reference beam is incident on the inside sphere wall but does not pass through the center of the sphere. The sample beam, on the other hand, passes through the center of the sphere and, for the calibration, is incident upon the sphere wall a short distance from the spot where the reference beam is incident. For this premeasurement calibration, the specimen is retracted slightly from the center of the sphere. The specimen is then translated into the center of the sphere for the actual reflectance measurement. In this geometry, the sample beam is incident upon the specimen, and only that energy which is reflected from the specimen is detected. Let the intensity of the reference beam which is incident upon the sphere wall be denoted by I_R, and let the intensity of the sample beam which is incident upon the specimen be denoted by I_S. The two beam intensities are identical: $I_R = I_S$. The portion of the sample beam which is reflected from the specimen onto the sphere wall is $\rho_\lambda I_S$, where ρ_λ is the spectral reflectance of the specimen. The ratio-recording detector develops a signal which is equal to $\rho_\lambda I_S / I_R = \rho_\lambda$, since $I_S = I_R$. Hence, the instrument provides an absolute measurement of the spectral reflectance, ρ_λ.

Heated Cavity Method. The test equipment and measurement method is, in principle, similar to that of the integrating sphere method except that instead of an integrating sphere (at room temperature), a heated cavity is used, and instead of the sample beam being compared to the reference beam reflected by a highly diffusing and reflecting surface, it is reflected by a platinum foil which is kept by the surrounding heated cavity at 815°C (1500°F).[33]

8-28. Measurement of Total Reflectance

Measurement of the total reflectance from a sample requires a light source, a detector, and a reflectance standard. Both the sample under test and the standard should have reasonably similar spectral reflectance characteristics to minimize test errors.[34]

ENVIRONMENTAL TESTING

8-29. Particle Radiation-testing

Solar cell radiation damage experiments are performed primarily with electrons, secondarily with protons, and, to a small extent, with neutrons. Special equipment is required to generate the particles and increase their speed until the desired particle energy is achieved.

Electron-testing. Electrons are typically produced by Van de Graaff generators. As an example of a typical radiation facility, the installation at the Jet Propulsion Laboratory, Pasadena, California, is described in the following paragraphs. The radiation laboratory is built around a 3 MeV Dynamitron accelerator, manufactured by Radiation Dynamics, Inc. This machine produces a useful electron beam in the range of energies between 0.6 and 2.3 MeV at electron beam currents up to 2 mA. This relatively high current capability makes possible the irradiation of large areas with high flux rates. The flux rate is adjustable from 1×10^9 $e \cdot cm^{-2}$/second to 1×10^{12} $e \cdot cm^{-2}$/second. The electron beam can be directed (horizontally) down a beam transport system into either one of two experimental areas. Patch panels installed in each area allow the routing of beam monitoring signals to a data acquisition area.

One experimental area is devoted to a semipermanent installation of a vacuum chamber designed for measuring radiation effects in solar cells. An AM0 solar simulator is coupled through Corning 7940 fused silica windows into the vacuum chamber for producing a beam of light on a 12×12 cm test plane. A temperature controlled block at the target area can be maintained between $-150°$ and $+150°$ C. Provision is made for the simultaneous irradiation of up to 14 solar cells on this target plane, with subsequent *in situ* measurement of their electrical parameters using the solar simulator. A thin aluminum or copper scattering foil is used to diffuse the electron beam uniformly over the target area. A small Faraday cup is mounted in the center of the target area for measuring the electron dose. All areas struck by the beam are water-cooled (including the scattering foil). A liquid nitrogen shroud in the chamber is used during solar cell radiations to trap diffusion and fore-pump oil (even though the pumping system is LN_2 trapped), and to cryopump the chamber.

An electromagnet may be used to direct the electron beam into the second experimental room. Here, the beam is brought out into the air through a water-cooled titanium foil. Various experimental arrangements may be set up independently of the first area. Irradiations may be done in the open air (an activated charcoal filter is provided for ozone removal), or the beam may be directed into a vacuum chamber through a titanium entrance window.

Electron Energy Spectrum-testing. Most electron radiation testing is performed using a mono-energetic beam of electrons which is incident perpendicularly on the solar cell surface. However, the JPL facility discussed above was used to generate an electron energy spectrum on occasion.

Proton-testing. Low-energy protons are produced by equipment similar to the proton source shown in Section 8-32, while high-energy protons are generated by cyclotrons. Tandem Van de Graaff generators produce protons having energies from 2 to 10 MeV, cyclotrons from 10 to 50 MeV, and synchro-cyclotrons in the range between 50 and 155 MeV, approximately.

Neutron-testing. Neutrons are usually obtained as by-products from nuclear reactors. One example of such sources is the Fast Burst Reactor at the White Sands Missile Range.

8-30. Ultraviolet Radiation-testing.

Ultraviolet test setups differ widely in appearance; however, their common characteristics are a strong source of ultraviolet (UV) radiation and evacuated volumes in which the test samples are contained: One typical UV test system is described below; another system is described in Section 8-32.

The UV test system uses a xenon compact arc lamp and a number of individually pumped sample chambers. In each such *in situ* vacuum test chamber, the sample is in contact with a temperature controlled (liquid), axially translatable base. The chamber walls consist of UV-transparent quartz tubes. The test samples are maintained in a high vacuum by sputter ion pumps connected to stainless steel tees. All-metal seals are used throughout to maintain ultra-high vacuum and to minimize the potential introduction of contaminants. The sample chambers are pumped down to a pressure of less than 10^{-6} torr using molecular sieve sorption pumps and the integral sputter ion pumps on each sample chamber. The construction of the *in situ* chambers permit the sample, while still in a vacuum enclosure, to be placed at the center of an Edwards type integrating sphere.

A number of individual sample chambers are placed radially around one xenon compact arc lamp located at the center. The chambers are movable along tracks in order to vary the lamp-to-sample distance. Thus, the irradiance on the sample can be set at any value from less than 1 "ultraviolet sun" ($\lambda < 0.4$ microns) to greater than 12 "ultraviolet suns." The lamps used typically range from 2.2 to 6.5 kW types. Other sources are available for degradation testing (e.g., the General Electric B-H6 high-pressure mercury arc), but the xenon arc source is preferred as a better simulation of the solar spectrum in the UV region (Fig. 8-26).

8-31. Far Ultraviolet Testing

In recent years, the *far ultraviolet* (FUV) region of the solar spectrum (below 200 nm) has been identified as being most damaging to organic spacecraft materials such as Kapton and Teflon. Radiant energy at these short wavelengths can be obtained from electrodeless "continuum" krypton or xenon lamps. The gas in these lamps is ionized by RF (radio frequency) fields. An RF input power of 120 W to the xenon lamp produces approximately 7 FUV suns (0.5×10^{14} photons/second) at a distance of approximately 1 m from the lamp. Typical relative spectra are shown in Fig. 8-27.

Another type of electrodeless krypton lamp, in use for FUV testing, is a "resonance" lamp. This lamp produces approximately 3×10^{15} photons/second in two single lines: 116.5 and 123.6 nm.

The FUV radiation from the lamps is reflected by special FUV mirror coatings (Fig. 8-28) and transmitted through magnesium fluoride (MgF_2) windows.

Photodiodes are available for detecting FUV radiation. The National Bureau of Standards provides calibration services in the FUV region of 120 to 254 nm. A typical detector has a rubidium-telluride cathode and a MgF_2 window.

8-32. Combined Environments-testing

In the actual space environment, UV and charged particle radiation (electrons and protons), encompassing large variations in energy, are simultaneously incident on solar cell array materials. Inasmuch as synergistic or anti-synergistic effects can be expected to occur in materials, the simultaneous exposure of solar cell array mate-

rials to various forms of radiation in a vacuum environment is desirable. Such simultaneous exposure is achieved with *combined environment* test setups. Pre- and post-exposure tests are performed *in situ* to prevent chemical changes from occurring in irradiated samples due to the effects of atmospheric oxygen or water vapor.

As an example of the many different systems of this type that are in existence, one of the facilities is described in the following for illustration.[40] A schematic drawing of this facility is shown in Fig. 8-29.

Vacuum System. The vacuum chamber is in the form of a horizontally oriented cylinder approximately 46 cm in diameter by 76 cm long with a corresponding test section volume of approximately 125 liters. The chamber materials are type 304 or 321 stainless steel for the chamber walls and flanges, and fused silica and glass for the windows. No polymeric or other organic surfaces are exposed to the vacuum environment. The ends of the chamber are closed with domed, flanged doors sealed with crushable copper wire rings. A rotatable cantilever end-door-support mounts on either end of the chamber for end-door removal. Numerous flanged ports of various sizes extend from the main chamber to provide access for vacuum pumping, environment components simulation, fluid, mechanical and electrical feedthroughs, viewports, etc.

A 36 cm diameter titanium sublimation pumping (TSP) well extends below the main chamber, and a 400 l/second ion pump mounts to the bottom of this well. The TSP well has fluid feedthroughs and a copper cold wall for increased pumping speeds. A four-filament titanium sublimator extends through the well wall and provides an estimated extra 1200 l/second pumping speed to handle peak gas loads during initial pumpdown and sample irradiation.

Pumping down to 1 to 10 μm of pressure is accomplished with a roughing system consisting of a dry vane mechanical pump and two sorption pumps operated sequentially. During rough pumping, the titanium filaments are outgassed. Upon reaching a pressure of 1 to 10 μm, the ion pump is started.

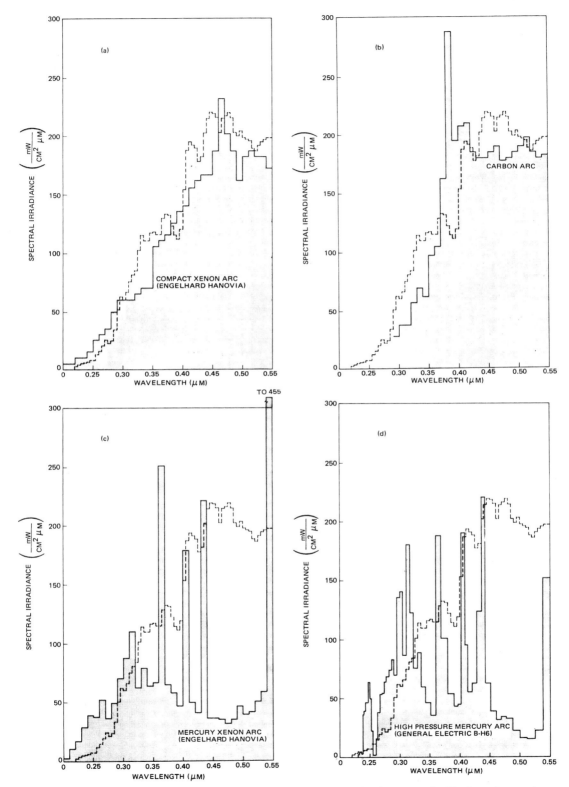

Fig. 8-26. Spectral energy distribution of ultraviolet sources (solid lines) compared with the solar spectrum (dashed lines); a,[35] b,[36] c,[35] d.[37]

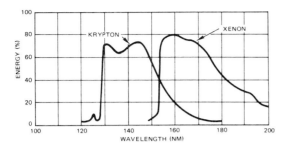

Fig. 8-27. Relative photon energy of krypton and xenon FUV lamps.[38]

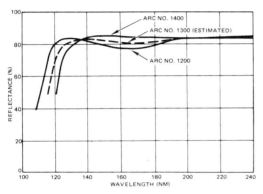

Fig. 8-28. Spectral reflectance for three Acton Research Corp. (ARC) FUV mirror coatings.[39]

Sample Holder and Transfer Mechanism. The sample holder and transfer system was designed to provide maximum capacity and adequate temperature control during exposure, and to permit accurate spectral properties measurements to be made. The design of the mechanical manipulators to transfer samples in the chamber is consistent with good ultra-high vacuum practice. Only inorganic or dry film lubricants are used.

Figure 8-30 illustrates the sample holder/transfer system. The system sample capacity, using a 1×2 cm rectangular sample size, is 28. Small individual sample holders (1) are spring-mounted on four fluid-cooled heat sink trays (2). The trays are vertically translatable using the externally driven spur gear-rack arrangement (4). Translation of the idler gear (3) from one rack gear to another allows horizontal movement of individual sample trays using the externally driven gear (5). Any particular sample may thereby be translated to the "pickup" position, removed from the tray (Fig. 8-31), and translated into the integrating sphere for spectral property measurements.

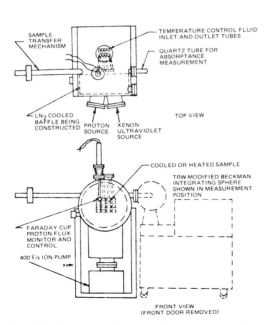

Fig. 8-29. Schematic drawing of a typical combined environment facility (CEF).[36]

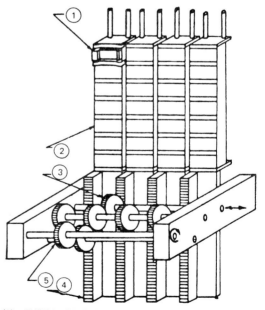

(1)   TYPICAL SAMPLE HOLDER
(2)   HEATER/COOLANT FLUID RESERVOIR
(3)   TRANSLATABLE IDLER GEAR
(4)   RACK GEAR FOR VERTICAL RESERVOIR MOVEMENT
(5)   DRIVE GEAR

Fig. 8-30. Sample holder-motion mechanism.[36]

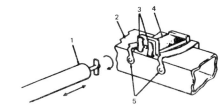

SPECIMEN HOLDER IN "PICK-UP" POSITION

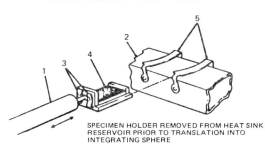

SPECIMEN HOLDER REMOVED FROM HEAT SINK
RESERVOIR PRIOR TO TRANSLATION INTO
INTEGRATING SPHERE

LEGEND:

(1) SPECIMEN PICK-UP/TRANSFER MANIPULATOR
    ARM (EXTERNALLY DRIVEN PUSH-PULL ROTARY
    MOTION FEEDTHROUGH)
(2) SPECIMEN COOLANT/HEATER RESERVOIR
(3) BERYLLIUM-COPPER SPRING CLIPS TO LATCH
    SPECIMEN HOLDER TO MANIPULATOR ARM
(4) 1 x 2 CM TEST SPECIMEN
(5) BERYLLIUM-COPPER SPRING CLIPS TO HOLD
    SPECIMEN HOLDER AGAINST RESERVOIR

Fig. 8-31. Illustration of specimen holder pick-up technique.[36]

The operation of removing a particular sample assembly from the heat sink once the sample has been moved to the "pickup" position, consists of 1) inserting the alignment pin on the end of the sample "pickup"/transfer manipulator shaft; 2) rotating the shaft through 90° to engaged the "propeller" into the spring clips; and 3) pulling the manipulator back to remove the sample holder from the springs holding it against the coolant tray. Since the transfer manipulator shaft can be rotated after the sample has been removed from the coolant tray, directional reflectance measurements are possible.

To replace a sample onto the coolant tray, one simply reverses the three steps above.

Proton Source. The charged particle accelerator consists of three basic components:

1. *Source*—the chamber in which hydrogen is ionized with an RF field and energized with a high potential anode;
2. *Mass separator*—a section in which the

ionized hydrogen is mass separated to provide a near-pure H_1^+ beam; and

3. *Particle detector*—a Faraday cup particle detector for measuring and monitoring the proton flux.

Source. High-purity hydrogen gas (99.999% H_2) is bled into the ionizing chamber through a variable leak valve. The ionizing chamber is a Pyrex bulb 15 cm in diameter by 9 cm long, closed on one end and sealed to a high-vacuum 15 cm port flange on the other end. A 10 MHz RF field is set up inside the bulb by passing an RF current through a copper tube coiled around its exterior. A portion of the hydrogen is ionized by this field and is then excited to higher energies by means of a high-potential anode ring mounted inside the bulb.

Mass Separator. Ions are extracted from the plasma and directed toward the target plane through a mass separator to eliminate other ions from the beam. The separator is basically a Bennett tube type RF mass spectrometer which has been enlarged to accept the full 12 cm ion beam and allow protons (H_1^+ ions) to flow undiverted into the test chamber. At the exit end of the mass separator, hot filaments inject thermal electrons into the beam to provide space charge neutralization.

Particle Detector. A Faraday cup particle detector is used to accomplish four operations: beam uniformity mapping, beam spread measurement, beam flux monitoring, and beam energy detection.

UV Source. A compact arc xenon lamp is used as the UV source. Focusing optics, consisting of a suprasil quartz lens assembly and first surface collection mirrors, are arranged inside a lamp projector housing, a shown in Fig. 8-32. The lamp is a 3.8 kW xenon lamp and is controllable from approximately 100 mW/cm² to 750 mW/cm² (below 400 nm) at the sample plane. The total irradiance has been measured with an electrically compensated, blackened foil radiometer. Filters are used with the radiometer to determine the UV content of the beam before and after a test.

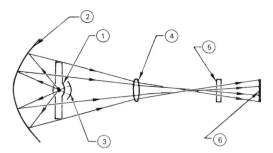

(1)   3.8 KW XENON ARC LAMP
(2)   FIRST SURFACE ELLIPSOIDAL PRIMARY MIRROR
(3)   FIRST SURFACE SPHERICAL SECONDARY MIRROR
(4)   FUSED SILICA LENS
(5)   QUARTZ CHAMBER WINDOW
(6)   SAMPLE PLANE

Fig. 8-32. Schematic drawing of ultraviolet source optics.[36]

Spectral Reflectance Measurements. Spectral reflectance measurements can be performed on any of the test specimens, at any time during the exposure period, by removing the desired sample from the heat sink with the sample manipulator and translating it into a fused silica test tube mounted on the wall of the vacuum chamber. A Beckman DK2A spectrophotometer with an integrating sphere of the Edwards type is positioned adjacent to the chamber with the quartz tube protruding into the sphere.

8-33. Temperature Cycling-Testing

Temperature cycling-tests are performed by two basically different methods: in vacuum, and in air. Temperature cycling in vacuum, also known as *thermal vacuum* or *vacuum thermal cycling*, generally provides good simulation of the space vacuum environment, but a sufficiently fast temperature decay and sufficiently low temperatures, as predicted for deployed solar cell arrays in geosynchronous or planetary orbits, are generally not obtainable.

The undesirably low rate of temperature decay is caused by three unavoidable conditions; namely, a relatively large thermal mass of structural elements and light sources in the space simulation chamber, a relatively high heat sink temperature ($-196°C$ for liquid nitrogen cooled walls instead of $-273°C$ for space), and the relatively inefficient heat transfer by radiation, especially at lower absolute temperatures.

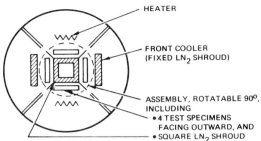

Fig. 8-33. Schematic top view of rapid thermal vacuum cycling equipment. (*Reprinted with permission of the IEEE.*[42])

Frequently, some liquid nitrogen vapors are introduced directly into the vacuum chamber to accelerate the temperature decay and provide a lower temperature for the array under test. The associated loss in vacuum is temporary and can be minimized by using high-volume vacuum pumps.

A different type of thermal vacuum-test setup that permits rapid temperature cycling in high vacuum is illustrated in Fig. 8-33.[41,42] Four solar panel test sections can be mounted with stand-offs to the outside walls of a liquid nitrogen-cooled rectangular cylinder, which, in turn, is able to rotate about its central axis by $90°$ and back. Two of the solar panels face tungsten filament heaters and the other two face liquid nitrogen-cooled walls. All cold walls and heaters are maintained at constant temperature. The liquid nitrogen is boiled off at ambient pressure to reach low cold wall temperatures. Temperature cycling of the solar panels is achieved by rotating the inner assembly into alternate positions. Two test specimens are heated and maintained at the upper equilibrium temperature, while the other two specimens are cooling to the lower test limit. Once this limit is reached, the inner assembly is rotated again and the heating and cooling process repeats on the opposite specimens. Solar panel test sections, as described in Section 7-14, carrying 250 interconnected 2×4 cm solar cell stacks each, and all other elements found on flight panels, reach $-110°C$ in 20 minutes and $-175°C$ in 2 hours. The upper temperature of $65°C$ is reached in about 20 minutes.[42]

More rapid temperature cycling than is possible in vacuum can be achieved with circulating air chambers. Typically, precautions are taken to eliminate moisture and oxygen from the chamber interiors; however, such methods are only moderately effective. With liquid nitrogen vapor-cooling and electric heating, forced air chambers can produce almost any desired temperature profile. Test costs and test durations can be as low as 1% of those for vacuum-tests; however, even well controlled air tests frequently show interconnector and joint failure rates much earlier in the simulated life and at a higher rate of incidence than vacuum tests show. Apparently, atmospheric effects play significant roles in fatigue life testing (see Section 6-22).

Electrical test results typically show solar cell output degradation, which usually is due to increased cell and interconnector series resistance. Depending upon the upper and lower temperature limits and the number of temperature cycles incurred, electrical output losses at the maximum power point are typically only a few percent.

SIGNIFICANCE OF TEST DATA

8-34. Errors

Any test data, no matter how carefully obtained, is subject to 1) being not absolutely correct (or true), and 2) coming out slightly different in a repeat test. The science of statistics can explain not only why this is to be expected, but also can quantize the amount of variation which can be expected.[43]

For simplicity of illustration, let us measure the short-circuit current (I_{sc}) of a solar cell under an AM0 solar simulator.[44] The I_{sc} being measured is called a *variable*. The recorded I_{sc} value from this test is called *data*. Assume further that, based on a light intensity measurement using a primary balloon standard solar cell, the light intensity was too low by 1%. Hence, the data is known to be in *error* by −1% and requires correction. After having corrected the data, the *result* is then reported in the test report. If this thusly measured solar cell is flown in space, its I_{sc} output will be the true output, denoted here by I'_{sc}. The value of the difference between the measured result of the I_{sc} and true I'_{sc} is the error of this *single-sample* experiment. How-

ever, prior to the space flight, the true I'_{sc} is not known, so then we only speculate as to what I'_{sc} might be. We say that the measured result of I_{sc} has associated with it an *uncertainty*. Since the value of the uncertainty is what one thinks the error might be, uncertainty is based on an estimate or assessment by the experimenter of all the possible errors that might be associated with a specific experiment. The errors can fall into any of the categories below.

- *Accidental errors*, such as a time lag in the solar simulator intensity stability control, or *x-y* recorder friction.
- *Fixed errors*, such as deviations in spectral distribution of the solar simulator from that of natural space sunlight.
- *Mistakes*, such as accidentally using a long-lead two-terminal connection to the solar cell under test instead of a four-terminal connection (see Section 8-19).

It has been found that most of the errors tend to be rather small, but, nevertheless, very large errors are possible, even if expected only rarely. The errors can be positive or negative.

In most experiments reported in the literature, uncertainty is typically taken as being identical to the *probable error*. The probable error is usually calculated by taking the square root of the sum of squares of the individual errors. The calculated probable errors found in different publications of test results usually differ from each other considerably, because some experimenters include more sources of errors than others; the given individual errors due to similar apparatus and equipment are usually quite consistent with each other.

8-35. Uncertainties

The user of the design and test data in this handbook is cautioned that each of the many different sets of data included were typically obtained by slightly different test methods and from different test specimens selected from different production lots. None of these differences can be fully ascertained from the available test documents, so it is not surprising to find that some of the data sets may not be mutually compatible with each other (as would be re-

Table 8-6. Typical Uncertainties in Predicted Array Performance.[44,45,46,47]

Project	Uncertainty or Difference from Prediction (%)
JPL Statistical Prediction, Mariner	± 3.8
General Electric, ERTS-1	2
TRW, Intelsat III	0 to 3
Hughes, Intelsat IV	1 to 2

quired, for instance, for comparative analyses and trade-off studies).

The total uncertainty (or probable error) for predicting solar cell array performance in space, based on ground testing of array subassemblies (solar panels, modules, or strings) and computer aided extrapolations to space, is in most cases on the order of a few percent and usually well below 5%. Some observed values of uncertainty are shown in Table 8-6. The uncertainty increases as the complexity of shadow patterns and the angle of non-normal incidence of sunlight increases.

8-36. Uncertainties in Inspection

Many solar cell array design and performance requirements and criteria are verified by inspection. Some examples of such inspections are concerned with the following:

- Cover alignment over solar cells
- Cracked and chipped solar cells and covers
- Adhesive voids and overflow
- Soldered joint quality
- Damaged interconnectors and wires.

Inspectors are inherently not capable of finding all existing defects, even after having received the proper training and orientation. The reasons for inspector errors are given below.[48]

- *Wilful errors*, including fraud and collusion; falsification for the convenience or to the advantage of the inspector; and falsification due to management pressure and deadlines.
- *Intermediate errors*, including inspector bias (usually affects borderline cases);

rounding off (related to readability of meter scales); and overzealousness.
- *Involuntary errors*, including blunders (usually caused by others rather than the inspector); fatigue; and human imperfection.

The accuracy, A, of an inspector can be defined by the percentage of defects he can identify correctly:[48]

$$A = \frac{d - k}{d - k + b}$$

where

d = number of defects reported
k = number of non-defective units rejected
b = number of defects missed.

The quantity $(d - k)$ is the true number of defects found by the inspector; $(d - k + b)$ is the true number of defects in the inspection lot.

Illustrative Example No. 8-1

Inspection lot: 10,000 cell stacks mounted to a solar cell panel.

Number of cracked covers found	92
Number of acceptable cracked covers	2
Number of cracked covers not found	10

From the equation above, the inspector's accuracy is

$$A = \frac{92 - 2}{92 - 2 + 10} = 90\%.$$

In the usual case, the true number of defects, $(d - k + b)$ is unknown because the number of defects missed, b, is unknown. Under the assumption of $k = 0$, an estimate of the total number of defects, denoted by $\hat{N}$, can be made from

$$\hat{N} = d/A$$

where d and A are as previously defined.
In the above example,

$$\hat{N} = 02/0.90 = 102$$

and $b = 102 - 92 = 10$ defects were missed. During a second inspection, either by the same or by a different inspector, $b_2 = b_1 \cdot A_2$ defects would be discovered (under the assumption that the defective covers are marked or recorded). In the above example, if $A_2 = 0.90$ also $b_2 = 10 \times 0.90 = 9$ defective covers would be discovered in addition, or $92 + 9 = 101$ defectives in both inspections together.

If an environmental exposure had been performed between these two inspections, the additionally discovered nine defective covers may not have been due to the environmental exposure.

In actual industrial settings, inspector accuracies are highly dependent upon the nature of the defects, ease of inspectability, clarity of the definitions of fail/pass criteria, available inspection tools (lighting, etc.), personal comfort or discomfort during inspections, boredom, fatigue, motivation, schedule pressure, general working conditions, time of day (relating to daily alertness and productivity cycles), training, and other factors. The actual accuracies for a given number of solar cell panel inspections can, therefore, be expected to be varying both from panel to panel and from one inspection to another inspection of the same panel.

Accuracies of inspectors of solar cell assemblies have not been found in the literature; however, they can be expected to be similar to the accuracies found in other industries, where they range from 50 to 100%, with 80 to 90% occurring quite frequently.

Recommended Practice. The above discussion suggests that a solar cell panel should be inspected prior to an environmental exposure at least twice, or at least as many times prior to the environmental exposure as it will be inspected after the exposure.

8-37. Significance of Sample Size

It is a well recognized fact that increasing the (random) sample size (the number of cells in a test sample selected at random from a population, or production lot) will permit a more accurate prediction of the mean behavior of the population. The estimated mean m of the population is always calculated from the measured mean $\bar{x}$ of the sample; however, there is a risk α that the estimated population mean m is off

from the true (but unknown) mean, by an amount d or greater. Or, conversely, there is $1 - \alpha$ confidence that the estimated population mean is different than the true mean by an amount less than d. If the potential error d is fixed, the confidence $1 - \alpha$ (or the risk α), depends upon the sample size n, and on the standard deviation σ of the population (or the spread in the test data s, if σ is unknown) in accordance with the Eq. 8-1.

$$n = \frac{z_p^2 \cdot \sigma^2}{d^2} \qquad (8\text{-}1)$$

The standard normal variable, z_p, where $p = 1 - \alpha/2$, is given in a statistical table of "Cumulative Normal Distribution Values of z_p."

In order to obtain an estimte of σ to use in Eq. 8-1, a number of sets of solar cell test data were reviewed.[36] It was found that the test samples are seldom selected at random from an entire production run and, therefore, rarely represent the entire population statistically. However, both the mean and the distribution of the entire population (many production lots) is reasonably well known from the cell manufacturer's quality control records, at least for electrical output under standard test conditions (28°C, one solar constant, AM0). Some large solar cell procurements made during the mid-1970's were designed to encompass the cell manufacturer's yield distribution as shown below.

Electrical Group No.	Minimum Output Current at 0.425 V for 0.004 A Intervals
1	0.235 A
2	0.239 A
3	0.243 A
4	0.247 A
5	0.251 A
6	0.255 A
7	0.259 A

Typical calibration and test repeatability was ±0.002 A, or one-half of the interval of an output group. From this, the population mean and the standard deviation were estimated to be:

$$m = 0.249 \text{ A}$$

$$\sigma = 0.005 \text{ A}$$

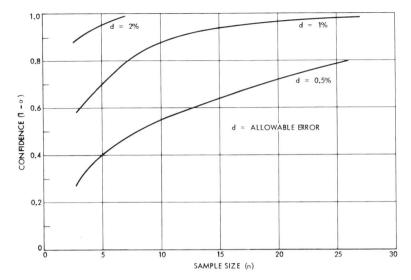

Fig. 8-34. Confidence in test data as a function of sample size with allowable error as a parameter.

where it was assumed that the 6σ limits ($\pm 3\sigma$) include the entire distribution ranging from 0.235 to 0.263 A. Knowing m, values of d can be selected corresponding to any desired uncertainty. For example, $d = 0.00249$ A corresponds to a $\pm 1\%$ uncertainty.

Using Eq. 8-1 and values for σ, z_p, and d, as discussed above, values for confidence $1 - \alpha$ were calculated as a function of sample size n and are plotted in Fig. 8-34. For a sample size n, Fig. 8-34 gives the confidence $1 - \alpha$ that the sample mean $\bar{x}$ is off from the population mean by an amount less than d.

REFERENCES

1. R. A. Marzek, "Survey and Study for an Improved Solar Cell Module, STOD Task No. 43," Document No. **900-270,** Jet Propulsion Laboratory, August 1969.
2. R. B. Larson, "Microjoining Processes for Electronic Packaging," in *Assembly Engineering*, Hitchcock Publishing Co., Wheaton, Illinois, October 1966.
3. R. Buhs *et al* in *Conference Records of the 11th IEEE Photovoltaic Specialists Conference*, 1975.
4. H. S. Rauschenbach and A. F. Ratajczak in *Conference Records of the 10th IEEE Photovoltaic Specialists Conference*, 1973.
5. H. G. Mesch in *Conference Records of the 10th IEEE Photovoltaic Specialists Conference*, 1973.
6. T. C. Eakins, "Results of Solar Cell Welded Interconnection Development," in *Proceedings of the*

7th Intersociety Energy Conversion Engineering Conference, 1972.
7. R. V. Elms, Jr., "Solar Array Welding Development," in *Proceedings of the 9th Intersociety Energy Conversion Engineering Conference*, 1974.
8. D. R. Lott, "Solar Array Flexible Substrate Design Optimization, Fabrication, Delivery and Test Evaluation Program," Final Report **LMSC-0384284,** Lockheed Missiles and Space Company, Inc., March 1975.
9. *Conference Records of the 10th IEEE Photovoltaic Specialists Conference*, 1973.
10. *Conference Records of the 11th IEEE Photovoltaic Specialists Conference*, 1975.
11. R. M. Jenkins *et al* in *Conference Records of the 10th IEEE Photovoltaic Specialists Conference*, 1973.
12. D. R. Lott *et al* in *Conference Records of the 11th IEEE Photovoltaic Specialists Conference*, 1975.
13. TRW Systems, previously unpublished data.
14. H. F. Sawyer and J. R. Mulkern, "In-process non-destructive Microweld Inspection Techniques," presented in Microelectronic Packaging Conference, Palo Alto, California, November 1968.
15. W. S. Griffiths and H. F. Sawyer "Non-destructive Weld Inspection Techniques," Contract **NAS 2-4166** by W. V. Sterling for NASA Ames Research Center; "Study and Development of Non-destructive Weld Inspection Techniques, Phase I Final Report," NASA CR-73, 207, Contract **NAS 2-4166** by W. V. Sterling, Inc., March 1968; and "Study and Development of Non-destructive Weld Inspection Techniques, Phase II Interim Report," NASA CR-73, 385, Contract **NAS 2-4166** by W. V. Sterling, Inc., October 1969.
16. F. S. Johnson, "The Solar Constant," (pp. 431–

439) in *Journal of Meteorology*, Vol. **II**, *No. 6*, December 1954.

17. Data Sheet for Spectrosun Model X-25 Solar Simulator, Spectrolab.

18. G. A. Work, "Pulsed Xenon Solar Simulator Description," TRW DSSG.

19. "LAPSS-III Solar Simulator," Data Sheet, TRW DSSG.

20. *Report and Recommendations of the Solar Energy Data Workshop Held November 1973*, National Science Foundation, National Oceanic and Atmospheric Administration, **PB-238 066**, September 1974.

21. *Proceedings of the ERDA Semiannual Solar Photovoltaic Program Review Meeting, Silicon Technology Programs Branch*, **CONF-770112**, January 1977.

22. *Proceedings of the Semiannual Review Meeting, Silicon Technology Programs*, U.S. Department of Energy, Solar Energy Research Institute, Golden, Colorado, April 1978.

23. L. B. Sidwell, "Results of the 1974 through 1977 NASA/JPL Balloon Flight Solar Cell Calibration Program," JPL Publication **77-82**, January 1978.

24. R. F. Greenwood and R. L. Mueller, "Results of the 1970 Balloon Flight Solar Cell Standardization Program," Technical Report **32-1575**, Jet Propulsion Laboratory, December 1972.

25. H. S. Rauschenbach, "Understanding Solar Measurements," Hoffman Electronics, Inc., Application Notes, 1959.

26. M. Wolf and H. Rauschenbach, *Series Resistance Effects on Solar Cell Measurements, Advanced Energy Conversion*, *Vol. 3*, (pp. 455–479) Pergamon Press, Elmsford, New York, 1963.

27. M. S. Imamura and P. Brandtzaeg (Martin Marietta Corporation) and J. L. Miller (NASA Marshall Space Flight Center), "Solar Cell Dark *I-V* Characteristics and their Applications," in *Proceedings of ENERGY 70 Intersociety Energy Conversion Engineering Conference*, 1970.

28. R. Stair *et al*, "Some Developments in Improved Methods for the Measurement of the Spectral Irradiances of Solar Simulation," NASA **CR-201**, April 1965.

29. H. K. Gummel and F. W. Smits, "Evaluation of Solar Cells by Means of Spectral Analysis," *The Bell System Technical Journal*, Vol. **XLIII**, *No. 3*, May 1964.

30. J. Mandelkorn *et al*, "Filter-Wheel Solar Simulator," NASA **TN D-2562**, NASA Lewis Research Center, Cleveland, Ohio, January 1965.

31. E. R. G. Eckert and R. M. Drake, Jr., *Heat and Transfer, 2nd Edition*, McGraw-Hill, New York, 1959.

32. D. K. Edwards *et al*, "Integrating Sphere for Imperfectly Diffuse Samples," (pp. 1279–1288) in *Journal of the Optical Society of America, Vol. 51*, 1961.

33. R. V. Dunkle *et al*, "Heated Cavity Reflectometer for Angular Reflectance Measurements," (pp. 541–567) in *Progress in International Research on Thermodynamics and Transport Properties*, American Society of Mechanical Engineers, 1962.

34. K. E. Nelson, E. E. Leudke, and J. T. Bevans, "A Device for the Rapid Measurement of Total Emittance," (pp. 758–760) in *Journal of Spacecraft Rockets, Vol. 3*, 1966.

35. "Hanovia Compact Arc Lamps," Hanovia Lamp Division of Englehard Hanovia, Inc., Newark, New Jersey.

36. TRW DSSG, previously unpublished data.

37. "High Brightness Mercury Arc Lamps Capillary Type A-H6 and B-H6 Application Data and Accessory Equipment," **GET-1248H**, General Electric, Hendersonville, North Carolina.

38. "The Electrodeless Lamp System," Ophthos Instrument Co., Rockville, Maryland.

39. Product Data Sheets, Acton Research Corporation, Acton, Massachusetts.

40. G. L. Brown, E. E. Leudke, and R. L. Hammel, "Combined Environment Simulation Facility," TRW DSSG.

41. W. Ley, "DFVLR Facility for Thermal Cycling Testing on Solar Cell Panels under Vacuum Conditions," in *Conference Records of the 12th IEEE Photovoltaic Specialists Conference*, 1976.

42. H. S. Rauschenbach *et al*, "The TDRSS Solar Array," in *Conference Records of the 13th IEEE Photovoltaic Specialists Conference*, 1978.

43. S. J. Kline and F. A. McClintock, "Describing Uncertainties in Single-Sample Experiments," in *Mechanical Engineering*, January 1953.

44. B. Anspaugh, "Uncertainties in Predicting Solar Panel Power Output," NASA **TM 33-673**, Jet Propulsion Laboratory, April 1974.

45. A. Kirpich et al, "Flight Performance of the ERTS-1 Spacecraft Power System," in *Proceedings of 1973 IEEE Power Electronics Specialists Conference*.

46. TRW data obtained from COMSAT Corporation.

47. E. Levy, Jr. and F. S. Osugi, "Design and Performance of Intelsat IV Power Subsystem," in *Proceedings of the 7th Intersociety Energy Conversion Engineering Conference*, 1972.

48. J. M. Juran *et al*, *Quality Control Handbook, 2nd Edition*, McGraw-Hill, New York, 1962.

9
Environments and Their Effects

9-1. The Solar Cell Array Environment

The total solar cell array environment is the complex of sunshine, climatic conditions, biotic factors, and, for space arrays, extraterrestrial phenomena. For convenience only, at the risk of oversimplification, the total environment is divided into the *terrestrial* and the *space* environment. Each of these is further subdivided into a number of *individual* environments. While some individual environments interact with each other, others do not. The interaction may be *synergistic* or *anti-synergistic*. Synergism results in a greater effect on the array from *combined* environments than the sum of the effects from each individual environment. Anti-synergistic effects partially nullify the individual effects.

Most environments have a detrimental effect on the long-term performance capability and reliability of solar cell arrays. The most significant environments against which terrestrial arrays must be protected include high wind, snow, and ice loadings, and corrosion aided by moisture, high temperature, and air-borne contaminants. The most significant environments against which space arrays must be protected include ground handling, launching, and space radiation. A significant, life reducing environment for both terrestrial and space array is temperature cycling, caused by periodic interruptions of the array's insolation by clouds, night-time, or solar eclipses. Many other environments also have deleterious effects on solar cell arrays.

Beneficial environments for terrestrial arrays include low air temperatures and moderate wind velocities that increase the solar cell operating efficiency.

SOLAR ENERGY

9-2. The Sun

The sun is a gigantic thermonuclear reactor emitting energy from its surface approximately like a black-body radiator at 6000°K. The emitted energy is mainly in the form of electromagnetic radiation, ranging from about 30 m short-wave radio waves to 10^{-10} m X-rays. However, most of the solar energy is in the visible and near-infrared wavelength range.[1]

The earth revolves around the sun in a slightly elliptic path which gives rise to annual variations in the solar intensity falling onto the earth's surface. The inclination of the earth's spin axis by 23.5° produces the summer/winter variation in sun elevation above the earth's horizon. Having a diameter of approximately 1.39×10^9 meters, the sun appears from the earth as a disk subtending a total angle of 31°59′ (as seen from the center of the earth), known as its *mean angular diameter*. Its seasonal variation is ±1.7%.

9-3. The Solar Constant

The total energy received from the sun on a unit area perpendicular to the sun's rays at the mean earth-sun distance, termed an astronomical unit (1.000 AU = 1.496×10^{11} m), is called the *solar constant*. The solar intensity at solar distances other than 1 AU is typically expressed as a fraction or a multiple of the solar constant.

The value of the solar constant has been revised many times. The most widely used values for solar array work during the period between 1958 and 1972 were 1400 W/m^2 and 1396 W/m^2, based on the work done by Johnson.[2] In 1971, the value of the solar constant was revised to a design value of 1353 W/m^2 or 1.940 cal · cm^{-2} · min^{-1}. It is taken for a mean earth-sun distance of 1 AU and in the absence of the earth's atmosphere. The estimated error is ±2.1 mW cm^{-2} or ±0.03 cal · cm^{-2} · min^{-1}. (The calorie is the thermochemical calorie and the milliwatt is 10^{-3} absolute joule/second.)[3]

Revisions in the value of the solar constant may only affect the predicted solar cell array temperature in orbit. There is no effect on the photovoltaic performance of the solar cell on the array, because solar cells are calibrated in near-space against the sun directly without having to know the solar intensity. Inasmuch as changes in the measured values of the solar constant do not alter the sun's actual intensity, they also do not alter the solar cell output obtained in space at a given distance from the sun. (For calibration techniques of solar cells, see Section 8-13.)

The term *total solar irradiance* refers to total radiant energy received at a given distance, whereas the term *solar constant* describes the same parameter at 1 AU. This handbook has adopted the generally accepted terms *solar illumination* and *solar intensity* instead of *solar irradiance* in order to minimize potential confusion with radiation effects (i.e., ultraviolet, charged particles, etc.).

On the basis of the value adopted for the solar constant, Table 9-1 gives the variation in total solar intensity with changes in earth-sun distance during the year. Table 9-2 gives the corresponding solar intensity values for the other planets of the solar system.

The spectral irradiance of the sun at the distance of 1 AU in the absence of the earth's atmosphere is given in Table 9-3 and Fig. 9-1. The estimated error in these values is ±5% in the wavelength range of 0.3 to 3.0 μm, and greater outside these wavelength limits. Figure 9-1 also shows terrestrial sunlight spectra and identifies atmospheric absorption bands.

Table 9-1. Variation of Solar Intensity with Earth-Sun Distance.[3]

Date	Solar Intensity* (mW · cm^{-2})	Relative**
January 3 (perihelion)	139.9	1.0340
February 1	139.3	1.0296
March 1	137.8	1.0185
April 1	135.5	1.0015
May 1	133.2	0.9845
June 1	131.6	0.9727
July 4 (aphelion)	130.9	0.9675
August 1	131.3	0.9704
September 1	132.9	0.9823
October 1	135.0	0.9978
November 1	137.4	1.0155
December 1	139.2	1.0288

*The changes in sun-earth distance for the same date from year to year are such that values may vary by ±0.1 mW cm^{-2}. For precise comparison, the table of radius vector given in the American Ephemeris should be consulted.

**Relative to 135.3 mW · cm^{-2}.

Table 9-2. Orbital Constants of the Planets and Solar Intensity at Planetary Distances.[3,4,5]

Planet	Semimajor Axis of Orbit (AU)	Semimajor Axis of Orbit (10^6 km)	Sidereal Period (days)	Eccentricity of Orbit 1971 (ϵ)	Solar Intensity at Distance of Semimajor Axis* Solar Constant	Solar Intensity at Distance of Semimajor Axis* mW·cm^{-2}	Ratio of Max to Min Intensity** $\left(\frac{1+\epsilon}{1-\epsilon}\right)^2$
Mercury	0.387 099	57.91	87.9686	0.205 629	6.673 5	902.9	2.303
Venus	0.723 332	108.21	224.700	0.006 787	1.911 3	258.6	1.028
Earth	1.000	149.60	365.257	0.016 721	1.000 0	135.3	1.069
Mars	1.523 69	227.94	686.980	0.093 379	0.430 7	58.28	1.454
Jupiter	5.2028	778.3	4 332.587	0.048 122	0.036 95	4.999	1.212
Saturn	9.540	1427	10 759.20	0.052 919	0.010 99	1.487	1.236
Uranus	19.18	2869	30 685	0.049 363	0.002 718	0.3678	1.218
Neptune	30.07	4498	60 188	0.004 362	0.001 106	0.1496	1.018
Pluto	39.44	5900	90 700	0.252 330	0.000 643	0.0870	2.806

*Solar intensity is $1/R^2$ in units of the solar constant and $135.3/R^2$ in mW · cm^{-2} where R is the semimajor axis of the planetary orbit.

**Values of eccentricity change with time; the ratio of solar intensity at perihelion to that at aphelion in the last column is computed on the assumption of constant eccentricity.

9-4. Albedo

The fraction of solar energy or sunlight reflected from a body in space is known as the body's *albedo*. The reflections may be from the surface, from clouds, or from scattering effects by the atmosphere. The effect of the albedo on the solar cell array is twofold: additional energy incident on the array increases its operating temperature, thereby lowering the solar cell's efficiency; and albedo energy falling on the solar cells will increase the cell's output only if the energy lies in the spectral range in which the solar cell is responsive. For the albedo light to reach the solar cells, the array must be properly oriented (see Fig. 9-2).

Figure 9-3 shows the calculated maximum albedo contribution to solar cell output as a function of altitude. For solar cells to receive this maximum albedo illumination, they must be oriented toward the earth. For this calculation, the earth was assumed to be a uniform diffuse reflector with an albedo of 0.34. The spectral characteristics of the reflected light were assumed to be similar to Air-Mass One (AM1) sunlight in the wavelength region of the solar cell's spectral response. On the dark side of the earth, the albedo is zero.[7]

9-5. Solar Radiation Pressure

As was shown in Section 2-26, the phenomenon of sunlight shining upon a surface is equivalent to the surface being bombarded with photons. In the collision process, the momenta (momentum = mass × velocity) of the photons are conserved, with the result that the radiation pressure acting on a highly reflecting surface is much greater than the pressure on a highly absorbing surface.

For illustration, consider the small surface area dA in Fig. 9-4. In the center of the area, a normal unit vector **n** has been erected and another unit vector **s** points toward the sun (a unit vector points in one direction only, and has a value of unity). The force on the area consists of two components: one acting opposite to **n**, denoted by vector **K**, and another one, **L**, acting in the plane of the area and attempting to push it sideways. The two force components add to the total force dF, which, in vector notation, is written as

$$dF = \mathbf{K} + \mathbf{L}$$

and where

$$\mathbf{K} = -P_s(1 + \rho)(\mathbf{s} \cdot \mathbf{n})^2 \mathbf{n} \, dA$$

Table 9-3. Solar Spectral Irradiance at 1 AU (Solar Constant of 135.30 mW · cm^{-2}).[3]

Wavelength, λ (μm)	Average Irradiance,* P_λ (W·cm^{-2}μm^{-1})	Area under curve, 0 to λ, A_λ (mW·cm^{-2})	Portion of solar constant with wavelength <λ, D_λ (%)
0.120	0.000010	0.00059993	0.00044
0.140	0.000003	0.00073000	0.00054
0.150	0.000007	0.00072000	0.00058
0.160	0.000023	0.00093000	0.00069
0.170	0.000063	0.00135000	0.00101
0.180	0.000125	0.00230000	0.00170
0.190	0.000271	0.00428000	0.00316
0.200	0.00107	0.010985	0.0081
0.210	0.00229	0.027785	0.0205
0.220	0.00575	0.067985	0.0502
0.225	0.00649	0.098585	0.0729
0.230	0.00667	0.131485	0.0972
0.235	0.00593	0.162985	0.1205
0.240	0.00630	0.193560	0.1430
0.245	0.00723	0.227385	0.1681
0.250	0.00704	0.263060	0.1944
0.255	0.0104	0.306660	0.2267
0.260	0.0130	0.365160	0.270
0.265	0.0185	0.443910	0.328
0.270	0.0232	0.548160	0.405
0.275	0.0204	0.657160	0.486
0.280	0.0222	0.763660	0.564
0.285	0.0315	0.897910	0.644
0.290	0.0482	1.09716	0.811
0.295	0.0584	1.36366	1.008
0.300	0.0514	1.63816	1.211
0.305	0.0603	1.91741	1.417
0.310	0.0689	2.24041	1.656
0.315	0.0764	2.60366	1.924
0.320	0.0830	3.00216	2.219
0.325	0.0975	3.45341	2.552
0.330	0.1059	3.96191	2.928
0.335	0.1081	4.49691	3.324
0.340	0.1074	5.03566	3.722
0.345	0.1069	5.57141	4.118
0.350	0.1093	6.11191	4.517
0.355	0.1083	6.65591	4.919
0.360	0.1068	7.19366	5.317
0.365	0.1132	7.74366	5.723
0.370	0.1181	8.32191	6.151
0.375	0.1157	8.90641	6.583
0.380	0.1120	9.47566	7.003
0.385	0.1098	10.0302	7.413
0.390	0.1098	10.5792	7.819
0.395	0.1189	11.1509	8.242
0.400	0.1429	11.8054	8.725
0.405	0.1644	12.5737	9.293
0.410	0.1751	13.4224	9.920
0.415	0.1774	14.3037	10.572
0.420	0.1747	15.1839	11.222
0.425	0.1693	16.0439	11.858
0.430	0.1639	16.8769	12.474
0.435	0.1663	17.7024	13.084
0.440	0.1810	18.5707	13.726
0.445	0.1922	19.5037	14.415
0.450	0.2006	20.4857	15.141
0.455	0.2057	21.5014	15.892
0.460	0.2066	22.5322	16.653
0.465	0.2048	23.5607	17.414
0.470	0.2033	24.5809	18.168
0.475	0.2044	25.6002	18.921
0.480	0.2074	26.6297	19.682
0.485	0.1976	27.6422	20.430
0.490	0.1950	28.6237	21.156
0.495	0.1960	29.6012	21.878
0.500	0.1942	30.5767	22.599
0.505	0.1920	31.5422	23.313
0.510	0.1882	32.4927	24.015
0.515	0.1833	33.4214	24.702
0.520	0.1833	34.3379	25.379
0.525	0.1852	35.2592	26.060
0.530	0.1842	36.1827	26.743
0.535	0.1818	37.0977	27.419
0.540	0.1783	37.9979	28.084
0.545	0.1754	38.8822	28.738
0.550	0.1725	39.7519	29.381
0.555	0.1720	40.6132	30.017
0.560	0.1695	41.4669	30.648
0.565	0.1705	42.3169	31.276
0.570	0.1712	43.1712	31.908
0.575	0.1719	44.0289	32.542
0.580	0.1715	44.8874	33.176
0.585	0.1712	45.7442	33.809
0.590	0.1700	46.5972	34.440
0.595	0.1682	47.4427	35.065
0.600	0.1666	48.2797	35.683
0.605	0.1647	49.1079	36.296
0.610	0.1635	49.9284	36.902
0.620	0.1602	51.5469	38.098
0.630	0.1570	53.1329	39.270
0.640	0.1544	54.6899	40.421
0.650	0.1511	56.2174	41.550
0.660	0.1486	57.7159	42.658
0.670	0.1456	59.1869	43.745
0.680	0.1427	60.6284	44.810
0.690	0.1402	62.0429	45.856
0.700	0.1369	63.4284	46.880
0.710	0.1344	64.7849	47.882
0.720	0.1314	66.1139	48.865
0.730	0.1290	67.4159	49.827
0.740	0.1260	68.6909	50.769
0.750	0.1235	69.9384	51.691
0.800	0.1107	75.7934	56.019
0.850	0.0988	81.0309	59.890
0.900	0.0889	85.7234	63.358
0.950	0.0835	90.0334	66.544
1.000	0.0746	93.9859	69.465
1.100	0.0592	100.676	74.409
1.200	0.0484	106.056	78.386
1.300	0.0396	110.456	81.638
1.400	0.0336	114.116	84.343
1.500	0.0287	117.231	86.645
1.600	0.0244	119.886	88.607
1.700	0.0202	122.116	90.256
1.800	0.0159	123.921	91.590
1.900	0.0126	125.346	92.643
2.000	0.0103	126.491	93.489
2.100	0.0090	127.456	94.202
2.200	0.0079	128.301	94.827
2.300	0.0068	129.036	95.370
2.400	0.0064	129.696	95.858
2.500	0.0054	130.286	96.294
2.600	0.0048	130.796	96.671
2.700	0.0043	131.251	97.007
2.800	0.00390	131.661	97.3104
2.900	0.00350	132.031	97.5838
3.000	0.00310	132.361	97.8277
3.100	0.00260	132.646	98.0384
3.200	0.00226	132.889	98.2180
3.300	0.00192	133.098	98.3724
3.400	0.00166	133.277	98.5047
3.500	0.00146	133.433	98.6200
3.600	0.00135	133.573	98.7239
3.700	0.00123	133.702	98.8192
3.800	0.00111	133.819	98.9057
3.900	0.00103	133.926	98.9848
4.000	0.00095	134.025	99.0580
4.100	0.00087	134.116	99.1252
4.200	0.00078	134.199	99.1862
4.300	0.00071	134.273	99.2412
4.400	0.00065	134.341	99.2915
4.500	0.00059	134.403	99.3373
4.600	0.00053	134.459	99.3787
4.700	0.00048	134.510	99.4160
4.800	0.00045	134.556	99.4504
4.900	0.00041	134.599	99.482195
5.000	0.0003830	134.63906	99.511500
6.000	0.0001750	134.91806	99.717709
7.000	0.0000990	135.05506	99.818965
8.000	0.0000600	135.13456	99.877724
9.000	0.0000380	135.18356	99.913939
10.000	0.0000250	135.21506	99.937221
11.000	0.0000170	135.23606	99.952742
12.000	0.0000120	135.25056	99.963459

*Spectral irradiance averaged over small bandwidth centered at λ:

0.3 to 0.75 μm (bandwidth, 0.01 μm)
0.75 to 1.0 μm (bandwidth, 0.05 μm)
1.0 to 5.0 μm (bandwidth, 0.1 μm)

Table 9-3. (Continued)

Wavelength, λ (μm)	Average Irradiance,[*] P_λ (W·cm^{-2}μm^{-1})	Area under curve, 0 to λ, A_λ (mW·cm^{-2})	Portion of solar constant with wavelength $<\lambda$, D_λ (%)
13.000	0.0000087	135.26091	99.971109
14.000	0.0000055	135.26801	99.976356
15.000	0.0000049	135.27321	99.980200
16.000	0.0000038	135.27756	99.983415
17.000	0.0000031	135.28101	99.985965
18.000	0.0000024	135.28376	99.987997
19.000	0.0000020	135.28596	99.989623
20.000	0.0000016	135.28776	99.990953
25.000	0.000000610	135.29328	99.995037
30.000	0.000000300	135.29556	99.996718
35.000	0.000000160	135.29671	99.997568
40.000	0.000000094	135.29735	99.998038
50.000	0.000000038	135.29801	99.998525
60.000	0.000000019	135.29829	99.998736
80.000	0.000000007	135.29855	99.998928
100.000	0.000000003	135.29865	99.999002
1000.000	0.000000000	135.30000	100.000000

[*]Spectral irradiance averaged over small bandwidth centered at λ:

0.3 to 0.75 μm (bandwidth, 0.01 μm)
0.75 to 1.0 μm (bandwidth, 0.05 μm)
1.0 to 5.0 μm (bandwidth, 0.1 μm)

$$L = -P_s(1 - \rho)(\mathbf{s} \cdot \mathbf{n})[\mathbf{n} \times (\mathbf{s} \times \mathbf{n})] \, dA$$

and ρ is the surface reflectivity and P_s is the solar pressure constant. The value of P_s is proportional to the solar constant and is approximately 4.5×10^{-6} N·m^{-2} (0.94×10^{-7} lb/ft^2) at a solar distance of 1.00 AU. The magnitude of $d\mathbf{F}$ and $\mathbf{K}$, modified by the reflectivity term $(1 + \rho)$, is seen to be twice as great when $\rho = 1$ (highly reflecting surface) as when $\rho = 0$ (black surface). In vector notation, $\mathbf{s} \cdot \mathbf{n} = \cos \theta$ so that the vertical component $\mathbf{K}$, proportional to $\cos^2 \theta$, is largest at normal incidence and falls off rapidly with misorientation.[1]

9-6. Terrestrial Sunshine

The earth's atmosphere is a spectrally selective filter which modifies the space sunlight described in Section 9-3. The optical path through the atmosphere to a point on the earth's surface at normal sea level, perpendicular to the

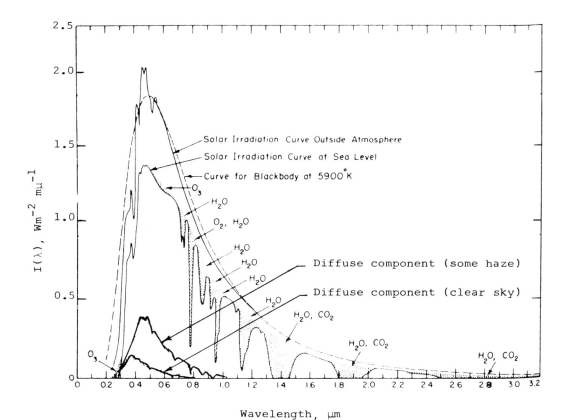

Fig. 9-1. Spectral distribution of sunlight.[6]

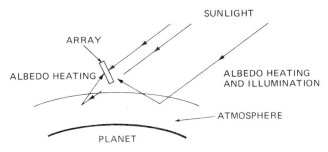

Fig. 9-2. Albedo effects on array.

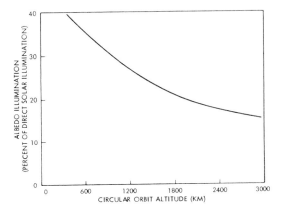

Fig. 9-3. Calculated maximum contribution of earth albedo illumination to solar cell output as a function of altitude for a uniform diffuse reflecting earth with albedo equal to 0.34.[7]

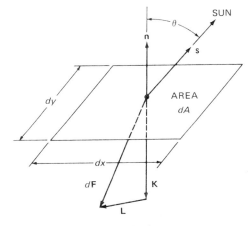

Fig. 9-4. Solar radiation pressure.

local mean earth surface, is said to have penetrated "Air-Mass One" or AM1. Other air mass values indicate the ratio of the optical path length through the atmosphere to the path length through AM1.

In the absence of any atmospheric attenuation or modification of the sun's radiation, the optical air mass is zero, denoted by "AM0."

The atmospheric attentuation due to an air mass is spectrally selective and non-linear with air mass as shown in Figs. 9-1 and 9-5. As an example, the direct solar intensity (i.e., without sky radiation) near sea level on a clear day near noon is approximately 100 mW/cm^2, while in free space (i.e., at AM0), the solar intensity is 135.3 mW/cm^2. The short-circuit current output of a silicon solar cell at AM0, however, will not be 135.3% of its near-sea level output, but only approximately 120%. The difference arises from the change in spectral distribution by the atmosphere that is most pronounced between AM0 and AM1, as shown in Fig. 9-5. This figure also illustrates that the silicon solar cell's energy conversion efficiency is higher for AM1 spectral conditions than for AM0 conditions. The AM1 spectrum is deficient in the short-wavelength or "blue" region of the spectrum, and, therefore, a relatively greater percentage of the incident total solar energy is in the larger wavelength region of the spectrum where the cell is spectrally more sensitive (see Figs. 9-1 and 4-26).

The actual amount of sunlight falling on a specific geographic location, known as *insolance*, is highly dependent upon the prevailing local climate, and varies primarily with general weather patterns. Secondary effects include the location's latitude, the seasonal variation of the earth-sun distance, and local air pollution levels and air mass variations. The amount of sunshine may be numerically expressed as an average of several years, of one year, of one month, or of one day, or it may show the

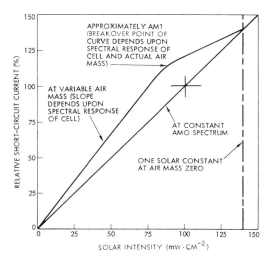

Fig. 9-5. Silicon solar cell short-circuit current output versus solar intensity (collimated sunlight perpendicularly incident on solar cell and on Eppley Normal Incidence Pyrheliometer).

instantaneous value throughout a typical day. Any of these numerical expressions, however, are by themselves insufficient to permit realistic sizing of solar cell arrays. What needs to be considered is the probabilistic nature of weather patterns as they vary over ten to fifty years, or even over longer periods. Presently, insufficient insolance data exists for the world to design solar cell arrays having the smallest possible size and, hence, the lowest possible cost. Rather, currently, photovoltaic systems, together with any energy storage devices, must be overdesigned based on worst-case assumptions of load, sunshine, and weather conditions. The worst-case assumptions cannot be backed up at the present time by statistically significant isolance data, so that each designer must take his own risk of meeting specific power delivery specifications.

Efforts are presently underway to upgrade the existing network of weather stations that record insolance. Most stations have recorded only the total solar energy falling on a horizontal surface, using broad-band radiometers. Only a few stations have measured the direct beam energy, or direct normal energy; so, for most stations, the direct normal energy must be calculated from the horizontally measured insolance, using estimates of the amount of diffuse, or sky, radiation that adds to the direct normal incidence radiation. The largest and presently most widely used insolance data are being accumulated by the Environmental Data Service of the National Climatic Center, National Oceanic and Atmospheric Administration (NOAA), U.S. Department of Commerce, Asheville, North Carolina. Their data have been analyzed widely, recently resulting in the Aerospace Insolation Data Base (AIDB) available from the Aerospace Corporation, El Segundo, California. This data base contains on magnetic tape hourly direct and diffuse solar and climatological data for the 33 cities across the U.S. (listed in Table B-1 of Appendix B).

The AIDB has been analyzed and simplified to provide monthly and yearly averages for the two-year time period 1962 to 1963 of solar energy falling on a flat plate or the entrance apperture plane of a concentrator system (as shown in Table B-2). The simplified data base[8] for the six apperture cases is shown in Table B-3. The monthly variations of the lowest and third to fourth highest station in the data base are illustrated in Figs. 9-6 and 9-7.

Inasmuch as photovoltaic convertors require a certain minimum of solar energy before they produce a practically useful output, it is necessary to know for how many hours sufficiently intense sunshine is available. The simplified data base was analyzed by breaking the solar energy received hourly into intensity level bands and finding the average numbers of hours per year during which the intensity is in one of the levels (the resulting data are shown in Table B-4). The actual variation of the solar intensity during one day is illustrated in Figs. 9-8 through 9-10 for a typical, clear day; a partly cloudy day; and a cloudy day; respectively.

For sizing the maximum heat load capabilities of certain array designs, the amount of maximum possible sunshine is of interest. Figure 9-11 illustrates the extreme insolance predicted for a geographic area that includes the northern Gulf of Mexico, Huntsville, Alabama, New Orleans, Louisana, and the Coastal areas of Florida.[9]

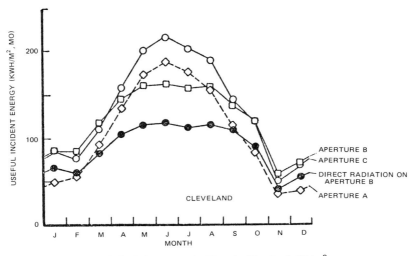

Fig. 9-6. Solar energy incident in Cleveland, Ohio.[8]

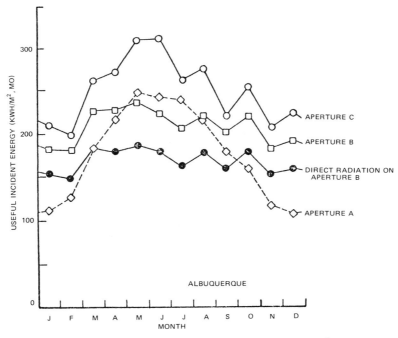

Fig. 9-7. Solar energy incident in Albuquerque, N.M.[8]

The angular position of the sun relative to a terrestrial array is discussed in Section 3-12.

9-7. Ultraviolet Radiation

Sunlight having wavelengths in the range between about 10 nm and 400 nm is defined as ultraviolet (UV) light. Visible light starts at the violet end of the spectrum at about 400 nm wavelengths and continues through blue, green, yellow, and red at about 700 nm. Infrared light has wavelengths greater than 700 nm.

The high UV content of space sunlight (see Table 9-3) is absorbed in the upper atmosphere,

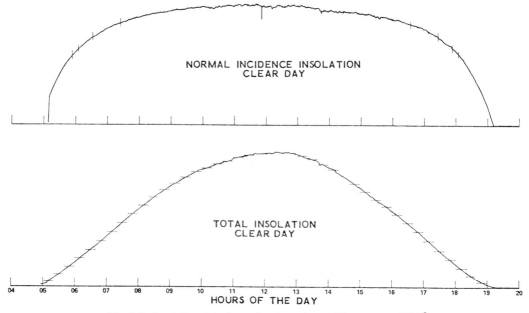

Fig. 9-8. Insolation data for a clear June day at Albuquerque, N.M.[8]

particularly by ozone, such that very little energy from wavelengths shorter than 0.3 μm (3000 Angstroms) reaches the earth. The small fraction of UV radiation that does penetrate the atmosphere accounts for widespread destruction of many materials on the earth.

Effect of UV Light on Materials. In space, damage to plastics materials from UV radiation is generally minor, because the presence of oxygen is essential for major damage to occur. The following materials have been studied under vacuum conditions while being irradiated with UV light (0.20 to 0.25 μm) and were found to exhibit insignificant damage: polyester, epoxy and phenolic laminates, aluminum oxide, and polyethylene. In the presence of oxygen, UV damage can be reduced by incorporating into the original material a UV inhibitor. In utilizing these types of inhibitors, a vacuum weight-loss study is necessary on the finished composition to determine whether their effectiveness would be lost by vaporization in outer space.

UV radiation darkens solar cell coverglasses and the cover adhesive. This darkening reduces the sunlight transmission to the solar cells. Solar cell and cover degradation due to UV

radiation is related to specific products that are discussed in Chapters 4, 5, and 10. Also, see Section 9-44.

UV Radiation Dose. For solar cell array work, the UV exposure dose is typically expressed in *equivalent sun hours*, abbreviated ESH. To be meaningful, such equivalence must always be associated with a wavelength band in which the equivalence was established. For example, a test specimen exposed to an intensity of two UV suns, as measured between 0.2 μm and 0.3 μm for 100 hours, is said to have been exposed to "200 ESH in the 0.2 to 0.3 μm wavelength band."

It should be noted that the accumulated UV dose on solar cell assemblies is a function of solar distance, illumination angle, and array configuration (approximately $1/\pi$ for cylindrical arrays).

TERRESTRIAL ENVIRONMENTS

9-8. Temperature—Terrestrial

In the terrestrial atmosphere, solar cell arrays attain temperatures that are determined by the heating or cooling effects of the surrounding

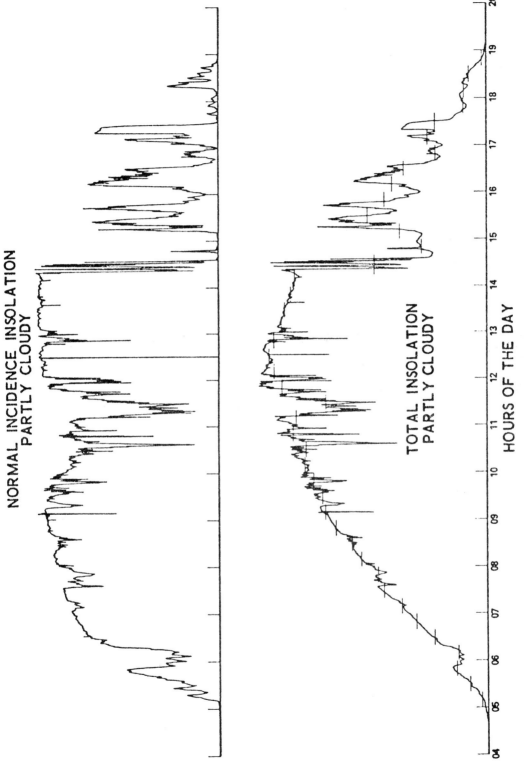

NORMAL INCIDENCE INSOLATION
PARTLY CLOUDY

TOTAL INSOLATION
PARTLY CLOUDY

HOURS OF THE DAY

Fig. 9-9. Insolation data for a partly cloudy June day, Albuquerque, N.M.[8]

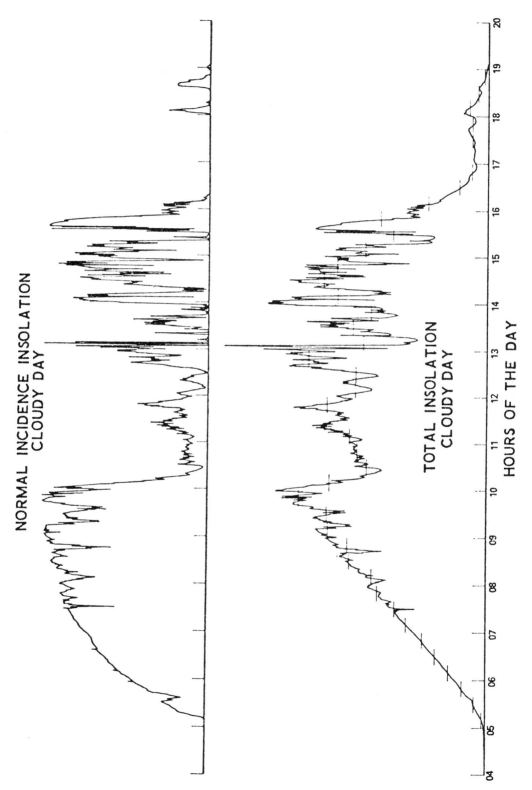

Fig. 9-10. Insolation data for a cloudy June day, Albuquerque, N.M.[8]

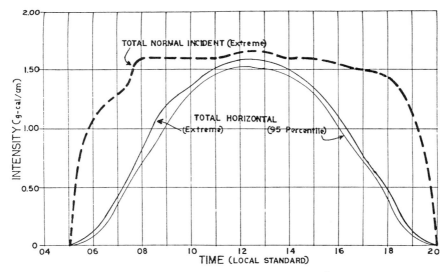

Fig. 9-11. Extreme insolance during June.[9]

atmosphere, by sunlight shining on it, and by the areas that radiate heat away. Additional cooling effects are introduced in systems that utilize external cooling facilities. In general, different surfaces of an array are at different temperatures, causing stresses to be set up in solar cells, solar cell interconnectors, potting materials, encapsulants, frames, support structures, and bearings of orientation systems. Surfaces are not necessarily at the same temperature as the surrounding air, depending upon the specific heat transfer mechanisms that prevail (see Sections 2-53 through 2-58).

Air Temperatures Near the Earth Surface.[9,10,11,12] The air temperature changes diurnally (cycles daily), reaching a maximum usually shortly after (or within a few hours after) local noon, and a minimum just before sunrise. Most of the world experiences temperature variations ranging from no less than −40°C in winter to no more than +45°C in summer.

Air temperatures above 45°C are usually limited to latitudes between about 45° South to about 55° North. Extremely high air temperatures above 50°C occur rarely and usually only in the following areas: the central deserts in the U.S. and Mexico (between about 15° N and 50°N latitude and between 80°W and 125° W longitude), the North African and Middle Eastern areas (between about 7° N and 37° N latitude and between about 15° W and 80° E

longitude), and an Eastern inland portion of Australia.

Air temperatures below −40°C occur on the North American continent, in Europe, and in Asia, above approximately 55° N latitude. Temperatures below −60°C occur usually only in arctic and antarctic regions. Extremely low air temperatures are believed to lie around −70°C, with −90°C being a possibility after prolonged periods of darkness.

Extremely low and extremely high temperatures tend to occur at zero (or low) air speeds, typically at less than 1 m/second. Extremely low temperatures can be reached practically only in low-temperature surroundings by radiation losses into a clear night sky. Extremely high temperatures require that hot air pockets form atmospheric (or "hot-house") effects to contain the hot air locally while the sun shines through a low air mass. It is therefore possible, but not generally occuring, that unexpectedly low or high temperatures are observed, at least for short periods of time, in areas where such temperatures would ordinarily not be expected. Furthermore, reflections and reradiations from the ground or other nearby objects or buildings may cause local "hot spot" air temperatures up to perhaps 70°C, at least for short periods of time.

Air Temperature at Higher Altitudes. See Section 9-15.

Surface Temperatures. See *Thermal Analysis* in Chapter 2 and *Thermal Design* in Chapter 3.

9-9. Humidity

The moisture content of the atmosphere is commonly expressed by the relative humidity, defined as the ratio of the actual vapor pressure of the water vapor contained in the air to the saturated vapor pressure of water vapor at the same temperature. Air with a constant water vapor content will experience a decrease in relative humidity with a rise in temperature. Another measure of atmospheric moisture content is the dew point. The dew point temperature, which is a function of the absolute quantity of moisture in the air, is the temperature to which the air must be lowered for water vapor to condense. Atmospheric moisture ranges from low relative humidity to precipitation.

Relative humidity is measured with hygrometers. Directly recording hygrometers are frequently used in solar cell array production areas where humidity control and its documentation are practiced.

Water vapor in the atmosphere is invisible to the human eye, but is "seen" by solar cells. The absorption bands visible in Fig. 9-1 at approximately 0.93 μm, 1.13 μm, and 1.38 μm wavelength, are primarily caused by water vapor.

The most humid areas of the world are all tropical areas between approximately 20° S and 25° N latitude (except for the Sahara and Arabian desert), the low-lying coastal areas of South America, Austrialia, North America, Northwestern Europe, Japan, and New Zealand. In these, as well as in most other regions, the relative humidity may reach 100% for a significant number of hours/day during a number of days/year. In certain desert areas, the relative humidity is believed to approach zero during periods of extremely high temperature.

Control of Humidity. The major control of humidity is achieved by modern refrigeration-type air-conditioning processes. In these processes, the naturally occurring increase in relative humidity associated with a decrease in air temperature is circumvented by condensing and removing from the air significant quantities of water. Typical relative humidity values in many modern plants lie below 60%.

Additional precautions are usually taken to protect humidity-sensitive solar cells having unprotected titanium-silver contacts (see Sections 9-17 and 9-26).

Effects of Humidity on Adhesives. Control of humidity during the assembly process may be required. Certain adhesives will not develop their highest adhesive strength in the presence of high humidity, while other adhesives may require a high humidity level for adequate curing. The specific manufacturer's recommendations for each adhesive to be used should be followed carefully.

Effects of Humidity. The primary effect of humidity on terrestrial solar cell arrays is corrosion, especially in the simultaneous presence of high temperature (see Section 9-17). Other effects, not necessarily negligible, include growth of fungus (see Section 9-19) and the formation of a "sticky" surface film of moisture that tends to "catch" dust and dirt particles (see Section 9-12). The use of improperly designed, fabricated, or treated solar cell arrays in high-humidity, high-temperature climates can be expected to result in premature solar cell output degradation and physical disintegration of the array.

A decrease of the temperature to the dew point or below will cause a condensation layer and/or droplets to form on surfaces. A continuing temperature decrease to the freezing point and below will cause ice to form on surfaces and in crevices, a process that may be destructive to the array package.

Effects of Humidity on Structural Components for Space Applications. A relatively large quantity of moisture trapped inside voids (such as in honeycomb panels, box beams, or resilient materials) will vaporize during and after the launch phase because of a loss of ambient pressure, as well as aerodynamic and solar heating. Structural damage can usually be prevented only by providing adequate vent openings.

9-10. Precipitation

Precipitation may occur in the form of rain, hail, snow, or ice.

Rain. This form of precipitation may occur anywhere in the world, ranging from essentially zero to several meters annual average. The effects of rain are usually beneficial, cleaning dirt off the solar cell array surfaces. Local rain patterns are usually of interest only for establishing proper drainage requirements.

Hail. Defined as solid precipitation in the form of ice balls or irregular lumps having at least 5 mm diameter and a density of between 0.60 and 0.92 g/cm^3, hail may occur almost anywhere, even though occurrences are infrequent. Smaller ice grains are called *small hail* or *ice pellets*. Small hail has a soft snow core that is covered by a thin ice crust. Ice pellets are solid and hard, rebounding from the hard surfaces (such as glass) upon which they fall. Hail stones of 8 to 13 mm diameter fall frequently; those over 50 mm in diameter fall only occasionally. The largest measured hail stone was 137 mm in diameter and weighed 0.68 kg. Typical hail stones have densities of around 0.80 g/cm^3 and fall in approximately 10 m/second winds at velocities of 20 to 30 m/second. Hail storms are relatively brief, typically lasting no more than 15 minutes and occuring between the early afternoon and evening hours, depositing no more than 50 mm of hail at a surface density of 2.4 kg/m^2 per cm layer thickness.

Larger hail stones can do significant structural damage to solar cell arrays. The impact loading can shatter the transparent glass and plastic solar cell array package windows and/or the underlying solar cells.

Snow. This category includes all forms of frozen precipitation other than hail and rime ice. Snow deposits usually weigh between 0.5 and 2.0 kg/m^2 per cm of depth. The maximum snowfall onto a horizontal surface during a single storm may exceed 1 m in high-snowfall areas, but tends to be less than 0.5 m. The typical design snow load on a nearly horizontal array covered with an 0.5 m thick layer of snow will be 50 kg/m^2, using a 1.0 kg/m^2 · cm density. Snow has some transparency for solar radiation, so that even thickly covered arrays will show some output.

Ice. Ice may form on solar cell arrays from a number of causes: freezing of condensation (see Section 9-9), freezing of precipitation, melting of earlier snow and ice deposits and subsequent refreezing, and direct precipitation from the air at high wind velocities (this is known as *rime ice*).

Ice and snow usually transmit significant amounts of solar radiation, so that even under heavy ice and snow loads the array produces power output. The real danger from ice build-up arises from the possibility of large pieces melting or breaking off from a higher structure and falling onto the array.

9-11. Wind

Wind is defined as the three-dimensional movement of air: in an east-west, north-south, and up-down direction. The direction of the wind is defined as the angle, measured clockwise from true North ($0°$), from which it is blowing. The strength of the wind is defined by its speed, measured with an anemometer at a standard height of 10 m above ground. Wind speed can be estimated from the Beaufort scale (Table 9-4).

Uneven heating of the atmosphere causes *prevailing* and *local* winds. The prevailing winds generally blow from the west (*Westerlies*) in two belts around the earth, extending from approximately $30°$ N to $60°$ N and from $30°$ S to $60°$ S latitude. In the belt between $30°$ S and $30°$ N latitude, the *Trade Winds* blow from the east and toward the equator. At around $30°$ S and $30°$ N latitude, winds come down from the upper atmosphere so that very little, if any, surface winds blow in those narrow, calm belts. At the equator, and about 1000 km on each side of it, warm air rises upward, causing another calm belt at the surface.

Local Winds. These include the relatively extensive monsoons in Asia and many smaller winds having either unusually low or unusually high temperatures. Other local winds are of the

Table 9-4. Beaufort Wind Scale.[10]

Beaufort Number	Identification	Wind Speed			Effect
		Miles/hour	Knots	m/second	
0	Calm	0 to 1	0 to 1	0 to 1	Smoke rises vertically
1	Light air	1 to 3	1 to 3	1 to 2	Smoke drifts with air
2	Light breeze	4 to 7	3 to 6	2 to 3	Wind felt on face; leaves move lightly
3	Gentle breeze	8 to 12	7 to 10	4 to 5	Leaves and twigs move; light flags extend
4	Moderate breeze	13 to 18	11 to 16	6 to 8	Small branches move; dust and paper gets picked up
5	Fresh breeze	19 to 24	17 to 21	9 to 11	Small trees sway; whitecaps form on lakes
6	Strong breeze	25 to 31	22 to 27	12 to 14	Large branches sway; umbrellas are difficult to use
7	Moderate gale	32 to 38	28 to 33	15 to 17	Whole trees sway; walking against wind is difficult
8	Fresh gale	39 to 46	34 to 40	18 to 21	Twigs break off trees; walking against wind is very difficult
9	Strong gale	47 to 54	41 to 47	22 to 24	Shingles blow off roofs; slight damage to buildings
10	Whole gale	55 to 63	48 to 55	25 to 28	Trees are uprooted; considerable damage to buildings
11	Storm	64 to 73	56 to 63	29 to 33	Widespread damage; very rare
12	Hurricane	$\geqslant 74$	$\geqslant 64$	> 33	Severe destruction

From *The World Book Encyclopedia*. © 1979. World Book–Childcraft International, Inc.

cyclone type and include twisters, whirlwinds, tornadoes, and hurricanes. Tornadoes tend to occur over the Central Plains of the U.S. and along its Eastern seacoast. They are characterized by the highest estimated wind speeds and largest air pressure differentials of any wind. Tornadoes possess the most destructive wind forces, but they are limited to relatively small areas (about 6 km²). Hurricanes affect much larger areas than tornadoes, ranging from one hundred to many hundreds of square kilometers. Hurricanes develop over most oceans in narrow belts centered at approximately 20° S and 20° N latitude.

9-12. Sand, Dust, and Dirt

Sand consists of loose, siliceous particles ranging in size from approximately 0.08 to 1.0 mm in diameter. Dust consists of multiple composite particles ranging from 0.1 to 80 μm in diameter. Dust particles may be electrically conductive and are usually soluble in water.

Sand and dust are most severe in low-humidity regions. Dust becomes air-borne with slight winds and may remain suspended for hours as dust clouds. During wind storms, dust particles penetrate almost any enclosure which is not hermetically sealed.

The effects of sand and dust on equipment and materials include increased friction between sliding surfaces, causing abrasion, excessive wear, and binding of parts; degradation of plastics and elastomers used for dynamic seals; clogging of orifices, such as vent ports; contamination of lubricants; erosion of paints, coatings, glass, plastics, and surface finishes; and potential short circuiting of electrical elements. Also, dust may be hygroscopic; its presence on metallic surfaces may aggravate corrosion.

A small amount of dust on the solar cell covers has a negligible effect on the sunlight transmission to the solar cells. Heavy layers of dust accumulation on terrestrial arrays may cause 10 to 20% reduction in output, potentially necessitating washing operations.

9-13. Earthquakes

Earthquakes are three-dimensional motions of the ground. They may manifest themselves as

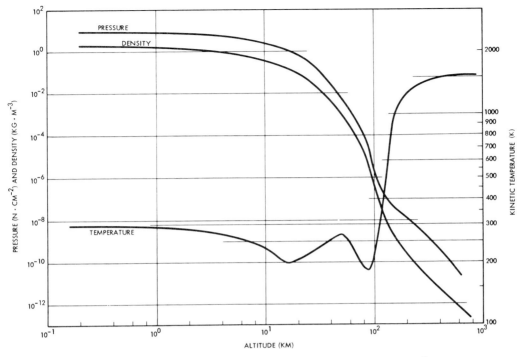

Fig. 9-12. Altitude variations of density, temperature, and pressure.[9]

sliding of portions of land past each other horizontally or vertically, or as vibrations. The ground may shake (vibrate) horizontally or may deform in wave-like fashion similar to the disturbance of a water surface by waves. The magnitude of an earthquake depends upon the source location, known as the *epicenter*, the distance from the epicenter, and the soil type through which the earthquake is transmitted.

Earthquake shocks and vibrations will be transmitted by the support structures to solar cell panels, potentially causing their destruction. Space arrays are capable of withstanding severe vibration environments, and terrestrial arrays can probably be designed readily to withstand severe earthquakes.

9-14. Gravity

The effects of gravity are primarily of concern to large solar cell panels and arrays. Hardware designed for space applications is usually not sufficiently strong to be handled safely in the terrestrial gravity field without the use of appropriate handling equipment. Large-sized

terrestrial panels may equally require handling equipment to prevent the panels from bending excessively when handled in a horizontal position.

9-15. The Atmosphere

The atmosphere is a gaseous envelope that surrounds the earth, extending from sea level to an altitude of several hundred kilometers. The upper limit of the atmospheric gas pressure decreases with increasing distance from the earth until it reaches the so-called interplanetary value of 10^{-11} newton/cm^2 near 20,000 km. The variations of temperature and pressure in the atmosphere are illustrated in Fig. 9-12.

At sea level, the dry atmosphere is made up of about 78% nitrogen, 21% oxygen, 1% argon, less than 0.1% carbon dioxide and neon, and less than 0.01% helium, krypton, xenon, hydrogen, methane, nitrous oxide, ozone, sulfur dioxide, nitrogen dioxide, ammonia, carbon monoxide, iodine, radon, and other components. Additional constituents, even in relatively high concentrations, may be present locally from industrial sources. Water vapor is usually present, even in dry climates.

The atmospheric composition changes with altitude. Between approximately 100 and 1000 km altitude, molecular oxygen (O_2), atomic oxygen (O), and ozone (O_3) dominate. Above 1000 km, only atomic and ionized hydrogen and helium are believed to exist.

At sea level, the density of the air is approximately 2.5×10^{19} gas molecules or atoms/cm^3. At an altitude of 30 km, the density drops to 4×10^{17}, and at 230 km, the density goes down to 10^{16} (molecules or atoms/cm^3). At 1000 km, 10^6 ions (ionized atoms or molecules)/cm^3 are found, dropping to 1000/cm^3 at 7400 km, and to 10 to 100/cm^3 at 26,000 km.[9, 10]

Electrical Arcing. Partial vacuum at high altitudes can cause flashover between electrical conductors. The breakdown voltage is a function of many parameters, including the conductor shape, size, composition, and temperature; the presence of illumination or other radiation; the composition and configuration of surrounding dielectrics; and other factors. Apparently, definitions of the electric field and the ionization potential of the surrounding air are insufficient criteria to assess the possibility of arcing. As an estimate, it may be assumed that the arc-over voltage at some low pressure may be only about 10% of the value obtained at sea level pressure.

Mechanical Effect of Pressure/Altitude on Space Arrays. During ascent, following launch, the solar cell array is subjected to rapid depressurization. The rate of this depressurization depends upon the rate of ascent and the rate of air leakage from the shroud, and therefore is highly mission dependent. Typical depressurization rates range from 1 to 10 minutes to reduce the initial ambient pressure to 1% or less.

Solar cell array components are generally not sensitive to such depressurization, except for elements containing gas filled voids. Such elements—for example, honeycomb substrates, box beams, or foams—must be vented with sufficiently large openings to prevent excessive internal net pressure from damaging these elements. An even more catastrophic result can be expected when a large amount of moisture is trapped inside inadequately vented voids, especially when the satellite protective shroud (nose cone) is ejected early and the array is subjected to high temperatures by aerodynamic and/or solar heating.

9-16. Atmospheric Electricity

Several atmospheric effects can endanger personnel or equipment at a terrestrial photovoltaic generator site, even if the system is not connected to the public utility grid and produces only low-voltage output. These effects may include the build-up of electric charges on solar panels and ungrounded structures and direct lightning strikes. Lightning, resulting from thunderstorm activities, may occur in almost any location on earth, even though the expected frequency may be very low in certain regions. Lightning occurs when the voltage breakdown of the air, about 3×10^6 V/m on the average, is exceeded. On the average, peak currents of 10,000 A can be expected, while currents exceeding 100,000 A are rare. The electrical energy of about 25 to 100 coulombs is discharged in about 20 microseconds. Electric current flow in the ground can cause voltage gradients in the ground sufficient to electrocute personnel and animals, and can induce relatively high voltages in electric circuits.[9]

Static electricity in the air, typically in the order of 300 V/m on clear days, will increase during periods of cumulus cloud development or thunderstorm activity, resulting in charge build-up of ungrounded equipment. Considerable currents, in the order of milliamps or amps, can flow even if there is no lightning strike. Frequently, corona is present while potential gradients are high.

9-17. Corrosion

The general phenomenon of deterioration, disintegration, or loss of material is called *corrosion*. Chemists differentiate between *chemical*, *electrochemical* (also known as *galvanic*), *electrolytic*, *oxidation and reduction*, *atmospheric*, and other corrosion processes. Corrosion affects primarily metals, but to a lesser degree also affects non-metals. Corrosion processes are accelerated by conditions of high humidity, high temperature, high concentrations of ionic compounds, and high mechanical stress.

Usually posing as the most severe environmental problem for solar cell arrays, electrochemical corrosion is related to dissimilar metals that are in intimate contact with each other. Consider, for example, steel bolts used in the assembly of aluminum structures, or brass screws and washers used to attach copper grounding wires to steel or aluminum frames. Dissimilar metals are differentiated by the relative positions they occupy in the so-called *electrochemical series*, as shown in Tables 9-5 and 9-6. The relative positions of the metals in the series are not fixed; they depend to a certain degree on the specific reaction that takes place. Hydrogen is arbitrarily used as the zero reference potential. The electrochemical series differs from the *galvanic series*; the latter gives the relative positions of metals when immersed in sea water, while the former is related to the ionization potential of the metal in an electrolyte.

Atmospheric Corrosion. Atmospheric constituents cause oxidation as well as corrosion of the surfaces of most metals. While the presence of humidity accelerates oxidation, it is necessary for corrosion to occur. Small quantities of ionizable substances, always present in the atmosphere, form an electrolyte with a humidity layer on a material's surface, as shown in Fig. 9-13. At locations where different materials are in contact with each other, a galvanic cell exists, causing an electric current to flow from the anodic material through the electrolyte to the cathodic material.

Table 9-5. Electrochemical Series of Pure Metals.[13]

Anodic End Least Noble Metal		
	Chromium	Silver
	Iron	Rhodium
	Cadmium	Palladium
Magnesium	Nickel	Platinum
Beryllium	Molybdenum	Gold
Aluminum	Tin	
Titanium	Lead	**Most Noble Metal**
Zinc	Copper	**Cathodic End**

Table 9-6. Electrochemical Series of Structural Metals.[13]

Anodic End	
Magnesium alloys	Lead and tin
Zinc and galvanized steel	Muntz metal
Aluminum 2S, 3S, 4S, 52 SH, 53S-T	Manganese bronze, naval brass
Alclad	Nickel and Inconel (A)
Cadmium	Brass, yellow, admirability, red
Aluminum 17S-T, A17S-T, 24S-T	Copper
Mild steel, wrought and cast iron	Bronze, silicon, G, M
Stainless steel, 13% Cr, 410 (A)	Nickel and Inconel (C)
Solder, lead-tin	Monel
Stainless steel, 18-8, 18-8-3, 304, 316 (A)	Stainless steel, 18-8, 18-8-3, 304, 316 (C)
	Cathodic End

NOTE: Cathodic (C) materials attack anodic (A) ones. Example: nickel (C) corrodes aluminum, but nickel (A) may be corroded by stainless steel (C).

Corrosion of Solar Cell Contacts.[16-22] The most important corrosion phenomena on solar cell arrays is the potential deterioration of titanium-silver (Ti-Ag) contacts on silicon solar cells in humid environments. Conditions of high temperature (generally above 40°C) and high humidity (generally above 60% relative humidity) can cause long-term deterioration of these contacts. Typically, higher temperatures and higher humidity levels accelerate the corrosion process, as may the presence of minute quantities of ionizable contaminants (such as salts).

It has been found that a thin interlayer of palladium (Pd) between the silver and titanium significantly reduces the corrosion rate of the contacts.[19] Most contemporary solar cells having solderless contacts use the Ti-Pd-Ag contact system.

Protection from Corrosion. The use of dissimilar metals is difficult, if not (at the present time) impossible, to avoid in the construction of highly efficient, long-lived solar cell arrays. Therefore, it is necessary to protect array components and assemblies from adverse environments such that corrosion processes are either avoided or slowed to a sufficiently low rate.

Terrestrial arrays are designed, constructed, and packaged such that the solar cells, interconnectors, and electrical circuit elements

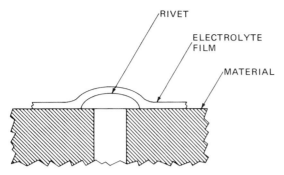

Fig. 9-13. Corrosion model.

are hermetically sealed in a weatherproof encapsulation. All exterior components are either made from corrosion resistant materials or are appropriately protected by surface treatments such as galvanizing or painting.

Space arrays are usually protected from adverse humidity/temperature conditions during their terrestrial life by storing them in air-conditioned rooms and in low-humidity containers. Desiccated plastic bags are frequently used for long-term storage, keeping the relative humidity inside the bag below 50%. Storage times in excess of five years under controlled conditions have not resulted in any space array electrical or mechanical degradation. There appears to exist no practical limit to array storage under room temperature, low-humidity, clean air conditions.

Protection of space arrays from adverse terrestrial environments by protective coatings or surface treatments, directly applied to the arrays, is usually not practical for weight reasons and because such protective treatments tend to be unstable in the space environment, resulting in undesirable outgassing and, subsequently, possible contamination of nearby thermal control surfaces and optical elements.

9-18. Ozone

Occurring naturally in the atmosphere, ozone (O_3) is produced mainly by a photochemical action of short wavelength, solar UV radiation (below 0.2537 μm) on molecular oxygen (O_2). It is also produced during electrical storms as a consequence of lightning. Man-made O_3 occurs mainly in the vicinity of metropolitan areas and is caused by UV light sources, motor and generator brushes, and photochemical processes

which produce smog. The UV radiation from solar simulators also produces significant amounts of O_3 locally.

High concentrations of O_3 are explosive and toxic; a concentration of 1 part per million (ppm) is lethal to man. Typical O_3 concentrations on the earth's surface range from near zero to normally less than 3 parts per hundred million (phm) and up to 6 phm during periods of intense smog. The O_3 concentration increases with altitude up to about 10 ppm at 30 km. High concentrations in solar simulator installations must be prevented by adequate ventilation.

Effects of Ozone. The cracking of natural rubber, butadiene-styrene (SBR), butadiene-acrylonitrile (NBR), and some other elastomers under stress are all caused by O_3. O_3 cracking resistance of an elastomer part is dependent on exposure time, temperatures, material strains, humidity, and O_3 concentration. Polymers classified according to O_3 resistance are presented in Table 9-7. To increase the resistance to O_3 anti-ozonants may be added to the materials. An anti-ozonant is a substance which inhibits cracking due to the action of air containing O_3 when the elastomer is subjected to tension strains. The effect of an anti-ozonant may be lost after exposure to high vacuum at room or elevated temperature.

Effects of Ozone on Solar Cell Arrays. The effects of O_3 on solar cell array materials are generally negligible for space arrays, but must be considered in the material selection for terrestrial arrays, especially for external wire insulation and weather seals. Special precautions are required for arrays that are to operate at the fringes of the earth's atmosphere.

9-19. Fungi and Bacteria

Micro-organisms such as fungus, mold, and bacteria grow on certain materials under high-humidity and high-temperature conditions. The growth rates are highest at relative humidity levels between 75% and 95% and at temperatures between 20° and 40°C. Materials such as wood, leather, organic adhesives, RTV rubbers and sealants, some plastic materials, paints, and even metals may support

Table 9-7. Elastomers According to Ozone Resistance.[23]

Inherently Ozone-Resistant	Ozone Resistant (if properly compounded)	
	Without Antiozonant	With Antiozonant

Acrylons
Hypalon
Vyram
Hycar 4021
LS-53
Kel-F elastomer
Poly FBA
Silicone
Vitron A
	Brominated butyl
	Butyl
	Neoprene
	Urethane (Genthane S)
		Buna N
		Carboxylic Buna N
		Butadiene-styrene (SBR)
		Vinyl pyridine
		Natural rubber
		Synthetic cis 1-4 polyisoprene
		  cis 1-4 polybutadiene
		Conventional polybutadiene
		Mercapan modified adducts
		  of polybutadiene
		Polysulfide
		Urethane (Adiprene B, C)

(Reprinted with permission of the Southwest Research Institute)

fungus and bacteria growth. The acidic secretions from these organisms aid in the corrosion processes. The growths themselves can severely interfere with light transmission to the solar cells.

Fungus and bacteria growth retardants and treatments are available for structural surfaces, but not for optical surfaces.

9-20. Salt Spray

Wind blowing over bodies of salt water will pick up small droplets that remain suspended in the air to altitudes of 3000 m for long periods of time and may be carried inland for several kilometers. Eventually, the salt will deposit on surfaces, coating them with sufficient thickness to cause large light transmission losses. In the presence of moisture, highly corrosive solutions will form.

The rate of salt deposited on exposed surfaces along the coast may range from 5 to 100 μm per day. The particle sizes may range from 0.1 to 20 μm.

9-21. Biotic Elements

Terrestrial solar cell arrays are subject to damage or degradation from small animals and insects. Rodents enjoy gnawing on certain types of electrical wire insulation materials and crawling into small openings in electrical equipment, especially into vent holes of heat-dissipating equipment. Certain types of flying and crawling insects tend to spread deposits on certain surfaces, or infest them for living or feeding purposes. Birds, especially gulls and pigeons, enjoy resting on elevated structures and covering them with droppings.

By proper design and installation, using fences, armored cabling, physical separation from trees and other tall plants, and closely spaced rods along the upper edges of solar arrays, most light reducing contamination and physical damage can probably be prevented.

9-22. Vandalism

Man has been found to be one of the more destructive terrestrial threats to solar cell arrays. Theft and the discharge of firearms have been common causes of damage. Throwing of rocks has also been reported as a damage mechanism. In several installations, a thin but strong wire mesh is now mounted in front of the arrays. The mesh is spaced several centimeters off the arrays so that flying rocks are bounced back. Mounting the mesh a larger distance from the array, say 10 to 20 cm, also has an advantage in terms of reducing solar cell shadowing (see Chapter 2).

HANDLING AND TRANSPORTATION

9-23. Handling and Assembly

Handling of solar cell panels during fabrication, assembly, test, transportation, loading and unloading, and field installation can be severely damaging to solar cell arrays. Typical handling damage includes breakage arising from the accidental dropping of tools, snagging of clothing on solar cell covers and interconnectors, pulling on wires and cables, bumping into arrays with other objects, and improper lifting.

Table 9-8. Typical Vibration Levels in Transportation.[24]

Source	Vibration Environment
Jet aircraft	Acoustical vibration due to jet wake and combustion turbulence. Frequency range up to 500 Hz and maximum amplitude approximately 25 μm.
Piston engine aircraft	Engine vibration range up to 60 Hz and maximum amplitude to 0.25 mm. Propeller vibrations range up to 100 Hz with maximum amplitudes to 0.25 mm. Amplitudes of vibration vary with location in aircraft.
Ships	Engine vibration in diesel or reciprocating steam types range up to 15 Hz with maximum amplitudes to 0.5 mm. Most vibrations are amplified. An amplification factor of 3 is usually acceptable.
Trucks	Suspension resonance of 4 Hz with maximum amplitude of 13 cm. Structural resonance above 80 Hz and maximum amplitude of 0.13 mm.
Passenger automobiles	Suspension resonance of 1 Hz and maximum amplitude of 15 cm. Irregular transit vibrations due to road roughness above 20 Hz and maximum amplitude of 50 μm.
Railroad trains	Broad and erratic frequency range. Isolation resonant frequency of 20 Hz has been successful in railroad applications.

9-24. Vibration and Acoustic Noise in Transportation

Solar panels transported by truck, railroad car, or aircraft are subject to long-duration vibrational stress. Panels shipped by aircraft may also be exposed to acoustic noise that has a similar effect as vibration. Typical vibration levels encountered in different transportation vehicles are given in Table 9-8.

9-25. Mechanical Shock in Transportation

Shock loads arise from dropping an object onto a hard surface. For example, briskly setting down a heavy solar cell panel on a concrete floor causes a shock loading of the panel at the point of impact that may be of sufficient magnitude to deform the panel edge. Metallic frames around the panel's edges should be designed to deform without relaying the deformation to the solar cells or the cell coverglass or other brittle encapsulant. Shock loads are usually expressed in multiples of "g" units (see Section 9-29; also see Section 9-30).

9-26. Storage

Solar cells and solar cell panels are believed to be storable for indefinite time periods as long as the storage environment is controlled. Deleterious storage environments include high temperature, high humidity, corrosive atmospheres, dust, and, to some degree, the ordinary atmosphere. These environments cause corrosion and light obscuration. Even the ordinary atmosphere

causes a film deposit ("makes glass blind") that reduces light transmission (see Sections 9-9, 9-12, and 9-19).

9-27. Pressure/Altitude in Transportation

Transportation of solar cell panels in nonpressurized compartments of aircraft are subject to a partial vacuum environment (see Section 9-15). Under reduced external air pressure, air or gas pockets contained and sealed within solar cell panels can exert great static forces on the panel's package, potentially causing its explosion, especially when dynamic transportation stresses are added (see Section 9-23, 9-24, and 9-25).

LAUNCH AND FLIGHT OF SPACE ARRAYS

9-28. Dynamic Forces During Launch and Flight

The launch and flight of a spacecraft is accompanied by a number of events that can cause significant mechanical stresses on the array, including acceleration, mechanical shock, vibration, and acoustic field exposure. Some or all of these "environments" can combine to lead to some temporary, very high mechanical stress levels. Additionally, even higher stress levels may occur when, at the same time, the array is at some very low or very high temperature (relative to room temperature).

Vibrational and shock forces are transmitted

to the solar cell array by structural members and, as long as it is sufficiently dense, by the surrounding air. The magnitudes and frequency spectra of the forces from their original sources are modified by the transmitting media before they reach the solar cell array. The vibrational amplitudes may be attenuated or amplified by the structure. Inasmuch as the actual forces acting on the array are very dependent upon the choice and the design of a specific launch vehicle, satellite, and structural spacecraft and array system, the data given in this chapter can serve as a general guide only.

The initial launch phase of a space vehicle is characterized by engine ignition and an intense acoustical field from the rocket engine exhaust, which builds up in intensity until the moment of launcher release. The acoustic field is reflected from the ground to the launch vehicle and diminishes as the launch vehicle rises. The acoustical excitation increases again sharply due to aerodynamic disturbances as the vehicle approaches the speed of sound. Once past the speed of sound, aerodynamic excitation diminishes until stage separation, when the vehicle is subjected to shock forces resulting from exploding bolts and/or second stage engine ignition.

Vibration and shock are generally negligible during space flight. However, in a mission which requires maneuvering for rendezvous or for transfer between orbits and/or soft landing by throttling, vibration and shock during space flight may be significant. Sources of dynamic forces may arise from the operation of maneuvering or landing engines (start-up, shut-down, random pulsing, and discrete frequency thrust variations), touchdown, or rendezvous. It should be noted that even though the solar cell array may not be operating at the time of the earth launch, it is usually electrically biased by an energy storage battery. Therefore, the array must be designed to withstand the adverse effects of acceleration and vibration loads without potentially short-circuiting or discharging the battery.

9-29. Acceleration

Acceleration forces are encountered during launch and in orbit when linear or angular velocities are changed. Acceleration forces are also inherent in mechanical shock and vibration.

Acceleration is commonly given in terrestrial g units where 1 g equals 9.8 m/second² (32.2 ft/second²). To obtain the forces on a body in a different gravitational field or under acceleration, the weight under a 1 g acceleration or terrestrial weight is multiplied by the number of g units. Typical acceleration values used in solar cell array design are given in Table 9-9.

Under high acceleration loads, parts not rigidly mounted will deflect from their 0 g or 1 g position. This deflection may be temporary or permanent, depending upon the softness of the mounting elements. For example, adhesive-mounted solar cell stacks will temporarily move slightly; and blocking diodes, supported only by their soft leads, may bend permanently. Inadequately supported conductors attached to solar cell contacts may pull the cell contacts off the silicon wafer.

To avoid potential problems caused by sustained acceleration, components should be oriented such as to nullify or minimize the effects of acceleration. Also, the avoidance of large moments by mounting each part close to its center of mass, providing adequate stress relief, and fastening wires at short intervals close to the substrate are all important.

9-30. Shock (Mechanical)

Shock, sometimes referred to as impulse or impact loading, may be defined as a suddenly applied load of short duration. The magnitude of a shock load is usually high, but the time duration of the loading is relatively small. The characteristic of a shock load which makes it different from a static load is the time required for the force to rise from zero to a maximum, compared to the natural period of vibration of the structure. If the time of load application is less than one-half the natural period of the structure, it is considered an impact load. If the time of load application is greater than three times the natural period of the structure, it is considered a static load.

The response of a solar cell array under shock conditions has characteristics similar to those of systems under acceleration and vibra-

Table 9-9. Typical Acceleration Levels.[24]

Table 9-9a. Typical g Forces During Launch/Ascent (Test Levels).

(Solar Cell Array Test Levels)

Launch Vehicle	Intensity (g)	Time
Saturn/Apollo Lunar Module	8 to 12	5 minutes in each of three mutually per- pendicular axes
Titan III	4.5	420 seconds
Thrust Augmented Delta	5 to 10	5 minutes each axis
Atlas Centaur	1 to 7.3	5 minutes each axis

Table 9-9b. Typical g Forces During Re-entry.

Planet	Direct Entry at Escape Velocity*			Direct Entry at Orbital Velocity*			Entry by Decay from Satellite Orbit
	$\theta = 5°$	20°	90°	$\theta = 5°$	20°	90°	
Venus	28.6	112	326	14.3	56	163	8.9
Earth	28.3	111	324	14.3	55.5	162	9.5
Mars	1.6	6.3	18.3	0.8	3.2	9.2	9.2

*Where θ is the re-entry angle with the horizontal, and decelerations are given in earth g's.

tion. The initial deformation of the structure is large; it then goes to zero as a damped harmonic oscillation. The intensity of the response of a structure to a pulse loading depends upon the natural frequency of the structure and the intensity and duration of the pulse.

In most cases, shock loads need not be considered for solar cell arrays which are located some distance away from the booster interface. If, however, the array attaches to the structure close to the booster interface or close to active deployment/latch-up or pyrotechnic elements, shock isolation may be required to prevent solar cell or coverglass cracking.

Sources of shock environment include:

• Transportation and handling
• Pyrotechnic (firing of explosive bolts, cable cutters, restraining mechanisms, etc.)
• Deployment (initial release, latch-up)
• Rocket engine ignition
• Rocket engine combustion instability

• Stage separation forces
• Satellite separation forces
• Impact loads due to meteoroid bombardment
• Docking loads
• Landing impact loads.

Typical values used in solar cell array design are up to 2500 g in close proximity of explosive bolts. The shock pulses have typical durations of 1 to 10 milliseconds.

9-31. Vibration

Vibration may be defined as a cyclically varying displacement of a body from its equilibrium position, or as the cyclically varying deformation of a body from its equilibrium shape. Vibration may be free or forced. Free vibration in an elastic system refers to a system free of impressed forces but under the action of forces inherent in the system itself. A freely vibrating system will vibrate at one or more of its natural frequencies. Forced vibration refers to a vibrating system under the excitation of an external force; i.e., a forcing function, which may be of a sinusoidal or a random frequency nature.

In general, the frequency, or frequency spectrum, of the exciting force is independent of the natural frequency of the system. However, the frequency (frequency spectrum) of a force actually driving a component may be severely altered by the elements which connect this component with the exciting force. This is particularly true for fixed solar cell arrays which are mounted via relatively long structural members to the spacecraft/booster interface elements, and for deployable arrays.

When the frequency of the driving force is near the natural frequency of the structure, resonance will occur. When no damping is available in the system and when the driving frequency is equal to the natural frequency, the amplitude of vibration increases until the system becomes non-linear. Non-linearity is often associated with permanent damage, such as deformation or bond separation. Avoiding or damping of resonance in the array support and in the array panels is a primary objective of the structural designers. The solar cell array designer, however, provides necessary inputs and interface considerations.

Vibrational exciting forces encountered during transportation, launch, and flight (see Tables 9-10 and 9-11) are almost always of a random frequency and random amplitude na-

Table 9-10. Typical Vibration Levels During Launch.[24]

Source	Vibration Environment
Rocket noise generated in exhaust stream	Usually most severe vibration environment in missiles. Results in random high amplitude vibrations during launch in atmosphere. Characterized by a broad spectral distribution coinciding with resonance frequencies of vehicle structure, skin, and equipment.
Space vehicles earth launch	Approximately 10 g's rms, 600 to 1600 Hz. Acoustical noise in field of payload 150 decibels for 60-second duration.
Space vehicles low earth orbit	Vibration range to 1000 Hz and up to 50 g's for 5-minute duration.
Space vehicles lunar orbit	Vibration range above 1000 Hz and up to 50 g's for 10-minute duration.
Lunar launch	Vibration levels up to 15 g's with frequency spectrum greater than 1000 Hz.
Lunar landing	Vibration levels up to 50 g's and frequency range from a few to several thousand Hertz.

Table 9-11. Typical Random Vibration Intensities During Launch/Ascent.[24]

(Solar Cell Array Test Levels)

Launch Vehicle	Frequency Range	Intensity
Saturn/Apollo Lunar Module	15 - 100 Hz	$0.01 \ g^2/Hz$ to $0.06 \ g^2/Hz$
	100 Hz - 1 kHz	$0.06 \ g^2/Hz$
	1 kHz - 2 kHz	$0.06 \ g^2/Hz$ to $0.015 \ g^2/Hz$
Titan III	20 - 800 Hz	$0.01 \ g^2/Hz$ to $0.4 \ g^2/Hz$
	800 - 1500 Hz	$0.4 \ g^2/Hz$
	1.5 - 2.0 kHz	$0.4 \ g^2/Hz$ to $0.3 \ g^2/Hz$
Atlas/Agena	20 - 150 Hz	$0.023 \ g^2/Hz$
	150 - 300 Hz	$0.023 \ g^2/Hz$ to $0.045 \ g^2/Hz$
	300 - 2000 Hz	$0.045 \ g^2/Hz$
Thrust Augmented Delta	20 - 2000 Hz	$0.07 \ g^2/Hz$ 11.8 g rms
Scout	20 Hz - 20 kHz	$0.07 \ g^2/Hz$ 11.8 g rms

ture. To permit design and test engineers to perform their functions, the natural vibration environment is idealized, and the system response is evaluated in simplified fashion, usually using sinusoidal vibration having a slowly varying frequency. The response of solar cell arrays is typically expressed in one of three quantities: *amplitude, acceleration,* and *mean-square acceleration density*; all of these are functions of frequency. Many other quantities are also used, the differences being either semantic or due to slightly different mathematical definitions.

Amplitude Frequency Spectrum. Usually expressed as *double amplitude*, this quantity gives the peak-to-peak deflection (response) of a point on the array relative to the tie-down (excitation) points plotted as a function of frequency. This maximum deflection must be limited by the design process for two reasons:

1. To prevent excessive bending of the array substrate with attendant potential structural damage of the substrate, solar cells, cell covers, or interconnectors; and
2. To prevent the array from touching other spacecraft components or the shroud, and damaging itself or these components.

Acceleration Frequency Spectrum. Usually expressed in g units (1 g is a force of 9.8 N created by the earth's gravitational field on a mass of 1 kg), it is also an "amplitude" type of quantity and is plotted as a function of frequency. Acceleration amplitude is typically measured by accelerometers placed at the excitation point and at various response points, especially where large vibrational amplification is expected. Acceleration amplitude is applicable only for the description of sinusoidal vibration, and is especially helpful to identify resonance frequencies. Both the peak and the rms amplitude of acceleration, A, is being used:

$$A_{rms} = \left\{ \frac{1}{T} \int_0^T [A_{peak} \sin (\omega t)]^2 \, dt \right\}^{1/2}$$

where $\omega = 2\pi f$, T is the period, and t is time.

For the special case of purely harmonic motion, this expression reduces to:

$$A_{rms} = \frac{\pi}{2\sqrt{2}} A_{average} = \frac{1}{\sqrt{2}} A_{peak}.$$

Mean-square Acceleration Density Spectrum. Usually expressed in units of g^2/Hz, this quantity is proportional to power density and is used to quantize the severity of random vibration. Random vibration is characterized by independent statistical variations of both amplitude and frequency as time passes. Thus, at each instant of time, there exists both a probability distribution for the acceleration amplitude and an associated continuous vibration frequency spectrum. To make this information useful, both the amplitude probability distribution and the frequency spectrum is required not for each instant of time, but rather for a longer time interval, such as for the entire launch phase during which vibration exists. As a most useful quantity, a mean-square spectral density function $W(f)$ has been defined such that

$$\int_0^\infty W(f) \, df = \lim_{T \to \infty} \frac{1}{T} \int_0^T \dot{f}^2(t) \, dt$$

where f is the frequency, T is the period, and t is time.

Minimizing the Effects of Vibration. The effects of vibration may be minimized by the techniques listed below.

- Provide solar cell array substrate isolation from the spacecraft structure.
- Change the natural frequency of the solar cell array by modifying its shape, mass, or stiffness, or break up larger areas into smaller ones or into modules.
- Dissipate energy and limit amplitude by the use of dampers, resilient pads, or additional tie-downs.
- Avoid sharp bends, fillets, notches, and long runs of unbonded (fastened) wire.
- Space wire spot bonds and interconnector joints at irregular intervals to prevent build-up of large deflections.
- Rivet members (rather than weld them) because they provide interface friction and, therefore, damping between members. Cold-driven rivets should not be loaded in tension because of residual stress concentration at the formed head.

- Lock bolts and nuts, since they tend to loosen under vibration and shock. Slippage of the joint due to excessive clearance in a bolt hole should be avoided by using close tolerance bolts or dowel pins. Bolts made from materials with low yield strengths, such as 18-8 stainless steel, tend to stretch and loosen under shock loads even though they have a high ultimate strength. The fatigue strength of bolts may be increased by cold working, such as rolling of thread, rolling of fillets near head, and shot peening the shank. Typical locking devices include threading of lock wires through holes in the nuts or bolts and then fastening them to the structure, friction nuts with a polymeric insert or distorted holes, and friction bolts with a polymeric insert in the threaded portion. Lock-washers should be used cautiously as locking devices when shock and vibration are present. Bolted structures provide friction damping between members and may be more desirable than a welded structure if damping is required.

9-32. Acoustic Field

An intense acoustic field is generated by two mechanisms during launch: first, by rocket engine exhaust and its reflection from the ground to the launch vehicle and the shroud that covers the payload; and second, by aerodynamic excitation of the shroud itself at high air speeds. The vibrating launch vehicle and shroud also generate an acoustic field inside the volume enclosed by the shroud, in turn exciting a vibrational response of the solar cell array. Acoustically induced vibration (random frequency distribution) of the solar cell array is especially high for body-mounted arrays that are in close proximity to the shroud. Frequently, the acoustically induced vibrations of the array are larger than vibrations transmitted to the array through structural components, so that meeting the acoustic field requirements becomes one of the important design aspects.

Typical failure modes during acoustic-testing are similar to those observed during vibration-testing and typically occur in the substrate rather than in the solar cells or their associated components. The design recommendations made in Section 9-31 to minimize the effects of vibration also apply to minimizing the effects of acoustic fields.

The acoustic field intensity is measured with microphones and is expressed in units of *dB sound pressure level*. The decibel (dB) scale is a logarithmic ratio of power levels, the square of force levels, the square of displacement levels, or the square of acceleration levels. If F is the measured acoustic field intensity (force per unit area), then the dB level is

$$dB = 10 \log_{10}(F^2/F_0^2) = 20 \log_{10}(F/F_0)$$

where F_0 is a reference sound pressure level, usually taken as 2×10^{-5} N/m^2 (0.0002 dynes/cm^2). Typical sound pressure levels are shown in Table 9-12 for test and design purposes. The expected flight level is generally 3 dB lower in each one-third octave band.

THE SPACE ENVIRONMENT

9-33. The Solar System

The solar system consists of the sun as a central body (with approximately 99% of the total mass), 9 planets, their 31 known satellites, tens of thousands of asteroids, and countless numbers of smaller objects which are occasionally observed as comets, meteors, or meteorites. All of these bodies revolve in different elliptical orbits about the sun. All of the planetary orbits can be bounded by a thin disk, having a diameter of 80 AU or one-eight-hundredth of a light-year.

The characteristics of the solar system are summarized in Table 9-13 and in Fig. 9-14. The properties of the sun are discussed below; its radiation is treated in Section 9-3. The orbital terminology and the orbits of artificial satellites are described starting in Section 9-41.

Asteroids. The asteroids (planetoids or minor planets) are small, irregularly shaped bodies of widely differing sizes (from 1 to 500 miles), the solar orbits of which lie principally between those of Mars and Jupiter, with mean distances

Table 9-12. Typical Acoustic Field Levels During Launch/Ascent.[24]

(Solar Cell Array Qualification Test Levels)*

1/3 Octave - Band Center Frequency (Hz)	1/3 Octave Band Sound Pressure Levels (dB)		
	Atlas Centaur	Titan IIIC	Titan IIID
5	98		
6.3	102		
8	105		
10	108		
12.5	111		
16	114		
20	117		
25	120		
31.5	122		
40	125	124	136
50	127	125.5	138
63	129	127	140.5
80	131	129	142.5
100	132	130.5	144
125	133.5	131.5	145
160	134.5	132.5	146
200	135.5	133.5	147
250	136	134	147.5
315	135.5	134.5	148
400	135	134.5	148
500	133.5	134	147.5
630	131	133.5	147
800	129	133	146.5
1,000	127	132	145.5
1,250	125	131	145
1,600	123	129.5	143
2,000	121	128.5	142
2,500	119	126.5	140
3,150	117	125	138.5
4,000	115	123	136.5
5,000	112.5	121.5	135
6,300	110	120	133.5
8,000	108	118	131.5
10,000	106.5		129.5
Overall SPL	146.0	145.0	158.0

*Reference level 2×10^{-5} N · m^{-2}

from the sun of 2.1 to 3.5 AU. Eight asteroids have perihelia smaller than that of earth, and one (Icarus) penetrates even closer to the sun than Mercury. It is estimated that there are 80,000 asteroids brighter than the nineteenth magnitude. Orbital elements are available today for about 2000 of them.

Comets. The observable aspect of a comet is the extensive atmosphere (coma, tail) which is

Table 9-13. Characteristics of the Solar System.[1,25]

Body	Semi-Major Axis to Sun (AU)*	Period Earth-Years (Earth = 1)	Mean Diameter (Earth = 1)	Relative Mass (Earth = 1)	Number of Natural Satellites	Equatorial Surface Gravity (Earth = 1)	Surface Temperature (°C)	Albedo	Surface Atmospheric Pressure (in atmospheres)	Atmospheric Composition
Sun			109.2	3×10^5		28	6500			
Mercury	0.387	0.241	0.379	0.055	0	0.380	400	0.06	≪1	Traces of heavy gases
Venus	0.723		0.956	0.815	0	0.893	430	0.76	16?	93 percent CO_2; possibly N_2 trace of water vapor
Earth	1.000	1.00	1.00	1.00	1	1.00	15	0.36	1	See Table 2.1-1
Mars	1.524	1.88	0.535	0.108	2	0.377	30 to -120	0.15	0.01	90 to 100 percent CO_2 remainder unknown, but upper limit for N_2 is possibly 3 percent
Jupiter	5.203	11.9	11.14	317.9	12	2.54	-140	0.51	≫1	
Saturn	9.539	29.5	9.47	95.1	10	1.06	-170	0.50	?	
Uranus	19.25	84.0	3.69	14.5	5	1.07	-210	0.66	?	NH_3, CH_4, H_2, He
Neptune	30.04	164.8	3.50	17.0	2	1.4	-220	0.62	?	
Pluto	39.64	247.7	1.1?	0.8?	0	0.7?	-220	0.16	?	Heavy gases?
Earth's Moon		0.075	0.272	0.012	0	0.165	-150 to 130	0.07	10^{-17}	Traces of very heavy gases

*1 AU = 92,959,670 miles = 1.4959789×10^{11} m.

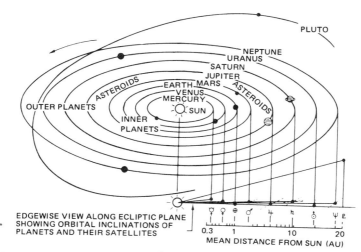

Fig. 9-14. The basic solar system.[1] (*Reprinted with permission of TRW, Inc.*)

developed and irretrievably lost during passage through the inner solar system. The source (an unobserved nucleus, probably a few miles in diameter) forfeits perhaps a thousandth part of itself in each passage. To date, some 550 different comets have been satisfactorily observed. The motion is found to be Keplerian and eccentric, the periods of the closed ellipses being long (thousands of years for about 450 objects) or short (6 or 8 years for fewer than 100 objects). Halley's famous comet is one of a few hybrids between these two classes. In spite of the prevalence of near-parabolic orbits, no fundamentally extrasolar object has yet been recorded.

9-34. The Space Vacuum

The vacuum of space consists of a low-density gas mixture, made up primarily of hydrogen, helium, protons, and alpha particles. The estimated gas pressure in interplanetary space is approximately 10^{-18} N $\cdot$ m^{-2} (10^{-16} mm Hg). In interstellar space, pressures lower than 10^{-27} N $\cdot$ m^{-2} may be encountered. The best vacuum obtainable in a laboratory ranges from 10^{-12} to 10^{-15} N $\cdot$ m^{-2}; however 10^{-12} N $\cdot$ m^{-2} is considered practical for the best commercial vacuum systems, with 10^{-8} N $\cdot$ m^{-2} (10^{-6} mm Hg) being more typical for space

chambers. The transition between the atmosphere and space is discussed in Section 9-15.

For design purposes, the following are typically recommended:

- Gas pressure 10^{-11} N $\cdot$ m^{-2}
- Density 10^{-23} g $\cdot$ cm^{-3}
- Kinetic gas temperature 2×10^{5} K.

Effects of Vacuum on Metals. Metals which might vaporize at an appreciable rate, if heated in the space vacuum environment, are magnesium, cadmium, and zinc. These should be avoided for outer space applications unless they are maintained at a low temperature, utilized in thick sections, or overcoated with some other material of lesser volatility. Of the above metals, magnesium was utilized on the exterior of the Midas II satellite. The problems associated with utilizing volatile materials are at least twofold: they are removed by the action of the space vacuum from the devices in which they are intended to be used; and they may condense on the cooler surfaces, possibly causing electrical short-circuiting, change of surface emissivities, or change in optical properties of mirrors and solar cell covers. Sublimation of the base material can be retarded by the use of surface coatings with low vapor pressures; for example, inorganic coatings such as oxides.

Table 9-14. Sublimation of Metals in High Vacuum.[26]

Element	Temperature (°C) at Which Given Sublimination Rate Occurs			Melting Point (°C)
	0.1 μm/yr	10 μm/yr	1 mm/yr	
Cadmium	38	77	122	320
Zinc	71	127	177	420
Magnesium	110	171	243	650
Silver	480	590	700	960
Aluminum	550	680	810	660
Beryllium	620	700	840	1280
Copper	630	760	900	1080
Gold	660	800	950	1060
Chromium	750	870	1000	1870
Iron	770	900	1500	1540
Nickel	800	940	1090	1450
Titanium	920	1070	1250	1670
Molybdenum	1380	1630	1900	2610
Tantalum	1790	2040	2320	2980
Tungsten	1870	2150	2480	3430

NOTE: To convert sublimation rate g in gm/cm^2 to cm/s, divide g by density in gm/cm^3.

In general, the weight loss rate in vacuum increases directly with increasing vapor pressure of the material. Table 9-14 presents a list of several metals and their corresponding sublimation rates for different temperatures.

The mechanical properties of materials in vacuum are different from those exhibited in air. Some metals tested in vacuum grow stronger, while others become weaker and have altered creep and fatigue properties.[27,28,29] The following two surface reactions in air are believed to be the controlling factors in these differences: 1) the surface of the material strengthens and hardens by oxidation or is altered by gas diffused into its interior; or 2) surface cracks form and adsorbed gases tend to wedge the crack. The material will be stronger in either vacuum or in air, depending upon which of these reactions is the controlling factor. Ordinary glass is three times as strong in a vacuum of 10^{-5} mm Hg as it is in air. Surface finishes can, therefore, be expected to control or significantly influence the strength of metals in vacuum.

Effects of Vacuum on Plastics. The high vacuum of outer space will cause volatile materials, plasticizers, and additives to vaporize.

The weight loss exhibited by organic polymers in vacuum is usually the result of the evaporation of relatively lower molecular weight fractions; unreacted additives; contaminants; and adsorbed (on surfaces) and absorbed (in bulk) gases, moisture, and other materials. The loss of these additives and contaminants, however, can change important properties of the polymers. For example, the loss of a plasticizer by evaporation in a vacuum environment will produce a more rigid or brittle part, with a corresponding decrease in elongation and an increase in tensile and flexure strength. Electrical components, such as capacitors, may change in value if the insulating materials used in their construction lose moisture or any other contaminants which are trapped during their manufacture.

The rate of weight loss at a given pressure and temperature varies as a function of time. The initial weight loss is usually high and is due to the loss of adsorbed gases, water, and other contaminants. During this stage, the total weight loss may be as great as 3% for some polymers. This relatively high initial weight loss will drop to a very low value when the loss of weight is due primarily to degradation of the basic polymer.

In general, polymers of relatively high molecular weight, such as Teflon, do not evaporate or vaporize in vacuum, but when supplied with sufficient thermal energy, they decompose or depolymerize. These polymers have such low vapor pressures that the thermal energy required to cause evaporation exceeds that required to break the chemical bonds of the polymer. Many polymers of engineering importance do not sublime or evaporate in high-vacuum environments, and the thermal stability of these polymers should be at least as good in a high vacuum as in the earth atmosphere (see also Section 10-13).

The additional points listed below should be noted.

- Weight loss rate and amount of weight loss are greatest early in the test period, when the materials at or near the surface evaporate. These loss factors decrease subsequently to a rate determined principally by diffusion rates through the polymer to the surface.

- Rigid plastics are, in general, preferred over flexible, elastomeric materials.

- Materials with a minimum number and quantity of additives and modifiers are preferred.

- Complete cure of the plastics must be obtained by extended time and/or elevated temperature post-curing to ensure the elimination of unreacted, low-molecular fractions in the product.

- Those materials exhibiting high loss rates but considered necessary for use on space vehicles because of special desirable properties should be preconditioned in vacuum at elevated temperature to reduce, as much as possible, the potential loss of the material to space.

Lubricants in Space Vacuum. Conventional lubricants are generally not suitable for use in the space vacuum because of their high vapor pressure, which results in loss of fluid by evaporation. Even if the rate of evaporation of a fluid lubricant is acceptable, the vapors may condense on cooler surfaces such as lenses, solar cell covers, and thermal control surfaces. Other problems associated with using a lubricant in a vacuum are 1) the absence of oxygen—essential to forming a metallic soap; and 2) the absence of absorbed water vapor—necessary for the lubricating properties of bearing materials, such as graphite.

9-35. Meteoroids

Interplanetary space contains many small particles called *meteoroids*. When a meteoroid passes through the earth's atmosphere, its luminous, incandescent body is called a "meteor." The remnants of meteoroids found at the earth's surface are termed *meteorites*.[1]

Meteoroids are classified according to their most likely origin and frequency of occurrence; they may originate either from asteroids or from comets. Cometary meteoroids may occur sporadically or in streams or showers, while asteroidal meteoroids occur only sporadically.

Asteroidal meteoroids are relatively dense (with an average of approximately $3.5 \text{ g} \cdot \text{cm}^{-3}$), stone-like, iron-rich, irregularly shaped particles. Cometary meteoroids are less dense (with an average of $0.5 \text{ g} \cdot \text{cm}^{-3}$) and frequently possess a dustball or porous structure. Even though most of the cometary meteoroids are less than 1 mm in diameter, their greater frequency and hypervelocity (an average of 20 km/second, and rarely as high as 72 km/second) may cause a threat to spacecraft and solar cell arrays.

The meteoroidal particle mass of most concern to solar cell arrays is estimated to lie between 10^{-6} g and 10^{-3} g, since particles with mass below 10^{-6} g, in general, do not have sufficient energy to cause significant damage, and since particles with mass greater than 10^{-3} g are less frequently encountered.

To assess the potential damage of meteoroids to solar cell arrays, the meteoroidal particle mass and frequency of occurrence must be known, as well as the probability of intercepting such particles in a given orbit at a certain date.[30,31]

Effects of Meteoroids on Solar Cell Arrays. The damage expected from meteoroid impacts on the solar array is primarily erosion of the cover-glass and the substrate rear surface thermal control coating.

Coverglass erosion would consist first of mechanical abrasion of the anti-reflective coating (typically magnesium fluoride) and then pitting of the cover itself (similar to sandblasting). Heavier particles impacting the solar cell cover at high velocity may cause the covers to crack; however, very few such particles, if any, are expected to impact an array in each earth orbit. Cracked covers typically do not affect the solar cell output.[31, 32, 33]

The orbital performance of satellites has not indicated significant damage due to meteoroids, so that the array output degradation due to meteoroids is usually assumed zero.

9-36. Deposits

One source of solar cell array output degradation in space may be contamination of the solar cell array surfaces by engine exhaust plumes and by condensation of outgassing products stemming from exposed non-metallic materials or from sublimating metals on the spacecraft. This contamination may cause solar cell array output degradation by two different mechanisms: 1) loss of light transmission to the solar cells, and 2) increased solar cell operating temperature. The increase in cell temperature is due to a deterioration in the thermo-optical characteristics of the cell covers and thermal control surfaces on the array back side. Attempts have been made to experimentally measure the impact of exhaust plumes on array power loss, but significant effects (probably in excess of 2%) were not found. Theoretical predictions of the effects of deposits from outgassing materials are more severe, and had been estimated to reach 10% for Skylab. The actual flight data of Skylab during 200 days in orbit has shown evidence of such deposits; however, their impact on solar cell array performance was not distinguishable from the small, but measurable, total array degradation due to all environmental effects, including UV and corpuscular irradiation.[34-40]

9-37. Gravity in Space

The gravitational potential, U, of the earth decreases approximately with the square of the distance from the center of the earth, r, as follows:

$$U = \frac{GE}{r^2}$$

where $GE = 398601.2$ (± 0.4) $km^3 \cdot second^{-2}$, the geocentric gravitational constant. Computations of satellite orbits require detailed considerations of the non-spherical shape and non-homogeneous mass distribution of the earth.[30]

Effects of Zero Gravity. The effects of zero gravity on solar cell array materials and assemblies are generally beneficial, especially when the array is large and of lightweight construction. However, absolute zero gravity rarely exists on actual solar cell arrays, due to a number of disturbing forces that may be caused by any of the following:

- Gravity gradients
- Spacecraft velocity and attitude changes
- Solar cell array reorientation
- Solar radiation pressure
- Spacecraft spinning or tumbling.

Simulation of zero gravity for the testing of larger, deployable, lightweight arrays is difficult to achieve but has been done repeatedly and successfully, utilizing so-called "zero-g" fixtures, water tanks, and aircraft.

Gravity Gradient Torques. Because the gravitational potential in an inverse square law field varies with altitude, the center of gravity of a body will not lie at its mass center. Unless the gravitational force passes through the mass center, a torque will result. Although this effect generally degrades attitude accuracy, it can provide control capability for a spacecraft which is properly configured.

9-38. Time in Space

In the past, typical satellite design lifetimes ranged from several months to three years. Recent successful spaceflights have prompted the planning of longer duration missions. Examples are communication satellites and manned earth-orbiting space stations for ten year durations and unmanned Grand Tour reconnaissance missions to Jupiter, Saturn, Uranus, and Neptune or Pluto, requiring mission durations of six to twelve years.

The effects of time in space are adverse, causing continuing degradation of the array due to the space radiation environment (see Section 9-49 and following). The probability of failure of the solar cell interconnecting system and/or soldered or welded joints by metal fatigue increases with exposure time, especially with the number of thermal cycles due to solar eclipses (see Sections 6-4 and following). Solar cell, cover, and adhesive damage due to the space radiation are cumulative functions of time.

9-39. Magnetic Fields

The earth's magnetic field, also called the geomagnetic or terrestrial magnetic field, origi-

nates in its center, but is neither coincident with the earth's geographic poles nor symmetrical to the earth's surface. The total strength of the geomagnetic field varies from approximately 3.0×10^{-5} to 3.5×10^{-5} tesla, T (0.30 to 0.35 gauss, G) at the equator to approximately 6.5 to 7.0×10^{-5} T (0.65 to 0.70 G) at the magnetic poles. With increasing altitude, the field strength falls off approximately with the cube of the distance from the center of the hypothetical earth's magnet (Fig. 9-15).

The geomagnetic field is disturbed by the solar plasma. The solar plasma also limits the extent of the geomagnetic field in the direction of the sun to approximately 10 earth radii.

The geomagnetic field strength at synchronous altitude is approximately 1.38×10^{-7} T (138 gammas). The magnetic field strength in interplanetary space is due to the solar plasma; its magnitude is about 5×10^{-9} T (5 gammas)

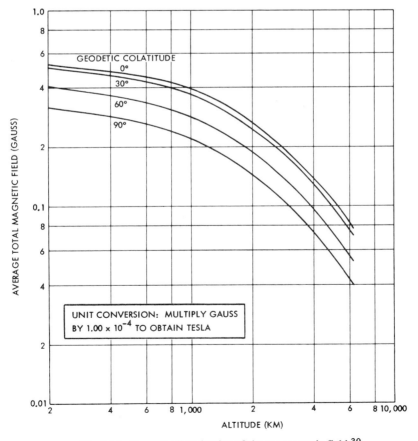

Fig. 9-15. Magnetic flux density of the geomagnetic field.[30]

at a distance of 1.0 to 1.5 AU from the sun. The interplanetary magnetic field strength temporarily increases by up to two orders of magnitude during periods of increased solar activity.[30] (See also Section 9-44).

Effects of Magnetic Fields. Magnetic fields produced by the solar cell array may have an impact on two other subsystems: attitude control and magnetic field experiments. For a spacecraft in an environmental magnetic field (such as the earth's magnetic field), the presence of residual magnetism or current loops will result in a torque on the vehicle. Occasionally, this phenomenon is purposely used for attitude control (e.g., Tiros, OAO), but most often the effect is undesirable. For this reason, especially on spacecraft carrying large solar cell arrays, the electrical solar cell circuits are laid out such that the current loops produce no net torque.

For missions flying sensitive magnetometers, the entire spacecraft and solar cell array designs may be restricted to the use of non-magnetic materials (potentially excluding Kovar and Invar for cell interconnector material) and require careful circuit layout, so that the magnetic fields induced by the spacecraft or the array have a negligible strength at the magnetometer location.

Magnetic fields produced by electrical current loops can be minimized by laying out the solar cell circuits such that fields from neighboring circuit loops cancel each other. Different degrees of field cancellation can be achieved by different methods, as described in Sections 3-38 and 3-39.

9-40. Temperature in Space

Interplanetary space consists of widely separated gas molecules, so that the concept of temperature environment in space is quite different from the concept of temperature as an environment in the atmosphere. Due to the extremely low density of the interplanetary gas mixture, it is necessary to consider temperature in terms of the kinetic theory of gases. Based on this theory, gas temperatures of several thousand degrees have been predicted. However, since these high-temperature gas

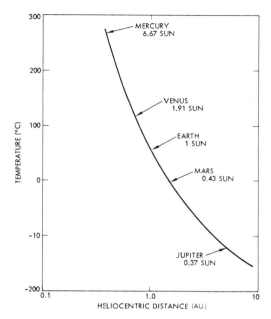

Fig. 9-16. Conventional mariner solar array temperature versus heliocentric distance at normal incidence (illustrative example).

molecules are so widely scattered, they have a negligible effect on the temperature of a solar cell array due to the small amount of heat energy involved. The temperature of a space vehicle, therefore, is determined not by the temperature of the surrounding atmosphere, but rather as a result of radiation from other sources, such as the sun, and re-radiation to the heat sink of space.

The primary external source of thermal energy for a solar cell array traveling within the solar system is direct radiation from the sun. The heat flux intensity varies inversely as the square of the distance from the sun (see Section 9-3), as illustrated in Fig. 9-16.

Another, secondary source of heat for bodies in close proximity to a planet is their reflected and emitted energy. The emission and reflectivity of heat energy from a planet depends on its temperature and *emissive* properties, and on its *albedo* (*reflective* properties). The albedo represents the percentage of incident energy reflected by a planet. The average albedo for several solar system bodies is given in Sections 9-4 and 9-33.

The steady-state temperature of a solar cell

array in space can be determined by an energy balance equation, as shown in Chapter 2. The effects of temperature on the solar cell array are of an electrical and mechanical nature, as described in Chapters 4 and 6, respectively.

9-41. Solar Cell Arrays in Orbit

The power output capability of a solar cell array is significantly affected by its orientation to the sun. This orientation is determined by mission-imposed requirements for attitude control and maneuverability, by the capability of the attitude control subsystem, and by the physical configuration of the solar array and the spacecraft body. The interaction of mission requirements and spacecraft design characteristics is illustrated in Table 9-15, which also contains examples of typical earth-orbiting spacecraft and descriptions of solar array orientation.

Solar cell arrays may be fixed relative to the spacecraft coordinate system or oriented toward the sun. Fixed arrays may be spacecraft body-mounted (approximating cylindrical, spherical, or tetrahedral shapes), or they may be in the form of deployed panels (or both). Oriented arrays are generally composed of flat panels that are driven and controlled in one or more axes. The array drive systems are designed to track the sun and are often capable of off-pointing part or all of the array to reduce excess power.

Table 9-15 does not describe all of the possible array-spacecraft configurations. Some possible configurations are limited to special applications because of constraints on field-of-view or power capability. For example, besides orienting the principal axis of a spin stabilized spacecraft perpendicular to the orbit plane, it is also possible to point the axis toward the earth or to fix it in inertial space. However, earth-pointing, spin stabilized spacecraft with cylindrical solar cell arrays usually require auxiliary solar panels to compensate for reduced power at satellite high noon (i.e., when the solar vector is parallel to the satellite spin axis).

Two-axis control of a flat panel is required to maintain its pointing directly to the sun. A solar cell array attitude control system such as that contained in the flexible rolled-up solar array (FRUSA) system (see Chapter 7) provides this control. Most other oriented solar cell arrays are, however, controlled in only one axis, with second axis control provided, if it is required, by rotation of the entire spacecraft. Table 9-15 shows spacecraft axis orientation for selected examples and, in each case, identifies the axis that is used for array control. It is seen from the table that various options exist for reducing the impact of spacecraft orientation on power output. For example, a yaw rotation performed twice per orbit permits substitution of a flexible harness for a set of slip rings. Canting the panels with respect to the array drive axis reduces the effect of seasonal changes of the angle between the sun vector and the orbit plane. In the case of a geosynchronous equatorial orbit, the canting of the oriented panels by 11.7°, coupled with seasonal yaw axis rotations, can provide an array power increase of approximately 4% over one year, for an array configuration that otherwise experiences the total effect of the ±23.4° inclination of the ecliptic plane.

Section 2-62 (and following) contains an analytic treatment of orbital mechanics and spacecraft configuration orientation analysis at a level of detail sufficient for the detailed calculation of the insolation intercepted by solar array surfaces.

9-42. Solar Eclipses

Whenever the view from the sun to the spacecraft is obstructed by a planet or one of its satellites, the spacecraft is said to be in an *eclipse*. If the sun is completely obscured by an object (as viewed from the spacecraft), the satellite finds itself in the *umbra*, or full shadow, of the object. If the sun is only partially obscured, the satellite is in the *penumbra*. When a spacecraft is in a penumbra shadow, the solar illumination is reduced by approximately the same percentage as the area of the solar disk (as it appears from the spacecraft) is obscured. The number of eclipses experienced over the lifespan of a spacecraft depends mainly upon the orbit altitude and eccentricity,

Table 9-15. Examples of Solar Array Orientation.

Solar Array Configuration	Method of Spacecraft Attitude Control	Spacecraft Axis Orientation			Orbit Inclination (deg)	Insolation Angle to Solar Array (deg)	Selected Examples	Comments
		Roll	Pitch	Yaw			Spacecraft	
Body-mounted, fixed cylinder	Spin stabilized	Direction of flight	Spin axis	Toward earth	0 102	±23.4 30 to 60 (reference pitch axis)	Intelsat IV Tiros	Geosynchronous altitude. Sun-synchronous orbit.
Deployed, fixed, orthogonal panels	Gravity-gradient	(See comments)	(See comments)	Toward earth	125	(see comments)	NTS-1	Variable insolation depending upon panel angle with respect to yaw axis, yaw angle, position in orbit and season.
Deployed, partially oriented (one-axis) panels	Reaction wheel	Array drive axis	Toward earth	Toward earth	90	0	POGO	180° yaw maneuver required twice per orbit; no array drive sliprings.
Deployed, oriented (one-axis) panels	Reaction wheel	Direction of flight	Array drive axis	Toward earth	0	±23.4	FLTSATCOM	Geosynchronous attitude; insolation angle does not include other pointing requirements.
		Toward sun	Array drive axis	Toward earth	32	0	OAO	Star pointing obtained by rotation about pitch axis.
		Direction of flight	Array drive axis	Toward earth	99	±6	ERTS-1	Sun-synchronous orbit; panels canted 33° to pitch axis.
Deployed, oriented (two-axis) panels	Reaction wheel	Array drive axis	Array drive axis	Toward earth	Any	0	FRUSA	Array system provides two-axis control independent of spacecraft attitude control.

being highest for circular orbits at the lowest practical altitudes. Figure 9-17 illustrates the relationship between the number of eclipses and the flight altitude for circular orbits.

Not all eclipses of a spacecraft in a given orbit are of the same duration. Variations are produced by the motion of the planet around the sun, resulting in changes to the angular relationship between the earth-sun line and the orbit plane. Fractional sun time of circular orbits is illustrated in Fig. 9-18. Subtraction of the fractional sun time from unity gives the fractional eclipse time. Figure 9-19 shows the eclipse duration in real time. The temperature variations due to eclipses of varying duration can be determined from the data given in Chapter 2.

THE RADIATION ENVIRONMENT
IN SPACE

9-43. Radiation Terms

Radiation may be classified as either *electromagnetic*, having zero rest mass, or *particulate* (also called *corpuscular*), having finite rest mass. Electromagnetic radiation includes UV light, X-rays, and gamma rays. Particulate radiation includes electrons, protons, neutrons, and alpha particles. The more frequently encountered radiation terms are defined below.

Alpha Particles (α). Positively charged particles whose properties are identical to all properties of the nucleus of a helium atom, consisting of two protons and two neutrons.

Beta Particles (β). Negatively or positively charged electrons emitted from a nucleus, and having an energy of approximately 1 MeV.

Photons. Quanta of electromagnetic radiation (see Section 2-26 for further details).

Bremsstrahlung. The secondary radiation induced by high-energy electrons which are deflected by another charged particle, such as a nucleus. The Bremsstrahlung photons are X-rays having energies near that of high-energy electrons, but which are more penetrating than the electrons themselves.

Cosmic Rays. High-energy particles or electromagnetic radiation originating in interstellar space.

Electrons (e). Elementary particles of rest mass $m = 9.109 \times 10^{-31}$ kg, and having a charge of 1.602×10^{-19} coulomb. An electron's charge may be positive or negative. A negative electron is also called a negatron, but the term electron is usually used. A positive electron is called a positron. Negative electrons occurring in space are designated by e^-.

Gamma Rays (γ). A form of electromagnetic radiation with wavelengths of approximately 10^{-8} to 10^{-11} cm. Gamma rays are highly penetrating, and are emitted by a nucleus in its transition from a higher to a lower energy state.

Protons (p^+). Positively charged particles of mass number one (having a mass of 1.672×10^{-27} kg) and a charge equal in magnitude to the electron. A proton is the nucleus of a hydrogen atom.

X-Rays. Electromagnetic radiation with wavelengths of approximately 10^{-8} cm. X-rays are highly penetrating and are usually formed by bombarding a metallic target in a high vacuum with a particle. X-rays are also called *Roentgen* rays, named after their discoverer.

Flux. Defines the number of particles, photons, or energy passing through a given area in a specified time, usually given in particles $\cdot$ cm^{-2} $\cdot$ second^{-1} or photons $\cdot$ cm^{-2} $\cdot$ second^{-1}. Flux may also be specified in terms of the number of particles per unit time passing through an area on the surface of a sphere enclosed by a solid angle. The units are particles $\cdot$ cm^{-2} $\cdot$ second^{-1} $\cdot$ sr^{-1}, where a steradian (sr) is defined as the solid angle which encloses a surface on a sphere equal in area to the radius of the sphere squared.

Fluence. Also known as time-integrated flux; the total number of photons or particles in any given time period.

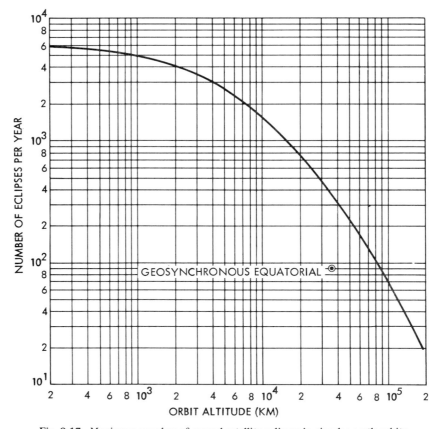

Fig. 9-17. Maximum number of annual satellite eclipses in circular earth orbits.

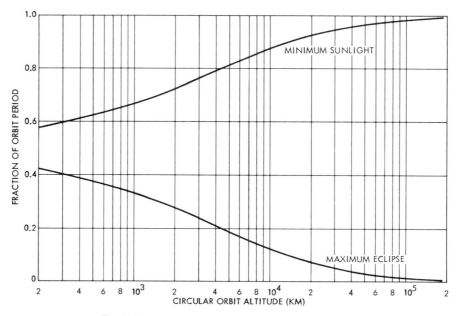

Fig. 9-18. Fractional sun time of circular earth orbits.

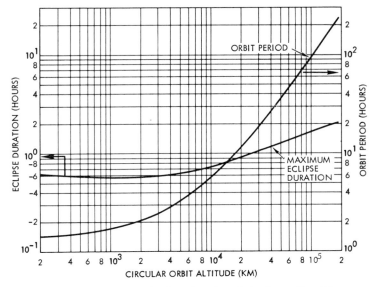

Fig. 9-19. Orbit period and eclipse duration of circular earth orbits.

Omnidirectional Flux. The number of particles of a particular type that would transverse a test sphere of 1 cm^2 cross-sectional area in 1 second (particles $\cdot$ cm^{-2} $\cdot$ second^{-1}).

Unidirectional Flux. The flux arriving at a test sphere per unit solid angle from any particular direction, having units of particles $\cdot$ cm^{-2} $\cdot$ second^{-1} $\cdot$ sr^{-1}. If the incident radiation is isotropic, the undirectional flux equals the omnidirectional flux divided by 4π (there are 4π steradians in a sphere). The conversion of omnidirectional into unidirectional flux in conjunction with solar cell damage calculations is more complex, however, and is discussed in Chapter 2.

Radiation Dose. This can be expressed either in terms of the exposure dose, which is a measure of the radiation field to which a material is exposed, or in terms of the absorbed dose, which is a measure of the energy absorbed by the irradiated material. Absorbed dose units are given below.

- *Joules/gram* is the energy expressed in joules absorbed by a gram of the irradiated material.
- *Rad* is the absorbed dose defined as 1 $\times$ 10^{-5} joules (100 ergs) of radiation energy of any

type absorbed per gram of any irradiated material. (See *Gray*.)
- *Gray* is a new unit replacing Rad. (1 Gy = 1 $\times$ 10^{-2} Rad.)
- *Roentgen (R)* is an exposure dose defined as the quantity of X- and gamma-radiation which will produce one electrostatic unit of electrical charge (3.335 $\times$ 10^{-10} coulombs) in the mass of dry air contained in 1 cm^3 at standard conditions of temperature and pressure (0.001293 gram). This amount of energy gives an absorbed dose of 87.7 $\times$ 10^{-7} joules of energy per gram of air.
- *Joules/gram carbon* or *joules/gram (C)* is an indirect measure of a gamma radiation field based on an absorbed dose, using carbon as a standard. One roentgen, R, of gamma rays is equivalent to approximately 87.7 $\times$ 10^{-7} joules/gram carbon.
- *Dose rate* is the rate of energy delivered or absorbed; e.g., R/month, R/year, rad/day.

Damage Equivalent Radiation Dose in Solar Cells. For convenient calculation of solar cell performance degradation in a corpuscular radiation environment and simplified laboratory radiation test methods, the concept of "normally incident damage equivalent 1 MeV fluence" was evolved. Particulate radiation damage to solar cells is dependent on the energy and type of the particle. Conversion into "1 MeV fluence" utilizes so-called "equivalent damage coefficients," as discussed in Chapter 2. The unit of equivalent fluence is 1 MeV electrons per cm^2, or, in brief, "e/cm^2" or "$e \cdot cm^{-2}$," for a specified time period, usually either 1 year or end-of-mission.

9-44. Space Radiation and its Effects

The radiation environment in space is characterized primarily by electrons and protons. Alpha particles and other charged particles are usually of negligible quantity as far as solar cell arrays are concerned.

The space surrounding the earth can be divided into a number of different regions, the boundaries of which are defined by natural phenomena that arise from interactions of the *solar wind* with the *earth's magnetic field*. Illustrated in Fig. 9-20, the earth's magnetic field distorts the otherwise uniform flow of the solar wind in the *interplanetary space* and deflects it around the earth. In the outer magne-

tosphere (the magnetosheath, high-latitude magnetotail, and plasma sheet), the solar wind, in turn, distorts the magnetic field lines emanating from the earth dipole ("bar magnet") and pushes them in a tail-like fashion away from the sun. In the immediate vicinity of the earth, up to a distance of about 8 earth radii (known as the *inner magnetosphere*), electrons and protons become *trapped* by the magnetic field lines in the so-called *radiation belts*. Current models of the various radiation environments are listed in Table 9-16.

The radiation particles possess energies over a wide range and propagate through space with different velocities. The presentation of the number of particles having a certain energy, measured over the entire range of energy from a few keV to many MeV or GeV, is known as the *energy spectrum* for that particle type. Different types of particles, and particles of the same type but of different energy, produce different types and amounts of damage in different materials.

Effects of Radiation on Solar Cell Arrays. Solar cells in orbit are *damaged* (i.e., their

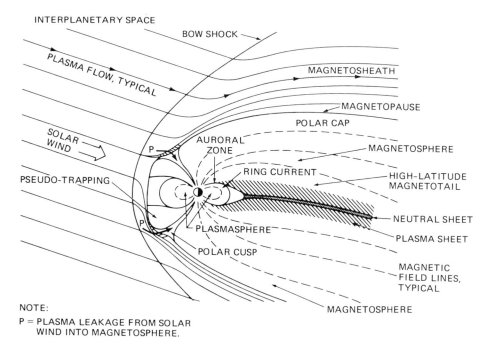

NOTE:
P = PLASMA LEAKAGE FROM SOLAR WIND INTO MAGNETOSPHERE.

Fig. 9-20. Regions of the magnetosphere shown in the noon-midnight meridian plane.[41]

Table 9-16. Current NSSDC Radiation Environment Models.[42]

Name of Model	Particle and Energy Range	L-Range	Remarks
AE-4	Electrons 0.04 to 4 MeV	2.8 to 11.0	Flux values for epoch 1964 and 1967 corresponding to solar minimum and maximum conditions. Solar cycle effects only occur between 2.8 ≤ L ≤ 5. Energies above 4 MeV are strictly exrapolations, and data above 1.9 MeV did not have proper calibration.
AE-5 (1975 projected)	Electrons 0.04 to 4 MeV	1.2 to 2.8	Flux values for October 1967, but Starfish residue subtracted and solar cycle effects used, so projected valid epoch is 1975, corresponding to solar minimum conditions.
AE-6	Electrons 0.04 to 4 MeV	1.2 to 2.8	Flux values for October 1967, but Starfish residue subtracted.
AP-8	Protons 0.1 to 400 MeV	1.17 to 6.6	Model has both solar minimum and maximum values; these changes occur only at low altitudes.
AEI-7	Electrons 0.04 to 5 MeV	2.8 to 11.0	Interim model with upper and lower limit for energies above 1.5 MeV to account for ATS 6 data at 3.9 MeV and OV1-19 data up to 5 MeV. Model is interim until discrepancies between Azur data at 4.5 MeV and OV1-19 data can be properly studied. At energies below 1.5 MeV, this model is same as AE-4 in the outer zone for solar maximum.

energy conversion efficiency is permanently degraded), mainly due to irradiation with electrons and protons. In lower earth orbits, both geomagnetically trapped electrons and protons may be of significance, while at higher altitudes, such as at synchronous altitude, during periods of high solar activity, solar flare protons may add significantly to the total cell-damaging fluence.

The radiation particles of significance to solar damage have approximately the following energy ranges when they impinge on the solar cell covers:

- Electrons—0.2 to 1 MeV.
- Protons—4 to 40 MeV.

The actual radiation environments seen by the solar cells differ from the naturally existing environment because the energy-flux spectra of the natural radiation environments are modified by the solar cell radiation shields, and the solar cells receive radiation both through the front shield (coverglass) and the back shield (substrate); i.e., the radiation environment seen by the solar cells is, in part, design related (see Chapters 2 and 4).

Effects on Solar Cell Covers. Solar cell covers are discolored (darkened) by particulate radiation, thereby absorbing some of the sunlight. This increased light absorption reduces solar cell output by two mechanisms: 1) reduction of the amount of sunlight that reaches the cell, and 2) increased array operating temperature (hence, a decrease in cell efficiency). (See Chapter 5.)

Effects on Other Array Materials. Organic materials, as a class, are the least stable in a radiation field. Radiation damage to organic materials is dependent upon the total energy absorbed and sometimes upon the radiation intensity. Damage is usually not dependent upon the type of radiation, but may be dependent on the particle energy. Radiation damage to polymers may occur because of the removal of bonded electrons, leading to bond rupture, free radicals, and discoloration. Polymers may be degraded by a loss in mechanical strength, an increase in vapor pressure and viscosity, and a reduction in molecular weight.

It is important to note that test data from radiation exposure in the presence of air and in a vacuum environment indicate that radiation damage is reduced considerably in vacuum. This is explained by the fact that the presence of an oxidizer in the environment causes oxidation of ionized polymers, which results in greater alteration of the molecular structure than in a chemically inert (vacuum) environment. Inert atmospheres available in the laboratory, having an oxygen content as high as 1 ppm, may be insufficiently pure of such tests. Vacuum of less than 10^{-6} torr (1.3×10^{-4} $N \cdot m^{-2}$) is usually mandatory.

Solar cell array materials and components other than solar cells and covers of special interest to radiation damage studies (in regard to both mechanical and electrical characteristics) are the following: electrical insulation on wires, terminals, connectors, and between the solar cells and a metallic substrate; adhesives, both exposed and lightly shielded; blocking diodes; shadow bypass diodes; Zener diodes; and temperature transducers.

It should be noted that the corpuscular radiation, even that from solar flares, travels in spiral orbits along geomagnetic flux lines and thereby becomes an "omnidirectional" flux, which impinges on all array sides.

Particulate and UV Radiation Combined. In most practical satellite orbits, corpuscular and UV radiation exists simultaneously. Divergent views exist regarding the effect of such combined radiation on solar cell assemblies. One view, supported by ground-testing, is that UV exposure bleaches some of the darkening induced by corpuscular radiation. The other view, supported by comparing ground-test data with orbital data, holds that the simultaneous exposure causes greater darkening than each exposure alone. However, the data of the very few ground-tests which have been performed are in question, orbital data analysis is not very accurate, and the darkening mechanism is not fully understood at this time. (See also *Orbital Performance* in Chapter 1.)

9-45. Radiation in Interplanetary Space

Interplanetary space is defined as the space between the planets, their moons, the stars, and the sun. Radiation in interplanetary space consists of the solar wind, solar flare radiation, and galactic cosmic rays.

The *solar wind* at a distance of one AU from the sun consists primarily of hydrogen, moving at a speed of typically near 450 to 500 km/second (but varying by a factor of up to four) away from the sun. The average flux is about 2×10^8 hydrogen atoms/cm²/second. The average density is about 5 hydrogen atoms/cm³. The flux and the density are believed to vary approximately inversely with the distance from the sun squared.

The solar wind also contains lower-energy electrons and protons in the quantities and with the energies shown in Figs. 9-21 and 9-22. Higher-energy electrons and protons of solar or galactic origin are also present, as shown in Fig. 9-23. Solar wind electrons, having energies up to 1 keV, constitute a reasonably isotropic flux; however, solar wind protons tend to arrive near the earth in bundles within a 20° cone angle. Fluxes of electrons above 1 keV energy, and fluxes of protons above 10 keV energy, tend to arrive near the earth sporadically, with their timing being related to solar activities.

Galactic cosmic rays, radiation of galactic origin, consist of protons (about 85 to 93%) and alpha particles (about 7 to 13%), along with about 2% of the nuclei of heavier elements. The energy of the protons is in the range of 5×10^8 to 2×10^{10} eV. Although the energies are quite high, the free space flux of particles is only 2.5 particles $\cdot$ cm^{-2} $\cdot$ second^{-1}. Since this flux is small, radiation damage to solar cell arrays due to cosmic rays can usually be neglected.

9-46. Solar Flares

Solar flares are eruptions of the sun that are not always associated with optical phenomena (called "sun spots"), but always with the emission of energetic particles. The emissions of importance to solar cell arrays are mainly protons and alpha particles. The frequency

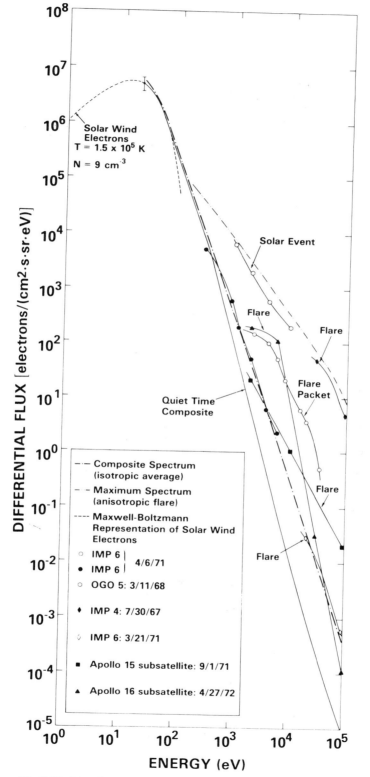

Fig. 9-21. Interplanetary electron spectra. (*Courtesy of NSSDC*.[42])

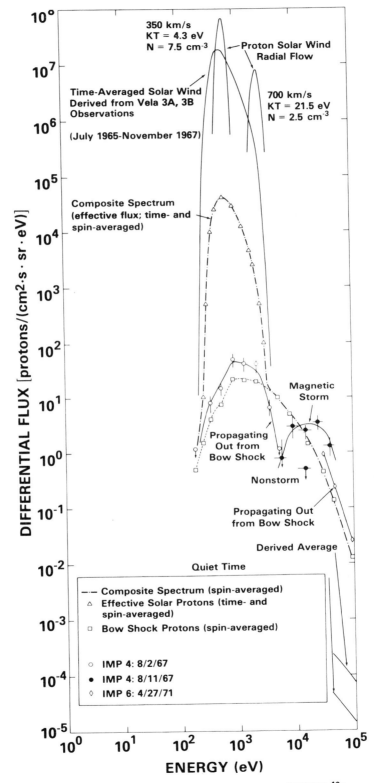

Fig. 9-22. Interplanetary proton spectra. (*Courtesy of NSSDC.*[42])

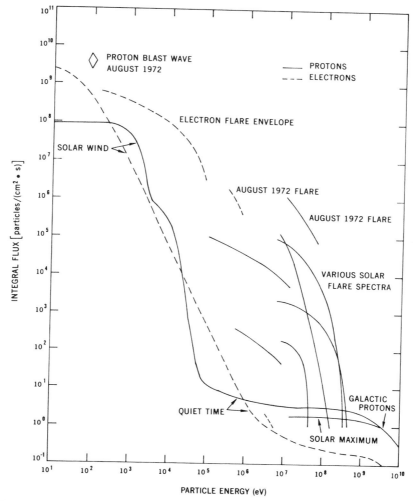

Fig. 9-23. Integral spectra of protons and electrons in the interplanetary medium. (*Courtesy of NSSDC.*[42])

with which sun spots occur increases to a maximum and decreases again during approximately eleven-year-long *solar cycles*. The duration of *solar maximum* is approximately seven years. The solar cycles of current interest are defined in Table 9-17.

Table 9-17. Solar Cycles.[43,44]

Solar Cycle No.	Period of Cycle	Duration of Maximum Activity
19	1953 to 1964	1955 to 1961
20	1964 to 1975	1965 to 1972
21	1976 to 1987	1978 to 1984

After its sudden eruption, the solar flare rapidly expands over an area of several million square kilometers of the solar disk, reaches a peak intensity, then gradually decays and completely disappears within a period of several minutes to several hours. Within a period of about half an hour or more following an eruption, energetic particles are detected at the earth, particularly in the polar regions inside the auroral zones. This radiation disappears within a period of one to three days. The constituent particles are electrons, protons, alpha particles, and very small numbers of medium nuclei (C, N, and O). The ratios of protons to alpha particles, and of protons to medium nuclei, vary considerably between different solar events, whereas the ratio of alpha particles to medium nuclei remains relatively constant. If has been found that solar flare events producing a large proton fluence tend to occur during the period of increasing or decreasing sunspot activity, rather than during solar maximum. Observed sunspot numbers for the previous solar cycles and the predicted numbers for the twenty-first cycle are shown in Fig. 9-24.

Solar flare particle fluxes measured near the earth are highly time dependent in intensity, spectrum, and isotropy (spacial uniformity), arriving from a highly preferred and fairly narrow direction in space from 30° to 60° west of the earth-sun line.

Many statistical analyses have been made of past proton events observed near or on the earth to predict the magnitude, spectrum, and timing of solar flare proton events. Unfortunately, the correlation between the prediction and observations has been poor. A Poisson distribution may appropriately describe the sunspot numbers and visually observable solar flares, but not solar flare proton events. The flares which are large enough to emit a large number of energetic protons to reach the earth belong in a special class of solar flare events. Phenomena observed during the nineteenth and twentieth solar cycles have indicated that most of the total proton flux during the past two solar cycles has occurred during one (or a few) anomalously large solar proton events. The number of these events is too small to warrant a meaningful statistical analysis for predicting the time of occurrence of anomalously large events. Table 9-18 shows all of the larger proton events observed during the twentieth solar cycle, grouped by year. According to this table, the annual relative solar flare proton flux was approximately as shown below.

| 1966 to 1971 | 5 % per year |
| 1972 | 70 % |

Therefore, a small degradation due to ordinary flare protons should be allowed for during the entire active solar period, even if no anomalously large flare events occur in some years.

Several observed and computed energy spectra from the nineteenth and twentieth solar cycles are given in Fig. 9-25. The most likely proton fluence to be encountered during the twenty-first cycle can be estimated from this graph.

Because solar flare proton clouds emanating from the sun enlarge upon their departure from the sun, the proton flux density within the

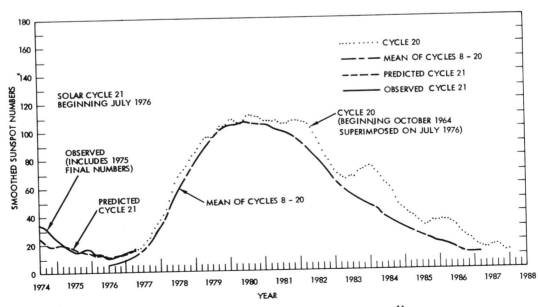

Fig. 9-24. Predicted and observed sun spot numbers.[41]

Table 9-18. Major Solar Flare Proton Events
During Twentieth Cycle.[41]

Year	Flux for $E > 10$ MeV ($10^7 p \cdot cm^{-2}$)	Percentage of Total Seven-year Flux Annual	Cumulative
1966	4 160 }	5.0	5.0
1967	75 66 3 }	4.4	9.4
1968	41 9 26 110 28 }	6.5	15.9
1969	6 4 150 87 }	7.5	23.4
1970	3 10 6 8 26 10 }	1.9	25.3
1971	150 3 38 }	5.8	31.1
1972	7 2250 }	68.9	100
	3280	100.0	

cloud decreases with distance from the sun. It is generally, but not universally, assumed that a solar cell array penetrating such a cloud will be exposed to a flux that is proportional to between D^{-2} and D^{-3}, where D is the array-sun distance.

9-47. Radiation Near Earth

The earth acts like a large magnetic dipole (bar magnet) with magnetic field lines connecting its poles. The axis of this magnetic dipole does not coincide with the earth's axis of rotation, but rather is inclined by $11.5°$ to it. A geo-

magnetic coordinate system, known as the B–L system, permits convenient expression of the magnetic field intensity, B, relative to the earth's location, using a distance parameter, L, that is related to measurements made of B at different geographic locations:

$$ B = \frac{M}{R^3} \left(4 - \frac{3R}{L} \right)^{1/2} $$

where R is the radial distance from the center of the coordinate system to the point in space at which B is to be calculated, M is the magnetic dipole moment of the earth, and L is related to R by $R = L \cos^2 \lambda$, where λ is the geomagnetic latitude.

The magnetic field lines will trap moving charged particles (but not electrically neutral particles) if the particles have the proper momentum and direction of travel relative to the magnetic field lines. The charged particles may have their origin in outer space or in a high-altitude nuclear explosion. They travel along helical paths of varying pitch until they reach so-called reflection (or mirror) points near the earth's magnetic poles just outside the earth's atmosphere. As the particles spiral back and forth in their latitudinal motion, they also drift around the earth in a longitudinal direction. Near the mirror points, the particles collide with upper atmosphere gas molecules, thereby gradually losing their energy until they fall into the lower atmosphere.

At some distance from the earth, the geomagnetic field is distorted by the solar wind, as shown in Fig. 9-20. The solar wind interacts with the geomagnetic field, resulting in the formation of a shock wave, and—behind the shock wave—turbulence in the magnetic field. There is a region of hot (high-energy) plasma near the earth-sun line on the day side. The solar wind deforms the geomagnetic field and squeezes it into a cavity called the magnetosphere, enveloped by the magnetosheath, which ranges from 10 to 14 earth radii.

The geomagnetic field lines just behind the magnetosheath are qualitatively similar to those associated with the simple dipole model, and they trap corpuscular radiation in the plasmasphere as described above (Fig. 9-20). During solar quiescence, a relatively steady flow of

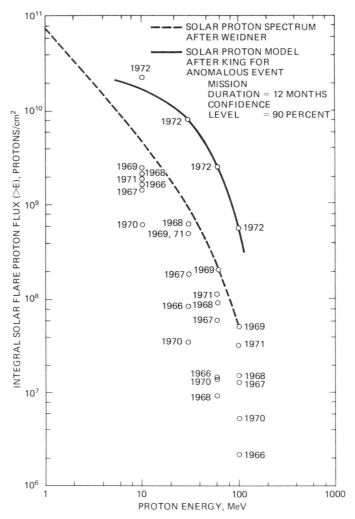

Fig. 9-25. Solar flare proton environment of solar cycle 20.[41]

solar wind tends to blow the field away from the sun, thereby causing an asymmetric shape of the radiation belt, compressed on the sun's side and forming the elongated tail of the magnetosphere and the thin neutral layer on the dark side of the earth. However, during periods of high solar activity, the entire quasi-equilibrium condition depicted in Fig. 9-20 becomes greatly disturbed.

Geomagnetically trapped radiation is confined by the outer boundary of the magnetosphere, which, on the sun side of the earth, is at a distance of 8 to 10 earth radii (50,000 to 64,000 km) from the earth.

The Auroral Zone. The auroral zone is located between approximately 60° and 65° geomagnetic latitude. Auroral displays (Northern Lights) are produced by low energy (less than 200 keV) electrons entering the atmosphere. Protons may also be present. The auroral particles are easily stopped and, consequently, do not present a serious radiation problem on the ground. Auroral displays are especially intense some time after a solar flare has occurred.

Geomagnetically Trapped Radiation. Both electrons and protons are trapped in the Van Allen radiation belts, as shown in Figs. 9-26

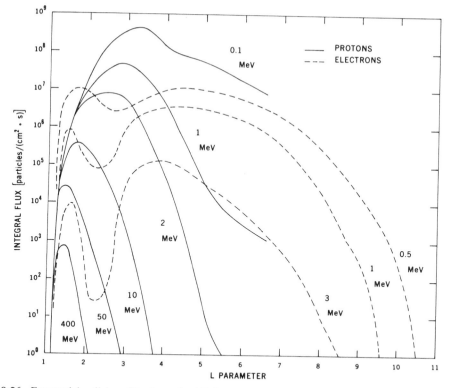

Fig. 9-26. Equatorial radial profiles from the AE-4, AE-6, and AP-8 Models. (*Courtesy of NSSDC.*[42])

and 9-27. (For the conversion of the natural environment to assess solar cell damage, see Chapter 2.)

The Outer Magnetosphere. The electrons and protons in the magnetosheath, plasmasheet, and magnetotail are shown in Fig. 9-28.

9-48. Radiation at Synchronous Altitude

Satellites in 24 hour orbits revolve around the earth with the same (i.e., synchronized) angular velocity as the earth so that the satellites appear to remain stationary over the earth's surface. Therefore, such orbits are called *synchronous* or *stationary* orbits. The prefix *geo*, sometimes used, indicates that the orbits are around the earth rather than about another planet. Synchronous satellites in circular orbit are at an altitude of approximately 35,807 km. For a variety of reasons, all stationary satellites actually move about slightly and require that

station-keeping maneuvers be performed from time to time.

Radiation at synchronous altitude includes trapped electrons and protons, solar flare protons and alpha particles, and the solar plasma. The effects of these particles on solar cell arrays include transmission degradation of optical elements, electrical degradation of solar cells, and material degradation, all as discussed in Section 9-44, and two additional phenomena: low-energy proton damage and electrostatic charging, as discussed in Sections 4-38 and 9-49, respectively.

In terms of contributing to total solar cell damage, the radiation environments at synchronous altitude rank as follows for most longer missions during periods of maximum solar activity:

1. Solar flare protons on station
2. Trapped electrons on station
3. Trapped electrons and protons during transfer orbits.

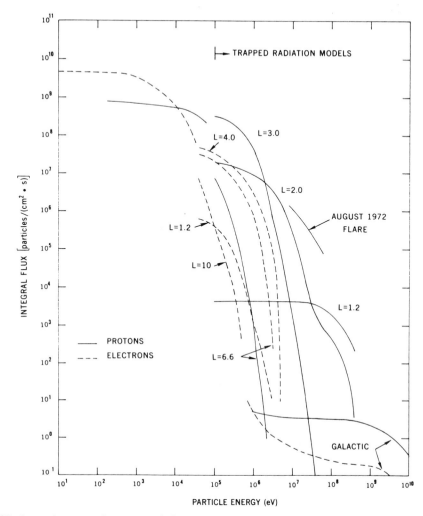

Fig. 9-27. Integral spectra of protons and electrons in the inner magnetosphere. (*Courtesy of NSSDC.*[42])

During periods of low solar activity, the solar cell damage due to solar flare protons moves from first place to third.

The total radiation environment causes two radiation components to enter the solar cell: one through the coverglass (front) and one through the substrate (back).

Solar Flare Alpha Particles. The alpha particle flux is typically neglected. At most, the alpha particle integral fluence is taken as 5% of the solar flare proton spectrum.

Trapped Electrons on Station. The trapped electron environment is defined by the AE4

Model[45] which, for synchronous altitude, can be approximated closely by the following set of equations for the integral electron spectrum:

$E \leqslant 0.3$:

$$\log_{10} \Phi_e(>E) = -3.0\,E + 7.7$$

$0.3 \leqslant E \leqslant 3.5$:

$$\log_{10} \Phi_e(>E) = -1.25\,E + 7.2$$

where Φ is in $e \cdot cm^{-2} \cdot second^{-1}$ and the energy E is in MeV.

The AE4 model supersedes the earlier AE3 model.[45] Compared with the AE4 model, the AE3 model showed a slightly higher electron flux at energies below 0.7 MeV and a lower

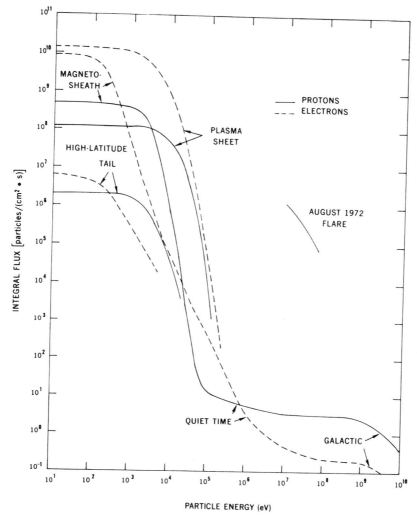

Fig. 9-28. Integral spectra of protons and electrons in the magnetosheath, magnetotail, and plasma sheet. (*Courtesy of NSSDC.*[42])

flux above 0.8 MeV. For most solar cell array designs, the damage equivalent 1 MeV fluence calculated from the two models is somewhat different, but the impact on predicted end-of-life power output is generally less than a few percent, depending upon time in orbit and specific array design parameters.

9-49. Geomagnetic Substorms

Relatively small activities of the sun, resulting in the emission of high-energy electrons, can cause the equilibrium condition of the geomagnetic field and the plasma sphere depicted in Fig. 9-20 to become distorted. As a consequence of this, satellites in geosynchronous orbit (at a distance of 6.6 earth radii from the earth) may find themselves in a localized area of geomagnetic field distortion such that the energetic electron stream can impinge on the spacecraft. This phenomenon, known as a geomagnetic *substorm* (as contrasted by a *major magnetic storm* caused by a major solar flare activity), can cause charging of spacecraft surfaces to large negative potentials relative to the surrounding plasma. Also, different surface dielectric materials may charge to different potentials, known as *differential charging*. As the spacecraft emerges from the dark side, photon-induced electron emission from illuminated dielectric and conductive surfaces will discharge these surfaces, while shadowed surfaces may remain charged. Unless these surfaces can quickly collect ions from the surrounding plasma, very large voltage potentials of up to 20 kV may exist between adjacent surfaces. The resulting arc discharges may cause radio interference and destruction of materials or components. Many satellites have experienced operational difficulties arising from geomagnetic substorms.[46,47]

REFERENCES

1. J. B. Kendrick, *TRW Space Data*, Third Edition, TRW Systems Group, © TRW, Inc., 1967.
2. F. C. Johnson, *Journal of Meteorology*, *Vol. 11, No. 6*, December 1954.
3. NASA Space Vehicle Design Criteria (Environment), Solar Electromagnetic Radiation, NASA **SP-8005**, May 1971.
4. Anon., *The American Ephemeris and Nautical Almanac*, U.S. Nautical Almanac Office, U.S. Government Printing Office, Washington, D.C., current annual edition.
5. C. W. Allen, *Astrophysical Quantities*, The Athlone Press, University of London, 1964.
6. *On the Nature and Distribution of Solar Radiation*, U.S. Department of Energy, **HCP/T2552-01, UC-59,62,63A**, March 1978.
7. W. E. Allen, "Design and Analysis of Solar Cell Array Configurations for Vertically Stabilized Satellites in Near-Earth Orbits," Technical Memorandum **TG-1066**, The Johns Hopkins University Applied Physics Laboratory, August 1969.
8. D. L. Evans, "Simplified Solar Irradiation Data Based on the Aerospace Insolation Data Base," Arizona State University, **ERC-R-77007**, 1977.
9. G. E. Daniels, "Terrestrial Environment (Climatic) Criteria Guidelines for Use in Space Vehicle Development, 1966 Revision," NASA Marshall Space Flight Center **TM 53872**, September 1969.
10. *The World Book Encyclopedia*, Field Enterprises Educational Corporation, Chicago, Ill., 1979.
11. *Guinness Book of World Records*, N. and R. McWhirter, Bantam, New York, 1976.
12. *Great World Atlas*, Readers Digest, Pleasantville, N.Y. 1963.
13. Military Standard, "Dissimilar Metals," MIL-STD 889 B, July 7, 1976.
14. *Reference Data for Radio Engineers*, Fourth Edition, International Telephone and Telegraph Corporation, New York, N.Y. 1956.
15. W. Luft, C. C. McCraven, and L. A. Aroian, "Temperature and Humidity Effects on Silicon Solar Cells," *Conference Records of the 7th Photovoltaic Specialists Conference*, 1968.
16. "Solar Cell Contact Development," Contract **NAS 5-11595**, Applied Sciences Division, Litton Systems, Inc.
17. W. H. Becker and S. R. Pollack, "The Formation and Degradation of Ti-Ag and Ti-Pd-Ag Solar Cell Contacts," *Conference Records of the 8th IEEE Photovoltaic Specialists Conference*, 1970.
18. C. J. Bishop, "The Fundamental Mechanism of Humidity Degradation in Silver-Titanium Contacts," *Conference Records of the 8th IEEE Photovoltaic Specialists Conference*, 1970.
19. H. Fischer and R. Gereth, "New Aspects for the Choice of Contact Materials for Silicon Solar Cells," *Conference Records of the 7th Photovoltaic Specialists Conference*, 1968.
20. M. Stern and H. Wissenberg, "The Electrochemical Behavior and Passivation of Titanium," *Journal of the Electrochemical Society* **106**, 755, 1959.
21. P. Berman and R. K. Yasui, "Effects of Storage Temperatures on Silicon Solar Cell Contacts," Technical Report **32-1541**, Jet Propulsion Laboratory, October 1971.
22. R. K. Yasui and P. A. Berman, "Effects of High-Temperature, High-Humidity Environment on Silicon Solar Cell Contacts," Technical Report **32-1520**, Jet Propulsion Laboratory, February 1971.
23. A. G. Pickett and M. M. Lemcoe, *Handbook of Design Data on Elastomeric Materials used in Aerospace Systems*, Southwest Research Institute, San Antonio, Texas, **ASD-TR-61-234**, January 1962.
24. Data from Various Project Documents and Equipment Specifications (no longer readily available for reference purposes).
25. *Handbook of Astronautical Engineering*, H. H. Koelle (Ed.), McGraw-Hill, New York, 1961.
26. R. V. Burry, "Final Report, Space Transfer Phase Propulsion System Study (Vol. 4, Appendices)," Report **R-3923**, Rocketdyne Division, North American Aviation, Inc., Canoga Park, California, NASA Contract **NAS 7-88**, February 1963.
27. "Vacuum Alters Materials," U.S. Army Ordnance, Frankford Arsenal, Philadelphia, Information Materials Engineering, July 1959.
28. H. M. Preston and N. E. Wahl, "Influence of Ultraviolet and Vacuum Environments on Structural Plastics," Institute of Environmental Sciences, 1960 Proceedings, Los Angeles, California, April 1960.
29. *First Symposium, Surface Effects on Spacecraft Materials, Palo Alto, California, May 1959*, F. J. Clauss (Ed.), John Wiley and Sons, New York, 1960.
30. D. K. Weidner, "Natural Environment Criteria for the NASA Space Station Program (Second Edition)," NASA **TM X-53865**, Marshall Space Flight Center, Alabama, August 1970.

31. R. T. Naumann, "The Near Earth Meteoroid Environment," NASA **TN D-3717**, November 1966.

32. F. A. Wade, "Martian Environmental Effects on Solar Cells and Solar Cell Cover Glasses," Report No. **3101**, Jet Propulsion Laboratory, Contract No. **952582**, Texas Tech University, August 1971.

33. J. A. Fager, "Effects of Hypervelocity Impact on Protected Solar Cells," AIAA No. **65-289**, July 1965.

34. J. Moses, E. Miller, J. Miller, and L. Zoller, "Contamination of Optical Surfaces by Solid Rocket Exhausts," NASA **TN-P&VE-P-67-2**, May 1967.

35. B. A. Sodek and C. Y. Chow, "Reaction Control System Rocket Engine Space Plume Flow Fields," Brown Engineering Report **RL-SSL-039**, April 1968.

36. N. Borson, "Rocket Plumes as Contamination Sources," Optical Contamination in Space Symposium, Aspen, Colorado, August 1969.

37. G. M. Arnett, "Lunar Excursion Module RCS Engine Vacuum Chamber Contamination Study," NASA **TM X53859**, July 1969.

38. P. J. Martinkovic, "Bipropellant Attitude Control Rocket (ACR) Plume Effects on Solar Cells, Optics and Thermal Paint," **AFRPL-TR-70-87**, Air Force Rocket Propulsion Laboratory, Directorate of Laboratories, Air Force Systems Command, United States Air Force, Edwards, California.

39. R. O. Rantanen and J. P. Thornton, "Deposited Contaminants Effects on Solar Array Power Loss," *Conference Records of the 10th IEEE Photovoltaic Specialists Conference*, Palo Alto, California, 1973.

40. "MSFC Skylab Mission Report—Saturn Workshop," NASA **TM X-64814**, Skylab Program Office, Marshall Space Flight Center, October 1974.

41. H. Y. Tada and J. R. Carter, Jr., *Solar Cell Radiation Handbook*, JPL Publication **77-56**, November 1977.

42. D. M. Sawyer *et al*, "A Review of the Near-Earth Radiation Environment," National Space Science Data Center, NASA Goddard Space Flight Center; also published in *Conference Records of the 13th IEEE Photovoltaic Specialists Conference*, 1978.

43. "The Earth's Trapped Radiation Belts," NASA **SP-8116**, March 1975.

44. "Interplanetary Charged Particle Models (1974)," NASA **SP-8118**, March 1975.

45. G. W. Singley and J. I. Vette, "The AE-4 Model of the Outer Radiation Zone Electron Environment," **NSSDC 72-06**, NASA GSFC National Space Science Data Center, August 1972; G. W. Singley and J. I. Vette, "A Model Environment for Outer Zone Electrons," **NSSDC 72-13**, NASA GSFC National Space Science Data Center, December 1972; and M. J. Teague and J. I. Vette, "A Model of the Trapped Electron Population for Solar Minimum," **NSSDC 74-03**, NASA GSFC National Space Science Data Center, April 1974.

46. *Proceedings of the Spacecraft Charging Technology Conference*, C. P. Pike and R. R. Lovell (Eds.), NASA **TM X 73537, AFGL-TR-77-0051**, February 24, 1977.

47. "Spacecraft Charging by Magnetospheric Plasmas," A. Rosen (Ed.), *Progress in Astronautics and Aeronautics*, *Vol.* **47**, Princeton University, 1975.

10
Material Properties

10-1. Where to Find the Data

The material properties and device characteristics data have been limited to the generally hard-to-obtain data that are of special interest to solar cell array design independent of its structural design. Data relating to solar cells are given in Chapter 4; solar cell cover and coating data are in Chapter 5; electrical component data can be found in Chapter 6; some substrate and mechanical support data are discussed in Chapter 7; assembly related material characteristics are covered in Chapter 8; environmental effects on materials are presented in Chapter 9; and all other material data are collected in this chapter. Specific material topics can be located quickly by referring to the Index.

Material properties data for common structural elements, such as substrates, frames, and support structures are well known and readily available from book stores, libraries, and professional groups.

10-2. Material Properties and the Designer

Material properties constitute the basic experimental data upon which the designer bases his designs. However, since material-testing is typically performed on standardized test specimen configurations, the resulting test data may not be applicable to a specific design or application. This is especially true in the areas of solar cell interconnector and adhesive bond design for long-lived arrays. Consequently, the designer will have to rely on additional tests to obtain confidence in his design or to establish adequate reliability.

GENERAL CHARACTERISTICS

10-3. Characteristics of Metals

Aluminum. Many different commercial grades of aluminum are available. However, only the industrially pure form, designated by A1100 with temper 0 (fully annealed) has been used for solar cell interconnectors.

A1100 is a soft, highly ductile material that can be readily worked by most commercially available processes and can be plated with silver or other metals to facilitate joining. A1100 can be welded and ultrasonically joined.

Beryllium-copper.[1] Beryllium-copper is an alloy that consists mainly of copper and usually of less than 3% cobalt, less than 2% nickel, and less than 1% beryllium. It is commercially available in several tempers, ranging from soft annealed to hard, and as a high-conductivity grade. Its most frequent application is for electric current carrying springs. It has occasionally been used as a solar cell interconnector material, presumably because it exhibits a higher ultimate strength than does pure copper.

Beryllium-copper can be worked readily by conventional processes and can easily be plated. It can be soft soldered and welded. Annealing is not recommended to be performed outside the mill, but hardening heat treatments are possible.

Beryllium-copper has been reported to be notch sensitive. Therefore, caution for the use of this material for solar cell interconnector expansion loops appears to be indicated.

Copper.[2] Many different commercial grades of copper are available, but it has been suggested that for solar cell interconnectors, only oxygen-free, high-conductivity (OFHC) copper would be an acceptable material. The lack of oxygen in OFHC copper retards the formation of fatigue cracks in bending, while the absence of other impurities increases the material's ductility and electrical conductivity.

OHFC copper is a soft, highly ductile material that can be readily worked and plated by most commercially available processes. It is easily solderable and weldable.

Invar.[3,4] Invar is a nickel-iron alloy with low thermal expansion properties. Of all the nickel-iron alloys, those with 36.0% nickel content exhibit the lowest thermal expansion for solar cell array applications. Two of such alloys are marketed as Invar "36" by Carpenter Technology Corporation, Carpenter Steel Division, Reading, Pennsylvania, and as Unispan 36 by Universal-Cyclops Specialty Steel Division, Cyclops Corporation. The typical chemical composition is shown in Table 10-1.

Invar can be cold- and hot-worked. For mild forming and blanking, a Rockwell hardness of B-90 is recommended. For sharper bending and deep drawing, such as for most solar cell interconnectors, a Rockwell hardness of B-75 is recommended.

Table 10-1. Typical Composition by Percent Weight.

Element	Kovar	Invar
Nickel	29	36.0
Cobalt	17	—
Manganese	0.45	0.35
Silicon	0.10	0.12 to 0.30
Aluminum	—	0.1
Carbon	0.02	0.04 to 0.12
Phosphorus	—	0.015
Iron	Balance	Balance

Cold-work stresses can be relieved by heating to temperatures above 540°C for 5 minutes, followed by air cooling. Higher annealing temperatures result in lower hardness; a 650°C anneal results in a Rockwell hardness of B-87 to B-88, while a 1040°C anneal results in a Rockwell hardness of B-66 to B-68.

Unplated Invar parts may be welded; however, the parts must be free of oxides, oil, and sulfur-containing substances before and during welding, although Invar interconnectors usually are plated with an electrically more favorable metal.

The heat treatment of Invar affects its thermal expansion characteristics. The following heat treatments have been reported to yield the lowest thermal expansivity: first, heat to 760° to 840°C (830°C typical); water (or oil) quench; stabilize low thermal expansivity by heating to 315°C for 1 hour, followed by air cooling; relieve quench-induced stresses and stabilize dimensions by heating to 95°C for 48 hours, followed by air cooling.[4,5]

The heating should be done in an inert or (better) a reducing atmosphere that is free of sulfur. The carbon content of the Invar should not exceed 0.15% to achieve the lowest thermal expansion properties.

Kovar.[6] Kovar is an alloy that was especially developed for making glass-to-metal seals. Because its low thermal expansion coefficient very nearly matches that of silicon, Kovar is of interest as a solar cell interconnector material. Kovar is a registered trademark of the Westinghouse Electric Corporation. The typical chemical composition is shown in Table 10-1.

After annealing in hydrogen for 1 hour at 900°C and 15 minutes at 1100°C, the average linear coefficient of expansion is typically quoted for a "gamma" crystalline structure. Like all other iron-nickel-cobalt alloys, Kovar is subject to a phase transformation at some temperature below −78.5°C. During the phase transformation, a part or all of the gamma crystalline structure changes permanently to an alpha structure, which has a considerably larger thermal rate of expansion than does the gamma structure.

The temperature of −78.5°C has been selected

for convenience, since this is the temperature resulting from an excess of dry ice in acetone. Production-testing by Kovar manufacturers or processors does not involve determination of the actual temperature of transformation of each heat. Tests of a large number of production heats, however, have indicated that the actual temperature of transformation is considerably below $-78.5°C$. On a special test of 14 production heats, actual determination of transformation temperatures was as follows:

- Six heats showed no transformation at $-269°C$
- Five heats showed partial transformation at $-196°C$
- Three heats showed partial transformation at $-120°C$.

For solar cell interconnector production requirements, special lots of Kovar can be obtained by selection to ensure meeting lower transformation points than those meeting the standard guaranteed value of $-78.5°C$.

Figure 10-1 shows the contraction of one particular heat of Kovar that partially transformed at $-120°C$ (Curve A) and the contraction of another particular heat, which showed no transformation at $-196°C$ (Curve B).

Standard machining practices can be used with Kovar, although relatively slow cutting speeds and high-speed steel or tungsten carbide tools are recommended. Recommended coolants are conventional compositions except that they should be sulfur-free.

The forming properties of Kovar are similar to those of mild steels. Kovar may be deep-drawn; however, the precautions given below are recommended.

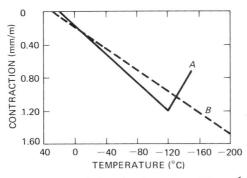

Fig. 10-1. Typical contraction curves of Kovar.[6]

1. Tooling should be designed to prevent over-stressing the metal.
   - Keep hold-down pressures to a minimum to ensure metal flow from the outside rather than stretching.
   - Open-end eyelets should be cupped with a closed end before final piercing.
   - On the initial draw, punch radius should be a minimum of four times material thickness. Reduce successively on redraws.
   - On the initial draw tools, the difference between die and punch diameter should be three times the thickness of the material.
   - Radius on final draw should be not less than material thickness. Sharper radii should be made by a subsequent coining operation.
2. Scratches and tool marks should be minimized.
   - On large parts, all defects must be removable by light polishing with 180-grit aluminum oxide abrasive cloth.
   - Surface defects of small parts must be removable by a nominal amount of tumbling.

The recommended annealing procedure for relief of stress and work hardening of Kovar parts appears below.

1. Wash and degrease parts.
2. Anneal in atmosphere-controlled furnace (atmosphere may be wet or dry hydrogen, dissociated ammonia, cracked gas, or a similar neutral atmosphere).
3. The annealing temperature is not critical, but high temperatures and long time periods promote large grain growth. Complete stress relief is obtained in the range of $700°C$ ($1290°F$) to $1100°C$ ($2012°F$), held for a minimum of 15 minutes after the parts have attained the temperature of the hot zone. Then the parts should be placed in the cooling zone before exposure to air. A typical schedule follows.
   - Hold at $870°C$ ($1600F$) for 20 minutes.
   - Place in cooling zone for half an hour

or until the parts are at less than 175°C (350°F) before removal to the air.

The foregoing intermediate annealing procedure is distinct from heat treatment for cleaning, strain relief, and degassing just prior to glass sealing. The latter should be done in a wet hydrogen atmosphere for a longer period; e.g., 1000°C for 30 minutes.

Kovar oxidizes readily and similarly to soft steels. Adequate protection from humidity is therefore required.

Kovar may be solder plated directly by dipping. Typically, however, the Kovar surface is "passivated" by a thin nickel strike, followed by a copper or silver plating (to enhance the electrical conductivity) and—if desired—a solder plating.

Molybdenum.[7] While primarily developed for high-strength, high-temperature applications, its low coefficient of thermal expansion makes molybdenum desirable for solar cell interconnectors. Pure molybdenum, also known as "moly," is brittle at and below room temperature and above 1000°C. Special alloys are available to reduce brittleness over a specific temperature range. Moly exhibits directional properties that call for consideration during bending operations. Smaller bend radii than twice the material thickness are not practical, even at elevated temperature. For shearing or stamping, blanking quality moly should be specified to prevent excessive lamination (spalling).

Experience with moly solar cell interconnectors gained by several organizations showed that the material should have been produced by an arc-cast process. Plating of moly has been a problem for years, but now several organizations offer reliable moly plating, usually by vacuum deposition of a Ti or Pd passivation coating followed by a silver layer. Humidity- and peel-tests have been found necessary to verify control of the plating process quality.

Moly can be obtained from the General Electric Company, Sylvania, and Metallwerk Plansee, Austria (U.S. distributor: Schwartzkopf Development Corporation, Holliston, Massachusetts).

Silver.[8] For use on solar cell arrays, "fine silver" (the commercially pure form of silver) is usually specified. Of all the metals, fine silver has the highest electrical and thermal conductivities. Its ductility and malleability are second only to those of gold. The "softness" of fine silver, especially in the form of thin, narrow ribbons or thin wires, often presents a major problem in manufacturing.

Fine silver is available in finenesses ranging from 999.0 to 999.99. (It is customary to express purity of silver in parts per thousand, and concentration of impurities in percent.)

Fine silver can be hot- or cold-worked. It work hardens at a lower rate than most metals; however, its low strength usually limits the degree of cold-work that can be done in one operation.

The absorption of oxygen in the silver undergoing processing at elevated temperatures leads to embrittlement of the material or the weld joints. The silver should be deoxidized before welding and shielded during welding by inert or reducing (hydrogen) atmospheres.

Silver does not oxidize in air, but tarnishes rapidly if sulfur is present in the atmosphere. Silver tarnish removers are commercially available and are recommended to be used prior to welding of silver. Also, silver tarnish preventers, such as "Silver Saver" paper, are commercially available.

Solder.[9] For soldering to silver or silver plated parts (such as the common Ti/Ag solar cell contacts), SN62 solder (62% Sn, 36% Pb, 2% Ag) is typically used. The silver content prevents an excessive amount of silver being scavenged from the cell contacts and dissolved in the solder. The solubility of silver as a function of solder alloy temperature is illustrated in Fig. 10-2.

For soldering to gold or gold plated parts, the scavenging of gold by the solder is reduced by adding indium to the solder.

10-4. Characteristics of Non-metals

Adhesives and Sealants. Two major adhesive systems are required for solar cell arrays. One system is used to attach the solar cells to the structure (substrate); the second is used to bond the solar cell coverglasses to the cells. The requirements for attaching the solar cells to the structure vary with the various arrays under

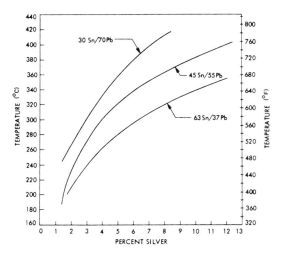

Fig. 10-2. Solubility of silver in tin-lead solders at various temperatures.[9]

consideration, but in general must have the following properties: high thermal conductivity, low outgassing in the vacuum environment, thermophysical and mechanical properties that are compatible with those of the solar cells and their support structure, repairability, and adequate strength to resist vibration and thermally induced stress.

The adhesive for bonding the coverglasses to the solar cells must be transparent to electromagnetic radiation in the wavelengths from approximately 0.35 to 1.1 μm and must not degrade appreciably under ultraviolet and particulate irradiation.

Additional adhesive systems are required for bonding insulating sheets to metallic substrates, for bonding wires and miscellaneous mechanical and electrical parts and connectors to the substrate, and for potting connectors.

The term "adhesive system" is typically used to describe, or at least imply, that an "adhesive" is more than just a simple product. "Adhesive systems" usually are comprised of the following:

- Surface preparations (cleaning, scrubbing, degreasing, etc.) of the components to be bonded
- Application and curing of a primer, if used, on a specified humidity/temperature/time schedule
- Measuring, mixing, and de-airing of multi-compound adhesives and control of shelf life

- Application and bonding within specified time limits to prevent skin-over
- Curing of the adhesive on a specified humidity/temperature/time schedule
- Clean-up, bake-out, pre-outgassing, etc., as and if required.

All adhesives, including the non-solvent types, produce volatile by-products upon curing. These by-products of adhesives currently used on solar cell arrays may be either of a gaseous acidic or alcoholic nature. The acidic by-products may combine with moisture from the ambient air and form acids that can, under severe conditions, corrode solar cell contacts. The susceptibility of a particular solar cell and array design to a potential corrosion mechanism should be determined by test.

For each specific adhesive, the manufacturer's recommendations should be followed closely and its data sheets should be consulted.

Epoxy-polyamide Adhesives. During the 1960's, several polymeric systems were considered. Most systems exhibited little energy absorbing capability. Epoxy-polyamide adhesives have been used on earlier solar cell arrays, such as on the IMP spacecraft and on the Mariner 1964 solar panels. Their performance in space has apparently been satisfactory.

Silicon Rubber Adhesives. Two generic types of RTV (room temperature vulcanizing) silicone rubbers, the methyl-phenyl silicones and the dimethyl silicones, have found use in bonding applications for solar cells. The methyl-phenyls have superior low-temperature properties, although the dimethyls have been more widely used in past space flights.

Conductive Adhesives. Potential applications for conductive adhesives include the attachment of solar cells to interconnectors and circuitry, especially during array repair, and the making of reliable interconnections between grounding straps and metallic surfaces and of flat conductors (in addition to mechanical fasteners).

Even though conductive adhesives have not been fully investigated for use in space and have not been widely used, they are a potentially attractive and, on a small scale, a necessary means of making reliable electrical interconnections for such applications as bolted-together, high-current bus bars, RF ground straps, and flat conductor interfaces between dissimilar metals. In these applications, the adhesive serves mainly as a conductive medium, while an additional structural element (bolt, rivet, etc.) provides the mechanical strength.

Kapton.[10] Kapton is a registered trademark of the DuPont Company for its flame resistant, transparent, gold colored polyimide film. Kapton does not melt, but it chars and decomposes above 800°C. There is no known solvent for the film.

Kapton is marketed by DuPont as Kapton "Type H" film; when combined with heat-sealable FEP-fluorocarbon resin ("Teflon"), Kapton film is called "Type HF." The Type H film is available in the thicknesses and widths shown below.

Nominal Thickness		Maximum Width	
inches	μm	inches	cm
0.0005	12.5	18	45.7
0.001	25	28	71.1
0.002	50	28	71.1
0.003	75	34	86.4
0.005	125	34	86.4

Kapton retains its physical properties and dimensional stability over a wide range of temperatures (see Table 10-2). Relative to other organic films, Kapton has a very high cut-through resistance and creep strength at elevated temperatures. Kapton has a relatively high resistance

Table 10-2. Strength of Kapton.[11]

T ($°C$)	E (GN/m^2)	3% Yield Strength (MN/m^2)	Ultimate Strength (MN/m^2)
-196	3.5	–	240
25	3.0	69	170
200	1.8	41	120

NOTE: Kapton has a 10,000 cycle folding endurance when tested per ASTM D-2176-63T. The Elmendorf propagating tear strength per ASTM D-1922-61T is 3.2 N/mm, and the Graves initial tear strength per ASTM D-1004-61 is 200 N/mm.

to tearing, but once a tear has started, it propagates easily under only a slight load. The FEP layer on Type HF film resists such tear propagation. Kapton has also excellent creasing and repeated foldability characteristics.

Kapton can readily be sheared, die-cut, laminated, metallized, punched, formed, and adhesive coated. Three-dimensional configurations can be fabricated only with difficulty by "heat forming" (i.e., creep at elevated temperature under high loading). When used as a wire insulator, it must be wrapped around the conductor and held in place with an adhesive or FEP-Teflon.

FEP-Teflon.[12] Teflon is a registered trademark of the DuPont Company for its fluorocarbon resins. FEP-Teflon is a non-flammable, transparent, colorless, thermoplastic, fluorocarbon film. FEP is abbreviated from fluorinated ethylene propylene. In contrast to FEP-Teflon, TFE-Teflon is of a milky-white color.

FEP-Teflon is inert to all known chemicals and solvents except for fluorine, compounds containing fluorine, and molten alkali metals. FEP-Teflon exhibits anti-stick properties and a low coefficient of friction. It has good impact and tearing resistance and is continuously usable up to 200°C. It melts at 260° to 280°C.

FEP-Teflon films are available in three types:

- *Type A*—heat seals to itself and to other materials (adhesives usually will not stick to its surfaces)
- *Type B*—one surface modified to permit its use in laminations using any of many commercially available adhesives
- *Type C20*—both sides modified to accept adhesives.

FEP-Teflon film is available in the thicknesses and widths shown below.

Thickness		Width	
inches	μm	inches	cm
0.0005	12.5	30	76.2
0.001	25	48	121.9
0.002	50	48	121.9
0.005	125	48	121.9
0.010	250	48	121.9
0.020	500	48	121.9

Because of its heat sealing capability, dielectric properties, optical qualities, and chemical stability, FEP-Teflon has found extensive use on spacecraft exteriors and in electronic equipment. The mechanical strength and dimensional stability of FEP-Teflon is significantly improved when it is laminated to Kapton film.

FEP-Teflon can readily be cut, sheared, punched, metallized, folded, formed, and adhesive coated (Types B and C20 only, see above) and laminated. One of its attractive properties for space applications is that it can be heat sealed directly to a variety of materials, including Kapton, metals, silicon, and glass, without the use of an adhesive or primer, except that a silane (siloxane) adhesion promoter may be required in certain applications.

Space radiation and ultraviolet exposure can severely degrade exposed FEP-Teflon film, especially when under tensile stress and at elevated temperature, typically above 60°C.

10-5. Density, Mass, and Weight

Mass is the physical measure of the inertial property of a body. Mass, denoted by m, offers a resistance to a force F that intends to change the velocity v of a body by an amount a, known as acceleration, such that $F = ma$. At small speeds of the body relative to the speed of light, mass is effectively invariant throughout the universe. At higher speeds, applicable primarily to charged particles, the mass depends upon the speed of the body relative to an observer as follows:

$$m = m_0 \left[1 - (v^2/c^2) \right]^{-1/2}$$

where m_0 is the value of the mass at or near rest, v is the body's speed, and c is the speed of light. Particles moving with speeds such that $m \neq m_0$ are also called *relativistic* particles. The unit of mass is the kilogram (kg).

Density. This is defined as mass per unit volume for both homogeneous and non-homogeneous bodies. Density is expressed either in g/cm^3 or in kg/m^3, or in unitless ratios relative to the density of pure water at 4°C. The unitless form of density is also known as *specific density* or as *specific gravity*.

Weight. This is the force exerted on a body of mass m by the gravitational force of the earth or another large body. Weight, w, of a body with mass m is defined as:

$$w = mg$$

where g is the acceleration of gravity. On earth, the value of g changes with distance from its center (altitude) and with geographic latitude. The unit of weight is the same as that of force and is the newton (N). The gravitational acceleration at the earth's mean sea level is 9.80665 m/second^2. For example, 1 liter = 1 dm^3 = 1 $\times$ 10^{-3} m^3 of water has a mass of approximately 1 kg and, at sea level, weighs 9.8 N.

Relative Density. Typical density values for several metals relative to the density of copper are shown in Fig. 10-3. The densities for various solar cell array materials are given in Tables 10-3a through 10-3c. Masses for several array parts are illustrated in Tables 10-4a and 10-4b.

10-6. Centroids, Moments of Inertia, and Radii of Gyration

The *centroid* is the center of an area or of a volume. For an area located in an x-y plane, the coordinates of the centroid are given by

$$\bar{x} = \frac{1}{A} \int x \, dA \quad \text{and} \quad \bar{y} = \frac{1}{A} \int y \, dA$$

where the integrals are taken over the entire area A. If a system of parallel forces is applied to a body from any direction, their resultant force will always pass through the centroid. In the special case where the gravitational field acting on a body is uniform over the entire body, the center of gravity coincides with the centroid. In general, the centroid of a body is the *center of mass* of this body. The coordinates of the centroid of a body located in an x-y-z orthogonal coordinate system can be found from:

$$\bar{x} = \frac{\sum m_i x_i}{\sum m_i} \quad \bar{y} = \frac{\sum m_i y_i}{\sum m_i} \quad \bar{z} = \frac{\sum m_i z_i}{\sum m_i}$$

where m_i are the masses of each of the i elements of the body, and x_i, y_i, and z_i are the respective coordinates of each of the i elements.

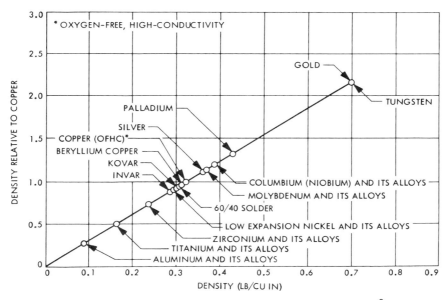

Fig. 10-3. Density of metals relative to copper.

UNIT CONVERSION: MULTIPLY LB/CU IN BY 27.68 TO OBTAIN G · CM^{-3}

The moment of inertia of a body is a measure of the body's rotational inertia about some specific axis. The moment of inertia of a body or system of bodies is defined as

$$I = \int r^2 \, dm$$

where r is the distance of each mass element, dm, from the axis of rotation, and the integral is taken over the entire mass of the body or system of bodies. The moment of inertia, I, is related to the net torque, τ, on the body about the same axis by the angular acceleration, α:

$$\tau = I\alpha$$

The radius of gyration, k, relates the moment of inertia, I, of a real body with total mass M about an axis to a hypothetical point mass M at a distance k from the same axis, such that

$$k = (I/M)^{1/2}.$$

Formulas for some commonly encountered space array configurations are given in Fig. 10-4.

MECHANICAL PROPERTIES

10-7. Stress, Strain, and Strength

Uniaxial Loading. An external force applied to a body that is restrained from moving (by a

Table 10-3a. Densities of Several Metals.[13,14,15]

Material	Density (g · cm^{-3})
Aluminum	2.70
Beryllium	1.85
Brass	8.47
Copper, annealed	8.89
Copper, hard-drawn	8.94
Gold	18.90 to 19.32
Indium	7.28 to 7.30
Invar	8.05
Iron, pure	7.86
Kovar	8.2
Lead	11.34
Magnesium	1.74
Molybdenum	10.2
Nickel	8.9
Palladium	11.4 to 12.0
Phosphor-bronze (4 Sn, 0.5 P, Cu)	8.9
Platinum	21.4
Silver	10.5
Steel	7.8 to 7.9
Tin	7.3
Titanium	4.5
Tungsten	18.6 to 19.3
Zinc	7.14
Zirconium	6.4

Table 10-3b. Densities of Several Non-metals.[15]

Material	Density $(g \cdot cm^{-3})$
Ceria-doped microsheet	2.62
FEP-Teflon	2.1 to 2.2
Fused silica	2.202
Germanium	5.46
Kapton	1.42
Korad	1.17
Microsheet	2.51
Silicon	2.32 to 2.40
TFE-Teflon	2.1 to 2.2

Table 10-3c. Densities of Several Polymers, Adhesives, Primers, Sealants, and Resins (Cured).[15]

Material	Manufacturer	Color	Density $(g \cdot cm^{-3})$
6-1104	Dow Corning	White, translucent	1.12
93-500	Dow Corning	Clear	1.08
RTV-40	General Electric	White	1.35
RTV-41	General Electric	White	1.31
RTV-118	General Electric	Clear	1.04
RTV-511	General Electric	White	1.20
RTV-560	General Electric	Red	1.42
RTV-566	General Electric	Red	1.51
RTV-567	General Electric	Clear	1.00
RTV-577	General Electric	White	1.35
RTV-580	General Electric	Red	1.49
RTV-602	General Electric	Clear	0.995
Silgard 182	Dow Corning	Clear	1.05
Silgard 184	Dow Corning	Clear	1.08
R6-3488	Dow Corning	Clear	1.05
R6-3489	Dow Corning	Clear	1.02

Table 10-4a. Mass of Solar Cells.

Size (mm × mm)	Thickness (mm)	Thickness (in.)	Solder Coating	Mass (g)
20.0 × 20.0	0.25	0.010	Thin	0.252
20.0 × 20.0	0.25	0.010	Medium	0.285
20.0 × 20.0	0.25	0.010	Thick	0.320
20 × 20	0.20	0.008	None	0.194
20 × 20	0.15	0.006	None	0.151
20 × 20	0.10	0.004	None	0.107

Table 10-4b. Mass of Various Array Parts.

Item	Material	Size (mm × mm × mm)	Mass (g)
Coverglass	Microsheet	20.2 × 19.2 × 0.15	0.140
Coverglass	Fused silica	20.2 × 19.2 × 0.32	0.310
Wire, insulated	Copper	AWG No. 28, per meter	~1.4
Wire, insulated	Copper	AWG No. 24, per meter	~3.0
Diode, blocking	Glass envelope	1 amp	0.275

second force of equal magnitude but acting in the opposite direction) tends to deform that body. The resultant internal force in the body that opposes the external force F is called *stress*, denoted by σ. Any deformation of the body that takes place as a result of the external force is called *strain*, ϵ. Both stress and strain may be tensile, compressive, or in shear, as illustrated in Fig. 10-5. The solid lines depict the body, a rectangular prism, before application of the force F, while the dashed lines illustrate, in a highly exaggerated manner, the deformations, or strains, of the body while the force is acting.

Let the bar in Fig. 10-5a and b have an initial length L_0 and an initial cross-sectional area A_0. Then let the external load, F, be applied. Since

F acts in the axial direction, let us denote the load by F_a. The stress in the bar, also in the axial direction, is

$$\sigma_a = \frac{F_a}{A_0}.$$

As a result of application of the force F_a, the bar has deformed: the length has changed by an amount ΔL, and the cross-section by an amount ΔA, to a new length $(L = L_0 + \Delta L)$ and a new cross-section $(A = A_0 + \Delta A)$. For compressive loading, ΔL is a negative and ΔA is a positive quantity. For tensile loading, ΔL is positive and ΔA is negative. The strain in the bar in the axial direction is

$$\epsilon_a = \frac{L - L_0}{L_0} = \frac{\Delta L}{L_0}.$$

For most materials and for relatively small values of strain, the strain is a linear function of the stress. The ratio between the stress and the strain is known as the *elastic*—or *Young's*— *modulus*, denoted by E or Y:

$$E = \frac{\sigma_a}{\epsilon_a}.$$

As the bar is stretched axially, it contracts in both lateral directions. The ratio of the lateral strain, ϵ_L, to the axial strain, ϵ_a, is known as

FIGURE	CENTROID	MOMENT OF INERTIA	RADIUS OF GYRATION
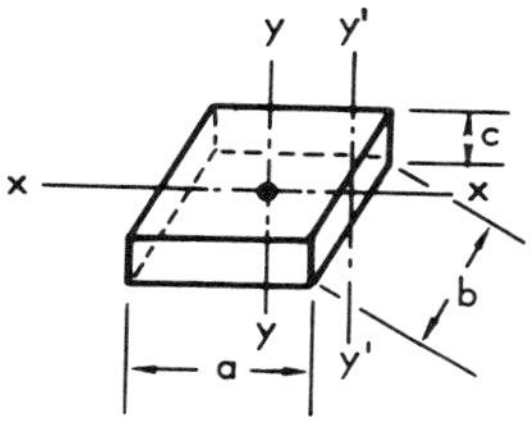 FLAT PLATE	0	$I_x = \dfrac{m(b^2 + c^2)}{12}$ $I_y = \dfrac{m(a^2 + b^2)}{12}$ $I_{y'} = \dfrac{m(4a^2 + b^2)}{12}$	$k_x = \left(\dfrac{b^2 + c^2}{12}\right)^{1/2}$ $k_y = \left(\dfrac{a^2 + b^2}{12}\right)^{1/2}$ $k_{y'} = \left(\dfrac{4a^2 + b^2}{12}\right)^{1/2}$
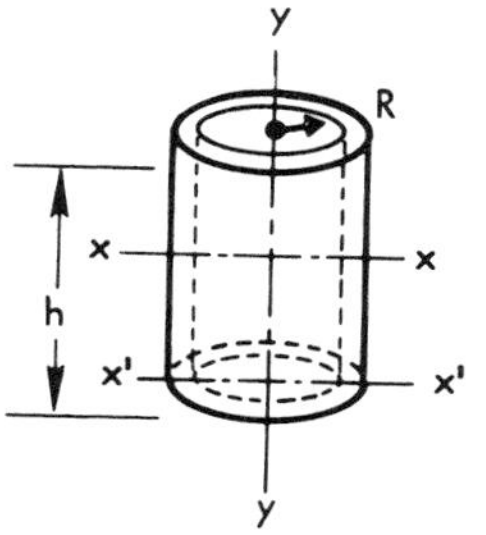 CYLINDRICAL SHELL	0	$I_x = \dfrac{m(6R^2 + h^2)}{12}$ $I_{x'} = \dfrac{m(3R^2 + 2h^2)}{6}$ $I_y = mR^2$	$k_x = \left(\dfrac{6R^2 + h^2}{12}\right)^{1/2}$ $k_{x'} = \left(\dfrac{3R^2 + 2h^2}{6}\right)^{1/2}$ $k_y = R$
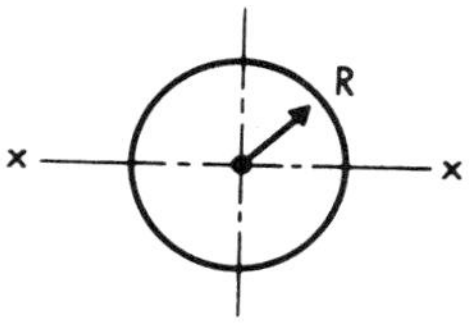 SPHERICAL SHELL	0	$I_x = \dfrac{2mR^2}{3}$	$k_x = R\left(\dfrac{2}{3}\right)^{1/2}$

Fig. 10-4. Centroids, moments of inertia, and radii of gyration (m = mass).

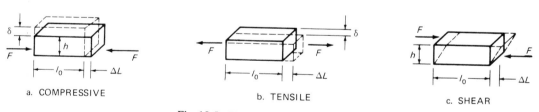

a. COMPRESSIVE   b. TENSILE   c. SHEAR

Fig. 10-5. Three types of stresses.

Poisson's ratio, v. For a laterally unrestrained bar,

$$v = \frac{\epsilon_L}{\epsilon_a}$$

and the axial strain is

$$\epsilon_a = \frac{\sigma_a}{E}.$$

Conversely, if lateral loads are applied to the bar tending to prevent the contraction, the in-crease in the axial strain is reduced. In particular, if all lateral contraction is prevented, the strain in the axial direction becomes

$$\epsilon_a = \frac{(1 - 2v^2)}{E}\, \sigma_a.$$

As the load on a laterally unrestrained bar is increased, the cross-sectional area, A, of the bar is reduced from the initial value of A_0. Thus, the actual stress or "true" stress, F/A, increases more rapidly than does the load F. The value of the stress computed based on A_0 is designated the *engineering stress*, since it is the stress used to compute the initial area required for a given load. In the linear elastic region, the difference between the two definitions is inconsequential, but it can be significant in the plastic region, as discussed below.

For larger strains, the concept of the *true strain*, ϵ', is used. The true strain equals the sum of the increments of strain, each increment being computed from the current value of length:

$$\epsilon' = \int_0^{\epsilon'} d\epsilon = \int_{L_0}^{L_f} \frac{dL}{L} = \ln \frac{L_f}{L_0} = \ln (1 + \epsilon).$$

As indicated in Fig. 10-6a, some materials will fail in tension by rupturing while still on the linear portion of the stress-strain curve. These are designated as *linearly elastic* and are generally thought of as brittle materials, such as glass and silicon.

Other materials are *non-linearly elastic*. After a certain stress level is reached, their stiffness reduces so that stress-strain curves become non-linear (Fig. 10-6b). On unloading, these materials essentially retrace their loading curve and regain their initial length. Their performance on successive load cycles is essentially unchanged. Typical examples are some rubbers and elastomers used for bonding.

Most metals are *elastic-plastic* (Fig. 10-6c). Above a critical stress, their stress-strain curves also become non-linear, but the increase in strain above the linear value, called the plastic strain, is not recoverable. The unloading stress-strain curve is linear and essentially parallel to the initial loading curve. For some metals (annealed, low-carbon steel), the transition to plas-

ticity is quite sudden; for others, it is more gradual (nickel-chromium stainless steels). Therefore, the stress at which metals become plastic, called the *yield stress*, is usually defined as the stress at which the deviation of the strain from the linear value equals 0.2%. Yielding in materials does not involve rupturing of the molecular bonds, but rather the movement of imperfections or "dislocations" along certain shear planes of the crystal lattice. The total deformation is the summation of these individual shearing deformations. Thus, plastic deformation does not involve any change in volume and the plastic value of Poisson's ratio is 0.5 for all materials.

As the load on the bar is increased past the yield value, the metal continues to deform uniformly along its length; however, at some critical load, the stretching becomes non-uniform and tends to concentrate in one or more local spots along the length. Due to the accompanying lateral contraction, these local spots of high axial strain have reduced cross-sectional areas called *necks*. The maximum value of the *engineering stress* (load divided by the initial area) occurs at the load at which necking commences and is defined as the *ultimate strength* of the material. The corresponding value of the strain is called the *uniform elongation*. As the stretching of the bar continues farther, the *true stress* (load divided by the minimum area of the neck) will continue to increase and can attain values considerably higher than the ultimate strength.

As necking progresses, the final *rupture strength* of the bar will be reached. The load at which this occurs may be considerably lower than the maximum load, depending on the necking behavior, but the true stress at failure

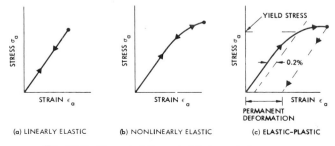

(a) LINEARLY ELASTIC   (b) NONLINEARLY ELASTIC   (c) ELASTIC–PLASTIC

Fig. 10-6. Characteristic material stress-strain curves.

will be considerably higher than the ultimate stress, as defined above.

The value of the strain at failure is called the *elongation*. Since the strain after necking is no longer uniform, the elongation is a function of the *gage length* or distance over which it is measured. Unless specified otherwise, this is usually taken to be 2 in. (51 mm). The shorter the gage length, the higher will be the measured value of the elongation. The maximum local value of the elongation occurs at the center of the necked area and can be determined most conveniently by measuring the reduction in area. Since most of the strain in the necked area is plastic, it can be assumed that the material is strained at constant volume ($\nu = \frac{1}{2}$). Therefore, if A_0 and A are the initial and final cross-sectional areas, respectively, then

$$AL = A_0 L_0 \quad \text{or} \quad \frac{L}{L_0} = \frac{A_0}{A}$$

and the true fracture strain is

$$\epsilon' = \ln \frac{L}{L_0} = \ln \frac{A_0}{A} = \ln \frac{1}{1 - R}$$

where $R = (A_0 - A)/A_0$ is defined as the *reduction in area*. The true fracture strain is often referred to as the ductility, D, and is an important parameter in calculating the low-cycle fatigue capability of a material.

Materials capable of sustaining large deformations without failure are said to be *plastic*, or to exhibit *plasticity*. Plasticity under tensile loading is referred to as *ductility*, and under compressive loading, as *malleability*.

Shear Loading. The loading case illustrated in Fig. 10-5c results in shear stress and shear strain,

$$\sigma_s = \frac{F}{A} \quad \text{and} \quad \epsilon_s = \frac{\Delta L}{L_0}$$

respectively, related by the *shear modulus*,

$$G = \frac{F/A}{\Delta L/L_0}.$$

The shear modulus is related to the elastic modulus by

$$G = \frac{E}{2(1 + \nu)}.$$

Compressibility. The *bulk modulus*, K, relates the change in volume, ΔV, of a body with volume V under hydrostatic pressure F/A as follows:

$$K = -\frac{F/A}{\Delta V/V} = \frac{E}{3(1 - 2\nu)}.$$

Work Hardening. When a metal which has been loaded beyond its yield strength is reloaded in the same direction, its yield stress will be increased to the value of stress to which it was previously loaded. The metal is then said to be strain hardened (Fig. 10-7a); if the load cycle is repeated, the metal will remain linearly elastic. However, if the metal is then loaded in the reverse direction (i.e., first tension, then compression), for many metals, the yield stress will be reduced below its original value (Fig. 10-7b); this is called the Bauschinger effect. If the load or strain cycling is continued in the yield region, a new symmetrical stress-strain curve will be developed (Fig. 10-7c) which may be stronger (higher yield stress) or weaker than the original material values.

Biaxial and Triaxial Loading. Consider an infinitesimal cube which is arbitrarily oriented with respect to three reference axes at a point, as shown in Fig. 10-8. On the three parallel pairs of surfaces located at right angles to each other, there are three normal stresses (stresses normal to the surfaces)—σ_x, σ_y, σ_z— and six shear stresses (stresses parallel to the surfaces)— τ_{xy}, τ_{xz}, τ_{yz}, τ_{yx}, τ_{zx}, τ_{zy}—where the first subscript refers to the outward normal to the surface and the second subscript refers to the direction in which the stress is acting. From the equations of moment equilibrium for the cube, it can be shown that $\tau_{xy} = \tau_{yx}$, etc., so that at any point, there are six independent stresses. At the cube, initially in the x, y, z coordinate system (both coordinate systems having a common origin), the values of the stresses acting on the surfaces change and their variation can be computed by the theory of elasticity. According to this theory, there is an orientation of the cube at which all three shear stresses are zero and the normal stresses achieve their maximum values. The three maximum normal stresses are designated as the *principal stresses*, σ_1, σ_2, and σ_3,

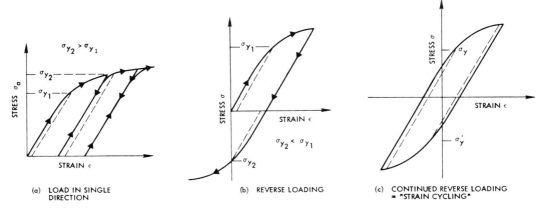

Fig. 10-7. Strain hardening characteristics.

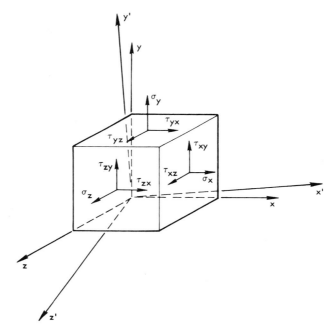

Fig. 10-8. Three-dimensional stresses on an infinitesimal cube of material subjected to an arbitrary external load.

and the stress state of the center of the elemental volume can be defined in terms of the values of the principal stresses and the angular orientations of the principal directions.

The average value of the principal stresses is called the *hydrostatic stress*,

$$p = \tfrac{1}{3}(\sigma_1 + \sigma_2 + \sigma_3)$$

and it acts as a pressure causing only uniform compression or expansion of the material, but no distortion. The differences between the principal stresses and the hydrostatic stress are called deviatoric stresses,

$$\sigma_1 - p, \sigma_2 - p, \sigma_3 - p$$

and they cause distortion of the element. Since yielding of a material is only a function of element distortion, it is a function of the deviatoric stresses. According to the generally accepted

Von Mises yield criterion, yielding of a material occurs when the *effective stress*, defined by

$$\bar{\sigma} = \left(\frac{(\sigma_1 - \sigma_2)^2 + (\sigma_2 - \sigma_3)^2 + (\sigma_3 - \sigma_1)^2}{2} \right)^{1/2}$$

exceeds the material's uniaxial yield stress. Notice that $\bar{\sigma}$ reduces to the uniaxial value when two of the three principal stresses are zero. Sometimes the Von Mises criterion is referred to as the *octahedral* shear stress, τ, which differs from the effective stress only by a constant. The *distortion energy* yield criterion is also equivalent to the Von Mises criterion.

For non-principal directions, x, y, z, the equation for the effective stress becomes

Until recently, the methods of analysis were limited for nonlinear problems, such as plasticity, so that solutions were available only under simplified conditions or were very approximate. However, with the continuing development and refinement of the finite element numerical solutions, many of these limitations are now being removed and more accurate plastic solutions require new, three-dimensional material properties which, heretofore, have not been investigated in any detail, as one-dimensional material properties have.

Linearly elastic or brittle materials generally fail when the maximum normal stress exceeds their ultimate strength. The maximum normal

$$\bar{\sigma} = \left(\frac{(\sigma_x - \sigma_y)^2 + (\sigma_y - \sigma_z)^2 + (\sigma_z - \sigma_x)^2 + 3(\tau_{xy}^2 + \tau_{yz}^2 + \tau_{zx}^2)}{2} \right)^{1/2} .$$

Since the addition of a hydrostatic pressure p has no effect on yielding, the individual stresses in a three-dimensional state of stress can be significantly higher than the yield stress. However, for the commonly assumed two-dimensional state of stress, called plane stress, in which the stresses in one direction, say z, are always zero, an arbitrary hydrostatic stress cannot be added. As a consequence, the maximum stress value can only be approximately 15% greater than the effective stress.

In determining the three-dimensional post-yield stress-strain curve, the effective strain, $\bar{\epsilon}$, corresponding to the effective stress is defined by

$$\bar{\epsilon} = \left(\frac{(\epsilon_1 - \epsilon_2)^2 + (\epsilon_2 - \epsilon_3)^2 + (\epsilon_3 - \epsilon_1)^2}{2} \right)^{1/2}$$

where ν has the elastic value for the elastic portion of the strain, and $\nu = \frac{1}{2}$ for the plastic portion. The value of the effective strain also reduces to the uniaxial value when two of the principal strains are zero. Thus, the multiaxial stress-strain curve can be obtained from the results of a uniaxial test up to the strain value at necking; i.e., up to the uniform elongation. Beyond that strain, the behavior in uniaxial and multiaxial stress conditions will differ due to the inhibiting of necking in the three-dimensional state of stress.

stress, however, may not occur in the directions of the coordinates in which a stress analysis is made; therefore, the maximum stress has to be calculated. For a three-dimensional stress analysis, the resulting equations are quite complex, but they simplify considerably if a two-dimensional analysis is performed in one of the principal planes. Thus, assuming σ_z is a principal stress, the maximum stress in the x-y plane is given by

$$\sigma_{max} = \frac{\sigma_x + \sigma_y}{2} \pm \sqrt{\left(\frac{\sigma_x - \sigma_y}{2} \right)^2 + \tau_{xy}^2} .$$

Similarly, the analysis can be carried out in the x, z, and y, z planes to find both the magnitude and direction of the maximum stress.

10-8. Stiffness and Bending Stress

A coil spring deforms (compresses or stretches) under the influence of a force. Similarly, a leaf spring bends and a straight wire stretches under the influence of a perpendicularly or axially applied force, respectively. The resistance offered by the material or structural element in response to the applied force, F, is known as its stiffness, k. In general, k is defined as a *spring constant*,

$$k = F/\Delta L$$

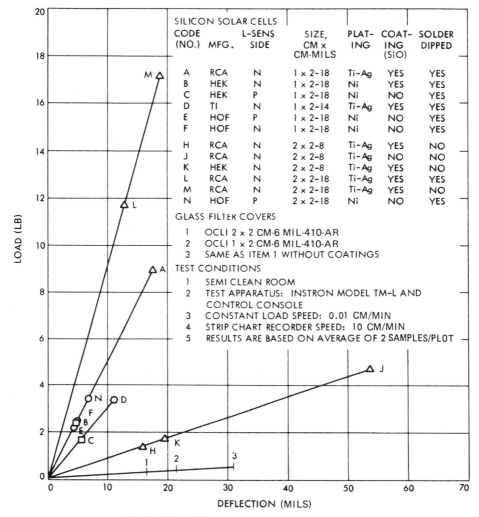

Fig. 10-9. Breaking strength in bending of silicon solar cells and coverglasses.[16]

where ΔL is the change in length due to the force of magnitude, F. The stiffness is related to the elastic modulus, E, and shear modulus, G, as follows:

$$k = EI \quad \text{in bending}$$

$$k = EA \quad \text{in axial loading}$$

$$k = GA \quad \text{in shear loading}$$

where A is the area as defined above and I is the moment of inertia as defined in Section 10-6. Within the elastic range, *Poisson's ratio*, ν, provides a measure of the body's stiffness:

$$k = \nu = \frac{\delta/h}{\Delta L/L_0} = \frac{1}{2} - \frac{E}{6K} = \frac{E}{2G} - 1$$

where the terms are defined in Fig. 10-5.

A frequent loading condition of solar cells and coverglasses is in bending. Figure 10-9 shows the experimentally obtained breaking strengths of a variety of small sample groups.

10-9. Mechanical Properties as a Function of Temperature

The mechanical properties of materials change with temperature. For space arrays, the very

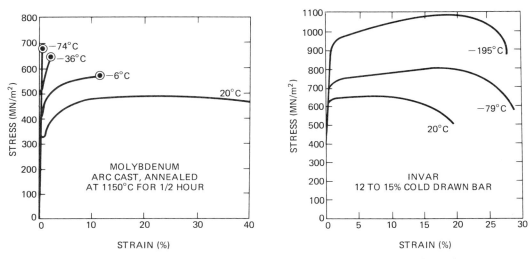

Fig. 10-10. Stress-strain behavior at different temperatures (molybdenum,[17] Invar[18]).

low-temperature behavior is of primary importance. For concentrator array types, moderately high-temperature properties are significant as well as low-temperature properties. Figure 10-10 illustrates the variations in the stress-strain curves with temperature for two commonly used solar cell interconnector materials. The values of the elastic modulus, yield strength, ultimate strength, Poisson's ratio, and shear modulus for typical solar cell array materials, as functions of temperature, are given in Figs. 10-11 through 10-15, respectively.

10-10. Elongation and Reduction in Area

Elongation and reduction in area are indicators of the ductility of a material. Both these parameters are determined by tensile-testing specimens of initial length L_0 and cross-sectional area A_0 until rupture occurs. Both parts of the fractured specimens are fitted together again, and the final length, L_f, and minimum cross-sectional area in the necked-down region, A_f, are measured (see Fig. 10-16). Elongation, EL, and reduction in area, RA, are calculated by

$$EL = (L_f - L_0)(100\%)/L_0$$

$$RA = (A_f - A_0)(100\%)/A_0.$$

Typically, initial length $L_0 = 2.0$ inches (5.08

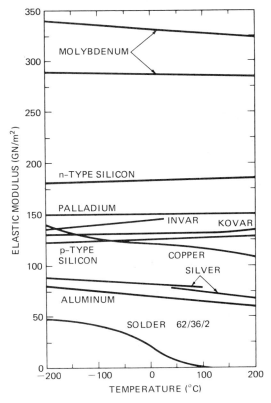

Fig. 10-11. Elastic modulus of several materials (molybdenum, upper curve,[20,21] lower curve;[19] silicon;[23] palladium;[19] Invar;[18,22] Kovar;[19] copper;[21] silver, upper left curve,[20] upper right curve,[21] lower right curve;[19] aluminum,[21] solder[19]).

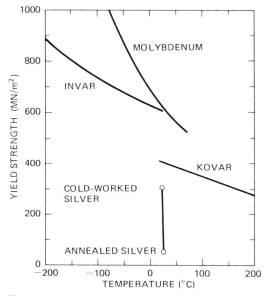

Fig. 10-12. Yield strength in tension of several materials (molybdenum,[26] Invar,[18] Kovar,[24],[25] silver[27]).

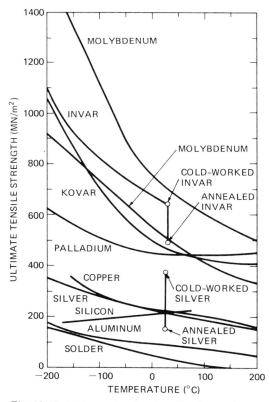

Fig. 10-13. Ultimate tensile strength of several materials (molybdenum, upper curve,[19] lower curve;[21] Invar curve,[18] 30°C points;[28] Kovar;[19] palladium;[19] copper;[21] silver curve,[19] 25°C points;[27] silicon;[23] aluminum;[21] solder[19]).

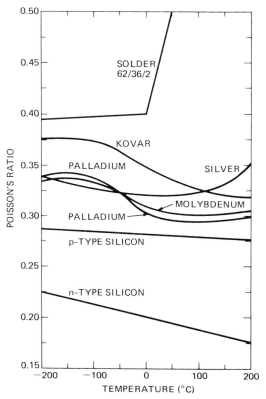

Fig. 10-14. Poisson's ratio of several materials (metals,[19] silicon[23]).

cm). Data for several materials are shown in Figs. 10-17 and 10-18.

10-11. Fatigue Strength

Fatigue failures and fatigue strength are related to cyclic application and removal of stress or strain (see Sections 6-19 through 6-22). Temperature influences the fatigue life as shown in Fig. 10-19. Non-metallic materials also exhibit fatigue life phenomena, as illustrated in Fig. 10-20.

10-12. Mechanical Properties of Elastomers

Non-metals may, depending upon their temperature, behave like elastomers, metals, or glasses. The stress-strain characteristics of elastomers are different from those of metals and glasses in that they can sustain relatively large plastic deformation without taking a permanent set. Most elastomers used for solar arrays have

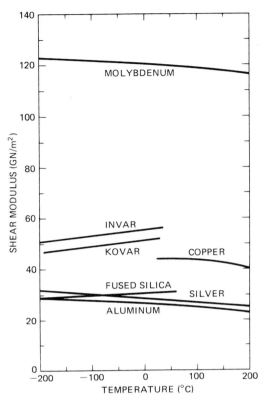

Fig. 10-15. Shear modulus of several materials (Invar,[18,21] fused silica,[23] silver,[21,29] all others[21]).

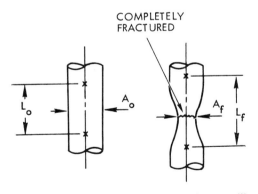

Fig. 10-16. Elongation and reduction in area illustrated.

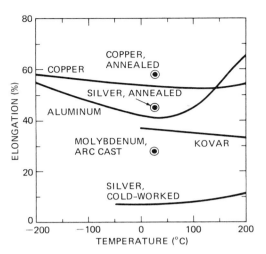

Fig. 10-17. Elongation of several materials (copper and molybdenum at $25°C$,[31] all others[21]).

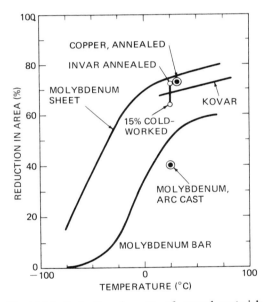

Fig. 10-18. Reduction in area of several materials (copper and molybdenum at $25°C$,[31] all others[26]).

stress-strain characteristics that show complete recovery of a large strain. The rate of recovery may be relatively slow for some materials, taking from minutes to hours.

Elastomers include such materials as room temperature vulcanizing (RTV) rubbers, silicone adhesives and sealants, and similar rubber-like organics and plastics. Figures 10-21 through 10-26 and Table 10-5 give properties for some frequently used elastomers.

10-13. Outgassing and Weight Loss

Organic materials in the space vacuum environment lose volatile components adsorbed on, absorbed in, or otherwise contained in these materials. The rate of outgassing and the total

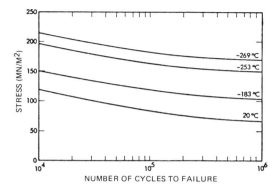

Fig. 10-19. Fatigue strength of annealed silver.[17]

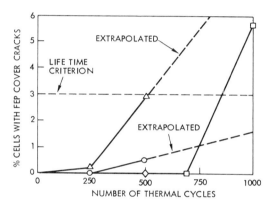

LEGEND:

△ EVALUATION TEST (IMTS), CONVENTIONAL CONTACT CELLS

○ EVALUATION TEST (IMTS), WRAPAROUND CONTACT CELLS

◇ DEVELOPMENT TEST, CONVENTIONAL CONTACT CELLS

□ DEVELOPMENT TEST, WRAPAROUND CONTACT CELLS

Fig. 10-20. Fatigue life of FEP-Teflon (0.125 mm thick on silicon).[34] (*Reprinted with permission of the IEEE*)

quantity of material outgassed depends upon the mobility of the outgassing substances through the material, the outgassing path lengths, the material temperature, and the time during which outgassing takes place. The total mass of material outgassed is measured by the weight loss.

The currently most acceptable outgassing-test method is the Stanford Research Institute (SRI) method. This method was developed under NASA-JPL sponsorship and consists of the equipment and test procedures below.

1. Preconditioning of the test samples (of about 0.1 to 0.3 g mass) for 24 hours in ambient air having 50% relative humidity.
2. Weighing of the test samples and collector plates (see below).
3. Placement of the test samples into cavities in a copper bar such that all volatiles must escape through an exit port (a 6.3 mm diameter hole) in a copper cover which is placed over each cavity, and placement of a chromium plated collector plate in direct line of sight of the exit port at a distance of 12.5 mm from the exit port.
4. Evacuation of the test apparatus and heating of the copper bar with test specimens to 125°C for 24 hours while maintaining the collector plates at 25°C.
5. Reweighing of the test samples and determining the percentage of the total mass loss (TML).
6. Reweighing of the collector plates and determining the percentage of the mass of the collected volatile condensable materials (CVCM), based on the initial mass of the samples.

The test results obtained by this (and any other) method depends to a large degree upon the mix ratios of two-part adhesives and their curing cycles. Table 10-6 gives data on commonly used spacecraft materials.

THERMAL PROPERTIES

10-14. Thermal Expansion

Physical bodies change their size with temperature. If they increase their size with increasing temperature, as they generally do, they exhibit a "positive" temperature coefficient. For a given change in temperature, a hole in a body changes its size by precisely the same amount as would a hypothetical body, made of the same material, which could be fitted precisely into the hole.

Coefficients of Linear Thermal Expansion. The coefficient of linear (as contrasted by area or volume) thermal expansion is defined in the following way. In Eq. 10-1, L is the length of a piece of material and T is the temperature.

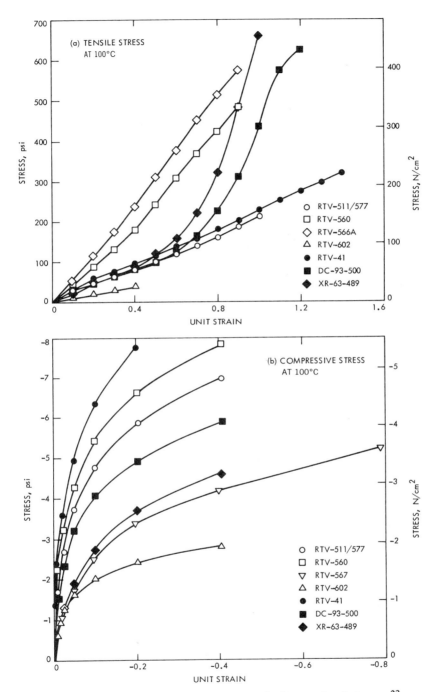

Fig. 10-21. Tensile and compressive stress-strain diagrams for elastomers.[23]

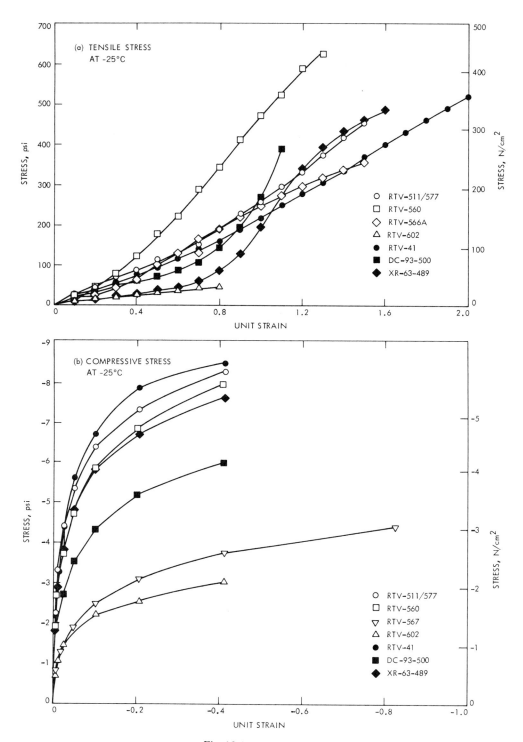

Fig. 10-21. (*Continued*)

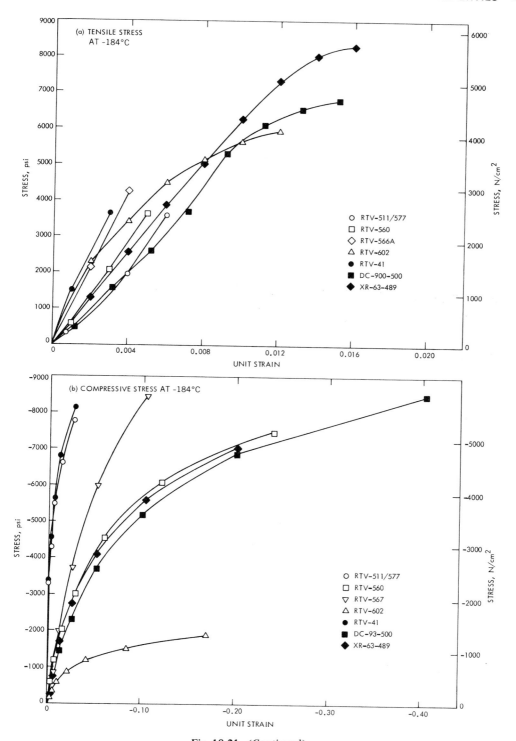

Fig. 10-21. (*Continued*)

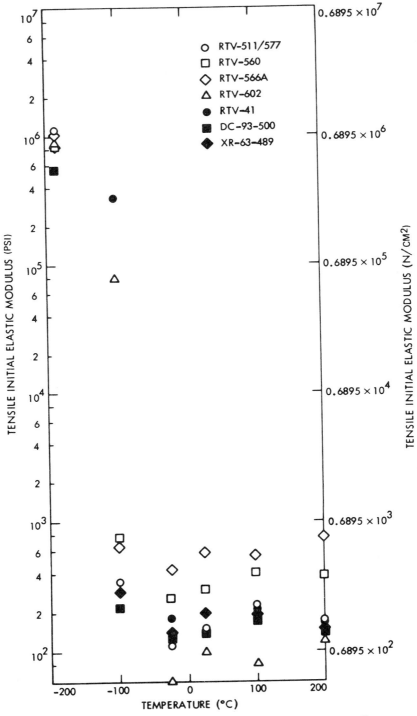

Fig. 10-22. Silicone rubbers–initial elastic modulus in tension.[23]

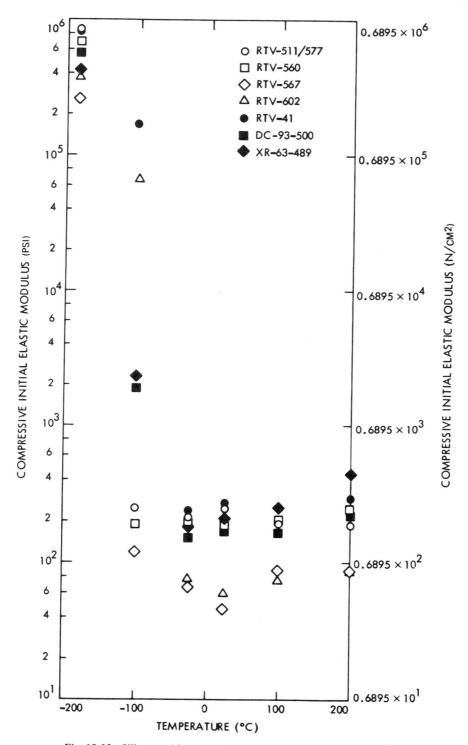

Fig. 10-23. Silicone rubbers—initial elastic modulus in compression.[23]

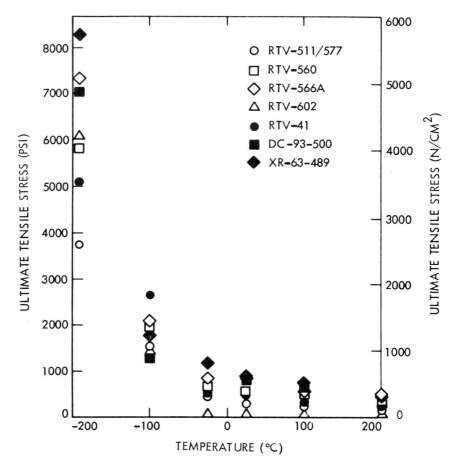

Fig. 10-24. Silicone rubbers—ultimate tensile strength.[23]

$$L_{T2} = L_{T1}[1 + \alpha(T_2 - T_1)] \quad (10\text{-}1)$$

Solving for α, we get Eq. 10-2.

$$\alpha = \frac{L_{T2} - L_{T1}}{L_{T1}(T_2 - T_1)} \quad (10\text{-}2)$$

The α in Eqs. 10-1 and 10-2 has been interpreted in the literature to express the following quantities:

- Instantaneous coefficients of expansion (α)
- Average coefficients of expansion ($\bar{\alpha}$)
- Normalized thermal expansion ($\Delta L/L$).

The normalized thermal expansion is not a coefficient, even though it is occasionally (but erroneously) called a coefficient in the literature. The three different meanings of Eq. 10-2 are illustrated in Fig. 10-27 and below.

Instantaneous Coefficients of Linear Expansion. The instantaneous coefficient, α, is determined experimentally by measuring a change in length, ΔL, of a specimen for a given change in temperature, ΔT. To make the data universally useful, the change in length is normalized by dividing by L_0, the initial specimen length at room temperature, T_0. For the instantaneous coefficient, Eq. 10-2 becomes, for the ith increment, Eq. 10-3.

$$\alpha_i \text{ (from } T_i \text{ to } T_{i+1}) = \frac{1}{L_0} \frac{(L_{i+1} - L_i)}{(T_{i+1} - T_i)}$$

$$= \frac{1}{L_0} \frac{\Delta L_i}{\Delta T_i} \quad (10\text{-}3)$$

The ΔT's in Eq. 10-3 are relatively closely spaced intervals. The data points (α_1, T_i) are

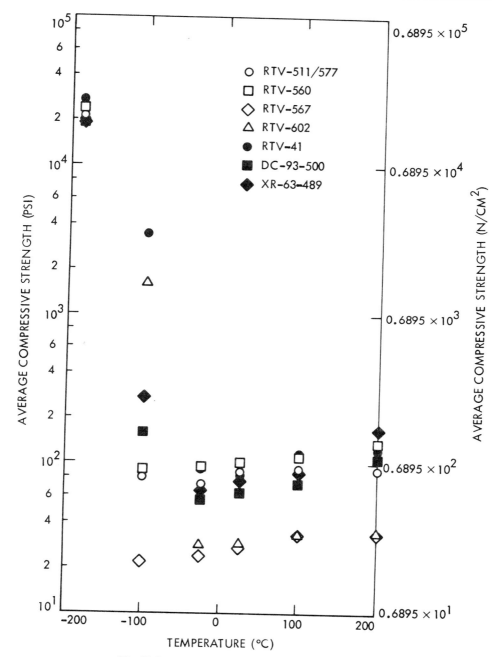

Fig. 10-25. Silicone rubbers—compressive strength.[23]

entered in a graph of α versus T and interconnected by a smooth curve (Fig. 10-27a). The value of α at a given T gives the instantaneous coefficient of expansion. In order to use the instantaneous coefficient in computations, it must be converted into an "average" coeffi-

cient, as defined below. Examples of instantaneous coefficients are shown in Fig. 10-28.

Average Coefficient of Linear Expansion. The average, or mean, coefficient of expansion is defined by Eq. 10-4.

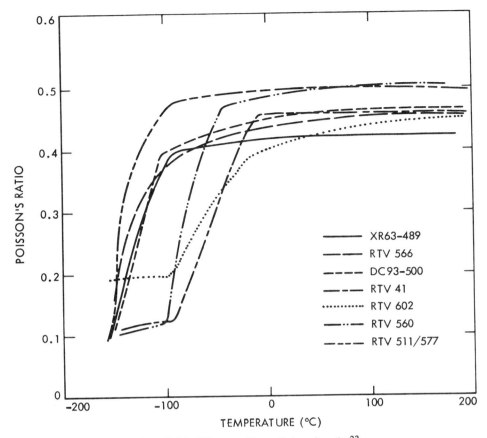

Fig. 10-26. Silicone rubbers—Poisson's ratio.[23]

Table 10-5. Properties of RTV 118.[11]

Temperature °C	α $10^{-6}/°C$	E MN/m^2	G MN/m^2	Yield Strength MN/m^2	Poisson's Ratio
−200	134	2070	690	83	0.45
−170	180	1200	345	69	0.45
−100	290	210	69	14	0.45
+20	440	0.21	0.07	1.4	0.45

$$\bar{\alpha} = \frac{1}{L_0} \frac{(L_j - L_0)}{(T_j - T_0)} \qquad (10\text{-}4)$$

This is accurate only for the specific T_j's measured (see Fig. 10-27b). The value of $\bar{\alpha}$ at any given T_j gives the average coefficient of expansion when the temperature changes from T_0 to T_j.

The temperature coefficients typically given in the literature are based on the average change in length from $T_0 = 0°C$ or $T_0 = 20°C$ to a given T. Hence, they are called average coefficients and are denoted by $\bar{\alpha}$. To calculate the change in length, ΔL, of an object, due to an increase in temperature from T_1 to T_2, Eq. 10-1 is applied twice (with a change of subscripts as indicated below), such that

$$\Delta L = L_{T2} - L_{T1} = L_{T0}[1 + \bar{\alpha}_2(T_2 - T_0)]$$
$$- L_{T0}[1 + \bar{\alpha}_1(T_1 - T_0)].$$

Table 10-6. Outgassing Properties of Some Solar Cell Array Materials.

Material	Mixing Ratio A/B by weight	Curing Cycle			TML (%)	CVCM (%)	Ref.
		Time	Temperature (°C)	Environment			
DC 6-1104	–	7 days	25	Air	0.19	0.01	35
		24 hours	25	Air	0.16	0.04	36
DC 93-500	10/1	7 days	25	Air	0.16	0.00	35
		24 hours	25	Air	0.29	0.00	35
		4 hours	65	Air	0.16	0.00	36
		8 hours	25	Air	0.10	0.01	36
Silgard 182	10/1	22 hours	100	Air	1.10	0.33	35
		22 hours	60	Air	1.03	0.23	35
		7 hours	25	Air	1.09	0.33	35
Silgard 184	10/1	4 hours +24 hours	65 150	Air Air }	0.92	0.40	35
		4 hours	65	Air	1.32	0.41	35
		2 hours	170	Air	1.01	0.48	35
DC 6-3488	10/1	4 hours	60	Air	1.42	0.74	35
		4 hours +24 hours	66 110	Air 10^{-3} torr }	0.83	0.40	35
		16 hours +4 hours +24 hours	25 65 110	Air Air 10^{-3} torr }	0.99	0.43	35
DC 6-3489	10/1	4 hours	60	Air	1.42	0.57	35
		4 hours +24 hours	65 110	Air 10^{-3} torr }	1.11	0.47	35
		4 hours +48 hours	65 110	Air 10^{-3} torr }	0.89	0.44	35
		4 hours +69 hours	65 130	Air 10^{-6} torr }	0.23	0.15	35
		69 hours	130	10^{-6} torr	0.36	0.17	35
Silastic 140	–	24 hours	25	Air	1.38	0.22	35
RTV 40/T-12	100/0.1	24 hours	25	Air	1.49	0.43	35
		7 days	25	Air	1.07	0.33	35
RTV 41/T-12	100/0.1	8 hours +4 hours	25 50	Air Air }	2.06	0.45	35
		8 hours +24 hours	25 150	Air Air }	1.09	0.60	35
		8 hours +24 hours	25 250	Air Air }	0.17	0.12	35
RTV 118	–	24 hours	25	Air	2.21	1.07	35
		24 hours +24 hours	25 125	Air 10^{-6} torr }	0.58	0.43	36
RTV 511/T-12	100/0.5	24 hours	25	Air	3.13	0.60	35
		3 days +16 hours	25 177	Air 10^{-5} torr }	0.09	0.00	35
RTV 560	100/0.5	7 days	25	Air	2.52	0.55	35

(Continued)

Table 10-6. (*Continued*)

Material	Mixing Ratio A/B by weight	Curing Cycle			TML (%)	CVCM (%)	Ref.
		Time	Temperature (°C)	Environment			
RTV 566	100/0.1	24 days	155	Air	0.14	0.02	35
		7 days	25	Air	0.07	0.00	35
	100/0.2	7 days	25	Air	0.27	0.00	35
	100/0.3	24 hours	25	Air	0.34	0.00	35
	100/0.5	24 hours	25	Air	0.41	0.01	35
		24 hours	25	Air	0.29	0.11	36
RTV 567	100/0.3	12 days	25	Air	0.18	0.07	35
	100/0.5	12 days	25	Air	0.27	0.07	35
	100/0.1	48 hours	25	Air	0.13	0.01	35
RTV 577/T-12	—	48 hours	25	Air	2.99	0.57	35
RTV 580/T-12	100/0.1	24 hours	25	Air }	1.81	0.81	35
		+24 hours	150	Air }			
RTV 602/SRC	100/0.25	24 hours	25	Air	3.10	0.96	35

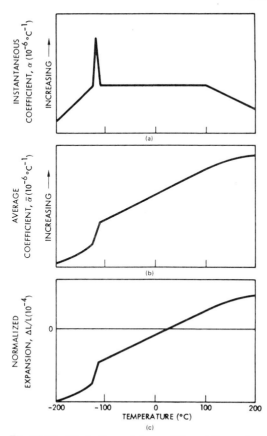

Fig. 10-27. Illustration of three different linear thermal expansion parameters (idealized silicone characteristics).

The subscripts of $\bar{\alpha}$ indicate that they are applicable only for the specific temperature range $T_2 - T_0$ or $T_1 - T_0$, respectively.

The average expansion coefficients for a number of materials are shown in Fig. 10-29.

Normalized Thermal Expansion. Since the temperature coefficients defined by Eq. 10-2 are cumbersome to use in engineering, the normalized thermal expansion, $\Delta L/L$, is frequently given as a function of temperature. The quantity $\Delta L/L$ is occasionally, but erroneously, labeled expansion coefficient. On a $\Delta L/L$ versus T curve, $\Delta L/L = 0$ at room temperature. The slope of the $\Delta L/L$ versus T curve is the temperature coefficient α of Eq. 10-2 as the quantity $(L_{T2} - L_{T1})$ approaches zero.

The *normalized thermal expansion*, also known as *unit expansion*, is shown for several materials in Figs. 10-30 and 10-31.

Conversion of Temperature Coefficients. The instantaneous coefficient is converted into the average coefficient by integration:

$$\bar{\alpha}_{(T_0 \text{ to } T_j)} = \int_{T_0}^{T_j} \alpha \, dT$$

where $\alpha = \alpha(T)$, as given by Eq. 10-3 or by a graph such as Fig. 10-27a.

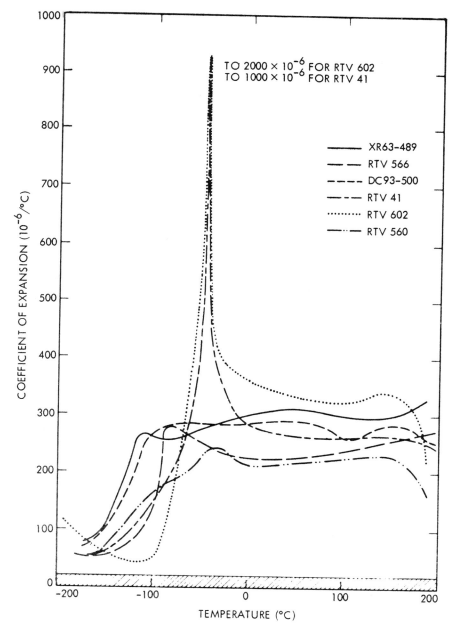

Fig. 10-28. Instantaneous coefficient of thermal expansion for six RTV type silicone rubber adhesives.[23]

The average coefficient is converted into the instantaneous coefficient by differentiation at each T taken from a graph (Fig. 10-27b):

$$\alpha = \frac{d\,\bar{\alpha}}{dT}.$$

The average coefficient is converted into the normalized expansion (Fig. 10-27c) by multiplication:

$$\frac{\Delta L}{L} = \bar{\alpha}(T - T_0)$$

where each $\bar{\alpha}$ and corresponding $(T - T_0)$ is taken from a graph such as Fig. 10-27b.

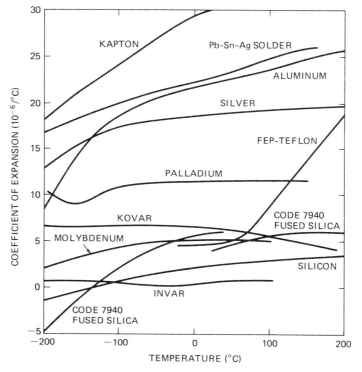

Fig. 10-29. Average coefficient of thermal expansion for several materials (Invar,[22,28] Kapton,[37] FEP,[38] all others[23]).

Units and Unit Conversion. The correct units of the instantaneous and average coefficients are "°C⁻¹," "°F⁻¹," or "°K⁻¹." Typically, the units are stated in the literature as "in./in. °F" or "cm/cm °C". Inasmuch as in./in. cancel each other, the values of

$$\frac{\text{in.}}{\text{in. °C}} = \frac{\text{cm}}{\text{cm °C}}.$$

The only change in the value of the coefficients occurs when the change is due to a different temperature unit (see below).

Multiply	by	to obtain
$°F^{-1}$	1.8	$°C^{-1}$
$°C^{-1}$	1.0	$°K^{-1}$
$°C^{-1}$	1/1.8	$°F^{-1}$

Relative Thermal Expansion. The average coefficients of thermal expansion of several metals relative to that of silicon is illustrated in Fig. 10-32.

10-15. Specific Heat and Heat Conductance

The *heat capacity* of a substance at constant pressure is defined as

$$c_p = \frac{dQ}{dT}$$

where dQ is the increase in stored heat energy in a substance due to an increase in absolute temperature, dT. The *specific heat capacity* of a substance is the heat capacity per unit mass. Typical values are shown in Fig. 10-33. The thermal mass of an object is defined by the product $c_p m$, where m is the total mass of that object.

The *thermal conductivity* or *heat conductivity*, k, of a substance is a measure of the transfer of a quantity of heat Q during a time interval t through a substance of thickness d and cross-sectional area A, due to a temperature difference ΔT across the thickness, such that

$$Q = k \frac{\Delta T \cdot A \cdot t}{d}.$$

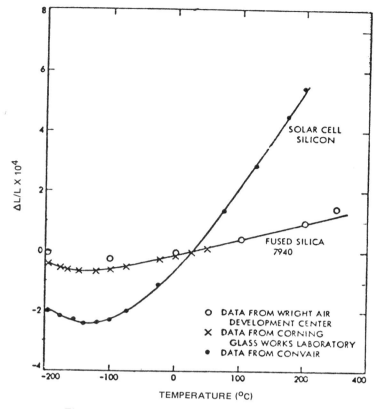

Fig. 10-30. Thermal expansion of several materials.[19]

Hence, k is a proportionality constant which depends upon the specific material. Metals have the highest heat conductivities of all known materials, and silver has the highest heat conductivity of all metals.

The heat conductivity of several metals relative to the heat conductivity of silver are given in Fig. 10-34. Several additional thermal parameters are given in Table 10-7.

ELECTROMAGNETIC PROPERTIES

10-16. Electrical Properties of Conductors

Resistivity. The absolute *volume resistivity*, ρ, is a material-peculiar proportionality constant which permits the calculation of the resistance, R, of a piece of conductor with cross-sectional area A and length L, such that

$$R = \rho L / A.$$

The units of ρ are ohm $\cdot$ m, but typically are given in μohm $\cdot$ cm or ohm $\cdot$ circular-mils/ft. Unit conversion factors are given in Appendix D. Values of resistivity are given in Table 10-8.

Temperature Coefficient of Resistivity. The temperature coefficient, α, of resistivity gives the ratio of the change in resistivity due to a change in temperature in °C relative to the resistivity at 20°C. The resistance, R, at any temperature T (°C), relative to the resistance R_0 measured at some reference temperature T_0, is

$$R = R_0 \left[1 + \alpha(T - T_0)\right].$$

For example, the resistance of an aluminum conductor of 1 m length and 1 mm² cross-sectional area at 20°C is $R_{20} = 28.3$ milliohms. At 120°C, the same conductor exhibits an approximate increase in resistance by $\alpha(T - T_0) = 0.35$ (or 35%) for a total resistance of $R_{120} = 28.3 \, (1 + 0.35) = 38.2$ milliohms.

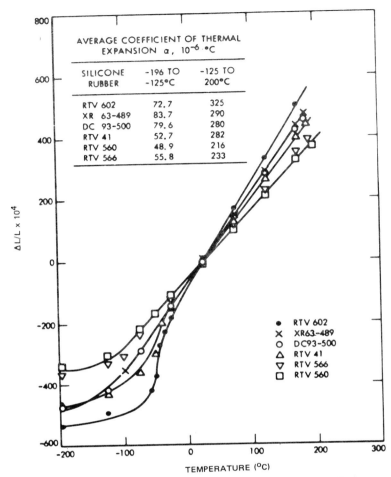

Fig. 10-31. Thermal expansion of silicone rubber adhesives.[19]

Conductivity. The conductivity, γ, is the inverse of the resistivity, ρ of a conductor:

$$\gamma = 1/\rho.$$

The recommended units of conductivity are $ohm^{-1}\ m^{-1}$; the use of "mho/m" is discouraged.

Relative Electrical Properties. Relative resistivity indicates the relative resistance of an otherwise identical conductor to that of one made from annealed copper at the same temperature. Typical values are also given in Table 10-8.

10-17. Electrical Properties of Dielectrics

Dielectric materials are electrical insulators. Aside from wire insulation, the main applica-

tion of dielectric sheets on solar cell arrays is to electrically insulate the solar cell rear contacts from metallic substrates. The primary electrical properties of dielectrics that are of interest to the array designer are the *voltage breakdown* characteristics of, and the electrical *current leakage* through, the dielectric material. The equivalent circuit of a dielectric of unit area is shown in Fig. 10-35. Both resistances, as well as the capacitance, are highly nonlinear with applied voltage. The leakage resistance is expressed as

$$R_L = \rho t / A$$

where ρ is the volume resistivity of the dielectric, t is the sheet thickness, and A is the area of the dielectric covered with solar cells and other non-insulated conductors.

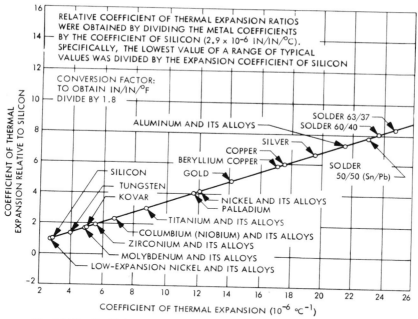

Fig. 10-32. Coefficient of thermal expansion of metals relative to silicon.[16]

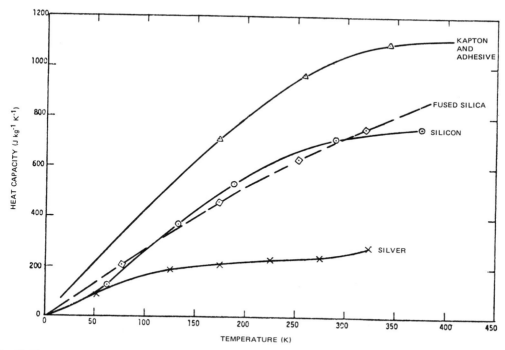

Fig. 10-33. Specific heat capacity for various materials (silicon,[39] silver,[39] fused silica,[40] Kapton and adhesive[41]).

In general, all dielectrics possess leakage paths under ambient terrestrial conditions. This leakage is due to imperfections in the material (pin holes) and due to moisture absorption by the dielectric. In addition to these two mechanisms, ionic conductions may contribute to leakage. Ionic conduction is caused by mobile ions that may be present in the dielectric material. The

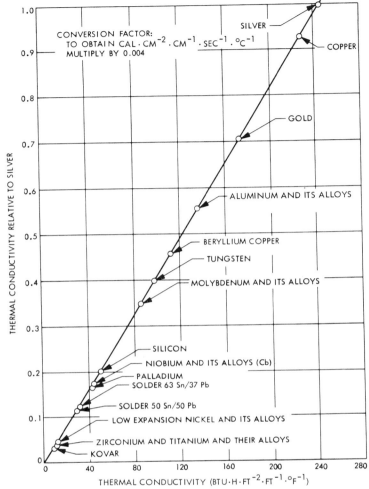

Fig. 10-34. Thermal conductivity of metals relative to silver.[16]

Table 10-7. Heat Capacitances of Different Metals.[42]

Material	Density, m (g/cm^3)	Specific Heat, c_p (J · kg^{-1} · °K^{-1})	Thermal Mass, $m \cdot c_p$ (J · cm^{-3} · °K)	Required Mass for Equal Heat Storage (g · J^{-1} · °K)
Beryllium	1.85	1920	3.55	0.52
Aluminum	2.70	920	2.48	1.1
Steel	8.0	500	4.00	2.0
Copper	8.9	380	3.38	2.6

concentration of mobile ions typically is greater in the softer resins than in harder resins and tends to increase with increasing water absorption in the dielectric and with increasing temperature.

The *dielectric strength* of an insulating material is defined as the ratio of its breakdown voltage to its thickness, also known as the maximum potential gradient that the material can withstand. In general, the dielectric strength

Table 10-8. Electrical Resistivity of Several Metals.[16]

Material	Resistance Relative to Copper	Resistivity at 20°C (μohm · cm)
Aluminum	1.64	2.65 to 2.83
Brass	3.9	6.7
Beryllium-copper	3.1	5.32
Constantan	28.45	49.1
Copper, annealed	1.00	1.7241
Copper, hard drawn	1.03	1.7758
Gold	1.416	2.42
Indium	9.0	15.5
Invar	47.6	82
Iron, pure	5.6	9.7
Kovar	28.4	49
Lead	12.78	22
Molybdenum	3.3	5.7
Nickel	5.05	6.84
Palladium	6.2	10.7
Silver	0.95	1.59 to 1.6
Tin	6.7	11.6
Titanium	47.8	42
Tungsten	3.25	5.6

(volts per unit thickness) increases with decreasing film thickness, and decreases with increasing time during which the electrical stress is applied. The effect of time under stress is significantly greater for applied ac voltages than for dc voltages. Dielectric strength ratings are usually based on the average breakdown voltage measured in tests; that is, when about 50% of the specimens under test have failed.

Dielectric properties for some widely used materials are shown in Figs. 10-36 through 10-41.

10-18. Magnetic Properties

All metallic alloys containing iron, nickel, or cobalt (such as Kovar or Invar) are "magnetic."

A "magnetic" material is loosely defined as a material that becomes measurably (in an engineering sense) magnetic when it is subjected to an external magnetizing force. This magnetizing force may result from a current carrying electric conductor. The degree to which a material becomes magnetic in response to a given magnetizing force is expressed by the material's magnetic susceptibility, χ.

For magnetic design work, the quantity of permeability, μ, is generally used to relate the magnetic flux density, B, created in a piece of magnetic material which is subjected to an externally applied magnetizing force, H, such that

$$B = \mu H.$$

The permeability, μ, (and, similarly, χ) varies with the applied magnetization, H, up to its saturation value, μ_m. The value μ also changes with temperature, decreasing with increasing temperature up to the Curie temperature, or Curie "point." Above the Curie temperature, materials essentially lose their magnetic properties.

The magnetic susceptibility, χ, is related to the permeability, μ, such that

$$\mu = \mu_0 + \chi$$

where μ_0 is the permeability of empty space. In vacuum, $\chi = 0$, $\mu = \mu_0$. Values of μ can be obtained by determining the slope of a magnetization curve on a B-H diagram, as shown in Fig. 10-42. This figure displays the resulting flux density, B, of the magnetism that is induced in a material by an external magnetizing force, H, when the magnetizing force alternates cyclically and is at least as great as to cause the induced magnetism (magnetic induction) to saturate in the positive and negative directions. If the magnetizing force, H, were returned to and left at zero after having magnetically saturated the material to B_s, the material would

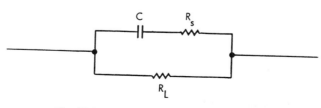

Fig. 10-35. Equivalent circuit of a dielectric.

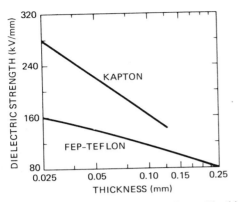

Fig. 10-36. Dielectric strength variation with thickness.[43,44]

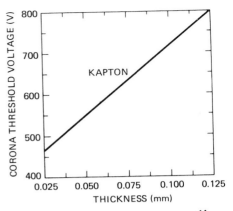

Fig. 10-39. Corona threshold voltage.[44]

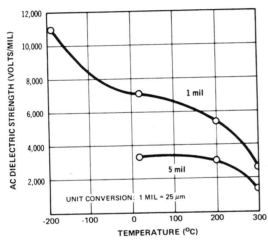

Fig. 10-37. Dielectric strength variation with temperature for Kapton.[44]

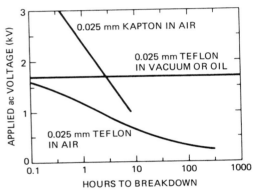

Fig. 10-40. Dielectric life.[43,44]

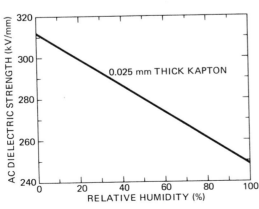

Fig. 10-38. Dielectric strength variation with humidity.[44]

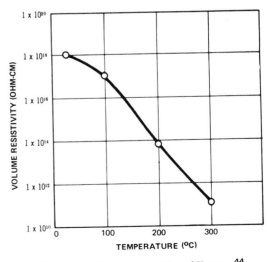

Fig. 10-41. Volume resistivity of Kapton.[44]

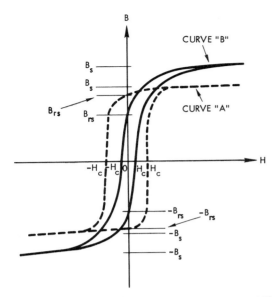

Fig. 10-42. Illustration of hysteresis loops on *B-H* diagram for magnetically "hard" (Curve *A*) and magnetically "soft" materials (Curve *B*).

Table 10-9. Magnetic Properties of Some Materials.[49,50,51]

Material	Induced Magnetic Flux Density (gauss)	
	Saturation (B_s)	Retentivity (B_{rs})
Alnico magnet material	8000 to 16,000	7000 to 13,000
Carbon steel (1% C)	Unknown	9000
Core iron	Up to 15,000	4000 to 9000
Kovar	17,000	Unknown
Invar	7000	Unknown
Copper	0	0

retain some magnetism, as denoted by the retentivity, B_{rs}.

The magnetizing force required to reduce induced magnetism to zero ($B = 0$) is referred to as the coercive force, H_{cs}. Magnetically "hard" materials, used for permanent magnets, exhibit relatively large values of H_{cs}. Magnetically "soft" materials, used for transformer cores and similar applications, exhibit relatively small values of H_{cs} (see Table 10-9).

The area enclosed by the hysterisis loop is proportional to the energy required to remagnetize the material in the opposite direction. This energy is dissipated in the form of heat in the material.

Effects of Magnetic Materials on Solar Cell Arrays. The two magnetic materials of current interest in solar cell interconnector design for space applications are Kovar and Invar. Both

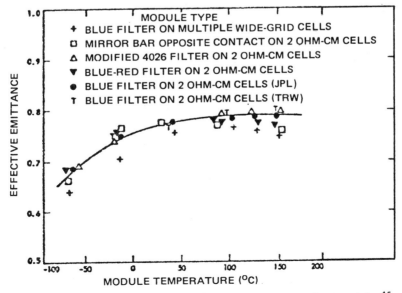

Fig. 10-43. Effective front surface hemispherical emittance of test modules.[45]

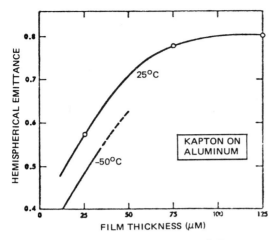

Fig. 10-44. Hemispherical emittance of Kapton on aluminum versus Kapton thickness.[46]

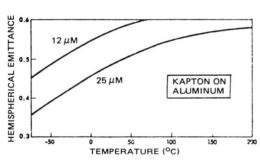

Fig. 10-45. Hemispherical emittance of Kapton on aluminum versus temperature.[46]

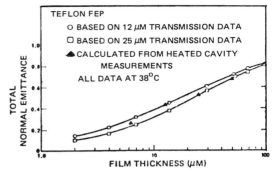

Fig. 10-46. Normal emittance for FEP-Teflon at 38°C versus Teflon thickness.[47]

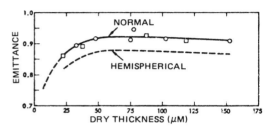

Fig. 10-47. Hemispherical and normal emittance of typical epoxy paints at room temperature versus dry paint thickness.[46]

of these materials are magnetically "soft" because they retain relatively little permanent magnetism after having been magnetized to saturation in a strong magnetic field.

10-19. Thermal Emittance

The emittance of several solar cell array materials is given in Figs. 10-43 through 10-49 and in Table 10-10. The conversion from normal to hemispherical emittance is discussed in Section 8-26.

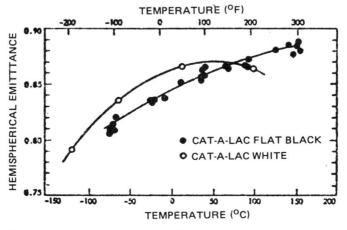

Fig. 10-48. Hemispherical emittance of Cat-A-Lac paints versus temperature.[45]

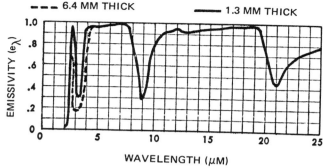

Fig. 10-49. Spectral normal emissivity of Corning fused silica code 7940.[48]

Table 10-10. **Hemispherical Emittance and Absorptance of Glassed Solar Cells.**[36,52]

Manufacturer	Surface	p$^+$	BSR*	AR Coating	Cover**	α_S	ϵ_H
AEG	Chem. Pol.	No	No	TiO_x	Fused silica	0.805	0.825
AEG	Chem. Pol.	No	No	TiO_x	Microsheet	0.850	0.850
AEG	Chem. Pol.	No	No	TiO_x	Ceria glass	0.872	0.850
OCLI, Spectrolab	Chem. Pol.	No	No	Ta_2O_5	Fused silica	0.852	0.781
OCLI	Chem. Pol.	No	No	Multilayer	Fused silica	0.874	0.782
Spectrolab	Chem. Pol.	No	No	Ta_2O_5	Ceria glass	0.854	0.815
OCLI, Spectrolab	Chem. Pol.	No	Yes	Ta_2O_5	Ceria glass	0.731	0.829
Spectrolab	Chem. Pol.	No	Yes	Ta_2O_5	Fused silica	0.739	0.779
Spectrolab	Chem. Pol.	Yes	Yes	Ta_2O_5	Fused silica	0.796	0.776
Spectrolab	Textured	Yes	Yes	Ta_2O_5	Fused silica	0.908	0.783
OCLI	Chem. Pol.	Yes	No	Ta_2O_5	Fused silica	0.852	0.784

*BSR = Back surface reflector.
**Cut-on wavelength 350 nm.

REFERENCES

1. Data Sheet, "Brush High Conductivity Beryllium Copper Strip," The Brush Beryllium Co., Cleveland, Ohio, July 1963.
2. D. R. Lott, "Solar Array Flexible Substrate Design Optimization, Fabrication, Delivery, and Test Evaluation Program," Final Report, NAS 8-28432, Report No. LMSC-D384284, Lockheed Missiles and Space Co., Inc., March 1975.
3. "Selection, Engineering and Fabrication of Car-Tech Alloys for Electronics, Magnetics and Electrical Applications," Product and Applications Brochure, Published by Carpenter Technology Corp., Reading, Pennsylvania, 1965.
4. "Unispan 36, Low Thermal Expansion Alloy," Product and Applications Brochure, Published by Universal-Cyclops Specialty Steel Division, Cyclops Corp., 1968.
5. B. S. Lement, C. S. Roberts, and B. L. Averbach, "Determination of Small Thermal Expansion Coefficients by a Micrometric Diletometer Method," *The Review of Scientific Instruments, Vol. 22, No. 3*, 1951.
6. Westinghouse Technical Data Bulletin No. 52-460, Westinghouse Electric Corp., Materials Manufacturing Division: Metals Plant, Blairsville, Pennsylvania, March 1965.
7. "How to Make Out with Moly," Schwartzkopf Development Corp., Holliston, Massachusetts, Brochure and Guide to the Use of Molybdenum.
8. "Alloy Digest," Published by Engineering Alloys Digest, Inc., Upper Montclair, New Jersey, June 1971.
9. R. A. Marzek, "Survey and Study for an Improved Solar Cell Module, STOD Task No. 43," Document No. 900-270, Jet Propulsion Laboratory, August 1969.
10. "DuPont Kapton Polyimide Film," Technical Information Bulletin H-1.

11. "Study to Establish Criteria for a Solar Cell Array for use as a Primary Power Source for a Lunar-based Water Electrolysis System," Phase III Technical Report, Contract No. **NAS 8-21189,** December 1970.

12. "DuPont Teflon FEP Fluorocarbon Film," Technical Information Bulletin **T-1C.**

13. *Handbook of Chemistry and Physics,* 13th Edition, Chemical Rubber Publishing Co., Cleveland, Ohio, 1948.

14. "Reference Data for Radio Engineers, 4th Edition, International Telephone and Telegraph Corp., 1957.

15. Supplier Catalogs and Brochures Included Elsewhere in this Handbook.

16. R. K. Yasui, "Summary of Work Accomplished in the Area of Photovoltaic's Supporting Development," Jet Propulsion Laboratory Document **320-31601-2-3420.**

17. R. D. McCammon and H. M. Rosenberg, "The Fatigue and Ultimate Tensile Strengths of Metals between 4.2 and 293°K," (pp. 203–211) in *Proceedings of the Royal Society*, London, *Vol.* **242,** 1957.

18. *Cryogenic Materials Data Handbook* (*Revised*), Air Force Materials Laboratory, **AMFL-TDR-64-280,** August 1968.

19. M. A. Salama *et al*, Technical Report **32-1552,** Jet Propulsion Laboratory, March 1972.

20. Von W. Koster, "Die Temperaturabhängigkeit des Elastizitätsmoduls Reiner Metalle," Unknown Journal, *Vol.* **39,** *No. 1*, 1944.

21. D. R. Lott, "Solar Array Flexible Substrate Design Optimization, Fabrication, Delivery and Test Evaluation Program," Final Report **LMSC D-384284,** Lockheed Missiles and Space Co., Inc., NASA Marshall Space Flight Center, Contract **NAS 8-28432.**

22. "Mechanical and Physical Properties of Invar and Invar-Type Alloys" Defense Metals Information Center Memo **207,** August 1965.

23. M. A. Salama, W. M. Rowe, and R. K. Yasui, "Thermoelastic Analysis of Solar Arrays and Their Material Properties," Technical Memorandum **33-626,** Jet Propulsion Laboratory, Pasadena, California, September 1973.

24. Westinghouse Technical Data **52-460,** March 1965.

25. Personal Communication of W. Luft, TRW Systems Group, with T. Lang, Carpenter Technology Corp., May 1972.

26. Manufacturer's Data Sheets, undated.

27. B. A. Rogers, I. C. Schoonover, and L. Jordan, "Silver: Its Properties and Industrial Uses," National Bureau of Standards Circular **C412,** 1936.

28. "Invar–36 Percent Nickel Alloys for Low Temperature Service," International Nickel Company Data Sheet, 1966.

29. D. B. Fraser and A. C. H. Hallitt, "The Coefficient of Lihnar Expansion and Gruneisen γ of Cu, Ag, Au, Fe, Ni, and Al from 4 to 300°K," in *Proceedings of the 7th International Conference on Low Temperature Physics, 1969,* University of Toronto Press, 1961.

30. A. Butts and C. Coxe, *Silver, Economics, Metallurgy, and Use*; Chapter 7: "The Physical Properties of Silver," and Chapter 9: "Mechanical Properties and Uses of Fine Silver," Van Nostrand Reinhold, New York, 1967.

31. T. Baumeister and L. S. Marks, *Standard Handbook for Mechanical Engineers,* 7th Edition, McGraw-Hill, New York, 1958.

32. P. Chevenard and C. Crussard, *Comput. Red., Vol.* **215,** p. 58, 1942; and *Vol.* **216,** p. 685, 1943.

33. W. Koster and J. Scherb, *Z. Metallkunde, Vol.* **49,** p. 501, 1958.

34. H. S. Rauschenbach *et al* (p. 162) in *Conference Records of the 11th IEEE Photovoltaic Specialists Conference,* 1975.

35. W. A. Campbell *et al*, "Outgassing Data for Spacecraft Materials," NASA **TN D-8008,** Goddard Space Flight Center, 1975.

36. Previously Unpublished Measurements Performed by TRW Systems Group, TRW, Inc.

37. DuPont Technical Information Bulletin **H-2.**

38. DuPont Technical Information on FEP-Teflon.

39. *Handbook of Chemistry and Physics,* 35th Edition, Chemical Rubber Publishing Co., Cleveland, Ohio, 1953.

40. Goldsmith, Waterman, and Hirschhorn, *Handbook of Thermophysical Properties of Solid Materials, Vol.* **3,** 1961.

41. Skylab Orbital Workshop, *Solar Array System, Critical Design Review Document, Vol.* **IV,** TRW Systems Group, TRW, Inc., 1971.

42. "Beryllium in Aero/Space Structures," The Brush Beryllium Company, Cleveland, Ohio.

43. "Teflon Fluorocarbon Resins, Mechanical Design Data," DuPont de Nemours and Co. (Inc.), Plastics Department, Wilmington, Delaware.

44. DuPont Kapton Polyimide Film, Technical Information Bulletin **H-4,** Electrical Properties.

45. R. G. Ross *et al*, "Measured Performance of Silicon Solar Cell Assemblies Designed for Use at High Solar Intensities," Technical Memorandum **33-473,** Jet Propulsion Laboratory, March 15, 1971.

46. Previously Unpublished TRW Data Provided by W. Luft.

47. A. E. Eagles and S. J. Babjack, "Hardened Thermal Control Coatings (U)," AF Technical Report **AFML-TR-69-241,** October 1969 (SRD).

48. Corning Glass Works Product Information Sheet on Fused Silica Code 7940.

49. D. G. Fink, *Standard Handbook for Electrical Engineers,* 10th Edition, McGraw-Hill, New York, 1969.

50. "CarTech Alloys for Electronic, Magnetic, and Electrical Applications," Product Information, Published by Carpenter Technology Corp. Reading, Pennsylvania, 1965.

51. Westinghouse Technical Data Bulletin No. **52-460,** Westinghouse Electric Corp., Materials Manufac-turing Division, Metals Plant, Blairsville, Pennsyl-vania, March 1965.

52. R. L. Crabb, "Evaluation of Cerium Stabilized Microsheet Coverslips for Higher Solar Cell Out-puts," *Conference Records of the 9th IEEE Photo-voltaic Specialists Conference*, 1972.

Appendix A.
Mathematics

This section is provided as an aid for the non-technical reader to the understanding of the mathematical notations used in this handbook.

Addition and Subtraction

Numerical quantities are designated by letters. Subscripts are used to clarify the quantities. For example, let R_n stand for the number of non-technical readers of this handbook and R_t for the number of technical readers. Then the total number of readers, designated by R, is the sum of both:

$$R = R_n + R_t$$

Examples. Evaluate the formula

$$A = a + b - c$$

for $a = 6$, $b = 3$, and $c = 4$.

$$A = 6 + 3 - 4 = 5.$$

Each of the letters, a, b, or c, could have been a negative quantity. For example, now let $a = 8$, $b = -2$, and $c = -5$. Then

$$A = 8 + (-2) - (-5)$$
$$= 8 - 2 + 5 = 11.$$

Multiplication

The volume V of a rectangular prism is calculated by multiplying the base b by the width w and by the height h, written as

$$V = b \cdot w \cdot h \quad \text{or} \quad V = bwh.$$

The order of multiplication is not important;

we can write

$$V = bwh = bhw = whb = wbh = hwb, \text{ etc.}$$

Examples. Calculate the volume for $b = 1$ in., $h = 10$ mm, $w = 2$ cm. First, the units are made alike by (arbitrarily) choosing centimeters: $b = 2.54$ cm, $h = 1$ cm, $w = 2$ cm. Then

$$V = 2.54 \times 1 \times 2 = 5.08 \text{ cm}^3.$$

Note that, in general, algebraic expressions involve positive and negative quantities: "Plus times minus = minus" and "minus times minus = plus." Now, evaluate $A = abcd$ for $a = 2$, $b = -3$, $c = -1$, $d = -0.5$. In step-by-step fashion:

$$A = 2 \times (-3) \times (-1) \times (-0.5)$$
$$= -6 \times (-1) \times (-0.5)$$
$$= 6 \times (-0.5)$$
$$= -3.$$

Division

Assume that the volume V, height h, and width w of the above rectangular prism are known and the base b is to be found: $b = V/wh$, also written as $b = B/wh$ or as $b = Vw^{-1}h^{-1}$. Again, w and h may be interchanged in position. In general, negative quantities are treated as in multiplication: "plus divided by minus = minus," "minus divided by plus = minus," and "minus divided by minus = plus."

Examples. Find A in $A = a/bcd$ for $a = 40$, $b = 2$, $c = -5$, and $d = -2$. In step-by-step fashion:

$$A = \frac{40}{2 \times (-5) \times (-2)}$$

$$= \frac{20}{(-5) \times (-2)}$$

$$= -\frac{4}{(-2)}$$

$$= +2.$$

If the problem were solved in a different order, such as $A = a/cbd$ or $A = a/cb$, the identical answer would result.

Parentheses

Mathematical expressions may have to use parentheses to indicate clearly the order in which calculations are to be performed. For example, if

$$A = \frac{a+b}{c+d}$$

is written in a single line, we must write

$$A = (a+b)/(c+d)$$

because multiplication and division has a higher priority for execution than does addition and subtraction. Without parentheses, the expression would be (incorrectly)

$$A = a + b/c + d.$$

For example, for $a = 5$, $b = 4$, $c = 2$, and $d = 1$, the correct solution is $A = (5+4)/(2+1) = 9/3 = 3$; the *incorrect* solution is $5 + 4/2 + 1 = 8$.

Exponents

The intensity of sunlight falls off with the square of the distance from the sun. This is equivalent to the statement that the intensity is proportional to inverse of the distance squared. If we let S stand for the solar constant at 1 AU (see Section 9-3) and S' (S-prime) equal the intensity at any distance from the sun (in astronomical units, AU), then $S' = S \div D^2$, also written as $S' = S/D^2$ or $S' = S \cdot D^{-2}$ or $S' = SD^{-2}$. In general, any number x raised to the ath power is $x^a = x \cdot x \cdot \cdots \cdot x$, a-times. If a is preceded by a negative sign, $x^{-a} = 1/x^a$, and $1/x^{-a} = x^a$.

Examples. Let $x = 2$ and $a = 3$. Then $x^a = 2^3 = 2 \cdot 2 \cdot 2 = 8$. But $x^{-a} = 2^{-3} = 1/2 \cdot 2 \cdot 2 = 1/8 = 0.125$.

Since fractional exponents indicate roots, $\sqrt{a}$ is also written as $a^{1/2}$. Similarly,

$$\frac{1}{\sqrt{b}} = b^{-1/2} \quad \text{and} \quad \sqrt[3]{c} = c^{1/3}.$$

Powers of Ten

Very small or very large numbers are expressed in *powers of ten*.

Examples. The number 6590 is written 6.59×10^3 or sometimes as 6.59 E3. The decimal 0.098 is written as 9.8×10^{-2} or sometimes as 9.8 E-2.

Some computer print-out formats write all numerals as decimal fractions in powers of ten. The above two examples would thus be printed as 0.659×10^4 and 0.98×10^{-1}, respectively.

Multiplication of Powers of Ten

To multiply powers of ten, we add the "powers": $(a \times 10^n) \cdot (b \times 10^m) = ab \times 10^{n+m}$.

Examples. Multiplying 1.2×10^6 times 3×10^8 gives 3.6×10^{14}. Other examples are as follows:

$$5 \times 10^6 \cdot 3 \times 10^3 = 15 \times 10^9 = 1.5 \times 10^{10}$$

$$0.3 \times 10^7 \cdot 0.2 \times 10^{-4} = 0.06 \times 10^3 = 0.6 \times 10^2.$$

Division of Powers of Ten

To divide, we subtract the "powers": $a \times 10^n \div b \times 10^m = ab \times 10^{n-m}$.

Examples. 1.2×10^6 divided by 3×10^8 equals 12×10^5 divided by 3×10^8, which gives 4×10^{-3}. Another example follows:

$$0.3 \times 10^7/0.2 \times 10^{-4} = (0.3/0.2) \times 10^{7-(-4)}$$

$$= 1.5 \times 10^{7+4} = 1.5 \times 10^{11}$$

Summation of Powers of Ten

To add or subtract numbers expressed in powers of ten, the numbers must first be converted into the same powers.

Examples.

$$1.65 \times 10^{15} + 2.0 \times 10^{13} = 1.65 \times 10^{15} + 0.02 \times 10^{15}$$
$$= 1.67 \times 10^{15}$$

$$8.8 \times 10^7 - 7.1 \times 10^8 = 0.88 \times 10^8 - 7.1 \times 10^8$$
$$= -6.2 \times 10^8$$

$$4.500 \times 10^{-3} + 6.2 \times 10^{-6} = 4.500 \times 10^{-3} + 0.00062 \times 10^{-3}$$
$$= 4.506 \times 10^{-3}$$

Trigonometry

Trigonometric functions are of paramount importance in solar cell array design and analysis work. Consider the right triangle in Fig. A-1, positioned at the center of a *rectangular*, or *Cartesian* coordinate system. The lengths of the sides a and b and of the hypotenuse c are related to the included angles as follows:

$$\sin \alpha = \cos \beta = a/c$$
$$\cos \alpha = \sin \beta = b/c$$
$$\tan \alpha = \cot \beta = a/b$$
$$\cot \alpha = \tan \beta = b/a$$
$$\sec \alpha = \csc \beta = c/b$$
$$\csc \alpha = \sec \beta = c/a.$$

The abbreviations are sin = sine, cos = cosine, tan = tangent, cot = cotangent, sec = secant, and csc = cosecant.

The sum of the angles $\alpha + \beta = 90$ degrees (90°), because $\alpha + \beta + \gamma = 180°$. Also, $c^2 = a^2 + b^2$, or $c = \sqrt{a^2 + b^2} = (a^2 + b^2)^{1/2}$. The squares of trigonometric functions are written by placing the exponent after the function name: $(\sin \alpha)^2 = \sin^2 \alpha$, and so on.

Vector Notation

A *vector* is a quantity that has both a magnitude and a direction. In contrast, all other quantities, having only magnitude, are *scalars*. For example, mass, speed, density, temperature, energy, power, and distance are scalars; weight, force, momentum, velocity, and magnetic field intensity are vectors, because the magnitude of each must be in a specific direction. Consider the vector r in three-dimensional space (Fig. A-2). This vector has three components: r_x, r_y, and r_z, that lie along the coordinate axis. The

magnitude of r, written as $|\mathbf{r}|$ or simply r, is given by

$$r = |\mathbf{r}| = \sqrt{r_x^2 + r_y^2 + r_z^2}.$$

The *direction* is defined as r_x, r_y, and r_z, or by the *direction cosines*, α, β, and γ. The direction cosines of r are defined as

$$\cos \alpha = r_x/r, \quad \cos \beta = r_y/r, \quad \text{and} \quad \cos \gamma = r_z/r.$$

It can be shown that

$$\cos^2 \alpha + \cos^2 \beta + \cos^2 \gamma = 1$$

where $\cos^2 x$ is the same as $(\cos x)^2$.

Vectors can be shifted around the space as long as their direction and magnitude is not altered. Vectors can be added and subtracted,

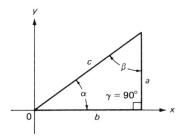

Fig. A-1. Trigonometric relationships.

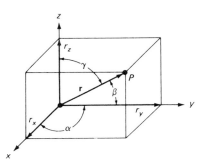

Fig. A-2. Vector definition.

and multiplied and divided by scalars according to these rules:

$$\mathbf{A} + \mathbf{B} = \mathbf{B} + \mathbf{A}$$

$$\mathbf{A} + (\mathbf{B} + \mathbf{C}) = (\mathbf{A} + \mathbf{B}) + \mathbf{C}$$

$$m \cdot \mathbf{A} = m\mathbf{A} = \mathbf{A}m$$

$$(m + n)\mathbf{A} = m\mathbf{A} + n\mathbf{A}$$

$$m(\mathbf{A} + \mathbf{B}) = m\mathbf{A} + m\mathbf{B}.$$

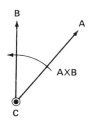

Fig. A-3. Vector cross-product.

Multiplication of vectors by other vectors involves either the *dot product*, also known as the *scalar product*, or the *cross-product*, also known as the vector product. They are defined as:

$$\mathbf{A} \cdot \mathbf{B} = AB \cos \theta$$

and

$$\mathbf{A} \times \mathbf{B} = \mathbf{u}AB \sin \theta.$$

where **u** is a unit vector pointing in a direction that is perpendicular to both **A** and **B** and points "out of the paper" in Fig. A-3, according to the "right hand rule."

Mathematical Nomenclature Definitions

Symbol	Definition
$a \neq b$	a does not equal b.
$x \rightarrow a$	the value of x approaches (becomes nearly equal to) the value of a.
$\bar{y}$	the average value of y.
$\exp(a)$	e^a, where $e = 2.718\ldots$
$\lvert a - b \rvert$	the magnitude of the quantity a minus b. $\lvert a - b \rvert$ is always positive, even if $b > a$.
$a > b$	a (is) greater than b.
$a < b$	a (is) less than b.
$I(V)$	I is a function of V. Denotes a general functional relationship between variables that is usually not simply expressible.
$\sin^{-1} x$	arc sin x. If $y = \sin^{-1} x$, then $x = \sin y$.

Appendix B.
Insolance Tables

The Aerospace Insolation Data Base (AIDB), discussed in Section 9-6, was analyzed and simplified for the 33 cities listed in Table B-1 for the solar cell array aperture configurations defined in Table B-2. The simplified insolance data is shown in Table B-3, and the corresponding solar energy received annually per hour in certain intensity level bands is given in Table B-4. (Illustrations of some insolation profiles are given in Section 9-6.)

These data were taken from D. L. Evans, "Simplified Solar Irradiation Data Based on the Aerospace Insolation Data Base," Arizona State University, Sandia Contract No. 02-7850, Report No. ERC-R-77007.

The insolance averages are for the two-year time period of 1962/63 and assume no shadowing of illuminated arrays.

Table B-1. AIDB Weather Stations.

Station	Lati- tude, N	Longi- tude, W	Abbreviation
Albuquerque, N.M.	35.05	106.62	Albuqu
Bismark, N.D.	46.77	100.75	Bismark
Blue Hill, Mass.	42.22	71.02	BluHil
Boise, Idaho	43.57	116.22	Boise
Charleston, S.C.	32.54	80.02	Charls
Cleveland, Ohio	41.40	81.85	Clevel
Dodge City, Kans.	37.77	97.97	Dodge C
Edwards AFB, Calif.	34.90	117.90	Edw. AFB
El Paso, Tex.	31.81	106.40	El Paso
Ely, Nev.	39.28	114.85	Ely
Fresno, Calif.	36.77	119.72	Fresno
Fort Worth, Tex.	32.83	97.05	Ft. Worth
Grand Junction, Col.	39.12	108.53	Grand J.
Great Falls, Mont.	47.29	111.21	Great Falls
Inyokern China Lake, Ca.	35.68	117.68	Inyokern
Lake Charles, La.	30.12	93.22	Lake Charles
Los Angeles Airport, Ca.	33.93	118.38	LAX
Los Angeles Civic Center, Ca.	34.05	118.23	LA Civic
Madison, Wis.	43.13	89.33	Madison
Medford, Ore.	42.37	122.87	Medford
Miami, Fla.	25.80	80.27	Miami
Midland, Tex.	31.93	102.20	Midland

Table B-1. (*Continued*)

Station	Lati-tude, N	Longi-tude, W	Abbreviation
Nashville, Tenn.	36.12	86.68	Nashville
Omaha, Neb.	41.37	96.02	Omaha
Phoenix, Ariz.	33.43	112.02	Phoenix
Riverside, Calif.	33.95	117.45	Riverside
Salt Lake City, Utah	40.78	111.92	Salt Lake
San Diego, Calif.	32.73	117.18	San Diego
Santa Maria, Calif.	34.90	120.45	Santa Maria
Seattle, Wash.	47.45	122.30	Seattle
Sterling, Va.	38.98	77.47	Sterling
Tucson, Ariz.	32.23	110.95	Tucson
Yuma, Ariz.	32.65	114.62	Yuma

Table B-2. Definitions of Solar Cell Array Aperture Type.

A. Plane horizontal in a fixed position, receiving both diffuse sky and direct solar radiation.

B. Plane tilted down from the horizontal position toward the south by an angle equal to the local latitude angle and fixed in position, receiving both diffuse sky and direct solar radiation, but no ground reflections.

C. Plane two-dimensionally tracking the sun such that the plane normal always points toward the center of the sun, receiving direct normal solar radiation only.

D. Plane one-dimensionally tracking the sun such that the axis of rotation lies horizontally in an east-west pointing direction, receiving only direct solar radiation.

E. Same as *D* except that the axis of rotation lies horizontally in a north-south pointing direction.

F. Same as *D* except that the axis of rotation is parallel to the earth's axis of rotation (i.e., the polar axis of the earth).

Table B-3. Average Monthly Insolance (kWh/m^2).

Station	Month	*A* Totally Horizontal	*B* Totally Tilted	*C* Direct Normal	*D* East/West Axis	*E* North/South Axis	*F* Polar Axis
Albuqu	1	111	183	210	172	145	197
	2	126	182	199	156	155	194
	3	186	227	263	184	233	262
	4	219	228	273	190	260	264
	5	257	236	310	220	304	281
	6	259	223	312	227	307	276
	7	229	206	263	194	258	236

Table B-3. (*Continued*)

Station	Month	A Totally Horizontal	B Totally Tilted	C Direct Normal	D East/West Axis	E North/South Axis	F Polar Axis
	8	224	221	276	195	267	259
	9	176	202	221	160	202	220
	10	162	220	254	184	211	251
	11	114	181	207	167	148	196
	12	108	190	224	183	149	206
	Ann. Avg.	2171	2499	3012	2232	2639	2842
Bismark	1	59	137	153	131	86	143
	2	69	123	130	105	89	127
	3	125	178	200	143	161	199
	4	149	167	200	134	181	190
	5	161	154	186	132	176	168
	6	205	179	253	179	241	216
	7	210	190	266	185	253	232
	8	194	202	265	178	246	245
	9	135	175	203	141	172	202
	10	100	167	185	142	135	183
	11	55	117	129	107	77	122
	12	44	111	122	108	63	113
	Ann. Avg.	1506	1900	2292	1685	1880	2140
BluHil	1	58	115	126	106	78	118
	2	75	123	130	105	93	127
	3	125	165	184	132	155	183
	4	152	165	190	131	175	182
	5	188	175	218	154	210	198
	6	190	167	213	156	207	189
	7	177	159	199	143	193	179
	8	162	165	199	138	188	186
	9	125	152	168	120	147	167
	10	104	156	170	131	130	168
	11	53	98	106	87	68	100
	12	59	122	132	115	75	122
	Ann. Avg.	1468	1762	2035	1518	1719	1919
Boise	1	60	120	125	109	72	117
	2	69	111	111	89	78	108
	3	126	168	179	132	148	179
	4	164	180	211	145	195	206
	5	205	191	248	173	238	226
	6	221	190	267	188	259	233
	7	256	227	330	228	319	292
	8	215	220	284	194	267	271
	9	162	202	230	165	206	236
	10	103	161	171	133	128	169
	11	55	102	104	88	64	99
	12	44	91	93	82	50	85
	Ann. Avg.	1680	1963	2359	1726	2024	2221
Charls	1	85	129	134	112	94	125
	2	100	135	136	108	108	133
	3	150	178	183	133	165	183
	4	187	194	214	153	206	210
	5	201	187	220	160	217	204
	6	173	153	180	135	177	162
	7	195	176	210	156	208	192

Table B-3. (Continued)

Station	Month	A Totally Horizontal	B Totally Tilted	C Direct Normal	D East/West Axis	E North/South Axis	F Polar Axis
	8	183	181	204	147	199	197
	9	148	166	170	126	157	169
	10	140	182	193	148	161	191
	11	98	144	150	124	110	143
	12	89	142	156	131	105	144
	Ann. Avg.	1749	1967	2150	1633	1907	2053
Clevel	1	48	86	84	73	50	78
	2	56	85	77	63	55	75
	3	93	119	112	84	94	112
	4	136	146	159	110	148	156
	5	174	162	201	140	194	184
	6	188	163	217	154	211	190
	7	177	158	203	142	197	181
	8	159	160	190	130	180	182
	9	115	138	145	102	128	145
	10	84	121	120	93	93	119
	11	35	58	50	43	31	47
	12	39	72	69	62	38	64
	Ann. Avg.	1304	1468	1627	1196	1419	1533
Dodge C	1	89	160	185	150	124	173
	2	108	162	176	137	133	171
	3	161	204	233	162	203	232
	4	190	201	238	164	225	228
	5	194	180	227	159	221	206
	6	213	182	255	180	249	222
	7	231	206	271	196	265	243
	8	208	207	265	181	254	247
	9	148	173	190	134	171	190
	10	130	183	206	152	167	204
	11	89	150	170	136	119	161
	12	79	154	188	151	123	173
	Ann. Avg.	1840	2162	2604	1902	2254	2450
Edw. AFB	1	102	169	191	157	131	179
	2	110	157	168	132	131	164
	3	171	209	232	167	205	231
	4	203	211	253	174	242	249
	5	240	219	294	205	288	270
	6	255	218	317	224	311	278
	7	260	228	327	228	321	292
	8	234	230	292	201	283	282
	9	190	218	259	178	238	258
	10	148	200	221	168	181	218
	11	105	166	187	151	134	177
	12	95	164	186	157	121	171
	Ann. Avg.	2113	2389	2927	2142	2586	2769
El Paso	1	127	195	222	181	160	208
	2	148	203	228	174	184	222
	3	200	237	271	190	245	270
	4	231	238	284	198	274	276
	5	266	243	325	229	320	295
	6	263	228	311	228	307	276
	7	237	213	265	198	261	239

Table B-3. (*Continued*)

Station	Month	A Totally Horizontal	B Totally Tilted	C Direct Normal	D East/West Axis	E North/South Axis	F Polar Axis
	8	230	226	273	195	267	258
	9	171	192	223	150	208	222
	10	173	225	259	189	221	256
	11	123	181	200	162	148	190
	12	114	182	209	174	143	193
	Ann. Avg.	2283	2563	3070	2268	2738	2905
Ely	1	94	175	199	166	128	186
	2	98	150	160	127	119	156
	3	168	215	243	174	209	242
	4	190	202	239	165	224	230
	5	213	196	256	177	248	231
	6	234	201	279	200	273	243
	7	260	230	325	228	316	288
	8	229	230	300	203	287	279
	9	184	219	258	179	231	257
	10	144	210	237	180	188	234
	11	97	171	194	159	131	184
	12	86	173	205	171	127	189
	Ann. Avg.	1997	2372	2895	2129	2481	2719
Fresno	1	69	113	117	97	78	109
	2	71	99	93	73	72	91
	3	150	186	201	145	175	200
	4	181	190	229	154	218	222
	5	218	202	255	182	248	235
	6	250	216	298	215	292	264
	7	269	239	330	235	323	296
	8	239	238	310	212	298	291
	9	181	211	244	170	221	243
	10	134	186	202	153	163	200
	11	78	125	131	108	90	124
	12	47	78	75	64	47	69
	Ann. Avg.	1887	2083	2485	1808	2225	2344
Ft. Worth	1	95	147	158	131	110	148
	2	108	149	157	122	124	153
	3	161	193	208	150	186	207
	4	156	163	170	123	163	166
	5	211	197	234	172	230	218
	6	211	184	235	174	231	210
	7	230	205	268	194	264	241
	8	220	216	271	188	263	255
	9	158	179	194	138	179	193
	10	138	181	199	148	167	196
	11	91	135	143	116	105	136
	12	81	130	141	118	95	130
	Ann. Avg.	1860	2079	2378	1774	2117	2253
Grand J.	1	79	141	150	129	95	141
	2	93	143	152	121	113	149
	3	149	190	208	150	180	208
	4	185	197	230	160	216	226
	5	220	202	271	187	263	246
	6	233	199	286	201	279	249
	7	236	209	293	204	285	261

Table B-3. (*Continued*)

Station	Month	A Totally Horizontal	B Totally Tilted	C Direct Normal	D East/West Axis	E North/South Axis	F Polar Axis
	8	202	202	251	173	240	241
	9	170	202	237	164	213	236
	10	133	192	211	162	167	208
	11	90	155	171	142	114	162
	12	74	142	155	135	92	143
	Ann. Avg.	1864	2174	2615	1928	2257	2470
Great Falls	1	47	110	118	103	64	110
	2	68	125	134	108	89	130
	3	123	178	199	143	160	199
	4	149	168	198	136	178	189
	5	174	164	211	146	200	187
	6	195	169	245	172	233	206
	7	210	190	270	188	256	230
	8	185	194	247	169	228	230
	9	130	170	196	136	165	195
	10	87	147	159	123	114	157
	11	50	109	118	99	69	112
	12	39	99	109	96	55	100
	Ann. Avg.	1457	1823	2204	1619	1811	2045
Inyokern	1	111	190	225	182	155	210
	2	124	179	195	153	152	191
	3	189	234	279	190	247	278
	4	229	239	299	203	285	289
	5	258	236	330	227	323	298
	6	268	229	333	237	326	291
	7	276	242	354	246	346	312
	8	246	243	330	220	318	307
	9	196	226	271	185	249	270
	10	154	211	244	179	200	240
	11	113	182	206	167	145	195
	12	102	186	224	184	148	206
	Ann. Avg.	2266	2597	3290	2373	2894	3087
Lake Charles	1	75	106	104	86	76	97
	2	103	136	137	107	111	133
	3	141	164	169	121	154	168
	4	156	161	166	119	161	163
	5	201	186	226	162	223	208
	6	176	154	193	140	190	171
	7	193	173	220	157	217	196
	8	176	171	207	140	203	196
	9	150	166	175	123	165	175
	10	139	176	184	141	157	182
	11	95	133	135	110	102	128
	12	78	115	120	100	83	110
	Ann. Avg.	1683	1841	2036	1506	1842	1927
LAX	1	99	158	168	138	117	157
	2	103	143	147	113	116	143
	3	173	214	242	166	215	241
	4	198	208	241	167	230	233
	5	207	194	233	165	228	216
	6	190	169	192	144	190	174
	7	234	210	259	193	255	238

Table B-3. (*Continued*)

Station	Month	A Totally Horizontal	B Totally Tilted	C Direct Normal	D East/West Axis	E North/South Axis	F Polar Axis
	8	223	223	260	184	252	247
	9	176	202	206	149	188	205
	10	127	172	189	140	156	186
	11	98	150	159	129	114	150
	12	92	154	176	146	118	162
	Ann. Avg.	1920	2197	2472	1834	2179	2352
LA Civic	1	91	148	165	135	114	154
	2	93	130	136	106	106	132
	3	162	199	227	157	202	227
	4	197	206	240	167	229	233
	5	195	183	218	155	213	204
	6	188	165	202	149	199	184
	7	252	226	289	214	284	265
	8	230	228	274	197	266	264
	9	176	202	225	161	206	224
	10	130	176	193	143	159	190
	11	98	152	169	136	121	159
	12	94	160	187	154	126	172
	Ann. Avg.	1906	2175	2525	1874	2225	2408
Madison	1	55	106	109	96	63	102
	2	69	114	117	95	82	114
	3	114	150	158	116	131	157
	4	164	179	207	145	190	203
	5	187	173	226	156	217	205
	6	214	183	260	183	252	227
	7	208	185	254	177	246	226
	8	191	195	247	169	233	235
	9	135	166	189	132	166	189
	10	101	155	163	128	122	161
	11	54	101	103	88	63	97
	12	48	100	104	93	56	96
	Ann. Avg.	1540	1807	2137	1578	1821	2012
Medford	1	52	99	105	88	65	99
	2	67	105	101	83	71	99
	3	119	156	161	119	134	160
	4	157	172	190	136	175	185
	5	190	179	212	155	204	195
	6	231	200	277	199	269	244
	7	250	224	307	219	297	276
	8	212	218	275	191	259	260
	9	160	196	222	159	194	222
	10	85	126	127	99	96	125
	11	47	81	79	66	50	75
	12	34	64	60	53	33	55
	Ann. Avg.	1604	1820	2116	1567	1847	1995
Miami	1	118	159	171	138	132	160
	2	134	168	182	137	155	178
	3	183	207	227	160	212	227
	4	200	202	224	160	220	220
	5	207	191	234	169	231	214
	6	179	158	199	145	196	176
	7	199	180	223	163	220	200

Table B-3. (*Continued*)

Station	Month	A Totally Horizontal	B Totally Tilted	C Direct Normal	D East/West Axis	E North/South Axis	F Polar Axis
	8	177	173	189	138	186	181
	9	144	155	158	113	151	157
	10	152	184	201	146	178	198
	11	114	150	156	126	123	148
	12	113	158	173	143	128	159
	Ann. Avg.	1920	2085	2337	1738	2132	2218
Midland	1	105	160	178	146	128	167
	2	122	166	179	139	143	174
	3	170	201	220	157	198	219
	4	192	196	227	158	219	223
	5	220	203	251	181	247	234
	6	224	194	265	191	261	235
	7	225	200	267	190	263	241
	8	219	214	261	182	255	254
	9	173	195	222	154	207	221
	10	149	192	207	157	175	205
	11	109	160	178	142	132	169
	12	87	137	149	125	102	137
	Ann. Avg.	1995	2218	2604	1922	2330	2479
Nashville	1	61	99	101	85	67	94
	2	81	116	113	92	85	110
	3	115	140	139	102	122	139
	4	152	161	169	123	160	165
	5	190	179	207	152	202	193
	6	173	154	177	134	174	161
	7	183	167	192	145	188	176
	8	174	174	193	142	186	186
	9	131	151	151	113	137	151
	10	120	163	167	132	135	165
	11	60	92	90	75	62	85
	12	57	95	95	82	61	88
	Ann. Avg.	1497	1691	1794	1377	1579	1713
Omaha	1	76	151	173	143	110	162
	2	81	127	131	105	95	128
	3	130	169	183	130	155	183
	4	160	173	198	137	184	190
	5	181	171	203	145	196	185
	6	207	181	235	172	228	208
	7	212	190	245	176	237	220
	8	184	187	227	158	215	214
	9	140	170	188	133	166	188
	10	119	178	195	148	151	193
	11	72	132	148	119	99	193
	12	65	133	149	128	86	137
	Ann. Avg.	1627	1962	2275	1694	1922	2148
Phoenix	1	112	177	199	164	139	186
	2	126	176	192	149	152	187
	3	185	223	253	178	226	252
	4	217	225	269	186	258	261
	5	248	227	299	211	293	272
	6	243	210	290	209	285	256
	7	240	213	285	204	280	256

Table B-3. (Continued)

Station	Month	A Totally Horizontal	B Totally Tilted	C Direct Normal	D East/West Axis	E North/South Axis	F Polar Axis
	8	213	211	256	180	249	242
	9	178	202	228	160	211	227
	10	159	211	242	178	203	239
	11	116	178	198	160	144	188
	12	106	177	206	170	139	189
	Ann. Avg.	2143	2430	2917	2149	2579	2755
Riverside	1	98	155	164	139	111	153
	2	106	146	149	119	117	146
	3	170	206	228	163	203	227
	4	206	215	249	176	239	243
	5	221	205	259	184	254	240
	6	227	197	261	191	258	235
	7	265	235	325	232	319	296
	8	239	235	306	209	297	291
	9	191	217	252	176	233	252
	10	150	200	222	166	183	219
	11	111	172	192	155	138	182
	12	109	186	220	181	148	202
	Ann. Avg.	2093	2309	2827	2091	2498	2686
Salt Lake	1	69	134	153	125	98	143
	2	83	129	132	106	96	129
	3	165	216	249	175	212	248
	4	181	195	224	151	209	213
	5	235	221	276	192	267	248
	6	242	210	281	205	274	245
	7	248	221	302	216	294	269
	8	223	224	305	201	290	280
	9	169	206	246	169	219	246
	10	137	206	237	176	186	234
	11	78	141	160	129	107	152
	12	57	114	128	108	77	118
	Ann. Avg.	1887	2217	2693	1953	2329	2525
San Diego	1	101	157	174	143	122	163
	2	106	146	153	121	120	149
	3	162	196	212	154	189	211
	4	189	196	223	156	214	220
	5	195	182	214	156	210	202
	6	184	162	197	147	194	180
	7	222	200	250	185	246	232
	8	213	211	242	177	235	235
	9	171	194	214	153	197	213
	10	138	183	191	149	157	188
	11	103	155	169	138	123	160
	12	98	160	180	150	122	166
	Ann. Avg.	1882	2142	2419	1829	2129	2319
Santa Maria	1	99	164	185	152	126	173
	2	101	144	155	120	121	151
	3	168	209	241	167	213	241
	4	209	220	265	182	252	255
	5	215	201	249	177	243	230
	6	223	196	247	185	243	224
	7	242	218	273	204	268	252

Table B-3. (*Continued*)

Station	Month	A Totally Horizontal	B Totally Tilted	C Direct Normal	D East/West Axis	E North/South Axis	F Polar Axis
	8	220	226	269	194	260	259
	9	172	199	218	157	198	218
	10	137	188	208	157	169	204
	11	100	159	177	144	126	167
	12	95	168	201	164	134	185
	Ann. Avg.	1987	2292	2688	2003	2353	2559
Seattle	1	37	81	83	71	47	78
	2	55	97	97	77	66	94
	3	96	135	140	101	112	140
	4	126	141	153	108	138	148
	5	184	176	217	155	204	199
	6	180	159	209	150	199	181
	7	192	176	231	165	219	206
	8	159	168	200	139	183	190
	9	121	157	171	123	144	170
	10	68	109	108	85	78	107
	11	33	67	66	56	39	63
	12	26	60	59	53	30	55
	Ann. Avg.	1277	1526	1734	1283	1459	1631
Sterling	1	70	126	138	114	89	129
	2	81	122	123	98	91	120
	3	137	174	191	135	165	190
	4	166	176	203	140	190	197
	5	192	180	215	155	209	198
	6	194	170	215	158	210	191
	7	197	178	223	162	217	202
	8	181	183	217	152	207	208
	9	132	157	168	119	150	168
	10	123	176	195	146	156	193
	11	70	120	130	106	88	123
	12	60	115	130	108	82	120
	Ann. Avg.	1603	1877	2148	1593	1854	2039
Tucson	1	118	182	205	167	146	192
	2	132	181	199	153	160	194
	3	192	229	260	182	235	260
	4	229	236	282	196	272	274
	5	255	233	309	218	304	281
	6	258	223	311	225	306	275
	7	223	200	254	186	250	229
	8	205	202	239	170	233	228
	9	178	200	227	158	211	226
	10	158	206	234	171	199	231
	11	114	171	191	153	142	181
	12	106	171	197	163	135	182
	Ann. Avg.	2168	2434	2908	2142	2593	2753
Yuma	1	114	179	204	167	145	191
	2	129	179	195	152	156	190
	3	186	221	249	177	224	249
	4	217	223	269	184	259	264
	5	252	230	304	214	299	281
	6	256	219	318	225	312	279
	7	255	225	317	222	311	284

Table B-3. (Continued)

Station	Month	A Totally Horizontal	B Totally Tilted	C Direct Normal	D East/West Axis	E North/South Axis	F Polar Axis
	8	230	225	280	195	274	272
	9	191	215	254	174	236	253
	10	162	213	235	179	197	232
	11	119	180	203	163	150	193
	12	106	174	205	169	141	189
	Ann. Avg.	2217	2483	3033	2221	2704	2877

Table B-4. Number of Hours/Year During Which the Solar Energy has a Given Value.

Station	Apper- ture Type	\u2264												

Station	Apper-ture Type	⩽0.1	0.15	0.25	0.35	0.45	0.55	0.65	0.75	0.85	0.95	1.05	1.15	>1.2
Albuqu	A	657	365	452	327	406	395	445	345	347	323	242	41	1
	B	620	369	283	424	203	343	288	291	369	408	482	224	41
	C	0	29	162	205	256	305	410	586	1077	867	131	1	1
	D	158	405	440	412	319	435	327	482	591	399	63	1	0
	E	0	65	188	266	359	616	671	724	809	319	14	0	1
	F	0	36	157	183	225	334	458	710	1198	555	67	1	1
Bismark	A	1038	660	540	460	403	329	319	288	217	97	5	0	0
	B	1010	468	355	448	246	367	260	323	313	356	179	28	5
	C	0	88	329	300	381	355	415	684	858	160	39	0	0
	D	187	492	549	394	370	357	375	417	374	77	15	0	0
	E	13	256	420	436	520	486	542	679	244	11	1	0	0
	F	0	94	330	290	352	338	474	864	598	111	23	0	0
BluHil	A	1097	649	476	397	425	322	301	281	191	106	29	2	0
	B	1133	463	373	382	267	310	272	295	297	265	168	46	3
	C	1	72	287	293	382	376	430	528	534	273	61	1	0
	D	197	426	466	363	345	329	327	339	286	130	27	0	0
	E	7	186	330	423	509	478	512	464	264	61	1	0	0
	F	1	88	277	303	346	391	500	540	461	223	21	0	0
Boise	A	608	680	500	478	379	368	309	278	302	211	22	1	0
	B	712	480	317	505	235	346	268	323	304	372	237	29	7
	C	0	75	325	244	254	288	416	678	1113	139	31	0	0
	D	144	375	590	396	391	371	360	416	445	64	11	0	0
	E	20	244	329	310	403	435	510	724	565	21	2	0	0
	F	0	89	331	232	233	295	476	864	864	63	23	0	0
Charls	A	955	557	394	380	370	364	417	335	279	218	61	1	0
	B	1050	374	381	349	267	351	274	327	328	313	226	82	9
	C	0	72	285	284	411	300	488	631	621	235	11	0	0
	D	211	406	472	335	413	366	392	366	348	113	6	0	0
	E	0	133	322	325	489	633	600	575	330	22	0	0	0
	F	0	83	264	304	411	405	571	676	514	141	5	0	0
Clevel	A	899	739	637	490	381	316	290	250	111	9	0	0	0
	B	1012	508	475	469	352	343	329	318	237	76	3	0	0
	C	0	138	458	287	419	573	770	461	26	1	0	0	0
	D	145	536	633	418	424	426	383	160	9	1	0	0	0
	E	15	344	446	447	489	533	616	240	5	0	0	0	0
	F	0	155	457	296	402	624	845	273	11	0	0	0	0

Solar Energy Band Centered at Given Energy with ±0.05 kWh/m^2 Band Width

Table B-4. *(Continued)*

Station	Apper-ture Type	≤0.1	0.15	0.25	0.35	0.45	0.55	0.65	0.75	0.85	0.95	1.05	1.15	>1.2
				Solar Energy Band Centered at Given Energy with ± 0.05 kWh/m² Band Width										
Dodge C	A	782	512	508	382	465	437	382	365	250	217	65	1	1
	B	766	384	403	366	300	372	308	424	341	382	248	64	9
	C	0	65	194	215	278	317	929	816	854	204	14	0	0
	D	186	398	541	398	459	404	535	451	420	88	4	0	0
	E	1	126	224	311	539	692	944	631	401	13	3	0	0
	F	0	75	198	204	254	617	698	970	634	130	7	0	0
Edw. AFB	A	531	267	499	402	533	484	466	310	402	347	64	0	0
	B	465	403	173	505	257	531	242	449	441	605	233	0	8
	C	0	5	128	150	378	319	438	1412	1349	0	0	0	0
	D	126	318	576	389	581	430	639	713	406	0	0	0	0
	E	0	30	224	274	654	589	610	1045	752	0	0	0	0
	F	0	8	151	167	343	282	775	1651	715	0	0	0	0
El Paso	A	610	378	442	284	376	352	436	406	344	349	338	48	0
	B	624	342	298	392	221	259	372	252	387	370	503	277	66
	C	0	35	164	198	281	465	401	452	955	1112	72	0	0
	D	197	414	486	372	323	504	234	527	607	441	30	0	0
	E	0	79	196	232	313	685	727	602	917	381	5	0	0
	F	0	42	169	188	233	483	440	581	1231	627	43	0	0
Ely	A	615	489	432	454	390	466	365	355	284	237	181	31	2
	B	637	399	273	425	263	275	407	239	413	305	421	217	41
	C	0	54	221	233	277	313	363	425	783	1166	107	0	0
	D	178	371	442	426	375	425	324	489	464	417	32	0	0
	E	1	117	265	313	455	560	550	538	727	398	19	0	0
	F	0	64	225	226	246	333	348	523	1142	664	57	0	0
Fresno	A	865	498	439	337	448	350	373	300	334	214	173	9	2
	B	855	484	296	415	216	388	263	347	396	325	301	53	15
	C	0	47	216	242	332	385	717	787	823	214	3	0	0
	D	176	499	501	410	352	465	417	438	387	118	1	0	0
	E	1	140	244	356	471	583	673	604	615	77	1	0	0
	F	0	57	200	231	290	404	850	817	750	51	1	0	0
Ft. Worth	A	886	483	441	348	402	348	419	307	309	239	141	8	0
	B	933	400	345	363	252	395	204	347	320	383	313	68	8
	C	0	59	252	303	340	349	463	740	909	204	10	0	0
	D	205	432	510	340	380	351	410	433	450	113	5	0	0
	E	0	120	275	340	423	630	657	646	485	53	0	0	0
	F	0	65	249	298	315	385	543	901	717	76	7	0	0
Grand J.	A	491	481	500	467	577	427	415	380	340	145	0	0	1
	B	558	358	259	505	283	463	282	498	474	454	91	0	21
	C	0	37	371	114	302	344	673	1613	567	0	0	0	0
	D	167	389	665	320	537	389	617	765	172	0	0	0	0
	E	0	177	290	307	655	621	820	961	190	0	0	0	0
	F	0	49	358	135	258	385	946	1479	319	0	0	0	0
Great Falls	A	1011	710	571	489	409	314	326	241	201	77	2	0	0
	B	1010	452	364	444	317	412	256	379	321	304	84	9	4
	C	0	76	320	375	427	435	560	860	553	43	6	0	0
	D	196	460	634	435	433	385	400	446	242	23	1	0	0
	E	14	284	477	516	517	552	573	602	114	5	1	0	0
	F	0	86	329	367	384	419	646	945	297	27	5	0	0
Inyokern	A	542	351	461	316	404	484	397	360	382	350	301	7	1
	B	461	442	234	456	175	280	374	270	485	464	511	190	33

Table B-4. (Continued)

Station	Aperture Type	≤0.1	0.15	0.25	0.35	0.45	0.55	0.65	0.75	0.85	0.95	1.05	1.15	>1.2
	C	0	9	85	111	179	315	506	713	1401	924	21	0	0
	D	122	351	553	402	371	412	388	572	768	319	6	0	0
	E	0	33	116	162	381	724	730	777	1013	325	3	0	0
	F	0	9	88	113	188	316	538	867	1571	444	9	0	0
Lake Charles	A	896	599	456	414	372	410	433	392	257	106	8	0	1
	B	1014	424	455	341	350	322	330	371	360	273	83	14	10
	C	0	80	288	308	425	491	762	748	294	49	8	0	0
	D	189	487	497	401	455	442	444	384	127	23	1	0	0
	E	0	153	311	351	490	731	835	479	97	3	3	0	0
	F	0	91	277	306	417	541	846	702	152	39	6	0	0
LAX	A	862	460	454	359	450	403	359	301	343	343	13	0	11
	B	816	418	341	379	256	385	264	381	369	472	226	31	16
	C	0	55	247	246	367	391	540	920	952	55	16	0	0
	D	194	444	526	357	407	372	484	608	379	18	0	0	0
	E	0	115	286	357	614	588	567	833	411	5	15	0	0
	F	0	68	246	262	347	432	623	1158	545	42	14	0	0
LA Civic	A	777	438	467	356	494	332	375	244	268	310	174	19	0
	B	760	376	319	432	215	373	285	311	389	339	341	101	10
	C	0	62	210	225	332	344	519	667	941	343	57	0	0
	D	175	404	465	352	371	442	387	488	485	122	8	0	0
	E	0	107	264	361	563	494	510	572	631	173	25	0	0
	F	0	67	220	241	301	425	547	763	875	177	43	0	0
Madison	A	576	717	615	588	413	307	306	286	256	64	0	0	0
	B	699	387	418	619	333	385	221	266	348	298	55	0	2
	C	8	79	942	94	249	310	543	1155	363	24	1	0	0
	D	197	525	933	309	371	344	444	519	113	10	1	0	0
	E	41	418	655	306	444	430	651	695	125	1	0	0	0
	F	4	129	881	98	243	324	771	1004	209	15	1	0	0
Medford	A	1003	678	488	380	358	294	286	242	270	235	58	1	0
	B	1049	511	351	444	227	357	217	285	251	315	265	20	3
	C	0	132	332	330	358	340	394	550	858	129	6	0	0
	D	205	496	523	379	358	325	318	362	402	59	1	0	0
	E	16	280	378	408	427	376	470	540	507	23	3	0	0
	F	0	142	332	311	328	345	459	644	742	34	3	0	0
Miami	A	722	544	436	429	386	399	422	356	301	235	109	15	3
	B	855	331	474	373	295	389	299	374	346	299	235	77	15
	C	0	86	295	376	454	515	621	665	673	119	19	0	0
	D	260	479	574	401	447	431	469	359	326	66	10	0	0
	E	0	134	342	420	524	698	716	563	375	44	7	0	0
	F	0	93	287	375	447	565	676	740	479	81	9	0	0
Midland	A	509	383	560	381	487	425	492	355	358	262	46	0	0
	B	518	369	314	510	328	444	234	455	382	523	181	0	5
	C	0	50	470	121	318	333	608	1345	811	0	0	0	0
	D	183	409	754	299	533	378	588	632	279	0	0	0	0
	E	0	195	374	210	463	688	837	953	336	0	0	0	0
	F	0	50	463	150	266	380	867	1392	428	0	0	0	0
Nashville	A	1058	614	399	395	353	368	329	285	255	117	9	0	1
	B	1155	418	395	280	322	301	296	323	299	256	116	21	8
	C	0	61	319	305	375	428	572	627	335	48	4	0	0
	D	178	432	398	339	414	355	407	358	172	21	1	0	0

Table B-4. (*Continued*)

Station	Aperture Type	≤0.1	0.15	0.25	0.35	0.45	0.55	0.65	0.75	0.85	0.95	1.05	1.15	>1.2
	E	0	158	325	408	526	551	525	478	98	5	1	0	0
	F	0	66	328	311	371	481	624	580	244	31	3	0	0
Omaha	A	940	613	499	413	442	337	324	271	257	204	13	0	0
	B	921	445	407	403	288	341	239	305	289	376	245	49	5
	C	1	79	320	303	370	355	449	569	862	236	21	0	0
	D	197	499	504	370	358	352	356	385	412	120	11	0	0
	E	5	199	362	366	549	579	567	615	313	9	0	0	0
	F	1	96	315	303	330	363	518	753	639	151	7	0	0
Phoenix	A	635	364	448	305	438	404	495	384	433	380	78	1	1
	B	638	352	301	372	219	415	246	408	386	571	362	80	31
	C	0	32	149	224	331	369	552	939	1301	258	6	0	0
	D	200	433	548	319	422	407	495	632	591	112	3	0	0
	E	0	67	184	267	467	750	849	918	639	19	1	0	0
	F	0	35	142	214	305	404	641	1264	895	154	4	0	0
Riverside	A	173	436	425	309	408	370	417	307	351	346	226	18	1
	B	712	418	264	431	188	286	326	243	395	398	482	164	23
	C	0	29	173	212	251	342	392	529	1252	686	13	0	0
	D	171	379	498	325	355	374	345	478	652	294	8	0	0
	E	0	64	201	278	382	653	557	610	928	204	1	0	0
	F	0	32	166	199	252	372	420	682	1359	314	8	0	0
Salt Lake	A	822	510	472	397	384	368	299	298	280	258	202	8	3
	B	784	479	287	422	263	252	359	197	359	276	406	183	41
	C	0	60	231	245	287	281	290	444	768	995	118	0	0
	D	164	394	444	454	351	366	284	424	455	355	28	0	0
	E	4	182	271	304	415	396	459	564	742	349	33	0	0
	F	0	69	237	241	268	271	335	513	978	627	66	0	0
San Diego	A	569	439	598	369	493	409	416	292	306	271	59	0	5
	B	549	445	340	449	373	368	221	377	385	520	192	0	0
	C	0	104	736	89	279	224	414	1190	893	0	0	0	0
	D	210	498	763	218	448	311	538	619	325	0	0	0	0
	E	0	252	643	185	469	617	591	756	417	0	0	0	0
	F	0	106	739	149	239	236	658	1328	465	0	0	0	0
Santa Maria	A	760	432	503	369	396	400	360	282	305	266	202	57	3
	B	689	424	324	425	256	320	290	275	404	394	340	164	27
	C	0	72	301	185	262	310	415	694	1125	464	42	0	0
	D	170	425	546	325	389	351	427	504	497	216	21	0	0
	E	0	148	319	245	513	587	519	631	692	202	16	0	0
	F	0	79	311	192	253	339	508	931	920	276	21	0	0
Seattle	A	1363	806	506	414	317	237	243	170	166	128	11	0	0
	B	1385	573	405	401	270	299	204	241	190	218	153	21	2
	C	0	147	415	372	366	310	348	442	531	112	8	0	0
	D	212	516	544	362	299	288	246	263	265	53	3	0	0
	E	38	310	471	463	391	354	376	416	222	10	1	0	0
	F	0	171	402	366	324	314	383	523	412	63	1	0	0
Sterling	A	1123	577	463	381	392	342	336	274	260	176	39	0	0
	B	1121	444	394	362	258	329	251	306	324	303	209	58	8
	C	0	69	276	323	352	382	475	609	688	214	14	0	0
	D	213	454	473	356	363	347	366	388	343	92	6	0	0
	E	2	163	330	386	496	544	596	567	306	11	3	0	0
	F	0	85	270	296	336	418	548	697	536	135	6	0	0

Table B-4. (*Continued*)

Station	Apper-ture Type	Solar Energy Band Centered at Given Energy with ±0.05 kWh/m² Band Width												
		≤0.1	0.15	0.25	0.35	0.45	0.55	0.65	0.75	0.85	0.95	1.05	1.15	>1.2
Tucson	A	630	372	462	296	437	407	469	356	397	329	203	3	0
	B	626	354	298	428	212	376	289	350	405	502	376	120	20
	C	0	52	150	235	313	351	442	877	1311	347	32	0	0
	D	202	404	521	356	405	418	437	617	606	131	14	0	0
	E	0	82	194	270	455	693	721	735	881	76	4	0	0
	F	0	53	151	216	289	350	560	1166	972	237	17	0	0
Yuma	A	493	250	488	301	508	476	547	329	432	373	103	0	0
	B	404	410	191	478	207	506	235	454	427	707	281	0	16
	C	0	10	115	87	293	203	420	1557	1511	0	0	0	0
	D	128	301	573	316	542	421	692	745	476	0	0	0	0
	E	0	39	120	207	461	705	680	1197	787	0	0	0	0
	F	0	13	116	132	200	281	688	1886	801	0	0	0	0

Appendix C.
Physical Constants

Table C-1. Names and Symbols of SI* Units.[1]

Quantity	Name of Unit	Symbol	
SI BASE UNITS			
length	meter	m	
mass	kilogram	kg	
time	second	s	
electric current	ampere	A	
thermodynamic temperature	kelvin	K	
luminous intensity	candela	cd	
amount of substance	mole	mol	
SI DERIVED UNITS			
area	square meter	m^2	
volume	cubic meter	m^3	
frequency	hertz	Hz	s^{-1}
mass density (density)	kilogram per cubic meter	kg/m^3	
speed, velocity	meter per second	m/s	
angular velocity	radian per second	rad/s	
acceleration	meter per second squared	m/s^2	
angular acceleration	radian per second squared	rad/s^2	
force	newton	N	$kg \cdot m/s^2$
pressure (mechanical stress)	pascal	Pa	N/m^2
kinematic viscosity	square meter per second	m^2/s	
dynamic viscosity	newton-second per square meter	$N \cdot s/m^2$	
work, energy, quantity of heat	joule	J	$N \cdot m$
power	watt	W	J/s
quantity of electricity	coulomb	C	$A \cdot s$
potential difference, electromotive force	volt	V	W/A
electric field strength	volt per meter	V/m	
electric resistance	ohm	Ω	V/A
capacitance	farad	F	$A \cdot s/V$
magnetic flux	weber	Wb	$V \cdot s$
inductance	henry	H	$V \cdot s/A$
magnetic flux density	tesla	T	Wb/m^2
magnetic field strength	ampere per meter	A/m	
magnetomotive force	ampere	A	
luminous flux	lumen	lm	$cd \cdot sr$
luminance	candela per square meter	cd/m^2	
illuminance	lux	lx	lm/m^2
wave number	1 per meter	m^{-1}	
entropy	joule per kelvin	J/K	
specific heat capacity	joule per kilogram kelvin	$J/(kg \cdot K)$	
thermal conductivity	watt per meter kelvin	$W/(m \cdot K)$	
radiant intensity	watt per steradian	W/sr	
activity (of a radioactive source)	1 per second	s^{-1}	
SI SUPPLEMENTARY UNITS			
plane angle	radian	rad	
solid angle	steradian	sr	

*Systeme International d'Unités; The International System of Units.

Table C-2. SI Prefixes.

Factor by which unit is multiplied	Prefix	Symbol
10^{12}	tera	T
10^{9}	giga	G
10^{6}	mega	M
10^{3}	kilo	k
10^{2}	hecto	h
10	deka	da
10^{-1}	deci	d
10^{-2}	centi	c
10^{-3}	milli	m
10^{-6}	micro	μ
10^{-9}	nano	n
10^{-12}	pico	p
10^{-15}	femto	f
10^{-18}	atto	a

Table C-3. Values of Important Constants.[1]

$\pi = 3.141\ 592\ 653\ 589$
$e = 2.718\ 281\ 828\ 459$
$\mu_0 = 4\pi \times 10^{-7}$ H/m (exact), permeability of free space
$\quad = 1.256\ 637\ 061 \times 10^{-6}$ H/m
$\epsilon_0 = \mu_0^{-1} c^{-2}$ F/m, permittivity of free space
$\quad = 8.854\ 185 \times 10^{-12}$ F/m

Table C-4. Values of Physical Constants.[1]

Quantity	Symbol	Value	Error ppm	Prefix	Unit
Speed of light in vacuum_____	c	2. 997 925 0	0. 33	$\times 10^8$	m s^{-1}
Gravitational constant_____	G	6. 673 2	460	10^{-11}	N m^2 kg^{-2}
Avogadro constant_____	N_A	6. 022 169	6. 6	10^{26}	kmol $^{-1}$
Boltzmann constant_____	k	1. 380 622	43	10^{-23}	J K^{-1}
Gas constant_____	R	8. 314 34	42	10^3	J kmol $^{-1}$ K^{-1}
Volume of ideal gas, standard conditions_	V_0	2. 241 36	_____	10^1	m^3 kmol $^{-1}$
Faraday constant_____	F	9. 648 670	5. 5	10^7	C kmol $^{-1}$
Unified atomic mass unit_____	u	1. 660 531	6. 6	10^{-27}	kg
Planck constant_____	h	6. 626 196	7. 6	10^{-34}	J s
	$h/2\pi$	1. 054 591 9	7. 6	10^{-34}	J s
Electron charge__ _____	e	1. 602 191 7	4. 4	10^{-19}	C
Electron rest mass_____	m_e	9. 109 558	6. 0	10^{-31}	kg
		5. 485 930	6. 2	10^{-4}	u
Proton rest mass_____	m_p	1. 672 614	6. 6	10^{-27}	kg
		1. 007 276 61	0. 08	_____	u
Neutron rest mass_____	m_n	1. 674 920	6. 6	10^{-27}	kg
		1. 008 665 20	0. 10	_____	u
Electron charge to mass ratio_____	e/m_e	1. 758 802 8	3. 1	10^{11}	C kg^{-1}
Stefan-Boltzmann constant_____	σ	5. 669 61	170	10^{-8}	W m^{-2} K^{-4}
First radiation constant_____	$2\pi hc^2$	3. 741 844	7. 6	10^{-16}	W m^2
Second radiation constant_____	hc/k	1. 438 833	43	10^{-2}	m K
Rydberg constant_____	R_∞	1. 097 373 12	0. 10	10^7	m^{-1}
Fine structure constant_____	α	7. 297 351	1. 5	10^{-3}	
	α^{-1}	1. 370 360 2	1. 5	10^{+2}	
Bohr radius_____	a_0	5. 291 771 5	1. 5	10^{-11}	m
Classical electron radius_____	r_e	2. 817 939	4. 6	10^{-15}	m
Compton wavelength of electron_____	λ_C	2. 426 309 6	3. 1	10^{-12}	m
	$\lambda_C/2\pi$	3. 861 592	3. 1	10^{-13}	m
Compton wavelength of proton_____	$\lambda_{C,p}$	1. 321 440 9	6. 8	10^{-15}	m
	$\lambda_{C,p}/2\pi$	2. 103 139	6. 8	10^{-16}	m
Compton wavelength of neutron_____	$\lambda_{C,n}$	1. 319 621 7	6. 8	10^{-15}	m
	$\lambda_{C,n}/2\pi$	2. 100 243	6. 8	10^{-16}	m
Electron magnetic moment_____	μ_e	9. 284 851	7. 0	10^{-24}	J T^{-1}
Proton magnetic moment_____	μ_p	1. 410 620 3	7. 0	10^{-26}	J T^{-1}
Bohr magneton_____	μ_B	9. 274 096	7. 0	10^{-24}	J T^{-1}
Nuclear magneton_____	μ_n	5. 050 951	10	10^{-27}	J T^{-1}
Gyromagnetic ratio of protons in H$_2$O__	γ'_p	2. 675 127 0	3. 1	10^8	rad s^{-1} T^{-1}
	$\gamma'_p/2\pi$	4. 257 597	3. 1	10^7	Hz T^{-1}
Gyromagnetic ratio of protons in H$_2$O corrected for diamagnetism of H$_2$O.	γ_p	2. 675 196 5	3. 1	10^8	rad s^{-1} T^{-1}
	$\gamma_p/2\pi$	4. 257 707	3. 1	10^7	Hz T^{-1}
Magnetic flux quantum_____	Φ_0	2. 067 853 8	3. 3	10^{-15}	Wb
Quantum of circulation_____	$h/2m_e$	3. 636 947	3. 1	10^{-4}	J s kg^{-1}
	h/m_e	7. 273 894	3. 1	10^{-4}	J s kg^{-1}

Table C-5.   Periodic Chart of Elements.[2]

(Reprinted with permission from [2]. Copyright The Chemical Rubber Co., CRC Press, Inc.)

Group

Period	1a	2a	3b	4b	5b	6b	7b		8		1b	2b	3a	4a	5a	6a	7a	0	Orbit
I — 2 Elements	1 H 1.00797																	2 He 4.0026	K
II — 8 Elements	3 Li 6.939	4 Be 9.0122											5 B 10.811	6 C 12.01115	7 N 14.0067	8 O 15.9994	9 F 18.9984	10 Ne 20.183	K–L
III — 8 Elements	11 Na 22.9898	12 Mg 24.312											13 Al 26.9815	14 Si 28.086	15 P 30.9738	16 S 32.064	17 Cl 35.453	18 Ar 39.948	K–L–M
IV — 18 Elements	19 K 39.102	20 Ca 40.08	21 Sc 44.956	22 Ti 47.90	23 V 50.942	24 Cr 51.996	25 Mn 54.9380	26 Fe 55.847	27 Co 58.9332	28 Ni 58.71	29 Cu 63.54	30 Zn 65.37	31 Ga 69.72	32 Ge 72.59	33 As 74.9216	34 Se 78.96	35 Br 79.909	36 Kr 83.80	–L–M–N
V — 18 Elements	37 Rb 85.47	38 Sr 87.62	39 Y 88.905	40 Zr 91.22	41 Nb 92.906	42 Mo 95.94	43 Tc (99)	44 Ru 101.07	45 Rh 102.905	46 Pd 106.4	47 Ag 107.870	48 Cd 112.40	49 In 114.82	50 Sn 118.69	51 Sb 121.75	52 Te 127.60	53 I 126.9044	54 Xe 131.30	–M–N–O
VI — 32 Elements	55 Cs 132.905	56 Ba 137.34	57 La 138.91	72 Hf 178.49	73 Ta 180.948	74 W 183.85	75 Re 186.2	76 Os 190.2	77 Ir 192.2	78 Pt 195.09	79 Au 196.967	80 Hg 200.59	81 Tl 204.37	82 Pb 207.19	83 Bi 208.980	84 Po (242)	85 At (210)	86 Rn (222)	–N–O–P
VII	87 Fr (223)	88 Ra (226)	89** Ac (227)																–O–P–Q

Transition Elements

Group 8

| *Lanthanides | 58 Ce 140.12 | 59 Pr 140.907 | 60 Nd 144.24 | 61 Pm (145) | 62 Sm 150.35 | 63 Eu 151.96 | 64 Gd 157.25 | 65 Tb 158.924 | 66 Dy 162.50 | 67 Ho 164.930 | 68 Er 167.26 | 69 Tm 168.934 | 70 Yb 173.04 | 71 Lu 174.97 | –N–O–P |
| **Actinides | 90 Th 232.038 | 91 Pa (231) | 92 U 238.03 | 93 Np (237) | 94 Pu (242) | 95 Am (243) | 96 Cm (245) | 97 Bk (249) | 98 Cf (249) | 99 Es (254) | 100 Fm (252) | 101 Md (256) | 102 No (254) | 103 Lw | –O–P–Q |

KEY TO CHART

50 Sn 118.69

Atomic Number (black) — Symbol (black) — Atomic Weight (red) — Oxidation States (green) — Electron Configuration (blue)

Numbers in parentheses are mass numbers of most stable isotope of that element.

Table C-6. Greek Alphabet.

alpha	α	A	nu	ν	N
beta	β δ	B	xi	ξ	Ξ
gamma	γ	Γ	omicron	o	O
delta	δ	Δ	pi	π	Π
epsilon	ϵ	E	rho	ρ	P
zeta	ζ	Z	sigma	σ ς	Σ
eta	η	H	tau	τ	T
theta	θ ϑ	Θ Θ	upsilon	υ	Υ
iota	ι	I	phi	ϕ φ	Φ
kappa	κ	K	chi	χ	X
lambda	λ	Λ	psi	ψ	Ψ
mu	μ	M	omega	ω	Ω

REFERENCES

1. E. A. Mechtly, "The International System of Units, Physical Constants and Conversion Factors," 2nd Revision, NASA **SP-7012,** 1973.

2. *Handbook of Chemistry and Physics*, 47th Edition, The Chemical Rubber Co., CRC Press, Inc., West Palm Beach, Florida.

Appendix D.
Conversion Factors and Formulas

Table D-1. Temperature Conversion.

Celsius to Kelvin: $T_K = T_C + 273.15$
Farenheit to Kelvin: $T_K = (5/9)(T_F + 459.67)$
Rankine to Kelvin: $T_K = (5/9) T_R$
Farenheit to Celsius: $T_C = (5/9)(T_F - 32)$

°K	°C	°F	°R
0	−273	−460	0
73	−200	−328	132
173	−100	−148	312
233	−40	−40	420
273	0	32	492
373	100	212	672

ΔT

°F or °R	°C or °K
1.8	1
1	0.5556

Table D-2. Addition of Mass per Unit Power.

The total system's mass per unit power is

$$M_s = \sum_{i=1}^{n} m_i = m_1 + m_2 + \cdots + m_n \quad \text{(kg/W)}.$$

The m_i are the masses per unit power of the components

$$m_i = \frac{M_i}{P} \quad \text{(kg/W)}.$$

M_i are the masses of the components and P is the power of total system.

Illustrative Example:

Power output: 600 W
Solar cells: 20 kg
Solar cell covers: 15 kg
Substrate: 25 kg

$$M_s = \frac{20}{600} + \frac{15}{600} + \frac{25}{600} = 0.10 \text{ kg/W}.$$

Table D-3. Addition of Power per Unit Mass.

The total system's power per unit mass, P, is calculated from:

$$\frac{1}{P} = \sum_{i=1}^{n} \frac{1}{p_i} = \frac{1}{p_1} + \frac{1}{p_2} + \cdots + \frac{1}{p_n} \quad \left(\frac{1}{W/kg}\right).$$

The p_i are the power outputs per unit mass of the components

$$p_i = \frac{P}{m_i} \quad (W/kg).$$

P is the total system's power output and m_i are the masses of the components.

Illustrative Example:

Power output: 600 W
Solar cells: 20 kg P_c = 600/20 = 30 W/kg
Solar cell covers: 15 kg P_g = 600/15 = 40 W/kg
Substrate: 25 kg P_s = 600/25 = 24 W/kg

$$\frac{1}{P} = \frac{1}{30} + \frac{1}{40} + \frac{1}{24} = 0.0333 + 0.0250 + 0.0417 = 0.10$$

P = 1/0.10 = 10 W/kg.

Table D-4. Conversion Factors—Solar Cell Array Units.

To Convert From	Into			By
W/kg	W/lb	Multiply	W/kg	0.45359
	kg/kW	Divide	1000	W/kg
	lb/kW	Divide	2204.6	W/kg
W/lb	W/kg	Multiply	W/lb	2.2046
	kg/kW	Divide	453.59	W/lb
	lb/kW	Divide	1000	W/lb
kg/kW	lb/kW	Multiply	kg/kW	2.2046
	W/kg	Divide	1000	kg/kW
	W/lb	Divide	453.59	kg/kW
lb/kW	kg/kW	Multiply	lb/kW	0.45359
	W/kg	Divide	2204.6	lb/kW
	W/lb	Divide	1000	lb/kW

Table D-5. Conversion Factors—Electrical.[1]

To Convert From	Multiply By	To Obtain
ohm·m	100	ohm·cm
μohm·cm	10^{-6}	ohm·cm
ohm·inch	2.54	ohm·cm
circular mils	0.7854	square mils
circular mils	5.067×10^{-6}	cm^2
circular mils/foot	1.662×10^{-7}	cm
ohm·circular mils/foot	1.662×10^{-7}	ohm·cm

Table D-6. Conversion Factors—Thermal. [2]

THERMAL CONDUCTIVITY

$cal \cdot s^{-1} \cdot cm \cdot cm^{-2} \cdot {}^oC^{-1}$	$Btu \cdot h^{-1} \cdot ft \cdot ft^{-2} \cdot {}^oF^{-1}$	$Btu \cdot h^{-1} \cdot ft \cdot in^{-2} \cdot {}^oF^{-1}$	$W \cdot cm \cdot cm^{-2} \cdot {}^oC^{-1}$
1	241.9	2,903	4.183
4.13^{-3}	1	12	0.0173
3.45^{-4}	0.0833	1	1.44^{-3}
0.239	57.8	694	1

HEAT TRANSFER COEFFICIENT

$watts \cdot cm^{-2} \cdot {}^oC^{-1}$	$cal \cdot s^{-1} \cdot cm^{-2} \cdot {}^oC^{-1}$	$Btu \cdot h^{-1} \cdot ft^{-2} \cdot {}^oF^{-1}$
1	0.239	1,763
4.183	1	7,373
5.67^{-4}	1.36^{-4}	1

Note: Exponents indicate powers of 10.

Table D-7. Conversion Factors—Physical.[2]

LENGTH

cm	in.	ft	mi	nm	km
1	3.937^{-1}	3.28^{-2}			
2.54	1	8.33^{-2}			
30.48	12	1			
		5280	1	8.685^{-1}	1.6093
		6080	1.1515	1	1.8531
		3281	6.214^{-1}	5.396^{-1}	1

VOLUME

cm^3	ft^3	liter	yd^3	gallon
1	3.531^{-5}	1.0^{-3}	1.308^{6}	2.642^{-4}
2.832^{4}	1	28.32	3.704^{-2}	7.481
10^{3}	3.531^{-2}	1	1.308^{-3}	2.642^{-1}
7.646^{5}	27	7.646^{2}	1	202
3.785^{3}	1.337^{-1}	3.785	4.951^{-3}	1

AREA

cm^2	in^2	ft^2
1	0.155	1.08^{-3}
6.45	1	6.94^{-3}
929	144	1

DENSITY

g/cm^3	lb/ft^3
1	62.43
0.016	1

VELOCITY

cm/s	ft/s	ft/h	mi/h
1	0.0328	118.1	0.0224
30.48	1	3,600	0.6818
8.47^{-3}	2.78^{-4}	1	1.89^{-4}
44.70	1.467	5,280	1

TIME

(BASED ON 24-HOUR DAY, 30-DAY MONTH, 12-MONTH YEAR)

s	min	h	day	week	mo	yr
1						
60	1					
3.6^{3}	60	1				
8.64^{4}	1.44^{3}	24	1			
6.05^{5}	1.01^{4}	168	7	1		
2.59^{6}	4.32^{4}	720	30	4.29	1	
3.17^{7}	5.18^{5}	8.64^{3}	360	51.4	12	1

PRESSURE

torr	mm Hg	micron (μ Hg)	P$_a$	N·m^{-2}
1	1	1^{-3}	133.322	133.322
7.501^{-3}	7.501^{-3}	7.501	1	1

MASS

See Table D-8

Note: Exponents indicate powers of 10.

Table D-8. Conversion Factors—Mass.

To Convert From	Multiply by	To Obtain
gram	10^{-3}	kilogram
lbm (pound mass)	0.4536	kilogram
ounce mass (avoirdupois)	0.02835	kilogram
slug	14.59	kilogram
gram/centimeter^3	10^{-3}	kilogram/meter^3
lbm/inch^3	27,680	kilogram/meter^3
lbm/ft^3	16.02	kilogram/meter^3
ounce mass/inch^3	1730	kilogram/meter^3
slug/ft^3	515.4	kilogram/meter^3
dyne	10^{-5}	newton
kilogram force	9.807	newton
kilopound force	9.807	newton
kip	4,448	newton
lbf (pound force)	4.448	newton
ounce force	0.2780	newton
poundal	0.1383	newton

Table D-9. Conversion Factors—Magnetic.

To Convert From	Multiply by	To Obtain
Magnetic Dipole Moments		
amp·turn·ft^2	6.86×10^{-6}	ft·lb/gauss
amp·turn·m^2	10.76	amp·turn·ft^2
pole·cm	1.00×10^{-3}	amp·turn·m^2
pole·cm	10.76×10^{-3}	amp·turn·ft^2
pole·cm	7.38×10^{-8}	ft·lb/gauss
weber·meter	$1.00 \times 10^{7}/4\pi$	amp·turn·m^2
weber·meter	$1.00 \times 10^{10}/4\pi$	pole·cm
Magnetic Fields		
gamma	1.00×10^{-9}	tesla
gauss	1.00×10^{-4}	tesla
gilbert	$10/4\pi$	ampere·turn
lines	1.00×10^{-8}	weber
maxwell	1.00×10^{-8}	weber
oersted	$1000/4\pi$	ampere·turn/meter
tesla	1.00	newton/(amp·turn·meter)
unit pole	1.2566×10^{-7}	weber
weber	1.00	volt·second
weber amp	1.00	joule
weber/m^2	1.00	tesla

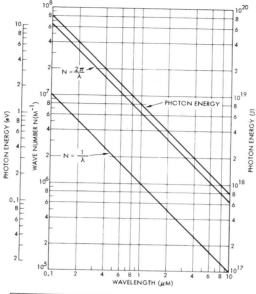

Applicable unit conversion factors are:

Multiply	by	to obtain
J (joules)	6.25×10^{18}	eV (electron volts)
eV	1.6×10^{-19}	J
μm	10,000	Å (Angstrom units)

Fig. D-1. Relationships between wavelength, wave number, and photon energy.

REFERENCES

1. *Reference Data for Radio Engineers*, 4th Edition, International Telephone and Telegraph Corporation, New York, 1956.

2. J. B. Kendrick, "TRW Space Data," 3rd Edition, TRW Systems Group, TRW Inc., 1967.

Appendix E.
1 MeV Fluence Tables

Damage equivalent 1 MeV fluence values for silicon solar cells have been predicted for solar flare protons in free space at a distance of 1 AU from the sun (Table E-1), and have been evaluated for geomagnetically trapped electrons and protons (Tables E-2 through E-5).[1,2] The 1 MeV fluence values are given for different fused silica shielding thicknesses and apply to the solar cell I_{sc} (or J_{sc}), V_{oc} and P_{mp} in the case of electrons, but for V_{oc} and P_{mp} only in the case of protons. The geomagnetically trapped electron and proton environments are for circular orbits of various altitudes and inclinations and are based on the AE3, AE4 and AE5 electron models and AP5, AP6 and AP7 proton models, respectively (see Section 9-44). The notation EX in the tables signifies 10^x; for example $3.2E09 = 3.2 \times 10^9$.

Table E-1. Free Space Solar Flare Proton Equivalent 1 MeV Electron Fluence (e/cm^2) for Various Cover Thicknesses.

Years	Cell Parameter	Cover Thickness (mm)					
		0.0764	0.152	0.305	0.509	0.764	1.52
1975–1977	J_{sc}	2.9E13	1.7E13	8.7E12	5.3E12	3.7E12	1.9E12
	V_{oc} and P_{max}	6.7E13	3.4E13	1.6E13	8.6E12	5.5E12	2.6E12
1978–1979	J_{sc}	1.5E14	1.3E14	4.4E13	2.6E13	1.8E13	9.7E12
	V_{oc} and P_{max}	3.3E14	1.7E14	8.0E13	4.3E13	2.7E13	1.3E13
1980–1982	J_{sc}	2.9E14	1.7E14	8.7E13	5.3E13	3.7E13	1.9E1
	V_{oc} and P_{max}	6.7E14	3.4E14	1.6E14	8.6E13	5.5E13	2.6E1
1983–1984	J_{sc}	1.5E14	1.3E14	4.4E13	2.6E13	1.8E13	9.7E1
	V_{oc} and P_{max}	3.3E14	1.7E14	8.0E13	4.3E13	2.7E13	1.3E1
1985–1987	J_{sc}	2.9E13	1.7E13	8.7E12	5.3E12	3.7E12	1.9E1
	V_{oc} and P_{max}	6.7E13	3.4E13	1.6E13	8.6E12	5.5E12	2.6E1

Table E-2. Annual Trapped 1 MeV Electron Fluence (e/cm^2) for 0.0764 mm (0.0003 inch) Thick Covers.

Altitude		Inclination 0°		Inclination 30°		Inclination 60°		Inclination 90°	
(N.M.)	(km)	Electrons	Protons	Electrons	Protons	Electrons	Protons	Electrons	Protons
150	278	0.	0.	5.51E08	8.50E11	1.32E11	5.99E12	1.34E11	4.36E12
300	556	1.11E08	6.69E10	1.55E11	3.32E13	3.37E11	4.85E13	3.08E11	3.57E13
450	834	3.00E10	4.00E13	1.54E12	2.20E14	1.08E12	1.93E14	9.22E11	1.45E14
600	1110	2.53E12	4.25E14	7.21E12	8.39E14	3.81E12	5.66E14	3.27E12	4.49E14
800	1480	4.19E13	3.32E15	2.86E13	3.41E15	1.50E13	2.04E15	1.28E13	1.68E15
1000	1850	1.33E14	1.17E16	6.79E13	9.86E15	3.62E13	5.47E15	3.10E13	4.61E15
1250	2320	2.44E14	3.47E16	1.09E14	2.67E16	5.84E13	1.42E16	4.98E13	1.20E16
1500	2780	2.64E14	8.28E16	1.10E14	5.85E16	5.85E13	2.93E16	4.99E13	2.47E16
1750	3240	2.22E14	1.82E17	9.34E13	1.12E17	5.11E13	5.70E16	4.33E13	4.84E16
2000	3710	1.70E14	3.43E17	7.50E13	1.89E17	4.24E13	9.29E16	3.56E13	7.98E16
2250	4170	1.34E14	5.22E17	6.06E13	2.51E17	3.51E13	1.29E17	2.92E13	1.11E17
2500	4630	1.14E14	6.32E17	5.17E13	2.90E17	3.15E13	1.53E17	2.59E13	1.31E17
2750	5100	1.01E14	6.91E17	4.52E13	3.10E17	2.87E13	1.61E17	2.33E13	1.38E17
3000	5560	8.69E13	6.76E17	3.89E13	2.91E17	2.59E13	1.53E17	2.08E13	1.31E17
3500	6490	5.93E13	5.19E17	2.89E13	2.22E17	2.15E13	1.13E17	1.66E13	9.69E16
4000	7410	4.21E13	4.79E17	2.42E13	2.11E17	1.98E13	1.08E17	1.50E13	9.30E16
4500	8340	3.53E13	4.10E17	2.42E13	1.76E17	2.00E13	9.06E16	1.52E13	7.72E16
5000	9260	3.02E13	2.87E17	2.63E13	1.18E17	2.12E13	6.09E16	1.60E13	5.26E16
5500	10200	2.87E13	1.81E17	3.14E13	7.10E16	2.34E13	3.73E16	1.82E13	3.19E16
6000	11100	3.22E13	1.05E17	3.88E13	3.92E16	2.63E13	2.07E16	2.08E13	1.78E16
7000	13000	5.10E13	3.21E16	5.68E13	1.22E16	3.41E13	6.47E15	2.75E13	5.56E15
8000	14800	7.07E13	8.90E15	7.39E13	3.25E15	4.09E13	1.76E15	3.37E13	1.52E15
9000	16700	9.91E13	1.52E15	9.07E13	5.61E14	4.75E13	3.00E14	3.94E13	2.57E14
10000	18500	1.29E14	2.46E14	9.71E13	9.97E13	4.95E13	5.48E13	4.18E13	4.60E13
11000	20400	1.44E14	1.78E13	9.97E13	7.31E12	4.95E13	3.74E12	4.11E13	3.14E12
12000	22200	1.48E14	1.19E12	9.14E13	4.70E11	4.64E13	2.60E11	3.92E13	2.25E11
13000	24100	1.31E14	1.14E10	7.90E13	5.83E09	3.99E13	3.18E09	3.39E13	2.70E09
14000	25900	1.15E14	2.13E08	6.51E13	8.35E07	3.26E13	4.70E07	2.77E13	4.10E07
15000	27800	9.89E13	4.11E07	5.27E13	1.53E07	2.65E13	8.12E06	2.26E13	7.01E06
16000	29600	7.80E13	1.57E07	4.01E13	6.51E06	2.01E13	3.38E06	1.72E13	2.78E07
17000	31500	5.97E13	9.59E06	2.96E13	4.45E06	1.49E13	2.19E07	1.27E13	1.80E06
18000	33400	4.48E13	1.01E07	2.11E13	3.66E06	1.06E13	1.79E07	9.13E12	1.54E07
19400	35900	4.77E13	0.	—	0.	—	0.	—	0.

Table E-3. Annual Trapped 1 MeV Electron Fluence (e/cm^2) for 0.152 mm (0.006 inch) Thick Covers.

Altitude		Inclination 0°		Inclination 30°		Inclination 60°		Inclination 90°	
(N.M.)	(km)	Electrons	Protons	Electrons	Protons	Electrons	Protons	Electrons	Protons
150	278	0.	0.	4.84E08	3.16E11	1.14E11	2.46E12	1.14E11	1.81E12
300	556	1.04E08	2.48E10	1.34E11	1.36E13	2.87E11	2.03E13	2.63E11	1.49E13
450	834	2.68E10	1.55E13	1.34E12	9.31E13	9.28E11	8.09E13	7.93E11	6.11E13
600	1110	2.24E12	1.76E14	6.31E12	3.57E14	3.32E12	2.39E14	2.84E12	1.91E14
800	1480	3.70E13	1.41E15	2.50E13	1.47E15	1.31E13	8.64E14	1.12E13	7.17E14
1000	1850	1.17E14	5.08E15	5.91E13	4.26E15	3.16E13	2.35E15	2.70E13	1.98E15
1250	2320	2.13E14	1.51E16	9.43E13	1.15E16	5.03E13	6.05E15	4.30E13	5.14E15
1500	2780	2.27E14	3.56E16	9.25E13	2.48E16	4.94E13	1.23E16	4.21E13	1.05E16
1750	3240	1.85E14	7.70E16	7.57E13	4.64E16	4.16E13	2.37E16	3.53E13	2.01E16
2000	3710	1.35E14	1.42E17	5.78E13	7.26E16	3.30E13	3.79E16	2.77E13	3.25E16
2250	4170	9.95E13	2.13E17	4.39E13	1.01E17	2.60E13	5.19E16	2.15E13	4.45E16
2500	4630	7.99E13	2.54E17	3.56E13	1.15E17	2.25E13	6.02E16	1.83E13	5.18E16
2750	5100	6.76E13	2.73E17	3.00E13	1.20E17	2.01E13	6.23E16	1.61E13	5.34E16
3000	5560	5.67E13	2.64E17	2.54E13	1.09E17	1.81E13	5.75E16	1.43E13	4.94E16
3500	6490	3.77E13	1.80E17	1.89E13	7.20E16	1.54E13	3.72E16	1.17E13	3.18E16
4000	7410	2.66E13	1.05E17	1.65E13	4.23E16	1.47E13	2.22E16	1.10E13	1.91E16
4500	8340	2.30E13	6.27E16	1.77E13	2.56E16	1.55E13	1.34E16	1.17E13	1.15E16
5000	9260	2.11E13	3.63E16	2.08E13	1.41E16	1.72E13	7.40E15	1.29E13	6.37E15
5500	10200	2.20E13	1.88E16	2.61E13	7.05E15	1.96E13	3.75E15	1.52E13	3.21E15
6000	11100	2.68E13	8.80E15	3.31E13	3.15E15	2.24E13	1.70E15	1.77E13	1.47E15
7000	13000	4.40E13	1.66E15	4.90E13	6.15E14	2.93E13	3.30E14	2.37E13	2.84E14
8000	14800	6.13E13	3.31E14	6.38E13	1.18E14	3.52E13	6.39E13	2.91E13	5.50E13
9000	16700	8.59E13	3.51E13	7.82E13	1.31E13	4.08E13	7.08E12	3.39E13	6.21E12
10000	18500	1.11E14	3.59E12	8.34E13	1.48E12	4.24E13	8.17E11	3.59E13	6.92E11
11000	20400	1.24E14	3.67E10	8.55E13	1.74E10	4.23E13	7.07E09	3.52E13	7.34E09
12000	22200	1.27E14	1.25E09	7.81E13	5.41E08	3.96E13	3.00E08	3.35E13	2.58E08
13000	24100	1.12E14	1.14E06	6.71E13	6.09E05	3.39E13	2.51E05	2.88E13	1.75E05
14000	25900	9.78E13	0.	5.49E13	0.	2.75E13	0.	2.34E13	0.
15000	27800	8.38E13	0.	4.42E13	0.	2.22E13	0.	1.90E13	0.
16000	29600	6.53E13	0.	3.32E13	0.	1.67E13	0.	1.42E13	0.
17000	31500	4.92E13	0.	2.42E13	0.	1.22E13	0.	1.04E13	0.
18000	33400	3.66E13	0.	1.70E13	0.	8.55E12	0.	7.37E12	0.
19400	35900	3.14E13	0.	—	0.	—	0.	—	0.

Table E-4. Annual Trapped 1 MeV Electron Fluence (e/cm^2) for 0.509 mm (0.020 inch) Thick Covers.

Altitude		Inclination 0°		Inclination 30°		Inclination 60°		Inclination 90°	
(N.M.)	(km)	Electrons	Protons	Electrons	Protons	Electrons	Protons	Electrons	Protons
150	278	0.	0.	3.17E08	1.87E11	6.82E10	4.51E11	6.80E10	3.37E11
300	556	8.12E07	1.58E10	8.39E10	5.13E12	1.72E11	4.28E12	1.57E11	3.30E12
450	834	1.82E10	6.88E12	8.55E11	2.86E13	5.72E11	1.77E13	4.87E11	1.42E13
600	1110	1.48E12	6.45E13	4.06E12	9.66E13	2.10E12	5.39E13	1.80E12	4.47E13
800	1480	2.43E13	4.29E14	1.60E13	3.58E14	8.39E12	1.93E14	7.17E12	1.63E14
1000	1850	7.61E13	1.35E15	3.77E13	9.17E14	2.01E13	4.85E14	1.72E13	4.14E14
1250	2320	1.37E14	3.36E15	5.89E13	2.09E15	3.15E13	1.09E15	2.69E13	9.27E14
1500	2780	1.41E14	6.23E15	5.53E13	3.68E15	2.97E13	1.83E15	2.53E13	1.56E15
1750	3240	1.08E14	1.08E16	4.19E13	5.89E15	2.33E13	3.01E15	1.98E13	2.57E15
2000	3710	7.13E13	1.69E16	2.85E13	7.98E15	1.67E13	4.19E15	1.39E13	3.59E15
2250	4170	4.48E13	2.21E16	1.82E13	9.86E15	1.15E13	5.13E15	9.38E12	4.41E15
2500	4630	2.96E13	2.33E16	1.23E13	1.02E16	8.74E12	5.36E15	6.92E12	4.61E15
2750	5100	2.03E13	2.23E16	8.66E12	9.62E15	7.09E12	5.04E15	5.43E12	4.32E15
3000	5560	1.46E13	1.95E16	6.64E12	8.27E15	6.25E12	4.35E15	4.68E12	3.73E15
3500	6490	8.42E12	1.41E16	5.04E12	5.69E15	5.90E12	2.92E15	4.18E12	2.50E15
4000	7410	5.83E12	9.58E15	5.34E12	3.64E15	6.32E12	1.93E15	4.50E12	1.65E15
4500	8340	5.67E12	4.77E15	7.15E12	1.83E15	7.35E12	9.71E14	5.37E12	8.35E14
5000	9260	6.63E12	1.94E15	1.01E13	7.35E14	8.95E12	3.88E14	6.61E12	3.34E14
5500	10200	9.53E12	7.93E14	1.45E13	2.95E14	1.10E13	1.57E14	8.46E12	1.35E14
6000	11100	1.49E13	3.19E14	1.97E13	1.15E14	1.32E13	6.22E13	1.04E13	5.34E13
7000	13000	2.68E13	4.78E13	2.99E13	1.77E13	1.76E13	9.51E12	1.43E13	8.21E12
8000	14800	3.82E13	7.98E12	3.90E13	2.85E12	2.12E13	1.55E12	1.76E13	1.33E12
9000	16700	5.35E13	7.61E11	4.72E13	2.85E11	2.44E13	1.54E11	2.04E13	1.33E11
10000	18500	6.69E13	7.19E10	4.93E13	2.95E10	2.49E13	1.61E10	2.11E13	1.36E10
11000	20400	7.38E13	0.	4.99E13	0.	2.46E13	0.	2.04E13	0.
12000	22200	7.47E13	0.	4.48E13	0.	2.27E13	0.	1.92E13	0.
13000	24100	6.44E13	0.	3.77E13	0.	1.90E13	0.	1.61E13	0.
14000	25900	5.50E13	0.	3.02E13	0.	1.51E13	0.	1.29E13	0.
15000	27800	4.65E13	0.	2.38E13	0.	1.20E13	0.	1.02E13	0.
16000	29600	3.48E13	0.	1.72E13	0.	8.66E12	0.	7.40E12	0.
17000	31500	2.52E13	0.	1.21E13	0.	6.09E12	0.	5.21E12	0.
18000	33400	1.82E13	0.	8.15E12	0.	4.12E12	0.	3.56E12	0.
19400	35900	1.12E13	0.	−	0.	−	0.	−	0.

Table E-5. Annual Trapped 1 MeV Electron Fluence (e/cm^2) for 1.52 mm (0.060 inch) Thick Covers.

Altitude		Inclination 0°		Inclination 30°		Inclination 60°		Inclination 90°	
(N.M.)	(km)	Electrons	Protons	Electrons	Protons	Electrons	Protons	Electrons	Protons
150	278	0.	0.	1.31E08	1.31E11	2.42E10	1.77E11	2.35E10	1.33E11
300	556	4.54E07	1.16E10	3.34E10	2.41E12	6.27E10	1.55E12	5.60E10	1.23E12
450	834	7.78E09	3.65E12	3.42E11	1.12E13	2.19E11	6.03E12	1.84E11	4.93E12
600	1110	6.02E11	2.81E13	1.63E12	3.40E13	8.28E11	1.77E13	7.09E11	1.49E13
800	1480	9.83E12	1.57E14	6.42E12	1.14E14	3.34E12	5.98E13	2.85E12	5.08E13
1000	1850	3.07E13	4.38E14	1.51E13	2.60E14	8.01E12	1.35E14	6.85E12	1.16E14
1250	2320	5.45E13	9.42E14	2.33E13	5.17E14	1.24E13	2.67E14	1.06E13	2.29E14
1500	2780	5.53E13	1.36E15	2.13E13	7.08E14	1.14E13	3.54E14	9.76E12	3.03E14
1750	3240	4.12E13	1.97E15	1.54E13	1.01E15	8.60E12	5.18E14	7.30E12	4.41E14
2000	3710	2.53E13	2.55E15	9.66E12	1.13E15	5.70E12	5.99E14	4.75E12	5.14E14
2250	4170	1.38E13	3.04E15	5.23E12	1.30E15	3.45E12	6.81E14	2.80E12	5.85E14
2500	4630	7.35E12	2.76E15	2.86E12	1.17E15	2.29E12	6.22E14	1.77E12	5.33E14
2750	5100	3.76E12	2.46E15	1.54E12	1.05E15	1.68E12	5.51E14	1.22E12	4.71E14
3000	5560	2.08E12	1.89E15	9.94E11	8.24E14	1.45E12	4.31E14	1.02E12	3.70E14
3500	6490	8.17E11	1.48E15	8.03E11	6.16E14	1.53E12	3.11E14	1.02E12	2.66E14
4000	7410	4.75E11	1.16E15	1.14E12	4.21E14	1.77E12	2.24E14	1.22E12	1.93E14
4500	8340	4.94E11	4.97E14	1.88E12	1.86E14	2.17E12	9.95E13	1.56E12	8.56E13
5000	9260	8.91E11	1.44E14	3.09E12	5.40E13	2.80E12	2.88E13	2.05E12	2.48E13
5500	10200	2.23E12	4.71E13	4.89E12	1.75E13	3.63E12	9.40E12	2.80E12	8.05E12
6000	11100	5.02E12	1.66E13	7.07E12	5.96E12	4.57E12	3.23E12	3.64E12	2.78E12
7000	13000	1.00E13	2.01E12	1.10E13	7.43E11	6.28E12	4.01E11	5.11E12	3.45E11
8000	14800	1.47E13	2.84E11	1.43E13	1.01E11	7.60E12	5.52E10	6.32E12	4.75E10
9000	16700	2.08E13	2.46E10	1.69E13	9.24E09	8.61E12	4.99E09	7.19E12	4.29E09
10000	18500	2.43E13	2.16E09	1.67E13	8.81E08	8.40E12	4.76E08	7.13E12	4.04E08
11000	20400	2.49E13	0.	1.60E13	0.	7.85E12	0.	6.55E12	0.
12000	22200	2.39E13	0.	1.37E13	0.	6.91E12	0.	5.87E12	0.
13000	24100	1.95E13	0.	1.10E13	0.	5.54E12	0.	4.71E12	0.
14000	25900	1.59E13	0.	8.41E12	0.	4.20E12	0.	3.58E12	0.
15000	27800	1.29E13	0.	6.32E12	0.	3.20E12	0.	2.73E12	0.
16000	29600	9.11E12	0.	4.34E12	0.	2.19E12	0.	1.87E12	0.
17000	31500	6.21E12	0.	2.88E12	0.	1.46E12	0.	1.25E12	0.
18000	33400	4.30E12	0.	1.84E12	0.	9.45E11	0.	8.10E11	0.
19400	35900	1.17E12	0.	−	0.	−	0.	−	0.

REFERENCES

1. H. Y. Tada and J. R. Carter, Jr., "Solar Cell Radiation Handbook," JPL Publication 77-56, November 1, 1977.
2. D. K. Weidner, "Natural Space Environment Criteria for 1975–1985, NASA Space Stations," NASA TM X53865, August 1969, Second Edition, 10 August 1970.

Index

Index